NATURAL SCIENCES IN AMERICA

NATURAL SCIENCES IN AMERICA

Advisory Editor
KEIR B. STERLING

BIRD BOOKS AND BIRD ART

BY

JEAN ANKER

ARNO PRESS
A New York Times Company
New York, N. Y. • 1974

Reprint Edition 1974 by Arno Press Inc.

Reprinted from a copy in The American Museum
   of Natural History Library

NATURAL SCIENCES IN AMERICA
ISBN for complete set: 0-405-05700-8
See last pages of this volume for titles.

Manufactured in the United States of America

Publisher's Note: The illustrations in this
book have been reproduced in black and white.
The pages have been reduced by 29%.

———————◆———————

Library of Congress Cataloging in Publication Data

Anker, Jean, 1892-1957.
   Bird books and bird art.

   (Natural sciences in America)
   Based on the collection of books in the University
library at Copenhagen.
   Reprint of the 1938 ed. published by Levin & Munks-
gaard, Copenhagen.
   Bibliography: p.
   1. Birds--Pictorial works--Bibliography. 2. Birds
--Bibliography--Catalogs. 3. Copenhagen. Universitet.
Bibliotek. I. Copenhagen. Universitet. Bibliotek.
II. Title. III. Series.
Z5335.A54 1974   016.5982   73-17795
ISBN 0-405-05705-9

BIRD BOOKS AND
BIRD ART

FRONTISPIECE

Fig. 1

Fig. 2

Fig. 3

Fig. 4

BIRD BOOKS AND BIRD ART

AN OUTLINE
OF THE LITERARY HISTORY AND ICONOGRAPHY OF
DESCRIPTIVE ORNITHOLOGY

BASED PRINCIPALLY ON THE COLLECTION
OF BOOKS CONTAINING PLATES WITH FIGURES OF BIRDS AND THEIR
EGGS NOW IN THE UNIVERSITY LIBRARY AT COPENHAGEN
AND INCLUDING A CATALOGUE OF THESE WORKS

WRITTEN AND COMPILED

BY

JEAN ANKER

ISSUED BY THE UNIVERSITY LIBRARY COPENHAGEN
TO COMMEMORATE THE INAUGURATION OF THE NEW BUILDING
OF THE LIBRARY

LEVIN & MUNKSGAARD . EJNAR MUNKSGAARD
COPENHAGEN 1938

Dedicated to the memory of

JOHAN FREDERIK CLASSEN

the great collector of books on

the natural sciences

LIST OF CONTENTS.

ACKNOWLEDGEMENT.

In the beginning of 1938 the section of the University Library devoted to natural sciences and medicine will take possession of a new, modern building. The desire to mark this great and happy event in the history of the Library suggested the issue of a publication which should convey an idea of the standard of its collections and also be of use to scientific research.

It would not, however, have been possible to bring out this book if the Library had not received financial aid from 'Det Classenske Fideikommis' and from 'Rask-Ørsted Fondet'. On behalf of the Library, therefore, I tender cordial thanks to the Trustees of both these institutions for the funds granted towards the preparation and publication of the book.

Svend Dahl
Librarian.

PREFACE.

This is a book about books and pictures.

It is divided into two parts, the first 'An outline of the literary history and iconography of descriptive ornithology' to some extent depending on the second 'A catalogue of the collection of books containing plates with figures of birds and their eggs now in the University Library at Copenhagen'.

When the Chief Librarian of the University Library at Copenhagen first suggested to the writer that he should produce a book on the ornithological literature in the library, careful deliberation of the reasons for and against the proposal became necessary. Trained and educated as a biologist and as a zoologist, and interested chiefly in zoological history and biology, he had to consider closely whether he could undertake a task that, although only theoretically, involved an intimate knowledge of a special branch of zoology. That in spite of preliminary hesitation the work eventually was undertaken is due firstly to the fact that literary and bibliographic experience could largely be employed in its fulfilment; secondly, an offer of expert ornithological assistance was received from *Finn Salomonsen,* the well-known ornithologist, who has been kind enough to identify the birds figured on the plates and to read through the manuscript of the first part of the book. The practical suggestions he thus made, and his advice, have materially assisted in the production of the work.

The subject matter is more fully treated in the part of the first section of the book dealing with the period up to 1800 than in that dealing with the subsequent period; for obvious reasons this is also the case as regards the sections on Scandinavian literature and its illustrations. It is hoped, however, that the general effect of the survey of the most important works on descriptive ornithology and its illustrations presented in this part will not be spoiled by these inequalities.

The accompanying catalogue contains short notes on the history and contents of the works listed in it, on the artist, or artists, responsible for the originals for the plates, and on the production of the plates themselves. The collection contains a number of valuable antique works in large format, of great interest bibliographically, and much in demand, among which is John James Audubon's 'The birds of America'. As must be the case in every large library of any age, there are also individual examples of rarities such as the original edition of Thomas Pennant's 'Indian zoology', of which only a few copies are known, and the folio edition of Johann Andreas Naumann's plates; the latter is incomplete, as are the majority of the few examples now in existence. An even greater bibliographic rarity is the copy of the first volume of the text to Naumann's plates as it contains all the title-pages issued for this volume, thus surely being unique.

Although the collection cannot compete with the more wealthy foreign libraries, that it contains so many antique works as it does is very largely due to that great patron of literature, Major-General *Johan Frederik Classen* (1725—92), an industrialist and a landowner whose name is especially connected with the development of the town called by him Frederiksværk. From comparatively modest circumstances this great man worked his way up to become one of the most important personalities of his country. Impelled by his interest in books he bought and bought, both at home and abroad, until he had formed a library so large that at his death it was valued at over 100,000 thalers and consisted of about 20,000 volumes. Although his collection was not, strictly speaking, that of a bibliophile, it gave Classen a position in the first rank of the contemporary collectors in his country in this the golden age for bibliophiles. In his will he left his whole library to the public, with funds for its development. In 1867, when the 'Classenske Bibliothek' had reached a total of about 30,000 volumes, it was broken up and the greater part of it — including, especially, the natural science section — incorporated in the University Library, which was thereby enriched with a number of valuable and important works. A great many of the large antique tomes illustrated with copperplates, and mentioned in the accompanying catalogue, originate from this source. The University Library still benefits from Classen's munificence, as it receives an annual sum from the 'Classenske Fideikommis' founded by him, with which it purchases works on natural science, for preference on zoology. It has thus been able to increase its collection of ornithological literature.

The composition of a book such as the present one necessitates assistance from many quarters. So many institutions and private persons in Denmark and abroad have been kind enough to contribute to it by supplying information of various kinds that space is not available to mention all of them. Of especial value in this respect was a visit the author and compiler was able to pay in the summer of 1936 to several German libraries. This was made possible by a donation from Dr. and Fru *V. Eilschou Holm,* for which most cordial thanks must here be expressed.

In addition to the courtesies which have already been acknowledged, special mention must be made of Dr. *Ejnar Munksgaard,* the publisher of the book, who has assisted in its publication in every possible way. Thanks must also be offered to the bird-painter *Johannes Larsen* for contributing the original watercolours reproduced in the frontispiece; to Hr. *Holger Jensen* of Messrs *Wendt & Jensen,* process-engravers, for the contribution of the blocks for two of the coloured plates in the book; and to Hr. *Johan Olsen* of *'Det Berlingske Bogtrykkeri',* for the gratuitous production of four of the coloured plates.

The already existing catalogues of collections of zoological literature have been of valuable assistance in the compilation of the catalogue, more especially the excellent 'Catalogue of the books, manuscripts, maps and drawings in the British Museum (Natural History)', 1903—33, J. T. Zimmer's admirable 'Catalogue of the Edward E. Ayer Ornithological Library', 1926, Casey A. Wood's 'Introduction to the literature of vertebrate zoology', 1931, and a number of others, each of which has in its own particular way facilitated the work.

Invaluable help in the laborious and tedious work of collation has been rendered by Frk. *Elisabet Graae,* and, in particular, by Fru *Fritze Smith,* both of the University Library, of whom the latter has been able to devote much of her time to this exacting work of precision. Various experts are responsible for the translation into English.

The names of the persons referred to in the text of the first part of the book are given so far as possible, with the Christian names or initials by which they are generally known, or which are in general use; initials are used in the catalogue. Full names and, so far as possible, dates of birth and death are shown in the index.

The catalogue does not include the books in the collection that are illustrated with photographic plates only, nor those with but few or indifferent plates.

The works included in the catalogue are listed under the names of the authors, with cross-references in cases of joint authorship.

When the ornithological matter in a work is not scattered, this part is listed wherever possible directly under its author. For the sake of brevity the following signs are used in the transcriptions of the titles. The insertion of - - denotes that what follows is taken from another page with a subordinate title or heading. The signs < > enclose headings, and also subordinate titles in which the name of the publisher and the place of publication is not mentioned, or in which — as compared with the title — one of these names is omitted. All titles connected with the section in question are thus included in the transcription, with the omission of any unnecessary repetition. The sign —➤ after a date or after the number of a volume, or a part of a volume, indicates that the set is in progress.

In the description of a work the designations for volumes and parts of volumes are all given in English.

The name of the publisher, or printer, is taken from the title-page and printed before the name of the place of publication. When the names of more than one publisher or more than one place of publication appear on the title-page, only the first is given.

Slight alterations from volume to volume in the general title of a work comprising more than one volume are shortly explained in parentheses.

No special mention is made in the second part of this work (the catalogue) when the plates are reproduced by the four-colour process, the expression 'three-colour process' covering both methods of reproduction.

The titles in the catalogue and in the bibliography are numbered consecutively. The figures in parentheses refer to these numbers.

UNIVERSITY LIBRARY, COPENHAGEN
January 5, 1938.

Jean Anker
Assistant Librarian.

PRINCIPAL ABBREVIATIONS USED, MORE ESPECIALLY IN THE CATALOGUE.

c. (circa) ...	about
cap. (capitulum) ...	chapter
cf. (confer) ...	compare
col. ...	coloured
del. (delineavit, delineaverunt) ...	drawn [by]
dir., direx. (direxit, direxerunt) ...	engraved under the supervision of
ed. ...	edition
e. g. (exempli gratia) ...	for example
exc., excud. (excudit, excuderunt) ...	printed [by], or engraved and printed [by]
f. ...	florins
fasc. ...	fascicle, fascicles
fe., fec. (fecit, fecerunt) ...	made [by]
fig. (figs.) ...	figure (figures)
fl. ...	flourished
fol. ...	folio
fold. ...	folded
front.	frontispiece, frontispieces
i. e. (id est) ...	that is [to say]
imp. (impressit, impresserunt, imprimé, imprimerie) ...	printed [by], printing establishment
in lap. (in lapidem) ...	on stone [by]
lit. (lith.)	lithographed [by]
no. (nos.)	number (numbers)
numb. ...	numbered
obl. ...	oblong
p. (pp.) ...	page (pages)
phot.	photographic
photograv.	photogravure
pinx. pinxt., pxt. (pinxit, pinxerunt) ...	painted [by]
pl. ...	plate (plates)
q. v. (quod vide) ...	which see
sc., sculp. (sculpsit, sculpserunt) ...	engraved [by]
seqq. (sequentia) ...	[and] the following
ser. ...	series
s. l. (sine loco) ...	without place
suppl. ...	supplement, supplements, supplementary
text-fig. (text-figs.) ...	text-figure (text-figures)
uncol. ...	uncoloured
unnumb. ...	unnumbered
vol. (vols.) ...	volume (volumes)

LIST OF ILLUSTRATIONS.

I.

AN OUTLINE OF THE LITERARY HISTORY AND ICONOGRAPHY OF DESCRIPTIVE ORNITHOLOGY

The Red-backed Shrike, *Lanius collurio* L., in a Sont-bush. Painting in the tomb of Chnemhetep. From a coloured plate (Pl. VII) by Howard Carter in the Archæological Survey of Egypt. Edited by F. L. Griffith. Seventh Memoir. Beni Hasan. Part IV. London 1900.

1. PICTURES AND RECORDS OF BIRDS UP TO THE INVENTION OF PRINTING AND THE DEVELOPMENT OF THE WOODCUT.

Among the many fellow creatures that man finds around him hardly any have had such power to attract his attention, occupy his thoughts, or fire his imagination as birds. There is, therefore, available a wealth of evidence of man's interest in birds right from the earliest times, even though this interest may have been inspired by the most diverse motives. Foremost among these are the attractions birds possess for earthbound man in their power of flight, and in the vitality and beauty expressed by their whole appearance and behaviour. Quite apart from the more esthetic satisfaction to which birds give rise, there is another very natural, and primitive, reason for close contact with the bird world. These creatures are fit quarry for the hunter, and various means are employed to effect their capture.

This fact may have induced man to produce the earliest pictures of animals on record, the figures created by the upper Palœolithic art of Southwestern Europe during the Ice Age, the first part of the Quaternary period. Many investigators think that these drawings may be taken to be magical figures, by means of which the hunter hoped to secure the animals thus depicted as his prey, or to protect himself against them (627; 628).

Bird pictures, it is true, form an insignificant part of upper Palœolithic art, as compared with its representations of the larger mammals which were hunted, but figures of birds are by no means rare in Palæolithic 'home' art, among the sculptures and outline drawings of which it has been thought possible to identify such birds as the Swan, the Wild Goose, the Wild Duck, the Crane, the Eagle, the Owl, the Raven, and the Black Grouse (591).

These small figures, made of, or on, such material as stone, bone, or reindeer-horn, cannot always have been intended for magical purposes, whereas this purpose is most often ascribed to the representations of animals found as mural decorations in caves, among which, however, figures of birds are rare (616, p. 86).

While birds are thus but seldom represented in the latter kind of Palœolithic art, it has been possible to identify a considerably larger number of species from drawings in a cave in Southern Spain, in fact probably no fewer than twelve species. Among these were forms such as those of the Great Bustard, the Crane, the Wild Duck, the Wild Goose, the Flamingo, the Glossy Ibis, and others; in other words, of birds that live in Spain to this day and, consequently were also natives of that country in the remote ages when the drawings were made, i. e. six or eight thousand years ago. For it is assumed that the drawings must be assigned to the Neolithic epoch (607, p. 3).

Animal figures dating from the later periods of the stone age have been found in other places, for instance in Russia and Scandinavia, where they occur in the shape of carvings on stones and rocks. Among these monuments of the past there are also figures of birds, such as swans and geese, and we have examples of a bird like the Great Auk serving as a model for a bone pendant (580, p. 59).

In addition to this evidence from the oldest times that birds have engaged the attention of man and stirred his imagination, we have other signs of his early interest in birds, to which their wings and power of flight, especially, have contributed. Numerous legends, myths, and supernatural ideas are associated with or draw their subject matter from the bird world, and some of them, by their wide distribution among the earliest civilised peoples, afford evidence of venerable age. This is instanced by the idea of the sun bird (765), the myth of a gigantic bird, such as the immense Garuda of the Indians, the Anka of the Arabs, and the Roc of the Arabian Nights, and the idea, so

1*

beautiful in itself, of the soul as a bird, a conception as old as ancient Egypt (908). Among the relics of the ancient civilisation of this and other countries we also find evidence of a real and more intimate knowledge of birds, for example in the form of figures as known from the Mesopotamian bas-reliefs, the bird figures of which are, however, so conventionalized that they are difficult to identify. On the other hand, ancient Egyptian art has produced no small number of birds (620) painted or in relief and executed with great fidelity. Among the pictures decorating Egyptian tombs in particular it is not unusual to find representations of birds. Some of these figures are of considerable age and are remarkable for their fine execution. One of the most famous is a fresco from the tomb of Ne-fer-Maat at Medum, showing six geese of three different species, according to Moreau (620, pp. 62—63), the Bean Goose (Anser fabalis), the Red-breasted Goose (Branta ruficollis), and the White-fronted Goose (Anser albifrons or erythropus) (738, pp. 120—121; 801, pp. 95—99). These birds are rendered in a very life-like way by the artist, who has succeeded in presenting their characteristic attitudes and movements. The painting dates from the earliest dynasty, and from so remote an epoch as 3000 B. C. at least. Figures of birds become more and more frequent in later Egyptian paintings, and other excellent pictures of birds might be mentioned (620; 780), for instance the frescoes of the tombs in Beni Hasan (Fig. p. 2), dating from c. 2000—1800 B. C. (726; 727; 826).

While pictures of birds dating from the earliest ages may thus be found in great numbers, written accounts of an ornithological nature are scarce until the Greeks became the leaders of ancient civilization. In the fourth century B. C. *Aristotle,* the greatest zoologist of the ancients, mentions several birds in his zoological writings, especially in Book IX of the work 'Historia animalium'. According to Sundevall (893), in addition to a score of doubtful species, he records over 150 forms which, however, are not discussed in detail. For in his writings 'the philosopher' attempted to elucidate especially anatomical conditions and the question of reproduction; and birds were not among the groups of animals in which he was particularly interested. The zoology of the ancients culminated with Aristotle. The succeeding period on the whole marks a deterioration, interrupted by some few bright points only, as will appear if we consider the contents of the big 'Historia naturalis' (37 books), written by *Caius*

Plinius Secundus in the first century of our era. He collected the material for his work somewhat indiscriminately from the writings of numerous predecessors. Adding nothing new of import, he recorded anything and everything about birds. Beginning with the Ostrich he treated them in Book X, and dwelt more especially on the real or fictitious traits of their habits and on their importance to man, with especial reference to their harmfulness or utility, for instance as food. But the natural history of Pliny became of very great importance to posterity as a source of knowledge of Nature. It was copied over and over again in the Middle Ages, by which procedure it was steadily reduced in value by clerical errors and misinterpretation.

The above-mentioned lack of discrimination becomes still more conspicuous among the authors of later antiquity. Thus *Aelian,* in the third century, gives random accounts of real birds as well as of imaginary creatures, and this downward path is followed until the final decay of the culture of antiquity caused by migration. After this the intellectual life of Europe steadily declined, reaching its lowest level about the year 1000.

That in spite of this retrogression the works of the ancient civilisations, including the scanty ornithological material, were not completely lost was due to the fact that relics of classical culture and of the early knowledge of Nature were saved from annihilation in three ways. First, by the copying of ancient works, especially in the monasteries, the Church using them as linguistic models and thus contributing to the preservation of the literary tradition. Secondly, indirectly, by the culture of the Arabs, who preserved part of the literary material of the ancients though, cramped as they were by unquestioning faith in the authorities, they were unable to add anything new of importance. To these must be added the direct contact of the West with what still survived of the ancient culture of Southern Europe, for instance in Sicily and especially in the near East, with which Western Europe came into contact during the crusades. A certain knowledge of the old literary works was preserved here and formed a source from which the Arabs, too, could draw their knowledge of and veneration for the science of antiquity.

There is also a good deal of ornithological material in the manuscripts of the Middle Ages, which were often illustrated with beautiful miniatures, characterized artistically by their lightness of touch and their freedom of execution. This material must have been largely derived from the remnants of a knowledge of Nature which had been transmitted from classical antiquity. The medieval figures representing animals were also in all probability influenced by Greek art in several ways, even though some of the pictures dealing with natural history which appear in the medieval and later writings were hardly transmitted directly from Greek and Roman antiquity. They date from a later age, which doubtless produced them without the old drawings as models, although these were not unknown in the works of antiquity. Thus Aristotle refers to illustrations in several passages in his writings, while Pliny, in a passage in his Natural History (book 25, chapter 2, section 4, § 8), criticises the coloured pictures of plants in works by Greek authors.

The custom of illustrating books is to all appearance derived from Egypt, the home of ancient book production, whence the Greeks not only adopted the material that originally formed the basis of bookmaking, papyrus, which was later replaced by parchment, but also the form in which the books appeared, the roll, as well as everything essential to the technique and decoration of books, including the use of painted pictures. Although no rolls of pictures have been transmitted from early times, illuminated manuscripts have come down to us from late antiquity and the early Middle Ages. They belong to the form of book which came into general use in the 4th century A. D. (605; 613). This was the codex, especially the vellum codex.

Thus the famous 'Wiener Dioskurides' or 'Dioscurides Constantinopolitanus', assigned to the year 512 A. D., is derived from the Byzantine sphere of culture. It is written in Greek on vellum and decorated with 507 pictures. This magnificent specimen, now in the Wiener Nationalbibliothek (Cod. Med. Gr. I), contains amongst other things (folia 474—485) a paraphrase of Dionysios' Ornithiaka, a work dealing with the catching of birds. Its author, besides describing methods of catching birds, also gives quite good descriptions of some of them. The paraphrase, which is reproduced in the second part of the facsimile of the manuscript (698) is ornamented with a number of pictures of birds, which àre often very beautiful. 23 of them are included in the text, while 24 are collected on a plate, the picture of a peacock bringing up the total number of miniatures to 48 (767; 8Ɖ5).

The natural history material in medieval writings often appears in a more or less corrupt form. This applies not least to the moral fables, mainly about animals and including several birds, related in an edifying publication 'Physiologus', originally written in Alexandria or in Syria in one of the first centuries A. D. It is a kind of collection of examples for the clergy, and in the course of the Middle Ages it obtained a wide circulation in many countries in several variations and was translated into most of the languages of civilised Christendom (781; 891; 910). Though 'Physiologus' is an edifying work rather than a book on natural history, it and its variations, the bestiaries (763), by their wide distribution acquired no little importance as a source of purely literary knowledge of Nature for laymen. Certain classes of the population, however, in spite of all their unquestioning faith in the authorities, obtained first-hand, though slight knowledge, in some directions.

Thus, within the domain of ornithology, falconry, a sport much in favour in the Middle Ages and supposed to be so old that it was practised in Persia 1700 years B. C., furnished opportunities for a certain direct interest in and observation of the birds within its range. Many illuminated manuscripts testify to the interest in this branch of sport shown by the upper classes of the Middle Ages. This occasionally led its devotees to a closer observation and a more thorough study of these birds. The classical example is the work on falconry written by the German Emperor *Frederick II of Hohenstaufen* in the 13th century, under the title 'De arte venandi cum avibus' (153). The Emperor had observed and studied birds for nearly thirty years before he made up his mind to commit his knowledge to writing, and it is clear that independent observations underlie his treatment of several of the subjects. The work not only describes the sport itself but also deals with questions relating to the anatomy, physiology, and habits, of the birds. The movements of migratory birds are discussed, as well as the mechanism of flying.

The text and the many hundreds of faithful colour sketches with which the work was illustrated testify to a close knowledge of birds gained through sedulous observation. Hence the sketches for the figures, which give reproductions of the flight of birds and the characteristic phases of their movement, are in all probability from the hand of the Emperor himself, for we know that he liked drawing. The final execution of the coloured pictures, however, as they appear in the manuscript preserved in the archives of the Vatican

(Pal. Lat. 1071), must be ascribed to artists at the Emperor's court. They occur in early copies of the work and reappear in later copies. It would seem natural to suppose that their execution may have been influenced by extant Persian, Arabian or antique drawings (766, pp. 332—336).

Our reason for dwelling on the work just mentioned is that it shows the Emperor to have been far in advance of his time as an observer and describer of Nature. He even permits himself to correct no less an author than Aristotle himself. His book towers above the majority of the works current in the Middle Ages, whose themes were taken entirely or partly from natural history. These were as a rule marked by their lack of independence and their unquestioning faith in the authorities. An example of this is the work which was usually employed as a textbook for instruction during the greater part of the Middle Ages, the encyclopedia compiled by Saint *Isidore of Seville* in the beginning of the 7th century under the name of 'Etymologiæ sive origines'. This embodied the learning of his time. The material had been collected from many sources, among which was Aristotle. Book XII, Of beasts and birds, is based mainly on the writings of Pliny and Solinus. Isidore's work was also widely used by other writers as a source. But it was gradually surpassed, the later medieval authors obtaining a closer knowledge of the writings of classical antiquity, amongst others of the works of Aristotle. These were especially utilised in the 13th century by the Dominican friar *Albertus Magnus* the first native of Western Europe to know the philosophy of the great Greek in its entirety. In the latter years of his life this learned man also occupied himself in writing works on natural history, here as in other domains basing his writings mainly on Aristotle. As the most prominent writer on natural history in the 13th century he composed a large work 'De animalibus' (665; 754; 873). Birds (768) are treated especially in Book 23, which contains independent material and, according to Carus (597, p. 235, cf. pp. 221—222), has much in common with the descriptions of birds in 'De naturis rerum', a work in 20 books written by a friar of the order of Albertus and his pupil *Thomas of Cantimpré*, presumably during the period 1233—1247 or 1248. The latter work, which enumerates 114 forms of birds, including however the bat, obtained wide circulation and became very popular. It was based on the works of many earlier authors, among these Isidore of Seville.

A German adaptation of Thomas of Cantimpré 's work was prepared in the years 1349—50 by *Conrad von Megenberg* who gave his work the title 'Buch der Natur', but did not include in his translation all there was in Thomas' original work, as 42 forms of birds are missing. As the first encyclopedia of natural science in the German language this work became one of the most popular and widely read books in the 14th and 15th centuries, as evidenced by the numerous manuscripts, sometimes furnished with illuminated figures, found especially in South German libraries.

2. THE ART OF PRINTING. WOODCUTS AND ENGRAVINGS. BELON AND THE ENCYCLOPEDISTS.

'Buch der Natur', together with other works current at the time and containing themes from natural history, belongs to the sphere of writings which were published in print soon after the invention of the art which at one stroke totally changed conditions for the spread of literary material. Manuscripts, being comparatively costly, had been reserved for the narrow circle of those who were able to obtain them; whereas the facility with which the printed book was duplicated meant that it could reach a far greater number of prospective buyers.

The first printed book containing material relating to animals was a work by *Rabanus (Hrabanus) Maurus,* Abbot of Fulda, later Archbishop of Mainz. He wrote many widely read, but not very original, books, among which was the above-mentioned work entitled 'De sermonum proprietate, seu de universo'. It is Rabanus' chief pedagogic work, a kind of encyclopedia in 22 books, based on the Etymologies of Isidore, and was printed in 1467 by Adolf Rusch at Strasbourg. The animals are treated in Book VII, in a series of chapters, one of which is entitled 'De avibus'. Other works with natural historical themes soon followed, thus the above-mentioned work by

Aristotle was issued in a Latin version, 'Libri de animalibus', by Theodorus Gaza at Venice in 1476, though a Greek edition did not appear till 1495.

While printing with movable type thus laid the foundation for the duplication of written works, it was the development of the woodcut that became the starting-point for the decoration of printed books with instructive pictures. The art of engraving figures on wooden blocks with or without writing, and printing them, was invented long before the art of printing. A similar technique was known in olden times, when plates, blocks, etc., were made with written characters for relief printing. At a later period pictures were even printed on stuffs by means of wooden models. This art probably came to Europe from the East in the beginning of the 13th century; but the process does not seem to have been employed for printing pictures on paper until about 1400 when printers, encouraged by the increasing demand for cheap pictures of this kind, used it especially for duplicating calendar pictures, devotional pictures, and playing cards, the production of which became common in Germany in the early part of the 15th century. From about 1418—50 cards were printed in that country from wooden blocks, while in the last quarter of the fifteenth century they were manufactured from engravings on copper, and on these, besides human figures, animals and plants denoted the various suits.

Through these channels woodcutting (604; 614), the earliest of the graphic arts, as well as the above-mentioned engraving on copperplates, which gained ground particularly in the 16th century, came to play a similar role in the diffusion of pictorial material to that played by printing in the dissemination of written records. As indicated above, woodcuts of German or Netherlandish provenance are known from the beginning of the 15th century in the shape of broadsheets or parts of blockbooks, though the earliest dated woodcut on record — a picture of Saint Christopher, now in the Rylands Library at Manchester — dates from 1423. Woodcuts at first consisted of simple line drawings, on which colours were subsequently laid; but this laying on of colours was given up to a large extent about the middle of the 15th century.

As regards technique, the relief process used for the woodcut much resembles the technique of book-printing, and soon after 1460 painted woodcuts first introduced into books printed with movable type. They gained greatly in importance in the earlier art of illustration precisely because they could be printed on the page of a book at the same time as the text. This method was first applied by the printer Albr. Pfister of Bamberg. The woodcut was soon also used for works of a zoological character printed in the earlier period of book-printing, being, in its most perfect form, unsurpassed at that time for the duplication of pictorial matter.

Conrad von Megenberg's 'Buch der Natur', referred to above, was first printed in this way at Augsburg in 1475 (dated 30th October) by Johann Bämler. He decorated the book, a folio volume, with twelve full-page woodcuts, the work being divided into 12 parts or books, to each of which belongs one woodcut (560, pp. 99—122; 585, pp. 73—79; 857, p. 14). The fourth part, 'Von den vögeln in einer gemein', is furnished with a woodcut containing 13 figures of birds (Pl. I, Fig.1). The popularity of the work, as a printed book too, appears from the fact that it was reprinted no fewer than six times before the year 1500. In the later reprints the woodcuts of the first edition appear with some changes, the number of them as well as of the figures in them being gradually increased until there are 14 figures of birds. The woodcuts may also be coloured, as in copies of the second edition (Augsburg 1478, Bämler), (588, p. 458).

The adornment of printed books with instructive or illustrative pictures of natural objects ultimately derives its origin from the custom of embellishing manuscripts with decorative pictures and ornaments. The pictures with natural historical subjects are not however so good or of such artistic freedom in these first prints as many of the ornaments in the manuscript literature. This may be due to a lack of ability on the part of the artists to copy the models presumably available in the manuscripts. Or it may result from the difficulty of having to represent objects of which the artist knew nothing, or had only such vague ideas that he had to produce his pictures by using his imagination to eke out the often very scanty and incomplete description, or with only the name of the natural object as a guide. This was especially the case when he had to produce pictures of foreign or fabulous animals and plants mentioned in the text. The result is to be seen in many of the odd-looking figures of animals which, in addition to the fabulous animals proper and several reproductions more true to nature, are met with in old natural histories dating from the infancy of the art of illustration.

A work of no small historical importance in illustrating the use of woodcuts for the reproduction of natural objects in the earliest period of book-printing is 'Hortus (Ortus) sanitatis', which may be characterised as the finest of the illustrated natural history works of the time. As indicated by the title, the 'Hortus sanitatis' ('Garten der Gesundheit' or 'Garden of Health'), is principally a medical work concerning remedies in which, therefore, mineral products, animals, and, in particular, many plants and their medical uses are mentioned. It is a compilation of the works of earlier authors or is based on medieval compilations presumably composed by a medical officer of Frankfurt, *Johann Wonnecke von Caub (de Cuba)*, who held this office from 1484 to 1503, or just at the time when 'Hortus sanitatis' was first printed. This was in 1485 (dated 28th March), when Peter Schöffer at Mainz printed the book in German under the name of 'Ortus sanitatis... ein gart der Gesuntheit' (facsimile edition, München 1924) (560, pp. 20—73; 585, pp. 79—90; 636). Several German editions were then published, some with coloured pictures. A considerably enlarged Latin edition was printed in 1491 (dated 23rd June) at the printing works of Jacob Meydenbach in Mainz. The adaptor of this work would seem to have wished to weld together the smaller German 'Hortus' and Conrad von Megenberg's then widely read 'Buch der Natur', the animals being treated in the same order as in Megenberg's work. The numerous editions and many translations at the close of the 15th and the first part of the 16th century testify to the popularity enjoyed by 'Hortus sanitatis'. The large amount of pictorial material which it brought into the market at a time when illustrated natural histories were rare doubtless contributed to its success.

The first edition of the smaller German version, the main part of which consists of 435 chapters, in which 25 animals and animal products are mentioned, is illustrated with 379 woodcuts made for the work. They are not very true to nature, none of them represents birds, and eleven only represent other animals. In the large Latin edition of 1491 several more animals are mentioned. This is divided into seven parts, of which the five that constitute the main part of the work, the discussion of the various remedies, consist of 1066 chapters, each of which is decorated with a woodcut, the illustrations being executed by different artists. In the fourth part of the work 'Tractatus de avibus',

which consists of 122 chapters, not only birds but also other animals of the air are dealt with, thus certain insects and bats, besides several fabulous creatures. Among the pictures in this part which, like the others opens with a full-page woodcut, there occur, in addition to the more credible and less striking (Pl. I, Fig. 2), some few which look rather mysterious, though they can still be explained without difficulty when due allowance is made for the scanty information from which the artist had to make his picture. Under the Ostrich (Strutio, Cap. 109) there is, thus, a peculiar picture representing two birds resembling, if anything, birds of prey, each holding a horseshoe in its beak (Pl. I, Fig. 4), a pictorial representation which survived for a long time, and is still found in Aldrovandi (cf. p. 11 ('De avibus', I, 1599, p. 591)). This was meant to illustrate the extraordinary digestive power of the stomach of the Ostrich, as fabled especially by Pliny (X, 1) (666). It is true that the same bird is mentioned immediately afterwards under the name of *Strutiocamelo,* a Greek name, meaning camel-sparrow. It is derived partly from the fact that the strange creature (Struthio camelus L.) has two toes provided with strong claws which may suggest the two hoofs of the camel, and partly from the fact that it cannot fly, though it has wings, but must be content to run on its long legs like the mammal in question. The name then suggested to the artist the novel picture of the Ostrich in which it is represented as a hoofed animal provided with wings.

The pictorial treasures of the first Latin edition of 'Hortus sanitatis' did not fail to stimulate artists to further efforts in the illustration of natural history, a contributory cause being the high degree of perfection attained by the art of woodcutting at the beginning of the 16th century through an improvement in technique, due especially to the work of such excellent artists as *Lucas Cranach* and particularly *Albrecht Dürer,* in drawing designs for woodcuts. The latter's interest in Nature often led him to chose models from life, as appears from the fact that he has depicted about 180 different plants and animals (769). In this way he and other artists such as *Sandro Botticelli* and *Leonardo da Vinci* helped to open people's eyes to the beauties of nature and to prepare the way for direct observation.

As regards the literary material on which the printers worked, it was still the older works that furnished matter for activity in the domain of zoology, such earlier pictures as were available generally serving as

PLATE I

Fig. 1. PEACOCK AND OWL. From woodcut in Conrad von Megenberg's 'Buch der Natur', 1475

Fig. 2. SWANS. From woodcut in 'Hortus sanitatis', 1491

Fig. 3. 'LAGEPUS'. From woodcut in 'Hortus sanitatis', 1491

Fig. 4. 'STRUTIO'. From woodcut in 'Hortus sanitatis', 1491

Fig. 5. THE GREAT AUK. *Pinguinus impennis* (L.). From engraving in 'Museum Wormianum', 1655

Fig. 6. BIRD OF PARADISE. *Paradisea apoda* L. From woodcut in J. E. Nieremberg's 'Historia naturæ', etc., 1635

Fig. 7. THE DODO. *Raphus cucullatus* L. From woodcut in J. Bontius' 'Historiæ naturalis & medicæ Indiæ orientalis libri sex', 1658

Fig. 8. PARROT. *Ara*. From woodcut in G. Marcgraf's 'Historiæ rerum naturalium Brasiliæ, libri octo', etc., 1648

PLATE I

Fig. 1

Fig. 2

Fig. 3

Fig. 4

Fig. 5

Fig. 6

Fig. 7

Fig. 8

models in the field of illustration. Thus, for instance, Albertus Magnus' work on animals, first printed in Rome — in Latin — in 1478, was published in the year 1545 by the printer Cyriacus Jacobi of Frankfurt in a richly illustrated folio edition entitled 'Thierbuch. Alberti Magni, von Art Natur und Eygenschafft der Thierer [sic] ... Durch Waltherum Ryff verteutsch'. The second part of the work, dealing with birds, is illustrated with more than 50 woodcuts, several of which are comparatively true to life (630).

A great many of these illustrations have been drawn from pictures of birds which a citizen of Strasbourg *Hans Weiditz,* and others, had made for various natural history books and pamphlets published by the well-known printer Christian Egenolff, who carried on his business in Strasbourg and later in Frankfurt. Other bird pictures in the work were drawn from figures in the Mainz edition of 'Hortus', 1491, for instance some of the foreign ones and the monstrous animal forms unknown to the German draughtsmen, e. g. the quaint picture of the Ptarmigan (Lagopus mutus Mont.), which is called Lagepus or Lagophus and is represented as a bird with the head of a hare (Pl. I, Fig. 3). The name Lagopus (Greek 'hare's foot') is derived from Pliny who wished to call attention to the fact that the legs look as if they were covered with woolly hair like the feet of a hare. The artists concerned therefore felt that this likeness justified them in producing these extraordinary pictures. The greater part of the other illustrations in the work were also drawn from models. Thus, many of the pictures of quadrupeds are said to be copied from the illustrations of a well-known work by Michael Herr 'Gründtlicher underricht, warhaffte und eygentliche beschreibung ... aller vierfüssigen thier', published by Balth. Beck in Strasbourg, and dated 1546.

Based as they were on the authorities of the past, the above-mentioned works had brought about no great advance in zoological research, but they had helped to widen the scope of the interest in the literary material, and had created a desire for a closer study of the animate kingdom by immediate observation. This first began in botany; but zoology soon followed, investigators also including birds in their endeavours to obtain knowledge of the fauna of their native country, drawing first on the writings transmitted from the past and passing later to personal observation and direct study. The simultaneous desire for more authentic pictorial material was gradually met as fully as

possible, several artists having in fact to some extent contributed towards it already.

While the description and representation of plants thus preceded the direct study of animals, botanical research being stimulated by the importance of plants for medical science, in zoology it was birds — and fishes — that were first subjected to renewed study based on original observation. One of the reasons for this was, presumably, that a certain practical knowledge of these two groups of animals had been constantly kept alive by fishing, fowling, and falconry, while the markets, also, as far as these animals were concerned, offered large quantities of easily accessible material for examination. Thus the Frenchman *Pierre Belon*(619, pp. 40—45; 670; 786), one of the founders of the renewed study of birds, used the markets in the foreign cities which he visited on his journeys as the basis of his study of birds and fishes. In his main work, 'L'histoire de la nature des oyseaux', a folio of about 400 pages divided into 7 books, published in Paris in 1555, he mentions about two hundred different birds, mainly European, but some foreign (883). He makes many original observations, although he frequently refers to earlier authors such as Aristotle and Pliny and seeks to identify the birds they treat. The material is given in a certain systematic order and might thus serve as an example to posterity, as would also his treatment of anatomical and morphological conditions. Here he even employed the comparative method, depicting the skeleton of a man and a bird opposite each other in the first book of this work and comparing them bone by bone in the text.

The text for each form of birds described is as a rule illustrated with a woodcut made from drawings executed for the work by various artists(Pl. II, Fig. 1), though in his preface Belon only mentions 'maistre Pierre Goudet Parisien, peintre vrayment ingenieux' as the author of the drawings. Judged by the woodcuts, however, this artist, whose real name was *Pierre Gourdelle (Gourdel)* (848), had his faults as a bird-painter, especially if we consider the execution in detail of the 144 pictures of birds and the somewhat peculiar position in which they often appear in them. But Belon and Gesner (p. 10) were nevertheless among the first to use original drawings of birds for their illustrations; the former may therefore with some justice boast in his preface of being the first to bring 'les naïfs portraicts... des oyseaux: le naturel desquels nul autre n'avoit encor fait voir avant nous'. Belon, however, has to share the credit for

Bird Books   2 taking an interest in pictures of birds with some of his contemporaries.

In accordance with the literary attitude still so prevalent at the time, the study of ornithology was mainly carried on by the efforts of students to procure descriptions as well as drawings or paintings of birds. Hence the ornithological collections of the time consisted of pictures and notes which the student tried to procure either by his own aid or from his correspondents (641).

One of the pioneers of ornithology, *William Turner*, an Englishman, (619, pp. 76—78; 621, I), known as 'the father of British ornithology', in the postscript to his work 'Avium præcipuarum, quarum apud Plinium et Aristotelem mentio est, brevis & succincta historia', etc. (Coloniæ 1544, 8vo), which is based partly on his own observations, invites his readers, therefore, to send him drawings of birds that are unknown to them. For the sake of completeness, however, it may be mentioned that Belon recognized preserved specimens brought home from America, and that he was the first to publish a method of preservation; but for the time being this method for preserving the bodies of birds, or rather their skins, met with no recognition.

In the same year as that in which Belon's work appeared, a still more comprehensive and richly illustrated description of birds was issued by the above-mentioned Swiss physician and polyhistor *Konrad Gesner*. Applying the principle of omitting nothing and repeating nothing, he attempted to embody in his great work 'Historia animalium' all that was known in his time about the animal kingdom. Published at Zürich in 1551—58, it comprised four large folio volumes, and was not completed till 1587, the last volume being devoted especially to snakes (739; 789; 871; 890).

The volume dealing with birds ('liber III. qui est de avium natura') was published in 1555. It gives descriptions and pictures of a large number of birds (altogether 217 figures) material for which was drawn from many different sources, not least from the writings of the earlier authors, dating even as far back as the Early Ages. But this volume also contains original observations made by the author or by his contemporaries and fellow zoologists, from whom he procured information by correspondence.

In order to facilitate its use, the material is arranged alphabetically, i. e. quite unsystematically; closely allied forms are, however, often treated under one

head. The treatment is highly erudite, and is so detailed that Cuvier called Gesner 'the German Pliny'. The volume on birds, the pictures of which, with brief explanations appended, were also published separately in 1555 under the title of 'Icones avium', cannot compare with that of Belon for originality, and lacks his touch as regards system and anatomy.

Gesner's encyclopedic work acquired such prestige and importance during the following period that it is often regarded as the starting-point of modern zoology. Its great reputation and wide circulation were largely due to the fact that it was decorated with so many pictures in the form of woodcuts that it marked a new departure in the field of zoological illustration. The models for these woodcuts were derived from many quarters, for Gesner spared no effort in the provision of pictorial material.

Some of the illustrations, however, are copied from material already available in the literature of the subject. Thus, to mention an example, a figure of the Bee-Eater is derived from a work by Belon, dated 1553. But Gesner used his acquaintance with European scholars to the benefit of the pictures, too, for from them he received drawings of rare animals, or of animals not hitherto figured. The material for illustration was thus collected in many ways and seems to have been executed by several artists.

The only artist referred to in 'Historia animalium' is mentioned in the first volume of the work. His name is *Lukas Schan* and he is described as a painter of Strasbourg who depicted most of the birds from life. He is said to have been just as experienced a painter as a fowler. This Schan is identical with the artist who, in the literature in question, is erroneously called *Schrön* or *Schön* (785). A number of his original pictures of birds were found, and are still to be seen, in the collection of water colours of natural objects made by *Felix Platter*, a medical officer and professor of Basle. The University Library of that city still possesses 35 pictures of birds from Platter's collection. They represent, however, the few remaining examples of the more than 300 bird-pictures which originally constituted the collection (815). In some of the copies of Gesner's book Froschauer, the printer, had the woodcuts coloured by a painter from the original water colours. The result arrived at was not of any great excellence, even though the extant specimens of the original paintings are said to be very effective. Besides Schan other artists may possibly have executed some few pictures for Gesner's work on birds, for instance *Johann* (Hans or Grosshans) *Thomann* (n o t *Thomas*), better known as a painter on glass, whom Gesner mentions once by the Latinised name of Joanne Thoma, and *Hans Asper,* who is sometimes said to be Gesner's principal illustrator.

Several of the woodcuts are marked with the initials F O, an artist who seems to have drawn the designs on the wood as well as carving them. He is possibly identical with the wood-engraver *Franz Oberrieter,* who is known to have lived in Strasbourg, and who died about 1599.

In parenthesis it may here be mentioned that in 1555, too, a famous and profusely illustrated work of importance for the knowledge of the natural history of the North, the work by Olaus Magnus, mentioned later (p. 16), was issued.

The nature of the pictorial material in Gesner's work is so heterogeneous that it will be readily understood that the figures must differ much in value both from an artistic and a zoological point of view. For, while some of the portraits of birds fulfil such zoological demands as can reasonably be made in the circumstances (Pl. II, Fig. 2), e. g. certain figures of ducks, and the pictures of the Waxwing, the Nutcracker, and the Cormorant, others are not so successful. This applies, for instance, to such figures as those of the Nightingale, the Hedge-Sparrow, and the Gannet. Gesner's picture of the Solan Goose is really so bad that it is not unjustly characterized by the French ornithologist M. J. Brisson (p. 31) as an 'icon pessima' (69, VI, p. 503).

About 230 species of birds were described in Belon's and Gesner's works, only 15 of which, however, were natives of extra-European countries. Though Belon had estimated the total number of bird forms in the world at only about 300, the desire for a collection of the whole of the zoological and natural historical knowledge of the time in some easily accessible form had not yet been fulfilled. Other encyclopedists, as the learned men who devoted their energies to this task are characteristically called, were therefore free to take up this work. One of these was *Ulisse Aldrovandi,* an Italian and a professor in his native town of Bologna from 1560. His work is even more voluminously planned and carried out than that of Gesner, his collected O p e r a on natural history filling 14 big folio volumes in the Bologna edition. In spite of his passion for natural history and his un-

remitting industry and energy he was only able to write some few volumes himself. The publication of these was begun in his venerable old age, the first being the section on birds ('Ornithologiæ hoc est de avibus historiæ libri XII'), which appeared in Bologna in three folio volumes published successively in 1599, 1600, and 1603. In this Aldrovandus, who is not unjustly called the P o n t i f e x m a x i m u s of natural history by his contemporaries, has collected in a very scholarly way an immense amount of material which, however, he has not treated so critically as Gesner nor with quite the latter's originality. On the other hand, it contains several forms, notably foreign, not mentioned by the Swiss encyclopedist. A certain systematic order is observed in the treatment of the birds and their anatomy is given some consideration.

This work, like that of Gesner, had great influence on the study of natural history up to the end of the 17th century, though Buffon (pp. 32—33), whose great work on natural history produced at the close of the 18th century (74) indeed surpasses it, also so far as ornithology is concerned, says of Aldrovandi's voluminous work (74, I, 1749, p. 26) 'on les réduiroit à la dixième partie si on en ôtoit toutes les inutilités & toutes les choses étrangères à son sujet.'

The value of Aldrovandi's ornithology is enhanced by its many original illustrations (Pl. II, Fig. 3), which are often good and are generally better than Gesner's though the printed reproductions of the woodcuts do not entirely justify the commendation expressed by Aldrovandi in the passage quoted below. No effort or expense was spared in obtaining the pictorial material on which, and on the provision of a large collection, Aldrovandi spent all his fortune. His collection, which does not seem to have contained birds, however, formed the nucleus of the natural history museum at Bologna, in which city, too, all Aldrovandi's manuscripts are preserved. These are stated to comprise no less than 300 volumes, besides many blocks with the woodcuts for his works and many volumes with the original coloured drawings from which the woodcuts were made. The latter are said to be much better than the reproductions (663; 691, pp. 17—19; 713). The reputation enjoyed by Aldrovandi's original pictures is shown by the fact that Napoleon had them transferred to the collection in the Museum of the 'Jardin des Plantes', where they remained until after 1814 (802, p. 35). Aldrovandi could therefore with some justice call himself the I l l u s t r a t o r o f N a t u r e. He

2*

records his own efforts ('Ornithologiæ', 1599, præfatio) and the great expense to which he went to procure good pictures of birds, describing how he had them painted in their true colours, drawn on and carved in blocks of pearwood, and finally printed. He himself tells us that for this work he paid a painter, who was unique in this art, 200 florins a year for over thirty years, and that he engaged eminent draughtsmen at his own expense, viz. the miniature and animal painter, *Lorenzo Bennini* of Florence and *Cornelius Svintus (Swint)* of Frankfurt. 'In order that the birds might be drawn with as great a skill as possible' he also employed *Jacob Ligotius (Giacomo Ligozzi),* who was court painter in Florence to the Grand Dukes of Toscana from 1575, and was a celebrated painter of natural objects, including mammals and birds, especially the exotic species. Works of this kind are still preserved in the Uffizi Gallery and in the University Library of Bologna which, amongst other drawings of his, possesses seven volumes with animal figures and one volume where animals are shown together with plants. While Bennini and Swint thus evidently drew the designs on the wood, they were carved by a wood carver from Nürnberg, *Cristoforo Coriolano,* and by a nephew of his who, according to Aldrovandi's statement in the preface to the ornithological work, executed the woodcuts 'so carefully, so elegantly, that they seemed to be carved, not in wood but in copper'.

With the immense amount of material embodied in the text and pictures of these works by Belon, Gesner, and Aldrovandi, ornithological literature had, for the time being, reached its zenith. The world appeared to be enriched with so much knowledge of this subject that there seemed to be no foundation on which to base any further independent work in the way of compiling and observing, at least on a larger scale. It was quite natural, then, that a certain decline should be noticeable in literary production as well as in that of printed pictures, though lovers of Nature who collected pictures of birds and other natural objects were still to be found. Thus, in the Preussische Staats-

bibliothek at Berlin, under the signature L i b r i p i c-t u r a t i A. 1 6 — 3 3, there is a great work on animals and plants consisting of 16 volumes in large folio. This was written by the well-known French naturalist *Carolus Clusius (Charles de Lécluse),* who eventually became professor of botany at Leyden. His books, for instance his work 'Exoticorum libri decem' etc., (Leyden 1605, folio), the fifth book of which is devoted to animals, assisted greatly in spreading knowledge of the fauna and flora of distant countries from which travellers had brought home information. Hyperborean birds from the Faroes are also included, the material being derived from the Norwegian, Henrik Højer, a physician of Bergen (631, 28, pp. 84—89).

The above-mentioned work in the library at Berlin contains 261 animal pictures and 1856 pictures of plants executed in good water colours, about one-third of which have served as models for figures in various printed works. Volume II contains pictures of birds executed from life or from skins. It is not always possible to say who was the artist, but the greater part of the plants were painted by *Pierre van der Borcht,* a painter, engraver, and designer of woodcuts, who supplied drawings for the illustrations in the works published by Plantin (907).

New life was, however, gradually infused into the production of ornithological literature and pictures through the direct study of the bird-life of native and foreign lands mentioned in the following chapter. This also gave rise to a desire for the comprehensive classification of this great mass of material.

At the same time, the woodcut lost its position as the leading form of reproduction. From about the middle of the 16th century on, the art of wood-engraving declined for want of suitable tasks and, being less and less used, notably during the religious struggles in the 16th and 17th centuries, it was gradually superseded by engraving. By the close of the 17th century it had fallen almost entirely into disuse, but was revived, however, at the end of the 18th century by Thomas Bewick (p. 35).

PLATE II

Fig. 1. TURKEYS. *Meleagris gallopavo* L. From woodcut in Pierre Belon's 'L'histoire de la nature des oyseaux', 1555

Fig. 2. THE AVOCET. *Recurvirostra avosetta* L. From woodcut in Konrad Gesner's 'Historiæ animalium liber III. qui est de avium natura', 1555

Fig. 3. THE RUFF. *Philomachus pugnax* (L.). (Male in breeding plumage). From woodcut in Ulisse Aldrovandi's 'Ornithologiæ hoc est de avibus historiæ libri XII', Vol. III, 1603

PLATE II

Fig. 1

Fig. 2   Fig. 3

3. THE PROGRESS OF ENGRAVING. THE FIRST WORKS CONTAINING ORNITHOLOGICAL PLATES. INFORMATION ABOUT FAUNA GIVEN IN DESCRIPTIONS OF COUNTRIES AND IN TRAVEL BOOKS UP TO THE LAST QUARTER OF THE 17TH CENTURY.

While the art of engraving designs on metal plates is an ancient one, it was only towards the middle of the 15th century that the process of taking impressions from such plates began to be adapted to artistic purposes. Masterpieces were soon produced by means of the new technique; and with Albrecht Dürer, in particular, the art of engraving entered upon a period of greatness in the beginning of the 16th century.

Engraving (614; 615), however, is not a suitable means of producing illustrations in the text, for the engraving cannot, like the woodcut, be reproduced by the printing press but, as an intaglio process, the earliest of its kind, must be printed in a special copperplate press. Nevertheless, the engraving replaced the woodcut as the principal means of illustration when the latter declined, and it was therefore the engraving which dominated the decoration of books considered worthy of artistic pictures. Illustrative figures nearly always accompanied the text in the form of inserted plates. These were often printed on especially good and stout paper and, as they differed from the printed pages, among which they appeared as an almost foreign element, they were not included in the pagination, but were generally provided with special numbers.

Though the organic unity of the book and its pictorial material is somewhat lessened when the pictures appear wholly or partly in the shape of plates, on the other hand, the addition of this new element means that great care can be exercised in the execution of the plates just because their reproduction is independent of the printing of the text. The development of the illustration of zoological literature is therefore most apparent, generally speaking, in the plates, and in them it achieves its finest results. As far as ornithological works are concerned, the increasing use of engraving meant that for more than 200 years (c. 1600—c. 1830) it and its varieties were with rare exceptions predominant among the finer kinds of ornithological illustration.

The first purely ornithological work illustrated with a considerable number of engravings in the form of plates or, if the expression be preferred, full-page figures was published in Rome at the beginning of the 17th century. This was the first edition of *Giovanni Pietro Olina*'s 'Uccelliera', etc. (380), the illustrations of which, characteristically enough, occupy a kind of middle position between the hitherto familiar form, the text-figures, and the future form of finer illustration, the plates proper.

One of the first books with any considerable number of plates of birds belongs to the old sort of encyclopedic works, the possibilities of which in their usual form were not exhausted before ornithology had accomplished its final rupture with unquestioning faith in authority. It was published in 1650 and written by *John Johnstone,* a physician of Scottish descent, who, however, had been born on the Continent, where he spent the greater part of his life, among other occupations practising medicine at Leyden for several years. His work on birds appeared as part of a comprehensive description of the animal kingdom and is not remarkable for originality, except perhaps in the purely practical arrangement of the subject matter. But it was very well thought of right down to the time of Linnæus, as is evidenced by the number of editions and translations of it which were published (234—238).

One of the real causes of this popularity was the numerous figures it contained on its plates, which were reproduced as late as the close of the 18th century. These figures are said to have been executed by two sons of the publisher Matthæus Merian, s e n i o r, of Frankfurt, the engraver Kaspar Merian and the painter-engraver Matthæus Merian, j u n i o r, the latter of whom took over and carried on the publishing business after the death of his father in 1650.

However, even at that period a more direct study of Nature had begun the movement that was to alter the course of the study of ornithology and of the other branches of biology. Johnstone's work, with its pictures of fabulous birds, such as the phoenix, the griffin, and the harpy, seems in comparison to be a breath from the past.

Ornithology, too, benefited from the new conception of Nature and felt the effects of the new method of research employed in natural science. This movement spread during the course of the 17th century and involved an increasing interest in the life with which Nature surrounds man. In the course of the century this gave rise to a number of works describing

individual countries and districts, their fauna and avifauna.

At the same time the custom, dating back to antiquity, of keeping live animals in 'menageries', as these
collections were called, was extended. Rare, foreign
animals were the gems of these collections, which were
owned mostly by rulers. The menagerie established by
Henry I, 1100—35, at Woodstock in Oxfordshire, later
transferred to the Tower of London, and that kept by
Philip VI in 1333 at the Louvre in Paris are early
examples. These collections, however, were doubtless
made not so much for scientific reasons or to aid
research, as for the fact that they were curiosities, or
because they shed lustre on the owner. This was the
case also with the deer parks which, at the time of
the Renaissance, belonged to the courts of several
wealthy Italian princes (792). Even though the above-
mentioned collections did not as a rule serve any practical purpose, they still helped to arouse an interest in
animal life. Occasionally the animals served as models
for artists, as for instance the birds in the famous 'Ménagerie Royalle du Parc de Versailles', founded by
Louis XIV, which were painted by *Nicolas Robert.*
Some of the pictures were published in 1676, and
re-issued in 1773—74, together with the above-mentioned work by Johnstone (238).

Robert, who in 1673 had already published the
work 'Diverses oyseaux dessignées et gravées d'après
le naturel' (Paris, 31 pl., folio), was the first to bear
the title 'peintre ordinaire du Roi pour la miniature'.
He founded the collection of paintings on parchment
('Collection des vélins') of natural objects, mainly animals and plants, especially the latter, now in the library of the Natural History Museum of Paris. This fine
collection now comprises 6500 paintings, and at the
close of the 17th century it already contained nearly
300 pictures of birds, but additions are not made to
it now. A number of noted painters of natural history
subjects attached to the museum have contributed
specimens to it during the course of time (682—685).
Robert's total work consists of 727 parchments, 252
of which represent birds, the others plants. By a freak
of fortune a collection of his paintings, or copies of
them, and other French miniatures, originally belonging to Colbert, has found a home in the National
Library of Vienna.

Some smaller collections of engraved plates containing figures of birds had appeared before the publication of Robert's pictures, for instance a work 'Avium

vivæ icones', etc., with from twelve to sixteen plates by
the Flemish engraver *Adriaen Collaert,* published c.
1610, or 1580, and re-issued several times. The painter
Albert Flamen, too, who worked in Paris, issued several
minor works there, such as — about 1650 — 'Cyriosa
raccolta di varie e diuersi uccelli' (100 pl., 12mo) (588,
p. 343), 'Livre d'oyseaux', etc. (Paris 1650, and 1659,
12 pl., obl. folio), and 'Diversæ avium specie', etc.
(Paris 1659, 13 pl., obl. folio), while the English animal painter *Francis Barlow* drew pictures of birds
which served as models for engravings, executed
amongst others by *Wenceslaus Hollar* for the work
'Multæ et diversæ avium species', etc. (1658?, 18 pl.,
4to). Other plates with figures of birds by Barlow
occur in 'Various birds and beasts drawn from the
life' (London 1660—70, 66 pl., obl. folio) and in 'A
collection of birds and beasts', new edition (London
1799, 36 plates, (24 with birds), obl. 4to).

As will appear from the above, animal painting
also derived benefit from the patronage of princes,
particularly of such rulers as were interested in science
and art, the Emperor Rudolf II at Prague, for instance. He surrounded himself with scientists, such as
Tycho Brahe and Kepler, and also kept up the menageries established by the Emperor Maximilian II at
Ebersdorf and Näugebäu near Vienna and the menagerie at Prague, which latter existed in 1558 (719).
Nor did he neglect art. He employed the Dutch
miniature painter and draughtsman *Georg Hoefnagel*
(Joris Hufnagel) who worked in Bavaria as an animal
painter and was subsequently — as later, c. 1604—
15, was his compatriot *Roelant Savery,* also known as
a painter of birds — called to the court at Prague and
Vienna. Here he painted for Rudolf II, amongst other
things a miniature work consisting exclusively of pictures of natural historical objects, in four 4to volumes.
The work contains altogether 227 leaves of fine pictures
of various groups of animals, in Vol. I mammals, in II
birds, in III fishes, and in IV beetles and butterflies
(696). The work still seems to be in existence though
scattered among private owners. Presumably the animals of the menageries provided models for it.

For the Archduke Ferdinand of Tyrol, Hoefnagel
executed one of his most important works, the magnificent 'Missale romanum', now in the National Library
of Vienna. It is decorated with nearly 500 miniatures,
among which are representations of plants and animals, including several birds (696; 770; 771). Another
of his works of interest in this connection is in the

museum of the history of art in Vienna. It is a large folio — 61:83 cm — with miniatures on 100 leaves of vellum, representing a series of animals, chiefly marine animals painted in water colour by means of body-colours, supposed to represent 'die naturwissenschaftliche Sammlung des Erzherzogs Ferdinand'.

His son, the miniature painter and engraver *Jacob Hoefnagel,* also worked for the Emperor Rudolf II, whose court painter he became in 1602. It was in his service that he executed the plates, or at any rate many of the plates, for the 'Museum des Kaisers Rudolf II', a work now in what was the Imperial Hereditary and Private Library. It consists of two folio volumes, each containing 90 parchments on which zoological pictures are painted in oils. The second volume is devoted to birds and some of its pictures are rarities, thus pictures of the Dodo, and the 'poule rouge' (Aphanapteryx sp. Frauenfeld) from Mascarene Islands (151; 696; 772). Certain objects belonging to another class of institution, referred to above, i. e. collections of natural and other objects which assisted in promoting the growth of ornithology, are depicted in the first volume. These collections are now known as 'Museums', a name which dates back to antiquity, though in the form in which we now know them they date from the Renaissance. From the close of the 15th century, first in Italy and later in other countries also, we meet with such varied collections. They mostly take the form of 'curiosity cabinets' founded by princes, though other wealthy men or people with special interests have established such collections. They often contained curiosities, such as natural objects of a particularly rare or remarkable kind. This made the name 'cabinet of curiosities', appropriate, as it testifies to the very casual character of the exhibits. People interested in Nature of course paid great attention to the collection of natural products; both Belon and Gesner and, as mentioned already, Aldrovandi, having had considerable collections of natural curiosities. Birds were, however, seldom found in these collections, for people had no knowledge of the right way of preserving them or of keeping them when preserved. At first only single specimens of preserved birds appeared in the natural history museums at the close of the 16th century. The numbers increased during the course of the 17th century when the number of collections rapidly grew, and several natural history museums later to become famous were founded. The 'Cabinet du Roi' in Paris, which dates back to 1635 is one of these.

Among the earlier collections known to have contained preserved birds we may mention the museum founded in Copenhagen by the learned Danish archæologist *Ole Worm.* It was described the year after his death in 'Museum Wormianum', etc., an illustrated catalogue published by his son Villum Worm (Amsterdam, 1655, 10 figs. birds, folio) (Pl. I, Fig. 5). After Worm's death his museum was incorporated in the collection of the king 'Kunstkammeret' which was described in 1696 in a fine catalogue 'Museum Regium', etc., (Hafniæ, 1 pl. birds, folio) illustrated with engravings and written by *Holger Jacobæus.* A revised and enlarged edition was published in 1710 by *Johannes Laverentzen* (3 pl. birds).

A similar work, published in 1666, was a description of the cabinet of curiosities belonging to the Duke of Holstein-Gottorp which was later incorporated in the collections of the Danish kings. This work, 'Gottorfische Kunst-Cammer, worinnen allerhand ungemeine Sachen, so theils die Natur', etc. (Schleszwig, 3 plates with birds, obl. 4to; new edition 1674), was written by *Adam Olearius* (properly Oelschläger), and a copy of the first edition is now rare. It contains a good deal of ornithological matter and is illustrated by plates which, however, are partly executed from the pictures in 'Museum Wormianum'. Olearius is also famous as a traveller; in 1635—39 he was a member of an embassy sent from Holstein to Persia. An acute and conscientious observer, he wrote a work on this journey which was formerly widely read and in great demand. The first edition of this 'Offt begehrte Beschreibung der newen orientalischen Reise', etc., (Schleszwig 1647, folio) is now very rare. It subsequently appeared in several editions under a somewhat altered title and was translated into a number of different languages. In it the author also deals with the physical features of the foreign regions visited and gives desultory information as to the avifauna.

Another early museum containing birds was the collection established in England by the horticulturist and naturalist *John Tradescant,* s e n i o r, a native of Holland, whose son, *John Tradescant,* j u n i o r, kept up the collection which formed the nucleus of the Ashmolean Museum at Oxford. He described it in the work 'Museum Tradescantianum', etc. (London 1656, 12mo).

Only a negligible part of the collections founded in the 17th century has, however, been preserved in some form or other until our day, and the birds they contained have been long since lost. But they are the forerunners of the museum system which has since rendered such invaluable services to ornithology (622; 858). This may also apply to another of the new formations of those times, the learned societies or academies, whose name and nature were derived from antiquity though, like the museums, they did not flourish in Europe until the 16th and 17th centuries. Learned men had already begun to meet in Italy in the 15th and 16th centuries for the discussion of problems of common interest, and from these meetings societies, such as the *Accademia Secretorum Naturæ,* founded in Naples in 1560, evolved. This latter became the prototype of the *Accademia dei Lincei* founded in Rome in 1603, while the *Accademia del Cimento* was established in Florence in 1657.

Other countries soon followed this example. The *Académie des Sciences* was founded in France in 1666, the *Royal Society of London* in England in 1662, and *Academia Naturæ Curiosorum,* later the *Academia Cæsarea Leopoldina,* in Germany in 1652 (744). These established the type of scientific societies and determined their activities, which greatly assisted the development of the study of natural history, especially through the publications they issued. Their influence became greater, however, so far as ornithology was concerned, when, much later, societies or associations were founded, modelled on the earlier ones and with special zoological or ornithological aims in view.

The spiritual conflict and unrest of the 17th century had thus resulted in the founding of new bodies devoted to the study of Nature and, as already mentioned, the revival of the observation of Nature brought about the publication of the first works dealing with local avifauna. The first work of this kind to deal with European fauna was written by the German physician *Caspar Schwenckfeld* and published at Liegnitz in 1603 under the title 'Theriotropheum Silesiæ', etc., (4to). It is in 6 books and has as its subject the fauna of Silesia, including birds, which are dealt with alphabetically in the fourth book in Latin. Literature on the birds of other European countries and regions soon followed, for instance the description of the neighbourhood of the Lake of Lucerne entitled 'Beschreibung dess berühmbten Lucerner- oder 4. Waldstätten Sees', etc., (Lucern 1661, 4to) written in 1645 by *Johann Léopold Cysat,* a native of Switzerland. In this the author, who was town clerk of Lu-

cerne, deals with the birds in the 26th chapter, enumerating 70 species (808). A little later the birds of England were subjected to literary treatment by *Christopher Merrett* in 'Pinax rerum naturalium Britannicarum', etc. (Londini 1666; two editions in 1667), a cyclopedia in 12mo, chiefly of botany and medicine. It contains the earliest printed list of British birds which, however, only fills 15 of the pages of the work, though about 170 species are mentioned (621, III). Here we may also mention the first Scottish fauna 'Scotia illustrata sive prodromus historiæ naturalis', etc. (471), published in 1684, and written by *Robert Sibbald* (227, I, pp. 17—67; 818).

From the Northern countries, in addition to the museum catalogues already referred to (p. 15), mention should be made of the work of the Swedish Catholic ecclesiastic, Archbishop *Olaus Magnus* who, in the same year that Gesner's and Belon's works appeared, produced a famous work illustrated with many woodcuts, the 'Historia de gentibus septentrionalibus', etc. (Roma 1555, folio). This book was issued when he was far from his native country, which he had to leave in 1524 because of the Reformation, to live as an exile the rest of his life. As the first extensively planned account of the Scandinavian countries and peoples, the work is of no little value, even though it is full of exaggerations. The author's credulity and lack of discrimination are displayed in several places and are the cause of a number of more or less fantastic statements. And yet he knew large parts of Scandinavia from personal observation on his numerous journeys and, despite its defects, his detailed presentation of their natural history, including birds (pp. 645—696: liber XIX) is valuable in several respects (649; 839). As a matter of fact his work was widely read, being translated into so many languages that in the course of a hundred years about 20 different editions had appeared. In our own times a Swedish version has appeared edited by Michaelisgillet (Uppsala 1909—25, 4 parts, 4to).

The earliest reliable first-hand information about the birds of Norway occurs in 'Een saare kortt, doch sandru Beskriuelse om Loffothen, Vestraalen', etc., written in 1591 by *Erik Hansen Schönneböl,* a Dane, who was sheriff of Lofoten and Vesteraalen (880). He gives a very vivid description of the fisheries at Lofoten and also some account of bird-life. Several manuscripts of the work are in existence and, of late years, several editions of it have appeared, for instance in 'Det kongelige norske Videnskabers Selskabs Skrifter i 19. Aarhundrede' (I, 1817, pp. 449—486) and one by Gustav Storm in 'Historisk-topografiske Skrifter om Norge', etc. (Christiania 1895, 8vo; pp. 177—218). At the beginning of the 17th century the Norwegian clergyman *Peder Claussøn Friis* (879) wrote a description of Norway which, however, was not published until 1632 when it was produced in Copenhagen by Ole Worm under the title 'Norriges oc omliggende Øers sandfærdige Bescriffuelse', etc., (4to; re-issued in 1727, 8vo, and in 1881 by Gustav Storm in his edition of Claussøn Friis' collected papers (879, pp. 243—409)). Bird life is touched upon and the birds of the Faroes are mentioned, as the work, which also appeared in German in 1685 and became the model for a number of topographical works, includes the Faroes, Iceland, and Greenland. Friis also wrote a lengthy account, completed in 1599, of the natural history of Norway, with long sections on its fauna; but this manuscript, which came into the possession of Worm, was lost in a fire in 1670. The Faroes, whose bird life early attracted attention (631), were described at this period by *Lucas Jacobsøn Debes,* head-master and dean of Thorshavn, who gave an account of the natural history of the islands in his work 'Færoæ et Færoa reserata', etc. (Kjøbenhavn 1673, small 8vo). Pp. 124—148 give a good deal of information about 28 species of birds and the peculiar way in which the natives catch them. A Latin summary of the natural historical part of the work, written by Thomas Bartholin, was published as early as 1672 in his periodical 'Acta medica & philosophica Hafniensia'. The original work, in Danish, was translated into English in 1676 and into German in 1757, while an edition in modern language has been published in our own times (Thorshavn 1903, 8vo). Dating from the close of the 17th century there is a manuscript entitled 'Dyvr her i Norden' written by the clergyman *Peder Syv,* well-known for his publication of Danish proverbs. It has later been published by Svend Dahl (703; 704) and includes the names of a number of Danish birds with short notes based partly on the author's own observations.

European birds and animals were not the only subjects to be observed and written of; the remote regions of the other continents which Europeans had visited also furnished zoological matter for literary works. With their world of exotic, hitherto unknown, creatures they became especially important to the study of natural history, just because they stimulated obser-

vation and investigation. A wider horizon was revealed to man when the doors to these parts of the world were thrown open by those great voyages of discovery, of similar or even greater importance to biology than Marco Polo's journeys in Western and Southern Asia in the 13th century. Portuguese expeditions in the 15th century brought home the first information about the avifauna of Africa (625; 638). Towards the close of the century Christopher Columbus established connection with America, while the Portuguese Fernando Magalhães (Magellan) was, until his death, the leader of the expedition sent out by Spain which made the first voyage round the world in 1519—22. Five ships with a crew of 237 men started, but the 'Victoria', with a crew of but 18, was the only vessel to return. Among the survivors was the historiographer of the expedition, the Italian knight, *Antonio Pigafétta.* His account of the journey, probably written in 1524, contains also some brief notes on birds, information which, though incomplete, is of considerable historical interest. Four early copies of Pigafétta's narrative of the voyage exist, one of which is in Italy and three in France. The work has since been published, by Amoretti under the title 'Primo viaggio intorno al globo' (Milano 1800), and has appeared in several other languages.

The centre of activity for the observation of Nature outside Europe was still, however, the New World (652). Its fauna was soon subjected to literary treatment in works, the first of which were, however, written by authors who were not naturalists by profession. This applies, for instance, to the Spanish historian *Gonzalo Hernandez (Fernandez) de Oviedo y Valdés.* Sent out by the Spanish rulers, he visited America several times, staying there altogether for 34 years, and being appointed historiographer to the new countries by Charles V. He presented the results of his studies in 'Sumario de la natural y general istoria de las Indias' (Toledo 1526, folio), and in his principal work 'La historia natural y general de las Indias, yslas y tierra firme del mar oceano', the two first parts of which were published in 1535 and 1557, in Seville and Valladolid respectively (folio). The publication of the second part was interrupted by the death of the author, and a collective edition in four volumes by José Amador de los Rios was not published until 1851—55 (Madrid, 4to).

The above-mentioned works, especially the latter, contain several first-hand details, which produce a strange effect in view of the somewhat uncritical form in which they are presented. This also applies to the material relating to birds, several remarkable forms of which are mentioned, among them the humming-birds, here for the first time presented to the reading public.

The fauna of South America, too, was soon in-cluded in the investigations. In 1578 the French priest *Jean de Léry*, published an account of an expedition to Brazil in which he had taken part, and in his book he mentions certain birds. But it was not until the next century that the first work on the natural history proper of the New World was published. It had been written by the Spanish physician and naturalist *Francisco Hernandez (Fernandez)*, called 'the third Pliny'. He was physician-in-ordinary to Philip II and was sent by that ruler on a voyage of exploration to Mexico, the natural riches of which he was to study, and which he described in Latin manuscripts. He is also said to have caused a series of drawings to be made, at great expense, to illustrate the work he had planned. These, however, seem to have been lost. His notes were not published until 1615, when they were edited by Francisco Ximenez in Spanish under the title 'Quatro libros de la naturaleza, y virtudes de las plan-tas, y animales que estan recevidos en el uso de medi-cina en la Nueva España' (Mexico, 4to; re-issued in 1888). Hernandez' work became highly esteemed as a source of information for later authors, and a Latin version of it was incorporated in 1649 in a larger work in folio illustrated with woodcuts, published in Rome under the title 'Rerum medicarum Novæ Hispaniæ thesaurus', etc., by members of the above-mentioned Accademia dei Lincei. An edition dated 1651 also exists, the second title-page of which runs 'Nova plan-tarum, animalium et mineralium Mexicanorum', etc. It consists of works written by various authors and terminates with a section 'Historiæ animalium et mi-neralium Novæ Hispaniæ liber unicus in sex tractatus divisus', appearing under Hernandez' name, in which more than 200 birds are enumerated and briefly com-mented upon. This section is not illustrated, although several pictures of birds are found in other parts of the work.

One of the authors who extols the contribution of Hernandez is the Spanish Jesuit *José d'Acosta,* who was a missionary in South America (Peru) for 17 years. In his famous work 'Historia natural y moral de las Indias', etc. (Sevilla 1590, small 4to), which was translated into several European languages, he deals with the natural history of Mexico and Peru and also gives some ornithological particulars.

The manuscripts of Hernandez, as well as other works, evidently furnished material for the literary activity displayed by another Spanish Jesuit, *Juan Eusebio Nieremberg,* a native of Tyrol and a compiler of the same kind as Clusius, mentioned above (p. 12). Of special note is his 'Historia naturæ, maxime pere-grinæ, libris XVI. distincta', etc. (Antverpiæ 1635, folio), which describes the world of Nature, principally in the newly discovered regions outside Europe. The work contains numerous woodcuts (Pl. I, Fig. 6) by the Dutch draughtsman, wood-engraver, and printer *Christoffel Jegher (Jeghers)*. In the history of books he is best known as an illustrator to the publishing firm founded by Plantin, which brought out Nieremberg's work. Book X, of this work is divided into 99 sections, and deals with birds — as well as bats — a small number of the former being figured.

Towards the close of the 17th century there ap-peared the first really significant contribution to our knowledge of the fauna of South America. It was writ-ten by the German naturalist and traveller *Georg Marcgraf* who went out to Brazil in company with the Dutch physician Willem Piso, explored the country, and described its natural features in a work, the text and pictures of which give an excellent preliminary in-sight into the natural history of South America. After Marcgraf's death it was published by Jan de Laet under the title 'Historiæ rerum naturalium Brasiliæ, libri octo', etc., and was incorporated with a medical work by Piso in a volume illustrated with more than 500 woodcuts and entitled 'Historia naturalis Bra-siliæ', etc. (Lugduni Batavorum 1648, folio). In 'Liber quintus. Qui agit de avibus' over 120 birds are mentioned, some of them being depicted in the 55 figures found in this part executed from drawings by the author (Pl. I, Fig. 8). The above-mentioned Piso later published a work illustrated with woodcuts 'De Indiæ utriusque re naturali et medica', etc. (Amstelædami 1658, folio), of which he himself wrote the principal part 'Historiæ naturalis & medicæ Indiæ occidentalis libri quinque'. Birds are dealt with on pp. 79—96 and — some few forms — on pp. 318 —327. The text and figures are evidently based mainly on Marcgraf's work. In the same work, as well as a minor work by Marcgraf, Piso published 'Historiæ naturalis & medicæ Indiæ orientalis libri sex', etc., by *Jacobus Bontius*, a Dutch physician who lived in the East Indian Islands from 1627 till his death in 1631. This edition of Bontius is not, indeed, equally trustworthy in all respects, owing to the ready credulity of Piso, but it gives us valuable information about natural conditions in the East Indies. Birds are dealt with in 8 small illustrated sections (pp. 62—72 in 'Liber V. Historia animalium' (Pl. I, Fig. 7).

Besides the works already mentioned several others appeared in the course of the 17th century which contributed to throw light on the avifauna of foreign countries. Among these was the first English work on the natural history of America, 'New-Englands rarities discovered', etc., (London 1672, 8vo, and later edi-

tions) by *John Josselyn*, who had explored the country between 1638 and 1671.

Another work that may be mentioned is an account of a voyage in the Arctic regions, illustrated with 16 engravings, by *Friedrich Martens*. It is entitled 'Spitzbergische oder Groenlandische Reise Beschreibung gethan im Jahr 1671' (Hamburg 1675, 4to; facsimile edition Berlin 1923, large 8vo), and was translated into several languages, but it mentions only a few forms of birds.

All this enterprise had, meanwhile, given an immense amount of new material to research, and there was consequently an increasing desire to collect it and present it in a lucid form. This task was undertaken by Willughby and Ray.

4. WILLUGHBY AND JOHN RAY. THE FIRST WORKS IN WHICH PLATES ARE PROMINENT. WORKS ON FAUNA AND JOURNEYS UP TO THE LAST THIRD OF THE 18TH CENTURY.

In spite of the comparatively abundant amount of literature relating to birds which had appeared up to about 1675, ornithology had hardly yet attained a truly scientific position. The foundation of scientific ornithology was first laid by the united efforts of the two Englishmen *Francis Willughby* and *John Ray* in their work 'Ornithologiæ libri tres', etc., 1676 (532), which marks an epoch in the history of ornithology. It contains the first rational ornithological classification, and thus forms the basis of the system, a field which was further developed by Linnæus. These two men came from widely differing classes of society, Willughby being a country gentleman of means and with a series of distinguished ancestors, while Ray (or Wray, as he originally spelt his name) was 'the poor son of a village blacksmith' (228, pp. 17—146; 619, pp. 99—134; 621, VII). But, after their studies had brought them together at Trinity College, Cambridge, their common interest in Nature led to their intimate co-operation in, amongst other pursuits, making collections and travelling. Dissatisfied with the status of natural history, they set themselves the common task of producing a systematic description of the whole organic world, Ray undertaking the plants, Willughby the animals. Ray's contribution which, so far as zoo-

logy was concerned, was based on Willughby's preparatory work, was a very valuable one. So much so that he, who is sometimes called 'the father of English natural history', laid the foundation of the whole of systematic biology and raised systematics to an independent branch of science (840; 841; 842).

The two friends explored not only their native country but in 1663—65 they also visited several countries in Western and Southern Europe in order to collect material for their work, including pictures of birds. For they did not possess actual collections of preserved birds, and had only occasional opportunities of examining 'dried' specimens. It was the wealthy Willughby who acquired the material collected; thus in 1663 he bought at Strasbourg a number of pictures representing birds and other animals together with a written account of them. These were obtained from the author of the collection, a river fisherman interested in Nature, one *Leonhard Baldner*, who had written the text himself. The pictures, with an English translation of the notes on them, are now in the British Museum (607, pp. 197—200). The above-mentioned copy of Baldner's work, which contains a description of 56 birds, is dated 1653, as is a similar copy in private ownership with pictures of 55 species of birds on 57 plates (838). Baldner's 'Bird-, fish-, and animal-book' was not, however, completed until 1666 and several copies dated in that year are still in existence. Of these the best and most beautiful is said to be the manuscript in the Public Library of Cassel (782; 783; 843). In the same year that Willughby and his party visited Strasbourg he bought at Nürnberg a volume of coloured pictures representing about eighty species of birds, and these plates are still in the possession of his descendants by whom they are kept at Wollaston Hall in Nottinghamshire. Willughby evidently purchased other pictures of birds, and he and Ray did not fail to inspect Aldrovandi's collection at Bologna, where they had an opportunity of admiring six volumes of coloured pictures of birds, beasts, and fishes, drawn exactly by the hand. Willughby, who was one of the original members of the Royal Society of London, did not live to prepare the material thus collected for publication. But on the basis of his notes and observations Ray wrote the above-mentioned work 'Ornithologiæ libri tres', of which an enlarged English edition was published in 1678. Its origin makes it impossible to distinguish between the shares of the two naturalists in this work. The birds are divided into two main groups 'land-fowl' and 'water-fowl', being then further subdivided according to their habits, size, and morphological characters. In this way the first practicable classification was created, though it was in part based on biological features. The division into the two main groups was long retained, until it was superseded not so long ago by a classification based on anatomical features. As regards the form and arrangement of the description of the birds the work also became archetypal, for an attempt was made to render the latter as clear and accurate as possible for each form. It may also be mentioned that Ray-Willughby rejected the fabulous birds that had hitherto figured in the literature on the subject. The engravings for the work were executed at the expense of Mrs. Willughby. They are somewhat mediocre, and their utility for the identification of the birds is further diminished by the comparative smallness of the individual portraits. There was a good deal of material for the illustrations to begin with, and Ray received a number of pictures for this purpose from various quarters. Thus Sir Thomas Browne of Norwich let him have several drawings of rare birds executed by Browne himself or by his artist, some of which are still in the British Museum (607, p. 214). Ray received other pictures of birds

from his pupil, Sir Thomas Skippon, who was one of Willughby's and Ray's companions on their journey abroad.

At his death Willughby left Ray an annuity of sixty pounds, which became his chief source of income for the rest of his long and active life that provided valuable contributions to the growth of the study of natural history. Among these his establishment of the concept of species deserves to be noticed. It was therefore with good reason that the Ray Society for the publication of writings on zoology and botany was founded in England in 1844 in honour of his memory. Another of Ray's ornithological works 'Synopsis methodica avium', etc., was completed in 1693 or 1694, but was only published in 1713 by W. Derham (London, 8vo), while a French version, considerably enlarged and decorated with engraved plates, was issued by *François Salerne* in 1767 (414). To the above-mentioned English edition a considerable appendix had been added which, amongst other innovations, contained a small section 'Mantissam hanc avium Maderaspatanarum', etc., or a catalogue of the birds about Madras (Fort St. George). The material for this was derived from *James Petiver,* an apothecary of London, one of the few who, after the Tradescants, founded an extensive collection, a large mixed museum, described in his 'Musei Petiveriani', etc. (London 1695—1703, 8vo).

From all parts of the world this man sought to enrich his collections. He paid captains and surgeons of ships to bring home specimens for him, and published the observations made by Father *Georg Joseph Camel* when he was collecting zoological specimens in the Philippine Islands at the close of the century (London 1703). He tried also to improve the methods of preservation, being the author of a method, very much used in the 18th century, of preserving birds by 'drying'.

After Petiver's death his collection was purchased by an even more famous collector, the English physician Sir *Hans Sloane,* who is said to have offered Petiver himself £ 4000 for it. He had from his youth collected natural objects and other curiosities, which became very useful to John Ray. Sloane himself had the opportunity of making studies and collections of natural objects in the West Indies, which had, however, already been visited by other travellers interested in natural history. He thus became one of the pioneers in the investigation of the flora and fauna of the New

World, to which Willughby also had planned to make a voyage for the purpose of studying animal life, a plan which death prevented him from carrying out. Sloane stayed in the West Indies for fifteen months from 1687 —89 as physician to the Duke of Albemarle, the Governor of Jamaica, and on this island he had the opportunity of collecting a great many natural objects, especially plants, of which he was able to bring home specimens of no less than 800 new species. He published his results in his main work 'A voyage to the islands Madera, Barbados, Nieves, S. Christophers and Jamaica', etc., (474) which appeared in two volumes in 1707 and 1725 respectively. Although the substance is mainly botanical, a number of birds are also described. Figures of some of these are given on the engraved plates, but as they are not very good they are therefore of no great value. Sloane is also noted for his activities in the Royal Society (909, I, p. 450), whose 'Philosophical Transactions' he edited for 20 years. He bequeathed his large collection, the ornithological part of which amounted to no less than 1172 exhibits at the time of his death, to the British nation, on condition that the sum of £ 20,000, not a very high price as compared with the value of the collection, should be paid to his estate. The arrangement was carried through in the very year of Sloane's death, and his collection came to form the nucleus of the British Museum, which was opened in Bloomsbury in 1759 (677, I, p. VII—VIII).

In the middle of the century the natural history of Jamaica was again treated, this time by the Englishman *Patrick Browne*. Educated as a physician, he lived for a number of years in the West Indies, especially on the above-mentioned island, whose physical conditions he described in 1756 in 'The civil and natural history of Jamaica' (London, folio; second edition 1769). In the first edition the avifauna is dealt with on pp. 466 —483. The work is illustrated by engravings, none of which, however, depicts birds.

Plates occupied a prominent position already in Sloane's work on the voyage to the West Indies. At about the same time other treatises were published in which illustrations in the form of plates played such a prominent part that the works may be said to have been produced just as much for the plates as for the texts. Indeed, the latter may even play quite a subordinate role in books such as these, which inaugurated a series of a similar kind. Artists and others who were not ornithologists, were therefore frequently active in

this field both then and later on. Many of these works not produced by, or in collaboration with, ornithologists are of more importance for the history of book-making and illustration than for that of ornithology.

Some of the first works of this kind, like most of the rest of the ornithological literature of the time, were mostly of a faunistic character; some dealt with birds in general. The two large folio volumes by the English naturalist *Mark Catesby* belong to the former category. They appeared in London in 1731 and 1743, respectively, under the title 'The natural history of Carolina, Florida and the Bahama Islands' (94; 95). Printed with both an English and a French text, they contain material for a first account of the flora and fauna of the United States (573, I, p. 171; 640, 1; 653; 877). After studying natural history in London, Catesby made a journey in the years 1712—19 in the southeastern part of North America, returning home with a valuable collection of plants. Supported and encouraged by Hans Sloane and other eminent naturalists Catesby in 1722 went again to North America where, assisted by Indians, he explored Carolina and the neighbouring parts, eagerly studying Nature and describing, drawing, and collecting the most interesting natural objects, especially plants and birds. Many of these later found their way to Sloane's collection. In 1726 Catesby returned to England where he began to prepare for the publication of his principal work, mentioned above, the vividly coloured plates in which he engraved himself, after learning the art with this object in view (Pl. III, Fig. 3). With its numerous coloured plates, over a hundred of which contain pictures of birds, and its information as to the natural history of distant North America, Catesby's work enjoyed a considerable vogue. It was, in fact, so much in demand that, revised by George Edwards, it could be re-issued twice. A selection from the plates, together with plates from the works by Edwards, mentioned below, were also copied later by *Johann Michael Seligmann* a draughtsman, engraver and art dealer of Nürnberg. These were published with a German as well as a French and a Dutch adaptation of the text (462; 463).

As communication with the other continents developed, more and more interest was taken in the investigation of their avifauna. This applies not only to America, as shown by the above-quoted examples, but also to other regions, especially the East Indies, where the Dutch in particular took the lead. From Holland the priest *François Valentijn* was sent to East India in 1685. He was ordered to go to Amboina, where he met the famous naturalist G. E. Rumphius, then staying there. From here he made journeys in the Indian archipelago. In 1695 he returned to Holland where he remained till 1705 busily occupied with his collections and working up his notes. In 1705, however, he resolved to return to India. This time he stayed till 1713, the governor dismissing him in 1712, because he refused to go to an unhealthy post. In 1714 he went home to Holland and now devoted all his time to his collections and the writing of his main work 'Oud-en nieuw Oost-Indiën', etc., which appeared in no fewer than eight large parts (five volumes) with 1050 plates in all (Dordrecht 1724—26, folio) (690). An abridged edition of the work by S. Keyzer was issued in 1856—58 ('s Gravenhage, 3 parts, 8vo; new title edition 1862).

Uncritically, and with no great feeling for general effect, Valentijn gathered together in his comprehensive work all the material about the East Indies procurable in his time. In spite of its defects, it is a mine of information about these parts. It also contains an illustrated section with three engraved plates of birds, which are dealt with in Part III, pp. 297—329. Of greater importance for ornithology as well as for iconography, however, was the activity in the domain of natural history displayed by a compatriot and contemporary of Valentijn, the apothecary *Albert Seba*, who had made a fortune out of medicaments. With the aid of ship-owners and captains he obtained natural historical specimens from overseas for the collection which he founded in his native city, Amsterdam and which he later sold to Peter the Great for 15,000 f. He did not, however, give up collecting on that account, but accumulated a still larger and richer museum, which was one of the biggest natural history collections of his time. This enhanced his reputation in naturalist circles to such a degree that he was made a member of several learned societies (680; 860). The real interest he took in natural history is indeed evidenced by a work on his museum 'Locupletissimi rerum naturalium thesauri accurata descriptio', etc., (454) which he published in 1734—65 in four large folio volumes, several scholars assisting in the composition of the letterpress. By its bi-lingual text, Latin-Dutch and Latin-French, the work exemplifies how national languages were beginning to supplant Latin as the language of science, a process which, even in

purely scientific works, was completed in the course of the 18th century. Several examples, as well as the present one, show that, during the period of transition, texts were often printed in the national tongue as well as in Latin, thus rendering them accessible to a wider circle. Seba's work, in which the birds were treated in the first volume, was abundantly illustrated with beautifully engraved copperplates. It became widely known, and attained no little fame, not least on account of its rich pictorial material.

However, it was not only the strange creatures of distant climes which tempted writers to describe them in texts and pictures; the fauna of the European countries was now also taken up for treatment in works abundantly supplied with plates. So extensive a subject as the natural history of the Danube was thus treated by a remarkable personality, *Luigi Ferd. Marsigli*, an Italian count born at Bologna. After a military career, which ended with his degradation from the rank of general, he took up scientific work, which he had pursued in his youth. In 1712 he presented the rich collections he had made to the senate at Bologna, and they became the nucleus of the 'Instituto delle scienze ed arti liberali' of that city, which was opened in 1714 (709; 714; 793; 824; 825; 915). His work on the Danube was published in six large folio volumes in 1724—26 under the title of 'Danubius Pannonico-Mysicus', etc. (326), and is illustrated by a series of plates which reappear in a French translation published in 1744.

The zoology of the Danube is treated in the three last volumes, Vol. V containing the ornithological matter in the form of pictures which, however, are rather defective. Thus the figure of the Cormorant (Pl. 36) is called by Brisson (69, VI, p. 512) 'icon pessima'. A brief description not only of the birds but also of eggs and nests is appended. Considering the period this is remarkable, for the first work to deal exclusively with birds' eggs and birds' nests did not appear till 1737. This was entitled 'Delle uova e dei nidi degli uccelli' (161), and is due to *Giuseppe Ginanni* (or *Zinanni*), a compatriot of Marsigli and his equal in rank. The drawings for the above-mentioned fifth volume of Marsigli's work were contributed by his fellow townsman the painter and miniaturist *Raimondo Manzini*, who was court painter to the Duke of Modena and the Margrave Ludwig Wilhelm of Baden-Baden, and who specialized in depicting animals and flowers in oils and in water-colour.

Nor do the pictures in the first collection of coloured plates, representing mainly British birds, stand very high from an artistic point of view. According to its title 'A natural history of birds', etc., (4; 5) the work in question should be of a more general character, but the author, *Eleazar Albin,* drew his material principally from British avifauna, which supplied the greater part of the models for the original pictures drawn for the plates by Albin himself and his daughter Elizabeth. This work, in three volumes, first published in 1731— 38, testifies to his somewhat superficial knowledge of the birds which he figured and described. For as an ornithologist he was an amateur, but he was more capable as an artist, being a painter in water-colours and supporting himself by giving lessons in that art. According to his own account, he was led to the study of natural history through noticing the beautiful colours of birds and flowers. He issued several works of coloured plates with subjects from the animal kingdom, among which was another book on birds called 'A natural history of English song-birds', etc. (7; 8), first published in 1737. Although Albin complains in the preface to one of his works of the length of the list of names of his relations as compared with the relatively brief list of those of his subscribers, his works on birds, and especially the last-mentioned, attained considerable popularity so that a French translation (6) of his principal work could be published. Though his nature studies were hardly very profound, he nevertheless endeavoured to procure as many British birds as possible and, in his preface to his History of Birds, he requested the reading public to 'send any curious Birds' they came across to his address 'near the Dog and Duck in Tottenham-Court Road'. According to his own statement in the same passage he did not copy pictures already available. He says of the drawings that they are all 'done from the Life, with all the Exactness I could'. The same is said to be true of the descriptions of which he says 'I have done those with all the Accuracy I could from the very Birds themselves'.

In Germany, too, the study of the native bird-world began to make progress during the first half of the 18th century, encouraged in the first instance especially by sportsmen and lovers of birds. Even at the beginning of that century there were excellent German ornithological experts and observers of the habits of birds. *Ferdinand Adam,* Freiherr *von Pernau* is considered by Stresemann (642) to have founded scientific biological ornithology with his book 'Unterricht, was mit

dem lieblichen Geschöpff, denen Vögeln auch ausser dem Fang nur durch die Ergründung deren Eigenschafften und Zahmmachung oder anderer Abrichtung man sich vor Lust und Zeit-Vertreib machen könne' (small 4to; cited from Stresemann (885 b, p. 689)), which was published in 1702 and subsequently re-issued several times in a revised and enlarged form. Another German pioneer was the clergyman *Johann Heinrich Zorn* with his work 'Petino-Theologie oder Versuch, die Menschen durch nähere Betrachtung der Vögel zur Bewunderung Liebe und Verehrung ihres mächtigsten, weisesst- und gütigsten Schöpffers aufzumuntern' (title from Part I), (Pappenheim (Vol. II: Schwabach) 1742—43, 2 vols., 8vo).

Even before the appearance of this work by Zorn, his principal one, the publication of a large ornithological work containing many plates had been begun in Germany. This was 'Vorstellung der Vögel Deutschlandes', etc. (155), issued in 1733—63. It is due to *Johann Leonhard Frisch,* who gained great credit through this work by stimulating the newly awakened interest in the avifauna of Germany. The polyhistor Frisch (633, pp. 507—525), known perhaps even better as a fine linguist than as a naturalist, was head-master of the Gymnasium 'zum Grauen Kloster' in Berlin. A vicissitudinous career had made him acquainted with many different regions and countries, and this had sharpened and developed his powers of observation and interest in natural history, as well as his great practical ability, which he turned to account in silk production and during a period of his life when he was a farmer. His interest in ornithology was of no recent date when he began the publication of his bird book, since he states on that occasion that several of the specimens in his collection were over twenty years old. From what we are told in the 'Vorbericht' to his work, he had collected specimens of most of the German birds. 'Er hatte sie vorher einige Zeitlang eingesperret, oder auf seinem Hofe ernähret, um mit desto mehrerer Zuverlässigkeit ihre Eigenschaften untersuchen zu können, und liess sie hernach ausstopfen, um ihre äussere Gestalt aufzubehalten'. This collection, the basis of his great work, thus consisted of mounted birds which, however, seem mainly to have been obtained from the province of Brandenburg. In the course of the 18th century taxidermy gradually replaced 'drying' as a method of preservation, and it was a further advance when the birds, as in Frisch's museum, were kept in tightly closed glass cases by which procedure the ravages of moths and other harmful insects were checked. This improvement was rendered possible by the growth of the glass industry towards the close of the 17th century (641, pp. 117—118). In Frisch's collection each bird stood in its own glass case, arranged 'nach dem Leben'. 'Durch welche', as it says in the 'Vorrede' to the work, 'vor den Augen stehende O r i g i n a l i a das Abzeichnen, der Kupferstich und das Illuminiren desto natürlicher und lebhaffter werden können'. Frisch himself made some drawings for the work, and also drew designs for the plates for his large work on the insects of Germany, issued in 1720—38. His death, which occurred after he had finished the fourth class of the bird book, did not stop the publication of the work, which became a family duty, the task of its completion being transmitted from father to son for three generations. It was continued first by the sons of Johann Leonhard. *Just Leopold Frisch,* an evangelical preacher in Silesia, assisted especially in the last sections by the Danzig naturalist Freiherr *Friedrich August Zorn von Plobsheim,* completed the text with its brief descriptions, while his two brothers, *Philipp Jacob Frisch* and *Ferdinand Helfreich Frisch,* undertook the illustrations. The latter, who was an engraver, sportsman, and naturalist, worked at their completion for 22 years, supported by the former, who was actually a lawyer by profession but cultivated the arts of painting and engraving and had executed the greater part of the illustrations for his father's work on insects, mentioned above. Finally, after the death of Ferdinand Helfreich, the last plates of the work were executed by his son, the painter *Johann Christoph Frisch,* who took up engraving in his youth. Supported as he was by Frederick the Great, he finally became Director of the Academy in Berlin. He is especially famous for the decorative paintings which he executed for various palaces, for instance, that in Potsdam.

The figures of the plates are rather fine for the period (Pl. III, Fig. 1), although objections might in certain instances be raised against the colouring and the position of the birds, which are here, as in many later examples, characterized by a certain stiffness and awkwardness, having been drawn from mounted specimens. This, however, does not prevent the pictures from displaying an accuracy hardly ever attained before.

The English naturalist *George Edwards* also stressed the accurate portrayal of the birds rather than the artistic execution of the pictures. In the year of Johann Leonhard Frisch's death he began to issue a series of coloured plates with figures of animals, chiefly birds, which from the very first were his favourite subjects. After travelling in various European countries, 1716—20, and having had the adventure in Norway in 1718 of being arrested under suspicion of espionage, he began to execute his coloured drawings, the first series of which, entitled 'A natural history of birds', etc., appeared in 1743—51 (124) and was soon issued in a French version (125). He is said to have been so painstaking in his endeavours to make his pictures as lifelike as possible that he often made three or four drawings of the same animal. He himself informs us that (Part I, p. XIV) he 'made the Drawings of these Birds directly from Nature', sometimes from living specimens. He even engraved the plates himself, at the request of Catesby (p. 21), whose principal work he re-edited; as he says (Part I, p. XVII) 'my good friend Mr. Catesby put me on etching my Plates myself'. He also informs us that 'many of the Plates were directly worked from Nature itselfs' (Part II, p. 112). His artistic and literary undertakings could quite well be combined with the post of librarian to the Royal College of Physicians in London (127) which he obtained on the recommendation of Hans Sloane (pp. 20 —21). He sold his first works at such good prices that he was encouraged to continue his production of pictures with a fresh series entitled 'Gleanings of natural history', etc., which appeared in 1758—64 (126), the text being printed in English and French. According to his own statement, Edwards coloured most of the plates himself, and he tells us in the 'Gleanings' (Part II, p. IX) that many of the plates in this work are coloured from Nature 'in their proper colours by my own hand: so that they may be deemed original drawings' (Pl. III, Fig. 2).

Later on, as mentioned in the notes on Catesby, a selection of plates from both works, together with plates from the principal work of the latter, were copied by Seligmann (462; 463). It is true that the publications of Edwards are of a somewhat nonscientific character, for he was actually trained as a businessman. But they have been of importance in encouraging others to publish plates (pp. 31, 33, 34), and also because their producer was a clever ornithologist and a careful describer and painter of birds, often of such as were new to science and were thereafter assigned a place in the Linnean system. Edwards, it may

PLATE III

Fig. 1. THE BEE-EATER. *Merops apiaster* L. From hand-coloured engraving (Pl. 222) in J. L. Frisch's 'Vorstellung der Vögel Deutschlandes', etc., 1763

Fig. 2. THE HOOPOE. *Upupa epops* L. From hand-coloured engraving (Pl. 345), by George Edwards, dated Septem. 1. A. D. 1753, in Edwards' 'Gleanings of natural history', etc., Part III, 1764

Fig. 3. THE BLUE JAY. *Cyanocitta cristata* (L.). From hand-coloured engraving (Pl. 15), drawn and engraved by Mark Catesby, in Catesby's 'The natural history of Carolina', etc., Vol. I, 1754

PLATE III

Fig. 1

Fig. 2

Fig. 3

be noted in passing, corresponded with Linnæus, and the great systematist himself made an index with Linnean names for the works mentioned here (311).

Edwards received material for his works from many quarters. Thus he dedicated Part III of the 'Gleanings' to Earl Ferrers in recognition of the fact that the latter — then Captain Shirley — had contributed a large number of birds intended for Madame Pompadour, but captured by him in a French prize. Another source from which Edwards drew for his 'Gleanings', used also for a time by others who wanted pictures of Indian birds, was a collection of drawings of animals and plants from Ceylon and the Malay Archipelago, which had been made by a Dutchman *Gideon Loten,* governor of Ceylon in 1752—57 (639; 716; 717; 760). Greatly interested in Nature and nature study, he, himself a draughtsman and painter, tried to secure pictures of the exotic natural objects by which he was surrounded. Whilst thus employed he discovered a Eurasian with a natural genius for painting, one *Pieter Cornelis de Bevere*[1]), whose grandfather was a Dutch officer, the rest of his relatives being Singalese. This man was admitted to the Governor's household and, though he had never been taught drawing or painting, whilst in his service made a collection of water-colours — though some may have been by Loten himself — 144 in all, 103 of which represented birds, 5 mammals, 7 fishes, 3 shellfishes, 3 cuttle-fishes, 10 insects, and 13 plants. The zoological pictures were all drawn from life or from animals just killed, and are said to be finely executed and yet to reproduce form and colour accurately. Later, Loten brought the collection home to Europe, where he lived in England for a time and allowed the naturalists in England to use the figures. One of them, a German *Johann Reinhold Forster,* to whom we shall refer later, affirms in the preface to his 'Indische Zoologie', 1781 (cf. 149) that the collection was lost in a shipwreck when Loten sent it to Holland; but this statement seems to have been made chiefly with a view to increasing the demand for the above-mentioned work, for, after having been long in Dutch ownership, the collection was acquired in 1925 by the British Museum (Natural History) (678, pp. 61—62).

Forster's treatise was not original but was mostly

a German version of a similar work 'Indian zoology', issued in 1769 (395) by the English traveller and naturalist *Thomas Pennant* (654; 761; 827), to whom must be assigned the credit of having published the first important work on British birds illustrated with coloured plates, i. e. the ornithological section of his 'British zoology' (392), first issued in 1761—66. An enlarged version of this work was published several times and a combined Latin-German version also appeared. Pennant (223, II, pp. 1—65; 607, pp. 228—235; 621, VI; 836) was a very prolific author, as will be seen from the great number of different plates engraved for his numerous works. According to his own statement they totalled no less than 802. His 'British zoology' with its brief and lucid descriptions filled a gap in the British literature of natural history and, together with the works of his friend, the above-mentioned Edwards (p. 24), served as a considerable stimulus to study, which was traceable in an increased production of ornithological literature in the British Isles. It was, therefore, much in demand, and so was the most important of his zoological works, the compilation 'Arctic zoology', 1784—85 (397), of which several editions and translations appeared.

The descriptions of his numerous journeys in Great Britain which he gave in his 'Tours' are, however, the best known of Pennant's works to-day. Illustrations for these were drawn by his fellow-traveller, the artist Moses Griffith, who also supplied designs for some of the plates in 'Arctic zoology'. Pennant's fame, however, is especially due to a secondary cause. As the leading zoologist of his country he was naturally one of the men to whom Gilbert White (p. 35) addressed some of the letters which became the basis of his famous account of the natural history of Selborne (526), letters whose material Pennant, we may note, freely used in the second and in the later editions of his 'British zoology'.

That Edwards in particular could embody so many new forms in his works was due to the fact that birds from foreign parts were brought in increasing numbers to Europe, especially to England and France, though other countries, too, received a modest share. Thus in Italy Marquis *Giovanni Gerini,* who was much interested in natural history, was able to collect a large number of Italian as well as foreign birds. From these *Xaverio Manetti,* the engraver and draughtsman *Lorenzo Lorenzi,* and *Violante Vanni* made a series of hand-coloured plates, which were not very good but

---

[1]) According to Ferguson (717). In 'Nieuw Nederlandsch biografisch woordenboek' (VIII, 1930, columns 91—92) the artist is called by the name of his Dutch grandfather, Willem Hendrik de Beveren.

4

which were published in the work 'Storia naturale degli uccelli', etc. (Firenze 1767—76, 5 vols., 600 col. pl., folio). The text is not very scientific and is bilingual like the title, having been written in Italian and French.

Journeys of exploration, wholly or partly for purposes of nature study, gradually became more and more common, notably after the time of Linnæus. The latter sent his pupils out to collect specimens, and one of the ablest, *Fredrik Hasselquist* from 1749 to his death in 1752 travelled in the Levant, especially Palestine, and made abundant collections and observations. Linnæus who admired the results of Hasselquist's work, published them himself in 1757 under the title 'Iter Palæstinum eller Resa til Heliga Landet' (Stockholm, 8vo). Published also in other languages, it mentions a series of birds on pp. 208—291. The year before the publication of Hasselquist's work a description of Aleppo, in Syria had appeared in London under the title 'The natural history of Aleppo', etc. (3 pl. birds, 4to), birds being mentioned on pp. 63—72. Its author, *Alexander Russell,* who had lived in Aleppo as a physician in 1742—53, was so successful with his work that a second edition and a German version could be brought out.

Several other journeys of exploration made by pupils of Linnæus might be mentioned; thus *Pehr Kalm* went to North America in 1747—51; *Pehr Osbeck* travelled as chaplain in a ship to China in 1750—52; and *Peter Forsskål* was a member, from 1761 to his death in Arabia, of the Danish expedition to the East, from which *Carsten Niebuhr* returned as the sole survivor. Printed accounts of these journeys or of their results are in existence.

Another of the pupils of Linnæus, *Johan Falck,* was, at the suggestion of Linnæus, given a post in Russia, where he took part in the natural historical exploration work carried out in that vast country during the 18th century, especially during its latter half. Considerable collections of ornithological material were secured and incorporated in the Zoological Museum of St. Petersburg. *J. G. Gmelin* and *G. W. Steller,* who were members of the 'Great Northern Expedition' to the regions round Bering Strait (Gmelin as early as 1733) which took place in the years 1734—41 under the leadership of the Dane *Vitus Bering,* had already secured no little scientific material in Siberia. An event of the greatest importance to the exploration of Russia and indeed of other countries was, however, the transit of Venus in 1769, on account of which Catherine II sent out an official Russian scientific expedition, or rather no less than 5 expeditions, in 1768. In the succeeding years they traversed the vast empire in all directions, partly to observe the transit of Venus, partly to describe the country and its natural history. The result was a number of works of which the one based on the material collected by the above-mentioned Falck (140) was not published till after his death, which occurred before he had completed the journey. Other members of the expeditions were *Ivan Lepechin,* whose treatise (286) appeared in 1774—83, *Johann Anton Güldenstädt* and *S. G. Gmelin.* The latter lived only long enough to publish the first three parts of his work with the expedition (issued in 1770—84) (162). Güldenstädt never published any of his material, but under the title 'Reisen durch Russland und im caucasischen Gebürge' (St. Petersbourg 1787—91, 2 vols., 4to) it was brought out by a German *P. S. Pallas,* the most famous member of the expeditions, who also edited Part IV of Gmelin's work. Pallas (851; 918) acquired a great reputation as an explorer, and his works (cf. 385—387), which appeared in 1766—1842, deserve to be noted, not so much on account of the plates they contain, as for their zoological importance. He gave excellent descriptions of the animals and gave them names, many of which have been retained to this day. On his scientific expedition in 1768—74 he travelled through various parts of the Russian empire, especially Siberia, and thus laid a solid foundation for the zoological investigation of Northern Asia. This journey also helped to establish his reputation as one of the most eminent explorers and most versatile scholars of the century, equally prominent in the faunistic and the floristic field. He gave an account of the journey in 'Reise durch verschiedene Provinzen des russischen Reichs' (St. Petersburg 1771—76, 3 parts, 3 pl. birds, 4to), which passed through several German editions and appeared in French in 1788—93 (new edition in 1794).

In Northern Europe, too, where Linnæus worked, the 18th century saw an increasing activity in the investigation of the avifauna. Linnæus and his pupils made numerous journeys to study the natural history of Sweden, and the master himself treated the fauna of his country in 'Fauna Svecica' (Stockholmiæ 1746, 8vo), in which 205 forms of birds (Nos. 45—249) are treated on pp. 16—93 in the section 'Classis II, Aves'.

In Norway, too, where Peder Claussøn Friis (p. 17) was the prototype, a series of works appeared which are of value for the information they give of the natural history of that country. The clergyman and historian *Jonas Ramus* dealt with the subject in his book 'Norriges Beskrivelse', etc. (Kjøbenhavn 1715, 4to). Pages 244—251 contain matter relating to a number of birds 'as well as flying insects', mentioned by their Norwegian names. Later, the physical conditions of the country were described by the learned Danish Bishop and Vice-Chancellor *Erich Pontoppidan* in 'Det første Forsøg paa Norges naturlige Historie' (Kiøbenhavn 1752—53, 2 vols., 4to), in which the birds are fairly thouroughly treated, about 100 forms being given in Part II, Chapters III—IV (pp. 91—166, 3 pl.). The book (882), creditable for its time, appeared soon after in German and English translations, in 1753—54 (and 1769), and 1755, respectively.

Shortly after the appearance of Pontoppidan's work the natural history of Northern Norway was treated by a clergyman and philologist, *Knud Leem,* in a work with the title and text in both Danish and Latin 'De Lapponibus Finmarchiæ', etc. (Kiøbenhavn 1767, 3 parts, 4to). The birds are dealt with on pp. 230—294. This noble work (882), a German version of which was issued in 1771, is decorated with many hand-coloured, engraved plates (1 pl. birds); the descriptions relating to natural history, including the ornithological ones, are augmented by extensive notes and details by Leem's compatriot, the learned bishop and naturalist *Johan Ernst Gunnerus,* who also contributed articles on natural history to the publications of learned societies, and acquired importance mainly by awakening the interest of his countrymen in the study of Nature (702; 736). As Bishop of Trondhjem he was one of the founders of the Royal Norwegian Society of Sciences and during his episcopal visitations in his large diocese he studied the flora and fauna of the country, thus gathering material for important works on many subjects, including ornithology. His contemporary and compatriot *Hans Strøm* a clergyman and naturalist, also contributed to the ornithological exploration of Norway by his writings in the publications of learned societies and his work on his native district entitled 'Physisk og oeconomisk Beskrivelse over Fogderiet Søndmør', etc., (Sorøe 1762—66, 2 parts, 4to; supplement 1784 in Vol. I (pp. 103—170) of 'Nye Samling af Det Kongelige norske Videnskabers Selskabs Skrif-

ter'), in which the birds are treated in Part I, pp. 215 —262. A later work, 'Physisk-oeconomisk Beskrivelse over Eger-Præstegiæld', etc., (Kiøbenhavn 1784, 8vo) has a small section on birds pp. 111—119 (881).

As regards Denmark's northernmost possession, Greenland, desultory information as to the avifauna of this region had appeared earlier, but the greatest progress was here due to the Danish missionary *Hans Egede,* who has given not a few particulars about the bird life of that country. In his works, especially in 'Det gamle Grønlands nye Perlustration', etc. (Kjøbenhavn 1741, 4to), a book translated into several languages, he enumerates a number of birds (pp. 35— 36 and pp. 51—55) as natives of the country (582; 611; 648). Information drawn from this work combined with communications from captains and from other sources was incorporated in a treatise by *Johann Anderson,* mayor of Hamburg, entitled 'Nachrichten von Island, Grönland und der Strasse Davis' (Hamburg 1746, 8vo) in which the birds of Iceland are dealt with on pp. 39—49 (1 pl.) those of Greenland on pp. 173—184, and of which numerous editions and translations appeared. The historian of the Hernnhut mission, *David Cranz,* who lived for a year in Southern Greenland from 1761—62, in his well-known discursive 'Historie von Grönland', etc. (Barby 1765— 70, 3 parts, 8vo; I: second edition, 1770), translated into several languages, also gave a brief list of the birds of these northern regions, which are treated in Part I, pp. 101—119.

Pontoppidan, already referred to above, in his work 'Den danske Atlas' (I, 1763, pp. 614—631) gave a general idea of the land and water birds in Denmark, which were shown on two plates. This was the first comprehensive list of Danish birds; 215 species (besides some domestic birds) are included. The first part of the Danske Atlas was translated into German and appeared in 1765. In the same year the natural history part of this translation was issued separately. The above-mentioned list is presumed to have been mainly made by *Morten Thrane Brünnich,* the founder of Danish faunistic zoology, to whom Linnæus once wrote in the style of the time, 'Would that we 'had more Brünnichs; natural history would then soon be perfect'. Although his work was partly entomological it is to him that credit must be assigned for having made the first Danish contribution of any importance to ornithology (567; 581; 610). He based his work mainly on the material in a collection of Northern birds belonging to Christian Fleischer, a judge-advocate, whose collection, by the way, also furnished material for Pennant's 'British zoology'. The collection itself is described by Brünnich in 'Ornithologia Borealis', etc. (Hafniæ 1764, 1 pl., 8vo), who also drew on it for his description of the Eiderduck in the compilation 'Eder-Fuglens Beskrivelse' (Kiøbenhavn 1763, 3 col. pl., 4to; the same year also in 8vo with uncoloured plates), which was published in the same year in German, and also was enlarged by a supplement.

A great many of the birds in Fleischer's collection had been obtained by *Johann Dieterich Petersen.* Living on Christiansø for 42 years he made observations and collections there (749). The only work he ever had printed is a small 12-page book, now very rare, entitled 'Verzeichniss balthischer Vögel, alle auf Christiansöe geschossen, zubereitet, und ausgestopft' (Altona 1766, 8vo), a catalogue of his collection of birds which he was offering for sale.

Iceland had already been included in the field of investigation by the middle of the century, first by *Niels Horrebow,* who wrote on its natural history in his main work 'Tilforladelige Efterretninger om Island', etc. (s. l., 1752, 8vo). Birds are mentioned on pp. 140—180. As the first authentic printed account of the country, this work, consisting largely of corrections to Anderson's above-mentioned book on Iceland, was translated into the three main European languages. In the meanwhile Horrebow was called home, and the investigation of the physical conditions of the country was entrusted to two Icelandic naturalists vice-lawman *Eggert Olafsson* and the district physician *Bjarni Pálsson.* From 1752—57 they explored Iceland under the auspices of the Royal Society of Sciences in Copenhagen. An account of their journey, based on their diaries, was given in 1772 in the classic work 'Reise igiennem Island' (377), of which German and French editions (378; 379) were published as well as extracts in English. The contents, which relate predominantly to natural history, also contribute information about the avifauna of Iceland.

In the western hemisphere British activity gradually asserted itself, the contributions of the British nation to the exploration of the globe becoming more and more perceptible. The English chemist and naturalist *Edward Bancroft* visited North and South America several times, collecting material for his work 'An essay on the natural history of Guiana', etc. (London 1769, 8vo), which contains some new information about the fauna, including birds, which are treated on pp. 152—187. The northern parts of the new world, Newfoundland and Labrador, were visited in 1766 by the famous naturalist and traveller Sir *Joseph Banks,* who thus commenced an activity which brought him valuable collections (667; 804). Banks also took part in one of the large sea-going expeditions that were sent out at the close of the 18th century. Originally of a political and economic character, they nevertheless became of great importance to the knowledge of the fauna and flora of the world, though the study of natural history was at first only a minor part of their programme. At the end of the 17th century the English navigator *William Dampier* completed a long and adventurous circumnavigation of the world. He described it in the work, so often re-issued later, 'A new voyage round the world', etc. (London 1697, 12mo), in which there are many references to birds. Certain ornithological observations were also made on the rapid voyage round the world in 1764—66 carried out by his compatriot Commodore, subsequently Admiral, *John Byron,* and described in 'A voyage round the world in His Majesty's ship the Dolphin', etc. (London 1767, 8vo).

The nation that competed especially with England in voyages of exploration during these years was France. In the same year that Byron finished his voyage an expedition with a large staff of scientists was sent out from France. Under the leadership of *de Bougainville* it made a voyage round the world which was brought to an end in 1769. It was the first to be carried out by a Frenchman, and de Bougainville gave an account of it in 'Voyage autour du monde', etc. (Paris 1771, 4to; second edition 1772, 2 vols.). The naturalist of the expedition, *Philibert Commerson,* was really principally a botanist, but he nevertheless made several valuable zoological and ornithological observations, especially of the avifauna and certain forms of birds, later extinct, in the Mascarene Islands, where he lived till his death. Though several of the birds collected arrived safely in France and were incorporated in the 'Cabinet du Roi', much of the material was unfortunately lost, fragments only being preserved, for instance in Buffon's 'Histoire naturelle des oiseaux' (74).

But the most important results during this period were obtained on the voyages round the world carried out by the famous English navigator *James Cook.* On the occasion of the transit of Venus in 1769, already mentioned, Cook started in 1768 for Tahiti accompanied by a staff of scientists. The naturalist of the expedition was the above-mentioned Banks (p. 28) who was assisted by one of Linnæus' most prominent pupils *Daniel Solander.* One of the artists was *Sydney Parkinson,* who before his departure had executed for Banks 40 copies of Indian animals drawn by de Bevere (p. 25). Fourteen of these copies were the originals for the plates in Pennant's and Forster's works (p. 25) on the zoology of India. Parkinson made many drawings during the voyage (677, II, pp. 173—179), but died in 1771 shortly before it came to an end. A wealth of material, though mostly of a botanical nature, was brought home by Banks who then, in 1772, made an expedition with Solander to Iceland which further added to his manuscripts and collections. Since 1827 these, like Banks' extensive library (563), have constituted part of the treasures of the British Museum, though the birds, which were all mounted, are no longer in existence. Some of the notes from the expeditions which these explorers made together have since been published, for instance, 'Journal of ... Sir J. Banks ... during Captain Cook's first voyage', edited by J. D. Hooker (London 1896, 8vo).

As has been mentioned, Banks' collection also included a number of birds which were collected during Cook's and other voyages. Several birds were also found in another English museum of natural curiosities, the famous collection made by Sir Ashton Lever, which was only broken up in 1806, after having been partly described in 1792—96 in Latin and English by *George Shaw* (467 (cf. 862b); 468) in the work 'Museum Leverianum', etc. (London, 6 parts, 72 col. pl., 4to). This was published at the instance of James Parkinson who in 1784 had won the collection in a lottery arranged by Lever (819).

Especially productive of results, though mostly from a geographical point of view, was Cook's second voyage round the world in 1772—75; the naturalists taking part in it were Reinhold Forster, mentioned above, (p. 25) his son *George Forster,* and, from 1773, one of Linnæus' pupils, Sparrman, who will be mentioned later (p. 39). The year before the expedition started, Reinhold Forster had published a work of importance for the knowledge of the North American avifauna, 'A catalogue of the animals of North America', etc. (London, 8vo). Several valuable observations were also made relating to the avifauna, especially of the Antarctic regions, on Cook's second voyage, of which an account 'A voyage round the world in H. M. sloop Resolution', etc., (London 1777, 2 vols., 4to) was written by George Forster who, during the voyage, made a set of drawings, which included several birds (677, II, pp. 179—199; 762). His father's description of the animals was published collectively by H. Lichtenstein in 1844 in 'Descriptiones animalium quæ in itinere ad maris australis terras ... 1772—74 suscepto collegit', etc. (Berolini, 8vo).

George Forster's work appeared in the same year as Cook's own extensive account of the voyage, but shortly before the latter. Sparrman, too, wrote an account of the voyage which was translated into several languages. Its title was 'Resa till Goda Hopps-Udden, södra pol-kretsen och omkring jordklotet', etc. (Stockholm 1783, 1802—18, 2 parts, 8vo).

As will appear from the above, the stimulating influence of the archiater Linnæus on the investigation of the fauna and flora of the world made itself felt in no small degree during the latter half of the 18th century. The part of his epoch-making contribution which influenced descriptive and systematic ornithology will therefore now be briefly mentioned.

5. PROGRESS IN DESCRIPTIVE ORNITHOLOGY, SYSTEMATICS AND NOMENCLATURE. LINNÆUS. BRISSON.

Right down to the close of the 18th century native and foreign birds were in many instances described and named from unpublished pictures, for it was not until this period that collections, formed mostly of preserved specimens, from which the descriptions could be made, became general. This was rendered possible by the progress of taxidermy. The various methods of preservation previously used, such as 'drying' by heat, preservation in alcohol, or even dipping in varnish, which were not very practical, were then abandoned.

Even *Carl von Linné (Linnæus),* the son of a clergyman from Råshult in Småland (Sweden), named and described several species of birds from the coloured figures in a collection of plates of Swedish birds which was never published. These had been produced during the period from the early sixteen-nineties to about 1710 by a predecessor of Linnæus in the professorial chair at Uppsala, *Olof Rudbeck,* j u n i o r, to whose household the young undergraduate Linnæus was admitted in 1730 as tutor to some of Rudbeck's younger sons. Some of the pictures of birds were executed by Rudbeck himself, while others were made by *A. Holtzbom,* his assistant draughtsman. Some of these plates (796; 797; 798; 829; 894), which seem originally to have amounted to 215 — besides some unfinished sketches — now exist in Sweden in two series, the original, containing about 206 plates, some with more than one figure, the other, a copy executed by Rudbeck himself, consisting of 108 bird pictures. They are stated to be carefully executed. Lönnberg says of them (797, p. 307): 'The colours are correct, and the different parts are often reproduced in their minute details.' A total of 153 different species is represented; in some cases the two sexes are shown, as are some species in their different plumages, which indeed in certain instances caused Linnæus to give the same species more than one name. The particular importance of the collection of plates lies in the fact that as the basis for some of the species in the tenth edition, 1758, of Linnæus' principal work, the 'Systema naturæ', it contains what must be regarded as the type-specimens of the species in question, the above-mentioned edition forming the accepted starting-point for zoological nomenclature, as all the earlier names are not accepted.

'Systema naturæ' first appeared in 1735 in Holland (Leyden, pp. 14, folio), to which country Linnæus had gone in 1734 on a journey which lasted till 1738. For a couple of years during that period he held the post of director of the splendid botanical and zoological garden in Hartecamp near Haarlem owned by the mayor of Amsterdam, George Clifford. The success of the 'Systema' was so great that 12 editions were issued during Linnæus' lifetime. In a kind of 13th and final edition, published by *J. F. Gmelin* in 1788—93, it had grown into a work of 3 volumes (in 10) with over 6000 pages. The number of the species in this edition had been greatly augmented owing to the large amount of material that had then been produced by descriptive zoology.

All through the tenth edition Linnæus made use of one of his most important reforms, which had indeed been attempted earlier not only by himself but also by others. This was the designation of each species by two names, the first of which was to denote the genus, the other the species. By the aid of this binomial system it was possible in a simple and easy way to name an animal (or a plant) which was thus definitely labelled. In fact, it rendered possible the further development of descriptive zoology (799), for it removed the confusion which had hitherto prevailed in the nomenclature. The pre-Linnean authors had no fixed rules for nomenclature, but named plants and animals, birds for example, sometimes by one name, and sometimes by two or three, or even by a long series of words, in the latter case amounting to a short description or diagnosis.

Linnæus, however, made a sharp distinction between the name and the description. As regards the latter he distinguished the brief diagnosis from the detailed description, and in his striving for clarity and brevity he was himself a master in making diagnoses that gave in a few words the typical features of each form, the chief characters, or the distinguishing features. This method also meant an advance of great practical importance, even though the brevity might be so exaggerated as to make the diagnosis insufficient.

Ray and Willughby in particular had begun the work of classifying and grading the multiplicity of natural objects. In this field Linnæus is the great leader. With his craving and ability for organization and order — on one occasion he is said even to have given his contemporary botanists military rank, as a joke, with himself as the general — he emphasised the importance of classification, and created a lucid and practicable system, firmly and logically built up with definite groups of a principal and a subordinate character, i. e. class, order, genus, and species, the principal groups of which also had their special names. In addition Linnæus also took into consideration varieties which he thought had arisen owing to the influence of environment and which he wished to class in their definite species.

The concept of species had previously been established by John Ray (p. 20), and the names relating to the divisions larger than species had indeed been used before, but not consistently nor in the exact sense in which they were employed by Linnæus. The introduction of the genus concept was an especially great improvement. Linnæus, abandoning Ray and Willughby's main division as to habitat, gradually divided the birds into six orders, which in the tenth edition of his 'Systema naturæ' were subdivided into 63 genera. It is true that this grouping, based mainly on superficial morphological characters, has long since been abandoned, but its main features long served as a convenient basis for research.

Although Linnæus (724) has chiefly been of importance to ornithology in the way of description, nomenclature, terminology and, to some extent, systematics, he was also alive to problems other than the purely formal ones. Thus he emphasized the importance of anatomical research and could recognize geographical and ecological problems. This appears for instance from his observations on the occurrence and his reflections on the migration of birds (679).

By a freak of fortune it was not his native country but England that acquired his valuable private collections, his library, and his letters, which became the basis of the 'Linnean Society' in London.

Linnæus' systematic efforts stimulated ornithologists to further activity in this field which, in his time, seemed fairly easy to survey, for the archiater himself thought there were only about 2000 species of birds, of which he gave 554 in 1758. The attempts of the period at systematization were not all equally happy, however, as will appear from the system of classification erected on external, especially numerical characters by *Jacob Theodor Klein,* town clerk of Danzig, whose treatises are just as dry as the birds he preserved by 'drying'. His literary works, some of which were published after his death, possess the advantage, however, of being illustrated by fairly good plates (254—257). A collection of 168 pictures of birds which belonged to Klein, and a number of which were executed in the period 1655—64 by the Danzig painter and engraver *Samuel Niedenthal* and other artists, are now in the Zoological Institute of the University of Erlangen (728).

Of much greater importance, especially as to the description of the birds, was the work executed by *Brisson* in France, where Edwards' treatises served as a stimulus, particularly as regards illustrations, though they were not long allowed to remain the only ones in the market. However, it was presumably Willughby who particularly influenced Brisson, an influence resulting in the rigid, and hence also somewhat monoton-

ous, construction of his large ornithology in 6 volumes, issued in 1760 (69), the text of which, like the title, was printed both in Latin and French to make the work more accessible. The birds in Brisson's work are divided into 26 orders, clearly and consistently distinguished, and comprising a total of 115 genera with altogether about 1500 forms. Binomial nomenclature had not been developed when Brisson began his work, and he did not employ it; but his classification of the birds, which of course is not now considered satisfactory, surpasses that of Linnæus (655). Of special merit are his introduction of a considerable number of genera and his detailed descriptions of the various forms, which were so accurate and exhaustive that Newton (623, p. 9) said of him: 'as a descriptive ornithologist the author stands even now unsurpassed'. Linnæus' brief diagnoses did not satisfy him, and it was not without reason that he could remark in his work (I, p. XI) 'ses caractères sont insuffisants.'

It was small wonder that Brisson's knowledge of birds surpassed that of Linnæus, for he had made a special study of this group and had much richer material at his disposal. A pupil of the versatile French naturalist *de Réaumur,* who is perhaps best known as an entomologist, Brisson became his collaborator and the keeper of his very valuable collection of birds, far-famed especially on account of its foreign birds. This had been collected largely by the renowned traveller *Pierre Poivre* from Cochinchina, the Philippine Islands, and particularly from Madagascar, and also by *Michel Adanson,* who brought home 33 species, which are described by Brisson, from his journey to Senegambia in 1748—53. Here, then, the latter had a rich field for his ornithological studies which, however, he abandoned for physics after his master's death, though he was actually one of the greatest ornithological experts of his time. His illustrator *Martinet,* who drew and engraved the considerable number of plates containing 500 pictures of birds, did not indeed produce any great artistic effect, though his plates surpass those of his predecessors in this respect, but as zoological documents the figures are fairly satisfactory. Martinet, who was actually an engineer but who worked as a draughtsman and engraver in Paris, was, however, to become engaged in a much greater task in connection with the immense collection of plates which was to accompany Buffon's account of the natural history of birds.

6. BUFFON AND THE 'PLANCHES ENLUMINÉES'. THE ORNITHOLOGICAL LITERATURE IN THE LAST THIRD OF THE 18TH CENTURY.

Although the impulses that emanated from Linnæus became very influential during the course of the 18th century, his views did not gain adherence in all quarters. Another of the famous biologists of the century, the Frenchman *Leclerc, Comte de Buffon,* who was born in the same year as Linnæus, held quite different views on living Nature and its literary treatment. Both belonged to a period in which naturalists, as well as other intellectual workers enjoyed an increasing social esteem and were amply supported in their activities by the upper classes. This invested scientific work with a halo, the light of which was reflected on its followers and improved their whole social position. Linnæus was raised to the nobility, Buffon was made a count, both receiving many other honours as well as great fame. Rousseau is even said to have kissed the threshold of Buffon's study. In 1739 Buffon had been appointed keeper of the 'Jardin du Roi', later the 'Jardin des Plantes', and the collection connected with it, the 'Cabinet du Roi'. Under his direction its collection of birds was considerably augmented, particularly by the efforts of his collaborator Louis Daubenton. The collection is stated to have comprised about 800 species, specimens being secured from exotic countries, for instance by the above-mentioned travellers Poivre and Commerson. In these surroundings Buffon from now on devoted himself chiefly to natural history, principally animals, and began the preliminary studies for his greatest work, the extensively planned and immense 'Histoire naturelle', etc., (74—77) in which he aimed at no less than embodying all that was known in his time about Nature. The first volume appeared in 1749, and publication proceeded steadily, Buffon, assisted by several other investigators, working at this book all the rest of his life. In 1770 he had got so far that he could publish the first volume of the section on birds. The quarto edition of this section was completed in 1783 (74), and was issued in several other formats (75—77). Buffon's collaborators in the ornithological part of his general natural history were: first *P. Guéneau de Montbeillard,* later Abbé *G. L. C. A. Bexon,* it is therefore not easy to distinguish between the shares of the leader and the collaborators. But the plan, the style, and the final editing must at any rate be ascribed to Buffon, who is said to have sometimes revised the

manuscripts five times in order to attain that excellence in the art of which he was master — purity of style in the treatment of the subject. He devoted so much attention to it that when he was admitted to the French Academy in 1753 he wrote the famous inaugural address 'Discours sur le style', in which occurs the well-known maxim 'le style est l'homme même', or as it was put later 'le style, c'est l'homme'.

From the very beginning Buffon's great work attracted much attention and it was received with almost universal favour by the literary world. Its popularity was primarily assured by Buffon's great literary ability which allowed him to present even the most difficult topics in such sparkling style, in such a universally understandable form, and so fascinating a manner that, as was said, even ladies found amusement in reading about them, a testimony of importance in 'le siècle de la femme'. No doubt the elegance and stateliness of his appearance also contributed to his success in the leading circles of the time. Hume said of him that he carried himself more like a marshal of France than like a writer, while Voltaire has said that Buffon had the mind of a sage in the body of an athlete (619, pp. 359—390; 695; 707; 721; 722; 784; 821; 822).

Apart from certain extreme ideas, affecting ornithology only as a part of natural history in general, the special merit of the work is principally due to the fact that — with the exception of some few predecessors — it was the first to create interest in Nature and natural history in wide circles. The numerous editions and translations afford striking evidence of this. Through it Buffon, became, in fact the prototype of a describer of Nature. On the other hand, the scientific treatment of the material was not on a level with the demands of the time, for strict systematization and description of species with brief Linnean diagnoses was far from Buffon's larger, more comprehensive view of Nature. For him there existed only individuals in the world of life varying from one another far more than is expressed by the larger or smaller groups into which the human mind subdivides them. For the forms vary from different causes, or to express it more precisely than Buffon did, and in more modern language: the species are not constant. He therefore did not use the rigid framework of systematics, but adopted another method, which he himself characterized in the introduction to the natural history of birds (the folio edition, I, p. XVIII) as follows 'au lieu de traiter les oiseaux un à un, c'est-à-dire, par espèces distinctes & séparées, je les réunirai plusieurs ensemble sous un même genre, sans cependant les confondre & renoncer à les distinguer lorsqu'elles pourront l'être; par ce moyen, j'ai beaucoup abrégé, & j'ai réduit à une assez petite étendue cette histoire des oiseaux'. Thus the treatment centres round selected, and often particularly striking, representatives of the 1500—2000 species of birds which Buffon assumed to exist. These are discussed at length often with sound individual observations concerning their habits, reproduction, and other biological features, while the allied types are more lightly touched upon. By this lack of systematic method Buffon found himself in opposition to the views defended by Linnæus and his circle, and the latter of course could not feel satisfied with Buffon's observations, which were often not very deep, or with his use of vernacular names, which caused later authors to give many of the species Latin names (76, note; 273).

In 1783 one of these, a Dutchman *Pieter Boddaert,* issued a list of the accompanying series of plates, the 'Planches enluminées' mentioned below, with their titles and names in Latin and the vernacular. Only a few copies of this list are known; it has therefore since, in 1874, been reprinted and edited by W. B. Tegetmeier. Its importance lies in the priority of many of Boddaert's generic and specific names over later accepted terms.

A fact that contributed to the success of Buffon's work on birds was that a large number of coloured plates were made for the two folio editions, probably because of the success Edwards had had with his plates. They were issued without any text, and about 500 of these 'Planches enluminées' had already been published when the first volume of the text appeared, the publication being begun in 1765 at the instance of Buffon. Under the supervision of E. L. Daubenton, Martinet, mentioned above, drew and engraved these pictures of animals, numbering more than 1000, the great majority representing birds (Pl. V, Fig. 2). A number of artists and assistants were also engaged on this gigantic task which was completed in the course of about 20 years. The plates do not, indeed, show any high artistic merit but, as zoological studies, they are on the whole good, and were in great demand for a long time, evoking a series of supplementary collections of plates as the knowledge of the forms of birds was extended (76, note).

Soon after the publication of the 'Planches enluminées' had been completed, Martinet himself began to issue a work with pictures of birds, which was, however, never completed, 'Histoire des oiseaux, peints dans tous leurs aspects apparents et sensibles' (Paris 1787—90, 9 vols., 483 col. pl., 8vo).

Buffon's natural history long retained its vitality and new editions were issued well into the 19th century. The first complete edition of the great Frenchman's works was published in 1798—1807 (80) by *C. S. Sonnini,* who travelled in South America in 1772 ---75 and in this way provided Buffon with information of the fauna of that land and the 'Cabinet du Roi' with specimens of South American species. After his return from South America Sonnini went to Egypt and thus obtained material for his work 'Voyage dans la haute et basse Égypte' (Paris 1799, 2 vols. text, 8vo, and 1 vol. atlas, 4to), in which he furnished contributions to the knowledge of the flora and fauna of this part of the dark continent.

Altogether, during the last third of the 18th century, interest in descriptions of the fauna and avifauna of various countries increased, whether they were based on travels in foreign countries or inspired by the Nature of the writer's native country or works on it. This interest was felt strongly in England, where Edwards and Pennant had been active, the stimulating influence of the latter seeming to have been of especial importance in starting a rich production of ornithological works. Some of these, however, were not very original, but had more the character of compilations (621, VI). They will therefore be only briefly mentioned, in so far as they have a certain book-historical interest, on account of their pictorial matter and their relative age.

To this series belong the various works issued by the artist and ornithologist *William Hayes,* who with his twenty-one children is said to have had great difficulty in making both ends meet by means of his artistic and literary activities, amongst the fruits of which were a series of plates which are neither exactly without value, nor yet very good. His 'Natural history of British birds, &c.' appeared in the first half of the seventeen-seventies (198). It also contained foreign birds, and these, predominantly rare and exotic species, were also depicted in his 'Portraits of rare and curious birds, with their descriptions, from the menagerie of Osterley Park' (London 1794—99, 2 vols., 100 col. pl., 4to), of which the first part of a new edition (4 col. pl.) with a slightly altered title is said to have appeared in 1822 (564, 1846, pp. 407—408), while another

collection 'Rare and curious birds' had already been
published in 1782 (66 col. pl., folio). In the same
category of works that do not range very high must be
included 'Synopsis of British birds' (London 1789—
92, 2 vols., 255 pl., 4to) by *John Walcott*, with plates
on which the descriptive text is printed below the picture, engraved by P. Mazell, for the most part from
the author's drawings from life. The work was also
published with coloured plates, but copies of this kind
are very rare. No great specific value, as far as the
text is concerned, can be attached to the large work,
seven volumes in folio, issued by the naturalist *William
Lewin* in the years 1789—94 under the title 'The birds
of Great Britain with their eggs, accurately figured'
(London, 323 col. pl.; second edition (306) 1795—
1801; re-issued in 1812). The text is a compilation,
and Lewin's plates are of varying quality; some are
good and clear, while others are badly coloured and
some of the figures are out of drawing. The preparatory work is said to have been in progress for twenty
years, during which time Lewin was under the patronage of, amongst others, the Duchess of Portland, from
whose collection he obtained material for the figures
of the eggs, receiving other material from John Latham
(p. 34), James Parkinson (p. 29), Thomas Pennant
(p. 25), and others. A work which, in spite of its
promising title, is of no ornithological importance was
issued by *Thomas Lord*. This was 'Lord's entire new
system of ornithology, or oecumenical history of British
birds', etc., (London 1791—93, 114 col. pl., folio);
but it is rarely found in a complete state and, when
it is, is therefore expensive. The year after the completion of Lord's work the self-educated *James Bolton*
(700) commenced the publication of his 'Harmonia
ruralis; or, an essay towards a natural history of British song birds', etc. (Stannary 1794—96, 2 vols., 81
col. pl., folio), a rather fine work for the period, with
illustrations drawn and engraved by the author himself, which met with some real measure of success (new
editions, 4to, London 1824, 1830, and 1845). *Edward
Donovan*, one of the main purchasers at Parkinson's
sale of the Leverian Museum in 1806 (p. 29), acquired from this about 500 lots, which enabled him to
open his own museum in London in the following
year. His extensive works on natural history do not,
however, attain any high standard from a scientific
point of view. Their value is to be found in the plates
which adorn them. These are quite good artistically,
for instance in his principal ornithological work 'The

natural history of British birds', etc. (London 1794—
1819, 10 vols., 244 col. pl., 8vo, also large 8vo; re-
issued 1815—20 (588, p. 322)); or his 'The naturalist's repository', etc., (London 1822—26, 5 vols.,
8vo; re-issued in 1834 (588, p. 323)) with 180 coloured plates, including some of rare and beautiful
foreign birds.

Of minor importance, too, was the supplement to
Edwards' works issued in 1776 by *Peter Brown*, flower
painter to the Prince of Wales, under the title 'New
illustrations of zoology', etc. (72), in which the artist
depicted mainly birds, while the text, which is of less
importance, was mostly due to Thomas Pennant. Ornithological subjects also predominated in a work, not
very important, but rather rare, issued in 1776—92
by the English draughtsman *John Frederick Miller*.
This was (867) 'Various subjects of natural history
wherein are delineated birds, animals and many curious plants' (London, 60 col. pl., large folio), a new
edition of which appeared in London in 1796 under
the title 'Cimelia physica. Figures of rare and curious
quadrupeds, birds, &c., together with several of the
most elegant plants', etc. Miller, who had accompanied
Banks and Solander as draughtsman on the voyage to
Iceland, engraved and coloured the plates himself,
41 of which contain figures of birds 'from the subjects
themselves', while the descriptive text for 'Cimelia
physica' is due to George Shaw (mentioned on p. 29),
who was employed at the British Museum, but devoted
his time less to the collections there than to the composition of his own works (467; 468), which were
mainly compilations. One of these, 'The naturalist's
miscellany' was continued by his successor at the Museum *William Elford Leach* (282).

Among the important British works at the close
of the 18th century special note must be made of
'The general synopsis of birds' (277), a practical and
very useful survey, issued with a Latin abstract and
supplements (278; 279) by the physician *John Latham*
in the years 1781—1801 (or 1802), a German adaptation being published by Bechstein (280). Latham
(811) was also interested in comparative anatomy —
he had studied anatomy under W. Hunter — and
was a most industrious man. Besides attending to his
practice he found time to compose this extensive work,
the plates in which he made himself. He collected a
large and fine museum and was in communication
with the leading ornithologists of his day, for instance
Thomas Pennant (p. 25), and also revised the orni-

PLATE IV

Fig. 1. THE STRAW-CRESTED FLYCATCHER. *Elaenia caniceps* (Sw.). From hand-coloured lithograph (Pl. 49) by W. Swainson in Swainson's 'A selection of the birds of Brazil and Mexico', 1841.

Fig. 2. THE BEARDED MANAKIN. *Manacus manacus* (L.). (Adult male). From hand-coloured lithograph (Pl. 26) by W. Swainson in Swainson's 'A selection of the birds of Brazil and Mexico', 1841

Fig. 3. THE FIELDFARE. *Turdus pilaris* L. From woodcut by T. Bewick in Bewick's 'History of British birds', Vol. I, 1804

Fig. 4. THE ROBIN. *Erithacus rubecula* (L.). From woodcut by T. Bewick in Bewick's 'History of British birds', Vol. I, 1804

Fig. 5. THE PUFFIN. *Fratercula arctica* (L.). (Summer plumage). From woodcut by T. Bewick in Bewick's 'History of British birds', Vol. II, 1804

Fig. 6. THE GREAT CRESTED GREBE. *Podicipes cristatus* (L.). From woodcut by T. Bewick in Bewick's 'History of British birds', Vol. II, 1804

PLATE IV

Fig. 1

Fig. 2

Fig. 3

Fig. 4

Fig. 5

Fig. 6

thological section in the posthumous edition of the latter's British zoology (399). Latham described several hundred birds for the first time and named nearly two hundred new forms. Most of these came from Australia, from where many animals were brought to England after the country had been settled in 1788, for instance by means of the voyage of the governor, Phillip, to Botany Bay. Latham described the birds in the work on this voyage published in 1789 (402), while George Shaw treated the birds in a work about a voyage to New South Wales by Surgeon-General *John White,* published in 1790 (527; 650). Some of Latham's descriptions in 'Supplement II' (1801 or 1802) to his 'Synopsis' are based on a series of 512 original water-colour drawings of objects in the neighbourhood of Port Jackson executed by *Thomas Watling* (813) in the period about 1788—92, and the figures in question therefore form the types of Latham's descriptions. These drawings are now in the Zoological Department of the British Museum, while a duplicate copy, called the 'Lambert' drawings, is in private ownership in England. There is another series of drawings by Watling in the British Museum, and some of the plates in White's work, just referred to, were executed from these.

Latham had amassed a fortune by his activities, but was so unfortunate as to lose a great deal of money in his old age, and this is said to have been one of the reasons why, when past eighty, he issued an adaptation of his main work. This had, however, already been contemplated. It appeared in its new, considerably enlarged shape in 1821—28 under the title 'A general history of birds' (279, note).

Another of the finest private collections in British ownership belonged to *Marmaduke Tunstall,* whose collection now forms the nucleus of the Museum of Newcastle. The ornithological collection, especially, was good. Tunstall, who was not content with acquiring and preserving dead specimens, had also a collection of live birds and animals. His ornithological interest manifested itself among other ways in his composition and anonymous publication of a not very large, but important work, 'Ornithologia Britannica', etc. (London 1771, folio), a catalogue, a few pages long, of British birds, whose names are given in Latin, English, and French. In 1880 it was re-edited by Alfred Newton with brief notes on the author (900). Ornithology benefited from the birds in his collections in other ways also. Peter Brown (p. 34) took the models for several of his drawings from it, and the famous reviver of the art

of wood-engraving, *Thomas Bewick,* had an opportunity of drawing several of the birds during his examination of the collection after the death of Tunstall.

Through the 'History of British birds', first published at Newcastle in 1797—1804 in two volumes, 8vo, which saw altogether eight editions, the last appearing in 1847, Bewick had great influence on the stimulation of interest in ornithology in Great Britain (621, VIII). It was not, however, as an ornithologist that Bewick (460, pp. 17—51; 673; 847; 897; 898) achieved his great success. The text, which is neither especially interesting nor valuable, was based on works that were available at the time, particularly Pennant's. Most of the first volume was written by the engraver *Ralph Beilby* who collaborated with Bewick, while the latter compiled the text for the last volume himself. Hence it is primarily the fine woodcuts with which Bewick illustrated the work that explain its wide circulation and popularity, for it is in this very bird book that the artist's best woodcuts are to be found (Pl. IV, Figs. 3—6). Of even greater influence, however, was the description which the clergyman *Gilbert White* gave in 1789 of the natural history of his native parish, in 'The natural history and antiquities of Selborne' (526; 757; 828). Based mainly on letters to Thomas Pennant and the Hon. Daines Barrington this work, of which numerous editions have been published (807), has attained a fame enjoyed by few other literary works in Great Britain, where, as R. Bowdler Sharpe tells us (526, I, p. XVIII), it 'has been given to most of us as a prize at school — it is included amongst the "hundred best books" which every one is expected to read in these days, or to gather into a standard library'. One of the classic works of British ornithology, it has, perhaps more than any other, acted as a stimulus and contributed to awaken and quicken the interest in the study of wild Nature in Great Britain. Helped by his great literary power its author must here have struck chords that echo deep in the hearts of the British people.

On the European continent, too, an increase in ornithological activity could be noticed which gradually tended to make the study of birds independent and to separate this branch of science somewhat from immediate connection with the general cultural development.

At the same time as Buffon, in 1770, began to issue his 'Histoire naturelle des oiseaux', a Dutch clergyman, *Cornelis Nozeman,* who took a great interest

5•

in natural history, started the publication of his main work, 'Nederlandsche vogelen', etc. (369), in which the entire avifauna of the country is for the first time described at length. The work, only completed long after his death, was published by the Amsterdam publishing firm Sepp, later Sepp en Zoon (779), founded by a son of *Christiaan Sepp,* who was also a bookseller and publisher and who studied natural history in his spare time, especially entomology. He was also a good draughtsman and a successful engraver and issued a famous work on Dutch insects which was completed by his eldest son, the *Jan Christiaan Sepp* referred to above. The latter had from his youth occupied himself not only with the book trade, but also with entomology and other branches of natural science, and was also a painter and engraver. This uncommon combination of accomplishments also proved of use to the bird book, father and son drawing and engraving the plates for it, which were fairly good. Its publication was continued after the death of Jan Christiaan Sepp by his son Jan Sepp, who carried on the business. For the last parts of the work material was obtained from the famous collection belonging to C. J. Temminck, since 'bijna al de Vogelen in dit laatste, en vele in het vierde deel afgebeeld, ontvingen wij daartoe van Zijn Ed.' (i. e. Temminck) (369, V, p. II). Nozeman, it is true, was most interested in the study of Dutch birds, but his activities can be traced in other fields as well, for example in the annotations with which he furnished a much debated Dutch translation (799, p. 29), entitled 'Geschlechten der vogelen' (Amsterdam 1758, 8vo; facsimile edition 1906), of the 'Avium genera', etc. (Bremæ 1752, 8vo), by *Paul Heinrich Gerhard Moehring* in which the author propounded a system of birds slightly different from that of Linnæus.

During this period the production of plates for the illustration of natural history works, as shown already in our account of British ornithology, became more and more common, and a large number of less important works of this kind saw the light. As an example we may mention the plates for the ornithology of Southern Europe which, under the title 'Ornitologia dell' Europa meridionale' (Parma 1769—73, folio), were issued by the animal painter *Clemente Bernini* of Rome, who worked at Parma as a teacher at the Collegio dei Nobili. The production of these plates, of which only about some twenty were published, was continued by Bernini's daughter Rosalba. They

are now in the Biblioteca Palatina of Parma. In Rome *Maddalena Bouchard*'s collection of mediocre plates in folio with figures of 133 birds was published (53), while at Nürnberg the engraver and publisher *Adam Ludwig Wirsing* engraved the plates for and published the work 'Sammlung meistens deutscher Vögel' (Nürnberg 1772—77, 2 parts, 50 col. pl., large folio), which is now very rare (855). Its text was written by *B. C. Vogel,* while the pictures were painted by one of the most industrious and able members of a well-known family of painters, draughtsmen, and etchers in Nürnberg, *Barbara Regina Dietzsch* who, besides birds, painted especially flowers and insects. Wirsing also engraved the not very valuable plates for a work published by him in 1772—86 with delineations of eggs and nests (537). The text was written by several authors, amongst others *Nathanael Gottfried Leske.*

In France Buffon's bird book with the plates belonging to it unquestionably overshadowed all others in this field. That, however, did not prevent others from issuing plates. Among these was the physician and naturalist *Buc'hoz,* a very industrious author of compilations of no particular value, which however, acquired a certain importance on account of the numerous plates of a companion work, his 'Centurie de planches', etc., begun in 1775 (73). Of minor importance, also, were two books with a series of coloured plates 'Elementa ornithologica', etc., (439) and 'Museum ornithologicum', etc. (440), issued in 1774 and 1789, respectively, by the German ecclesiastic *Jacob Christian Schaeffer,* superintendent at Regensburg, who displayed a lively literary activity in many fields and, amongst other works, composed a series on zoological and botanical subjects. In somewhat the same category of less important treatises may be included the 'Beyträge zur Geschichte der Vögel' (220) written by *Joseph Franz Jacquin* chiefly on the basis of material from the West Indies, as also the 'Beyträge', six in all, which were issued under the title 'Beytrag zur Naturgeschichte der Vögel' (Wien 1790—95, 271 col. pl., folio) by *Joachim Johann Spalowsky,* a regimental surgeon of Vienna who took an interest in natural history.

Of greater value for the progress of ornithology than these heterogeneous works, in which the plates play a conspicuous or dominant role, were the contributions to the knowledge of the avifauna of various countries of the European continent, which saw the light in this period, for instance the 'Gli uccelli di

Sardegna' (Sassari 1776, 6 pl., 12mo; German translation 1784) by the Italian abbot *Francesco Cetti,* in which several new species are described, the 'Versuch einer Naturgeschichte von Liefland' (Leipzig 1778, 8vo; second edition, 2 vols., Königsberg 1791) by *Jacob Benjamin Fischer,* an accountant to an orphanage in Riga, with Fischer's additions to this work in *J. J. Ferber*'s 'Anmerkungen zur physischen Erdbeschreibung von Kurland' (Riga 1784, 8vo), and finally a small work on the birds of Kurland (40), by the philosopher and jurist *Johann Melchior Gottlieb Beseke.*

In Germany, especially, where Frisch and his predecessors had acted as a stimulus, birds became the subjects of more animated research towards the close of the century, and interest in this section of the fauna of the country greatly increased. In 1791—95 the ornithological section of 'Gemeinnützige Naturgeschichte Deutschlands', etc., was issued (second edition 1805—09 (30)). Its author *Johann Matthäus Bechstein* here gave an account of the natural history of the birds of his native country, and described a number of new species and genera. In his 'Ornithologisches Taschenbuch', etc., 1802—12 (29) he treated the subject in a more condensed form. Bechstein attached no little weight to observation and description of the habits of birds, and by his own writings as well as his translations contributed to heighten interest in the natural history of his native country. He saw clearly that individual natural phenomena form part of a connected whole, and this was probably one of the reasons why he applied himself to the science of forestry, which had hitherto had few devotees in Germany. At his death he was director of the Institute of Forestry in Dreissigacker near Meiningen (669; 756). His productions cannot, however, compete with the great and famous work on the birds of Germany begun by *Johann Andreas Naumann.* The latter, the 'alte Naumann', belonged to a family which had owned an estate in Anhalt near Dessau from the time of the Thirty Years' War and had always been interested in the bird life there. Naumann, who had to take part in the management of the estate from his fifteenth year, had had ample opportunity of studying not only the land and forest birds but also the water birds that settled in certain parts of the district during some wet years. The water partly ruined the fields of the estate and was a hindrance to Naumann's farming but, on the other hand, it gave him plenty of leisure to devote himself to his favourite occupation, the study

of birds. In 1795 he could, then, begin the publication of his principal work (354), which was not completed until 1817 when several supplements had been added, and which contains an abundance of accurate observations concerning the natural history of birds. In collecting his material he received great assistance from his sons (664; 788), especially from *Carl Andreas Naumann,* who from his 10th year took part in this work and was therefore called by his father 'my chasseur'. In the years 1816—43 he shot or caught no less than 48,932 birds (!), and he was also an excellent observer of the life and habits of the birds. With his great experience and his knowledge of birds he was a valuable aid to his eldest brother *Johann Friedrich Naumann,* the most renowned member of the family (743; 745; 776). When little more than 10 years old the latter began to paint birds from life under the supervision of his father. From his 15th year he took part in his father's ornithological observations, and he was co-editor of the last parts of his ornithological work issued in 1803—17. On account of his talent for drawing and painting he was given as many birds as possible to delineate and, despite his youth, was entrusted with the drawing and painting of all the bird pictures and with the engraving of most of the plates for the work under consideration. When he was older, however, he was far from satisfied with his early efforts, the folio plates, and for this reason he perhaps withdrew as many copies of them as he could. This would explain the rarity of these plates. He gradually collected so much material about bird life that, supported by his brother Carl Andreas' great knowledge in this field, he could begin in 1820 to issue a new edition (355) of his father's work which, however, was so extensively revised that in its new shape it has almost the character of an independent treatise. The great undertaking was at last finished in 1860. With its accurate observations and descriptions and its accounts of the natural history of birds it exercised an immense influence on the development of German ornithology. As one of the best bird books of Germany it also quickened the interest in the study of birds outside Germany, for instance in Denmark. This was also the case with the earlier works of Naumann, whose influence on his age may best be compared to that of Gilbert White's and Bewick's works in England. Johann Friedrich Naumann was highly thought of by his contemporaries. He was made an honorary professor and became a

member of many learned societies, and he lived to
see the periodical of the German Ornithological Society appear under the name of 'Naumannia' (358).
Another striking proof of the esteem in which Naumann's achievements were held by German orneitho-
logists is the fact that the publication of a quite new
and extensively revised edition (356), a kind of third
edition of the elder Naumann's work, was begun a
hundred years after the publication of the first edition started. This edition is not satisfactory in all respects, one of the reasons being that it was the result
of a collaboration between many different experts on
birds.

A more comprehensive presentation of ornithology
as a whole saw the light in France during this period.
This was the immense undertaking 'Encyclopédie
méthodique' in which the bird group was treated in
1782—1823 (134; 870), first by *Mauduyt*, then by
Bonnaterre, who at the beginning of the Revolution
retired to his native district, so that the work had to
be finished by *L. P. Vieillot*, to whom we shall refer
later.

In Northern Europe it was still largely the pupils
of Linnæus who were the leaders of natural historical
research. One of these, *Peder Ascanius*, a native of
Norway, was, as professor at the University of Copenhagen, the first official representative in Denmark of
the study of natural history as a branch of science
independent of medicine. Nevertheless he did very
little for zoology, and indeed, rumour has it that he
obtained his post in return for his silence over some
secret escapade in which he had surprised the king.
His principal work 'Icones rerum naturalium', etc.
(Kiøbenhavn, Part I, 1767, 10 col. pl. (2 col. pl.
birds), obl. folio; re-issued in Part I of a new edition
1772—1805: 5 parts, 50 col. pl. (3 col. pl. birds);
fresh reprint of the four first parts 1806) must, from
its very brief text, be characterised as mainly a zoological picture book, in which even the plates of Part I
are not very well executed. Nor did the famous zoologist *Otto Friderich Müller*, though otherwise a pioneer in his branch of science, add greatly to the knowledge of Denmark's birds in his 'Zoologiæ Danicæ
prodromus', etc. (Havniæ 1776, 8vo), in which the
list of birds is largely evolved from the works of Brünnich and others. The more comprehensive Danish zoology which Müller began in 1777 with the issue of
a folio number containing 40 coloured plates was
never completed. In all 160 plates were published in

the four parts issued, the last of which, published in
1806 (348) contains four plates with pictures of as
many birds.

The bird life of the Faroes, in the North Atlantic,
which had been fairly well investigated previously
(pp. 12 and 17), was studied during this period by *J.
C. Svabo*, a Faroese of exceptional powers who explored his native isles in 1781—82; but his detailed account of his journey with its lengthy list of birds and
the few colour plates belonging to the ornithological
section were never printed (631, 28, pp. 105—112).
Svabo's studies of the avifauna together with other material, including the contributions of Mohr, to whom
we shall refer later, were utilised by a clergyman, *Jørgen Landt* in his 'Forsøg til en Beskrivelse over Færøerne' published in 1800 (Kiøbenhavn, 8vo; English
edition 1810) in which the birds are treated on pp.
243—273. After the appearance of Olafsson's and
Pálsson's work on Iceland (p. 28; 377) *Olaus Olavius*
(*Ólafur Olafsson*) travelled in that island in order to
procure material for a supplement to the account of
the two first-mentioned authors, but the zoological
gains of this journey were small. The results were
published in 'Oeconomisk Reise igiennem de nord-
vestlige, nordlige, og nordostlige Kanter af Island'
(Kiøbenhavn 1780, 2 parts, 1 pl. birds, 4to; German
translation 1787; new edition of this translation 1805).
At the same time when Olavius was exploring Iceland, *N. Mohr* a Faroese naturalist and linguist, made
a voyage of exploration to the Faroes in 1776—78,
the results of which were of use to other authors,
including the above-mentioned Svabo, his friend and
fellow-student. In 1780—81 he travelled in Iceland,
where he collected observations on the natural history
of the country. The results were embodied in a treatise,
not strictly scientific, entitled 'Forsøg til en islandsk
Naturhistorie', etc. (Kiøbenhavn 1786, 8vo), in which
the birds are dealt with on pp. 18—55 of a section
illustrated with 3 handcoloured plates engraved by
Fridrich. Two of the drawings for these plates were
executed by the Icelandic engraver *S. M. Holm*, who
also made the coloured drawings for Svabo's work.
The ornithological section of Mohr's book on Iceland,
which contains valuable information about the habits
of birds, was translated into German by Frederik
Faber and published in Brehm's 'Ornis', Parts I—III,
1824—27. It was completed in Oken's 'Isis', 1829.

Still farther north the singular features of the ice-clad
shores of Greenland attracted explorers though several

contributions had already been made to their investigation (582; 611; 648). The first general and detailed description of the avifauna of Greenland, however, we owe to a Danish clergyman, *Otto Fabricius* (747; 777), who worked for five years as a missionary in that country. In 1780 his 'Fauna Groenlandica', etc., appeared (Hafniæ, 8vo; Danish version of the introduction and the section on mammals and birds by O. Helms, 1929). It was part of an unfinished work which was to deal with the natural history, geography, and history of Greenland. It contained a description and a name for all the Greenland animals he knew, and brief notes on their habits. In this work, which is the foundation of the study of Greenland's fauna and is therefore frequently cited, the birds, 53 species in all, are treated under Linnean names on pp. 53—124. Information given by Fabricius is, we may note, already found in Otto Friderich Müller's above-mentioned work on the Danish fauna issued in 1776. Fabricius also subsequently furnished contributions to ornithology.

Naturally, the influence of Linnæus was chiefly felt in Sweden where, however, at the close of the 18th century a good many descriptions of districts appeared, with information about the fauna (596). Among the pupils and immediate successors of Linnæus there are several who have furnished contributions to ornithology, e. g. the versatile theologian *Samuel Ödmann; 4. J. Retzius,* professor at the University of Lund; the physician *P. G. Tengmalm,* who took a particular interest in ornithology and collected a great many birds, *C. P. Thunberg* and *Anders Sparrman,* the two latter being famous as explorers.

Sparrman, who has previously been mentioned (p. 29), had brought home from his travels material which added to the great collection, including birds, founded by the Swedish magistrate *Gustaf von Carlson,* president of Åbo hovrätt, on his estate Mälby in Södermanland. He caused the rarest of the species to be drawn by *J. Carl Linnerhielm,* a draughtsman who, after having been a government official, held among other posts that of State Herald. Some of these coloured drawings were published in 1786—89, with texts by Sparrman, in the earliest monumental pictorial work on ornithology published in the North, 'Museum Carlsonianum', etc. (481). After Carlson's death his collection was dispersed, but most of the ornithological material finally found its way to the Natural History Museum at Stockholm, as stated by J. C. Sundevall.

in his critical treatise on the birds in the work just mentioned (794; 892, pp. 1—15). In the next century Sparrman began to publish a work with pictures of Swedish birds (482), but though this undertaking was in progress from 1806—17, it was never completed. Sparrman, however, who held a professorship at Stockholm, is undoubtedly most famous as an explorer. In 1772 he set out for the Cape with support from Linnæus. As already mentioned (p. 29), he became a member there of Cook's second expedition and, after his return to the Cape, travelled for some months in the country of the Hottentots and Kaffirs. As one of the pioneers of African exploration (625; 638) he was therefore able to bring home representatives of the fauna of the dark continent, whose western regions, i. e. Senegambia, he visited on another journey in 1787—88. His countryman, the famous botanist and traveller C. P. Thunberg, also visited the Cape and the adjacent districts. His journey, on which he set out in 1770, lasted nine years, and took him to the East Indies, Ceylon, and Japan as well as South Africa. On this, or rather, these journeys, which he described in a work which was translated into the chief European languages, entitled 'Resa uti Europa, Africa, Asia, förrättad åren 1770—1779' (Upsala 1788—93, 4 parts, plates, 8vo) he discovered many new forms of plants and animals which were incorporated in the system. He was also able to bring home many specimens with which he enriched his valuable collection of natural objects, which he presented in 1775 and 1785 to the University of Uppsala, where he held a professorial chair from 1784 (899). Although his collection was especially rich in plants, his gift of 1775 also contained a number of birds. Thunberg himself made several contributions to ornithological research.

Quite another part of Africa, Abyssinia, was explored in 1768—73 by the Scotch traveller *James Bruce* (495, I, pp. 17—84). He did not return to England till 1774, after his travels had taken him to the source of the Blue Nile. The doubt with which his account of his journey was met, amongst other reasons because he said that the natives ate raw meat, delayed the publication of his 'Travels to discover the source of the Nile', etc. (London, 5 vols., 8 pl. birds, 4to) until 1790, after which it was at once published in French and German versions. The ornithological results presented are, however, sparse, though the journey was made especially for the study of natural history.

The actual founder of African ornithological research was, however, the Frenchman *François Levaillant*. He set out for the Cape in 1781, and from then until 1785 made two journeys in South Africa, which he described in two accounts of his travels published in 1790 and 1795 and translated into different languages (495, II, pp. 17—31; 859). He devoted himself principally to ornithology, collecting many birds and making numerous observations on bird life. The disturbed political conditions following upon the Revolution in his native country rendered difficult the sale to the French government of the valuable collections he had brought home, part of which were later combined with those of Temminck. Levaillant's collections were however finally purchased by the Republican government, but they were· paid for with duplicate books from the National Library. Owing to these difficulties, therefore, Levaillant thought that he had better publish his results in a large work, abundantly provided with plates, which appeared in 1796 —1812 under the title 'Histoire naturelle des oiseaux d'Afrique' (297—299). This book, which forms the foundation of our knowledge of the avifauna of Africa, contains a great many observations about birds, particularly their biology, but suffers from the absence of system and a Latin nomenclature. Later authors, notably Vieillot (p. 46), have, however, remedied this deficiency. Furthermore, Levaillant, who sometimes wrote from memory, allocated species to Africa which did not belong to that continent, and his work also contains references to certain birds which must be regarded as fictions, all of which has been explained by Sundevall in his penetrative criticism of the work (831; 892, pp. 16—60).

Noteworthy drawings for the illustration of the book were made by *J. Lebrecht Reinold* who, in spite of the resemblance in name, should not be considered as identical with *Johann Friedrich Leberecht Reinhold*, of Gera, known especially as a portrait painter.

The plates were executed as colour-printed engravings, just then beginning to come into vogue in French zoological illustration, and one of the pioneers in this field, J. B. Audebert (pp. 42 and 46) assisted in making those for the first parts. Besides this, his principal, work Levaillant issued a series of ornithological works (300—305), partly supplementing one another, and adorned with colour-printed plates from drawings by *Jacques Barraband* (or *Barraban*), who principally painted birds and flowers. This artist acquired no small reputation as a painter of birds, but his pictures from mounted specimens suffer from the stiffness and unnaturalness that disfigure such reproductions. He also drew illustrations for Sonnini's edition of Buffon's 'Histoire naturelle' (p. 33) and worked as a draughtsman for the porcelain factory at Sèvres and for the tapestry factories. Several of his paintings with representations of birds were seen after his death at the Paris exhibitions and were exhibited at Lyon where he was a teacher of flower painting at a newly founded Academy of Art from 1807.

It is small wonder that Levaillant had many difficulties to overcome before he could publish his works, particularly during the Revolution. The more stable conditions preceding it facilitated matters for his countryman the naturalist *Pierre Sonnerat,* who from 1768 to 1805 made several journeys in the East Indies and adjacent regions, collected natural historical material and made many observations which he utilised in his accounts of his travels. His first journey, which he described in 1776 in 'Voyage à la Nouvelle Guinée', etc., (475; 651) was to the Philippine and adjacent isles, but did not take him to the island mentioned in the title. He drew the illustrations for his works himself and described a considerable number of birds in them which, however, are mentioned by their vernacular names. From a later voyage to the East Indies and China 1774—81, of which he gave an account in 1782 (cf. 477; 478), he brought home valuable collections of plants and animals, especially insects, fishes, and mammals, as well as 300 different species of birds, to enrich the royal museum which was nationalized during the Revolution in 1793 and was given the name Muséum d'Histoire Naturelle (787).

An unfortunate fate affected the results of a couple of large French expeditions sent out at the close of the century. The first of these set out in 1785 under the leadership of Count *Lapérouse* on a great voyage of exploration to the Pacific, of which many little known regions were visited, valuable results being obtained. Nothing was heard of the expedition after its visit to Botany Bay in New South Wales in January-February 1788, and it was only later discovered that the ships had evidently been wrecked on an island north of the New Hebrides. However, on the basis of the material, sparse from an ornithological point of view, sent home by Lapérouse, a large work on the expedition could be published in 1797 (276). In spite of revolution and unrest, 'la grande nation' had still sufficient strength left in 1791 to send out another great expedition to search for the lost one. The journey, under the leadership of *d'Entrecasteaux,* failed in its purpose, but the southwest coast of Australia and other little known areas of these waters were explored before the expedition, after the death of its leader in 1793, was abruptly ended by the surrender of its ships to the Dutch in Java. The naturalists of the expedition were *L. A. Deschamps* and *Labillardière,* who, held captive by the Dutch, were not allowed to return home till 1795, when Labillardière was able to write a work, published in 1800, about the expedition (274), in which some ornithological material also is treated. His zoological collections had been taken to England, but Sir Joseph Banks (pp. 28—29), President of the Royal Society of London, saw that they were sent back undamaged.

Constantine John Phipps visited quite different parts of the world, as will appear from the title of his work 'A voyage towards the North Pole ... 1773' (London 1774, 4to). The animals and plants observed are described in an appendix, among them, on pp. 186—189, twelve birds from Spitsbergen given under Latin names.

While Australia was visited especially by English expeditions (p. 35), the fauna of parts of North America was dealt with, amongst others, by the excellent observer *Benjamin Smith Barton* (640, 3) in his 'Fragments of the natural history of Pennsylvania' (Philadelphia 1799, folio; re-issued by O. Salvin 1883). This remarkable work contains heterogeneous ornithological material with sundry observations on birds given under binomial names. Barton based his work largely on the 'Travels through North and South Carolina, Georgia, East and West Florida', etc., (Philadelphia 1791, 8vo) by his friend and predecessor *William Bartram* (640, 2; 878). It contains a good deal of ornithological material, and several editions and translations were published.

While the above-mentioned works form a transition to the more extensive treatment of the avifauna of North America which commenced at the beginning of the 19th century, part of the avifauna of South America had been treated in 1782 by the Abbé *Giovanni Ignazio Molina* in his classic work 'Saggio sulla storia naturale del Chile' (Bologna, 8vo). This was republished in 1810 in a largely revised folio edition, and numerous translations appeared, for it was of no little importance to the knowledge of the natural history of South America of earlier times, and to ornithology also, which it enriched by descriptions and names of a number of birds.

7. A BRIEF SURVEY OF THE LITERATURE AND ICONOGRAPHY OF DESCRIPTIVE ORNITHOLOGY IN THE 19TH AND 20TH CENTURIES.

A retrospective view of the literary history of ornithology from the earliest times to the close of the 18th century will show that it began to assert its scientific independence only at the end of that period. At the beginning of the 19th century ornithology had become practically a separate and specific study which had made itself freer from its immediate connection with general cultural development than it had been previously. Its progress from now on was determined by scientific students of birds. At the same time there was a great increase in the quantity of literary material, caused by the growing democratization of science. The production of illustrations executed by hand also became greater in the early and middle 19th century than ever before or after.

Retrospection also emphasizes another fact, the gradual change that had taken place in the character of ornithological publications. Until collections of birds became more common and more comprehensive ornithologists wrote largely from memory or based their works on the reports of others, not least on the accounts of earlier authors. The landmarks in the development of ornithology are, then, chiefly the works offering more independent treatment of the material, or based on original observations. These latter now became more and more common as the ornithological material was augmented, especially by collection in foreign countries, as was the case as early as the close of the 18th century. But it was notably in the 19th century that the material collected on exploring expeditions increased so greatly. At the same time the methods of preservation gradually developed until the present stage was reached, and it is now possible to keep bird-skins for an almost unlimited time. The result of this was that the publications of descriptive ornithology came gradually, and increasingly, to be based on accurate descriptions of such specimens as were procured on expeditions; or they took the shape of monographs reviewing the collective knowledge of separate groups of birds. Works in which ornithological material from journeys and expeditions was treated therefore came to play no small part in ornithological literature, and such material also appeared more frequently in periodicals, especially as publications of this kind confined to zoology or even to ornithology alone, gradually came into being. Just as learned societies of a general or natural scientific kind began to issue periodicals containing zoological material (p. 16), so also zoological and ornithological societies now gradually arose and became the mainspring of the periodicals for these subjects. Zoological societies were formed on account of the gradually increasing desire for collaboration between zoologists which strengthened as their numbers grew. The first to come into existence was the Zoological Society of London, founded in 1826 (817). This society was, particularly in the 19th century, of no small importance for ornithology, for in its 'Transactions', issued from 1833 (548), and especially in its 'Proceedings' (547), published since 1830, important ornithological material appeared both in the text, and — in the 'Proceedings' from 1848 — also in the shape of pictures drawn by the best ornithological artists of the time.

The first periodical exclusively devoted to ornithology was 'Ornis' published from 1824—27 at Jena by *Ludwig Brehm,* but of which only three numbers appeared. The next to appear was 'Rhea', published at Leipzig by *Friedrich August Ludwig Thienemann.* It was also the mouth-piece of the meetings, started in 1845, of German ornithologists who had combined to form the ornithological section of 'Gesellschaft deutscher Naturforscher und Ärzte'. 'Rhea', however, only lasted a short time, two numbers only appeared, those for 1846 and 1849. Its place was taken by 'Naumannia' in 1849 (358), edited by *Eduard Baldamus.* This became the organ of the first ornithological society 'Deutsche Ornithologen-Gesellschaft', founded in 1850 and later the 'Deutsche Ornithologische Gesellschaft', whose periodical 'Journal für Ornithologie' (239) is the oldest of the current ornithological journals, since it was first issued in 1853. Other countries, however,

soon came into the field. 1858 saw the foundation of the 'British Ornithologists' Union' (595; 637), which in the following year began to issue 'The Ibis' (219; 595), while the leading American journal 'The Auk' (20) which was published by the 'American Ornithologists' Union' (624), founded in 1883, only dates from 1876 even if its predecessor (p. 78) be included. Altogether the number of societies and periodicals gradually increased so greatly that practically every country has now at least one. These organs, of which, however, only a small number can be mentioned in the survey which follows, have become a storehouse for a very large part of original ornithological literature, especially the three last mentioned. A series of plates executed from originals by leading ornithological artists adorn in particular the volumes of the British periodical, which in its stable and practical form is archetypal, and by its valuable contents has been of great importance to the growth of ornithology.

Engraving was still the sole form used for the production of plates at the beginning of the 19th century, but certain changes in execution had occurred during the course of the 17th and 18th centuries, traces of which can be found in ornithological illustration towards the close of the latter century. This is evidenced by Levaillant's works (p. 40), the plates of which were, as previously mentioned, printed in colour, thus to some extent avoiding the tiresome process of colouring by hand. It was in Paris that colour prints proper were made, the process being that of printing from several superimposed copperplates, a process invented by *Jacob Christoph Le Blon,* who used from three to five plates, each with its own colour. After his death others developed his methods, but there were many difficulties to overcome, and often the finished plates had to be retouched by hand. This, too, was the case in printing from one plate with several colours, a method much used in the production of colour-plates for zoological works. Audebert, to whom we shall refer later (p. 46), must be mentioned as a promoter of the use of engravings printed in colour in the production of plates for zoological and ornithological works. He also introduced the method of using oils for colouring the plates. Towards the close of the 18th century, however, copperplate engraving proper was superseded by the many simpler methods that had been invented, of which aquatinting, the invention of which is ascribed to the painter *Le Prince,* rendered possible the use of copperplates which possessed the properties necessary for the production of successful colour-prints. Progress in these various directions resulted in a rapid rise in the production of colour-prints in France, and especial mention may be made of Langlois and Rémond, who were well known printers of ornithological plates of this kind.

Just as colour prints from engravings were produced especially in a certain locality, so were they restricted to a certain period. Like engraving in general, they were overshadowed in their position as fine ornithological illustrations by quite a new form of picture printing, lithography (603; 606). This, which in contrast with wood-engraving and engraving is a planographic process, was invented between 1796 and 1798 at Munich by *Aloys Senefelder,* who in the main evolved the technique in its various forms. It made such rapid progress that from towards the middle of the 19th century to the introduction of modern methods of reproduction it was predominant as a process for the production of plates for the illustration of ornithological works.

In the period of transition between the epoch of engraving and that of lithography we occasionally meet with works in which some of the plates have been executed by the former, others by the latter method (cf. 194; 246). Just as copperplate engraving generally formed the foundation of the subsequent colouring, the hand-coloured lithograph was also the form in which this print was generally used, until it met with a rival in the colour-printed lithograph, the chromolithograph. This, however, did not come into prominence until the latter half of the 19th century, but only enjoyed a comparatively short vogue for, in the 20th century, it was gradually superseded, chiefly by the photo-mechanical methods of reproduction called the three- and four-colour processes, which yield very fine results. In the 19th century the colour-printed woodcut was used as a rare exception, while another photomechanical method, the collotype, which was developed in the same period as chromo-lithography, and by which particularly fine prints are produced, found, and still finds, a limited use in cases where the finest possible result is desired.

During the first half of the 19th century the development of zoology as a whole was influenced by the Frenchman *Georges Cuvier,* more especially by his fundamental works on comparative anatomy and palæontology. In the former field, in particular, his activities became of great importance to ornithology.

In the year 1800 he began the publication of his famous 'Leçons d'anatomie comparée', etc., (Paris 1800—05, 5 vols., 8vo), a preparatory work to one on general comparative anatomy, and the first of a series of works by means of which Cuvier founded modern comparative zoology (662; 710; 712; 720). As far as the class of birds was concerned he did not, however, add anything essentially new, for his classification was in the main an improvement on that of Linnæus the birds being arranged in six main groups according to purely external characters, more especially the appearance of the feet and the form of the beak. This grouping Cuvier had already introduced in 1798 in his first survey of the animal kingdom 'Tableau élémentaire de l'histoire naturelle des animaux' (Paris, 3 pl. birds, 8vo), which he issued because the Republican government had introduced the study of natural history into public education. The main groups mentioned above were retained under the name of orders in the work on which the fame of Cuvier especially rests, his classic 'Le règne animal distribué d'après son organisation', etc., (110; 111). The plates for the ornithological section of the "Disciples' edition" of this famous work (111) were executed from drawings by *Edouard Traviès,* a distinguished bird painter, known as a painter of animals and still life in water colour, who also issued ornithological atlases himself.

Even though Cuvier did not succeed in making his anatomical principles, so important for the development of zoology, the basis of his classification of birds, yet his system of classification, owing to its practicability, and the great authority of its originator, was much used for some length of time.

In the meanwhile anatomical tendencies were making themselves felt in ornithology too from the beginning of the 19th century and yielded good results which could be utilised in the endeavour to invent a more natural system of classification to replace the earlier artificial ones. In this work a number of investigators took part, each in his own way helping to elucidate important anatomical facts, and thus contributing to the development of the system of classification which led towards an arrangement based on the natural affinities of the different groups of birds, a classification which attempts are nowadays made to achieve by consideration of the anatomical characters. For the orders, whose numbers have increased considerably, it is based on many distinguishing features, so

6*

that several groups formerly believed to be closely allied, have now been separated from each other.

These efforts at systematization were greatly influenced by the doctrine of evolution. Starting from that doctrine, investigators often attempted to arrive at a system of classification giving the presumed course of evolution. Important contributions to classification were made in 1888 by *Max Fürbringer* on the basis of extensive morphological investigations (cf. 41, note). This school of research, which revises the arrangement of the superior groups has, however, passed its zenith (643). Systematists nowadays often work on the lines of the subdivision of the Linnean species into geographical races which we shall discuss below, or seek to combine the species into larger groups, or series of forms which substitute each other geographically, a field of research in which the work of a German, Pastor *Otto Kleinschmidt,* the founder of the Formen-kreis-theory (887) deserves mention.

Descriptions and diagnoses, too, have assumed more stable forms, increasing attention being paid to the growing knowledge of the anatomy of birds, so that it becomes possible, in a comparatively brief form which may, however, seem somewhat stereotyped and abrupt, to give an exhaustive characterization of the larger or smaller groups within the class of birds.

As knowledge of the forms of birds increased, investigators gradually realised that all specimens of the same Linnean species were not identical, for not a few deviations from type were found. In the first two decades of the 19th century an attempt was made to explain these as varieties, due largely to the influence of Cuvier's views (885 c). However, from about 1820 under Ludwig Brehm's leadership (p. 47) the view gained ground that even forms which merely deviate very slightly from each other must be regarded as independent species if their distinguishing characters are constant. This involved a more extensive division into species.

This view, which most fortunately caused increased investigation of the varieties within the Linnean species, was contested by other ornithologists, for instance by *Frederik Faber* (746; 748), who contended that the species vary under the influence of the climate, and that the races originating in this way must be subordinated to the species, while *Constantin Lambert Gloger* in 'Das Abändern der Vögel durch Einfluss des Klima's', etc., (Breslau 1833, 8vo) suggested that climatic varieties should be given special names. But

this idea was not applied consistently until 1844 when it was adopted by *Hermann Schlegel* (p. 55) in his 'Kritische Uebersicht der europäischen Vögel' (Leiden, 2 parts, 8vo). Here he designated the subspecies or geographical races by three names: one generic name, one specific name, and a name for the subspecies. The use of this ternary nomenclature did not, however, become common in Europe until the latter half of the century, after it had taken root in America (874; 885 c) where John Cassin (p. 78) in 1854 (92, note) and Spencer F. Baird, especially after 1858 (22, note), were instrumental in introducing it. Nowadays this nomenclature has become of great importance, for the study of the subspecies now occupies a prominent place in ornithology, immensely increasing our knowledge of the geographical forms of birds. It must further be added that the habits of birds which, apart from certain circles of German ornithologists, were not previously much heeded, are now eagerly studied. Migrations, variations, and changing plumages of birds in particular also engage attention. Generally speaking, biological subjects are coming more and more into the foreground, as evidenced, amongst other things, by the incipient use of experiment in ornithology, and the greater prominence of ecological considerations in the field of zoogeography.

The brief survey which follows must be viewed against the background here sketched in. Owing to the overwhelming amount of material, only the most important works will be mentioned for the purpose of throwing some light on the course of development.

During the greater part of the early and middle 19th century the main ornithological interest was centred in the discovery and description of new species. A number of large works were produced, principally in France, in the first part of the century. They were illustrated profusely with plates, usually in the form of colour-printed engravings based on the available collections or the results of the many important journeys and expeditions sent out from France during this period. These expeditions often took the form of voyages round the world, from which a large amount of material was brought home and treated in extensive publications. Besides many which are mentioned in the accompanying catalogue (references p. 124), we may here mention 'Voyage autour du monde ... exécuté sur ... l'Uranie et la Physicienne ... 1817—20', etc., by *Louis de Freycinet,* an important report published in Paris in 1824—42 (7 vols. text (in 10), 4to; and

PLATE V

Fig. 1. PALLAS' SAND-GROUSE. *Syrrhaptes paradoxus* (Pall.). From hand-coloured engraving (Pl. 95), by J. G. Prêtre, in C. J. Temminck and M. Laugier de Chartrouse's 'Nouveau recueil de planches coloriées d'oiseaux', Vol. I, 1838, large folio

Fig. 2. THE COMMON PELICAN. *Pelecanus onocrotalus* L. (Adult male). From hand-coloured engraving (No. 87), by Martinet, in Daubenton's 'Planches enluminées', large folio

PLATE V

Fig. 1

Fig. 2

4 vols. atlas, large folio). The zoological section of this work (1 vol. text and 1 vol. atlas with 96 plates (71 col.)) was written by *Quoy* and *Gaimard*. It appeared in 1824—26 and contains a good deal of ornithological material which is illustrated in the atlas by 27 coloured plates (numbered 13—39). The results of another French voyage round the world under the command of *Laplace* were treated in 'Voyage autour du monde par les mers de l'Inde et de Chine exécuté sur ... la Favorite ... 1830—32', etc., which was published in Paris in 1833—39 (5 vols. text, 8vo; and two vols. atlas, folio). The zoological report forms the fifth volume of the text, which was issued in 1839 as a reprint of various papers in the 'Magasin de zoologie', in which periodical the ornithological portion, written by *Fortuné Eydoux* and *Paul Gervais* was published in 1836 and 1838. Of the 70 plates belonging to the zoological section (61 col.) and included with the text in the volume, 16 are ornithological (15 col.). The great French sea-going expeditions followed in rapid succession. A new voyage round the world under the command of *Abel du Petit-Thouars* was described in 'Voyage autour du monde sur ... la Vénus ... 1836—39' (Paris 1840—64, 11 vols. text, 8vo; and 4 vols. atlas, large folio), the zoological volume of the report being published entire in 1855. The birds were treated by *Florent Prévost* and *Oeillet Des Murs,* mentioned again later (p. 46), in a section which appeared in 1849, while the 10 plates (9 col.) belonging to it were published in 1846. Finally the results of a famous expedition under the command of *J. Dumont d'Urville* are treated in 'Voyage au Pôle Sud et dans l'Océanie sur ... l'Astrolabe et la Zélée ... 1837—40' (Paris 1841—54, 23 vols. text (in 22), 8vo; and atlas 7 vols. (in 5), large folio). The birds are dealt with in the third volume, 1853, of the zoological portion of the complete report by *Jacques Pucheran,* with a single contribution by *Honoré Jacquinot.* The plates belonging to the ornithological section, 37 (36 col.) in all, were published in 1842—46. Works of the same kind as those mentioned here are listed in the accompanying catalogue, for instance the reports, important from an ornithological point of view, on the voyages of 'la Coquille', 1822—25 (288), 'l'Astrolabe', 1826—29 (410), and 'la Bonite', 1836—37 (138). These works were illustrated in accordance with the highest requirements of the time by bird painters such as *J. G. Prêtre,* who at the beginning of the 19th century was frequently employed as a zoological artist in Paris (Pl. V, Fig. 1);

Antoine Bévalet; Nicolas Huet, who like Prêtre worked for the commission which issued the large description of Egypt (15; 438); *Alphonse Prévost;* Edouard Traviès, mentioned already above; and *Paul Oudart,* all reputed and prolific illustrators, more especially Prêtre. The pictures of the last named, however, like the bulk of the earlier bird pictures, lack the naturalness of execution attained in more recent times, which have freed themselves from the stiffness that pervades reproductions from mounted specimens. Most of these artists, as later *Nicolas Maréchal* and *J. C. Werner,* worked as painters for the Jardin des Plantes, and added to the above-mentioned (p. 14) collection of pictures belonging to the Museum ('Collection des vélins') (684; 685). In spite of all their proficiency, hardly any of them could compete with Madame *Pauline Knip* (née *de Courcelles*) who illustrated the first large monograph on a single group of birds, the 'Histoire naturelle des tangaras', etc., (116) by *Anselme Desmarest,* which appeared in 1805—07 in Paris where the artist, who was married for several years to the Dutch painter and etcher Jos. Aug. Knip, lived and worked. She was a pupil of the above-mentioned Barraband (p. 40), among whose works we may here mention the originals for the plates in *F. M. Daudin*'s 'Traité élémentaire et complet d'ornithologie', etc., 1800 (112). Madame Knip applied herself with great success to her speciality, the painting of birds, as evidenced by her bird-pictures in the Paris Salon in 1808—14. She also worked as a porcelain painter for the factory at Sèvres and here, too, she used birds for models; but her fame rests mainly on the very beautiful and carefully executed portraits of birds, which she supplied as models for coloured copperplates in ornithological works (Pl. VI). Her collaboration with the well-known Dutch ornithologist *C. J. Temminck* was less successful. In Temminck's opinion she illegally appropriated his work on pigeons which she was to illustrate (cf. 261, note; 501, note), issuing it as the second of the series of monographs, to which she later added another volume (261). Temminck, through his father, was in communication with Levaillant, with whom he associated and whose collection was partly combined with Temminck's large museum. This was acquired by the state in 1820 and combined with other collections to form the Royal Natural History Museum at Leyden, whose director Temminck became the same year (668; 872; 902). He wrote the first European avifauna, 'Manuel d'ornithologie', etc. (Amsterdam 1815, 8vo; second much enlarged edition,

Paris 1820—40, 4 vols., 8vo), for which the above-mentioned J. C. Werner (p. 45) in 1826—42 issued a series of illustrations (523). He was a very industrious man and an ornithologist of note whose activity has left permanent traces. His and Laugier's continuation in 1820—39 of Buffon's 'Planches enluminées' (884) with plates by Huet and Prêtre (502; 503) may be viewed as a kind of external expression of his varied relations with ornithology in France (Pl. V, Fig. 1). In the middle of the century a continuation of Buffon's and Temminck's plates entitled 'Iconographie ornithologique', etc., (cf. 76, note) appeared in France. It was issued by the above-mentioned Oeillet Des Murs with plates from drawings by Alphonse Prévost and Oudart.

Des Murs wrote the section on birds in the large work 'Historia fisica y politica de Chile', etc., (Paris 1843—71, 28 vols. text, 8vo; 2 vols. atlas, folio) by *Claudio Gay.* This part is to be found in the first volume on zoology (1847, pp. 183—496, 14 pl. (13 col.)). In another large and valuable work dealing with the natural history of South America, the 'Expédition dans les parties centrales de l'Amérique du Sud... 1843—47' of Count *Francis de Castelnau,* which appeared in Paris in 1850—59 (14 vols. (in 13), 8vo, 4to, and folio), Des Murs also wrote a section on birds entitled 'Oiseaux' (1855, 20 col. pl., 4to). He described European birds, their eggs, and nests, in a richly illustrated, though hardly satisfactory, catalogue entitled 'Musée ornithologique illustré', etc. (Paris 1886—87, 4 vols. (in 5), 345 col. pl., 4to), the plates in which are, however, based on those in the works of F. O. Morris (p. 58; 346) and C. R. Bree (59). In 1860 he had shown his interest in general oology in 'Traité général d'oologie ornithologique', etc. (Paris, 4to), in which he tried to utilise birds' eggs in the service of classification.

In the de luxe series of French ornithological works we may mention 'Oiseaux dorées', etc., (14) by *J. B. Audebert* and *L. P. Vieillot,* a highly expensive work when it appeared in 1802. Its contents are heterogeneous, but the book is beautifully produced, with many of the individual plates printed from several copperplates and with an abundant use of gold to enhance the effect. Vieillot was fairly fertile as an author. He issued several large works decorated with plates, some of which are listed in the accompanying catalogue (514—516). As an ornithologist he was not without importance, as will be evident from his 'Ornithologie

française', etc., 1823—30 (516) and from 'Faune française', etc. (Paris 1820—30, 8 vols. text, 8vo, and 4 vols. atlas, 4to), started under his editorship, but in which, however, only Vieillot's text for the birds is complete. He thus contributed to the enrichment of the knowledge of the avifauna of France which has since been carried on by other investigators (570), of whose works we may mention some few examples — for instance the unfinished 'Ornithologie provençale', etc., (431) by *Polydore Roux,* which appeared in 1825—30, 'Ornithologie du Gard', etc., (Nismes 1840, 8vo) by *Jean Crespon,* 'Ornithologie de la Savoie' (text, Paris 1853—54, 4 vols., 8vo; atlas, Chambéry 1855—56, 110 pl. by J. Werner) by *J. B. Bailly,* and 'Richesses ornithologiques du midi de la France', etc. 1859—62 (230), said to have been written entirely by *J. B. Jaubert* (594, p. 40), although the name of the director of the Natural History Museum of Marseilles, *Barthélemy Lapommeraye* also appears on the work. French ornithologists have also produced a series of monographs. Thus in the earlier period some minor works are issued by *R. P. Lesson* (289—296) a very active ornithological writer whose works are of importance because he characterized and described a number of birds in them. In a later period we meet with *Alfred Malherbe's* revision of the woodpecker group, 1859—63 (321) and 'Histoire naturelle des oiseaux-mouches', etc., (Lyon 1873—79, 4 vols., and supplement, 120 col. pl., large 4to) by *Etienne Mulsant,* and *Édouard Verreaux.* This branch of French science, besides investigating native avifauna has also devoted no little attention to the avifauna of foreign regions, of recent times especially in the French colonies. The results have been embodied in reports on expeditions or in faunistic accounts. Besides those already referred to (pp. 44—46) mention may be made of *Alcide d'Orbigny's* (671; 849) works in the 1830's and 1840's on the birds of South America (382) and Cuba (383); the ornithology of the Canaries (522) in 1841 by *P. Barker Webb* and others in the great work 'Histoire naturelle des Îles Canaries', etc.; 'Oiseaux de l'île de la Trinidad (Antilles)' (Port d'Espagne 1866, 8vo) by *A. Léotaud,* the first general account of the avifauna of the island; *Victor Loche's* treatment of the birds in 'Exploration scientifique de l'Algérie' (313), as well as the ornithological portion of the large work on Madagascar, published since 1875, under the title 'Histoire physique, naturelle et politique de Madagascar', etc. (Paris, 4to), in which

PLATE VI

THE TURTLE-DOVE. *Streptopelia turtur* (I.). From colour-printed engraving (Pl. XLII), painted by Mme Knip, in Knip's 'Les pigeons', 1811

PLATE VI

the section on the birds (1876—85, 4 vols., 400 pl. (164 col.)), illustrated by J. G. Keulemans (p. 55) and others, was written by the editor *Alfred Grandidier* and *A. Milne Edwards.* As a further example we may mention 'Les oiseaux de la Chine' (113), published in 1877, by the Abbé *Armand David* and *Emile Oustalet,* David (672) being known as an indefatigable traveller in remote regions in the interior of China, which he explored on four large expeditions while he was in the country as a missionary.

After a period of a somewhat less lively activity present-day French science has again yielded important contributions to ornithology, for instance in the shape of works relating to the avifauna of foreign countries. As an example may be mentioned the work illustrated by Grønvold (p. 59) 'Les oiseaux de l'Indochine française' (Paris 1931, 4 vols., 67 pl., 4to), by *Jean Delacour* and *Pierre Jabouille,* which followed several predecessors. Further, as examples of French ornithologists writing on the avifauna of other parts of the world we may mention *Auguste Ménégaux* and especially *Jacques Berlioz* of the Muséum National d'Histoire Naturelle, who has issued not a few important treatises on this subject. The polar regions, too, have been explored by the French in our century under the leadership of *Jean Charcot* who conducted two expeditions to the Antarctic, in 1903—05 and 1908—10 respectively. The birds from the first French Antarctic expedition were all, apart from some dealt with in a small work by *R. Anthony,* treated by Ménégaux in the section on birds in the report on the scientific results of the expedition (Paris 1907, 12 pl., 4to), while one of the members of the other expedition, *Louis Gain,* presented the ornithological material from it in the section 'Oiseaux antarctique' of the scientific report of the expedition (Paris 1914, 15 pl., 4to).

The birds of France, too, have of course been treated in our day, for instance in minor works by Ménégaux (330) and *Paul Paris.*

As will appear from the above, there was a tendency in the beginning of the 19th century not least in France, but also, as we shall mention later, in other countries, to publish expensive works with series of coloured plates, a tendency which was presumably stimulated by the prevailing fashion of collecting and describing. It is true that these works are of interest as examples of book-production and the art of illustration, but for the growth of ornithology their significance was often problematic. When we add to this their costliness, it can be understood that this phenomenon might cause a certain annoyance to ornithologists, as pointed out by Newton (623, pp. 23—24), and as expressed in 1845 by *J. J. von Tschudi* (511, pp. 7—8), who says, 'Es haben sich der Ornithologie mehr als irgend eines andern Zweiges der Naturwissenschaften unglücklicher Weise Naturalienhändler, Dilettanten und Maler bemächtigt... Die Maler... bieten... dem Studium der Ornithologie bedeutende Schwierigkeiten dar. Ihre Werke, welche grössentheils prachtvoll ausgeführt sind, erreichen einen Preis, der selbst von den grössern Bibliotheken nicht mehr bezahlt werden kann. In ganz Deutschland sind nur noch drei Bibliotheken, deren Hülfsmittel ausreichen, solche Prachtwerke anzuschaffen, deren wirklicher Gehalt gewöhnlich ungemein gering ist, denn den schönen Kupfertafeln sind meistentheils Beschreibungen und Diagnosen beigegeben, die durchaus keinen wissenschaftlichen Werth haben, ja sogar unverständlich oder den Abbildungen widersprechend sind ... Die Herausgeber jener Werke haben es sich also selbst zuzuschreiben, wenn von ihren Arbeiten keine Notiz genommen wird; die Naturforscher sollten sich sogar vereinigen, dieselben nie zu benutzen, um auf diese Weise jenem literarischen Unfuge Einhalt zu thun'.

This not unjust pronouncement illustrates the way in which certain sections of book and picture production were, from the natural historical point of view, going astray. The various countries did not, however, contribute equally to this part of ornithological literature which, be it noted, could only prosper where, as in France, there 'was plenty of money available and a public with great purchasing power. In certain places scientists entered upon paths which opened up to wider prospects, for instance in Germany, where a circle of ornithologists centring round the above-mentioned investigators Ludwig Brehm, Friedrich Naumann, Gloger, Eduard Baldamus and Friedrich August Ludwig Thienemann, who is well-known for his works on the reproduction of birds (506; 507), contributed to the development of ornithology by the previously mentioned studies on the variations and habits of birds. Brehm (755), who was a clergyman at Renthendorf and father of the noted Alfred Brehm (p. 49), amongst other works wrote one on German birds 1831 (66) in which he utilised his thorough knowledge of them, a knowledge which also found

visible expression in his outstanding collection of about
10,000 specimens of birds. This collection, which was
especially valuable in that it represented so many variations within the species, and which was bought in
1897 by Walter Rothschild for the Museum at Tring
(741), consisted primarily of German and almost
exclusively of European birds. These latter, too, were
described by Brehm in 1823—24 in 'Lehrbuch der
Naturgeschichte aller europäischen Vögel' (Jena, 2
vols., 12mo). Gloger began a work on the same subject in 1834 with the title 'Vollständiges Handbuch
der Naturgeschichte der Vögel Europa's', etc. (Breslau,
8vo), of which, however, only the first part, entitled
'Deutsche Landvögel', appeared.

These examples are quoted to show the course of
development in Germany where, in addition, a number
of greater or smaller works, abundantly provided with
ornithological plates, saw light. Thus in the beginning
of the 19th century we have a larger and a smaller
work on German birds by *Bernhard Meyer* and *Johann Wolf* (336; 337) and a book on the same
subject with the text by *Borkhausen* and others and
plates by *J. C. Susemihl* and members of his family
(52). Susemihl, a Hessian draughtsman and engraver,
began these plates in 1795. Later he applied himself
to steel engraving and in 1839 began the issue of a
series of fine colour-printed plates in 'Abbildungen
der Vögel Europas, herausgegeben, gezeichnet und in
Stahl gestochen von J. C. Susemihl... und E. Susemihl', etc. (Darmstadt 1839—52, 36 parts, 108 col.
pl., 8vo and 4to). This work was never completed,
its text, based on Temminck's 'Manuel d'ornithologie'
and other sources was adapted by *F. Gergens* and H.
Schlegel. The first 100 pages of the latter's text with
the corresponding 44 plates were also issued separately
in 1845 under the title 'Die europäischen Tag-Raub-
vögel', etc. (Darmstadt, 4to). Another industrious
producer of ornithological atlases was *Carl Wilhelm
Hahn,* who delineated and described the birds of his
native country, for instance in 1830—35 — together
with *Jakob Ernst von Reider* — in the work 'Fauna
Boica', etc. (194), and further in 1819—36 published
'Die Vögel aus Asien, Africa, America, und Neu-
Holland', etc. (Nürnberg, 2 vols., 120 col. pl., 4to),
of which the text for the first volume appeared in a
revised edition in 1823. He likewise began an atlas,
which was continued by *Heinrich Carl Küster,* viz.
'Ornithologischer Atlas oder naturgetreue Abbildung
und Beschreibung der aussereuropäischen Vögel. Erste

Abtheilung. Papageien' (Nürnberg 1834—41, 17
parts, 136 col. pl., 8vo).

Even before the last-mentioned work of Susemihl
was finished the Director of the Natural History Museum at Dresden, *L. Reichenbach,* had begun to issue
a long series of publications of a compilatory kind
known under the collective title of 'Die vollständigste
Naturgeschichte des In- und Auslandes', etc. A great
many pictures of birds, but predominantly copies, are
to be found in the ornithological section of this
work 'Abtheilung II. Vögel' (Dresden (later: Berlin)
1845—63, 13 vols., 1028 pl. (922 col.), 4to) (816).

After these examples of earlier pictorial works
produced by German ornithology, mention will be
made of some of the more recent German ornithological works, dealing with European avifauna, treating of
the class aves as a whole, or of greater or larger groups
of birds. In this connection we shall mention *F. J. W.
Baedeker's* work of 1855—63 on the eggs of European birds (21), *Oskar von Riesenthal's* monograph
of 1876—78 on the birds of prey of his own country
(422), the account of the natural history and cultural
history of European birds of prey and falconry by *Fritz
Engelmann* under the title of 'Die Raubvögel Europas',
etc. (Neudamm 1928, 36 pl., 4to), the series of coloured plates with descriptions of parrots published
by *Anton Reichenow* under the title 'Vogelbilder aus
fernen Zonen', etc. (Kassel 1878—83, 33 col. pl.,
folio), and the long series of plates found in the two
last editions of Naumann's ornithological work (355;
356), the last of which gave the bird artists of Germany and indeed of other countries an opportunity
to exercise their powers in the production of a number
of original pictures. The figures of the eggs were
painted by *Alex. Reichert* from Eugène Rey's collection and were published separately (419) in 1899—
1905 in one of the best pictorial works on European
birds' eggs. The same year as this work was completed,
the publication of another handsomely illustrated series
of plates with figures of eggs and with a text in German and English was begun, 'Oologia universalis pa-
læarctica' (Stuttgart 1905—13, 78 parts, 158 col. pl.,
4to) by *Georg A. J. Krause,* a work planned to consist of 150 parts, which, however, was never completed.

We cannot leave the subject of German works
on eggs without recording that *Alexander Koenig,* to
be mentioned again below (p. 50), has issued a large
catalogue of his collection under the title 'Katalog der
Nido-Oologischen Sammlung (Vögeleiersammlung) im

Museum Alexander Koenig in Bonn a. Rhein' (Bonn 1932, 3 vols. text, 1 vol. plates, 20 pl. (18 col.), 4to) with plates executed from drawings by *Paul Preiss*. The chief part of the collection consists of eggs from Europe and North Africa, of which many have been collected by Koenig himself or under his direction.

German zoological artists such as Gustav Mützel and others found a special range for their activities in *Alfred Brehm*'s famous 'Tierleben' (62—65). One of them, the animal painter *Robert Kretschmer*, whom Brehm met on a journey to Abyssinia, indeed became of immediate importance to him by helping him with this work, which scored an immense success. It soon entered on its triumphal progress round the world and, despite the relatively high price, a new edition could be issued fairly soon. It became popular through those descriptions of animal life which the author gives in masterly style, drawing mostly on his own rich experience, and which fascinate the reader and have contributed much to spread the knowledge and love of animals in wide circles (676; 778; 823). In the two last editions of the work one of the illustrators was the well-known painter and etcher *Wilhelm Kuhnert*, who preferred to take as his subjects animals in their natural environment which he had studied on many journeys. He understood how to give a particular brilliance to his pictures, such as is not achieved by those actual ornithologists who take up illustrative work, though they, on the other hand, attain other effects which seem to them to be more desirable. Among such artists may be mentioned Otto Kleinschmidt. Some of his pictures appear in the periodical 'Berajah', ect., (258), edited by him since 1905, and in 'Journal für Ornithologie', a journal which, together with others such as the 'Ornithologische Monatsberichte' (Berlin, 8vo), founded in 1893, contains a considerable part of the material published by German ornithologists since the middle of the 19th century, although of course a number of works have been issued separately. To take a few present day examples we might mention the distinctive account, published in 1924—33, of the avifauna of Central Europe (202), written by the director of the Berlin Aquarium *Oskar Heinroth* and his wife *Magdalena Heinroth,* and the famous and momentous work 'Die Vögel der paläarktischen Fauna', etc., (Berlin 1903—22, 3 vols., large 8vo) by *Ernst Hartert,* who was for many years the chief of the ornithological department of the Museum of Tring. In the work mentioned above he pro-

duced a hand-book of great value, especially for the study of the subspecies, to which supplements have later been added (Nachtrag I 1923; Supplements I—V by Ernst Hartert and *Friedrich Steinbacher,* 1932—36). Hartert, who was an eminent ornithologist, indeed one of the leaders at the time in this field, displayed within his province a fruitful activity of no little importance for the growth and progress of ornithology.

A modern hand-book on the birds of Germany is now in progress under the title 'Handbuch der deutschen Vogelkunde' (Leipzig, 8vo). The completion of this work, the first volume of which came out in 1937, is intended, with a second volume, to be issued in the same year. It is edited by *Günther Niethammer* for the Deutsche Ornithologische Gesellschaft. For the sake of completeness it should also be mentioned that several accounts of bird life in various local districts have of course appeared in Germany. *Herman Shalow*'s 'Beiträge zur Vogelfauna der Mark Brandenburg', etc., (Berlin 1919, large 8vo) is one recent example (885 a).

Of more comprehensive recent works we may mention a handbook of systematic ornithology, 'Die Vögel', etc., (Stuttgart 1913—14, 2 vols., 8vo) by Anton Reichenow, which has perhaps already been superseded owing to the growth of ornithology. The work of Fürbringer referred to above (p. 44) has as its only analogue the section on birds in H. G. Bronn's 'Klassen und Ordnungen des Thier-Reichs'. This appeared under the subtitle 'Vögel' (Leipzig [1869—] 1891—93, 2 vols., 59 pl., 8vo) and was commenced by *Emil Selenka,* but was composed principally by *Hans Gadow,* who lived in England from 1880. Another contribution to ornithology as a whole is to be found in the 'Lieferungen' dealing with birds in the great work entitled 'Das Tierreich'. This great undertaking is composed of a series of monographs in which animals now in existence are briefly described. It was begun in 1896 by the 'Deutsche zoologische Gesellschaft', and is now issued by the 'Preussische Akademie der Wissenschaften'. In this connection mention must be made of the great survey of the natural history of birds by the Berlin professor, *Erwin Stresemann* in Willy Kükenthal's 'Handbuch der Zoologie' (Vol. VII, Part 2, Berlin 1927—34, large 8vo (size as 4to)).

In his 'Avifauna Macedonica', etc., (München 1920, 8vo) Stresemann has treated the ornithological results of Franz Doflein's and L. Müller-Mainz' expeditions to Macedonia in 1917 and 1918, an example of the valuable contributions made by German ornithologists to the investigation and description of bird life in other parts of the world, not least in Africa. The northeastern part of that continent was explored in the first part of the 19th century by *Eduard Rüppell,* who thus procured material for several illustrated works (433—435). The first of these was an atlas in which the ornithological section, published in 1826, was illustrated by *F. H. von Kittlitz,* a naturalist and an artist, and others. He accompanied Rüppell on part of his journey after taking part in 1826—29 as a naturalist, especially an ornithologist, in the Russian voyage round the world in the frigate 'Senjavin', whereby he secured material for ornithological works which he illustrated himself (1). The most important of Rüppell's treatises, however, the 'Systematische Uebersicht der Vögel Nord-Ost-Afrika's' (435) was illustrated by the eminent zoological artist *Joseph Wolf,* who must be regarded as one of the best animal painters that have ever lived (833). This artist, who was greatly influenced at the beginning of his career by the Dutch ornithologist Hermann Schlegel (p. 55), also known 'as a bird artist, did not however remain long in his native country, where he had worked for a time as a lithographer. In 1848, after a short stay in Holland, he went to London where he soon made a secure position for himself as a draughtsman and painter of animals in water colours. He obtained plenty of work as an illustrator of ornithological and other zoological writings, for instance for the Zoological Society's publications and 'The Ibis'. His masterly and lifelike pictures of scenes from animal life, which were greatly in demand, also form the essential part of several independent works, such as his 'Zoological sketches', etc. (539). Wolf studied his models in their natural state, and the knowledge of animals and their habits which he thus acquired contributed to the naturalness that distinguishes his pictures (Pl. VIII). He had such remarkable powers of observing nature that the English animal painter Archibald Thorburn said of him (509, p. V) that he was 'the most original observer of wild animal life I have ever known'.

Among other German ornithologists who contributed to the knowledge of the avifauna of Africa we may call to mind *Gustav Hartlaub.* In the latter half of the 19th century he made a particular study of the birds of Western Africa (197), publishing in 1857 his 'System der Ornithologie Westafrica's' (Bremen,

8vo), and in 1861 dealing with the birds of Madagascar. In collaboration with *Otto Finsch* (718) in 1870, he dealt with the birds from Baron Carl Claus von der Decken's journey in East Africa in 1859—65 (143), by which the knowledge of the birds of that region was much enlarged. Of special importance to our insight into the ornithology of Northeast Africa was, however, *M. Th. von Heuglin* through his large and valuable work on the birds in that part of the continent published in 1869—73 (209), while later the above-mentioned Reichenow issued a systematic descriptive treatise of the birds in part of East Africa in 'Die Vögel Deutsch-Ost-Afrikas' (Berlin 1894, 4to), crowning his work in 1900—05 by his large monograph on the birds of Africa (416). Finally, in our century Alexander Koenig has treated the birds of Egypt in a series of monographs which he called 'Avifauna Aegyptica' (266—269), a name reminiscent of his 'Avifauna Spitzbergensis' (265) published in 1911, and dealing with the birds in that archipelago of the Arctic regions. Heuglin had also contributed to its ornithology in 1874 in Part III of the work 'Reisen nach dem Nordpolarmeer... 1870 und 1871' (Braunschweig 1872—74, 3 parts, 5 pl. birds, 8vo), in which birds from Spitsbergen and Novaya Semlya are treated in pp. 79—201. In 1904 the avifauna of the Arctic regions was further dealt with by Herman Schalow in 'Die Vögel der Arktis' (Jena 1904, folio), part of the work 'Fauna Arctica', while the birds from other Northern countries, for example Iceland, were described by *Bernhard Hantzsch* (656) in his 'Beitrag zur Kenntnis der Vogelwelt Islands' (Berlin 1905, 8vo).

German ornithologists have also been active in South America. *J. B. von Spix,* who explored Brazil in 1817—20 in company with K. F. P. von Martius, published an account of the birds in that region in 1824—25 (483). The same country had been visited in 1815—17 by *Maximilian, Prince zu Wied,* who brought home a large and valuable collection of birds which, in conjunction with other matter, afforded material for several works (cf. 530). He also travelled in North America in 1832—34, while *Hermann Burmeister,* professor of zoology at Halle, made a scientific expedition in 1850—51 through the Brazilian provinces Rio de Janeiro and Minas Geraes, the results of which he dealt with in his 'Systematische Uebersicht der Thiere Brasiliens', etc. (Berlin 1854—56, 3 vols., 8vo), with special reference to the birds in the two last volumes. In 1856 he set out for South

America again and for the next four years travelled through vast, partly unknown, regions and reaped a rich scientific result, on which he based his 'Reise durch die La Plata-Staaten', etc. (Halle 1861, 2 vols., 8vo), a work very valuable for the knowledge of the Argentine fauna. In 1861 his longing for Argentina again took him to South America where he founded a zoological museum in Buenos Ayres, whose director he became.

The German naturalist *Jean Gundlach* worked in Cuba for many years. In 1855—75 he published valuable contributions to the ornithology of the island in the 'Journal für Ornithologie' under the titles 'Beiträge zur Ornithologie Cubas' and 'Neue Beiträge zur Ornithologie Cubas', of which a Spanish version with supplements appeared in 1873—76 under the title 'Contribucion á la ornitologia Cubana' (Habana, 4to). In Brazil, after Goeldi, to whom we shall return later (p. 53), had left Pará a German lady, Fräulein *Emilie Snethlage*, became keeper of the zoological department of the museum there and later of the whole museum. In order to explore the country she made many daring journeys, during one of which she had a finger bitten off by the 'piraya' (Serrasalmo piraya), a much dreaded fish living in the Brazilian rivers. These journeys gave her material for several contributions to the ornithology of the country, such as her 'Catalogo das aves Amazonicas', etc. (Burg 1914, 6 pl., 8vo), issued as 'Boletim do Museu Goeldi VIII'. Another German naturalist, *Hermann von Ihering,* who went out to Brazil in 1880, became director of the State Museum of São Paulo in 1893. He became one of the leading naturalists of South America and contributed much information about the fauna of this part of the world, as for instance in his useful list of Brazilian birds in 'Catalogos da fauna Brazileira. Vol. I. As aves do Brazil' (São Paulo 1907, 8vo), a work in which he collaborated with *Rodolpho von Ihering,* the custos of the above-mentioned museum (Museu Paulista).

German scientists have also made quite recent scientific investigations in South America. Under the leadership of Professor Hans Krieg of Munich the Gran Chaco expedition took place in 1925—26, its ornithological results being dealt with by *Alfred Laubmann* under the title 'Vögel' in the first volume of the scientific report of the expedition (Stuttgart 1930, 8vo), while in 1914, in the mathematico-physical section of the 'Abhandlungen' of the Bavarian Academy,

Laubmann dealt with the birds from G. Merzbacher's journey in Central and Eastern Tian-Shan in 1907—08, as well as from E. Zugmayr's journey in Baluchistan in 1911. In the same periodical *Carl Parrot* in 1907 published his 'Beiträge zur Ornithologie Sumatras und der Insel Banka', a memoir chiefly based on birds collected in Banka by B. Hagen, with some other material added.

We might add numerous other examples of the world-wide activity of Germany, as of other great nations, in this field. Thus we have 'Die Avifauna von Timor' by *C. E. Hellmayr* in the first 'Lieferung' of 'Die Zoologie von Timor' (Stuttgart 1914, 1 col. pl., large 8vo), or his 'A contribution to the ornithology of Northeastern Chile' in the publications of the Field Museum in 1929, in which he also published in 1932 'The birds of Chile', largely based on material from an expedition in 1922—24. The ornithology of Central Polynesia was treated by Hartlaub and Finsch in 1867 (141), the latter being also noted for his monograph 'Die Papageien', etc., 1867—68 (142). Among present-day German ornithologists *Wilhelm Meise* must be mentioned as a writer on the birds of foreign regions. Finally it may be mentioned that contributions have been made to the investigation of the avifauna of the oceans by large-scale German sea-going expeditions for oceanic exploration, viz. the 'Deutsche Tiefsee-Expedition' in 1898—99 in the 'Valdivia' and the 'Deutsche Südpolar-Expedition' in 1901—03 in the 'Gauss'. The scientific results have been published in a series of noble volumes in which the birds have been treated by Reichenow.

Austria sent the frigate 'Novara' on a voyage round the world in 1857—59, during which a good deal of ornithological material was collected. This was treated by *August von Pelzeln* (391) among whose works we may also mention 'Zur Ornithologie Brasiliens', etc. (Wien 1868—71, 8vo), which is one of the most important books relating to the avifauna of that country, based as it is on the first extensive collection made by Johann Natterer on his travels in 1817—35. In collaboration with *Emil Holub,* well-known for his travels in Africa, he subsequently wrote a work, based mainly on the results obtained by the latter, entitled 'Beiträge zur Ornithologie Südafrikas', etc. (Wien 1882, 5 pl. (3 col.), 8vo). Within the empire-monarchy then in existence a comparatively prolific ornithological activity grew up during the course of the 19th century (586). Of its productions we may further call to mind

7*

'Naturgeschichte der Vögel Europa's' (152), issued in 1852—70 by the Czech *Anton Fritsch,* director of the natural history department of the Zoological Museum of Bohemia at Prague. This activity is also manifested by the publication of the periodical 'Ornithologisches Jahrbuch', etc., issued in German Austria in 1890—1918 (Hallein, 8vo) under the editorship of *Victor* Ritter von *Tschusi zu Schmidhoffen.* The chief ornithological periodical of Austria was, however, published in that country by the 'Ornithologische Verein in Wien', founded in 1876. This was the 'Mittheilungen' of this society (Wien, col. plates, 4to), which were begun in 1877 and from 1889 also had the title 'Die Schwalbe'. After a life full of vicissitudes, reflected in the changes of title and format, it ceased however to exist.

In the Hungarian part of the former empire *J. Salamon von Petényi* (401, pp. V—XXII) who corresponded with leading ornithologists in Western Europe such as H. Schlegel, L. Brehm, J. F. Naumann, and E. Baldamus, is considered to be the actual founder of the scientific ornithology of the country (751). Recently the Hungarian ornithologists have presented the majority of their results in the periodical 'Aquila' (12), the organ of the Hungarian Ornithological Central-Bureau, founded in 1893, and for many years edited by the founder of the Bureau, *Otto Herman.* In this journal the ornithological artists of Hungary have also had an opportunity of showing their abilities, for example the admirable bird artist, *Stefan von Necsey,* and one of the editors, the ornithologist *Titus Csörgey.* Another journal 'Zeitschrift für die gesammte Ornithologie' (545) had a very short life. It was edited in 1884—88 by the director of the collection of birds in the Royal Hungarian National Museum, *Julius von Madarász,* who was himself a successful bird artist. His chief work is an account of the natural history of Hungarian birds entitled 'Magyarország madarai', etc. (Budapest 1899—1903, 9 col. pl., 4to). A work with a similar title, but referring especially to the importance of birds for agriculture, was issued in 1899 (Budapest, 2 vols. in 3, 51 pl., 4to) by one of the editors of 'Aquila', *Stefan von Chernel,* and has greatly influenced Hungarian ornithology, helping as it did to create an interest in birds in wider circles. As a complete Hungarian ornithography it has, together with the corresponding work by Madarász, been the firm foundation from which Hungarian ornithological research grew up (634).

As an example of a monograph on birds in remoter parts of Europe we may mention *Robert* Ritter von *Dombrowski's* 'Ornis Romaniæ', etc., (Bukarest 1912, large 8vo), in which the birds of Roumania were subjected to a systematic and biologico-geographical description, while the birds of the Balkans were dealt with in 1894—1905 (417) by the Austrian *Othmar Reiser,* curator of the Museum of Serajevo. Of Reiser's other works may be noted his treatment of the ornithological results of the zoological expedition sent out by the Academy of Sciences in Vienna to Northeast Brazil in 1903, published under the title 'Vögel' in the section for mathematics and natural science in the Academy's 'Denkschriften' (Vol. 76, 1926, pp. 107—252).

In Russia ornithology carried forward the traditions of earlier times by concentrating on the study of the native fauna, as well as the avifauna of Northern Asia, the latter being investigated on a series of journeys, the scientific results of which were treated in works of which a great many are enumerated in the accompanying catalogue (references p. 188). A voyage round the world, which yielded amongst other things ornithological results in the shape of pictures (742), was sent out from Russia in 1803—06 under the leadership of *A. J. von Krusenstern* (272), while we find eloquent testimonies to ornithological activity in publications concerning various journeys, in certain monographs, such as *Sergius Alferaki's* work on the geese of the Palæarctic region (9), and especially in works dealing with local faunas, such as the Siberian explorer *Gustav Radde's* work from 1884 on the birds of the Caucasus (412), a subject also treated in 1887 by *Th. Lorenz* (316). The latter also started a work in 1910—11, which was never completed, with the title 'Die Birkhühner Russlands', etc. (Wien, 24 col. pl., folio). A traveller known especially for his journeys in Asia is N. M. Prževal'skij, who brought home very important results from his various expeditions to Central Asia, the ornithological part being treated in 1889—1905, first by *Th. Pleske,* director of the Zoological Museum at St. Petersburg, and later by *V. Bianchi* (405). Pleske, in addition, began in 1889 an 'Ornithographia Rossica' (404), which was never completed. Bianchi also treated certain birds in the large work on the fauna of Russia, 'Faune de la Russie', etc., in which ornithological subjects are also dealt with by *M. A. Menzbir* (332), among whose other works was an uncompleted large local fauna

'Ornithologie du Turkestan', etc. (Moscou 1888—94, 15 col. pl., 4to). Pleske, whom we have already mentioned above, later treated a number of the birds of the Arctic region in his 'Birds of the Eurasian Tundra' (Boston 1928, 33 pl. (6 col.); Memoirs of the Boston Society of Natural History 6, No. 3, pp. 109—485), a work which is based principally on collections made during the Russian Polar Expedition in 1900—03 under the leadership of Baron E. von Toll. Another Russian ornithologist G. *Gorbunov* partly on the basis of his own observations has described the birds of the Arctic regions in a work written in Russian 'Die Vögel von Franz-Joseph Land' (Leningrad 1932; Transactions of the Arctic Institute, USSR, 4, pp. 1—244).

Polish ornithologists have also taken part in the exploration of Siberia, partly by collecting expeditions, partly by the elaboration of the material brought home from such journeys, as will appear for instance from the work 'Faune ornithologique de la Sibérie orientale', published in 1891—93 in the 'Mémoires' of the St. Petersburg Academy (Sér. VII, Tome XXXIX, Parts 1—2, 4to). Its author, *Władysław Taczanowski,* was director of the zoological museum of the University of Warsaw, which owned valuable collections of birds from Eastern Siberia, procured especially on collecting journeys made by *Benedykt Dybowski* and his various travelling companions, such as *Victor Godlewski* and others, whose results Taczanowski utilised in his work. The avifauna of quite a different part of the world, South America, was also treated by Taczanowski in the very important monograph 'Ornithologie du Pérou' (Rennes 1884—86, 4 vols., 8vo), based especially on the observations and collections of *Constantin Jelski* and *Jan Sztolcman.* The latter visited various parts of South America in 1865—73 and in 1873—84.

Other regions of South America, the La Plata countries and Paraguay, then almost entirely unknown, had already been explored in 1781—1802 by the Spanish naturalist Don *Felix de Azara* in his capacity as an officer in the army. He collected a great deal of material relating to the fauna of these tracts, not least the birds, treating these latter in a Spanish work published in three volumes in Madrid in 1802—05 but especially known in its French version, translated by Sonnini and published in the work 'Voyages dans l'Amérique méridionale' (Paris 1809, 4 vols. text, 8vo, and atlas, folio), of which it forms the two last volumes.

Another well-known traveller in South America

was the Swiss naturalist *J. J. von Tschudi*. In 1838— 42 he explored Peru, and in 1857—59 besides other regions, Brazil, where he was his country's ambassador in 1860—62. He issued a large work in 1844—46 (511) on the fauna of Peru, while the fauna of Brazil, including the birds, has been described in more recent times in several works (164; 165) by his compatriot *Emil August Goeldi,* who worked in that country for many years (901). In Switzerland itself several minor works relating to its avifauna had been published after Gesner's and Cysat's time (602), while a larger work 'Ornithologia Helvetica' (3 vols., 4to) by Pastor *Daniel Sprüngli* in Stettlen, appointed professor of natural history at the Academy of Bern in 1789, exists in a manuscript dating from about 1800 belonging to the Natural History Museum at Bern. The city library of that town possesses a 'Vogelbuch', a manuscript which at one time belonged to Sprüngli and which, besides some pictures of animals, contains 172 handcoloured figures of Swiss birds executed by unknown artists about 1650 (602, p. XXVI, note 4; p. XXVII, note 4).

At the beginning of the 19th century the avifauna of Switzerland was studied by *Friedrich Meisner,* a native of Germany, who was professor of natural history in Bern. In 1804 he issued 'Systematisches Verzeichniss der Vögel welche die Schweiz', etc. (Bern, 12mo), a minor work, of which an enlarged edition was issued in 1815, with the assistance of *Heinrich Schinz,* as a descriptive catalogue of the birds of Switzerland, entitled 'Die Vögel der Schweiz', etc. (Zürich, 8vo), since then further enlarged by additions published in periodicals. Schinz, who contributed several works of information about the fauna of his country, also added to the then prevalent production of ornithological picture works a book, published in 1818—30, on Central European, especially Swiss, birds' nests and eggs (441). In 1830—33 he brought out a folio work, later re-issued several times, also in a revised form, under the title 'Naturgeschichte und Abbildungen der Vögel' with 144 coloured plates by *K. Joseph Brodtmann.* A work which helped to increase the interest in the fauna of the Alps deserves to be mentioned, though popular in form. This is the fascinating book 'Das Thierleben der Alpenwelt' (Leipzig 1853, 8vo) by *Friedrich von Tschudi,* of which numerous editions and translations have subsequently been published.

Of recent Swiss ornithological authors we may

mention especially *Victor Fatio,* among whose works must be noted 'Histoire naturelle des oiseaux' (Genève 1899—1904, 2 vols., 4 pl. (3 col.), 8vo) or the second volume of 'Faune des vertébrés de la Suisse', the most complete account of the birds of Switzerland, in which the author gives elaborate descriptions of the avifauna of his country. In collaboration with *Th. Studer* Fatio, in 1889, commenced a detailed catalogue of the birds of Switzerland which was issued both in French and in German, in the latter language under the title 'Katalog der schweizerischen Vögel' (from 1918: 'Die Vögel der Schweiz') (Basel, 8vo). In 1907 the work, the 16th 'Lieferung' of which appeared in 1930, was taken over by *Gustav von Burg,* being carried on after his death by *Walter Knopfli.*

The painter *Léo Paul Robert* is well-known especially for his pictures of birds in their natural surroundings. He was awarded a gold medal for the bird pictures which he painted for the International Exhibition in Paris in 1878, and his water colours and drawings embellish, for instance, a work 'Les oiseaux dans la nature', etc., with a text written by *Eugène Rambert,* issued the same year and in the succeeding years (Paris 1878, 110 pl. (60 col.), folio; Lausanne 1879—81, 3 vols., 60 col. pl., folio). Robert's plates were published in Germany in 1880—83 (424) with a text by Oskar von Riesenthal, and 20 of the plates with a text by *J. E. Harting* appeared in London in 1880 (423). In our century, also, editions of Robert's plates with Rambert's text have been published in Switzerland, in French as well as in German; but the paintings from which these plates were made were only the beginning of a larger production of bird pictures, of which the artist intended to produce more than 800, a plan never fully carried out (846).

In Italy *F. A. Bonelli,* director of the Zoological Museum of Torino issued in 1811 a local fauna entitled 'Catalogue des oiseaux du Piémont'. Others followed his example, for instance *Paolo Savi* with his work 'Ornitologia Toscana' (Pisa 1827—31, 3 vols., 8vo). The year after this book had appeared the publication of an iconography, completed in 1841, concerned with the vertebrate fauna of Italy (48), was begun by Prince *Charles Lucien Bonaparte* (706, pp. 96—98) who, however, is especially noted for his continuation of Wilson's American Ornithology (p. 77; 47), and of Madame Knip's work on pigeons (261), as well as for his 'Conspectus generum avium' (Lugduni Batavorum 1850—57, 2 vols., 4to). At the

close of the 19th century Italian avifauna was investigated and described largely under the leadership of *Enrico Hillyer Giglioli,* professor and director of the Zoological Museum of Florence, among whose works we may note 'Avifauna Italica', etc. (Firenze 1886, 8vo), an annotated list of importance, for it is the first fairly complete list of the birds of the country. A revised and enlarged edition in three volumes appeared in 1889—91 at Florence, the first being re-issued in 1907. A large pictorial work was published by Giglioli under the title 'Iconografia dell' avifauna Italica', etc., (Prato 1879—94, folio) with fine illustrations on a large number of plates executed from designs by *Alberto Manzella,* while as an example of a beautifully illustrated local fauna we may mention the 'Storia naturale degli uccelli che nidificano in Lombardia', etc., (Milano 1865—71, 2 vols., 120 col. pl., large folio) by *Eugenio Bettoni,* the plates being due to *Oscar Dressler.* The birds of Europe were described and figured by another well-known Italian ornithologist, Count *E. Arrigoni degli Oddi* in the treatise 'Atlante ornitologico', etc. (Milano 1902, 50 col. pl., 4to). The same author treated the avifauna of his country in the 'Manuale di ornitologia italiana', etc. (Milano 1904, 12mo), and in the larger, and more complete, modern work based on it, entitled 'Ornitologia italiana' (Milano 1929, 36 col. pl., 4to). In the meanwhile another important book on the avifauna of Italy had appeared. This was 'Gli uccelli d'Italia' (Milano 1906, 6 col. pl., 4to) by the director of a collection of birds in Milan, Professor *Giacinto Martorelli,* a revised edition of which was issued by *Edgardo Moltoni* and *Carlo Vandoni* (Milano 1931, 16 col. pl.). Martorelli also gave an account of the Italian birds of prey in 'Monografia illustrata degli uccelli di rapina in Italia' (Milano 1895, 4 col. pl., 4to). Of other ornithologists who have described the birds of Italy, special mention may be made of the eminent ornithologist *T. Salvadori,* vice-director of the Zoological University Museum at Torino. As one of the leading ornithologists of Italy he deserves especial credit for those works of his that are of wider scope, for instance his collaboration in the making of the catalogue of the birds in the British Museum (70, XX, XXI, XXVI), and his treatment of birds in foreign countries, for example the birds of the East Indies and the ornithology of Abyssinia. The latter work was based on the material of Italian expeditions. In this connection, however, we must make especial note of his greatest achievement 'Ornitologia della Papuasia e delle Mollucche' (Torino 1880—82, 3 vols., 4to; with 'Aggiunte', etc., 1889—91, 3 parts), a monumental work which is the principal basis for the knowledge of the birds in these regions, including New Guinea.

That island as well as the East Indies, which partly belonged to Holland, naturally became the object of Dutch ornithologists' activities in so far as the elucidation of the avifauna outside their own country was concerned. Temminck's successor (p. 45) in this domain was the eminent ornithologist *Hermann Schlegel,* a native of Germany, who after the death of Temminck was put in part charge of the Museum at Leyden, of which he later became the sole director (856; 872). His contribution to ornithological literature consists of a number of larger or smaller works, some of which are given in the accompanying catalogue, and among which, besides some books on the Dutch avifauna (443; 445), will be found his and Temminck's treatment in 1844—50 of the birds in the first great work on the fauna of Japan (504). The catalogue also includes the periodical 'Bijdragen tot de dierkunde' (41) to which Schlegel contributed several treatises, and also his treatment, in collaboration with the German *Sal. Müller,* of the birds in the large work edited by Temminck on the natural history of the overseas possessions of the Netherlands (351), whose avifauna Schlegel, indeed, has partly dealt with in 'De vogels van Nederlandsch Indië', etc. (Leiden 1863 —66, 3 parts, 50 col. pl., 4to; new edition 1876), which was furnished both with a Dutch and a French text. He treated the collections of the Museum in a critical review 'Muséum d'Histoire Naturelle des Pays-Bas' (Leide 1862—80, 8 vols., 8vo) consisting of 41 monographs which with one exception all deal with birds, and of which only a single one has not been written by Schlegel.

Schlegel could draw birds very ably himself, and utilized this skill chiefly as an illustrator of his own works. He also showed his interest in the production of natural history pictures by writing in 1847 a prize essay on the vexed question — What must be demanded of a natural history drawing for it to satisfy both the naturalist and the connoisseur in art? In this essay, for which he was awarded the prize, he especially recommends the chalk lithography just then coming in (635). Schlegel, however, was of special importance to ornithological picture production by stimulating men of talent like Wolf, mentioned above (p. 50), and

his own compatriots *Joseph Smit* and *J. G. Keulemans* who both, when still comparatively young, emigrated to England after working for a short space as illustrators in Holland. Keulemans illustrated the periodical 'Notes from the Leyden Museum' (307) founded by Schlegel in 1879, while of works from Keulemans' Dutch period may be noted the ornithological plates in a treatise on the mammals and birds of Madagascar, published in 1867—68 (446). In England the two young Dutchmen soon found abundant employment as zoological artists, not least in the service of the Zoological Society and 'The Ibis', especially Keulemans, who had moved to England in 1869, and there became a celebrated ornithological artist. His plates, which are always harmonious and attractive, soon procured wide recognition for him in this field. Faithful to the principles indicated by Schlegel, he used lithography with great ease, being a master of this mode of reproducing his plates, the number of which is countless (Pl. IX). After his arrival in England we find them ornamenting most of the numerous illustrated ornithological works published in that country until the beginning of our century. During this and at the close of the previous century Holland has continued the exploration of her overseas possessions, sending also several excursions into other countries. A Swiss, *Johannes Büttikofer,* conservator of the ornithological department of the Leyden Museum and later director of the Zoological Gardens at Rotterdam, took part among others in this work, exploring Liberia for Schlegel and later visiting the Dutch East Indies and Borneo. A very full and systematic treatise, abundantly illustrated, on the birds of the three Guianas has been issued by the brothers *Frederick Paul Penard* and *Arthur Philip Penard* under the title 'De vogels van Guyana', etc. (Paramaribo 1908—10, 2 vols., 8vo) while since 1906 a large work in 4to on New Guinea has been in course of publication at Leyden. It is entitled 'Nova Guinea', etc., and embodies the results of Dutch expeditions carried out in 1903 and succeeding years; some ornithological material has been treated in a section of the ninth volume, published in 1909, by *E. D. van Oort,* who is noted especially for his great work on the birds of Holland, completed in 1935 (381), the first large illustrated work on the subject since the days of Schlegel. Of other publications of our own day may be mentioned a work containing pictures of the eggs of Dutch breeding birds, *A. A. van Pelt Lechner*'s 'Oologia Neerlandica', etc., 1910—14 (390), and also 'A monograph of the cranes', etc.

(Leiden 1897, 22 col. pl., large folio), only printed in 170 copies, a slightly older, handsomely illustrated account of the family of the cranes by *F. E. Blaauw*, noted for his travels in South America and Africa. It may also be mentioned that *A. C. Oudemans* in his 'Dodo-studiën', etc., 1917 (384) has reviewed the material relating to the Dodo produced in the 16th and 17th centuries.

During the first half of the 19th century a special study of the birds of Belgium was made by *Edmond de Selys Longchamps*, who treated them in a section of the first part of his 'Faune belge' (Liège 1842, 8vo). In his famous museum at Longchamps he collected over 3000 specimens of birds from Europe and from other continents. After his death these were listed by Julien Fraipont in Fascicle XXXI (Bruxelles 1910, 2 col. pl., 4to) of the systematic and descriptive catalogue published under the title of 'Collections zoologiques du Baron Edm. de Selys Longchamps' at the instance of de Selys' sons. A comprehensive work consisting of a series of monographs each by a different author and dealing with the various families of birds, was edited at the beginning of our century by *P. Wytsman* under the title 'Genera avium', etc. (Brussels 1905—14, 44 col. pl., 4to), but publication ceased after 26 parts had been issued. While the plates play a subordinate part in this work, they are more prominent in some works issued by *Ch. F. Dubois*, who executed the illustrations himself. The first of these, 'Ornithologische Gallerie, oder Abbildungen aller bekannten Vögel' (Aachen 1834—39, 22 parts, 124 (some copies 145) col. pl., 4to), is planned on a large scale; the next 'Planches coloriées des oiseaux de la Belgique et de leurs oeufs' (Bruxelles 1851—60, 3 vols., 429 col. pl., large 8vo), with its sequel 'Les oiseaux de l'Europe et leurs oeufs', etc. (Bruxelles 1861—72, 2 vols., 319 col. pl., large 8vo), constitutes an illustrated European avifauna, the latter work describing European birds that are not found in Belgium. In the writing of this Ch. F. Dubois was helped by his son *Alphonse Dubois*, who completed the book after the death of his father and later issued an illustrated account of the birds of his own country in 'Faune illustrée des vertébrés de la Belgique. Sér. II. Les oiseaux' (Bruxelles 1876—94, 2 vols. text, 2 vols. plates, 8vo), and a checklist of all known birds: 'Synopsis avium', etc. (Bruxelles 1899—1904, 2 vols., 16 col. pl., 4to). In 1905 he contributed to the ornithology of the Congo state (122), which has also been partially treated by the Director of the Congo Museum at Tervueren, *H.*

Schouteden, in a report entitled 'Contribution à la faune ornithologique du nord-est du Congo belge' (Tervueren 1936; Annales du Musée du Congo belge, pp. 1—156). In 1905 came the first volume of a treatise on Belgian birds by *Marcel de Contreras* entitled 'Les oiseaux observés en Belgique', etc. (Bruxelles 1905—07, 2 vols., 8vo), while a useful up-to-date manual of Belgian birds 'Les oiseaux de la faune belge', etc. (Bruxelles, 8vo), was issued in 1928 by *G. van Havre*.

The Belgian treatise on European birds referred to above was soon followed by an English one which still holds its own as the largest and most complete of its kind, *H. E. Dresser*'s immense monograph published in 1871—96 (120). It is illustrated with a great number of fine plates, one of the artists being Keulemans. Dresser, who was actually a businessman, never failed on his numerous journeys to look after his ornithological interests, and secured an excellent collection of eggs and about 12,000 skins, almost exclusively of Palæarctic birds, which he later presented to the Manchester Museum. In addition to treating the birds of that region in his principal work mentioned above, he also dealt with them in 'A manual of Palæarctic birds' (London 1902—03, 2 vols., 8vo). Of his other works note must be made of his treatise on the eggs of the birds of Europe and other Palæarctic regions, published in 1905—10 (121) as a kind of sequel to his principal work, and also of his monographs on two groups of birds, 'A monograph of the Meropidæ', etc., (London 1884—86, 34 col. pl., 4to) and 'A monograph of the Coraciidæ', etc. (Farnborough 1893, 27 col. pl., 4to).

Dresser's works are mentioned here as an introduction to the following brief sketch of the literary history and iconography of British ornithology in the period under consideration, because they give some idea of, and may be considered to be representative of, the part played by British ornithology during the 19th and 20th centuries. Aided by a lively interest in ornithological research and by favourable external conditions, ornithologists in Great Britain and the British possessions overseas have produced such a number of considerable works and such a vast and excellent pictorial material that they have taken the lead in this field. The overwhelming mass of writings that should be treated here cannot, however, be dealt with in a limited space. It must therefore be represented by examples which will show the importance of British ornithology.

The study of the avifauna, not least of the British

PLATE VII

HUMMING-BIRDS. *Threnetes ruckeri* Bourc. From hand-coloured lithograph (Pl. 11), drawn and lithographed
by J. Gould and H. C. Richter, in Gould's 'A monograph of the Trochilidæ', etc., Vol. I, 1861

PLATE VII

Isles themselves, found many devotees, especially after Bewick's and Gilbert White's works, as already stated, had created an interest in it (574). This is reflected in an imposing series of books dealing with the entire British avifauna among which was the 'Ornithological dictionary', etc. (London 1802, 2 vols., 8vo), by Colonel *George Montagu* (621, VIII; 701), an alphabetical synopsis of British birds augmented by a supplement in 1813 (344). This work which is regarded as one of the best accounts of British birds, was for many years a highly valued guide to the subject and appeared in a number of editions.

So great a popularity that it could be issued in more than one edition was not attained by the valuable work 'A history of British birds', etc., (London 1837—52, 5 vols., 8vo) by *William Macgillivray* (621, IX; 803), for it was thrown somewhat into the shade by a richer and more handsomely illustrated work with the same title which was published simultaneously and scored a much greater success. This was 'A history of British birds' (London 1837—43, 3 vols., 8vo) by *William Yarrell* (621, IX), which became the standard work in this field. It was enlarged in 1845 and 1856 respectively by two supplements, and four editions of it have appeared, the last of which was published in four volumes in 1871—85 by *Alfred Newton* and *Howard Saunders*. After its completion Saunders condensed the material in his classic handbook 'An illustrated manual of British birds' (London 1889, 8vo; second edition 1899), which gave the same pictorial material and which was so popular that a third revised and enlarged edition could be issued in 1927 by *William Eagle Clarke*. As a quite modern and highly useful work on the subject we must mention 'A practical handbook of British birds' (London 1919—24, 2 vols., 30 pl. (8 col.), 8vo) by *H. F. Witherby* and others. Finally Witherby's periodical, 'British Birds', of which the first volume was issued in 1907, must be mentioned as a source of information about British avifauna.

The fauna of the constituent parts of the British Isles has also been investigated by a series of observers, whose activities can be seen in accounts of the natural history of local districts and in a series of works dealing with local faunas, of which we shall, however, only mention 'The birds of the west of Scotland', etc., (Glasgow 1871, 15 pl., 8vo) by *Robert Gray;* the series of volumes on the vertebrate fauna of Scotland which was edited and the majority of which was written in 1887—1906 by *J. A. Harvie-Brown;* 'The verte-

brate fauna of North Wales' (London 1907, 28 pl., 8vo), by *H. E. Forrest*, to which the author has supplied some corrections and additions in a handbook with a title similar to that of the main work (London 1919, 8vo); the three first volumes, Birds, in 'The natural history of Ireland' (London 1849—51, 8vo) by *William Thompson;* and a standard work on the same subject entitled 'The birds of Ireland', etc. (London 1900, 7 pl. (1 col.), 8vo) by *Richard J. Ussher* and *Robert Warren*. As regards British works dealing with local faunas reference may be made to a bibliography on the subject (575); as an example from recent years, however, we may mention *Claud B. Ticehurst*'s 'A history of the birds of Suffolk' (London 1932, 19 pl., 8vo).

While in the works hitherto mentioned the pictorial matter, if any, is subordinated to the text, as is the case too in *T. C. Eyton*'s 'A history of the rarer British birds' (London 1836, 8vo), which is a supplement to Bewick (p. 35), British avifauna was at the same time given no small place in works in which illustrations in the form of plates are prominent. This applies for instance to 'The portraits of British birds', etc., (London 1808—16, 120 col. pl., 4to) by *Charles Hayes,* a son of William Hayes (p. 33), a rare work which was perhaps never completed. It was almost contemporaneous with a couple of other works of a similar type, viz. 'British ornithology', etc., (London 1811—21, 3 vols., 144 col. pl., 8vo; second edition issued also with uncoloured plates, 1821) by *George Graves,* and the rare and incomplete 'British ornithology' etc., (Norwich 1815—22, 3 vols., c. 192 pl. (180 col.), 8vo) by *John Hunt.*

On a much higher level than the three above-mentioned works, about whose authors we know very little, is the ornithologist *Prideaux John Selby*'s 'Plates to Selby's Illustrations of British ornithology' (Edinburgh 1821—34, 2 vols., 218, some copies 222, pl., large folio). This atlas, whose plates, with the exception of some few, are coloured, appeared in several editions, and was also issued with uncoloured plates. It was accompanied by an explanatory text in 4to, now very rare, which was replaced in 1825 by the first part 'Land birds' of 'Illustrations of British ornithology' (Edinburgh, 8vo), of which a second edition appeared in 1833 together with the second volume of the text entitled 'Water birds'. The plates for this work were engraved by *W. H. Lizars* and give life-size portraits of the birds in beautiful hand-coloured reproductions, the greater part of which were executed from drawings by Selby himself made from specimens in his own collection, while the rest were drawn by his brother-in-law Admiral *R. Mitford*. In addition to this his principal work, which may be compared to Audubon's work on the birds of America (p. 77), Selby is especially noted for his collaboration with *William Jardine* (p. 60) and his contributions to the latter's 'The Naturalist's Library' (224), in which Jardine, who was a prominent ornithologist and often drew illustrations for his own works, published a work on British birds, 1838—43 (227). These had already in 1835—41 been depicted again in a very fine and complete collection of lithographs, published by an Englishman of Dutch descent *H. L. Meÿer* under the title 'Illustrations of British birds' (London, 313 col. pl., large 4to), whose figures were executed by Meÿer himself, who was a professional artist, with the assistance of his family and in particular of his wife. The plates, whose number is somewhat variable, were re-issued several times, the last issue being in 1838—44, when they were accompanied by a fragmentary text which has been incorporated in the text of the 8vo-edition of Meÿer's 'Coloured illustrations of British birds and their eggs' (London 1842—50, 7 vols., 432 mostly coloured pl.; new edition 1853—57). The second series of the original work was really to have been published in conjunction with Yarrell's 'History of British birds' (p. 57) as illustrations to it. This, however, was never done. To mention an example of a work depicting eggs, a notable one with coloured and exact figures of eggs, intended to be a sequel to Yarrell's, was issued by *William C. Hewitson* under the title 'British oology', etc. (Newcastle upon Tyne 1831—42, 2 vols., and supplement (London), 169 col. pl., 8vo). This was re-issued in London in 1842—46 and 1853—56 under the title of 'Coloured illustrations of the eggs of British birds', etc. The last edition was published at the same time as another work on the eggs of British birds, the Rev. *Francis Orpen Morris'* 'Natural history of the nests and eggs of British birds' (London 1853—56, 3 vols., 223 col. pl., 8vo), of which several editions have appeared. Morris's main work, the popular 'A history of British birds' with many coloured plates, first published in 1850—57, achieved its fifth edition in 1903 (346). This work, however, does not equal in popularity the Rev. *C. A. Johns'* 'British birds in their haunts', etc. (232), first published in 1862 with woodcuts by *Josiah Whymper*

designed by J. Wolf, and since issued in a great many editions.

The impressive series of works with coloured portraits of British birds has since been continued. Thus we have the large work 'Rough notes', etc., (51) handsomely illustrated from drawings by *Edward Neale,* which was issued in 1881—87 by *E. T. Booth,* noted for the considerable museum he had collected at Brighton. An important and original work on British birds with coloured figures of their eggs was issued in 1882—85 by the ornithologist *Henry Seebohm* (457, pp. V—XIV), a steel manufacturer at Sheffield noted especially for his monographs (p. 62). Its title was 'A history of British birds', etc. (456), and its plates are different from the plates in Seebohm's posthumous 'Coloured figures of eggs of British birds', etc. (457), edited by R. Bowdler Sharpe in 1896.

The zenith of the iconographical description of the birds of the British Isles was, however, — as well as in the work on this subject by John Gould (p. 60) — reached in a work in seven volumes (308), illustrated with more than 400 handsome plates by the best artists, such as Keulemans and Archibald Thorburn. This was issued in 1885—98 by Lord *Lilford* (729), one of the original members of the British Ornithologists' Union. Lilford, who was keenly interested in wild animal life, had one of the finest collections of live birds in England, and also possessed an excellent collection of stuffed birds composed exclusively of British species (708).

The possibilities of enterprise in the field covered by Lilford's fine work had not, however, been exhausted with its appearance. This was evidenced by the subsequent publication of more popular works, such as one on the same subject (88), published in 1896—98, written by *Arthur G. Butler* and others and illustrated by *F. W. Frohawk,* an ornithological artist who pursued independent zoological studies in addition to his activities as an illustrator. Of recent years we may also mention 'The birds of the British Islands' (London 1906—11, 5 vols, 318 pl., 4to) by the military surgeon *Charles Stonham* and illustrated by *Lilian M. Medland;* the 'British bird book' (245) edited in 1910—13 by *F. B. Kirkman* with contributions by several authors, the plates of which were used in 1930 by Kirkman and the Rev. *C. R. Jourdain* in a work entitled 'British birds' (cf. 245, note); and also 'British birds', first issued in 1915—16 (508) by the eminent bird artist *Archibald Thorburn,* who has published several other zoological works which are, like this one, render-

PLATE VIII

The Greenland Falcon. *Falco rusticolus candicans* Gm. From hand-coloured lithograph (Pl. **XXX**), drawn from Nature by Joseph Wolf, London 1868, in D. G. Elliot's 'The new and heretofore unfigured species of the birds of North America', Vol. II, 1869

PLATE VIII

ed attractive by the beautiful illustrations from the hand of the author. Archibald Thorburn was the son of a miniature portrait painter Robert Thorburn, and even though the American Fuertes (p. 81) and the Dane Johannes Larsen (p. 75) can hold their own against him, he must be regarded as one of the best bird-painters of our day. His pictures adorn a series of the most recent and most beautifully illustrated ornithological works. He worked mostly in water colours and, inspired by his observations of Nature, he painted pictures of birds in their natural surroundings, which contributed to increase the life and charm which he knew how to communicate to his well-drawn pictures with their beautiful colouring (Pl. X, Fig. 2).

Thorburn issued special examples of his art in 1919 in the work 'A naturalist's sketch book' (509), while another bird artist, *Philip Rickman,* has issued a pictorial work with plates showing figures of British birds in his book 'A bird painter's sketch book', etc. (London 1931, 34 pl. (11 col.), folio; cheaper edition, 1935, 4to), a work the first edition of which appeared in different issues.

Single groups of British birds were of course also depicted in larger or smaller works, for instance, from a somewhat earlier period, the rare book 'A treatise on British song-birds', etc., (Edinburgh 1823, 15 col. pl., 8vo and 12mo) by the drawing-master and flower-painter *Patrick Syme,* published also with uncoloured plates; 'The British warblers', etc., (London 1823—32, 8vo) by the horticulturist *Robert Sweet,* a treatise generally found with 16, but also occurring with 6, coloured plates. Very rare is 'The resident song birds of Great Britain', etc., (London 1835, 2 parts, 33 col. pl., large 8vo; second issue in one volume 1836) by *John Cotton.* In addition to these works, noteworthy especially for their illustrations, may also be mentioned Macgillivray's 'Descriptions of the rapacious birds of Great Britain' (Edinburgh 1836, 2 pl., 8vo) and, among special works depicting eggs, the unfinished but fine work on the eggs of the British wading birds issued in 1895—96 (406) by *Frank Poynting.*

As members of a sporting nation, British ornithologists have turned no litle of their attention to game birds, which is exemplified by a series of works such as 'British game birds and wildfowl', 1855 (345) by *Beverley R. Morris* brother of the Rev. F. O. Morris. This work scored such a success that it could appear in 1895 in a fourth edition (2 vols., large 8vo) revised and corrected by *W. B. Tegetmeier,* who is

known especially for his works on pigeons and poultry, among which may be mentioned his book on pheasants (500) first published in 1873. One of the illustrators of the later editions of this work is *J. G. Millais,* known for his beautifully illustrated works, mostly on game animals and birds, for instance his fine books on British ducks (340; 342). To satisfy his zest for shooting he explored large parts of the world and thus became acquainted with the life of animals at first hand. He also obtained material for his extensive writings, in which he showed unflagging energy, and for his paintings which he exhibited three times in London. Evidences of his artistic activity are also found in the shape of illustrations for several other works, for instance in his own 'Game birds and shooting-sketches', etc. (London 1892, 34 pl. (16 col.), folio; second edition 1894, 18 pl., 8vo), and its sequel 'The natural history of the British game birds' (London 1909, 35 pl. (18 col.), folio). Millais, in collaboration with several others wrote 'British game birds and wildfowl' (London 1912, 36 col. pl., 4to). Among the authors of that book was *W. R. Ogilvie-Grant,* who had himself published a work on game birds in 1895—97 (371), while Thorburn, also, has displayed his ability in this field in his work 'Game birds and wild-fowl of Great Britain and Ireland' (London 1923, 30 col. pl., folio).

In the series of beautifully illustrated monographs on British birds we must not forget to mention *H. Eliot Howard*'s 'The British warblers', etc. (213), published in 1907—15; its plates were drawn by *Henrik Grønvold.* This much employed ornithological artist had from his youth studied bird life in the open in his native country, Denmark, where he began to draw and paint animals, an example of his work being a final plate for Kjærbølling's bird book (103) (Pl. X, Fig. 1). In 1892 he went to London where he obtained employment at the British Museum (Natural History). A couple of years later he began his work as a draughtsman and painter for zoological publications such as those of the Zoological Society of London. After taking part in a short collecting expedition to the Salvages Islands in 1895, he continued his work as a bird painter and has since supplied such a large number of beautiful and lifelike illustrations for zoological works that he is now a leading artist in that province.

In England Grønvold obtained a much richer and more extensive field of work than he could have had in his own country, for British ornithologists, besides treating the birds of the British Isles, have contributed very largely to promote the study of ornithology in general. With the position of the island kingdom as the centre of a world-wide empire, there were great possibilities for investigating bird life in many foreign tracts of the earth. Collections of birds from all parts of the world were brought home and, favoured by these excellent external conditions, British ornithology could tackle tasks of unparallelled scope and range.

One of the investigators who realized how best to exploit these rich possibilities of producing ornithological literature and pictures, which are also to some extent valuable from a scientific point of view, was *John Gould*. For many years he occupied a leading position among British ornithologists. From his youth he had lived in intimate intercourse with Nature and had learned to know the value of its beauties. But it was only after he had been appointed to a post at the Museum of the Zoological Society in London that he entered the field which he subsequently continued to cultivate— the production of magnificent ornithological works richly illustrated with beautiful plates. In London, where he married the artist Miss Coxen in 1829, he acquired a collection of bird-skins from the Himalaya Mountains and on this he based his first work, published in 1831—32 (168), with fine plates drawn by Mrs. Gould from her husband's sketches. The work scored such a great success that Gould continued for the rest of his life to publish large uniform monographs and faunas all on the same lines (169—182). A work on British birds, published in 1862—73 under the title 'The birds of Great Britain' (London, 5 vols., 367 col. pl., large folio), was not lacking among these. The total result of Gould's activities was a series of more than 40 large folio volumes, containing altogether over 3000 plates, by which he has left behind him a memorial unequalled by any other in this field. One of his greatest works is 'The birds of Australia', published in 1840—48 (174; 179), for which he collected part of the material on journeys through various parts of that country in 1838—40. The year after his return from Australia his wife died. This was a great loss to him, even though he was able to enlist the help of other collaborators in the illustration of his works, for instance, at an early period, Edward Lear, and later on the lithographer *H. C. Richter, W. Hart* — from 1851 — and occasionally J. Wolf. The imposing array of plates of birds from all quarters of the world which we meet in Gould's works, is on the whole most impressive, produced as they are with a distinct sense of

effect. This may, especially perhaps in the later works, give the figures a somewhat unnatural appearance, both as regards drawing and colour, the latter seeming to be excessively vivid. One of the groups of birds in which Gould was particularly interested was that of humming-birds (Pl. VII), which he described in a large monograph(177;182). He possessed a famous collection of these birds which was bought after his death by the British Museum for a sum of £ 3000, together with the rest of his ornithological collections. His unique collection of Australian birds had previously been sold to America (853; 861; 905). The entire stock of Gould's works and copyrights was purchased by the firm of Henry Sotheran & Co., who took in hand the completion of the unfinished works, R. Bowdler Sharpe undertaking the work of writing the text. A single one has not been completed, 'A monograph of the Pittidæ', etc., of which one part only was published in 1880 (cf. 178, note).

Gould's monographs of individual groups of birds (170; 171; 176; 177) belong to the category of works, the theme of which is not limited locally, but has a more comprehensive topographical character. Of such more general works published during the beginning of the 19th century we may mention 'Zoological illustrations', etc. (London, 8vo; first series 1820—23, 3 vols., 182 col. pl.; second series 1829—33, 3 vols., 136 col. pl.), a series of pictures and descriptions of new, rare, and interesting animals by *William Swainson* (645, pp. 338—352), an English naturalist and a great traveller. Upon the advice of his friend W. E. Leach he learnt the art of lithography, and designed and executed most of the plates for his works himself. In this way they were very handsomely illustrated, Swainson being one of the best ornithological artists of the time (Pl. IV, Figs. 1—2). Adopting writing as a profession, he issued a series of works among which, as evidence of his interest in systematics, mention may here be made of his survey of the whole class of birds, 'On the natural history and classification of birds' (London 1836 —37, 2 vols., 8vo). He also contributed to 'The Naturalist's Library', 1833—43 (224), a popular scientific description of many groups of animals, edited, as already mentioned, by Sir William Jardine, in which the volumes on birds occupy a prominent place. Jardine, who wrote a number of these volumes himself, was especially interested in ornithology, for which reason he had a collection of birds numbering 6000 species in his museum at Jardine Hall. He too, drew illustrations for his works himself, while his daughter *Catherine Dorcas Maule,* married to the ornithologist *H. E. Strickland* (889), assisted in lithographing many of the plates for 'Contributions to ornithology', 1848—53 (229). A series of fine handcoloured plates are found in Jardine and Selby's 'Illustrations of ornithology', 1826—43 (222), while a similar series of fine plates with figures of new, rare, and strange animals was issued under the title 'Illustrations of zoology', etc., (Edinburgh 1828—31, 36 col. pl. (20 pl. birds), folio) by Jardine's friend *James Wilson,* a Scotsman. Another Scot, Captain *Thomas Brown* (812), issued or commenced several large illustrated ornithological works, among which we may here mention the unfinished 'Illustrations of the genera of birds', etc. (London 1845—46, 59 pl. (56 col.), folio).

A particularly good basis for the writing of ornithological works of a more extensive character was afforded by the rich collections in the British Museum, that of birds gradually growing to be the largest in the world (677, II, pp. 79—515). The staff at that institution had of course special opportunities for exploiting the treasures stored there, as was done by the eminent ornithologist *G. R. Gray,* who became assistant in the zoological department of the museum in 1831. Among his works we find the forerunner of the famous 'Catalogue of the birds', etc., of that museum (pp. 61—62), as well as a complete list of all the genera of birds and their subdivisions, the 'Hand-list of genera and species of birds', etc., (London 1869—71, 3 parts, 8vo) in which 2915 genera and subgenera and 11,162 species are given, but which became obsolete comparatively quickly and was superseded in 1899—1909 by R. B. Sharpe's work of the same title (p. 62).

The industrious and painstaking Gray was the first to adopt the now generally accepted principle that the only valid name for a living form must be that which was first used, starting from the 10th edition, 1758, of Linnæus' 'Systema naturæ' and discarding all earlier names. As early as in 1844—49 he had issued his main work, 'The genera of birds', etc. (London, 3 vols., 360 pl. (185 col.), large 4to), a large systematic work based on the collections in the British Museum. It was handsomely illustrated by *D. W. Mitchell,* secretary of the Zoological Society, J. Wolf, and others, and was of no little importance to the progress of ornithology. G. R. Gray's brother, *John Edward Gray,* was also

interested in ornithology and, amongst other works, issued in 1846 the first part of the atlas 'Gleanings from the menagerie and aviary at Knowsley Hall' (189), in which, however, but few birds are depicted. In the previous year *Louis Fraser* commenced the publication of his 'Zoologia typica', etc. (150), with figures of animals from the gardens of the Zoological Society of London, or of animals described in the Proceedings of that society.

In 1831 the nineteen year old *Edward Lear,* was appointed draughtsman to the gardens of the society. This artist had already begun in the previous year the issue of his series of fine handcoloured lithographs with figures of parrots (283). This work thus precedes the first work by Gould, whom we may note he assisted as a draughtsman (p. 60). He also helped Sir William Jardine and others, and in 1832—36 he designed the fine plates for J. E. Gray's above-mentioned work. The following year, however, he left England on account of bad health. He visited the country now and again later on and still enjoyed such a high reputation that in 1845, on the occasion of one of these visits, he had the honour of giving drawing lessons to Queen Victoria.

Among accounts of individual groups of birds we may, besides those already noted, mention T. C. Eyton's monograph of the Anatidæ, 1838 (139). We may also note that one of England's most eminent ornithologists, *Philip Lutley Sclater,* who contributed to the progress of ornithology during the last half of the 19th century by his extensive production (595, pp. 129—137; 732), issued in 1857—58 and 1879—82 a couple of works belonging to this category (448; 451). His interest as an ornithologist was directed in no small degree towards America, as will appear from his writings (pp. 67—68) and his large collection of skins of American birds (449). The latter was transferred to the British Museum, of whose 'Catalogue of the birds', etc., 1874—98 (74), illustrated amongst other pictures by nearly 400 coloured plates, he wrote several volumes. The life and soul of this undertaking, which is one of the most important recent works in ornithology and has had great influence on the development of the science, was R. Bowdler Sharpe, one of the most industrious ornithologists England has produced. The son of a publisher, he came to London at the age of 16 and entered the service of Bernard Quaritch. Later on he was librarian to the Zoological Society and, after G. R. Gray's death in 1872, became his successor at the British

Museum, whose collection of birds was thus committed to his keeping, under which it grew from 35,000 specimens to half a million. The great number of species thus represented in the collection makes its catalogue, of which Sharpe wrote a long series of volumes entirely or in part, the greatest work extant on systematic ornithology. The unique collection at the British Museum also made another work by Sharpe very important, 'A hand-list of the genera and species of birds', etc. (London 1899—1909, 5 vols., 8vo), to which his collaborator at the Museum, W. R. Ogilvie-Grant, issued a general index in 1912. Sharpe's work, which superseded Gray's Hand-list, is written on the same lines as the latter. It may further be mentioned that Sharpe, as already noted, completed several of Gould's works, and also some others, such as a couple of works by Seebohm, and he assisted Dresser with the first parts of his 'Birds of Europe' (p. 56). He also wrote some monographs — his first work 'A monograph of the Alcedinidæ', etc., 1868—71 (464), which he began when he was about seventeen; 'A monograph of the Paradiseidæ ... and Ptilonorhynchidæ', etc. (London 1891—98, 2 vols., 79 col. pl., folio); as well as 'A monograph of the Hirundinidæ', etc. (London 1885—94, 2 vols., 104 col. pl., 4to), a work written in collaboration with Claude W. Wyatt.

Ogilvie-Grant, referred to above, was also an eminent ornithologist. From 1913—18 he was Assistant Keeper of Zoology in the British Museum (Natural History) and like Sharpe and in conjunction with him he added to and improved the collection of birds so that, as already mentioned, it became the finest in the world, attaining under Ogilvie-Grant a size of nearly 800,000 specimens. He himself made several collecting expeditions and was especially active in the economic organisation of such journeys. These expeditions furnished him with material for several works (pp. 66 and 69). He also worked at the 'Catalogue of the birds', (70) and completed the corresponding work on the collection of birds' eggs in the Museum (71), published in 1901—12.

Another man who made several journeys both at home and abroad in order to add to his valuable collection of birds' eggs was John Wolley (595, pp. 157—171; 911), whose collection was bequathed to his friend, the above-mentioned Alfred Newton (595, pp. 107—116; 916), and forms the basis of the latter's well known work 'Ootheca Wolleyana', etc., 1864—1907 (541). Newton's vast insight into ornithology won for him a world-wide reputation as a writer in this field and was especially manifested in 'A dictionary of birds', etc. (London 1893—96, 4 parts, 8vo).

Of other works published at the close of the 19th century may further be noted the fine monograph of the Capitonidæ (324) issued in 1870—71 by C. H. T. Marshall and G. F. L. Marshall; the 'Ornithological miscellany' (432), which was edited in 1875—78 by George Dawson Rowley, who wrote much of it himself, and in which many rare birds are depicted; and 'A monograph of the Nectariniidæ', etc., (London 1876—80, 121 col. pl., 4to) by Captain G. E. Shelley, who retired from military service to devote himself to nature study and is noted for his books on the ornithology of Africa (p. 68). J. G. Keulemans supplied the handsome illustrations for his monograph on the family of the sunbirds. Deserving of notice are also 'The ornithological works' (513) of the Marquis of Tweeddale (513, pp. XIII—LXII), published in 1881, and various monographs (455; 458) by the above-mentioned Seebohm, who also contributed to the 'Catalogue of the birds in the British Museum' (74). A monograph on a single species, Sula bassana, by J. H. Gurney, j u n i o r, is found in 'The Gannet', etc. (London 1913, 5 pl. (2 col.), 8vo), while extinct birds were treated in 1907 in a fine work by Walter Rothschild (430), and the story of the extinct Garefowl was told by Symington Grieve in 'The Great Auk', etc. (London 1885, 4 pl. (2 col. pl. eggs), 4to). The Dodo and other extinct birds were described in 1848 by H. E. Strickland and A. G. Melville in 'The Dodo and its kindred', etc. (486), a theme which was also treated by the famous anatomist Richard Owen in 'Memoir on the Dodo', etc., (London 1866, 12 pl. (2 col.), folio) with a historical introduction by W. J. Broderip. In this connection we may also mention Owen's well-known 'Memoirs on the extinct wingless birds of New Zealand', etc. (London 1879, 1 vol. text, 1 vol. plates (128 pl.), large 4to), in which osteology is given a prominent place.

As an example of an account of the entire group of birds may be noted the ninth volume, 'Birds' of the 'Cambridge Natural History' (London, 8vo 1899 and later editions) by A. H. Evans, an excellent work containing a wealth of information. An admirable work on the brush-tongued parrots, with fine hand-coloured plates by J. G. Keulemans, was issued in 1896 by St. George Mivart under the title 'A monograph of the lories', etc. (London, 61 col. pl., 4to) while Frederick Du Cane Godman (595, pp. 81—92)

PLATE IX

Fig. 1. HEUGLIN'S COURSER. *Rhinoptilus cinctus* (Heugl.). From hand-coloured lithograph (Pl. XII), by J. G. Keulemans, in Henry Seebohm's 'The geographical distribution of the family Charadriidæ', etc., 1887

Fig. 2. THE GREY FORK-TAILED PETREL. *Oceanodroma furcata* (Gm.). From hand-coloured lithograph (Pl. 11), drawn and lithographed by J. G. Keulemans, in F. Du Cane Godman's 'A monograph of the petrels', etc., 1907—10

PLATE IX

Fig. 1

Fig. 2

wrote a monograph of the petrels, published in 1907—10 (163) (Pl. IX, Fig. 2), a work projected by his friend Osbert Salvin. Finally, *H. Kirke Swann*, besides writing 'A synopsis of the Accipitres', etc., 1921—22 (497), had in 1924 commenced 'A monograph of the birds of prey', etc. (London, col. plates, large 4to), with illustrations by H. Grønvold, a work now — after the death of Kirke Swann — issued by Alexander Westmore (pp. 84—85). Fourteen parts have appeared, the first six having been completed by the original author.

The activities of British ornithologists have not only borne rich fruit in the literature relating to their native avifauna or to single groups of birds but they have also largely concerned themselves with investigations of the avifauna outside the British Isles, not least in the British possessions beyond the seas, whose ornithological literature on the larger areas will be treated here, while Canada will be mentioned under America.

European birds were not only, as previously mentioned, described by Dresser (p. 56), but also by John Gould in 1832—37 (169), while *C. R. Bree* in 1859—67, in a work illustrated with fine coloured woodcuts by *B. Fawcett,* treated the birds of Europe that had not been observed in the British Isles (59), thus producing a kind of supplement to Morris' 'A history of British birds' (346). The wilds of Scandinavia have had a certain fascination for adventurous and sport-loving Englishmen. Thus a devotee of field sports, *H. W. Wheelwright,* 'an old Bushman', as he calls himself on the title pages of his books, spent a number of years in Sweden and furnished contributions towards the knowledge of the avifauna of that country in a couple of books entitled 'A spring and summer in Lapland', etc. (London 1864, 8vo; second edition 1871, 6 col. pl. birds), and 'Ten years in Sweden', etc. (London 1865, 8vo). *L. Lloyd,* who came to Sweden at the age of 31 to shoot and fish, and stayed there for the rest of his life, published among other works a book in 1867 on the game birds and wild fowl of Sweden and Norway (312). During the years 1871, 1872 and 1875 Northern Europe was visited by the above-mentioned J. A. Harvie-Brown who collected material for his work Travels of a naturalist in Northern Europe', etc. (London 1905, 2 vols., 25 pl. (2 col.), large 8vo), in which birds from Norway, Archangel, and Petchora are mentioned. From quite another part of Europe, too, we have examples of the enterprise of British ornithologists. *L. Howard L. Irby* (595, pp. 187—191) during

his service at Gibraltar was able to collect material for his sound 'The ornithology of the Straits of Gibraltar' (London 1875, 8vo; second edition 1895, 14 pl. (8 col.), large 8vo), which he is said to have issued at the instance of Lord Lilford. *William Tait,* who was born and educated in England, but afterwards lived in Portugal, had such ample opportunities of studying bird life in that country that he could give an account of it in 'The birds of Portugal' (London 1924, 10 pl., 8vo), in which, however, the subject was not exhausted.

In the ornithological exploration of the world the British nation has further taken part by means of a number of major or minor journeys and expeditions, some of which have been mentioned in the appended catalogue (references p. 132). We may here mention some of the larger seagoing expeditions, such as Captain Beechey's voyage in the 'Blossom' in 1825—28 to the Pacific and the Bering Strait, in the zoological report of which, 1839, the birds are treated by *N. A. Vigors* (517). Considerable ornithological results, of no little importance for the knowledge of the avifauna of South America, were the outcome of the famous voyage of the 'Beagle' in 1832—36 in which Darwin took part, and the zoological results of which he edited in 1838—43, the birds being treated in a richly illustrated section (173) by John Gould, Darwin, and G. R. Gray, while the report on the ornithological results from the voyage of the 'Erebus' and 'Terror' under the command of Sir James Clark Ross in 1839—43 were issued in 1844—75, first by G. R. Gray and later by R. Bowdler Sharpe (185). The most renowned of all the larger British expeditions is, however, doubtless the voyage of the 'Challenger' in 1873—76. It was of fundamental importance for the development of oceanography but also obtained some ornithological results which were treated by a number of investigators. Among these was P. L. Sclater, who edited the report on the birds in 1880 (452).

The British nation has made considerable contributions towards the exploration of the Antarctic regions which, of course, have also yielded ornithological results. We may mention a couple of examples, first the voyage of the 'Southern Cross' in 1898—1900, under the leadership of the Norwegian Antarctic explorer *Carsten Borchgrevink,* who had in 1894—95 already visited the Antarctic. The zoologist of the expedition, the Norwegian *Nicolai Hanson,* died in 1899; but the material that had been collected relating to birds was treated by R. Bowdler Sharpe, the account being published in conjunction with extracts from the private diary of Hanson in the report on the natural history collections (London 1902, 4 col. pl., 8vo). Another noted Antarctic expedition is the voyage of the 'Discovery' in 1901—04, under the leadership of *R. F. Scott,* among the results of which we may here note that a number of birds were observed and collected, the material being treated in 1907 in the natural history report of the expedition by *Edward A. Wilson* (535).

British ornithologists have interested themselves in birds in all parts of the world and dealt with foreign avifauna in an imposing series of works. The birds of Asia formed the subject of one of John Gould's works which was published in 1850—83 (178). As already mentioned, this prolific author started his unique literary career with a work on the birds of the Himalaya Mountains. The southwestern part of China — Western Yunnan — was visited in 1868 and 1875 by two expeditions, of the zoological results of which *John Anderson* gave an account in a large work in which there is also a section on birds (10), while the journeys of the Persian Boundary Commission in 1870—72 supplied material for a work issued in 1876 by *W. T. Blanford* on Eastern Persia, in the second volume of which the zoology is treated and a considerable contribution made towards the knowledge of the avifauna of the country (45). A well-known work on the fauna and flora of Palestine published in 1884 (510) contains a large amount of ornithological material, its author, the Rev. *H. B. Tristram,* Canon of Durham, being well-known as one of the founders and original members of the British Ornithologists' Union. Finally we may mention the journeys of *Ferdinand Stoliczka* in Central Asia, where he lost his life in 1874, the report on his ornithological collection from the second Yarkand Mission after a checkered fate being at last written by R. Bowdler Sharpe and published in 1891 (465). The previous year Henry Seebohm had made an attempt to describe in monographic form the birds of a part of East Asia in 'The birds of the Japanese Empire' (London 1890, 8vo). Drawing his material from the accounts of two visits to Siberia, previously published, in 1875 and 1877 he also treated birds of that area in 'The birds of Siberia', etc. (London 1901, 8vo), while the birds of the coastal regions of China were studied by *Robert Swinhoe,* who was born in Calcutta and lived for many years in China. The birds in a part of that country have since been dealt with in a recent monograph entitled 'A handbook of the birds of Eastern China', etc. (London 1925—34, 2 vols., 25 pl., 8vo). Its author, *J. D. D. La Touche* was born in France, brought up in England, and lived for nearly 40 years in China. The birds in local districts of that country have also been subjected to more comprehensive treatment, for instance by *E. S. Wilkinson* in 'Shanghai birds', etc. (Shanghai 1929, 23 col. pl., 8vo), a useful local fauna relating to the bird life of that city and the surrounding districts.

Of course the areas in Southern Asia, where British interests are so largely represented, were early explored by British naturalists, who described the avifauna of these tracts in larger or smaller works. Thus the quadrupeds and birds of Java and the neighbouring islands were described and depicted in 1821—24 in a large work by *Thomas Horsfield* (212; 830) who, in collaboration with *Frederic Moore,* issued the important museum publication 'A catalogue of the birds in the Museum of the Hon. East-India Company' (London 1854—58, 2 vols., small 4to), while J. E. Gray in 1830—35 delineated a series of Indian birds in the atlas 'Illustrations of Indian zoology' (187; 773).

A collection of illustrations of Indian birds with notes entitled 'Illustrations of Indian ornithology' (231) was issued in 1843—47 by *T. C. Jerdon,* assistant surgeon in the Presidency of Madras. He wrote several other works on the zoology of India, among them an extensive and exhaustive survey entitled 'The birds of India', etc. (Calcutta 1862—64, 3 vols., small 4to), his best book, which was reprinted and republished several times. For twenty-two years *Edward Blyth* was curator of the Calcutta Museum. While he held this post he devoted himself to the study of the natural history of British India as well as displaying a vigorous activity in relation to the affairs of his institution. Of his works we may here notice a valuable catalogue entitled 'Catalogue of the birds in the Museum Asiatic Society' (Calcutta 1849[—52], small 4to). *Allan Hume* contributed several works which increased the knowledge of Indian birds. He collaborated with C. H. T. Marshall in the treatise 'The game birds of India, Burmah and Ceylon' (Calcutta 1879—81, 3 vols., 144 col. pl., 4to) and wrote 'The nests and eggs of Indian birds' (Calcutta 1873—75, 8vo; second edition edited by E.W. Oates (p 65) London 1889—90, 3 vols., 9 pl., 8vo). Collaborating with *George Henderson* he treated the natural history of the countries traversed (London 1873, 57 pl. (4 col.), 8vo) in a report of a scientific expedition 'Lahore to Yarkand', etc., and herein presented a considerable amount of ornithological material in a section edited by R. Bowdler Sharpe and containing a number of illustrations including 32 coloured plates by J. G. Keulemans. Hume (906), who held various high posts in India, collected a large Museum at Simla comprising 62,000 bird-skins and 19,000 eggs. He rendered a great service to England by presenting this collection to the Natural History Museum at South Kensington. For a number of years Hume edited an important journal of ornithology for India and its dependencies. This was 'Stray Feathers', etc. (Calcutta (Vols. 11—12 edited by Charles Chubb: London) 1873—99, 12 vols., col. plates, 8vo), the contents of which were in great part written by the editor himself. It is a source of information about the birds of Southern Asia. A comprehensive account of bird life in part of this area is found in 'The avifauna of British India and its dependencies', etc., (London 1888—90, 2 vols., 37 pl. (19 col.), 4to) by *James A. Murray*, who embodied a selection of the material from this work in 'The avifauna of the island of Ceylon', etc.(London 1890, 4 pl. (2 col.), 4to), while the above-mentioned *Eugene W. Oates* wrote the first two volumes of 'The fauna of British India, including Ceylon and Burma. Birds' (London 1889—98, 4 vols., 8vo). This is an excellent and a complete monograph on the birds of these countries, the two last volumes being written by W. T. Blanford. Oates, who in 1901 commenced the catalogue of the collection of birds' eggs in the British Museum (71), had already in 1883 issued 'A handbook to the birds of British Burmah', etc. (London, 2 vols., 8vo), while a so-called second edition of the volumes on birds, just referred to, in 'The fauna of British India', but in reality an entirely new work, was issued by *E. C. Stuart Baker* in 1922—30 (London, 8 vols., 37 col. pl., 8vo). This industrious author, who served in the Indian police, has recently described the eggs, nests, and breeding biology of Indian birds in 'The nidification of birds of the Indian Empire' (London 1932—35, 4 vols., 29 pl., 8vo) and has also issued a series of other works dealing with the avifauna of India, for instance 'The Indian ducks and their allies' (London 1908, 30 col. pl., large 8vo). A revision of that work appeared in the first volume of The game-birds of India, Burma and Ceylon' (London 1921—30, 3 vols., 80 pl. (60 col.), 8vo), of which his 'Indian pigeons and doves' (London 1913, 27 col. pl., folio) is a sister-work. A work on Indian birds, in-

tended for wider circles, is *Hugh Whistler*'s 'Popular handbook of Indian birds' (London 1928, 17 pl. (4 col.), 8vo; second edition 1935, 20 pl. (5 col.)), in which the common forms of the birds of the country are described. The picturesque bird life of Ceylon was treated in 1878—80 by *W. Vincent Legge* in a complete and important monograph, of which a second edition was published in 1880—81 (284), but which is now obsolete. The lack of a modern and supplementary work in this domain was remedied by the issue of the excellent 'Manual of the birds of Ceylon' (Colombo 1925, 20 pl., 4to) by *W. E. Wait,* published by the Ceylon Government. For this book a series of plates by *G. M. Henry,* with a short description of each bird by Wait, was published in 1927—30 under the title 'Coloured plates of the birds of Ceylon', etc. (Colombo, 3 parts, 48 col. pl., 4to). Special experience of the birds of the Malay Peninsula was gained by *Herbert C. Robinson* who in 1903 was appointed curator of the Museum at Kuala Lumpur and later became director of the Federated Malay States Museums. In 1926 he retired and settled in London, where he produced his great work 'The birds of the Malay Peninsula' (London 1927 →, col. plates, 4to), which was illustrated by Grønvold but of which Robinson only lived to issue two volumes, each with 25 plates. Vol. III (25 col. pl.) was edited in 1935 by *Frederick N. Chasen,* curator of the Raffles Museum in Singapore, who was also to issue the two volumes intended to complete the work.

First among the investigators of animal and bird life in the Malay Archipelago in the last half of the 19th century must be mentioned the renowned *Alfred Russel Wallace* (806; '903) who, while he was staying in the East Indies to which he had gone in 1854 and where he lived for eight years, simultaneously with Darwin emphasized the importance of the struggle for existence for the evolution of the organic world. During his stay in the archipelago he procured a great deal of material for the elucidation of its fauna, including 8000 specimens of birds, which group of animals he treated in several papers. He also secured material for the work 'The Malay Archipelago', etc. (London 1869, 2 vols., 8 pl., 8vo). Of his other works note may be made of the famous book 'The geographical distribution of animals', etc. (London 1876, 2 vols., 21 pl., 8vo), and 'Island life', etc. (London 1880, 3 pl., 8vo).

As the avifauna of the islands has been more closely

studied and subjected to literary treatment, important ornithological works relating to the islands of the archipelago have gradually appeared, for instance the important 'The birds of Celebes and the neighbouring islands', etc. (Berlin 1898, 2 vols., 45 pl. (42 col.), 4to) by the German ornithologist *A. B. Meyer,* a native of Hamburg, who had travelled in the island in 1870 —71. He was director of the Royal Museum of Zoology etc. at Dresden, and began his career as a scientific traveller and naturalist early. He wrote the work on Celebes in collaboration with his English assistant *Lionel W. Wiglesworth,* who actually wrote the greater part of this important work, which is one of the most complete and exhaustive monographs ever written on the birds of a geographical area. Another of the islands, Borneo, was visited by *John Whitehead* who in 1887—88 explored its northern part, particularly the region round Mount Kina Balu, about which expedition he published in 1893 a large work containing a good deal of ornithological material treated by Whitehead, R. B. Sharpe, and others (528).

Light has also been thrown on the avifauna of Polynesia through a series of reports on journeys made by various ornithologists and collectors in these regions. In addition to the above-mentioned work (p. 51) by Hartlaub and Finsch, there is a systematic catalogue of the birds of Polynesia entitled 'Aves Polynesiæ' (Dresden 1892, 4to) by Wiglesworth, referred to above. The birds of Hawaii especially have been treated in large works, such as the 'Aves Hawaiienses', etc. (536), issued in 1890—99 by *Scott B. Wilson* and A. H. Evans, a valuable work based partly on material gained during a couple of voyages to the islands. It is the only illustrated monograph of the Hawaiian birds, if we except Walter Rothschild's 'The avifauna of Laysan', etc., 1893—1900 (429), which contains a complete history up to the date of publication of the birds of the Hawaiian possessions. Rothschild, who collected a great number of birds from foreign countries at his famous museum at Tring (886), in this way contributed much to the knowledge of the avifauna of Polynesia, the Malay Archipelago, and Australia, not least through the medium of the journal of the Museum 'Novitates Zoologicæ', etc. (368), the publication of which was begun in 1894. This journal also contributed to throw light upon a region treated in one of John Gould's treatises (181) and in Salvadori's (pp. 54—55) large work, New Guinea and the adjacent areas. These regions, interesting from a zoological point of view,

have been explored by various expeditions of which we may mention the British Ornithologists' Union Expedition and the Wollaston Expedition in Dutch New Guinea in 1910—13, the results of which were edited in 1914—16 by W. R. Ogilvie-Grant, who wrote the section on the birds himself (373; 374) and thus made an important contribution to the ornithology of the island.

The fauna of the neighbouring Australian continent had early been studied by British naturalists (p. 35), and in the 19th century the accounts of the birds were continued, for instance in 'Birds of New Holland', etc. (London 1808, Vol. I, 18 col. pl., folio), with pictures painted from nature by *John William Lewin,* a son of William Lewin (p. 34). These plates were accompanied by a descriptive text, the work appearing in 1813 in a new edition entitled 'Birds of New South Wales', etc., and under the title 'A natural history of the birds of New South Wales', etc. (London 1822, 26 col. pl., folio; new edition by T. C. Eyton 1838). Soon after the appearance of the latter edition the publication of John Gould's large work on the birds of Australia (174) commenced. The author issued a kind of handbook to it called 'Handbook to the birds of Australia' (London 1865, 2 vols., 8vo), the text of which is largely the text of the main work and its supplements. It found a companion in the semi-popular work 'The ornithology of Australia', etc. (Brisbane 1866—70, 2 vols., 126 col. pl., large 4to; re-issued with an altered title in 1877, 123 col. pl.) by *Silvester Diggles.* The Australian birds in the Australian Museum at Sydney were treated by the curator of the museum *E. P. Ramsay* in 'Catalogue of the Australian birds in the Australian Museum', etc. (Sydney 1876—94, 4 parts, and supplement, 8vo), Part IV of which was edited by *Alfred J. North,* ornithologist of the museum, who in 1898 also prepared an unfinished second edition of which only the first two parts appeared. A new pictorial work on Australian birds saw light in 1887—91. This was *Gracius J. Broinowski's* 'The birds of Australia', etc. (Melbourne, 6 vols., 302 col. pl., folio), a semi-popular but comprehensive treatment of the subject illustrated by chromolithographs by the author. The same North, just referred to, described the eggs and nests of Australian birds in his 'Descriptive catalogue of the nests and eggs of birds found breeding in Australia and Tasmania' (Sydney 1890 (dated 1889), 21 col. pl.; supplement, 2 parts, 1891—92, 8vo; second edition 1901—14, 4 vols., 20 pl. nests, 25 pl. eggs, folio), while nearly the same subject was treated in an excellent and handsomely illustrated account by *Archibald James Campbell* under the title 'Nests and eggs of Australian birds', etc. (Sheffield 1901, 2 vols., 145 pl. (28 col.), 8vo), a book in which 765 birds are mentioned.

The greatest work on the birds of Australia is, however, *Gregory M. Mathews*' work in 12 volumes published in 1910—27 (328). Additions to it are found in the same author's 'The birds of Norfolk and Lord Howe Islands', etc., published in 1928, and in 'A supplement to The birds of Norfolk', etc., 1936 (cf. 328, note). This author, in collaboration with *Tom Iredale*, also treated the birds of Australia in a scientific handbook entitled 'A manual of the birds of Australia' (London 1921—25, 4 vols., 36 col. pl., 8vo), with plates by *L. Medland*. An excellent popular handbook, very useful to those to whom Mathews' large work is not available, has been issued by *A. H. S. Lucas* and *W. H. Dudley Le Souëf*, director of the Melbourne Zoological Gardens, under the title 'The birds of Australia' (Melbourne 1911, 6 col. pl., 8vo). It is also illustrated with good figures in the text, many of which are derived from the official organ of the Australasian Ornithologists' Union which, founded in 1900, has appeared in Melbourne and other places under the title 'The Emu', etc., (col. plates, 8vo) as a quarterly magazine to popularise the study and protection of native birds.

A guide to the birds of Australia has been issued by *Neville W. Cayley* under the title 'What bird is that?' (Sydney 1931, second edition, 44 pl., 8vo), an excellent and cheap handbook, whose success appears from the fact that it has been issued in several editions (fourth edition, 1933).

The first list of the birds of New Zealand is due to G. R. Gray and was published in 1843, but the leading authority with regard to the ornithology of the two islands was Sir *Walter L. Buller*, who was born in New Zealand where he lived most of his life and — a lawyer by profession — held several public posts. As early as 1865 he issued his first paper dealing with the ornithology of New Zealand, while his main work 'A history of the birds of New Zealand', first appeared in 1872—73, and has since been re-published and enlarged by supplements. Mathews, in the work of 1936 just referred to, made additions to Buller's work (85). Buller's survey of the subject in 'Manual of the birds of New Zealand' (84) in 1882 also deserves to be noted, while in addition an excellent though popular treatise

has been written in our day by the director of the Dominion Museum in Wellington *W. R. B. Oliver* under the title 'New Zealand birds' (Wellington 1930, 5 col. pl., 8vo).

In the New World, where indeed the young North American community's own scholarship gradually began to assert itself more and more in the exploration of the country, British naturalists have also in the 19th and 20th centuries made contributions to the treatment of the ornithological conditions, largely on the basis of material and observations collected on journeys and expeditions. Thus the northern part of North America was explored by Sir John Franklin on two land expeditions in 1819—22 and 1825—27, in which Dr. *John Richardson* took part as a surgeon and naturalist. In 1829—37 he edited his 'Fauna Boreali-Americana', etc., in which Richardson himself dealt with the birds in collaboration with the above-mentioned William Swainson in one part of the work which, published in 1831 (493), was handsomely illustrated by Swainson. The above-mentioned Thomas Brown (p. 61), too, contributed to America's ornithology in the rare 'Illustrations of the American Ornithology of Alexander Wilson and Charles Lucien Bonaparte', etc. (Edinburgh 1831—35, 124 col. pl., folio), which contains 523 figures of birds, among which are several not found in the works of the authors mentioned in the title. Brown's 'Illustrations' must be regarded as a companion to the edition of Wilson's 'American ornithology', etc., which appeared in Edinburgh in 1831. The industrious Philip Lutley Sclater in 1861—62 issued an important catalogue of his collection of American birds (449), while his son *W. L. Sclater* contributed to the ornithological literature relating to North America by his 'A history of the birds of Colorado' (London 1912, 17 pl., 8vo), a useful handbook, the material for which was, however, partly a compilation. British ornithologists have also been active in the West Indies and Central America, as will appear from 'The birds of Jamaica' (London 1847, 12mo) by *Philip Henry Gosse* (733), an Englishman engaged in commerce who visited Jamaica in 1844 and who, in writing his work, could rely on notes by *Richard Hill*, who was staying in the island. To illustrate his work Gosse later issued a series of plates executed from his own drawings under the title 'Illustrations of the birds of Jamaica' (London 1849, 52 col. pl., 4to). A very important monograph on the birds of Central America was issued in 1879—1904 by Osbert Salvin and Frederick Du

9*

Cane Godman. It formed the ornithological part of the great work on the flora and fauna of Mexico and Central America edited by the two authors under the title 'Biologia Centrali-Americana' (437), for which some of the material, including a large collection of birds, was secured by them on their several visits to the area in question.

Some rare and particularly interesting Mexican and South American birds were depicted by Swainson in an atlas published in 1834—41 under the title 'Ornithological drawings', etc., or 'A selection of the birds of Brazil and Mexico' (494) (Pl. IV, Figs 1—2). Classical studies on the natural history of the Amazon area were made in the middle of the 19th century by the above-mentioned Wallace, who explored the country in company with his compatriot *Henry Walter Bates*. In 1848 they went to South America in order to collect natural objects in this district, whence Wallace returned in 1852, though he unfortunately lost the greater part of his collections and notes in a fire on board the ship in which he was travelling. Nevertheless he was able the year after to issue an account of the journey in 'A narrative of travels on the Amazon and Rio Negro', etc. (London 1853, 8 pl., 8vo), in which many species of vertebrates are described. Bates, on the other hand, stayed in the Amazon country until 1859 and on his journeys during these eleven years collected a vast amount of material consisting of specimens of 14,712 species of different animals, especially insects, over half of which were new to science. Of birds, however, only 360 species were obtained, and these were dispersed before any complete report on the collection could be made. Some material relating to birds is, however, found in Bates' famous, but not specifically orthological, work 'The naturalist on the River Amazons', etc. (London 1863, 9 pl., 8vo), of which a number of editions have appeared (fifth edition 1879; revised edition in one volume 1892).

A late continuation of Buffon's 'Planches enluminées' with pictures of Neotropical birds was issued by Philip Lutley Sclater and Osbert Salvin in 1866—69 under the title 'Exotic ornithology', etc. (450), while Sclater and Salvin also issued the first systematic list of Neotropical birds, viz. 'Nomenclator avium neotropicalium', etc. (Londini 1873, folio). Finally, Sclater collaborating with *W. H. Hudson* made a descriptive catalogue of birds of the Argentine republic in the work 'Argentine ornithology', etc. (London 1888—89, 2 vols., 20 col. pl., 8vo), the plates of which

are due to J. G. Keulemans. The book was issued by Hudson in 1920 in a revised edition furnished with new plates under the title 'Birds of La Plata' (216). The birds of Tierra del Fuego, which are closely allied to the Argentine avifauna, have been treated by Captain *Richard Crawshay* in a beautiful work 'The birds of Tierra del Fuego' (London 1907, 44 pl. (21 col.; by Keulemans), 4to) which, however, is not a monograph but deals with the species the author collected or observed in the year 1904. It may also be mentioned that Walter Rothschild and Ernst Hartert in the fifth volume, 1899, of 'Novitates Zoologicæ' have dealt with the avifauna of the Galapagos Islands in a lengthy treatise entitled 'A review of the ornithology of the Galapagos Islands', etc., while an unfinished monograph relating to the birds of South America was commenced in 1912 by Lord *Brabourne* and *Charles Chubb* (56), a work intended to be illustrated with plates by Grønvold, some of which were issued separately in 1915—17 (56, II). Chubb made a further contribution to the ornithology of South America in 'The birds of British Guiana', etc. (100), published in 1916—21.

A detailed review of the birds of the Ethiopian region was commenced in 1896 by the above-mentioned G. E. Shelley in the large work 'The birds of Africa', etc. (470), the last part of which was completed after the death of Shelley and edited in 1912 by W. L. Sclater, mentioned above. As director of the South African Museum at Cape Town, Sclater acquired a special insight into African avifauna, as was evidenced by several works, such as his systematic catalogue of the birds of the Ethiopian region 'Systema avium Æthiopicarum', etc. (London 1924—30, 2 parts, 8vo), a splendid check-list, in which 4439 forms are given. Shelley's first considerable ornithological work was 'A handbook to the birds of Egypt', issued in 1872 (469). The same subject was dealt with by *Charles Whymper* in 1909 in a semi-popular treatise 'Egyptian birds', etc. (529), a richly illustrated work dealing especially with birds seen in the Nile Valley, while a modern and complete systematic work on the avifauna of Egypt was issued in 1930 by Colonel *R. Meinertzhagen*. This was entitled 'Nicoll's Birds of Egypt' (363), and was based on collections and notes for a projected work on the subject by *Michael Nicoll*, mentioned in the title, who was for a number of years assistant director of the Zoological Gardens at Giza. As regards the avifauna in other regions of North Africa we may mention that the English ornithologist *J. Whitaker* has described the birds of Tunisia in a book in two volumes published in 1905 (525), while birds from another region of Africa, Abyssinia, were dealt with by the above-mentioned (p. 64) W. T. Blanford in 1870 in a work (44) based on material and observations collected by a British expedition in 1867—68. Another British expedition visited a part of Equatorial Africa in 1905—06, the mountain Ruwenzori discovered by Stanley, and obtained a large amount of zoological material, of which the birds were treated in 1910 by W. R. Ogilvie-Grant (372). An earlier work on the birds of West Africa by the oft-mentioned William Swainson was published in 1837 and formed two volumes of Jardine's 'Naturalist's Library' (495), while an excellent compendium entitled 'Handbook of the birds of West Africa' (London 1930, 1 pl., 8vo) has been written by *George Latimer Bates,* who has been living in tropical Africa since about 1900. Finally, a large work on the birds in part of West Africa is in progress under the title 'The birds of tropical West Africa' (London 1930 →, col. plates, 8vo), of which up to 1936 Volumes I—IV have appeared (52 col. pl.), i. e. the main part of the six volumes intended to complete the work. Its author, *David A. Bannerman* has previously issued the work 'The Canary Islands', etc. (London 1922, 47 pl. (3 col.), 8vo), in which he gave an exhaustive account of an ornithologist's observations in these islands, of the natural history of which, not least the birds, the book contains much information. As regards Africa it may further be mentioned that Rear-Admiral *H. Lynes,* whose review of the genus Cisticola, 1930, is listed in the accompanying catalogue (320), has also dealt with the birds of Darfur in the work 'On the birds of North and Central Darfur', etc., published in 'The Ibis', 1924—25. He has also treated the ornithology of the Southern Tanganyika Territory (Berlin 1934, 15 pl.; Journal für Ornithologie 82; Sonderhefte), while Captain *Cecil D. Priest* describes the birds of a part of South Africa in an as yet unfinished work entitled 'The birds of Southern Rhodesia', four volumes of which have appeared (London 1933—36, 40 col. pl., 8vo), the fourth volume completing the general account of the birds, while the author promises a fifth volume as an appendix.

South Africa had already early attracted the attention of naturalists and ornithologists and investigations were continued in the 19th century, for instance by an expedition into the interior of the country in the years 1834—36. A great number of natural objects were collected, on which the 'Illustrations of the zoology of South Africa', etc., (London 1838—49, 5 vols., 270 col. pl., 4to) by *Andrew Smith* was mainly founded. It consisted of a series of figures with descriptions appended, of which Volume II, which deals with the birds, contains 114 coloured plates by Ford (904).

A fundamental monograph on the birds of South Africa was issued by *Edgar Leopold Layard* in 1867 under the title 'The birds of South Africa', etc. (Cape Town, 1 pl., 8vo). It was re-issued in 1875—84 in a revised and enlarged edition by R. Bowdler Sharpe (281), while a son of the above-mentioned L. Lloyd (p. 63), *Charles John Andersson* (737), who became the most renowned Swedish explorer of Africa, left so many notes relating to the birds of South-West Africa when he died that *J. H. Gurney* (595, pp. 95—99) could publish 'Notes on the birds of Damara Land', etc. (London 1872, 4 pl., 8vo), based on Andersson's note-books. These two works provide a fairly complete general view of the avifauna of South Africa. In our century the subject has been treated in a compendium 'The birds of South Africa' (London 1900—06, 4 vols., 8vo), a complete account of the birds of the country south of the Zambesi and Cunéné rivers. It constitutes part of 'The fauna of South Africa', a work in 6 volumes published in 1900—06, the two remaining volumes of which deal with the mammals. The first volume of the section on birds was written by *Arthur C. Stark,* while the three last volumes have been completed and edited by W. L. Sclater who edited the second volume from Stark's manuscript and wrote the two last volumes with the aid of Stark's notes. Finally it may be mentioned that the game birds and water fowl of South Africa were treated in 1912 in a handsomely and profusely illustrated work (211) by Major *Boyd Horsbrugh.*

Portugal, too, has contributed to the knowledge of African avifauna, for instance in the work 'Ornithologie d'Angola', etc. (Lisbonne 1877—81, 10 col. pl., 8vo), an important monograph on the birds inhabiting the Portuguese possessions of Central and West Africa, written by *J. V. Barboza du Bocage,* director of the National Zoological Museum of Lisbon, while J. G. Keulemans has supplied the designs for the plates.

The journeys made by Andersson, referred to above, show that Sweden has carried on her traditions of earlier times in the field of African exploration, a domain to which attention is also given in our day by Swedish ornithologists such as Professor *Yngve Sjöstedt,* an African explorer known especially as an entomologist. In 1890—92 he made a journey in the Cameroons, collecting material which formed the main basis of his 'Zur Ornithologie Kameruns', etc. (472), published in 1895, and in 1904 he described his journey in a more generally accessible form (473). A new zoological expedition to Kilimanjaro, Meru and the surrounding regions of East Africa was conducted by Sjöstedt in 1905—06. The ornithological result, which consisted of 1546 specimens of birds of 402 species, was treated by Sjöstedt in the third section of the first volume of the report on the scientific results of the expedition (Stockholm 1910, 5 pl. (2 col.), 4to). British East Africa was explored in 1910—11 by another Swedish expedition, the ornithological result of which was 885 bird-skins of 299 species, which were dealt with in a treatise entitled 'Birds collected by the Swedish zoological expedition to British East Africa 1910—11' (Uppsala 1911, 5 pl. (2 col.), 4to), published in the first volume of the report on the scientific results of the expedition, and in the 'Handlingar' of the Swedish Academy of Sciences. The author is the eminent Swedish zoologist Professor *Einar Lönnberg,* director of the department of vertebrates in the Natural History Museum of Stockholm in 1904—32, to whom we shall return below. Under the leadership of Prince Wilhelm of Sweden an expedition went to Central Africa in 1920—21. It explored the Birunga Mountains, the volcanic region north of Lake Kivu on the borders of Belgian Congo and collected specimens in the Congo forest north of Ruwenzori. Nearly 1700 birds were collected, and these were dealt with in a large treatise (pp. 326, 2 col. pl.), published in 1924 in the 'Handlingar' of the Swedish Academy of Sciences as part of the scientific results of the expedition. The author was the zoologist Count *Nils Gyldenstolpe,* who travelled for zoological purposes in different parts of Sweden, and who made scientific journeys of exploration in the above-mentioned part of Africa, in Algeria in 1910 and, as we shall soon mention, in Siam. Another expedition, the Swedish Mount Elgon Expedition, set out in 1920 under the leadership of Director *S. A. Lovén* with the exploration of the old giant volcano, Mount Elgon, on the boundary between Uganda and Kenya Colony as its main object. The zoologist of the expedition was Lector *Hugo Granvik* who collected the bulk of the birds and treated the material in his

work 'Contributions to the knowledge of the East African ornithology', etc. (184), published in 1923. The eastern, and later the northern part of Siam as well as the Malay Peninsula were explored in 1911—12 and 1914—15 by the above-mentioned Gyldenstolpe, who treated the material — 191 and 353 forms of birds respectively — in two papers, published in the 'Handlingar' of the Swedish Academy of Sciences in 1913 (pp. 76, 1 col. pl.) and 1916 (pp. 160, 4 pl. (2 col.)). Quite another part of Asia, the northeastern region, has recently been visited by the Swedish explorer *Sten Bergman,* who in 1920—23 explored Kamchatka, and in 1929—30 the Kurile Islands; on these journeys he gathered material for the useful work 'Zur Kenntniss nordostasiatischer Vögel', etc. (Stockholm 1935, 8vo), in which he gives an account of the birds of the areas visited, dealing with systematics, biology, and distribution. Swedish enterprise in the field of ornithology has also been displayed in other parts of the world, for instance in Australia. In 1910—13 this continent was explored by Swedish zoological expeditions under the leadership of *Eric Mjöberg.* On the expedition in 1910—11, 820 birds were collected, the ornithological results being treated by the ornithologist *Rudolf Söderberg* in 'Studies of the birds in North West Australia' (Stockholm 1918, 5 pl. (1 col.), 4to), published in the 'Handlingar' of the Swedish Academy of Sciences. Other parts of the world have also been explored by Swedes, for instance the southern and, especially, the northern Polar regions. As an example may be mentioned the great Vega Expedition under the leadership of the famous *Adolf Erik Nordenskiöld* who was the first to make the North-East Passage in 1878 —79, an achievement which greatly added to our knowledge of the Arctic Ocean. The scientific results were published in 5 volumes, large 8vo, in 1882—87. Several scientists collaborated in this work, among them the Finnish professor *Johan Axel Palmén* (759), who in 1887 set forth the ornithological results in the fifth volume (pp. 241—511) of this work under the title 'Bidrag till kännedomen om sibiriska ishafskustens fogelfauna', etc., a work which contains a mine of information about Arctic avifauna. Palmén, who was especially interested in faunistic-geographical questions such as the distribution of Finnish birds, conducted an expedition to the Kola peninsula himself in 1888. The birds of the Arctic regions were also studied by the Swedish zoologist and explorer *Gustaf Kolthoff,* who made three summer voyages to these northern regions, as a member of A. E. Nordenskiöld's expedition to Greenland in 1888 and of A. G. Nathorst's expedition to Spitsbergen and King Charles Land in 1898, and finally as the leader of a polar expedition made exclusively with zoological objects in view in 1900. On the basis of his studies on these voyages Kolthoff, who was custodian at the University of Uppsala, wrote a treatise of 104 pages on the mammals and birds of the Arctic regions, 'Bidrag till kännedom om norra polartrakternas däggdjur och fåglar', published in the 'Handlingar' of the Swedish Academy of Sciences in 1903. The birds are dealt with on pp. 31—104. The avifauna of the Arctic regions has since been treated in the work 'Arktiska fåglar' (Stockholm 1936, 2 col. pl., 8vo) by *Hialmar Rendahl,* mentioned on p. 72, and the Danish Greenland hunter and zoologist *Alwin Pedersen.*

Native avifauna was also subjected to close study on the part of Swedish ornithologists during the 19th and 20th centuries, as evidenced by a series of miscellaneous writings (565; 569; 576). In 1806, the same year as Sparrman (p. 39) commenced to issue his 'Svensk ornithologie', etc., (482) another Swedish work on that country's fauna was begun 'Svensk zoologi', etc. (388), which was edited by *Johan Wilhelm Palmstruch,* who was both a botanist and a zoologist. A work of fundamental importance for the faunistic study of animal life in Sweden was carried out by *Sven Nilsson,* Professor at the University of Lund, who is well-known both as a naturalist and an archæologist. He issued a treatise on Swedish birds, 'Ornithologia Svecica', in 1817—21 (364) and issued a completely revised Swedish edition of it which first appeared in 1824—28 as part of his 'Skandinavisk fauna', etc., and was republished in 1835 and 1858. A supplementary atlas 'Illuminerade figurer till Skandinaviens fauna' was published in 1829—40 (365). The drawings for it were supplied by *Magnus Körner,* draughtsman to the University of Lund. He is noted especially as a zoological artist, and in 1839—46 issued an ornithological atlas himself entitled 'Skandinaviska foglar', etc., (271). In 1828 the publication of an important atlas with pictures of Swedish birds had been begun (543), the plates for which were executed by the two Finnish brothers *Magnus von Wright* and *Wilhelm von Wright* (790; 791; 795), who belonged to a family that came from Scotland. Magnus' bird pictures created an interest in zoological circles in Stockholm, to which city Wilhelm had also come at his brother's instance. The two brothers were entrusted

by Count Nils Bonde with the task of issuing the above-mentioned work 'Svenska foglar', etc., at the Count's expense. With its fine hand-coloured plates it was much appreciated and admired. Magnus von Wright, however, returned to Finland, where he held several posts, among others as drawing-master and custodian at the University of Helsingfors, whose collection of birds he especially enriched. Subsequently he issued the beginning of a work on the birds of Finland (p. 73), and though his art never went beyond the zoological plate he is still regarded as one of the pioneers of Finnish art. Wilhelm von Wright, who was exclusively an animal painter, began when only 17 years of age to assist his brother in making the plates for the work on the Swedish birds, and the latter even then considered him his master. He became a zoological artist of note, whose excellent plates for his work on the fishes of Scandinavia, published in 1836—57, are especially admired. For some years he was draughtsman to the Royal Swedish Academy of Sciences and also a member of the Academy of Arts. A third brother, *Ferdinand von Wright,* who began to draw pictures of birds at the age of 8, lived for some years in Sweden painting natural objects. He also painted landscapes and portraits and obtained official recognition of his art in that he was granted a life-pension from the Finnish state in 1885. He must, as a matter of fact, be regarded as the best artist of the three brothers; he painted excellent bird pictures with vivid characterization and fresh colouring. It is a testimony to the quality of the bird pictures of the brothers von Wright that it has been possible to issue them in our century in a new edition with a text by Einar Lönnberg, all the bird plates of the three brothers which are suitable for the purpose, together with some new ones, being included (544).

Soon after the middle of the 19th century Swedish birds were presented in a considerable work, 'Svenska foglarna', etc. (490), begun in 1856 and illustrated with coloured plates. This was written by Professor *Carl Sundevall,* Intendant of the Natural History Museum of Stockholm, whose works deal especially with ornithological themes, for instance his 'Conspectus avium picinarum' (Stockholmiæ 1866, 8vo). a review of Malherbe's 'Monographie des picidées', 1859—62 (321). He is also known in ornithology as a systematist. Another Swedish ornithological author, *August Emil Holmgren,* whose work, however, was especially of importance for its information on noxious insects, issued in collaboration with Hjalmar Widegren a handbook of zoology, thus testifying to the wide extent of his interests, in which amongst other sections he wrote one entitled 'Skandinaviens foglar' (Stockholm 1867—71, 2 parts, 9 pl., 8vo).

Of more specialized works we may mention the 'Skandinavisk oologi', etc. (Stockholm 1867, 1 pl., 8vo) by *Carl Westerlund*. It deals with the distribution of the birds of Sweden and Norway, their nests and their eggs; and the same author's 'Skandinaviska foglarnes fortplantningshistoria' (Lund (supplement II by Westerlund and *Otto Ottosson:* Stockholm) 1878— 1905, 2 parts and 2 supplements, 8vo), as well as his 'Skandinavisk oologi. Indledning till Skandinaviska foglarnes fortplantningshistoria' (Stockholm 1905, 8vo). We may also note a couple of works dealing with local faunas, 'Göteborgs och Bohusläns fauna, ryggradsdjuren' (Göteborg 1877, 9 pl. (4 col.), 8vo) by *August Wilhelm Malm,* Intendant of the Zoological Museum of Göteborg, which deals with birds on pp. 24 — 49, and pp. 161—364; and 'Gotlands fåglar', etc., (Uppsala 1907, 8vo; second edition 1909) by *Henrik Hasselgren*. Brief descriptions and an account of the habits, occurrence, and other facts concerning birds are found in 'Sveriges fåglar', etc., (Lund 1894, 8vo) by *Aug. Carlson,* who has also treated Sweden's gamebirds in 'Sveriges jagtbara foglar', etc. (Jönköping 1878, 8vo), a subject also dealt with in several sections of the work 'Vårt villebråd', etc. (Stockholm 1896, 2 parts, 8vo; new edition 1914), published as 'Bibliotek för jägare... 3' under the editorship of Kolthoff. The latter wrote a good deal about birds in it himself, for he was a keen sportsman and a great lover of Nature. As such, he had an extensive knowledge, especially of the birds and mammals of Sweden, a knowledge which he could utilise in his popular work 'Nordens fåglar', etc. (270), which he issued in 1895—1902 in collaboration with *Leonard Jägerskiöld*. It was called a revised edition of Sundevall's 'Svenska foglarna', and was so much in demand that it could be issued again in a new edition with new plates in 1911—26 (221), Rudolf Söderberg acting as a collaborator. As a professor in 'Göteborgs Högskola' Jägerskiöld has had great influence on the development of the Natural History Museum of Göteborg and, by his popular writings, he has contrived to create an interest in and a love for Nature in his own country, for instance by his account of the higher vertebrates of Sweden in a handbook for the Swedish people entitled 'Sveriges Rike',

etc. (Stockholm 1899—1900, 2 parts, 4to; birds: Part II, columns 117—126, 153—301). He has treated the same subject in a work of popular biological literature, 'Sveriges djurvärld' (Stockholm 1903, 8vo; second edition 1911; a new work with the same title edited by Torsten Pehrson 1930, 2 parts) originally edited in conjunction with Einar Lönnberg and *Gottfrid Adlerz*. Lönnberg has also described the birds of Sweden in a popular handbook on a scientific basis 'Sveriges ryggradsdjur. Del II. Fåglarna' (Stockholm 1915, 8vo). Of the Swedish ornithological literature of our day we must not forget the numerous books by the zoologist, writer, and bird-photographer, *Bengt Berg* which, embellished by his admirable photos of birds, have contributed to widen the interest in the animal world. Another Swedish bird-photographer is the ornithologist *Paul Rosenius,* a physician of Malmö, who has published a series of pictorial nature-books and accounts of travels. His principal work, 'Sveriges fåglar och fågelbon' (427), a handsomely produced description of the birds of Sweden, their breeding places and nests, was begun in 1913 but has not yet been completed. The latest handbook on the birds of Sweden was published in 1935 by the director of the vertebrate department of the Natural History Museum of Stockholm, Professor Hjalmar Rendahl, under the title 'Fågelboken' (418); all species occurring in the country are treated there in brief and lucid form.

In Norway the study of birds did not attract much attention in the first half of the 19th century (569; 580), but soon after the middle of the century ornithology gained a keen student in *Robert Collett* (699) who actually took a degree in law, but soon turned his attention to his main interest, zoology, to which he devoted himself so eagerly and so successfully that he became professor of zoology and, in conjunction with G. O. Sars, director of the Zoological Museum of the University of Oslo. The branch of science in which he was most interested was ornithology. In 1864 he issued his first large work on birds, 'Oversigt over Christiania Omegns ornithologiske Fauna' (Christiania, 8vo) reprinted as a separate book from the journal 'Nyt Magasin for Naturvidenskaberne'; and in 1869 his 'Norges Fugle', etc., dealing especially with the distribution of birds in Norway, appeared in the 'Forhandlinger' of the Christiania Society of Science 1868 (pp. 116—193; supplement in the same periodical 1871, pp. 52—61). Altogether he made essential contributions to the avifauna of Norway by a number of papers, such as his 'Mindre Meddelelser vedrørende Norges Fuglefauna', published in the above-mentioned journal in 1877, 1881, and 1894. He also helped to increase interest in natural history by his popular books in which he gave standard descriptions of animals. About 1908 he planned the publication of a large work on all the vertebrates of Norway, of which, however, he only lived to complete the part on the mammals; nor did he finish the large work on the birds of Norway for which he had collected abundant material. After his death the University, therefore, entrusted Ørjan Olsen, better known as an explorer, with the task of writing the book in collaboration with A. Landmark. It appeared under the title 'Norges Fugle' (Kristiania 1921, 3 vols., 107 pl., 8vo) and gave rise to some controversy.

Another notable Norwegian ornithologist, Leonhard Stejneger, began his career as a lawyer, but soon turned his attention to ornithology. He wrote a number of papers on birds while he was in his own country and as his first ornithological work issued a brief description of the species of birds observed in Norway in a little book 'Norsk ornitologisk ekskursjonsfauna', etc. (Kristiania 1873, 4 pl., small 8vo). However, in 1881 he emigrated to America where he has occupied various posts in the Smithsonian Institution of Washington, and has since displayed a fruitful ornithological activity (p. 86). Other accounts of Norwegian birds have later been issued by H. Tho. L. Schaanning, keeper of the natural history department of the Museum of Stavanger, who has given a systematically arranged description in popular form of all species of birds known to be found in Norway in 'Norges fuglefauna', etc. (Kristiania 1916, 8vo). He also founded the journal 'Norsk ornitologisk Tidsskrift'. A minor account of common Norwegian birds and their habits will be found in 'Fugleboken' (Oslo 1926—29, 3 parts, 8 pl., 8vo) by Sophus Aars, which has been re-issued several times. More specialized works of interest to ornithology have of course also appeared in Norway, for example an investigation of the Willow Grouse, made in 1921—27, the results of which were presented in 1928 (233), and also several other writings on game birds, for instance 'Norges Fuglevildt', etc., (Kjøbenhavn 1881, 8vo) by J. B. Barth. Literature dealing with individual localities is by no means lacking. To mention a few examples there are 'Stavanger Omegns Fugle' (Stavanger 1866; supplement 1870; second supplement 1887) by Henrik E. S.

Bahr, published in an annual school publication, and the same author's 'Aves regionis Stavangeriensis', which appeared in the annual report of the Stavanger Museum for 1895 (pp. 29—152), as well as Schaanning's 'Østfinmarkens fuglefauna', etc., in 'Bergens Museums Aarbok' (1907, No. 8, 3 pl.). Finally it must be mentioned that Norwegians have participated in journeys and expeditions to, or made investigations in, Antarctic as well as Arctic regions, the latter especially, and have brought home ornithological material. As authors in these fields may be mentioned Robert Collett and, recently, Schaanning and Sigurd Johnsen.

In Finland, also, ornithological research was not very prominent in the first part of the 19th century (569), until the above-mentioned brothers von Wright began to be active. Magnus von Wright published in 1859 the first part of a work on the birds of Finland entitled 'Finlands foglar', etc. (Helsingfors, 8vo), in which the birds are described chiefly according to their plumages. However, he did not live to finish the second part of this work, but after his death it was edited by J. A. Palmén (Helsingfors 1873, 8vo) from von Wright's manuscript very carefully revised, particularly as regards the distribution of the birds. Finnish literature is not rich in ornithological atlases, though some such works may occur. Thus Gösta Sundman used his talent for drawing and painting in the service of zoology and published several atlases, for the production of which he set up a lithographic printing press. His atlas, containing 234 figures of eggs of Finnish birds and entitled 'Finska fogelägg' (491), issued in 1879—88, is the first atlas with chromo-lithographic plates published in Finland. A text for it was written by J. A. Palmén and issued in Swedish and Finnish as well as in German and English, but was never completed. Sundman also showed his unquestionable powers as a zoological painter in a well-produced ichthyological atlas, complete in 12 parts, issued in 1884—93, and entitled 'Finlands fiskar', while in 1894 he commenced a new atlas with figures of Finnish birds of prey, of which, however, only a single part appeared under the title 'Finlands roffoglar' (Helsingfors, 5 col. pl., folio). Finnish ornithology has of course produced more specialized literature, for instance on the avifauna in various parts of the country; of larger works it will, however, suffice to mention a book of 1142 pages with descriptions of all the species and races of birds found in Finland, 'Ornitologisk handbok' (Helsingfors 1929, 8vo) by Ivar Hortling, lector at

Helsingfors, and really a philologist. Of other Finnish ornithologists of our day may be mentioned *Pontus Palmgren,* who has made valuable contributions towards the knowledge of the avifauna of his country.

In Denmark, too, ornithology languished during the first part of the 19th century, though a series of descriptions of local districts appeared in which there often occurred information of considerable interest about birds (567; 569; 581; 610). Apart from their value, these more specialized works cannot be mentioned here, however, though there is reason to dwell on Frederik Faber, whom we have previously noticed (p. 44) as one of the greatest ornithologists Denmark has ever produced. Though he died at the early age of 31, he did valuable work in the field of research in which he was so keenly interested. He was actually a lawyer, and at his death held the office of paymaster and judge-advocate, a post to which he was appointed on his return in 1821 from a journey to Iceland for purposes of study, which lasted 2½ years. The first results of this journey he presented in 'Prodromus der isländischen Ornithologie', etc. (Kopenhagen 1822, 1 pl., 8vo; 'Nachtrag' in Oken's 'Isis', 1824), a history of the birds of Iceland which was followed in 1824—27 by a closer study, published in 8 parts in Oken's 'Isis' under the title 'Beyträge zur arktischen Zoologie'. Faber's principal work, however, and indeed one of the main works in Danish ornithological literature, is his 'Über das Leben der hochnordischen Vögel' (Leipzig 1826, 2 parts in 1 vol., 8vo), a handbook on the conditions of life of Northern birds which shows his great thoroughness and his wide knowledge, as did everything from the hands of Faber. We must not fail to mention that he wrote a number of minor works on Danish avifauna, which he seems to have intended to treat in a larger work, though he only wrote a single book about it, 'Ornithologiske Noticer som Bidrag til Danmarks Fauna' (Aarhus 1824, 8vo). In 1828, the year that Faber died, the publication of the first large atlas with pictures of Danish birds was commenced, 'Nordisk Ornithologie', etc. (521), in which a great number of birds were depicted, partly from life, in a long series of plates. Some of the figures are remarkably good. The author of this work, the painter and engraver *Johann Ernst Christian Walter,* was born at Ratzeburg and came to Copenhagen in 1817, where for a number of years he was caretaker at the Royal Collection of Paintings. Walter began two other atlases in the same year as the above, 'Vögel aus Asien, Africa, America und Neuholland', etc. (519), and a work

with pictures of beautiful birds and mammals entitled 'Pragtfugle og Pattedyr', etc. (520). These works, like that mentioned above, are very rare in complete form; the plates are often quite good, but seem chiefly to have been copied from foreign works.

Of leading zoologists who dealt with ornithology there were really only two in the early and middle 19th century. These were Professor *Johannes Reinhardt* and his son *Johannes Theodor Reinhardt,* who both included in their writings the birds of Greenland (582; 611; 648). Thus the elder Reinhardt reviewed at length the increase of the avifauna of Greenland since the publication of Fabricius' 'Fauna Groenlandica' (p. 39) in the first part (pp. 88—105, 3 pl.) of the paper 'Ichthyologiske Bidrag til den grönlandske Fauna', published in the 'Skrifter' of the Royal Society of Sciences in 1838. This paper also contained information about the material sent to the Museum in Copenhagen by the Danish governor of a colony in Greenland, *Carl Peter Holbøll,* who after 1822 had ample opportunities of collecting the birds of Greenland. He himself wrote a copious work on that subject, dated 1840 and published under the title 'Ornithologiske Bidrag til den grønlandske Fauna' in the journal 'Naturhistorisk Tidsskrift', 1842—43 (pp. 361—457). This also appeared later in German under the title 'Ornithologischer Beitrag zur Fauna Groenlands', etc. (Leipzig 1846, 1 col. pl., 8vo).

Important contributions to the ornithology of the Faroes also appeared about the middle of the 19th century (631; 632). Thus the Faroese pastor and author *Peter Alberg Holm* issued in 1848 in 'Naturhistorisk Tidsskrift' (1846—49, pp. 465—525) his 'Ornithologiske Bidrag til Færøernes Fauna', which was based on observations he had been making for many years and contained valuable new matter. The best of the works hitherto published on the birds of the Faroes, however, is due to *Hans Christopher Müller* who was 'Sysselmand' in the islands and had a close knowledge, gained by self-study, of their avifauna. The work in question, 'Færøernes Fuglefauna', etc., was published in 1862 in 'Videnskabelige Meddelelser fra den naturhistoriske Forening i Kjøbenhavn' (pp. 1—78; German translation in Journal für Ornithologie 1869). Extracts from Müller's ornithological notes from 1862—97 were edited in the same periodical in 1901 by *Knud Andersen* referred to below.

While Walter's atlas with pictures of Northern birds did not meet with much success, the work on the same subject which was commenced towards the middle of

PLATE X

Fig. 1. BAILLON'S CRAKE. *Porzana intermedia* (Herm.). From hand-coloured lithograph, drawn by H. Grøn-vold, lithographed by C. Cordts, in J. Collin's 'Ny Tavle III til »Skandinaviens Fugle«', 1888

Fig. 2. THE COMMON PHEASANT. *Phasianus colchicus* L., *subsp.* From four-colour print (Pl. 30), painted by Archibald Thorburn, in Thorburn's 'A naturalist's sketch book', 1919

PLATE X

Fig. 1

Fig. 2

the century by *Niels Kjærbølling* acquired great importance. As the first complete account of Denmark's birds it created and stimulated a general interest in the study of them. Kjærbølling was originally a teacher, later a horticulturist, and in his own country he is known especially as the founder of the Zoological Gardens in Copenhagen as well as for his book on birds (657). The publication of this was begun in 1847, and with its text and enlarged by supplements it was completed in 1856 (246—248). Kjærbølling, who associated himself with the circle of German ornithologists centred in 'Naumannia' (774), did not indeed produce anything very original either in the way of text (837) or plates, for which he drew the originals himself, but his book was very popular and was so much in demand that a new title edition of the plates could be published in 1858—65 (249) and the entire work re-issued by *Jonas Collin,* the text in 1875—77 (251), the plates augmented by two new ones in 1872—79 (250). A third new plate drawn by Henrik Grønvold (p. 59) was issued in 1888 (103) (Pl. X, Fig. 1), and Collin wrote three supplements to the text (101; 102; 104).

A good many other people studied ornithology in Denmark in the latter half of the 19th century (562), among them the politician *J. C. H. Fischer* who was for a time minister of education, and the well-known zoologist *Herluf Winge,* among whose works may be mentioned a popular account of the mammals and birds of Denmark in 'Danmarks Natur' (Kjøbenhavn 1899, 4to; columns 353—476) as well as a larger work on the birds of Greenland which was published under the title 'Grønlands Fugle' in 1898 in 'Meddelelser om Grønland'.

Bird life in the Faroes was studied about 1900 amongst others by two Faroese, *Peter Ferdinand Petersen,* a taxidermist and merchant, and *Samuel Niclassen,* a teacher, who both made valuable notes which were developed by the above-mentioned Knud Andersen under the title 'Meddelelser om Færøernes Fugle', published in 1898—1905 in six series in 'Videnskabelige Meddelelser fra den naturhistoriske Forening i Kjøbenhavn'.

Andersen left his native country and was later employed at the museum of Prince Ferdinand of Bulgaria and at the British Museum. Other Danish ornithologists, however, carried on the study of birds in the 20th century. Among these was *Otto Helms,* of whose works may be mentioned 'Fuglene ved Nakkebøllefjord' (Kjøbenhavn 1919, 8vo), an account of the birds in the neighbourhood of the sanatorium where he was physician-in-chief for many years, and also his three books with the title 'Danske Fugle', etc. (203—205), which are especially intended as a guide to those who wish to know the birds in their natural environment. Other modern books dealing with the birds of Denmark are *Gerhard Heilmann* and *A. L. V. Manniche*'s 'Danmarks Fugleliv' (201), a larger and more popular treatment of the subject, published in 1926—30, and three volumes on Danish birds by *R. Hörring* published respectively in 1919, 1926, and 1934, in the series of small illustrated handbooks in 8vo which have appeared in Copenhagen since 1907 under the general title 'Danmarks Fauna'.

The most extensive and hitherto unsurpassed treatment of the birds of Denmark in text and pictures is, however, the very important work 'Danmarks Fugle' etc. (442), commenced by the ornithologist *E. Lehn Schiøler,* a stockbroker, in 1925. It was planned to comprise eight volumes, but only three have appeared, the last one posthumously, since Lehn Schiøler himself only lived to see the two first volumes published. He was the owner of an imposing collection consisting of bird-skeletons and 25,000 bird-skins, and was an eminent authority on the avifauna of Denmark, Greenland, and Iceland, who utilised his insight in the production of his great work which — though incomplete — remains as a monument to his efforts. On the pictorial side, also, Schiøler's main work occupies a prominent place in ornithological literature, one of its illustrators being the excellent Danish painter *Johannes Larsen* (764), who was interested in birds as a child, and in whose art birds and bird life early began to occupy an increasingly prominent place (Front.). Thus in many of his landscapes birds are introduced as characteristic adjuncts, and they constitute an important part of the whole atmosphere of the pictures. He favours vivid, clear colours, employed with a peculiar, primitive taste, and his art is intimately associated with the scenery and animal life of his country. As early as 1895 he executed a series of excellent water-colours of dead birds, and evidence of his capacities as an illustrator is found in the form of woodcuts and drawings of animals and scenery in various books as well as in Schiøler's work. The illustrations for that work are good examples of the artist's characteristic pictures, which place him in the first rank as a bird painter.

In our day Danish ornithologists have treated

10*

especially the birds native to Denmark's northernmost possessions. Thus the birds of Greenland have been studied on journeys and expeditions and treated in works published in 'Meddelelser om Grønland' by Manniche (323) 1910, O. Helms, *Bernt Løppenthin* and *Finn Salomonsen*. Another of the younger Danish ornithologists, *Knud Paludan,* has, for instance, treated the ornithological material from an expedition to the French Sudan and Nigeria in 1927 in a paper published in 1936 in 'Videnskabelige Meddelelser fra Dansk naturhistorisk Forening i København'.

A thorough account of all the 155 species of birds occurring in Iceland has been given by *Bjarni Sæmundsson,* adviser to the fisheries in Reykjavik, in part of a work on the fauna of Iceland. This part bears the title 'Íslensk dýr III, Fuglarnir. (Aves Islandiæ)' (Reykjavík 1936, 8vo), and must be regarded as the most considerable contribution to the knowledge of Iceland's avifauna produced since the above-mentioned work by Hantzsch (p. 50). Finally, we may note an excellent work on the ornithology of the Faroes, Finn Salomonsen's 'Aves' (Copenhagen 1935, 8vo), part of the work 'Zoology of the Faroes', in which the author, partly on the basis of his own investigations, treats the 199 forms of birds occurring in the islands.

Until the 19th century the Americans, as already shown, had not made any large contribution to the investigation of the birds of the New World, although some few American authors of the 18th century had dealt with this subject (573). Examples are the above-mentioned writings of William Bartram and Benjamin S. Barton (p. 41). But as early as the first decade of the 19th century, in 1808, the publication was commenced in America of a large work on American birds entitled 'American ornithology', etc. (533), which was of fundamental importance for the study of birds in North America. It came into existence in difficult and peculiar circumstances. Its creator, *Alexander Wilson* (227, IV, pp. 17—50; 533, IX, pp. XIII—XLVIII; 534, I, pp. IX—CVII; 640, 4; 686; 735; 832; 834; 895; 913), who is often called the 'Father of American ornithology', was born in Paisley in Scotland. He was apprenticed to a weaver, but after a few years he gave up this trade to wander about Scotland as a pedlar. At the same time he cultivated his considerable powers as a rhymer and composed several poems, of one of which as many as 100,000 copies are said to have been sold in a few weeks.

Disturbances in the labour market and the resulting unpleasantness induced Wilson to emigrate to America in 1794, where he landed after a rather uncomfortable crossing, equipped only with a gun and some few shillings in his pocket. After some years he came into contact, in Philadelphia, with the above-mentioned naturalist William Bartram and his countryman the engraver *Alexander Lawson* (601; 687; 697) who both helped him, each in his own way, the former by stimulating his interest in nature, the latter by teaching him drawing, colouring, and etching. Encouraged in this way, Wilson could in 1805 begin to realize his great plan of depicting and describing North American birds in a large work, already mentioned above, of which the first volume was published in the autumn of 1808. The following winter he set out on his wanderings to seek birds and subscribers and, in spite of the high cost of the work, he managed to complete most of it before his death in 1813. Two volumes, however, remained; these were issued the next year by *George Ord,* who has also later added to and edited the work (715) which, considering the time and the circumstances in which it was produced, is a very valuable performance (688). As a matter of fact it became widely read and, together with Bonaparte's sequel (p. 77), has appeared in a number of editions (533, note). Wilson, who studied bird life in the open, gives good and exact descriptions and his figures, too, are on the whole good for the period, although the first ones especially may appear somewhat stiff and the postures a little unnatural. Through his friendship with Wilson the above-mentioned Lawson came to engrave plates for the book. Like Wilson he had emigrated to America from Scotland at the beginning of the seventeen-nineties, and displayed considerable activity in Philadelphia as the leading American engraver of the time, amongst other work engraving the plates for natural history works.

Wilson's influence on the development of ornithology in North America was very considerable. He initiated a more extensive investigation of the avifauna of the country and soon had successors, so that the Americans effactually took over the investigation of the ornithological conditions in the northern part of the New World. A rich growth was the result and an immense literature arose which can only be summed up in its main features here, especially as surveys already exist, for instance in publications by Allen, 1876 (592), and Stone, 1933 (584).

As in other parts of the world, an abundant periodical literature on ornithology is gradually growing up in America. After the middle of the 19th century it found a home, amongst other places, in a series of ornithological journals of which, besides some that will be mentioned later, we may here notice a magazine 'The Wilson Bulletin', which has been published under various names since 1889. This journal has in the course of years, as one of the most important American periodicals devoted to ornithology, issued material very valuable to all who are interested in the subject.

Wilson's work had not of course exhausted the theme. Therefore a sequel in four volumes could be issued in 1825—33 under the title 'American ornithology', etc. (47), by Charles Lucien Bonaparte (845), whose work deals with the birds of the United States not already treated by Wilson. Bonaparte, whom we have previously mentioned (p. 54), did considerable work as an ornithologist (674; 706, pp. 96—98) both in America and Europe, especially as a systematist and classifier. He was the eldest son of the Emperor Napoleon's second brother, Lucien Bonaparte. In company with Joseph Bonaparte, his uncle and father-in-law, he had gone to America at the age of about twenty. Settling in Philadelphia, he applied himself to the study of the avifauna of the country, so that besides the sequel to Wilson's book he could publish several large ornithological papers in scientific periodicals. In 1828 he returned to Europe and continued his scientific work in Italy, and later in France, his activities manifesting themselves in a series of larger and smaller works, examples of which have been given above (p. 54). Though of princely descent, he was an enthusiastic republican. In the revolution of 1848 he was the leader of the republican party in Rome, and in 1849 he was elected vice-president of the constituent assembly at Bologna. After the French had suppressed the revolution he fled to Paris, where he lived from 1850 till his death in 1857. In 1854 he was made director of the Jardin des Plantes.

All that had hitherto been produced of pictorial material relating to the birds of North America was, however, surpassed by a work of gigantic dimensions which was issued in London in 1827—38 under the title 'The birds of America', etc., (17) by *John James Audubon* (658a; 658b; 659; 660; 661; 681; 689; 752; 820; 835; 850; 852). This famous animal painter and ornithologist was born at Las Cayes, Santo Domingo, now Haiti, in 1785. He was the son of a

French naval officer and was educated in Paris where, amongst other subjects, he was taught painting, one of his teachers being J. L. David. At the turn of the century he went back to America and spent some time on a farm in Pennsylvania. He then applied himself to the study of the fauna of North America through which he roamed, eagerly occupied in studying nature and especially in drawing birds. In 1826 he again went to Europe where he made the acquaintance of some of the most renowned naturalists of the time, such as Cuvier, Humboldt, and St. Hilaire. The year after his arrival he could begin to issue his above-mentioned work with coloured plates of American birds. During succeeding years he was sometimes in Europe and sometimes in America until, in 1841, he bought an estate which he called "Minnie's Land", situated on the Hudson. The house which he built is still to be seen in New York City. In 1808 he had married Lucy Bakewell, who was a splendid help to him through years of financial difficulties and after her husband's death described his life from his diaries (661).

In the handsomely executed plates in Audubon's work the birds are shown in their natural size, and the figures are admittedly good, though there may be something unnatural or excessively sprightly in their postures (Pl. XI). Some of the first plates were executed by the Scotch painter and engraver *William Lizars*, though the bulk of them were prepared by the English painter, engraver, and publisher *Robert Havell, s e n i o r*, of whose engravings these very plates are the most important. He was in business in London with his son *Robert Havell, j u n i o r* (775; 912), until the latter emigrated to America in 1828, and he also traded in natural history specimens.

Audubon's plates were issued without a text, but this was published in 1831—39 in five octavo volumes under the title 'Ornithological biography', etc. (18), in which the birds are given in no systematic order, the sequence being the same as in the atlas. A systematic classification of the birds treated in the two works with references to the plates as well as the text was, however, issued by Audubon in 1839 under the title 'A synopsis of the birds of North America' (Edinburgh 1839, 8vo). Later on Audubon included the plates, which were modified and reduced, with the text in one work 'The birds of America', etc. (New York 1840—44, 7 vols., large 8vo), of which many editions have been published (19; 675; 753; 800; 844; 875).

Audubon's famous giant atlas which Cuvier called

'le plus magnifique monument que l'art ait encore élevé à la nature', has always been much coveted by collectors, especially, as is only natural, in America, where Audubon's memory is held in high honour. This will appear amongst other things from the existence of a number of 'Audubon Societies', whose official organ is the important periodical 'Bird-Lore', etc., the publication of which was begun in 1898. Fine pictures, too, have been published by this periodical, among them a series of coloured plates of American birds, part of which have been issued separately in a work bearing the title 'The warblers of North America', etc. (New York 1907, 32 pl. (24 col.), 8vo), of which several editions have appeared, with a text written mostly by the editor of 'Bird-Lore', *Frank M. Chapman,* and plates by Fuertes mentioned below (p. 81), and *R. Bruce Horsfall.*

While the publication of Audubon's work was still in progress there appeared in America a well-written account of the avifauna of that country. This was 'A manual of the ornithology of the United States and of Canada' (Cambridge, Mass. (Vol. II: Boston) 1832—34, 2 vols., 12mo) by *Thomas Nuttall,* the first volume of which deals with the land birds, the second with the water birds. This manual, which attained a well-deserved popularity, has later been re-issued, and in a revised shape carried right down to our century. It was, we may note here, the 'Nuttall Ornithological Club' of Cambridge, Mass. which in 1876 commenced the publication of that 'Bulletin' which was continued in 1884 as the leading ornithological periodical of America, 'The Auk' (p 42).

Towards the middle of the 19th century the knowledge of the birds of North America had increased so much that a desire was felt for a work which might supplement that of Audubon. The task was taken up by *John Cassin,* who in 1853—56 issued his 'Illustrations of the birds of California', etc. (92), and soon afterwards became collaborator in an important work on the birds of North America, to which we shall return below. Cassin, who was actually a business man, lived from 1834 in Philadelphia. After the death of Mr. Bowen, the principal engraver of that town, he took over the management of his establishment, which supplied illustrations for scientific publications and executed plates for several ornithological works. At Philadelphia Cassin had ample opportunities for cultivating in his leisure hours his special interest, ornithology, by means of the abundant literature and

large collection of birds in the academy there. However, he not only studied birds indoors but also in the open, for he was a great lover of Nature, and acquired a vast knowledge of ornithology. In this domain he did not keep to the fauna of his own country alone, for he had also a sound knowledge of the birds of the Old World, as is evidenced in his treatment of the ornithological material from various expeditions (p. 84). 'Cassinia', an annual devoted to the ornithology of Pennsylvania and New Jersey and published by 'The Delaware Valley Ornithological Club', of Philadelphia, is named after him.

The larger work, relating to the birds of North America on which Cassin was engaged, was the big volume on birds published in 1858, and forming Vol. IX of the Pacific Railroad reports of explorations and surveys (22), written by *Spencer F. Baird,* Cassin, and *George N. Lawrence.* The soul of this undertaking was Baird (705), whose contributions to ornithology have greatly enlarged our knowledge of the ornithological faunistics of North America. Baird's interest in ornithology had been especially aroused by Audubon, and he assiduously cultivated this interest, though as a professor of natural history, a chair to which he had been appointed in 1845, he had to lecture on several branches of natural science. The large field he thus had to cover gave a broad foundation to his researches, as is evidenced in part by his numerous papers, both long and short. Up to and including 1882 the number of these exceeded 1000 (731), and most of them are concerned with ornithology. His work in this domain greatly influenced the evolution of American ornithology, particularly after he had been appointed assistant-secretary in 1850 of the Smithsonian Institution of Washington, where he became secretary in 1878. In this post he had every opportunity of displaying his administrative talent and his powers as an organizer of scientific co-operation. He established the United States National Museum as a repository for specimens of all birds belonging to the American Government, and gave valuable assistance in promoting the investigation not only of North American avifauna but also of the whole vertebrate fauna of the country. The material for this purpose was secured especially by the great exploratory surveys which preceded the building of the railways between the eastern and western states, which was intended to develop the western part of the United States. Thus the material for the above-mentioned great work of 1858 was derived from

PLATE XI

THE BLACK-WINGED HAWK [= WHITE-TAILED KITE]. *Elanus leucurus* (Vieill.). From aquatint (Pl. CCCLII), drawn from Nature by J. J. Audubon, engraved, printed and coloured by R. Ravell, 1837, in Audubon's 'The birds of America', Vol. IIII, 1835—38

PLATE XI

these surveys, for Baird sent out naturalists with the different survey parties by whom large collections were secured, especially of mammals and birds. These also furnished material for a series of special 'Reports' written by Baird and his collaborators (references p. 207). The reports were accompanied by coloured plates, and such plates are also found in Baird's report on birds published in 1859 in Vol. II of 'Report on the United States and Mexican Boundary Survey' (Washington 1857—59, 2 vols., 25 col. pl. birds, 4to). The plates from these two sources were in 1860 incorporated in Baird, Cassin, and Lawrence's 'The birds of North America', etc. (24), a work whose text is mostly derived from the three authors' large book of 1858 (876).

Baird issued another, though unfinished, work on the birds of America as a whole in his 'Review of American birds in the Museum of the Smithsonian Institution' (Part I, Smithsonian Miscellaneous Collections, 181, Washington 1864—72, 8vo). In collaboration with *T. M. Brewer* and *Robert Ridgway,* who will be mentioned later, he also wrote a very important work on the birds of North America, 'A history of North American birds. Land birds' (25), published in 1874. The corresponding work on the water birds by the same three authors appeared in 1884 (cf. 25, note).

Brewer, who is known as an editor of Wilson's 'American ornithology' (p. 76), made oology his special study, which was of great benefit to the work just referred to. In 1857 he issued the first part of his 'North American oology', etc. (67), of which, however, only this part appeared. But the task was resumed by Bendire in 1892 (p. 80), and since 1919 has been carried on by Bent (p. 80).

The illustrations on plates in the last-mentioned works do not play a predominating part. On the other hand, in *Daniel Giraud Elliot* (711), for a time curator of zoology in the Field Columbian Museum at Chicago, America obtained an ornithologist who emphasized the iconographic part of his works. He himself supplied original designs for some of the plates in the first of these, for instance for 'The new and heretofore unfigured species of the birds of North America' (129), which was published in 1866—69 and was in the main planned as a kind of supplement or sequel to Audubon's and Wilson's pictorial works. Like Audubon's work, it was issued in a large format and

gives life-size representations of the birds (Pl. VIII). Elliot, we may note, also issued a number of monographs, which will be mentioned later on (p. 82).

The birds in the western part of the United States were studied by *J. G. Cooper* (917). The son of Audubon's friend, the naturalist William Cooper, he had been in touch with natural history from his childhood. Trained for the medical profession, he took part as surgeon and naturalist in several exploratory journeys in his country, thus in 1853 he became surgeon to the northern division of the Pacific Railroad Survey, where he also served as a naturalist and accomplished much by collecting natural objects (106; 107). In the Geological Survey of California, conducted by J. D. Whitney, he collected material relating to bird life. His manuscript and notes were given to Baird, who then edited Cooper's work under the title 'Ornithology. Volume I. Land birds' (Cambridge, Mass. 1870, 4to), which forms Vol. I of the Zoological Reports of the Geological Survey of California, an important manual of the birds west of the Rocky Mountains. Towards the close of the 19th century ornithology in this part of the United States benefitted by an important organ, a 'Magazine of Western Ornithology', published by the 'Cooper Ornithological Club of California', organised in 1893. Since 1900 this journal has been entitled 'The Condor'.

Of other general ornithological works dealing with the birds of North America on the basis of the different surveys of the territories of the United States, we may mention *Henry W. Henshaw*'s (750) ornithological portion of the Report upon geographical and geological explorations west of the one hundredth meridian (207), published in 1875, and the 'Birds of the Northwest', etc., (Washington 1874, 8vo) by *Elliott Coues,* a number of the 'Miscellaneous Publications of the United States Geological Survey'. As a handbook of the ornithology of the region drained by the Missouri River and its tributaries this work is an important manual on the subject. Coues (896), who, we may note, was an eminent bibliographer (561), had previously published his classical and much used work 'Key to North American birds', etc. (Salem 1872, 6 pl., 4to), a manual of the birds of North America north of Mexico which proved so useful that it was possible to publish several editions (sixth revised edition 1927).

A report on the avifauna of the region situated

between Sacramento, California, and Salt-Lake City, Utah, was published in 1877. It formed Volume IV, Part III, (pp. 303—669) of the Report of the United States geological exploration of the fortieth parallel (Washington, 4to). Its author was the above-mentioned Robert Ridgway (740), who was the zoologist to the expedition in question which took place in 1867—69. Ridgway was one of America's leading ornithologists. For nearly 50 years he was curator of the division of birds in the United States National Museum. His province was systematic ornithology, within which he did valuable work, as will be shown by examples which follow later. At the same time he was an excellent bird artist, as evidenced by pictures in his own works and those of others (598; 644). A condensed but complete account of the birds of North America was given by Ridgway in 'A manual of North American birds' (420), published in 1887, a work extremely useful for the identification of the different species, and one of which several editions have appeared. It was followed in 1901—19 by the as yet unfinished big systematic work 'The birds of North and Middle America', etc. (421), which deals very thoroughly with the subject and is one of the greatest ornithological faunal works ever published.

To quite another category belongs the popular account of North American birds, a compilation which was published under the title 'Studer's popular ornithology. The birds of North America', etc. (Columbus, Ohio 1874—78, 119 col. pl., folio), by *Jacob H. Studer.* This is a great favourite, and has appeared in several editions illustrated by chromo-lithographs from drawings by *Theodore Jasper.*

Another popular and more general account of the birds of North America was issued by *Heinrich Nehrling,* a German-American who was for some time curator of the Milwaukee Public Museum. It appeared under the title 'Die nordamerikanische Vogelwelt', etc. (Milwaukee 1889—91, 36 col. pl., 4to), with illustrations by Robert Ridgway, A. Goering, and Gustav Mützel and was long the only German bird book dealing with the birds of North America. This voluminous work, which in its own time contributed much to spread a knowledge of North American birds in German circles, also appeared in an English version entitled 'Our native birds of song and beauty', etc. (Milwaukee 1889—96, 2 vols., 36 col. pl., 4to).

A useful book on North American oology, and one of the earliest dealing with this subject, was issued by *Oliver Davie* under the title 'An egg check list of North American birds', etc. (Columbus 1885, 8vo). It has since been republished in several editions in an enlarged form with illustrations entitled 'Nests and eggs of North American birds', etc. Soon afterwards *Charles Bendire* resumed the work commenced by T. M. Brewer (p. 79), giving in 1892—95 an account of the reproduction of North American birds in his 'Life histories of North American birds', etc. (32—35), of which, however, only two volumes appeared, *Arthur Cleveland Bent* subsequently continuing the work in 1919 (36; 37).

The birds occurring east of the Mississippi River, between the Arctic Circle and the Gulf of Mexico, were treated by *Charles J. Maynard* in a work entitled 'The birds of Eastern North America', etc. (Newtonville, Mass. 1881, 32 col. pl., 4to), which was published in 1889—95 in a revised edition. Maynard has also, in addition to several other works, issued an ornithological atlas relating to the same subject, 'An atlas of plates for the Directory of the birds of Eastern North America' (West Newton, Mass. [1910], 51 col. pl.), which, dated 1906, was published in a limited edition.

A manual of the birds of Eastern North America, which became a standard work within its province and was much in demand, is Frank M. Chapman's 'Handbook of birds of Eastern North America', etc. (New York 1895, 20 pl., 12mo). Several editions of this have appeared with a gradually increasing pictorial material, for example a revised edition in 1927 with 24 coloured plates by Fuertes, to whom we shall refer later (second revised edition 1932, 29 col. pl.). A couple of years after the publication of the work just referred to, Chapman published a popular guide to the study of the common birds of Eastern North America under the title 'Bird-life', etc., (New York 1897, 75 col. pl., 8vo) with plates by *Ernest Thompson Seton,* while Mrs. *Florence Merriam Bailey* in her 'Handbook of birds of the western United States', etc., (Boston 1902, 33 pl., 8vo) produced a work corresponding to Chapman's 'Handbook'. It has appeared in several editions, and Fuertes was one of its illustrators.

Other works of a more general type are two manuals by *Ralph Hoffman,* director of the Santa Barbara Museum of Natural History, California. These are 'A guide to the birds of New England and Eastern New York', etc. (Boston 1904, 4 pl., small 8vo; new edition 1923), and 'Birds of the Pacific States', etc.

PLATE XII

THE NILE HELMET SHRIKE. *Prionops concinnata* Sundevall. From lithograph (offset), painted by L. A. Fuertes (dated April 6, 1929), in Fuertes' 'Abyssinian birds and mammals', 1930

PLATE XI

15 MILES WEST
OF
LAKE T'SANA.
APRIL 6, 1929-

Prionops cincinnata

(Boston 1927, 10 col. pl., 8vo). There are also several other works dealing with the avifauna in some of the larger areas of North America, for instance the 'Birds of the Pacific coast', etc. (New York 1923, 56 col. pl., 8vo), by *Willard Ayres Eliot,* a popular account of the birds of the Pacific Coast states.

Iconographically, too, North American avifauna has been treated by an increasing number of artists (644). A few of these only will be mentioned below, for space allows the inclusion of but a very limited number of recent American illustrators who have embellished ornithological publications with a series of excellent pictures of birds. In these the birds are free from the stiffness and pose of the earlier period, and are shown in their natural surroundings as a living part of them (608). A gigantic task in that field has been taken up by *Rex I. Brasher,* who for a number of years has devoted himself to the task of painting every species of North American bird from sketches executed directly in the field under natural conditions. He has executed an extensive series of paintings, good both from an artistic and a scientific point of view and has published them in life-size hand-coloured plates since 1929 under the title 'Birds and trees of North America' (Kent, Conn., c. 70 col. pl. in each volume, folio).

Of further works of a general type may be mentioned the long list of America's birds which is in progress under the title 'Catalogue of birds of the Americas', etc., and appears in the Publications of the Field Museum of Natural History, Chicago (Zoological Series 13). This great undertaking was commenced by *Charles B. Cory,* who in 1918—19 issued Part II, while Hellmayr, whom we have previously mentioned (p. 51), has brought out the sequel (Parts III—X, issued 1924—37), based partly on Cory's preliminary studies.

A profusely illustrated account of the American avifauna was issued under the title 'Birds of America' (New York 1917, 3 vols., 110 col. pl., 4to). This work, which contains a complete review of American birds, was written by several authors with *T. Gilbert Pearson* as editor-in-chief. As a book for bird lovers, written in plain language, it was issued in a single volume in 1936 (389). The illustrations in both editions included 106 coloured plates from Eaton's 'Birds of New York' referred to below. These plates are executed from the originals by the oft-mentioned *Louis Agassiz Fuertes,* one of the best and most popular American bird

painters of our time, whose handsome life-like pictures of birds adorn a great deal of the ornithological literature published in America from about 1900 to 1927, in which year he was killed in an accident. He was of Spanish descent and from his earliest years was interested in drawing and painting birds, an interest which increased under the influence of the ornithologist Elliott Coues, already referred to (p. 79), and the artist and colourist Abbott H. Thayer. On numerous journeys and expeditions, chiefly in the company of Frank M. Chapman (694), to various parts of North and South America and on his last journey to Abyssinia with Wilfred H. Osgood in 1926—27 (725), he studied birds in their natural environment and in so doing gained experience which he utilized so well in his numerous bird pictures that he became the leading bird artist of his country (Pl. XII). His knowledge of birds was also of advantage in other ways, for from 1922 he was lecturer in ornithology in Cornell University, Ithaca. A series of his plates has been published in the "Farmers' Bulletin" 513 (U. S. Department of Agriculture) under the title 'Fifty common birds of farm and orchard' (1913, 8vo), while after 1913 other series of his pictures of North American birds have appeared in the 'National Geographic Magazine' with a text by Henshaw. They have since been issued separately by the National Geographic Society in 'The book of birds', etc., (Washington, D. C. 1925, 8vo) with 331 coloured portraits of birds. Earlier editions also exist. The above-mentioned magazine, which is noted for its fine pictures, has issued many plates by other ornithological artists, for instance in a recent series of articles on American birds illustrated, sometimes with coloured plates, by Major *Allan Brooks,* another of America's fine bird artists. He was born in India and spent some time in England, while of late years he has lived chiefly in Canada, here as everywhere engrossed in the study and observation of wild bird life. He has thus acquired a first-hand knowledge of his models, which he places naturally in their scenery in pictures at times reminiscent of those of Joseph Wolf.

Besides the works dealing with the birds of the whole of North America or larger parts of it, a great number of the individual states of the United States possess a state bird book. Some of these are handsomely and richly illustrated works, occasionally consisting of several volumes. It is not possible to mention all these books here, but we give some examples of the most prominent works dealing with the birds of individual states. The oldest state bird book illustrated by coloured plates is Part II, 'Birds', of *James E. De Kay's* 'Zoology of New York', etc. (115), which was published in 1843—44 with 141 hand-coloured plates. It was only at the close of the 19th century that these works dealing with local faunas became more common, thus we may mention from this period *B. H. Warren's* 'Report on the birds of Pennsylvania' (Harrisburg 1888, 50 pl. (49 col.), 8vo; second edition 1890, 100 pl. (99 col.)), whose plates (lithographs) are, however, copies from Audubon's 'Birds of America'. In the 20th century, on the other hand, a number of works of this kind have appeared, profusely illustrated with original pictorial material, such as the 'Birds of New York' (Albany 1910—14, 2 vols., 106 col. pl., 4to), by *Elon Howard Eaton,* whose plates, due to Fuertes, formed part of the above-mentioned work 'Birds of America' issued by Pearson and others. The avifauna of California has been treated by *William Leon Dawson* in 'The birds of California', etc. (San Diego 1923, 4 vols., 260 pl. (110 col.), 4to), a popular account which was published in different issues with plates chiefly by Allan Brooks. The edition mentioned here is the most abundantly illustrated one. Another book worthy of notice is 'The birds of Florida', etc., (Baltimore, Md. 1925, 76 col. pl., 4to) by *Harold H. Bailey,* which appeared in a limited edition with plates by *George M. Sutton* of whose art as an illustrator examples may be seen in his 'Birds in the wilderness', etc. (New York 1936, 8vo), which is decorated with his own drawings in pencil and field sketches in colour. Fuertes and Allan Brooks supplied the designs for the handsome plates in 'Birds of Massachusetts and other New England states' (Boston 1925—29, 3 vols., 113 pl. (93 col.), 8vo) by *Edward Howe Forbush* (814). The same two artists illustrated 'Birds of New Mexico' (Washington, D. C. 1928, 79 pl. (25 col.), 8vo) by the above-mentioned Mrs. Bailey, while *Francis L. Jaques* of the American Museum of Natural History, a painter of water-fowl especially, has supplied the original pictures for the plates in 'Florida bird life' (New York 1932, 58 pl. (37 col.), 4to) by *Arthur H. Howell.* Several of the works referred to give figures of all the species of birds treated, as does 'The birds of Minnesota' (Minneapolis 1932, 2 vols., 92 col. pl., 4to; 2. edition, revised, 1936) by *Thomas S. Roberts,* an excellent handbook of the avifauna of that state, the plates in which are reproduced by the offset litho-

graphic process from originals by Allan Brooks, *Walter A. Weber, Walter J. Breckenridge,* and others. As has often been the case with recent American bird books, the plates of this work have been published separately under the title 'Bird portraits in color; 295 North American species', etc. (Minneapolis 1934, 92 col. pl., 4to), and in 1936 under the title 'Two hundred and ninety-five American birds', etc.

Individual groups of North American birds have also been treated in smaller or larger monographs. Thus the above-mentioned Elliot (p. 79) wrote three uniform popular and scientific accounts of this kind, chiefly illustrated by *Edwin Sheppard,* 'North American shore birds', etc. (New York 1895, 72 pl., 4to; second edition 1897), 'The gallinaceous game birds of North America', etc. (London 1897, 46 pl., 8vo; second edition 1897), and 'The wild fowl of the United States and British Possessions', etc. (New York 1898, 63 pl., 8vo), of which the last contains plates by J. Wolf as well as by Elliot himself. A series of works of this kind might be mentioned, for instance Chapman's book on the warblers of North America, mentioned above (p. 78). No little attention has been paid to the native North American birds that may in one way or another be considered to be of economic importance. These have been subjected to investigation by ornithologists working with practical purposes in view and the results embodied in several works. A couple of examples which may be mentioned on account of their pictorial material are *A. K. Fisher's* comprehensive bulletin on 'The hawks and owls of the United States in their relation to agriculture', published in 1893 (144) and Frank M. Chapman's 'Economic value of birds to the state' (New York 1903, 12 pl., 4to), published by the New York State Forest, Fish, and Game Commission and illustrated by Fuertes. As shown by the examples already mentioned, game birds have for obvious reasons attracted the attention of lovers of sport in America no less than in other countries. For which reason they have been treated in a great many larger or smaller publications which have been listed by *John C. Phillips* in a voluminous catalogue (578). We shall here mention only a few examples of works of this kind, such as 'Upland game birds and water fowl of the United States' (New York 1877—78, 20 col. pl., obl. folio) by *Alexander Pope* and *Ernest Ingersoll;* the well-written account 'Upland game birds' (New York 1902, 9 pl., 8vo; re-issued 1904, 1924), a popular work by *Edwyn Sandys* and *T. S. van Dyke.*

one of the illustrators of which was Fuertes who also illustrated the companion volume 'The waterfowl family' (New York 1903, 20 pl., 8vo) by *L. C. Sanford, Louis Bennett Bishop* and van Dyke. An excellent report on the game and shore birds of New England is found in 'A history of the game birds, wild-fowl and shore birds of Massachusetts and adjacent states', etc. (Boston 1912, 37 pl. (1 col.), 8vo; second edition 1916) by the above-mentioned Forbush, while the game birds of California were described in 1918 in a detailed account (190) by *Joseph Grinnell, Harold Child Bryant* and *Tracy Irwin Storer*. Finally, it may be mentioned that John C. Phillips and *Frederick C. Lincoln* in their work 'American waterfowl', etc., (Cambridge, Mass. 1930, 7 pl., 8vo) have reviewed the present situation and the outlook for the future of the birds in question. A pictorial work on game birds has been issued by *R. E. Bishop* under the title 'Birds. Etchings of water fowl and upland game birds' (Philadelphia 1936, folio), which appeared in a limited edition with 73 etchings reproduced in aquatone.

Canada has also produced a fairly rich ornithological literature dealing with larger or smaller groups of the avifauna of the Dominion. Of works of the more extensive kind may be mentioned the older 'Ornithologie du Canada', etc., (Quebec 1860, 2 vols., 12mo; re-issued 1861) by *J. M. le Moine,* a small systematic work which was followed about ten years later by a minor work by *Alexander Milton Ross* under the title 'The birds of Canada', etc. (Toronto 1871, 8vo; second edition 1872), an annotated list of species. For a long time the principal work on the birds of Canada was Swainson and Richardson's 'Fauna Boreali-Americana' (493) published in 1831, and not until the beginning of the 20th century was a larger work produced on the ornithology of the country, 'Catalogue of Canadian birds' (Ottawa 1900—04, 3 parts, 8vo; second edition, enlarged and revised, 1909). This gives a full account of all the Canadian birds and appeared in 1916 in a French version entitled 'Catalogue des oiseaux du Canada' (Ottawa, 8vo). The author of this work was the Irishman *John Macoun* who had emigrated to Canada in 1850 where he became naturalist to the Geological Survey and was noted especially as a botanist. His collaborator in the second edition of the catalogue was his eldest son *James M. Macoun,* also a botanist and, like his father, employed in the Geological Survey of Canada. A modern manual on the birds of the Dominion has been written by *P. A. Taverner* in two books, 'Birds of Eastern Canada' (499), first issued in 1919, and the complementary volume 'Birds of Western Canada' (Ottawa 1926, 84 col. pl., 8vo; second edition, revised, 1928). The plates for the latter work have been executed from drawings by Allan Brooks and the illustrator of the former work, *Frank C. Hennessey.* The material of the two works has been embodied by Taverner in 'Birds of Canada' (Ottawa 1934, 87 col. pl., 8vo), in which the author treats the birds of Canada as a whole, while some of the coloured plates are new and some are derived from the two preceding works. Birds in local parts of the Dominion have also been dealt with, for instance in 'The birds of Ontario', etc. (1886, 8vo; second edition, Toronto 1894), an account of all the species of birds found in the district concerned, written by *Thomas McIlwraith,* while of other local faunas we may mention 'Birds of Newfoundland Labrador' (Cambridge, Mass. 1932, 4to) by *Oliver Luther Austin* published as 'Memoirs of the Nuttall Ornithological Club', No. VII.

In this connection it may further be noted that bird life in Alaska has engaged no little of the attention of American ornithologists for whom it has afforded material for a number of literary works. Of these we shall here mention only *E. W. Nelson's* 'Birds of Alaska', 1887 (360) in 'Report upon natural history collections made in Alaska 1877—81' (730), and the contemporaneous treatise by *Lucien M. Turner* which was published in 1886 under the title 'Birds' in his 'Contributions to the natural history of Alaska' (512).

American ornithology, whose valuable contributions to the investigation of the avifauna of North America will in some degree have been illustrated by the above account has not of course confined itself to that task alone, but has, in addition, contributed largely to the growth of ornithology by more extensive as well as smaller works on the birds of foreign regions and by general ornithological works or monographs on individual groups of birds.

Within the latter domain we must first call to mind the large monographs of the earlier type, written by the above-mentioned Elliot, who provided his great books with abundant pictorial matter, mostly in the shape of coloured plates. Among his monographs we may note, besides those given in the accompanying catalogue (128; 130; 131), 'A monograph of the Pittidæ', (New York 1861—63, and 1867, 31 col. pl., large folio; second edition 1893—95, 51 col. pl.); 'A monograph of the Bucerotidæ', etc. (London 1877—82, 60 pl. (57 col.), folio and 4to); and 'A classification and synopsis of the Trochilidæ' (Washington 1878—79, large 4to).

Of the long series of monographs produced especially in the 20th century by American ornithologists, we shall here merely mention the largest and most important, among which especial note must be made of 'A monograph of the pheasants' (31), the principal work on the birds in question of recent years. It was published in 1918—22 and was written by Captain *William Beebe*, curator of birds of the New York Zoological Park and director of the Tropical Research Station in British Guiana. The author collected material on his research journeys, especially in the tropics, not only for his ornithological works but also for many entertaining and instructive books on natural history. Another important monograph has been written by John C. Phillips, to whom we have already referred (p. 82). This is 'A natural history of the ducks', etc., (Boston 1922—26, 4 vols., 102 pl. (74 col.), 4to) with plates from drawings by *Frank W. Benson,* Allan Brooks, and Fuertes. There may also be reason to mention 'The gulls (Laridæ) of the world', etc., by *Jonathan Dwight*, which was published in the 'Bulletin of the American Museum of Natural History' (62, 1925, pp. 63—401, 11 pl. (5 col.)), and Alexander Wetmore's previously noted (p. 63) continuation of H. Kirke Swann's 'A monograph of the birds of prey'.

Finally, of works dealing with the group of birds as a whole we may note the 19th century bird volume of the 'Standard Natural History' (Boston 1886, 8vo), an excellent semi-popular treatise, written chiefly by Stejneger, and in the 20th century the excellent popular account 'Birds of the world', etc. (New York 1909, 16 col. pl., large 8vo), written chiefly by *Frank H. Knowlton*. Mention must also be made of a work in the domain of nomenclature 'Check-list of birds of the world', of which three volumes have been issued 1931—37 (Cambridge, Mass., 8vo) by the excellent ornithologist *J. L. Peters.*

Of earlier times John Cassin must be mentioned as an especial example of an American ornithologist who published works on the birds outside North America, of which he had an extensive knowledge, as is evident from his treatment of the material from several expeditions. He wrote and issued in 1855 the section on birds, principally those of Chile, in the report on the 'United States Naval Astronomical Expedition to the Southern Hemisphere, 1849—52' (Washington 1855, Vol. II, pp. 172—206, col. pl., folio). He also described the birds, 1856, in the 'Narrative of the expedition of an American squadron to the China Seas and Japan ... 1852—54' (93) and issued 'Mammalogy and ornithology', forming Volume VIII (Philadelphia 1858, folio; atlas (large folio), 42 col. pl. birds) of the edition in 24 volumes of the complete report on the 'United States Exploring Expedition ... 1838—42. Under the command of Charles Wilkes', which, in a voyage round the world, made investigations in the South Sea and other places. This section, of value for its information about the fauna of Polynesia, was originally written by the chief zoologist of the expedition *Titian R. Peale,* an American painter in water-colours and illustrator and painter of animals, who took a great interest in natural history and drew the original designs for several of the plates in Cassin's report. This report replaced the suppressed volume written by Peale, which had been published in 1848 without the plates under the title 'Mammalia and ornithology' (2 parts, 4to) (810).

Since Cassin's time American ornithologists have continued to occupy themselves with the study of birds not only outside North America, but also, though only of late and then in increasing degree, outside the western hemisphere altogether; and the results of their studies have often appeared in various museum publications. As regards the avifauna of foreign regions, the birds of the West Indies and Central America, and recently especially of South America, have of course primarily been investigated and treated by North American ornithologists, as is shown by a noble series of works. Among the more outstanding of those dealing with the West Indies we may mention Charles B. Cory's 'Birds of the Bahama Islands', etc. (Boston 1880, 8 pl. (col. in some copies), 4to; revised edition 1890), a popular account of the 149 species recorded from the islands; the same author's works relating to West Indian birds, for instance his 'The birds of the West Indies', etc. (Boston 1889, 8vo); and his monograph 'The birds of Haiti and San Domingo' (Boston 1884—85, 23 pl. (22 col.), 4to). In our century the enlargement of our knowledge of the avifauna of the West Indies has been continued through such works as 'The birds of the Isle of Pines', etc., (Pittsburgh, Pa., 1916, 6 pl.; Annals of the Carnegie Museum 10, pp. 146—296) by *W. E. Clyde Todd,* with field notes by Gustav A. Link; 'Birds of

Cuba' (Cambridge, Mass. 1923, 4 pl., 8vo; Memoirs of the Nuttall Ornithological Club No. VI), by *Thomas Barbour;* Alexander Wetmore's 'The birds of Porto Rico and the Virgin Islands' (New York 1927, 11 pl., 8vo; Scientific survey of Porto Rico and the Virgin Islands of the New York Academy of Sciences 9, Parts 3—4 (pp. 243—598)); and also 'The birds of Haiti and the Dominican Republic' (Washington 1931, 25 pl., 8vo) by Wetmore and *Bradshaw H. Swales.* The sporadic material on the birds of the West Indies has been briefly summarised by *James Bond* in a handbook on the avifauna of the group, entitled 'Birds of the West Indies', etc. (Baltimore 1936, 1 pl., 12mo).

Of works dealing with the avifauna of Central America some of the most important may be mentioned, for instance 'An annotated list of the birds of Costa Rica', etc., (Pittsburgh, Pa., 1910; Annals of the Carnegie Museum 6, No. 4, pp. 314—915) by *M. A. Carriker,* j u n i o r; Frank M. Chapman's 'My tropical air castle', etc. (New York 1929, 47 pl., 8vo), a well written account of the bird and animal life of Barro Colorado in the Panama Canal Zone, the illustrations to which include drawings by Francis L. Jaques; 'The distribution of bird life in Guatemala', etc., (New York 1932, 8vo) by *Ludlow Griscom; Witmer Stone*'s 'The birds of Honduras', etc. (Philadelphia 1932, 8vo; Proceedings of the Academy of Natural Sciences of Philadelphia 84, pp. 291—342); and also Ludlow Griscom's check list 'The ornithology of the Republic of Panama' (Cambridge, Mass. 1935, 8vo; Bulletin of the Museum of Comparative Zoölogy at Harvard College 78, No. 3 (pp. 261—382).

As previously mentioned, American ornithologists have especially made valuable contributions to the investigation of South American ornithology. The results appear in a long series of works of which some of the most noteworthy may be mentioned, for example William Beebe's 'Tropical wild life in British Guiana', etc. (New York 1917, 8vo), based on the results of the work at the Tropical Research Station of the New York Zoological Society, which were also treated in the publication 'Jungle peace' (New York 1918, 16 pl., 8vo; several re-issues and reprints) intended for a wider public. We may next mention several works by Chapman, 'The distribution of bird-life in Colombia', etc., 1917 (96); 'The distribution of bird-life in the Urubamba Valley of Peru' (Washington 1921, 8 pl., 8vo); his 'The distribution of bird-life in

Ecuador', etc., 1926 (97), and finally 'The upper zonal bird-life of Mts. Roraima and Duida' (New York 1931, 8vo; Bulletin of the American Museum of Natural History 63, pp. 1—135).

Another valuable publication on the birds of South America is W. E. Clyde Todd and M. A. Carriker's 'The birds of the Santa Marta region of Colombia', etc. (Pittsburgh, Pa. 1922, 9 pl.; Annals of the Carnegie Museum 14). Mention may also be made of *Elsie M. B. Naumburg*'s 'The birds of Matto Grosso, Brazil', etc., 1930 (359); 'Birds of the Marshall Field Peruvian Expedition, 1922—23' (Chicago 1930, 8vo; Field Museum of Natural History, Publication 282, Zoological Series 17, No. 7, pp. 231—480) by *John T. Zimmer;* 'The avifauna of the Galapagos Islands' (San Francisco 1931, 8vo) by *Harry S. Swarth; Robert Cushman Murphy*'s 'Bird islands of Peru', etc. (New York 1925, 32 pl., 8vo), and the same author's 'Oceanic birds of South America', etc., 1936 (352). To this impressive series may finally be added Alexander Wetmore's 'Observations on the birds of Argentina, Paraguay, Uruguay, and Chile' (Washington 1926, 20 pl., 8vo) and *William Earl Dodge Scott,* R. Bowdler Sharpe, and Witmer Stone's contribution to the ornithology of Patagonia (453) published in 1904—27 in the Reports of the Princeton University Expeditions to Patagonia 1896—99; and we must here recall Hellmayr's works on the Neotropical birds (p. 51), the author of which lived for a number of years in America. Finally, the birds of a part of Brazil have been treated by *Oliverio M. de O. Pinto* in a Portuguese book entitled 'Aves da Bahia', etc. (São Paulo 1935, 8vo; Revista do Museu Paulista 19, pp. 1 —325), an excellent work based on the results of a collecting expedition in 1932—33.

As previously indicated, American ornithologists have only recently begun to contribute to the literature on the birds of the Old World. Africa has been visited in our century by several American expeditions which have furnished material for valuable works, for instance 'Birds collected by the Childs Frick Expedition to Ethiopia and Kenya Colony. Part I. Non-Passeres' (Washington 1930, 8vo) by *Herbert Friedmann,* and the very important 'The birds of the Belgian Congo' (Part I, New York 1932 [1933], 11 pl., 8vo) written by *James P. Chapin* and based on results and material from expeditions sent out by the American Museum, especially from the Congo expedition sent out by this Museum. As has previously been stated, the bird painter Fuertes was a member of an expedition to Abyssinia and executed a number of pictures, some of which were published posthumously in the atlas 'Abyssinian birds and mammals', etc., 1930 (157).

The birds of Hawaii have been dealt with, for instance by H. W. Henshaw in the semi-popular work 'Birds of the Hawaiian Islands', etc. (Honolulu 1902, 8vo) which is a very useful handbook, while contributions to the knowledge of the birds of Siberia have been made by Stejneger in his 'Results of ornithological explorations in the Commander Islands and in Kamtschatka', 1885 (485). The same author has written a series of papers (I—IX) on the birds of Japan which, under the title 'Review of Japanese birds', and illustrated with coloured plates, were published in 1886—88 in the 'Proceedings of the United States National Museum'. Southern Asia and the Malay Archipelago also belong to the areas whose birds have been subjected to literary treatment by American ornithologists. As examples we may mention 'The birds of the Natuna Islands' (Washington 1932, 8vo) by Harry C. Oberholser, and 'A manual of Philippine birds' (Manila 1909—10, 2 parts, 8vo) by Richard C. McGregor, a complete and valuable monograph. Many other examples could be mentioned of the investigation of the avifauna of Asia and other foreign regions by American ornithologists such as J. H. Riley. However, what has already been stated must suffice to convey an impression of conditions in this field, though it may finally be mentioned that the avifauna of Southern New Guinea has been treated by Ernst Mayr and A. L. Rand in 'The birds of the 1933—34 Papuan Expedition' (New York 1937, 1 pl., 8vo; Bulletin of the American Museum of Natural History 73, pp. 1—248) or 'Results of the Archbold Expeditions, No. 14', the work being largely based on the collection made by the American Museum's Papuan Expedition in 1933—34 led by R. Archbold.

The birds of the Philippine Islands, we may note, have also been described by a Japanese scientist, the Marquess Masauji Hachisuka, in a recent work in course of publication under the title 'The birds of the Philippine Islands', etc., (London 1931 →, Part I →, 8vo), a monograph illustrated with handsome coloured plates of which, up to 1935, Parts I—IV have appeared. Altogether Japanese ornithologists have recently displayed no little activity, especially in the investigation and description of the birds of their own

country and of East Asia, as is evidenced by a series of works such as Nagamichi Kuroda's 'A contribution to the knowledge of the avifauna of the Riu Kiu Islands', etc. (Tokyo 1925, 8 col. pl., 4to), and the same author's useful work on the birds of Java with the title 'Birds of the island of Java' (Tokyo 1933—36, 2 vols., 34 col. pl., folio) with excellent plates, each of them with many figures, from drawings by Shigekazu Kobayashi, who is commonly regarded as the leading bird artist of Japan. Evidence of Japanese activity on the Asiatic continent is found in the Report on the First Scientific Expedition to Manchoukuo in 1933, in which the 'Birds of Jehol' were treated in 1935 by a number of authors (498). Of works on the birds of Japan mention may be made of Kuroda's 'A monograph on the pheasants of Japan', etc. (Tokyo 1926, 15 pl. (12 col.), 4to), a complete account of the subject illustrated by Kobayashi and Yokoyama, and last, but not least, Prince Nobusuke Taka-Tsukasa's largely planned 'The birds of Nippon' (Tokyo 1932 →, Part I →, 4to), intended to fill five volumes. It is illustrated with coloured plates and, up to November 1936, Parts 1—6 have appeared. The ornithological literature of Japan has also a modern work with figures of eggs, 'The eggs of Japanese birds' (Kobe 1929 →, Part I →, col. pl., folio) by Keisuke Kobayashi and Takeo Ishizawa. It is issued in a limited edition which it is thought will consist of 20 parts, of which Parts 1—9 have appeared up to 1934.

This brief survey cannot be concluded without some few remarks on the literary fruits of the more official international collaboration in the province of ornithology.

The first international ornithological congress was held at Vienna in 1884 and at the same time the International Ornithological Committee was established as an institution of a permanent character. In the following year this Committee was able to issue the first volume of its special organ 'Ornis', etc., which, being an international journal, has been published in various places, and of which 13 volumes have appeared up to 1910, Volume XIV forming the 'Proceedings of the Fourth International Ornithological Congress', London 1905. International congresses and the publication of their proceedings were continued fairly regularly till the Great War, the second congress being held at Budapest in 1891, the third in Paris in 1900, the fourth, as already mentioned, in London in 1905, and the fifth in Berlin in 1910.

With the Great War, however, the activity of the International Committee ceased, and it was not until several years after the war had stopped that a new Committee, under the leadership of Ernst Hartert, who had worked assiduously for international co-operation, could make arrangements for the sixth International Congress, held in Copenhagen in 1926, while the seventh took place at Amsterdam in 1930, and the eighth and so far the last, at Oxford in 1934.

A retrospective view of the last and largest section of this survey will show that the various nations that are at all active scientifically have to a greater or less degree made contributions to the part of ornithological literature and iconography of the period after 1800 discussed here. The English-speaking part of the world has not been the least active in this respect. This is perhaps ultimately due to the favourable external conditions under which ornithologists have been able to work in these countries during the 19th and 20th centuries. One of the results of this is, then, a comprehensive knowledge of the forms of birds and an increasing insight into the biological conditions and geographical distribution of the species and subspecies. A great many excellent handbooks and monographs are now available, especially in faunistic literature. These cover the avifauna of virtually all the world, though areas such as China, the Malay Archipelago, and Polynesia can hardly compete with the rest of the globe in this respect.

As far as pictorial material is concerned there has been such an extensive production during the 19th and 20th centuries that a great part of the birds of the world may now be said to be more or less satisfactorily depicted. In most countries, however, a noticeable decline in the production of coloured plates set in at the close of the 19th and in the 20th century. One article on the book market belongs especially to the past, the huge and unpractical ornithological atlas. Its publication is not justified in our day and it is now chiefly in demand by libraries and collectors. The perfection of photographic pictures and their increasing employment as a basis for the pictorial material in ornithological works has in some degree thrown hand-made pictures into the shade. Fortunately, however, even colour photographs have not been able to stop the personal production of pictures. Executed by the hand of an artist, these will always have their advantages and retain their importance. It is to be hoped that they will continue to hold their own in ornithological works, and will add to them something which no other process can equal or replace, now that reproductive technique has reached its present high standard, attained thanks to the development of the three- and four-colour processes, the collotype, and the offset lithographic process which is so popular in America.

II.

A CATALOGUE OF THE COLLECTION
OF BOOKS CONTAINING PLATES WITH FIGURES
OF BIRDS AND THEIR EGGS NOW IN THE
UNIVERSITY LIBRARY AT COPENHAGEN

ABBOT, H. L.
1857. Reports of explorations and surveys ... for a railroad from the Mississippi River to the Pacific Ocean ... 1854—55 ... Vol. VI. Report of Lieut. Henry L. Abbot ... upon explorations ... from the Sacramento Valley to the Columbia River ... 1855. Part IV. Zoological report. No. 2. Report upon the zoology of the route. pp. 73—110: Chapter II. Report upon the birds. *See Newberry, J. S.*

ABILDGAARD, P. C.
1806. Zoologia Danica seu animalium Daniæ et Norvegiæ rariorum ac minus notorum descriptiones et historia. Vol. IV ... *See Mueller, O. F.*

ACADEMIA CÆSAREA LEOPOLDINO-CAROLINA NATURÆ CURIOSORUM.
1834. Nova Acta. Vol. XVI. Supplement. I. pp. 59—124: Beiträge zur Zoologie, gesammelt auf einer Reise um die Erde. Vierte Abhandlung. Vögel. *See Meyen, F. J. F.*

ACADÉMIE IMPÉRIALE DES SCIENCES DE ST.-PÉTERSBOURG.
1770—74. Reise durch Russland zur Untersuchung der drey Natur-Reiche. *See Gmelin, S. G.*
1786. Beyträge zur topographischen Kenntniss des russischen Reichs. Vol. III ... pp. 326—410: Zweite Klasse. Vögel. *See Falck, J. P.*
1831—42. Zoographia Rosso-Asiatica ... Aves. *See Pallas, P. S.*
1853. Reise in den äussersten Norden und Osten Sibiriens ... 1843 und 1844 ... Vol. II. Zoologie. Part II. Säugethiere, Vögel und Amphibien. pp. 124—246: B. Vögel. *See Middendorff, A. T. von.*
1860. Reisen und Forschungen im Amur- Lande ... 1854—56 ... Vol. I. pp. 215—567: Part II. Vögel des Amur-Landes. *See Schrenck, P. L. von.*
1889—92. Ornithographia Rossica ... Vol. II. Sylviinæ. *See Pleske, T. D.*
1889—1905. Wissenschaftliche Resultate der von N. M. Przewalski nach Central-Asien unternommenen Reisen ... Zoologischer Theil. Vol. II. Vögel. *See Pleske, T. D.*
[1830—] 1831—35. Mémoires présentés à l'Académie Impériale des Sciences de St.-Pétersbourg par divers savans et lus dans ses assemblées. Imprimerie de l'Académie Impériale des Sciences. *St.-Pétersbourg. Vols. I—II. plates. maps. 4to.*
The first two volumes of this series, which comprises altogether nine volumes published in 1830—59, contain the following ornithological treatises by F. H. v. Kittlitz, illustrated with coloured plates,

Vol. I, pp. 173—194: Über einige Vögel von Chili. 12 col. pl. (read 1830).
Vol. I, pp. 231—248: Über die Vögel der Inselgruppe von Boninsima. 4 col. pl. (read 1830).
Vol. II, pp. 1—9: Über einige noch unbeschriebene Vögel von der Insel Luzon, den Carolinen und den Marianen. 11 col. pl. (read 1831).
Vol. II, pp. 465—472: Über einige Vögel von Chili. Fortsetzung. 5 col. pl. (read 1834).
The plates (engravings coloured by hand) accompanying these papers were executed from drawings by the author.

Mémoires de l'Académie Impériale des Sciences de St.-Pétersbourg.
1835. Sixième série. Vol. III. (Sciences naturelles. Vol. I). pp. 443—543: Monographie de la famille des Myiotherinæ ... *See Ménétriés, E.*
[1839] 1840. Sixième série. Vol. V. (Sciences naturelles. Vol. III). pp. 239—275: Tentamen monographiæ zoologicæ generis Phaëton [Spicilegia ornithologica exotica. Fasc. I]. *See Brandt, J. F.*

Musée zoologique de l'Académie Impériale des Sciences de St.-Pétersbourg (1916: Petrograd).
1836. Descriptiones et icones animalium Rossicorum novorum vel minus rite cognitorum. Aves. Fasc. I. *See Brandt, J. F.*
1916. Faune de la Russie ... Rédigée par N. V. Nasonov. Oiseaux (Aves). Vol. VI. Falconiformes. Part I. *See Menzbir, M. A.*

ACADÉMIE DES SCIENCES DE L'INSTITUT DE FRANCE. PARIS.
1757. Der Herren Perrault, Charras und Dodarts Abhandlungen zur Naturgeschichte der Thiere und Pflanzen. Vols. I—II. *See Perrault, C.*

ACADEMY OF NATURAL SCIENCES OF PHILADELPHIA.
1841 → Proceedings of the Academy of Natural 2. Sciences of Philadelphia. Printed for the Academy (1871 →: (The) Academy of Natural Sciences). *Philadelphia. Vol. I → text-figs. plates. 8vo.*
From 1857 to 1900 the volumes of this periodical are unnumbered. The earlier volumes (up to 1875), to which contributions of an ornithological character were made by authors such as John Cassin, S. F. Baird, A. L. Heermann, G. N. Lawrence, D. G. Elliot, and Elliott Coues, contain a number of plates (more than 20), chiefly coloured, showing figures of birds executed in lithography coloured by hand (H. L. Stephens and Otto Koehler del.; some were drawn on stone by Wm. E. Hitchcock; J. T. Bowen (later Bowen & Co.) lith. & col., Philada.).
1847—1918. Journal of the Academy of Natural 3. Sciences of Philadelphia. Printed for the Academy. *Philadelphia. Second series. Vols. I—XVI. text-figs. plates. maps. fol.*

The academy was founded in 1812, and the publication of the 'Journal' started in 1817, Vols. I—VIII appearing in 1817—42 (8vo).

John Cassin contributed a good deal of ornithological matter to the first five volumes, 1847—63, of the second series, and in these volumes a number of coloured plates are published with figures of birds executed from drawings by H. L. Stephens and Otto Koehler (several drawn on stone by Wm. E. Hitchcock; most of them lith., printed & col. by J. T. Bowen (later Bowen & Co.), Philada.).

AKADEMIE VAN WETENSCHAPPEN TE AMSTERDAM.

1917. Verhandelingen. Tweede sectie. Deel XIX. No. 4. Dodo-studiën ... See Oudemans, A. C.

AKADEMIE DER WISSENSCHAFTEN. WIEN.

1865. Reise. der österreichischen Fregatte Novara um die Erde ... 1857—59 ... Zoologischer Theil. Vol. I ... 2. Vögel. See Pelzeln, A. von.

ALBIN, E.

4.   *1738. A natural history of birds. Illustrated with ... copper plates, curiously engraven from the life. And exactly colour'd by the author, Eleazar Albin. To which are added, notes and observations by W. Derham. W. Innys and R. Manby. London. 2 vols. 205 col. pl. 4to. — Vol. I. pp. [VIII] + 96 + [4]. 101 col. pl. (numb. 1—101). Vol. II. pp. [VIII] + 92. 104 col. pl. (numb. 1—104).*
A third and last volume of this work was issued in 1740 as a supplement (5), under which entry the work as a whole is more closely described.

5.   *1740. A supplement to the natural history of birds. Illustrated with ... copper plates, curiously engraven from the life; and exactly colour'd by the author, Eleazar Albin. Being the third and last volume. W. Innys and R. Manby. London. pp. [VIII] + 95 + [1]. 101 col. pl. (numb. 1—101). 4to.*
The third and last volume of a work, the first two volumes of which (4) appeared in 1738. According to Mullens and Swann (574, pp. 8—9), the original issue of the whole work appeared in London in 1731—38 under the title 'A natural history of birds. Illustrated with ... copper plates, curiously engraven from the life. Published by the author Eleazar Albin, and carefully colour'd by his daughter and self, from the originals, drawn from the live birds.'

In 1738 all three volumes were re-issued under the above-mentioned somewhat altered title and with Derham's notes, which are to be found on a leaf at the end of the first volume. In the present copy Vol. III appears as a supplement, published in 1740.

The figures of the birds, mainly British, were drawn by the author or his daughter Elizabeth, who also assisted him in colouring the plates. The latter are not distinguished by any particularly fine execution, either as regards drawing or colouring.

A French translation of the work was published in 1750 (6).

6.   *1750. Histoire naturelle des oiseaux, ornée de ... estampes, qui les représentent parfaitement au naturel, dessinées & gravées par Eleazar Albin, et augmentée de notes & de remarques curieuses, par W. Derham. Traduite de l'Anglois. Pierre de Hondt. La Haye. 3 vols. 306 col. pl. 4to. — Vol. I. pp. [X] + 87 + [1]. 101 col. pl. (numb. 1—101). Vol. II. pp. [IV] + 70. 104 col. pl. (numb. 1—104). Vol. III. pp. [IV] + 44. 101 col. pl. (numb. 1—101).*
A French translation of the edition of 1738 with Derham's notes. There are two copies of this edition in the Library.

1759. A natural history of English song-birds, and 7. *such of the foreign as are usually brought over and esteem'd for their singing. To which are added, figures of the cock, hen, and egg of each species, exactly copied from nature, by Eleazar Albin, and curiously engraven on copper. Also a particular account how to order the canary-birds in breeding; likewise their diseases and cure. The third edition. C. Ware. London. pp. [IV] + 96 + [4]. 23 pl. small 8vo.*
The first edition of this work, which is a popular treatise on these birds, appeared in 1737, a second edition appeared in 1741, and a new edition in 1779, all with coloured and uncoloured plates. Several anonymous pirated editions also appeared, according to Mullens and Swann (574, p. 9) in 1754, reprinted in 1776 (8), and in 1791.

1776. A natural history of singing birds: and par- 8. *ticularly, that species of them most commonly bred in Britain. To which are added, figures of the cock, hen, and egg, of each species, exactly copied from nature, and elegantly engraven on copper. Together with the figure, description, and use of the day-net, and the manner of catching small birds of all kinds. By a lover of birds. J. Wood. Edinburgh. pp. VII + [I] + 120 + [4]. 21 pl. (19 pl. birds). 12mo.*
A reprint of an anonymous piracy (published in 1754) of Albin's 'A natural history of English song-birds' (7).

ALEMBERT, J. LE R. D'.

1751—77. Encyclopédie, ou dictionnaire raisonné des sciences ... See Encyclopædias.

ALFERAKI, S. N.

1905. The geese of Europe and Asia. Being the 9 *description of most of the old world species. By Sergius Alphéraky. With ... coloured plates by F. W. Frohawk and frontispiece by P. P. Sushkin. Rowland Ward. London. pp. IX + 198. text-figs. 25 col. pl. (front. + Nos. 1—24). 4to.*
An English translation by John Marshall, M. A., of the author's 'Gusi Rossi', which was published in Russia in 1904.

All the known species and subspecies of Palæarctic geese are described and figured, which justifies the alteration of the title.

The text consists of an introduction with a general account of the group of birds dealt with, a key to the genera, species, and subspecies, and a discussion of the individual species or subspecies, in all 22, with a brief diagnosis (or differential diagnosis) of the ten genera into which the author divides the group.

A comprehensive synonymy is given under the individual forms as well as a description of the adult birds of both sexes, a review of their geographical distribution and habits, together with a description of the young birds.

Two appendices complete the text, I (pp. 185—190) 'Mr. G. F. Göbel on the eggs of Russian geese' and II (pp. 191—195) 'Extract from the diary of the visit to Kolguev in 1902 of Mr. S. A. Buturlin, kindly communicated by the author'.

Plates 1—24 (Lith. Tva. I. N. Kušnerev i Ko., Moskva, from drawings by F. W. Frohawk) show figures of the birds, Pl. 1—21, and of their bills, 22—24.

ALLEN, J. A.

1884—1911. See Auk.

ALLEN'S NATURALIST'S LIBRARY. Edited by R. Bowdler Sharpe.

1894—97. A hand-book to the birds of Great Britain. See Sharpe, R. B.

1895—97. A hand-book to the game-birds. See Ogilvie-Grant, W. R.

ALLGEMEINE DEUTSCHE ORNITHOLOGISCHE GESELLSCHAFT.

1876—95. See Journal fuer Ornithologie. Jahrgang XXIV—XLIII.

ALPHÉRAKY, S. N. *See Alferaki, S. N.*

AMERICAN MUSEUM OF NATURAL HISTORY.

1936. Oceanic birds of South America. A study ... based upon the Brewster-Sanford collection in the American Museum of Natural History ... *See Murphy, R. C.*

Bulletin.
1917. Vol. XXXVI. The distribution of bird-life in Colombia ... *See Chapman, F. M.*
1926. Vol. LV. The distribution of bird-life in Ecuador ... *See Chapman, F. M.*
1930. Vol. LX. The birds of Matto Grosso, Brazil ... *See Naumburg, E. M. B.*

AMERICAN ORNITHOLOGISTS' UNION.

1884 → See Auk.

AMSTERDAM. KONINKLIJK ZOÖLOGISCH GENOOTSCHAP 'NATURA ARTIS MAGISTRA'. *See Koninklijk Zoölogisch Genootschap 'Natura Artis Magistra'. Amsterdam.*

AMSTERDAM. KONINKLIJKE AKADEMIE VAN WETENSCHAPPEN. *See Akademie van Wetenschappen te Amsterdam.*

ANDERSON, J.

'0.   *1878 [1879].* Anatomical and zoological researches: comprising an account of the zoological results of the two expeditions to Western Yunnan in 1868 and 1875; and a monograph of the two cetacean genera, Platanista and Orcella. By John Anderson. Bernard Quaritch. *London. 2 vols. large 8vo.* — Vol. I. Text. *< - - pp. 565—702:* Aves. List of species collected on the two expeditions to Western Yunnan >. Vol. II. Plates. *10 col. pl. birds (numb. XLV—LIV).*
     Vol. I (pp. XXV + 984) of this work, in addition to vertebrates, mainly the work of Anderson, deals with Mollusca, Insecta, and Crustacea, which groups are treated by other authors. Vol. II (pp. XI + 29, 84 pl.) contains in all 51 coloured plates.
     The section on birds comprises 233 species. R. Bowdler Sharpe gave assistance in its preparation by verifying the identification of the birds, and by compiling the literature.
     Nine of the plates with figures of birds (hand-coloured lithographs, printed by Banks & Co., Edinr.) are signed J. G. Keulemans lith.

ANONYMOUS.

1774—85. Naturgeschichte der Vögel aus den besten Schriftstellern mit Merianischen und neuen Kupfern. *See Decker, J. M.*
1776. A natural history of singing birds ... *See Albin, E.*
1828. Atlas des oiseaux ... *See Lesson, R. P.*
1.   *1863.* Afbildninger til Fuglenes Naturhistorie med oplysende Text. Hempel. *Odense. pp. 17. 30 col. pl. (fold.) (numb. I—XXX).*
     This ornithological picture-book has been reproduced from

'Naturgeschichte der Vögel in Bildern', the first issue of which appeared in 1841. The text is printed in double columns, and gives brief and popular information about the birds figured.

APLIN, O. V.

1898. British birds with their nests and eggs. Vol. VI. Order Pygopodes. *See Butler, A. G., 1896—98.*

AQUILA.

1894 → Aquila. A magyar ornithologiai központ fo- 12. lyóirata. Szerk. Herman Ottó (1894—1914), Csörgey Titus (1915, 1922 →), Chernel István (1916—21). Magyar Ornithologiai Központot. *Budapest. I → Évfolyam. text-figs. maps. plates. 4to (1915 → 8vo).*
     This periodical of ornithology is edited by the Hungarian Central-Bureau for Ornithological Observations (later the Royal Hungarian Institute of Ornithology).
     The title quoted above originates from Jahrgang 1, and subsequently underwent minor alterations. From 1894—1914 the journal had the subtitle 'Periodical of Ornithology. Journal pour Ornithologie. Zeitschrift für Ornithologie', and the text of these series is, as a rule, printed in Magyar and German, or exceptionally English or French, in parallel columns. Upon the change of the size of the periodical in 1915 the subtitle was altered to 'Zeitschrift der Königlichen Ungarischen Ornithologischen Zentrale' (from 1919: '... des Königlich Ungarischen Ornithologischen Institutes'), and at the same time the double columns disappeared from the text, the individual papers or articles being from that date printed in one language only, Magyar or German.
     Many important contributions not only to the ornithology of Central Europe but also to the natural history of birds in general have been published, notably by Hungarian ornithologists, in this important periodical. In addition to the editors Otto Herman, Titus Csörgey, and Stefan Chernel, ornithologists such as J. v. Madarász, O. Kleinschmidt, O. Finsch, O. Heinroth, O. Helms, and Hjalmar Rendahl may be counted among its contributors.
     A number of plates, more than 20 of which are coloured, have been issued in the periodical.
     In the first annual series the coloured plates were executed by lithography (Mintern Bros. imp.; Litho. W. Greve, Berlin, and others), while from 1902 they have been produced by the three-colour process. The originals have been supplied by J. G. Keulemans and Steph. Nécsey, and others, later on by Titus Csörgey in particular. One of the coloured plates has, however, been executed from a photograph.

ARCHIVES DU MUSÉUM D'HISTOIRE NATURELLE, PARIS. *See Muséum D'Histoire Naturelle, Paris.*

ASTROLABE, Voyage of the [French corvette].

1830—33. Voyage de ... l'Astrolabe ... 1826—29 ... Zoologie. Oiseaux. *See Quoy, J. R. C.*

ASTROLABE, Voyage of the [French frigate].

1797. Voyage de La Pérouse autour du monde ... rédigée par M. L. A. Milet-Mureau. *See Lapérouse, J. F. de G. de.*

ATKINSON, J. C.

1892. British birds' eggs and nests, popularly 13. described. By J. C. Atkinson. Illustrated by W. S. Coleman. Nineteenth edition. George Routledge and Sons. *London. pp. VIII + 182 + [10]. 12 col. pl. eggs (numb. I—XII). 8vo.*
     The first edition of this once very popular book for beginners appeared in 1861. Subsequently a number of editions have been issued in addition to the present one, viz. in 1861, 1862,

1866, 1870, 1886. The book was revised and re-issued in 1898, and in 1904.

The principal aim is to give 'accounts of the nest and nesting-sites, the eggs, and any ascertained nesting or breeding season peculiarities of every undoubtedly British species'. In an appendix (pp. 171—178) an account is given of the habits of nidification, and of the nests and eggs of several birds which, though they occur in the British Isles, do not breed there.

The plates show pictures of a large number of eggs, characterized by varied colours and markings.

AUDEBERT, J. B.

14.   [1800?—] 1802 (An XI). Oiseaux dorés, ou à reflets métalliques. (Par J. B. Audebert et L. P. Vieillot). (Desray). *Paris. 2 vols. 190 col. pl. fol. —* Vol. I. Histoire naturelle et générale des colibris, oiseauxmouches, jacamars et promerops. *pp. [IV] + X + 128 + 8 + 28. 70 + 6 + 9 col. pl. (numb. 1—70; 1—6; 1—9).* Vol. II. Histoire naturelle et générale des grimpereaux et des oiseaux de paradis. *pp. [IV] + 128 + 40. 89 + 16 col. pl. (numb. 1—88, 26 bis; 1—16).*

In the present copy of this work the text and the plates have been bound separately. The first 128 pages of Vol. I comprise 'Histoire naturelle des colibris', pp. 1—40, 'Histoire naturelle des oiseaux-mouches', pp. 41—118, and 'Supplément á l'Histoire naturelle des colibris', pp. 119—128. Then follows 'Histoire naturelle des jacamars', pp. 8, and 'Histoire naturelle des promerops' (pp. 28 including table of contents). Before his death Audebert only managed to complete the section on the colibri, after which the work was continued by Vieillot on the basis of Audebert's drawings and his notes concerning the 'oiseaux mouches'.

Vol. II contains 'Histoire naturelle des grimpereaux souïmangas', pp. 128, with 'Discours préliminaire' by Camille of Geneva; 'Histoire naturelle des oiseaux de paradis' (with 'Discours préliminaire' by Camille) and 'Supplément', pp. 1—34, and Index, pp. 35—40.

The plates belonging to each section are numbered separately. They are beautiful, and are printed by a method devised by Audebert and already used in his work on monkeys.

The material for this well-known work was procured from French and foreign collections, and the pictures of the birds were executed by Audebert and 'les plus habiles peintres de Paris et de Londres', while Louis Bouquet, 'Professeur de dessin' assisted in the colouring of the plates which Audebert himself engraved and which were printed in oil-colours by Langlois.

The colours of the birds and their handsome appearance have evidently been the cause of their selection for inclusion in the book. The plates with the bird portraits are in beautiful colours; in this respect they are among the best colour prints found in ornithology.

200 copies of the work were printed, the legends of the plates being printed in gold, as in the present copy; but there also exist twelve copies in folio in which the text is printed in gold, for to imitate the metallic lustre of the birds a large amount of gold had to be used for the plates. A single copy was printed in gold on 'Peau-velin'. Finally, 100 copies[1]), large 4to, were printed on 'Papier velin' with the letterpress of the plates in black.

The original drawings for this work de luxe came into the market too. The ordinary folio edition was issued in 32 livraisons, at 30 francs each, while the price of the gold text copies was 120 francs per livraison, the 4to edition costing 18 francs (in all 500 francs).

The price of the folio edition with the inscription in letters of gold is at present about £ 45 (Bernard Quaritch's Catalogue No. 540, 1937, p. 85).

In a letter from John Cassin to the Ibis (693) the Philadelphia Academy offered for sale the engraved copper-plates for this work and for Vieillot's 'Oiseaux de l'Amérique septentrionale' (515) 'at the price here of refuse on old copper. My aversion to their destruction I cannot overcome, however un-

----

[1]) According to Graesse (568, I, p. 251) 300 copies.

reasonable it may be; ... Of the "Oiseaux Dorés" there are many plates, as the work was printed in colours: frequently several copper-plates were used in printing one bird'.

An Italian impression of the work was issued at Milan in 1830—40 (2 vols., fol.) under the title 'Storia naturale generale dei colibri degli uccelli mosca, della galbule e dei promeropi di G. B. Audebert e L. P. Vieillot; prima traduzione Italiana con note di Guiseppe de Ceresa'.

AUDOUIN, J. V.

15.-   [1826]. Description de l'Égypte, ou recueil des observations et des recherches qui ont été faites en Égypte pendant l'expédition de l'armée française, publié par les ordres de sa majesté l'empereur Napoléon le Grand. Histoire naturelle. Vol. I. < - - Part IV. - - *pp. 251—318:* Explication sommaire des planches d'oiseaux de l'Égypte et de la Syrie, publiées par Jules-César Savigny, membre de l'Institut; offrant un exposé des caractères naturels des genres, avec la distinction des espèces, par Victor Audouin >. Imprimerie Impériale. *Paris. large 4to.*

To this text, which is found in Part 4 of the volume, belongs 'Table des matières. Oiseaux' (Part 4, pp. 332—336).

In 1825 Audouin, on the recommendation of Cuvier, was entrusted by the French government with the task of completing the zoological section of the large work 'Description de l'Égypte', as its author, Savigny, was prevented by illness from doing so. However, as early as 1809, in a section of 'Description de l'Égypte', the latter had treated the birds in the text accompanying the plates (438). Audouin, in his turn, deals systematically with the birds portrayed in the 42 figures of the fourteen plates.

The second, almost unaltered, edition of the present work appeared in 1828 in Vol. XXIII of the octavo issue, published by Panckoucke 1820—30.

A reprint of the latter edition was issued by the Willughby Society in 1883 (16).

16.   1883. The Willughby Society. Audouin's Explication sommaire des planches d'oiseaux de l'Égypte et de la Syrie. Publiées par Jules-César Savigny. Edited by Alfred Newton. *London. pp. VII + 139. 8vo.*

A reprint of the dated octavo, second, edition of this paper, the first edition of which was published in 1826 (15).

The original pagination, pp. 302—430, 450—456, is preserved, and to this is added, besides the preface, pp. III—VIII, an Index, p. 139, of the scientific names of the birds and references to both editions.

AUDUBON, J. J. L.

17.   1827—38. The birds of America; from original drawings by John James Audubon. Published by the author. *London. 4 vols. 435 col. pl. double elephant fol. —* Vol. I. 1827—30. *100 col. pl. (numb. I — C).* Vol. II. 1831—34. *135 col. pl. (numb. CI—CCXXXV).* Vol. III. 1834—35. *95 col. pl. (numb. CCXXXVI—CCCXXX).* Vol. IIII. 1835—38, June 20. *105 col. pl. (numb. CCCXXXI—CCCCXXXV).*

The plates of this gigantic work without text (for which see 'Ornithological biography' (18)), whose immense format is due to the fact that the birds are represented in their natural size, were issued in 87 numbers, each containing five plates. The total number of figures is 1065, representing 489 supposed species. The reason why the plates are not accompanied by any text is said to be that the duty of sending presentation copies to the public libraries of England was thereby avoided. The plates are outstanding examples of English aquatinta and are, as a rule, beautiful both in drawing and colour. The birds were not drawn from stuffed but from living specimens or from specimens just killed and posed carefully and naturally for painting.

In the present copy on Pl. 64 the usual 'Drawn from Nature by J. J. Audubon, F. R. S., F. L. S.' is replaced by 'Drawn from Nature by Lucy Audubon' (775) ; Pl. 1—2, 6—7 were engraved by W. H. Lizars, retouched by R. Havell, jun. ; Pl. 8 and 9 were engraved by W. H. Lizars ; Pl. 3—5, 108, 110 were engraved, printed and coloured by R. Havell, jun. ; Pl. 10—107, 109, 111—435 were engraved, printed and coloured by R. Havell ; Pl. 136 is numbered CXX.

According to Stone (875) and other sources the extant copies of the work differ greatly ; Lizars was originally to have prepared the first ten plates (Parts 1 and 2) ; but, as he worked very slowly and the colouring was unsatisfactory, the task was entrusted to Robert Havell, London, who later on had some of Lizars' plates retouched or redrawn.

The work was intended to comprise 80 numbers (i. e. a total of 400 plates) (844), but this estimate was exceeded by 35 plates, and even then it proved necessary to depict from two to six species on the last few plates. The subscribers naturally resented the crowding, and it can be understood that some of them lost patience and refused to continue their subscriptions (18, IV, pp. XXI—XXII). The only attempt at a new folio edition is 'The birds of America ; from original drawings by John James Audubon ... Reissued by J. W. Audubon' (New York, Roe Lockwood and Son, 1860, 1 vol., (all published), double elephant folio) with 106 plates, in chromolithography, by J. Bien, 180 Broadway, corresponding to 151 of the plates of the original edition.

An edition with the plates reproduced in full colour by the offset lithographic process, but in reduced form, is now (autumn 1937) being issued (500 col. pl., 4to). The accompanying descriptive letterpress has been written by the editor of 'Bird-Lore', William Vogt.

In Vol. I, 1832, of the author's 'Ornithological biography' mentioned below (18) the following prospectus is found concerning the original edition of the folio plates : —

'Under the special patronage of her most excellent majesty, Queen Adelaide. *The birds of America*, engraved from drawings made in the United States and their territories. By John James Audubon ... Published by the author ; and to be seen at Mr. R. Havell's, jun., the engraver, 77, Oxford Street, London' (1831, pp. 16, large 8vo).

The small booklet contains a prospectus, the table of contents of Vol. I, extracts from reviews, and the names of the subscribers.

The price of each number, consisting of five plates, was 2 guineas, and it was planned that five numbers should appear annually.

The price of this immense work has since risen so considerably that at the present day about £ 1000 is asked for a copy of it (£ 950, Wheldon & Wesley's Cat., N. S. 22, 1929, p. 76).

18. 1831—39. Ornithological biography, or an account of the habits of the birds of the United States of America; accompanied by descriptions of the objects represented in the work entitled *The Birds of America*, and interspersed with delineations of American scenery and manners. By John James Audubon. Adam Black (Vols. II—V: Adam and Charles Black). *Edinburgh. 5 vols. text-figs. large 8vo.* — Vol. I. 1831. *pp. XXIV + 512.* Vol. II. 1834. *pp. XXXII + 588.* Vol. III. 1835. *pp. XVI + 638.* Vol. IV. 1838. *pp. XXVIII + 618.* Vol. V. 1839. *pp. XXXIX + 664.*

Vol. V is erroneously dated MDCCCXXXXIX on the title-page ; the preface is dated 1st May, 1839.

As stated in the title, this work is the text for the folio edition of the author's atlas 'Birds of America', 1827—38 (17). William Macgillivray contributed to this text by describing the species and many of the anatomical features of some of them. In another copy of the work, in the possession of the University Library of Copenhagen, Vol. I is seen to have been issued at Philadelphia in 1832 by E. L. Carey and A. Hart, Chesnut Street, and printed by James Kay, Jun. & Co. No. 4, Minor Street. This volume further contains the above-mentioned 'Prospectus' (17, note) of 1831 relating to 'The Birds of America'.

Besides the editions mentioned above, the following American issues of separate volumes are stated to exist, (cf. Braislin (675) and Loomis (800)) :

Vol. I, Philadelphia, Judah Dobson and H. H. Porter, 1831 ;
Vol. I, Philadelphia, Judah Dobson and H. H. Porter, 1832 ;
Vol. II, Boston, Hilliard, Gray, and Company, 1835.

In 1839 Audubon issued his 'A synopsis of the birds of North America' (Edinburgh, 8vo), a methodical catalogue of all the species at that time known to inhabit North America north of Mexico, intended to serve as a systematic index to the present work, and to the 'Birds of America' (17).

1856. The birds of America, from drawings made *19.* in the United States and their territories. By John James Audubon. Published by V. G. Audubon. (R. Craighead, electrotyper and stereotyper). *New York. 7 vols. text-figs. 500 col. pl. large 8vo.* — Vol. I. *pp. VIII + 11—246. col. pl. 1—70.* Vol. II. *pp. VII + 11—199. col. pl. 71—140.* Vol. III. *pp. VIII + 9—233. col. pl. 141—210.* Vol. IV. *pp. VIII + 9—321. col. pl. 211—280.* Vol. V. *pp. VIII + 9—346. col. pl. 281—350.* Vol. VI. *pp. VIII + 9—456. col. pl. 351—420.* Vol. VII. *pp. VI + 9—372. col. pl. 421—500.*

After Audubon's death his sons Victor and John issued several editions of the 'Birds of America'. In the present edition the first of these, or the second of the 8vo editions of Audubon's 'Birds', the background of the plates is coloured, while in the original 8vo edition, issued by Audubon in 1840—44, New York and Philadelphia, it was uncoloured. The text, with a few alterations, is the same as in 'Ornithological biography', 1831—39 (18). The plates of the original 8vo edition, with the exception of 17, were the same as those in the folio edition 1827—38 of 'Birds of America', whose figures were reduced by means of a camera lucida by John W. Audubon. In the present edition some of the plates are stated to be redrawn. The plates bear the inscription: lithogr., printed and col. by J. T. Bowen, Philadelphia.

In course of time the following editions of this work were issued (753):

1859. Issued by V. G. Audubon. Roe Lockwood and Son. (R. Craighead, printer, stereotyper, and electrotyper). (New York, 7 vols., 500 col. pl., text-figs., large 8vo). —
1860. Issued by V. G. Audubon. Roe Lockwood and Son. (New York, 7 vols., 500 col. pl., text-figs., large 8vo). —
1861. Reissued by J. W. Audubon. Roe Lockwood and Son. (New York, 7 vols., text-figs., large 8vo. Text only). —
1861. Reissued by J. W. Audubon. Roe Lockwood and Son. (New York, 7 vols., 500 col. pl., text-figs., large 8vo). —
1865. (New York, 8 vols., 8vo. Text only?). —
[1871]. George R. Lockwood, late Roe Lockwood and Son. (New York, 8 vols., 500 col. pl., text-figs., large 8vo.

According to Coues (561, I, p. 666) this edition of the work should presumably be assigned to the series of re-issues of the 8vo edition of the 'Birds of America' just enumerated : —
'The birds of North America: a popular and scientific description of the birds of the United States and their territories. New edition'. (New York 1863).

AUK.

1884 → The Auk. A quarterly journal of orni- *20.* thology. Editor J. A. Allen (1884—1911), Witmer Stone (1912 →). Associate editors, Elliott Coues, Robert Ridgway, William Brewster, and Montague Chamberlain (1884—87), C. F. Batchelder (1888—93), Frank M. Chapman (1894—1911). Published for (1901 →: by) the American Ornithologists' Union. Estes & Lauriat, *Boston* (1884—85) ; L. S. Foster, *New York* (1886—1900) ; *Cambridge, Mass.* (1901—19) ; *Lancaster, Pa. (1920 →).* Vol. I → *text-figs. plates. maps. 8vo.*

One of the leading ornithological periodicals, and the principal journal of this kind in the United States. It forms a continuation of the 'Bulletin of the Nuttall Ornithological Club' (Vols. I—VIII, 1876—83), a fact mentioned on the title-page, on which the number of the volume, too, is stated, e. g. Old Series, Vol. IX →, and New Series, Vol. I →.

Four volumes of a general index have been published ; in

1908 to the Bulletin (Vols. I—VIII), 1876—83, and 'The Auk' (Vols. I—XVII), 1884—1900; in 1915 to Vols. XVIII—XXVII, 1901—10; in 1929 to Vols. XXVIII—XXXVII, 1911 —20; and in 1934 to Vols. XXXVIII—XLVII, 1921—30.

Naturally, the birds of the western hemisphere are dealt with especially in the periodical, but a great amount of matter relating to the bird-life of other regions and questions of a more general character have been published in its columns by well-known ornithologists, principally American.

A number of plates (between 700 and 800) have also been published in the periodical. Most of these are from photographs, though some (about 80) are from drawings; more than half of the latter are coloured. The coloured plates are chiefly found in the volumes of the 1890's, and are executed in chromo-lithography (lith. A. Hoen & Co., Baltimore, or Ketterlinus, Phila.); since the beginning of this century they have been executed by the three-colour process. Among the artists, especial mention should be made of R. and J. L. Ridgway, Ernest Thompson, L. A. Fuertes, and Allan Brooks.

AUSTRIA-HUNGARY. Voyages.

1865. Reise der österreichischen Fregatte Novara um die Erde ... 1857—59 ... Zoologischer Theil. Vol. I ... 2. Vögel. *See Pelzeln, A. von.*

BAEDEKER, F. W. J.

21.   *1855—63.* Die Eier der europaeischen Voegel nach der Natur gemalt von F. W. J. Baedeker. Mit einer Beschreibung des Nestbaues gemeinschaftlich bearbei-tet mit L. Brehm und W. Paessler. J. Baedeker. *Leip-zig. 4 vols. in 2. 80 col. pl. fol.* — Vol. I. Accipitres. *pp. [XVI] + [50]. 15 col. pl.* Vol. II. Oscines. *pp. [142]. 17 col. pl.* Vol. III. Grallæ. *pp. [88]. 20 col. pl.* Vol. IV. Natatores. *pp. [106]. 28 col. pl.*

This work was published in ten parts (Part I, 1855; 2—7, 1857—61; 8—10, 1862—63), each consisting of eight coloured plates with accompanying text written by L. Brehm. In this Brehm assisted by the oologist Pastor Paessler of Brambach. The text is not confined to a description of the eggs but also gives information as to the distribution of the birds and describes, as far as possible, the history of reproduction by means of an account of the nests and the relation of the parent birds to eggs and young. In addition to the eggs of European birds the work mentions several fairly rare eggs of birds from regions outside Europe.

The title-pages are undated; a lith. title is found in Vol. I, and Vol. IV (Lieferung 8—10) contains 'Zusätze und Be-richtigungen' to Lieferung 1—7. The title-page and the beauti-fully executed plates are lithographed by Arnz & Co., Düssel-dorf.

A supplement of 16 pages was issued in 1867.

BAIRD, S. F.

22.   *1858.* Reports of explorations and surveys, to as-certain the most practicable and economical route for a railroad from the Mississippi River to the Pacific Ocean ... 1853—6 ... Vol. IX. <- - Part II. General report upon the zoology of the several Pacific Railroad routes. - - Birds: by Spencer F. Baird. With the co-operation of John Cassin and George N. Lawrence >. Beverley Tucker. (Senate Ex. Doc., No. 78). *Washing-ton. pp. LVI + 1005. 4to.*

In this volume the text to Baird and his collaborators' 'Birds of North America' was first published; it deals with the mate-rial collected on the different expeditions and on the Mexican Boundary Survey. The ornithology of the latter was treated by Baird in the 'Report on the United States and Mexican Boundary Survey', Vol. II, Part 2 (Washington 1859, pp. 32, 25 col. pl., 8vo). The plates from this report with one exception, were later incorporated in an edition of Vol. IX, issued in 1860 under the title 'The birds of North America' (24; 876), which also contained — sometimes in a slightly altered form — most of the 38 plates which were published together with other re-

ports of the Explorations and Surveys, especially in Vol. X, 1859 (24).

Of Baird's collaborators, John Cassin wrote the section on the Raptatores, Grallæ and Alcidæ, while George N. Lawrence wrote the articles on the Longipennes, Totipalmes, and Colym-bidæ.

Trinomials are used in this work to designate geographical races, the word 'variety' being, however, inserted in front of the third name, as in John Cassin's 'Illustrations of the birds of California', etc., 1853—56 (92).

1859. Reports of explorations and surveys, to as-   23. certain the most practicable and economical route for a railroad from the Mississippi River to the Pacific Ocean ... 1853—6 ... Vol. X. <- - Report of Lieut E. G. Beckwith ... upon explorations for a railroad route, near the 38th and 39th parallels of north latitude, by Captain J. W. Gunnison ... and near the forty first parallel of north latitude by Lieut. E. G. Beckwith ... 1854. - - Zoological report. 1857. - - pp. 11—16: No. 2. Report on birds collected on the survey. By S. F. Baird >. Beverley Tucker. (Senate Ex. Doc., No. 78). *Washington. 7 col. pl. (numb. XII—XV, XVII, XXXII, XXXV). 4to.*

The zoological report, the ornithological section of which is dealt with here, forms a continuation of a report commenced in Vol. II, 1855, of the series.

The present article contains a brief description of 25 species with references to the pages of the General report on birds, Pacific Railroad Survey, Vol. IX, where the species are described in detail (22).

The greater number of the plates (lithographs coloured by hand) were reproduced in a slightly altered form in Baird, Cassin, and Lawrence's 'The birds of North America' (24).

1860. The birds of North America; the descriptions   24. of species based chiefly on the collections in the mu-seum of the Smithsonian Institution. By Spencer F. Baird, with the co-operation of John Cassin, and George N. Lawrence. With an atlas of ... plates. J. B. Lippincott and Co. *Philadelphia. 2 vols. 4to.* — Text. *pp. LVI + 1005.* Atlas. *pp. XI. 100 col. pl.*

The text of this work is an almost unaltered reprint of Vol. IX, 1858, of 'Reports of explorations and surveys ... for a railroad from the Mississippi River to the Pacific Ocean ... 1853—56' (22), in which Baird in co-operation with Cassin and Lawrence treated the birds of North America north of Mexico. There are only a few alterations and additions in the first section of the text, pp. I—LVI. The book gives a complete account of the birds of the above-mentioned part of North America with descriptions of all the known species, thus carry-ing on the work of Audubon and Wilson.

The plates of the atlas (lithographs coloured by hand, most of them with the signature, Bowen and Co. lith. and col. Philada.) show 148 new or hitherto unpictured species of North American birds. About half of the 100 plates were prepared for the present work, the remaining number, as stated above (22, note), being derived from the ornithological illustrations of reports from the United States and Mexican Boundary Sur-vey and the Pacific Railroad Survey written by S. F. Baird, 1859 (23), J. G. Cooper, 1860 (107), A. L. Heermann, 1859 (200), C. B. R. Kennerly, 1859 (243), and J. S. Newberry, 1857 (362). All the plates, however, are said to have been carefully retouched with this edition in view; several of them were re-drawn entirely from better and more characteristic specimens of the birds. The plates are numbered as follows: I—XXXVIII (the majority — 33 — of these with the inscription: U. S. P. R. R. Exp. & Surveys, the remainder (the five numbers XV, XXVI, XXXII, XXXIII, and XXXV) with the inscription: Birds of North America), I—XXIV (with the inscription: United States & Mexican Boundary), and LXIII—C (with the inscription: Birds of North America). The work was re-issued in 1870 (Salem) in an almost unaltered form.

1874. A history of North American birds. By S. F.   25.

Baird, T. M. Brewer, and R. Ridgway. Land birds. Illustrated by ... colored plates and 593 woodcuts. Little, Brown and Co. *Boston. 3 vols. 64 col. pl. 4to. —* Vol. I. *pp. XXVIII + 596 + VI. text-figs. 26 col. pl. (numb. I—XXVI).* Vol. II. *pp. [V] + 590 + VI. text-figs. 30 col. pl. (numb. XXVII—LVI).* Vol. III. *pp. [V] + 560 + [I] + XXVIII. text-figs. 8 col. pl. (numb. LVII—LXIV).*

This work contains a description of the birds of North America north of Mexico, including Greenland and Alaska. The main stress is laid on an account of the life history of the species, to which is added information about the geographical distribution of the birds and a brief description of the eggs and the individual species.

Baird and Ridgway supplied the descriptive parts of the work, while Dr. Brewer dealt with the habits of the birds. Theodore N. Gill contributed the part of the Introduction which explains the difference between the bird group and other vertebrates and, finally, Coues tabulated orders and families and added a glossary of technical terms in Vol. III.

The plates (woodcuts coloured by hand) contain merely figures of the heads of the birds, drawn by Henry W. Elliott and Ridgway and engraved by Hobart H. Nichols of Washington.

The work was also issued with uncoloured plates, and appeared in 1875 with coloured plates, but otherwise in unaltered form. A new edition was issued at Boston in 1905.

The corresponding work on water-birds, produced by the same three authors, was issued in 1884 as Vol. XII of 'Memoirs of the Museum of Comparative Zoology at Harvard College' under the title 'The water birds of North America'. (2 vols., col. text-figs. (woodcuts coloured by hand), 4to). An edition with uncoloured figures was issued at the same place and in the same year, large 8vo.

BALDAMUS, A. C. E.

1850—58. See Naumannia.

1860. J. A. Naumann's Naturgeschichte der Vögel Deutschlands. Fortsetzung der Nachträge, Zusätze und Verbesserungen. *See Naumann, J. A.,* 1822—60.

1860—66. See Journal fuer Ornithologie.

1892. Das Leben der europäischen Kuckucke. Nebst Beiträgen zur Lebenskunde der übrigen parasitischen Kuckucke und Stärlinge. Von A. C. Eduard Baldamus. Mit ... Farbendrucktafeln. Paul Parey. *Berlin. pp. VIII + 224 + [1]. 8 col. pl. eggs (numb. I—VIII). 8vo.*

In this work the Cuckoo and other parasitic birds are described.

The volume falls into three sections, the first of which deals chiefly with Cuculus canorus L., the second with 'Die nichteuropäischen Schmarotzerkuckucke', and the third with Indicatorinæ and Molobrinæ.

The plates (W. A. Meyn ad nat. chromolith.) show a number of eggs of various parasitic birds and their hosts.

BARKER-WEBB, P. *See Webb, P. B.*

BARROWS, W. B.

1912. Michigan bird life. A list of all the bird species known to occur in the State together with an outline of their classification and an account of the life history of each species, with special reference to its relation to agriculture. With ... full-page plates and 152 text figures. By Walter Bradford Barrows. Special Bulletin of the Department of Zoology and Physiology of the Michigan Agricultural College. Michigan Agricultural College. *pp. XIV + 822. text-figs. 70 pl. (numb. I—LXX). 8vo.*

The total number of species which, according to this work,

have been found in the state of Michigan amounts to 326 as against 336 species and subspecies in A. J. Cook's 'Birds of Michigan', two editions of which were issued in 1893, forming Bulletin 94 of the Michigan Agricultural Experiment Station. The main features of the life history of each bird are given, special attention being paid to the species of economic importance; the information is given in such a form that it can be understood by laymen. In addition, the work contains keys to the particular characteristics of the birds, their technical description, popular synonyms, and information about their general distribution, migration, and occurrence in the state of Michigan.

Some of the figures of the plates have been reproduced from photographs, others have been taken from other works, while thirteen have been executed from original drawings by P. A. Taverner, and one from a drawing by the artist W. F. Jackson, of Mayfield.

BATCHELDER, C. F.

1888—93. See Auk.

BEAGLE, Voyage of H. M. S.

1838—41. The zoology of the voyage of H. M. S. Beagle ... 1832—1836. Part III. Birds. *See Gould, J.*

BEAL, F. E. L.

1911. U. S. Department of Agriculture. Biological *28.* Survey. Bulletin No. 37. Food of the woodpeckers of the United States. By F. E. L. Beal. Government Printing Office. *Washington. pp. 64. text-figs. 6 col. pl. (numb. I—VI). 8vo.*

This paper contains the results of the examination of the stomachs of 3,500 woodpeckers, representing 22 species and about 30 subspecies, taken in all parts of the United States, and also a few species from Canada.

The number of stomachs of each form examined varies from one to 723, and the total amount of animal food in relation to plant food in the main part of the material (3,453 stomachs) comes to 64,26 per cent., consisting chiefly of ants, and then beetles, both in the form of insects, wood-boring grubs, eggs, and pupæ.

These two groups of insects together constituted very nearly 50 per cent. of the total food, which shows the importance of the woodpeckers as factors in the campaign against the insects that attack trees.

The plates (chromo-lithographs) show seven species, drawn by L. A. Fuertes (Breuker & Kessler Co. Lith. Phila.).

BECHSTEIN, J. M.

1793—1812. Johånn Lathams allgemeine Uebersicht der Vögel. Aus dem Englischen übersetzt und mit Anmerkungen und Zusätzen versehen von Johann Matthäus Bechstein. *See Latham, J.,* 1793—1811.

1802—12. Ornithologisches Taschenbuch von und *29.* für Deutschland oder kurze Beschreibung aller Vögel Deutschlands für Liebhaber dieses Theils der Naturgeschichte von Johann Matthäus Bechstein. Mit ... illuminirten Kupfern. Carl Friedrich Enoch Richter (Part III: Johann Friedrich Gleditsch). *Leipzig. pp. XXXIV + 1—550 + IV + 551—612. 46 pl. (39 col., 7 uncol. (numb. I—VII)). 12mo.*

This small work is divided into three parts, the first two of which appeared in 1802—03 (the title-page dated 1803), while Part 3 appeared in 1812. 'Erster Theil, welcher die Landvögel enthält' takes up pp. 1—250, 'Zweiter Theil, welcher die Wasservögel enthält', pp. 251—550. The last part of the volume (pp. IV + 551—612), 'Dritter Theil, mit 7 Kupfertafeln, welcher Zusätze und Verbesserungen zu dem 1sten und 2ten Theile und die Abbildungen der Gattungs-Kennzeichen der Vögel enthält', consists of additions to the preceding parts of the work and an explanation of the seven uncoloured plates (engravings) engraved by J. Nussbiegel. These plates are folded and contain

7

figures of the heads and the feet of the birds. The coloured bird portraits (engravings coloured by hand) belong to the first and second parts; they seem somewhat insignificant, partly because, due to the format of the book, they are so small. It appears from the preface that the book was planned to contain still more illustrations: 'Um der Deutlichkeit willen habe ich eine Anzahl *Abbildungen von Vögeln* beygefügt, die neu, selten, oder auf eine andere Art merkwürdig sind, und ich wünschte nichts mehr, als dass ich von allen seltenen Vögeln eine Zeichnung hätte liefern können; allein viele meiner seltensten sind mir, ehe ich sie mahlen lassen konnte, durch die Unvorsichtigkeit einer Magd verbrannt'.

A later edition is sometimes quoted (cf. Allgemeines Bücher-Lexikon, 5, 1817, column 45) dated 1811—13: 2. Auflage, Johann Friedrich Gleditsch, Leipzig, 3 parts, small 8vo, 3rd part with the title 'Gattungskennzeichen der Vögel', etc.

30. *1805—09.* Gemeinnützige Naturgeschichte Deutschlands nach allen Art Reichen ... Zweyte vermehrte und verbesserte Auflage. Vols. II—IV. - - Gemeinnützige Naturgeschichte der Vögel Deutschlands für allerley Leser, vorzüglich für Forstmänner, Jugendlehrer und Oekonomen von J. M. Bechstein. Siegfried Lebrecht Crusius (Vol. IV: Fr. Chr. Wilh. Vogel). *Leipzig. 91 pl. 8vo.* — Vol. II (I). 1805. Welcher die Einleitung in die Naturgeschichte der Vögel überhaupt, und die Beschreibung der Raub-, sprechtartigen und krähenartigen Vögel Deutschlands enthält. *pp. XXXIV + 1346. 24 pl. (front. + Nos. I—VI, VIIa, VIIb, VIII—XXXI).* Vol. III (II). 1807. Welcher die sperlingsartigen, Sing- und schwalbenartigen Vögel, die Tauben und hühnerartigen Vögel Deutschlands enthält. *pp. XXX + 1486. 34 pl. (front. + Nos. I—IV, Va, Va (bis), Vb, VI—XLV).* Vol. IV (III). 1809. In zwey Abtheilungen, welche die Sumpf- und Schwimm-Vögel Deutschlands nebst dem Register enthalten. [Part I]. *pp. XXIV + 528. 33 pl. (front. + Nos. I—XXXVII).*

The first edition of this work, Vol. I of which deals with mammals, appeared in 1789—1795. In the present second edition, the first volume of which appeared in 1801, the number of the plates has been increased and the text enlarged. Ornithology was 'von jeher in der ganzen Naturgeschichte mein Lieblingsfach' says Bechstein, which statement is indeed confirmed by his treatment of the birds in this work. In this edition he has abandoned Linnæus' system of classification, following instead, though with alterations and improvements, the method of J. Latham. He was familiar with this from his translation of one of the works of this author, 'J. Lathams allgemeine Uebersicht der Vögel', 1793—1812 (280). Bechstein admits, however, that his arrangement of the birds does not come closer to the natural system than that of Linnæus, but suggests that it may be helpful as a good index.

The plates (engravings), which were also produced in colour, were drawn and engraved by Capieux, a number of them from oil-paintings by Salzmann and others.

The second part of Vol. I of the section on birds (pp. 284—470) is concerned with J. L. Frisch's work 'Vorstellung der Vögel Deutschlandes', 1833—63 (155), the figures of birds in this work being 'erläutert und bestimmt' (pp. 284—451) and 'Nach dem Linnéischen Systeme aufgestellt' (pp. 451—470).

The second part of Vol. IV (pp. 529—1282) includes two supplements (pp. 1163—1210 and pp. 1211—1220).

An unfinished work with notes on the present treatise was issued in 1812—13 by J. P. A. Leisler under the title 'Nachträge zu Bechsteins Naturgeschichte Deutschlands'.

BECKWITH, E. G.

1859. Reports of explorations and surveys ... for a railroad from the Mississippi River to the Pacific Ocean ... 1853—56. Vol. X. Report of Lieut. E. G. Beckwith ... upon explorations ... near the 38th and 39th parallels ... and near the forty first parallel of

north latitude ... 1854. Zoological report. 1857. pp. 11—16: No. 2. Report on birds collected on the survey. *See Baird, S. F.*

BEEBE, C. W.

1918—22. A monograph of the pheasants. By William Beebe. Published under the auspices of the New York Zoological Society by Witherby & Co. (Vols. II—IV: H. F. and G. Witherby). *London. 4 vols. 177 pl. (90 col., 87 photograv.). 20 maps. large 4to.* — Vol. I. 1918. *pp. XLIX + 198. col. pl. I—XIV and XVI—XX. photograv. pl. 1 and 1A—15. maps I—V.* Vol. II. 1921. *pp. XV + 269. col. pl. XXI—XLIV. photograv. pl. 16—39. maps VI—X.* Vol. III. 1922. *pp. XVI + 204. col. pl. XLV—LXVIII. photograv. pl. 40—60. maps XI—XIV.* Vol. IV. 1922. *pp. XV + 242. col. pl. XV and LXIX—XC. photograv. pl. 61—87. maps XV—XX.*

The material for this admirable work on pheasants was collected by the author from, among other sources, his study of the collections of type specimens in the museums of London, Tring, Paris, and Berlin, and on a journey of several months' duration to South and East Asia. He thus had an opportunity of studying these birds in their natural habitats, many fine photographs of which are represented in photogravure on the plates of the work, which is very handsomely produced in every way. It contains a complete account of each species and subspecies, both as regards the appearance of the birds and their geographical distribution and habits. The introduction (Vol. I, pp. XIX—XLIX) consists of a brief general account of pheasants and a description of their daily life.

The coloured plates are executed in various ways, such as chromo-lithography and collotype (the latter executed by Albert Frisch, Berlin), from drawings or paintings by L. A. Fuertes, H. Grønvold, H. Jones, C. R. Knight, G. E. Lodge, A. Thorburn, and — a single one — E. Megargee. The original paintings from which the reproductions were executed are water-colours, except those of Knight, which are in oils. The plates are beautifully and accurately reproduced, some on smooth paper, others on 'egg-shell'. The work was issued in 600 copies, of which the present copy is No. 336. In 1926 an abbreviated edition with fewer plates was issued under the title 'Pheasants, their lives and homes' (Garden City, New York, Doubleday, Page and Co., 2 vols., 64 pl. (31 col.), 4to) in an ordinary edition and also in a limited and more expensive de luxe autographed edition (re-issued in one volume 1936).

Another of Beebe's books, too, is derived from his large work on pheasants, 'Pheasant jungles', 1927 (New York, Putnam, 58 pl., 8vo), new edition (Blue ribbon books) 1932; but it contains no pictures of pheasants.

BEECHEY, F. W.

1839. The zoology of Captain Beechey's voyage; compiled from the collections and notes made by Captain Beechey ... in H. M. S. Blossom, under the command of Captain F. W. Beechey ... 1825—28 ... pp. 13—40: Ornithology. *See Vigors, N. A.*

BEKKER, Junior.

1800—09. Teutsche Ornithologie ... *See Borkhausen, M. B.*

BEKKER, C. W.

1800—09. Teutsche Ornithologie ... *See Borkhausen, M. B.*

BELCHER, E.

1843—44. The zoology of the voyage of H. M. S. Sulphur under the command of Captain Sir Edward Belcher ... 1836—42 ... (Nos. III—IV). Birds. *See Gould, J.*

BELEM (PARÁ). MUSEU GOELDI (MUSEU
PARAENSE) DE HISTORIA NATURAL E
ETHNOGRAPHIA. *See Museu Goeldi (Museu
Paraense) de Historia et Ethnographia. Belem
(Pará).*

BELL, T.
1824—26. See Zoological Journal, The, 1824—35.

BENDIRE, C. E.
2.   *1892.* Smithsonian Contributions to Knowledge.
Vol. XXVIII. - - Life histories of North American
birds with special reference to their breeding habits
and eggs, with ... lithographic plates. By Charles
Bendire. Government Printing Office. *Washington.
pp. XI + X + 446. 12 col. pl. eggs (numb. I—XII).
large 8vo.*
This work is based largely upon the collections in the
U. S. National Museum, with which Bendire was associated as
curator of the department of oology. Spencer F. Baird desired
that the subject should be treated in a comprehensive work;
however, beyond Baird, Brewer, and Ridgway's 'History of
North American birds' (25), Brewer's volume of 1857 on hawks
and owls, etc. (67) was actually the only large work as yet
published to give a detailed account of the oology of North
America. It was not continued for want of material.
The present initial volume deals with gallinaceous birds,
pigeons, and birds of prey, altogether 146 species and subspecies.
As regards classification, synonymy, and nomenclature, the Code
and Check List of the American Ornithologists' Union is followed. Under each species or subspecies are described not only
eggs and nests, but also geographical distribution, life history,
migratory and breeding ranges, nesting habits, and food.
The excellent plates (chromo-lithography: Ketterlinus Printing Company, Philadelphia) have been reproduced from original
water-colour drawings by John L. Ridgway, and contain in all
185 figures of eggs.
This memoir was issued at the same time as a Special Bulletin of the U. S. National Museum (33), and continued in 1895,
when a second part was issued (34; 35).

1892. Smithsonian Institution. United States Na-
tional Museum. Special Bulletin No. 1. Life histories
of North American birds with special reference to their
breeding habits and eggs, with ... lithographic plates.
By Charles Bendire. Government Printing Office.
*Washington. pp. VIII + 446. 12 col. pl. eggs (numb.
I—XII). large 8vo.*
Another edition of this work, issued at the same time as
Vol. XXVIII of the Smithsonian Contributions to Knowledge
(32).

1895. Smithsonian Contributions to Knowledge.
Vol. XXXII. - - Life histories of North American
birds, from the parrots to the grackles, with special
reference to their breeding habits and eggs. By
Charles Bendire. With ... lithographic plates. Smithsonian Institution. *City of Washington. pp. XI + IX
+ 518 + [14]. 7 col. pl. eggs (numb. I—VII). large
8vo.*
The present volume is the second part of this work, and is
based in all essentials on material from the same source as the
first part issued in 1892 (32; 33), the subject, too, being treated
similarly.
Altogether 197 species and subspecies are dealt with, while
196 figures of eggs are found on the handsome plates executed
with the same technique and by the same artist and printers as
the plates of the preceding volume.
Like the latter, the present work was also issued as a Special
Bulletin (No. 3) of the U. S. National Museum (35).
The continuation of the work was interrupted by the death
of Bendire, but the publication was resumed later on by A. C.
Bent (36; 37).

1895. Smithsonian Institution. United States National Museum. Special Bulletin (No. 3). Life histories
of North American birds, from the parrots to the
grackles, with special reference to their breeding habits
and eggs. By Charles Bendire. With ... lithographic
plates. Government Printing Office. *Washington. pp.
IX + 518 + [14]. 7 col. pl. eggs (numb. I—VII).
large 8vo.*
A separate edition of this work, also published in the Smithsonian Contributions to Knowledge, Vol. XXXII (34).

BENT, A. C.
1919. Smithsonian Institution. United States Na-   36.
tional Museum. Bulletin 107. Life histories of North
American diving birds. Order Pygopodes. By Arthur
Cleveland Bent. Government Printing Office. *Washington. pp. XIII + 245. 55 pl. (numb. 1—55; 12
col. pl. eggs (numb. 44—55)). 8vo.*
A continuation, more broadly planned, of the work commenced in 1892 by Charles Bendire under the title 'Life histories
of North American birds' (32).
The present volume deals with the families Colymbidæ, Ga-
viidæ, and Alcidæ, the life history of each species being described in the following sequence: Spring migration, courtship,
nesting habits, eggs, young, sequence of plumages to maturity,
seasonal moults, feeding habits, flight, swimming and diving
habits, vocal powers, behaviour, enemies, fall migration, winter
habits, and distribution.
The greater number of the plates are reproductions from
photographs of nests and breeding places, while a number of
eggs are figured on the coloured plates (three-colour prints).
A continuation of this work, prepared on the same plan,
was published in a series of numbers of the U. S. Nat. Mus.
Bull., the immediately succeeding part in No. 113, 1921 (37).

1921. Smithsonian Institution. United States Na-   37.
tional Museum. Bulletin 113. Life histories of North
American gulls and terns. Order Longipennes. By Arthur Cleveland Bent. Government Printing Office.
*Washington. pp. X + 345. 93 pl. (numb. 1—93; 16
col. pl. eggs (numb. 78—93)). 8vo.*
A continuation of the work, the preceding part of which
was published in 1919 (36). It is arranged on the same plan,
the majority of the plates containing reproductions of photographs of breeding places and eggs, while a number of eggs
are figured on the coloured plates (colour prints, A. Hoen &
Co., Baltimore).
The continuation of the work followed in a series of numbers of the bulletins, illustrated by photographs, as follows:
121, 1922, 'Life histories of North American petrels and
pelicans and their allies. Order Tubinares and order Steganopodes', 69 pl.;
126, 1923, 'Life histories of North American wild fowl.
Order Anseres (Part)', 46 pl.;
130, 1925, 'Life histories of North American wild fowl.
Order Anseres (Part)', 60 pl.;
135, 1926, 'Life histories of North American marsh birds.
Orders Odontoglossæ, Herodiones and Paludicolæ', 98 pl.;
142, 1927, 'Life histories of North American shore birds.
Order Limicolæ (Part 1)', 55 pl.;
146, 1929, 'Life histories of North American shore birds.
Order Limicolæ (Part 2)', 66 pl.;
162, 1932, 'Life histories of North American gallinaceous
birds. Orders Galliformes and Columbiformes', 93 pl.;
167, 1937, 'Life histories of North American birds of prey.
Order Falconiformes (Part 1)'.

BERAJA.
1905. Beraja, Zoographia infinita. *See Kleinschmidt, O.*

BERGENS JÆGER- OG FISKERIFORENING.
Rypeundersøkelsen 1921—27.
1928. Draktskiftet hos lirypen (Lagopus lagopus
Lin.) i Norge. *See Johnsen, S.*

7*

BERGENS MUSEUMS ÅRBOK.
1929. Naturvidenskapelig rekke. Nr. 1. Draktskiftet hos lirypen (Lagopus lagopus Lin.) i Norge. *See Johnsen, S.,* 1928.

BERLEPSCH, H. H. von.
38.   *1900.* Der gesamte Vogelschutz, seine Begründung und Ausführung. Von Hans von Berlepsch. Mit ... Chromotafeln und siebzehn Textabbildungen. Zugleich in englischer, französischer, italienischer, russischer und schwedischer Sprache. Vierte Auflage. Elftes bis fünfzehntes Tausend. Fr. Eugen Köhler. *Gera-Untermhaus. pp. II + 89 + [I]. 8 col. pl. (numb. 1—8). 8vo.*
      A popular account of the ways and means of protecting birds, issued in many editions and in several languages. The coloured plates (chromo-lithographs) are executed by H. Pforr, E. de Maes, and J. C. Keulemans, chiefly from the originals for Hennicke's edition of Naumann's 'Vögel Mitteleuropas' (356), issued by the same publishers.

BERNARD, P.
39.   *1842.* Le Jardin des Plantes. Description complète, historique et pittoresque du Muséum d'Histoire Naturelle, de la Ménagerie, des serres, des galeries de minéralogie et d'anatomie, et de la vallée suisse. Moeurs et instincts des animaux, botanique, anatomie comparée, minéralogie, géologie, zoologie. Par P. Bernard, L. Couailhac, Gervais et Emm. Lemaout, et une société de savants attachés au Muséum d'Histoire Naturelle. L. Curmer. *Paris. pp. [VI] + XXIV + 416. 16 pl. birds (9 col.). 4to.*
      A description of this famous Paris garden, opening with a historical survey (pp. I—XXIV), after which follows an account, divided into six sections, of the garden and its different sections (pp. 1—396), while in conclusion a 'Classification générale des trois règnes de la nature' is given (pp. 397—414). The zoological gallery is treated in the sixth chapter (pp. 361—394).
      Two of the uncoloured plates with figures of birds (in the open) are steel-engravings (one, signed L. Marvy del. et sculp., the other Ch. Jacque). The rest of the uncoloured plates are woodcuts (signed Levy del. et sc., H. Delacroix, or H. Delacroix et Daubigny del., Delduc, sc.). The coloured plates are executed in lithography coloured by hand, and are found also in a slightly different form in Le Maout's 'Histoire naturelle des oiseaux', 1853 (285). A second volume by Le Maout alone was published in 1843.

BERTHELOT, S.
      1841. Histoire naturelle des Iles Canaries ... Vol. II. Part II ... Ornithologie canarienne. *See Webb, P. B.*

BESEKE, J. M. G.
40.   *1792.* Beytrag zur Naturgeschichte der Vögel Kurlands mit gemalten Kupfern. Nebst einem Anhange über die Augenkapseln der Vögel. Von Johann Melchior Gottlieb Beseke. Auf Kosten des Verfassers und in Kommission. *Mitau. pp. 12 + 92. 8 pl. (6 col. (numb. 1—7 (3—4 on one leaf)); 2 uncol. (numb. 8—9)). 8vo.*
      An enumeration and description of all the birds which have been found in Courland, made chiefly on the basis of the author's own collection of stuffed birds. Linnæus and Gmelin's system is followed in the text. The coloured plates of especially remarkable new birds are engraved by C. Müller and W. Waitz. They are not particularly good, and give the impression of having been made from stuffed specimens.

The book was subsequently issued with a new title-page: Neue Auflage, Schöne, Berlin 1821, pp. 92, 8 pl. (6 col.), 8vo.

BEXON, G. L. C. A.
      1780—86. Histoire naturelle des oiseaux. *See Buffon, G. L. L. de,* 1770—86.

BIANCHI, V. L.
      1905. Wissenschaftliche Resultate der von N. M. Przewalski nach Central-Asien unternommenen Reisen ... Zoologischer Theil. Vol. II. Vögel. Part 4. *See Pleske, T. D.,* 1889—1905.

BIBLIOTHÈQUE DE POCHE DU NATURALISTE.
      VII, IX. 1898. Atlas de poche des oiseaux de France, Belgique et Suisse utiles ou nuisables. *See Hamonville, J. C. L. T. d'.*

BICHENO, J. E.
      1826—35. Illustrations of ornithology ... Vols. I—III. *See Jardine, W.,* 1826—43.

BIJDRAGEN TOT DE DIERKUNDE.
      1848—1929. Bijdragen tot de dierkunde. Uitgegeven door het Koninklijk Zoölogisch Genootschap Natura Artis Magistra. M. Westermann & Zoon (later: Tj. van Holkema). *Amsterdam.* (From 17e Aflevering: E. J. Brill. *Leiden*). *Aflevering 1—26. col. plates birds. 4to.*   41
      This important zoological periodical appeared at varying intervals, in instalments with somewhat irregular pagination.
      Several valuable contributions to ornithology have been published in its columns; for instance, Max Fürbringer's 'Untersuchungen zur Morphologie und Systematik der Vögel' (Aflevering 15, 1—2, 1888). Mention may also be made of J. H. Kruimel's 'Onderzoekingen over de veeren bij hoenderachtige vogels' (Aflevering 20, Stuk 2, 1916); it should also be mentioned that in the first eight instalments several ornithological papers were published, accompanied by a number of coloured plates (lithographs coloured by hand) with figures of birds. These were written by such well-known ornithologists as H. Schlegel and C. J. Temminck.

BILLBERG, G. J.
      1806—25. Svensk zoologi. *See Palmstruch, J. W.*

BLACKBURN, Mrs. H.
      1895. Birds from Moidart and elsewhere. Drawn   4 from nature by JB. Mrs. Hugh Blackburn. David Douglas. *Edinburgh. pp. VIII + 191. 88 pl. (front. + Nos. (in text) I—LXXXVII; 2 col. (Nos. XIV, LVII)). 8vo.*
      A series of descriptions, pictorial and literary, of bird-life in the southwestern corner of Inverness-shire, Scotland.
      According to the statements of the authoress, the figures have been drawn from nature, most of them from life, or in certain cases from newly killed specimens placed in their natural positions and surroundings.
      Some of the plates (lithographs) had previously been published in 'Birds drawn from nature' by the same authoress, a work in folio which appeared for the first time in 1862 with 22 plates, an enlarged edition of the same format with 45 plates appearing in 1868.

BLACKWELDER, E.
      1907. Research in China. ... Vol. I. Part II ...
      <-- *pp. 479—507:* Section V. Zoology. By Eliot

Blackwelder >. Carnegie Institution of Washington. *Washington. 6 col. pl. birds (numb. LVIII—LXIII). 4to.*
The zoological section of the report on an expedition to China sent out by the Carnegie Institution of Washington in 1903—04 under the direction of Bailey Willis. The report was published in 1906—13 in three vols., 4to, and an atlas, large folio, as Publication No. 54 of the Carnegie Institution. It deals chiefly with geologico-geographical and palæontological questions, the investigation of which was the main object of the expedition.
The greater part of the present zoological section (pp. 483—506) is devoted to the birds, of which 64 specimens, representing 49 species, were collected. Charles W. Richmond has studied and identified the specimens, which are now deposited in the U. S. National Museum. The collection has been supplemented with descriptions of 81 additional species, examples of which were examined or observed on the expedition. In the annotated list of birds thus produced one new subspecies is mentioned.
The plates (colour prints, A. Hoen & Co., Baltimore) have been executed from drawings by J. L. Ridgway.

BLAINVILLE, H. M. D. de.
1840—41. Dictionnaire des sciences naturelles ... Supplément. *See Dictionaries, 1816—41.*
1841. Voyage autour du monde exécuté ... 1836—37 sur la corvette la Bonite ... Zoologie. Oiseaux. *See Eydoux, J. F. T.*

BLANCHARD, C. É.
1857—58. Iconographie des perroquets non figurés dans les publications de Levaillant et de M. Bourjot Saint-Hilaire ... *See Souancé, C. de.*

BLANFORD, W. T.
4. *1870.* Observations on the geology and zoology of Abyssinia, made during the progress of the British expedition to that country in 1867—68. By W. T. Blanford. *< - - pp. 285—443:* Class aves >. Macmillan and Co. *London. 6 col. pl. (numb. II—VII). 8vo.*
The ornithological section of a work which, as may be briefly described as follows: pp. XII + II + 487, text-figs., 13 pl., 1 map.
Pp. 207—477 of the volume are devoted to zoology. The ornithological part, which refers to 293 species, consists of a list with short synonymy and with brief data. Six of the species were new to science and these, together with a seventh species, are figured on the accompanying plates (lithographs coloured by hand), which were drawn and lithographed by J. G. Keulemans, and printed and coloured by P. W. M. Trap, Leyden.
5. *1876.* Eastern Persia. An account of the journeys of the Persian Boundary Commission 1870—71—72. Vol. II. The zoology and geology by W. T. Blanford. *< - - pp. 98—304:* Aves >. Published by the authority of the government of India. Macmillan and Co. *London. text-figs. 10 col. pl. (numb. IX—XVIII). 8vo.*
This work, of which the ornithological section is mentioned here, consists of two volumes.
The zoological section of Vol. II (pp. 1—431, 28 pl. (18 col.)) gives an outline of the vertebrate fauna of Persia. The material for this account is mainly derived from two collections, mostly made by Major O. B. C. St. John and by Blanford himself. The collection of birds in its entirety consisted of 1236 specimens representing 248 species. In addition to these species the ornithological section of the work mentions all the other species collected or observed by previous travellers in Persia, thus providing a complete survey of the whole Persian avifauna, which therefore so far as is known consists of 384 species.
The plates (J. G. Keulemans del., Mintern Bros. lith.) are executed in lithography coloured by hand.

BLASIUS, J. H.
1860. J. A. Naumann's Naturgeschichte der Vögel Deutschlands. Fortsetzung der Nachträge, Zusätze und Verbesserungen. *See Naumann, J. A.,* 1822—60.

BLOSSOM, Voyage of H. M. S.
1839. The zoology of Captain Beechey's voyage ... in H. M. S. Blossom ... 1825—28 ... pp. 13—40: Ornithology. *See Vigors, N. A.*

BLUMENBACH, J. F.
[1796—] 1810. Abbildungen naturhistorischer Ge- **46.** genstände herausgegeben von Joh. Fried. Blumenbach. Nro 1—100. Heinrich Dieterich. *Göttingen. 19 pl. birds (numb. 8, 16, 24, 25, 34, 35, 45, 46, 55, 56, 64, 65, 75—77, 85, 86, 96, 97 in text; 9 col. (Nos. 8, 16, 35, 45, 56, 65, 76, 85, 96)). 8vo.*
The copperplates, of which the ornithological ones are noted here, were issued in ten parts of ten plates each and contain figures of rare and curious natural objects, chiefly animals, which are figured from nature, from drawings found in Blumenbach's collection executed by various artists, or from rare publications. The figures, of which only some few are coloured (engravings coloured by hand), represent objects which have never or but rarely been depicted, for instance the Dodo; whereas animals whose pictures are found in generally known works, such as Buffon's, are not included. To each plate belongs an unpaginated leaf with a descriptive text, the book also containing a 'Systematisches Verzeichniss der Abbildungen' (pp. 6).

BLYTH, E.
1853. Contributions to ornithology ... *See Jardine, W.,* 1848—53.

BONAPARTE, C. L. J. L., Prince of Canino.
1825—33. American ornithology; or, The natural **47.** history of birds inhabiting the United States, not given by Wilson. With figures drawn, engraved, and coloured, from nature. By Charles Lucian Bonaparte. Samuel Augustus Mitchell (Vols. II—III: Carey, Lee and Carey; Vol. IV: Carey and Lee). *Philadelphia. 4 vols. 27 col. pl. fol. —* Vol. I. 1825. *pp. VI + [I] + 105. 9 col. pl. (numb. 1—9).* Vol. II. 1828. *pp. VII + [I] + 95. 6 col. pl. (numb. 10—15).* Vol. III. 1828. *pp. [III] + 60. 6 col. pl. (numb. 16—21).* Vol. IV. 1833. *pp. [III] + 142. 6 col. pl. (numb. 22—27).*
This work (845) is a supplement to Wilson's 'American ornithology,' 1808—14 (533), and, according to the author's statement, was not commenced until he had made sure that no one but himself was willing to complete Wilson's work. The bird portraits have been 'drawn from the recent bird, not from the preserved specimen' by Titian R. Peale (pl. 1—9, 23—24), A. Rider (pl. 11—22, 25—27), and John J. Audubon & A. Rider (pl. 10). The drawings have been engraved by Alexander Lawson, who also engraved the plates for Wilson's ornithology, 'with the birds always before him', and the colouring of the plates has been executed from nature by A. Rider.
The work was originally planned by the author to comprise altogether three volumes, and formed part of several of the editions of Wilson's ornithology (533).
1832. American ornithology ... *See Wilson, A.*
1832—41. Iconografia della fauna italica per le **48.** quattro classi degli animali vertebrati di Carlo L. Bonaparte. Vol. I. Mammiferi e uccelli. *< - - pp. [147 —280]:* Uccelli >. Dalla Tipografia Salviucci. *Roma. 24 col. pl. fol.*
This work, the ornithological section of which is cited here, consists altogether of three volumes with a total of 180 coloured

plates. It was published in thirty parts whose dates of publication are stated in a 'Specchio generale dell'opera' in Vol. I. This volume, like the rest, contains an analytic index giving the species treated as well as a reference to the part in which the section on the individual species is published.

The year of publication for Fasc. I—XXX may also be found in a paper by Tom. Salvadori (854).

The plates (lithographs coloured by hand) have been lithographed by Battistelli, most of them from drawings by Carolus Ruspi and Petrus Quattrocchi.

49.   1850. Monographie des Loxiens. Par Ch. L. Bonaparte et H. Schlegel. Ouvrage accompagné de ... planches coloriées, lithographiées d'après les dessins de M. Bädeker et autres naruralistes [sic]. Arnz & Comp. Leiden. pp. [V] + XVII + 55. 54 col. pl. (numb. 1—54). 4to.

In addition to the genus Loxia (Lin.), the following genera are mentioned in the present monograph: Corythus (Cuv.), Carpodacus (Kaup.), Pyrrha (Cabanis), Erythrospiza (Bonap.), Uragus (Blas. et Keyserl.), Montifringilla (Brehm), Linota (Bonap.), Acanthis (Blas. et Keyserl.) and some few others.

Schlegel's plates (lithographs coloured by hand, executed by Arnz & Co.) are beautiful, and the reproductions of the birds and their colours are good.

1857—58. Iconographie des perroquets non figurés dans les publications de Levaillant et de M. Bourjot Saint-Hilaire ... See Souancé, C. de.

BONHOTE, J. J. L.

50.   1907. Birds of Britain. By J. Lewis Bonhote. With ... illustrations in colour selected by H. E. Dresser from his 'Birds of Europe'. Adam and Charles Black. London. pp. X + [I] + 405 + [4]. text-fig. 100 col. pl. (numb. 1—100 in 'List of illustrations'). 8vo.

A popular handbook on British birds, with notes on their haunts and habits made from direct observations in the open. The book mentions all species known to occur in Great Britain, and describes them in such a way that it should be easy to identify them. The plates (three-colour prints) have been selected with a view to supplying figures of the most typical species. They are reproduced from Keulemans' illustrations in the work by Dresser, cited in the title (120), and contribute to increase the attractiveness and usefulness of the book, even though the colours are not quite natural in all cases.

This popular work has been reprinted several times, e. g. in 1912, 1914, 1917, and 1919. In 1923 it was issued under the title 'Birds of Britain and their eggs' (pp. VII + 405, 33 col. pl.), with three plates of eggs not found in the original issue.

1910—13. The British bird book ... See Kirkman, F. B. B.

BONITE, LA, Voyage of the [French corvette].

1841. Voyage autour du monde exécuté ... 1836—37 sur la corvette la Bonite ... Zoologie ... Oiseaux. See Eydoux, J. F. T.

BONNATERRE, J. P.

1790—92. Encyclopédie méthodique ... Tableau encyclopédique et méthodique des trois règnes de la nature. Ornithologie. Par Bonnaterre, et continuée par L. P. Vieillot. Vol. I. See Encyclopædias, 1782—1823.

BONPLAND, A. J. A.

1812—33. Voyage de Humboldt et Bonpland. Deuxième partie ... Recueil d'observations de zoologie et d'anatomie comparée ... 1799—1803. Vols. I—II. See Humboldt, F. H. A. von.

BOOTH, E. T.

51.   1881—87. Rough notes on the birds observed during twenty-five years' shooting and collecting in the British Islands. By E. T. Booth. With plates from drawings by E. Neale, taken from specimens in the author's possession. R. H. Porter. London. 3 vols. 114 col. pl. large fol. — Vol. I. pp. VII + [III] + [234]. text-figs. 35 col. pl. Vol. II. pp. V + [I] + [264]. 31 col. pl. 1 map. Vol. III. pp. V + [I] + [224]. text-figs. 48 col. pl. 1 map.

A series of accounts of the habits of birds published in fifteen parts in the series of years stated. A summary of the dates and contents of the parts has been given by Zimmer (589, I, p. 80), according to whom the parts appeared as follows: 1, 1881; 2, 1882; 3—5, 1883; 6—8, 1884; 9, 1885; 10—13, 1886; 14—15, 1887. The text concerning each of the forms treated has a separate pagination.

The beautiful plates (lithographs coloured by hand) show the birds in different plumages.

BORKHAUSEN, M. B.

52.   1800—09. Teutsche Ornithologie oder Naturgeschichte aller Vögel Teutschlands in naturgetreuen Abbildungen und Beschreibungen. Herausgegeben von Borkhausen, Lichthammer und Bekker dem jüngern (und, Parts II—XVIII: C. W. Bekker & Lembcke). Im Verlage der Herausgeber. Darmstadt. 18 parts. 108 col. pl. large fol.

The first eighteen parts of a work by which it was attempted to create a German parallel to the sumptuous ornithological works of other countries, notably of France, e. g. Levaillant's works, to which it was compared at that time (Allgemeine Literatur-Zeitung, 1803, No. 327), and with which it is quite comparable on account of its beautiful plates. These were drawn, engraved, printed, and coloured, by J. C. Susemihl in co-operation with his brother J. Th. Susemihl, and later on his son, Eduard Susemihl. The originals, which are executed in gouache, are to be found in the gallery of Darmstadt (577, p. 16).

The ornithological collaborators are the circle of naturalists mentioned above as editors of the work. This was issued in parts appearing at irregular intervals, which, largely because of the Napoleonic wars, became longer and longer, though the editors had promised four parts annually. Each part consists of six unnumbered plates with accompanying unpaginated text, in which each species is treated on a separate leaf. A brief Latin text is found after the German one, Part 14 containing in addition a French text. The editors remark that they are willing to supply the French text to the thirteen parts already issued if a sufficient number of subscribers apply, which has evidently not been the case.

In addition to the eighteen parts of the present fragmentary copy, whose title is derived from the covers of the parts — a title-page is lacking in many copies — mention is very frequently made, up to 1811, of a further three parts, by which the number of the plates is increased to 126. A 22nd part, published in 1817, was intended to complete the work, which thus consists of altogether 132 plates.

A later edition is quoted 'Deutsche Ornithologie, etc., herausgegeben von Bekker, Lichthammer, C. W. Bekker und Lembcke. Neue Ausgabe' (Darmstadt 1837—41, 22 parts, fol.) with 43 leaves of text and 132 figures, engraved by C. Susemihl and coloured under his supervision.

BOSNISCH-HERCEGOVINISCHES LANDES-MUSEUM IN SARAJEVO. See Sarajevo. Bosnisch-Hercegovinisches Landesmuseum.

BOUCHARD, M.

53.   [1771—] 1775. Recueïl de cent-trente-trois oiseaux, des plus belles espèces, gravés sur ... planches et colorés [sic] d'après nature par d'habiles maîtres. Bouchard et Gravier. Rome. 87 col. pl. (numb. 1—87). large fol.

No text accompanies these plates, which were engraved by Maddalena Bouchard; the names of the birds only are given, in three languages, French, Latin, and Italian. The plates are not of any great excellence, either as regards drawing or colour.

BOURJOT SAINT-HILAIRE, A.

4. *1837—38.* Histoire naturelle des perroquets, troisième volume (supplémentaire), pour faire suite aux deux volumes de Levaillant, contenant les espèces laissées inédites par cet auteur ou récemment découvertes. Ouvrage destiné à compléter une monographie figurée de la famille des Psittacidés, le texte renfermant la classification, la synonymie et la description de chaque espèce; suivi d'un index général des espèces décrites dans tout l'ouvrage; Par Al. Bourjot Saint-Hilaire. Les figures lithographiées et coloriées avec soin par M. Werner. F. G. Levrault. *Paris. pp. LVI + [I] + [259]. text-figs. 111 col. pl. (numb. 1—100, 3bis, 11bis, 35bis, 44bis, 53bis, 55bis, 71bis, 72bis, 75bis, 75ter in 'Table du troisième volume'; 1 pl. [42bis] not listed). large 4to.*

A continuation of the work 'Histoire naturelle des perroquets' (303) issued by Levaillant in 1801—05. The present work is evidently also cited under the title 'Collection de perroquets', etc., a work which appeared in 29 parts, in 1835—39 (589, I, p. 84).

The section of the text paginated with Roman numerals contains, besides the 'Préface', an 'Introduction' (pp. XI—XXXIV) with a general description of the group, and an 'Index generalis Psittacorum' (pp. XXXV—XLVIII) with the names of all the species figured in the three volumes of the work, 'Table du troisème volume' (pp. XLIX—LIV), and 'Liste des auteurs principaux' (pp. LX—LVI). Then follows, on an unpaginated folded leaf, a 'Synopsis Psittacorum'.

The text in which the birds figured are treated is unpaginated; it describes each species, in French and Latin, gives synonyms and information about geographical distribution. The plates are coloured by hand (Lith. de Benard, or Benard & Frey).

In the present copy the text and the plates are bound separately. A large folio edition of the work was also issued (55 a), while a supplement by C. de Souancé was published in 1857—58 under the title 'Iconographie des perroquets' (479).

In 'Table du troisième volume' (pp. XLIX—LIV) a total of 115 plates is mentioned, whereas the volume, as stated above, contains 111 plates only. In the list of the plates the number 42 bis is lacking; the facts concerning the promised and published plates appear from the following letter, which is glued to the volume of plates, from the publisher F. G. Levrault, dated Paris, June 27th, 1838:

'La table des planches du 3. volume de l'histoire naturelle des Perroquets indique un nombre total de   116
Mais il n'en a été fait que   111

différence   5 qui n'ont jamais existé, parcequ'elles auraient fait double emploi.
Les 111 planches dont l'ouvrage doit être composé et qu'il a réellement coûté sont les Nos 1 à 100   100
celles bis 3, 11, 35, 42, 44, 53, 55, 71, 72 & 75, en tout 10
enfin le 75 ter   1

total des planches composant ce 3. vol.   111
Il est dont inutile de chercher les Nos 8, 12, 57 bis
35 et 72-ter
faisant la différence desdits 5 non figurés.'

1. *1837—38.* Histoire naturelle des perroquets, troisième volume (supplémentaire), pour faire suite aux deux volumes de Levaillant, contenant les espèces laissées inédites par cet auteur ou récemment découvertes. Ouvrage destiné à compléter une monographie figurée de la famille des Psittacidés, le text renfermant

la classification, la synonymie et la description de chaque espèce; suivi d'un index général des espèces décrites dans tout l'ouvrage; Par Al. Bourjot Saint-Hilaire. Les figures lithographiées et coloriées avec soin par M. Werner. F. G. Levrault. *Paris. pp. XL + [I] + [220]. text-figs. 111 col. pl. large fol.*

A copy of this work in a large folio format. The 'Synopsis Psittacorum' is printed on the back of the subtitle 'Index generalis Psittacorum'; but otherwise the text of the work does not seem to differ from the text of the 4to edition (54). The plates are possibly executed with somewhat greater care than the plates of the 4to edition.

BOUSSOLE, LA, Voyage of the [French frigate].

1797. Voyage de La Pérouse autour du monde ... rédigé par M. L. A. Milet-Mureau. *See Lapérouse, J. F. de G. de.*

BØVING-PETERSEN, J. O.

1900—03 [—04]. J. O. Bøving-Petersen og W. Dreyer: Vor Klodes Dyr. Det Nordiske Forlag. *København. 3 vols. text-figs. 27 col. pl. birds. 4to.*

A popular account of the animal life of the world arranged according to zoogeographical regions. The illustrations include 84 coloured plates (three-colour prints). The original drawings for the plates with figures of birds were executed by W. Kuhnert.

55b.

BRABOURNE, W. W. K.-H., Third Baron.

1912 [1913]—17. The birds of South America. By Lord Brabourne and Charles Chubb. *London. 2 vols. large 8vo, and (Plates) large 4to.* — Vol. I. 1912 [1913]. A list of the birds of South America. R. H. Porter. *pp. XIX + 504. 1 map.* Vol. II. (Plates). [1915—] 1917. Illustrations of the game birds and water fowl of South America. By H. Grönvold. John Wheldon. *pp. 11. 38 col. pl. (numb. 1—38).*

56.

The text of the volumes mentioned here is the only part of the text of this work which ever appeared. It was planned by the authors to comprise 16 volumes with 400 hand-coloured plates, but publication ceased on the death of Brabourne. According to a statement on the covers of the plates, the volume was issued in 1913, but the cover, which has been kept, and the introduction are dated December 1912.

However, there existed a fine series of plates by Grönvold, already finished and partly printed, intended to illustrate the second and third volumes of the 'Birds of South America'. These plates were therefore issued under the half-title· 'The birds of South America, Vol. II (Plates)' by H. Kirke Swann, who added short notes on some of the species.

The beautiful plates (lithographs coloured by hand, Bale & Danielsson imp.), which are among the best ever produced by Grönvold, were issued in several parts, the first of which, comprising 19 plates, was issued in 1915, as will appear from the original cover in which these plates are found in the present copy. The remaining plates also exist with an original cover, which is dated in ink 'May 1916' and — also in ink — is stated to contain four plates.

BRANDT, J. F.

1836. Descriptiones et icones animalium Rossicorum novorum vel minus rite cognitorum. Auctore Joanne Friderico Brandt. Aves. Fasc. I. Jussu et sumptibus Academiæ Scientiarum. Graeff. *Petropoli. pp. 64. 6 col. pl. (numb. I—VI). 4to.*

57.

This volume, whose title has been taken from the cover, is evidently all that was issued of an intended work on the birds of Russia. The plates were lithographed by J. Beggrow from drawings by Zagorsky and W. Pape, and were coloured by hand. In the literature of the subject references may be found to other plates which were evidently never published (328, VII, p. 446).

The present volume, the text of which is printed in Latin, deals with members of the orders Anseres and Steganopodes, the notes on each species being grouped under the headings: Character essentialis, Synonymia, Descriptio, Mensuræ, and Tabulæ explicatio.

58. *1839.* Spicilegia ornithologica exotica. Auctore Joanne Friderico Brandt. Fasc. I ex Actorum (Mémoires VI. Série sciences nat. Tom. V. P. II.) separatim impressus. Graeff. *Petropoli. pp. [III] + 37. 5 pl. (numb. I—V; 4 col. (numb. I—IV)). 4to.*

This reprint is derived from 'Mémoires de l'Académie Impériale des Sciences de Saint-Pétersbourg', Sér. VI, Vol. V, Part 2 (Sciences naturelles, Vol. III), 1840, where it appeared (pp. 239—275) under the title preserved in the copy as a heading, 'Tentamen monographiæ zoologicæ generis Phaëton'. The paper (lu le mars 1838) is paginated 1—37 in the separate copy, but the original pagination is added in parentheses to the new.

The text is printed in Latin, and deals with the genus Phaëton under the following headings: Character naturalis, Anatome, De vita et patria Phaëthontum and Phaëthonthum [*sic*] usus, while the matter concerning the three species treated is arranged under the headings: Character essentialis, Synonymia, Descriptio, Mensuræ, and Patria et Vita. In addition five formæ dubiæ are treated.

The plates (W. Pape ad nat. del.) are executed in lithography, I—IV are coloured by hand.

BREE, C. R.

59. *1859—63 [—67].* A history of the birds of Europe, not observed in the British Isles. By Charles Robert (Vol. IV: C. R.) Bree. Groombridge and Sons. *London. 4 vols. 238 col. pl. 4to.* — Vol. I. 1859. *pp. IV + 206. 60 col. pl. (15 pl. eggs).* Vol. II. 1860. *pp. IV + 203 + 117* + *203. 60 col. pl. (16 pl. eggs).* Vol. III. 1862. *pp. IV + 247. 60 col. pl. (15 pl. eggs).* Vol. IV. 1863. *pp. XV + 250 + [1]. text-figs. 58 col. pl. (12 pl. eggs).*

This work was published in parts, and seems to have been completed in 1867. It appears with differently dated title-pages, such as (552, I, p. 228) Vol. I, 1863; Vols. II—IV, 1867; Vol. I, 1866; or (589, I, pp. 87—88) Vol. II, 1863; Vol. III, 1864. The title-pages dated 1867 seem to have been issued at the completion of the work, which was rounded off by the 'Appendix' (Vol. IV, pp. 185—222), 'List of European birds', Bibliography, Index, and Errata (Vol. IV, pp. 223—250 + [1]).

The matter is arranged in the main according to the system of Temminck. The generic characters are given, the synonymy, specific characters, description of the various plumages, and information about the geographical distribution and habits being briefly stated under the individual forms.

The plates (wood-engravings printed in colour) were executed by B. Fawcett, the printer of the work.

The work forms a kind of supplement to F. O. Morris' 'A history of British birds', 1903 (346).

A new edition was issued in 1875—76 (5 vols., 253 col. pl., 4to).

BREHM, A. E.

60. *1871.* Fuglenes Liv, populairt fremstillet af A. E. Brehm. Paa Dansk udgivet af P. Mariager. Med 23 Farvetryk, 2 Chromolithographier og 170 Textbilleder. P. G. Philipsen. *Kjøbenhavn. pp. XXXII + 699 + [1]. 25 col. pl. (numb. I—XXI, A, B, X.B, XV.B). 8vo.*

A Danish edition of Brehm's 'Illustriertes Thierleben. Volks- und Schulausg. II. Die Vögel', 1869, the contents of which have been rearranged according to the current system. The text is somewhat abridged on certain points, but enlarged on

others; the Nordic bird fauna, especially, is more fully treated than in the German original.

The colour prints, which are not particularly valuable, are chiefly from drawings by Robert Kretschmer and have, with some few exceptions, been taken from Brehm's 'Das Leben der Vögel', the first edition of which appeared in 1861.

Two copies of this work are in the possession of the Library. A second edition was issued in 1876 (61).

61. *1876.* Fuglenes Liv ... Med 2 Kromolithografier, 26 Farvetryk (Iristryk) og 193 Textbilleder. Andet forøgede Oplag. P. G. Philipsen. *Kjøbenhavn. pp. XL + 758 + [1]. 28 col. pl. 8vo.*

The second, somewhat enlarged, edition of the preceding one of 1871 (60).

62. *1891—92.* Brehms Tierleben. Allgemeine Kunde des Tierreichs. Mit 1910 Abbildungen im Text, 12 Karten und 179 Tafeln in Farbendruck und Holzschnitt. Dritte, gänzlich neubearbeitete Auflage. Herausgegeben von Pechuel-Loesche. Vols. IV—VI. - - Die Vögel. Von Alfred E. Brehm. Unter Mitwirkung von Wilh. Haacke neubearbeitet von Pechuel-Loesche ... Bibliographisches Institut. *Leipzig. 3 vols. 57 pl. (29 col.). 8vo.* — Vol. IV [I]. 1891. *pp. XIV + 770. 19 pl. (10 col.).* Vol. V [II]. 1891. *pp. XIV + 713. 18 pl. (9 col.).* Vol. VI [III]. 1892. *pp. XIV + 740. 20 pl. (10 col.). 3 maps.*

The first edition of this famous work was issued in 1863—69 under the title 'Illustriertes Tierleben' in six volumes with 37 plates with figures of birds from drawings by Rob. Kretschmer and E. Schmidt. Brehm had already shown his ability as a popular scientific author in the accounts of his travels, published previously. In the present work, his chief one, he describes in a masterly manner the lives of animals, paying less attention to their structure and appearance, which have otherwise generally been given prominence.

The work did not fail to score a success; it was translated into nearly all the civilised languages, was issued in a popular edition, by Friedr. Schödler, 1868—70, in 3 vols. (Vol. II, Vögel), 8vo, and in spite of its comparatively high price (99,75 marks bound in linen) a second edition could be issued as early as 1876—80, in 10 vols. (IV—VI: Vögel, 1878—79, illustrated with woodcuts on 55 plates and as text-figs., from drawings by G. Mützel, Rob. Kretschmer, A. Göring, L. Beckmann, and Ch. Kröner), 8vo.

In the present, third, edition, which appeared in ten volumes in 1890—93, all polemic passages have been omitted, and the work has been revised in accordance with the increased knowledge of the bird world at the time.

The plates, some printed in colours, were executed from drawings by Robert Kretschmer, Wilhelm Kuhnert, Gustav Mützel, Friedrich Specht, Ludwig Beckmann, and others.

The fourth edition of the work was issued in 1911—18, the ornithological section in 1911—13 (63).

63. *1911—13.* Brehms Tierleben ... Mit 1803 Abbildungen im Text, 633 Tafeln in Farbendruck, Kupferätzung und Holzschnitt und 13 Karten. Vierte, vollständig neubearbeitete Auflage herausgegeben von Otto zur Strassen. Vols. VI—IX. - - Die Vögel. Von Alfred Brehm. Neubearbeitung von William Marshall, unter Mitwirkung von F. Hempelmann und O. zur Strassen ... Bibliographisches Institut. *Leipzig. 4 vols. 191 pl. (106 col.). 8vo.* — Vol. VI [I]. 1911. *pp. XVI + 498. 50 pl. (27 (1 pl. eggs) col., 15 phot. pl.).* Vol. VII [II]. 1911. *pp. XIV + 492. 50 pl. (28 (1 pl. eggs) col., 11 phot. pl.).* Vol. VIII [III]. 1911. *pp. XII + 472. 40 pl. (24 (1 pl. eggs) col., 8 phot. pl.).* Vol. IX [IV]. 1913. *pp. XVI + 568. 51 pl. (27 (2 pl. eggs) col., 9 phot. pl.). 3 maps.*

The ornithological section of the fourth edition of this work, which appeared in its entirety in 13 volumes in 1911—18.

Death prevented Marshall from completing the revision

of the ornithological part of this new edition, in which the birds are arranged according to Gadow's system in Bronn's 'Klassen und Ordnungen des Thier-Reichs'. Sections on domestic birds and on the prehistory of birds are inserted. Eugène Rey, the specialist in eggs, assisted in the preparation of the sections on eggs and nests.

Several of the illustrations in this edition, naturally enough, were executed from photographs. The drawings for the non-photographic plates were executed by W. Kuhnert and also by R. Kretschmer, G. Mützel, L. Beckmann, W. Heubach, A. Reichert, Ch. Kröner, Fr. Specht, and others. The coloured plates are executed by the three-colour process.

Sixty of the plates of the ornithological section by Wilh. Kuhnert and Walter Heubach were issued separately under the title 'Brehm's Tierbilder. 2. Teil. Die Vögel', etc. (Leipzig 1913), with text by Victor Franz.

64. *1922—26.* Brehms Tierleben ... Neudruck der vierten, vollständig neubearbeiteten Auflage. Vols. VI— IX. - - Die Vögel ... Bibliographisches Institut. *Leipzig.* An unaltered reprint of the fourth edition 1911—13 (63).

65. *1928.* Brehm Dyrenes Liv ... Vol. II. < - - Part 3. Fuglene Ved P. Jespersen >. Gyldendal. *København. pp. 236. text-figs. 14 pl. (12 col., 2 phot. pl.). large 8vo.*
The ornithological section of a Danish adaption of Brehm's Tierleben which appeared in its entirety in three volumes in 1927—29. It is illustrated with many photographs and with coloured plates (three-colour prints) from drawings by Kuhnert.

BREHM, C. L.
1825—30. Systematische Darstellung der Fortpflanzung der Vögel Europa's ... Parts I—IV. See *Thienemann, F. A. L.,* 1825—38.

56. *1831.* Handbuch der Naturgeschichte aller Vögel Deutschlands, worin nach den sorgfältigsten Untersuchungen und den genauesten Beobachtungen mehr als 900 einheimische Vögel-Gattungen zur Begründung einer ganz neuen Ansicht und Behandlung ihrer Naturgeschichte vollständig beschrieben sind. Von Christian Ludwig Brehm. Mit ... ganz treu und sorgfältig nach der Natur gezeichneten illuminirten Kupfertafeln. Bernh. Friedr. Voigt. *Ilmenau. pp. XXIV + 1085 + [3]. 47 col. pl. (frönt. + Nos. I—XLVI). 8vo.*
In this handbook, Brehm's chief work, the author gives his opinion on the system of Linnæus, which is rejected as being too unnatural. The birds are divided into 23 orders which are again subdivided into genera, 'species', and 'subspecies' (Gattungen), by which the author understands birds resembling each other and mating with each other ; whereas birds belonging to the same 'species' certainly bear a great resemblance to each other in most respects, but do not regularly mate with each other. Thus he went a step further than any other contemporary ornithologist in the division of the birds into species.
The plates give figures of all genera with the exception of three. The bird portraits were drawn by Bädeker and Th. Götz, and engraved by Wilh. Müller, of Weimar, and Schwanzl.

1855—63. Die Eier der europäischen Voegel ... See *Baedeker, F. W. J.*

BRENCHLEY, J. L.
1873. Jottings during the cruise of H. M. S. Curaçoa among the South Sea Islands in 1865. By Julius L. Brenchley ... pp. 353—394: Birds. See *Gray, G. R.*

BREWER, T. M.
7. *1859.* Smithsonian Contributions to Knowledge. Vol. XI. - - North American oölogy. By Thomas M. Brewer. Part I. Raptores and Fissirostres. Smithsonian

Institution. *City of Washington. pp. VIII + 132. 5 pl. eggs (numb. I—V). 4to.*
This work was originally published separately in 1857 under the title 'Smithsonian Contributions to Knowledge. North American oölogy ; being an account of the habits and geographical distribution of the birds of North America during their breeding season ; with figures and descriptions of their eggs'. The second title runs as the title of the present later reprint, in which the original first title has been reduced to the heading on page 1 by the omission of the words 'habits and'.
The text deals with the groups Raptores, Caprimulgidæ, Hirundinidæ, Cypselidæ, and Alcedinidæ. Altogether sixty species are treated ; their geographical distribution, nests, and eggs are discussed, with a brief account of their habits during the breeding season, and a list of synonyms.
The eggs of 49 species are shown in the 74 figures of the plates (Bowen & Co. Lith. Philad.), the originals for which were drawn by Otto Knirsch.
The original edition, 1857, differs from the present one in that the figures of the plates are coloured.
Only the first part of this work appeared, its production, however, being resumed in 1892 by C. E. Bendire (32—35).

1874. A history of North American birds. Land birds. See *Baird, S. F.*

BREWSTER, W.
1884—87. See Auk.

BRICKA, G. S.
68. *[1883—] 1884.* Illustreret Haandbog i Fjerkræavl. Af Georg St. Bricka. Med ... kolorerede Billeder og i Texten trykte Illustrationer. Magnus A. Schultz. *Aalborg. pp. [VIII] + 196 + [2]. text-figs. 30 col. pl. 4to.*
The present work was published in parts, the first two of which, each comprising 16 pages of text and two plates, appeared early in 1883. The book is divided into three sections, the first of which (pp. 1—130) deals with fowls, the second (pp. 131—167) with other poultry (turkeys, guinea-fowls, ducks, and geese), the third (pp. 168—196) with poultry diseases. The matter has been largely compiled from the works of foreign authors, such as L. Wright's 'Illustrated book of poultry', 1873 (542), whence also the illustrations are derived. The plates are executed in chromo-lithography (Vincent Brooks Day & Son, lith.).

BRISSON, M. J.
69. *1760.* Ornithologie, ou méthode contenant la division des oiseaux en ordres, sections, genres, espèces & leurs variétés. A laquelle on a joint une description exacte de chaque espèce, avec les citations des auteurs qui en ont traité, les noms qu'ils leur ont donnés, ceux que leur ont donnés les différentes nations, & les noms vulgaires. Par Brisson. Ouvrage enrichi de figures en taille-douce. Cl. Jean-Baptiste Bauche. *Paris. 6 vols. 261 pl. 4to.* Added title-page in Latin. — Vol. I. *pp. XXIV + 526 + LXXIII + [I]. 37 pl. (numb. I— XXXVII).* Vol. II. *pp. [IV] + 516 + LXVII + [I]. 46 pl. (numb. I—XLVI).* Vol. III. *pp. [IV] + XCI + [I]. 37 pl. (numb. I—XXXVII).* Vol. IV. *pp. [IV] + 576 + LIV + [I]. 46 pl. (numb. I— XLVI).* Vol. V. *pp. [IV] + 544 + LV + [I]. 42 pl. (numb. I—XLII).* Vol. VI. *pp. [IV] + 543 + LXV + [II]. 47 pl. (numb. I—XLVII).* < Supplément ...> (in Vol. VI). *pp. 146 + XXII + [I]. 6 pl. (numb. I—VI).*
The text is printed in Latin and French in parallel columns. Written by one of the greatest connoisseurs of birds of the time, the work deals with 1336 species in addition to 150 'varieties' distributed over 115 genera, which are again grouped

14

in 26 orders. Brisson knew by sight more than 800 of the species he described. He did not use the binomial system and his systematical classification of the birds differed from that of Linnæus, surpassing it and being less artificial. The descriptions of the species are careful, though somewhat lengthy.

The plates, which are folded, were drawn and engraved by Martinet. Both artistically and as accurate detail studies they are better than those of most of his predecessors (655).

In 1788 a new edition was issued: Paris, Treuttel & Würtz, plates, 4to.

A new, somewhat abridged, edition of the Latin text of the present 4to edition appeared at Leyden in 1763 (2 vols., 8vo) under the title 'Ornithologia sive synopsis methodica sistens avium divisionem in ordines, sectiones, genera, species, ipsarumque varietates'.

BRITISH MISCELLANY.

1804—06. The British miscellany: or coloured figures of ... animal subjects ... *See Sowerby, J.*

BRITISH MUSEUM (NATURAL HISTORY).

70.   *1874—98.* Catalogue of the birds in the British Museum. Printed by order of the Trustees. *London. 27 vols. text-figs. 387 col. pl. 8vo.* — Vol. I. 1874. Accipitres, or diurnal birds of prey. By R. Bowdler Sharpe. *pp. XIII + 479 + [1]. text-figs. 14 col. pl. (numb. I—XIV).* Vol. II. 1875. Striges, or nocturnal birds of prey. By R. Bowdler Sharpe. *pp. XI + 325 + [1]. text-figs. 14 col. pl. (numb. I—XIV).* Vol. III. 1877. Passeriformes, or perching birds. Coliomorphæ, containing the families Corvidæ, Paradiseidæ, Oriolidæ, Dicruridæ, and Prionopidæ. By R. Bowdler Sharpe. *pp. XIII + 343 + [1]. text-figs. 14 col. pl. (numb. I—XIV).* Vol. IV. 1879. Passeriformes ... Cichlomorphæ. Part 1, containing the families Campophagidæ and Muscicapidæ. By R. Bowdler Sharpe. *pp. XVI + 494 + [1]. text-figs. 14 col. pl. (numb. I—XIV).* Vol. V. 1881. Passeriformes ... Cichlomorphæ. Part 2, containing the family Turdidæ (warblers and thrushes). By Henry Seebohm. *pp. XVI + [I] + 426 + [1]. text-figs. 18 col. pl. (numb. I—XVIII).* Vol. VI. 1881. Passeriformes ... Cichlomorphæ. Part 3, containing the first portion of the family Timeliidæ (babbling-thrushes). By R. Bowdler Sharpe. *pp. XIII + 420 + [1]. text-figs. 18 col. pl. (numb. I—XVIII).* Vol. VII. 1883. Passeriformes ... Cichlomorphæ. Part 4, containing the concluding portion of the family Timeliidæ (babbling thrushes). By R. Bowdler Sharpe. *pp. XVI + 698 + [1]. text-figs. 16 col. pl. (numb. I—XV).* Vol. VIII. 1883. Passeriformes ... Cichlomorphæ. Part 5, containing the families Paridæ and Laniidæ (titmice and shrikes), and Certhiomorphæ (creepers and nuthatches). By Hans Gadow. *pp. XIII + 385 + [1]. text-figs. 9 col. pl. (numb. I—IX).* Vol. IX. 1884. Passeriformes ... Cinnyrimorphæ, containing the families Nectariniidæ and Meliphagidæ (sun-birds and honey-eaters). By Hans Gadow. *pp. XII + 310 + [1]. text-figs. 7 col. pl. (numb. I—VII).* Vol. X. 1885. Passeriformes ... Fringilliformes. Part 1, containing the families Dicæidæ, Hirundinidæ, Ampelidæ, Mniotiltidæ, and Motacillidæ. By R. Bowdler Sharpe. *pp. XIII + 682. text-figs. 12 col. pl. (numb. I—XII).* Vol. XI. 1886. Passeriformes ... Fringilliformes. Part 2, containing the families Cœrebidæ, Tanagridæ, and Icteridæ. By Philip Lutley Sclater. *pp. XVII + 431. text-figs. 18 col. pl. (numb. I—*

XVIII). Vol. XII. 1888. Passeriformes ... Fringilliformes. Part 3, containing the family Fringillidæ. By R. Bowdler Sharpe. *pp. XV + 871 + [1]. text-figs. 16 col. pl. (numb. I—XVI).* Vol. XIII. 1890. Passeriformes ... Sturniformes, containing the families Artamidæ, Sturnidæ, Ploceidæ, and Alaudidæ. Also the families Atrichiidæ and Menuridæ. By R. Bowdler Sharpe. *pp. XVI + 701 + [1] + 8. text-figs. 15 col. pl. (numb. I—XV).* Vol. XIV. 1888. Passeriformes ... Oligomyodæ, or the families Tyrannidæ, Oxyrhamphidæ, Pipridæ, Cotingidæ, Phytotomidæ, Philepittidæ, Pittidæ, Xenicidæ, and Eurylæmidæ. By Philip Lutley Sclater. *pp. XIX + [I] + 494 + [1]. text-figs. 26 col. pl. (numb. I—XXVI).* Vol. XV. 1890. Passeriformes ... Tracheophonæ, or the families Dendrocolaptidæ, Formicariidæ, Conopophagidæ, and Pteroptochidæ. By Philip Lutley Sclater. *pp. XVII + [I] + 371 + [1] + 8. text-figs. 20 col. pl. (numb. I—XX).* Vol. XVI. 1892. Picariæ. Upupæ and Trochili, by Osbert Salvin. Coraciæ, of the families Cypselidæ, Caprimulgidæ, Podargidæ, and Steatornithidæ, by Ernst Hartert. *pp. XVI + 703 + [1] + 17. text-figs. 14 col. pl. (numb. I—XIV).* Vol. XVII. 1892. Picariæ. Coraciæ (contin.) and Halcyones, with the families Leptosomatidæ, Coraciidæ, Meropidæ, Alcedinidæ, Momotidæ, Todidæ, and Coliidæ, by R. Bowdler Sharpe. Bucerotes and Trogones, by W. R. Ogilvie Grant. *pp. XI + 522 + [I] + 17. text-figs. 17 col. pl. (numb. I—XVII).* Vol. XVIII. 1890. Picariæ. Scansores, containing the family Picidæ. By Edward Hargitt. *pp. XV + 597 + [1] + 8. text-figs. 15 col. pl. (numb. I—XV).* Vol. XIX. 1891. Picariæ. Scansores and Coccyges, containing the families Rhamphastidæ, Galbulidæ, and Bucconidæ, by P. L. Sclater; and the families Indicatoridæ, Capitonidæ, Cuculidæ, and Musophagidæ, by G. E. Shelley. *pp. XII + 484 + [1] + 17. text-fig. 13 col. pl. (numb. I—XIII).* Vol. XX. 1891. Psittaci, or parrots. By T. Salvadori. *pp. XVII + 658 + [1] + 17. text-figs. 18 col. pl. (numb. I—XVIII).* Vol. XXI. 1893. Columbæ, or pigeons. By T. Salvadori. *pp. XVII + [I] +676 + 17. text-figs. 15 col. pl. (numb. I—XV).* Vol. XXII. 1893. Game birds (Pterocletes, Gallinæ, Opisthocomi, Hemipodii). By W. R. Ogilvie-Grant. *pp. XVI + 585 + [1] + 17. text-fig. 8 col. pl. (numb. I—VIII).* Vol. XXIII. 1894. Fulicariæ (Rallidæ and Heliornithidæ) and Alectorides (Aramidæ, Eurypygidæ, Mesitidæ, Rhinochetidæ, Gruidæ, Psophiidæ, and Otididæ). By R. Bowdler Sharpe. *pp. XIII + 353 + [1] + 17. 9 col. pl. (numb. I—IX).* Vol. XXIV. 1896. Limicolæ. By R. Bowdler Sharpe. *pp. XII + 794 + [1] + 19. text-figs. 7 col. pl. (numb. I—VII).* Vol. XXV. [1895] 1896. Gaviæ (terns, gulls, and skuas) by Howard Saunders. Tubinares (petrels and albatrosses) by Osbert Salvin. *pp. XV + 475 + [1] + 19. text-figs. 8 col. pl. (numb. I—VIII).* Vol. XXVI. 1898. Plataleæ (ibises and spoonbills) and Herodiones (herons and storks), by R. Bowdler Sharpe. Steganopodes (cormorants, gannets, frigate-birds, tropic-birds, and pelicans), by R. Bowdler Sharpe. Pygopodes (divers and grebes), Alcæ (auks), and Impennes (penguins), by W. R. Ogilvie-Grant. *pp. XVII + 687 + [I] + 20. text-figs. 14 col. pl. (numb. I—VIII, IA—C, IIA, Va, Vb).* Vol.

XXVII. 1895. Chenomorphæ (Palamedeæ, Phoenicopteri, Anseres), Crypturi, and Ratitæ. By T. Salvadori. *pp. XV + 636 + [1] +19. 19 col. pl. (numb. I—XIX).*

This survey, in which the titles of the individual volumes are somewhat abridged, shows that many of the volumes of this work, so important for systematic ornithology, were written by R. Bowdler Sharpe who, according to the original plan, was to have prepared the whole catalogue ; this, however, proved impossible, and he was therefore assisted by ten other ornithologists. His direct share in the undertaking may be seen from the fact that of the 11,617 species distributed over 2255 genera that are described in the catalogue, 5181 are treated in the parts written by him.

The immense collection of birds found in the British Museum forms the basis of the catalogue which, however, also makes use of the material in other public and private collections or described in the literature. It is therefore understandable that the work is characterized as 'one of the most important aids to the study of Systematic Ornithology which has ever been produced' (70, XXVI, p. V), nor is it too much to say that it is a landmark in the history of ornithology.

The work on the catalogue was commenced in 1872, and it is therefore natural that the first volumes should be less valuable, if only on account of their age, than the subsequent ones — the number of specimens in the Museum increased from about 35,000 in 1872 to nearly 400,000 in 1898. The origin of the binomial nomenclature adopted in the work — trinomials were not in use for the designation of subspecies at the time the catalogue was commenced — is generally the twelfth edition of Linnæus' 'Systema naturæ', while later on the tenth edition of this work has generally been used as a basis for zoological nomenclature.

The plates (lithographs, Vols. I—XIII mainly coloured by hand, later chiefly chromo-lithographs) are mostly printed by Mintern Bros. They are executed from drawings by J. G. Keulemans and J. Smit, while a smaller number are due to Peter Smit and W. Hart. The species reproduced, 540 in all, had not been figured previously, at any rate not satisfactorily, and in nearly all cases the drawings were executed from the types of the species.

An alphabetical index of the generic names used in the catalogue was prepared by F. H. Waterhouse and published in 1899 under the title 'Avium generum index alphabeticus' as Volume IX of the 'Bulletin of the British Ornithologists' Club'.

Information concerning the dates of publication of the first ten volumes of the catalogue has been given by Sherborn 1891.

'1.   *1901—12.* Catalogue of the collection of birds' eggs in the British Museum (Natural History). Printed by order of the Trustees. *London. 5 vols. 79 col. pl. 8vo.* — Vol. I. 1901. Ratitæ. Carinatæ (Tinamiformes—Lariformes). By Eugene W. Oates. *pp. XXIII + 252 + 23.·18 col. pl. (numb. I—XVIII).* Vol. II. 1902. Carinatæ (Charadriiformes—Strigiformes). By Eugene W. Oates. *pp. XX + 400 + 24. 15 col. pl. (numb. I—XV).* Vol. III. 1903. Carinatæ (Psittaciformes—Passeriformes). By Eugene W. Oates. Assisted by Savile G. Reid. *pp. XXIII + 349 + 24. 10 col. pl. (numb. I—X).* Vol. IV. 1905. Carinatæ (Passeriformes continued). By Eugene W. Oates. Assisted by Savile G. Reid. *pp. XVIII + 352 + 25. 14 col. pl. (numb. I—XIV).* Vol. V. 1912. Carinatæ (Passeriformes completed). By W. R. Ogilvie-Grant. *pp. XXIII + 547 + 30. 22 col. pl. (numb. I—XXII).*

With the exception of those in the exhibition galleries, this catalogue deals with all the eggs found in the collection of the Museum, whose eggs of British birds had previously been treated by G. R. Gray in his 'Eggs of British birds' (London 1852, 12mo).

This catalogue may be regarded as a kind of supplement to the British Museum's 'Catalogue of the birds', 1874—98 (70), and in the main follows this work and the arrangement

and nomenclature of Bowdler Sharpe's 'Hand-list of the genera and species of birds' (London 1899—1909, 8vo).

In the five volumes altogether 69,828 specimens of eggs are mentioned, distributed among 3890 species. Under each species there are references to the literature and to good figures of the eggs, a description of them, a list of the specimens, the localities in which they were found, and the source whence they have come to the collection, whose increase from about 1842 is dealt with in the Introduction to Vol. I. The manuscript for Vol. V was commenced by E. W. Oates, but was never completed. Nearly the whole volume was therefore subsequently re-written by Ogilvie-Grant.

The fine figures of the eggs were drawn by H. Grønvold, and the plates were executed, in chromo-lithography, by Pawson & Brailsford, Sheffield.

The Library possesses two copies of the first four volumes of this work.

1907. National Antarctic Expedition 1901—04. Natural history. Vol. II. Zoology … II. Aves. *See Wilson, E. A.*

1919. Economic Series. No. 9. Birds beneficial to agriculture. *See Frohawk, F. W.*

BRITISH ORNITHOLOGISTS' UNION.
1859 —> See Ibis.

1915 & 1916. Report on the birds collected by the British Ornithologists' Union Expedition and the Wollaston Expedition in Dutch New Guinea. *See Ogilvie-Grant, W. R.*

BROUWER, G. A.
1935. Ornithologia Neerlandica. De vogels van Nederland. Vol. V … voltooid door G. A. Brouwer. *See Oort, E. D. van, 1918—35.*

BROWN, P.
1776. New illustrations of zoology, containing fifty 72. coloured plates of new, curious, and non-descript birds, with a few quadrupeds, reptiles and insects. Together with a short and scientific description of the same. By Peter Brown. B. White. *London. pp. [VIII] + 136. 42 pl. birds. (numb. I—XLII in text; some plates numb.). 4to.* Added title-page in French.

Brown's plates for this work, which is a kind of supplement to Edwards' 'A natural history of birds', 1743—51 (124), and 'Gleanings', 1758—64 (126), were executed from animals that had not previously been drawn in the collections belonging to Marmaduke Tunstall (twelve of the figures of birds) and other private collectors, the British Museum, and the Royal Society. However, some of the 50 plates in the work are copies from drawings which the former Dutch governor of Ceylon, Mr. Gideon Loten, during his stay on Java and Ceylon, had caused to be made from living models, chiefly by the native artist P. C. de Bevere.

The plates (engravings coloured by hand) form the most important part of the work, while the descriptive letterpress in French and English, written principally by Thomas Pennant, is subordinate and rather brief. The ornithological part of this text covers pp. 1—104.

BRYANT, H. C.
1918. The game birds of California … *See Grinnell, J.*

BUC'HOZ, P. J.
[1775—] 1781. Première (& Seconde) Centurie 73. de planches enluminées et non enluminées représentant au naturel ce qui se trouve de plus intéressant et de plus curieux parmi les animaux, les végétaux, et

14*

les minéraux. Pour servir d'intelligence à l'histoire générale des trois règnes de la nature. Par Buc'hoz.
Lacombe. *Paris.* (Later: Marc-Michel Rey. *Amsterdam). 2 vols. 52 pl. birds. (26 col.). large fol.*

This collection of altogether 400 plates (200 coloured) was
published in twenty decades, and contains figures of the rarest,
most remarkable, and most interesting phenomena of the three
kingdoms of nature, each part being devoted to one of them.
The engravings relating to the animal kingdom are found in
Decades 1, 4, 7, and 10 in both volumes. The plates (engravings) are double, each being presented in an uncoloured
and a hand-coloured form. The ornithological plates were
drawn by Desmoulins and engraved by him, by Vin. Van-
gelisti, Fessard, Vidal, or others. The natural objects figured
are described in the author's 'Histoire générale et économique
des trois règnes de la nature' (Paris 1777, or 1789, fol.). In
addition to the 2 × 200 plates of which this work usually consists, the first 20 plates of a third hundred are quoted by
Quérard (579, I, 1827, p. 549). The plates of the present collection are also found in other works by the same author; thus
the following work appeared in Nürnberg in 1785, 'Abbildungen
der Vögel, welche in seinem grossen Werke von den drey
Reichen der Natur vorkommen' (40 col. pl., fol.) (564, I, 1846,
p. 386).

BUFFON, G. L. L., Comte de.

74. *1770—83.* Histoire naturelle, générale et particulière, avec la description du Cabinet du Roi. Vols.
XVI—XXIV. - - Histoire naturelle des oiseaux. Imprimerie Royale. *Paris 9 vols. text-figs. 262 pl. (separately numb. in each vol.). 4to.*

The ornithological section of the first edition of Buffon's
famous 'Histoire naturelle', which appeared in its entirety in
44 volumes in 1749—1804.

The plates (engravings) in the section on birds were drawn
by de Seve and engraved by C. Baron, Blanchon, Levillain,
L. Le Grand, C. Haussard, M. T. Rousselet, J. Mansard, M. R.
veuve Tardieu, and several others.

Information about other editions and about the text is
found below (76).

75. *1770—85.* Histoire naturelle, générale et particulière, avec la description du Cabinet du Roi. Vols.
XIV—XXXI. - - Histoire naturelle des oiseaux. Imprimerie Royale. *Paris. 18 vols. plates. 12mo.*

The section on birds in the first 8vo edition of Buffon's
'Histoire naturelle', which appeared in 1752—1805 in altogether
90 volumes (71 volumes if the anatomical sections are not included). The plates in this edition are reduced copies of the
corresponding ones in the 4to edition, 1770—83 (74).

Information about other editions and about the text is given
below (76).

76. *1770—86.* Histoire naturelle des oiseaux. Imprimerie Royale (Vols VII—X: Suivant la copie de
l'Imprimerie Royale). - *Paris 10 vols. 1008 col. pl.
(973 pl. birds). fol.* — Vol. I. 1770. *pp. [VI] + XXII
+ 313 + [2]. 76 pl. (75 col.).* Vol. II. 1772. *pp. [VI]
+ 488 + [2]. 53 col. pl.* Vol. III. 1774. *pp. [VIII] +
282 + [2]. 98 col. pl.* Vol. IV. 1777. *pp. [XI] + 405
+ [3]. 97 col. pl.* Vol. V. 1778. *pp. XI + 363 + [2].
98 col. pl.* Vol. VI. 1783. *pp. XII + 582 + [2]. 102
col. pl.* Vol. VII. 1783. *pp. XII + 435 + [2]. 142
col. pl.* Vol. VIII. 1783. *pp. VIII + 412 + [2]. 140
col. pl.* Vol. IX. 1784. *pp. VIII + 423 + [2]. 109
col. pl.* Vol. X. 1786. *pp. IV + 562 + [1]. 94 col. pl.*

The text of this work, with some alterations, has been
printed in three other formats besides the present folio edition,
large folio, 1771—83 (77); 4to, 1770—83 (74); and 12mo
1770—85 (75), (76, VII, p. II), the two latter of which entered
as the section 'Oiseaux' into the 'Histoire naturelle', where they
were illustrated by a series of black and white plates, drawn
by de Seve, because the coloured plates were too few (and too

expensive?) for all would-be purchasers to acquire a set of them
(76, I, p. IX).

The two folio editions of the text were intended to accompany the hand-coloured plates, which were drawn and engraved
by F. N. Martinet under the supervision of E. L. Daubenton
('D. le cadet'), who was a relation of L. J. M. Daubenton, Buffon's collaborator in 'Histoire naturelle', and was for many years
connected with and held an appointment at the Cabinet du Roi.

Under the direction of Buffon, Martinet had commenced in
1765 to draw, engrave, and paint animal portraits, which were
published in parts of 24 plates each by Panckoucke under the
title 'Collection de planches d'histoire naturelle enluminées'.
There was no accompanying text except the vernacular names of
the birds. The collection, which is cited under the title 'Planches
enluminées d'histoire naturelle par Martinet, executées par d'Au-
benton le jeune' (564, I, 1846, p. 158), was called 'Daubenton's Planches enluminées', or under Buffon's name, when it was
called 'Buffon's Planches enluminées', or simply 'Planches enluminées'. During the first five years about 500 plates were
published, and more than eighty artists and assistants engaged
on the work.

Publication went on till about 1783, when 42 cahiers comprising a total of 1008 plates had been published, 973 of which
contained figures of birds, while the remaining 35 plates represented other animals, notably insects, more especially butterflies and beetles, and also toads, reptiles, and corals (78, I, p.
XVII, note 8).

The collaborator for the first six volumes of the text was
Ph. Guéneau de Montbeillard, who also wrote the section 'Hiron-
delles' in Vol. VII. The Abbé G. L. C. A. Bexon then assisted
with the remainder of the bird section, so that Montbeillard
could devote himself entirely to the insects.

The text of all four formats is based on and refers to the
figures in 'Planches enluminées' for, as is stated in the Preface
(76, I, p. IX), 'Dans le vrai, les planches enluminées sont faites
pour cet Ouvrage, & l'ouvrage pour ces planches'.

The 35 plates which are not concerned with birds, are not
mentioned in the text, but are included in the total number of
plates given in Vol. VII, p. II.

A great number of species are enumerated and described in
this work, which is one of the chief works of ornithological
literature.

The birds are dealt with under their vernacular names; subsequently, however, other authors have given many of the
species binomial names, for instance Johann Hermann in 'Tabula affinitatum animalium', etc. (Argentorati 1783, 4to), and
Pieter Boddaert in his rare index to Buffon's great atlas 'Table
des Planches enluminées d'histoire naturelle, de M. d'Aubanon-
ton', etc. (Utrecht 1783, fol.), reprinted and edited by W. B.
Tegetmeier, 1874, 8vo. Other indices to the work are found
in Thomas Pennant's 'Histoire naturelle des oiseaux par le
Comte de Buffon, and the Planches enluminées, systematically
disposed' (London 1786, 4to), and in Kuhl's 'Buffoni et Daubentoni figurarum avium', 1820 (273).

For continuations of the 'Planches enluminées', see C. J.
Temminck, 1820—39 (502), and P. L. Sclater, 1866—69 (450).
A supplement to Buffon's and Temminck's plates was issued in
1845—49 by Oeillet Des Murs under the title 'Iconographie
ornithologique', etc. (Paris, 12 parts, fol. and 4to, 72 col. pl.),
while J. W. von Müller, 1853—66, issued a supplement to the
same two works under the title 'Description de nouveaux oiseaux
d'Afrique', etc. (Stuttgart, 5 parts, 16—20 col. pl., fol.).

77. *1771—83.* Histoire naturelle des oiseaux. Imprimerie Royale (Vol. VI: Suivant la copie de l'Imprimerie Royale). *Paris. 6 vols. text. 10 vols. atlas. 1008
col. pl. (973 pl. birds). large fol.*

Part of the text (Vols. I—VI), accompanied by the 'Planches enluminées', of a copy of the impression in large folio
format of Buffon's 'Histoire naturelle des oiseaux', which first
appeared in 4to, 1770—83 (74), in 8vo, 1770—85 (75), and
in folio, 1770—86 (76).

Apart from the large size of paper and the ornamental
border surrounding the letterpress on each page, this edition
corresponds to the corresponding volumes of the folio edition.
The title-page of the first volume is dated 1771.

The plates belonging to this copy seem in general to be better
executed than the corresponding plates of the smaller folio format.

78.   *1772—1809.* Herrn von Buffons Naturgeschichte der Vögel. Aus dem Französischen übersetzt, mit Anmerkungen, Zusätzen, und vielen Kupfern vermehrt, durch Friedrich Heinrich Wilhelm Martini (from Vol. VII: durch Bernhard Christian Otto). Pauli. *Berlin. 35 vols. and 2 suppl. vols. 1683 pl. 8vo.*
This work was published in two different issues, one being printed on writing paper ('pap. fort.') and with coloured plates, the other on ordinary paper with black and white plates (as in the case of the present copy). The paper and the print are poor, and the same applies to the plates. Reference is made to the figures in 'Buffon Planches enlum.', 1770—86 (76). The bird portraits on the plates of the work itself are derived partly from Buffon's original work, partly from other sources, such as the figures in the works of Catesby, Edwards, and Frisch. They have been drawn by Krüger jun. and others, and engraved i. a. by Glassbach and J. D. Philippin, née Sysang. A Vol. 36, 1829, is sometimes quoted, too (564, I, 1846, p. 387).

       1774—85. Naturgeschichte der Vögel aus den besten Schriftstellern mit Marianischen und neuen Kupfern. *See Decker, J. M.*

9.   *1775—82.* Allgemeine Historie der Natur nach allen ihren besondern Theilen abgehandelt; nebst einer Beschreibung der Naturalienkammer Sr. Majestät des Königs von Frankreich. Mit einer Vorrede Herrn ... Albrecht von Haller. Vols. IX—XI. - - < Naturgeschichte der Vögel >. Aus dem Französischen mit Anmerkungen und Zusätze. Hermann Heinrich Holle (Vols. X—XI: Johann Samuel Heinsius). *Leipzig. 3 vols. in 6. 146 pl. 4to.*
The ornithological section of a German edition of Buffon's 'Histoire naturelle' (74) which appeared in its entirety in 1750 —82 in 11 volumes (in 14).
The translation of the section 'Oiseaux' has been done by Carl Joseph Oehme, who wrote the Preface, 'Von den vornehmsten ornithologischen Büchern und Systemen', and provided the text with annotations and additions, partly from Martini's German translation, 1772—1809, of the same French ornithological work (78).
The production of the book is of moderate quality, as is also the execution of the plates, which are engraved by J. D. Philippin, née Sysang.

).   *1800—02 (An VIII—X).* Histoire naturelle, générale et particulière, par Leclerc de Buffon; Nouvelle édition, accompagnée de notes ... rédigé par C. S. Sonnini. Vols. XXXVII—LXIV. <- - Histoire naturelle ... Des oiseaux >. F. Dufart. *Paris. 28 vols. 256 col. pl. (numb. I—CCLVI). 8vo.*
Sonnini's well-known edition of Buffon's 'Histoire naturelle', which appeared in its entirety in 1799—1808 in 127 volumes (64 vols. + Suites, 63 vols.).
The section on birds has been provided with notes and additions by the editor and J. J. Virey. Vol. 64 further contains (pp. 129—158) 'Vues générales sur les quadrupèdes vivipares, les oiseaux, et sur la nature organisée, par J. J. Virey', and (pp. 159—341) 'Exposition méthodique d'ornithologie. Méthodes d'ornithologie. Par Brisson, Lacépède, Latham', edited by F. M. Daudin, and Buffon's preface to his various editions of Hales' 'Statique des végétaux' and Newton's 'Méthode des fluxions'.
The plates (engravings, printed in colour) were drawn by Barraband and de Seve, and engraved by Duhamel, E. Voysard, and several others.
The work was also issued with plain figures and on papier vélin with double figures, plain and printed in colour, and retouched by hand.

       1820. Buffoni et Daubentoni figurarum avium coloratarum nomina systematica. *See Kuhl, H.*

       [1852—?53]. Oeuvres complètes de Buffon, mises en ordre et précédées d'une notice historique, par Richard, suivies de la classification comparée, d'après Cuvier, Lesson, etc., etc. Vols IV—V. <- - [Oise-

aux] >. Chez l'éditeur. (Typ. de Mme Dondey-Dupré). *Paris. 2 vols. 37 col. pl. large 8vo.*
The ornithological section of one of the many editions of Buffon's works, which appeared under the title 'Oeuvres complètes'. In 1825—28 Achille Richard issued one with a preface, reprinted in the present edition which consists of 5 volumes, the first of which appeared in 1851₁
The text is provided with additions and notes, and is printed in double columns. The plates are drawn by Edouard Traviès, engraved by Massard, Fournier, Manceau, and others, and retouched by hand (Imp. de Laurent).

BUHLE, C. A. A.
       1818—28. Die Eier der Vögel Deutschlands ... *See Naumann, J. F.*

       [1832—35]. Die Naturgeschichte in getreuen Ab- 82. bildungen und mit ausführlicher Beschreibung derselben. Vögel. Carl Brüggemann. *Halberstadt. pp. 354 + [4]. 184 pl. (numb. 2—21, 20 [=22], 21 [=23], 24—85, 67 [=86], 68 [=87], 88, 71 [=89], 90, 75 [=91], 92—119, 119bis—142, 133 [=143], 144—155, 156a, 156b, 157—183; 70 partly col. (numb. 2—19, 25—27, 29, 35—41, 44, 46, 52—54, 72—76, 93—96, 99, 103—106, 110—114, 116, 130, 145, 148—151, 155, 156b, 157, 158, 166, 167, 174, 177, 181, 183); engraved title). small 4to.*
The ornithological section of a general account of natural history, which was published in its entirety in 1829—45 (zoological section 1829—41). The present section was issued in 27 parts, 1—4, in 1832; 5—10, 1833; 11—19, 1834; and 20—27, 1835, and in its text gives a fairly detailed description of the different birds. With their small figures the plates, a number of which are partially coloured (by hand), are of no particular value.

       [1842—] 1845. Naturgeschichte der domesticirten 83. Vögel in ökonomischer und technischer Hinsicht. Ein Hand- und Hülfsbuch für Jedermann besonders für Stadt- und Landwirthe. Von Chr. Adolph Buhle. Ed. Heynemann. *Halle. 6 vols. in 1. pp. 56 + 67 + 70 + 67 + 105 + [1] + 135. 6 col. pl. 8vo.*
Each of the six parts of this handbook on domestic birds deals with its own part of the subject, — birds which may be grouped with the swan; the goose and the duck; the peacock, the turkey, and the guinea fowl; the domestic hen; the dove, and finally cage-birds.
The plates (lithographs coloured by hand: Druck von C. C. Böhme, Leipzig) were executed from drawings by J. F. Naumann, and are without any particular value.

BULLER, W. L.
       1882. (New Zealand). Colonial Museum and Geo- 84. logical Survey Department. Manual of the birds of New Zealand. By Walter L. Buller. George Didsbury, Government printer. *Wellington. pp. XII + 107 + [1]. text-figs. 38 pl. (front. + Nos. I—XXXVII). 8vo.*
This manual, to be used in the study of the bird-life of New Zealand, was based on a list published in 1871, 'Catalogue of the birds of New Zealand, with diagnoses of the species' by F. W. Hutton. The total number of species described in the manual amounts to 176. Of fresh matter added, mention may be made of the brief sketches inserted relating to the life-histories, almost exclusively derived from the author's 'History of the birds of New Zealand', the second edition of which appeared in 1887—88 (85).
The plates are chiefly reduced reproductions in photo-lithography of Keulemans' coloured drawings for the work just mentioned, four, however, being copied from other sources.

       [1887—] 1888. A history of the birds of New Zea- 85. land. By Walter Lawry Buller. Second edition. Published by the author. *London. 2 vols. 50 pl. (numb.*

in 'Table of contents'; 48 col.). large 4to. — Vol. I. *pp. LXXXIV + 250 + [6]. text-figs. 24 col. pl. (Nos. I—XXIV). Vol. II. pp. XV + 359. text-figs. 26 pl. (Nos. XXV—L; 24 col. (Nos. XXV—XLVIII)).*

The first edition of this work was issued in four parts in 1872—73 in London and was provided with 36 plates, 35 of which (lithographs coloured by hand) were reproduced from drawings by Keulemans, containing altogether 70 figures of New Zealand birds. The impression was limited to 500 copies which were sold by private subscription, for which reason the price of the work soon rose. The author therefore set about preparing the issue of the present second edition, for which he had been able in the interval, which he spent in New Zealand, to collect a great deal of valuable material in the form of additions and of alterations. Of the 13 parts of the new edition the first two appeared in 1887, while the remaining parts were issued in the course of 1888 (328, VII, p. 447). Each part contains four lithographs printed in colour from coloured drawings by Keulemans, to whose skill as a bird-artist they testify. Keulemans himself has drawn or superintended the drawing of the colour-stones, the printing of the plates being carried out by Judd & Co. The whole issue amounted to 1000 copies, and of these only about 250 were available for Europe and America.

The text gives a very complete synonymy for each species, describes both sexes and every condition of plumage, and tells the life-history of each bird from personal observations made by the author during a period of twenty years.

After the lapse of seventeen years Buller issued a 'Supplement to the birds of New Zealand', (London 1905—06, 2 vols., 12 col. pl., text-figs., large 4to) in which he embodied the material relating to the subject that had been collected in the meantime, and in which he deals with all the known species of the birds of New Zealand. As in the chief work, the plates are lithographs executed from drawings by Keulemans.

Additions to this work and to Mathews' 'The birds of Norfolk and Lord Howe Islands', etc., were made by Mathews in 1936 (328, note), so that all the bird species of New Zealand should now be depicted in coloured figures.

BULLETIN OF THE AMERICAN MUSEUM OF NATURAL HISTORY. *See American Museum of Natural History.*

BURDICK, J. E.
1936. Birds of America ... *See Pearson, T. G.*

BURMEISTER, C. H. C.
86.   *[1859—]* 1860. Zoologischer Hand-Atlas zum Schulgebrauch und Selbstunterricht, mit besonderer Rücksicht auf seinen 'Grundriss' und sein 'Lehrbuch der Naturgeschichte' entworfen von Hermann Burmeister. Zweite Ausgabe. Mit 42 Kupfertafeln. Besorgt durch C. G. Giebel. < - - *pp. 37—67: 2. Klasse. Vögel Aves >. Georg Reimer. Berlin. 8 col. pl. (numb. 10— 17). 4to.*

This popular atlas for educational use was first issued in 1835—43. Burmeister's second journey to Brazil prevented him from preparing the present edition and Giebel therefore undertook the task. The work was published in 1858—61 in 6 Lieferungen, each with seven copperplates, and consists in all of [III] + 192 plates and 42 plates (41 col., engravings coloured by hand). The ornithological section of the text and plates was published in Lieferung 2 and 3. Many animals are figured on each plate, some few figures of the plates having been replaced by better ones in the present edition. The ornithological plates were engraved by J. C. Richter and C. E. Weber.

BURROUGHS, J.
87.   1902. Smithsonian Institution. Harriman Alaska Series. (Edited by C. Hart Merriam). *City of Washington. 1910. - -* Harriman Alaska Expedition with cooperation of Washington Academy of Sciences.

Alaska ... Doubleday, Page & Co. *New York.* — Vol. I. - - < *pp. 1—118:* Narrative of the expedition. By John Burroughs >. *text-figs. 6 col. pl. birds. 1 map. 8vo.*

According to an advertisement on the back of the first title-page, dated July, 1910, the publication of the series of volumes on this expedition, up to the present. printed privately, was transferred to the Smithsonian Institution, and the volumes were therefore provided with the special Smithsonian title-pages.

The expenses of the expedition, which took place in the summer of 1899, were defrayed by Edward H. Harriman, who invited as guests three artists, among whom was L. A. Fuertes, and twenty-five scientists, among whom were John Burroughs, Daniel G. Elliot, A. K. Fisher, Charles A. Keeler, C. Hart Merriam, and Robert Ridgway. The important collections included a series of birds from the coastal region.

The present section of Vol. I contains several particulars which throw light on bird-life. The fine paintings of birds were executed by L. A. Fuertes from living or freshly killed specimens and are excellently reproduced on the plates (three-colour prints and chromo-lithographs, executed by the Heliotype Co., and A. Hoen & Co., Baltimore).

1936. Birds of America ... See Pearson, T. G.

BUTLER, A. G.
[1896—98]. British birds with their nests and eggs. 8 Illustrated by F. W. Frohawk. Brumby & Clarke. *Hull. 6 vols. 4to.* — Vol. I. 1896. *pp. [IV] + 208. 56 pl. birds. egg pl. (col.) I—III.* Vol. II. *[1896—]* 1897. *pp. [IV] + 192. 51 pl. birds. egg pl. (col.) IV—VII.* Vol. III. 1897. *pp. [IV] + 175. 45 pl. birds. egg pl. (col.) VIII—XIII.* Vol. IV. 1897. *pp. [IV] + 219. 55 pl. birds. egg pl. (col.) XIV—XV.* Vol. V. 1898. *pp. [IV] + 178. 62 pl. birds. egg pl. (col.) XVI— XVIII.* Vol. VI. 1898. *pp. [IV] + 252. 49 pl. birds. egg pl. (col.) XIX—XXIV.*

In this work an account is given of the occurrence and distribution of the birds in the British Isles, their habits and their breeding conditions. The text, which has been written for both the scientific and the popular world, is due to several authors, whose contributions are distributed as follows:

Vols. I and II. Order Passeres. By Arthur G. Butler.
Vol. III. Order Picariæ. By Arthur G. Butler. Orders Striges and Accipitres. By Murray A. Mathew. Order Steganopodes. By Henry O. Forbes.
Vol. IV. Orders Herodiones and Odontoglossæ. By Henry O. Forbes. Order Anseres. By John Cordeaux. Orders Columbæ and Pterocletes. By W. B. Tegetmeier.
Vol. V. Orders Gallinæ, Fulicariæ, and Alectorides. By W. B. Tegetmeier. Order Limicolæ. By Henry H. Slater.
Vol. VI. Order Gaviæ. By Henry O. Forbes. Order Pygopodes. By O. V. Aplin. Order Tubinares. By H. A. Macpherson.

H. O. Forbes' contributions are partially written by Mrs. Anna Forbes, as appears from the introduction to the individual sections.

Nearly all Frohawk's drawings of the birds on the 318 plates in black and white are from skins; in many cases, however, they are combined with sketches from life. Three drawings only are executed from mounted specimens. The coloured plates of eggs (chromo-lithographs, Brumby & Clarke, Lithos.) supply for the first time a coloured reproduction of the eggs of the Great Auk (Vol. VI, Pl. 23). In the present copy the number of the coloured plates of eggs in the separate volumes does not agree with the table of contents.

A reprint of the first two volumes with the addition of new plates was issued under the title 'Birds of Great Britain and Ireland. Order Passeres. Illustrated by H. Grönvold and F. W. Frohawk' (London 1907—08, 2 vols., 115 col. pl., large 4to).

Frohawk's plates of the eggs reappear in the author's 'Birds' eggs of the British Isles' (London, 4to, 1904 and later editions); Butler had also issued a book on this subject previously, 'British birds' eggs', etc., (London 1885—86, 38 col. pl., 8vo).

1899. Foreign finches in captivity. Second edition.

By Arthur G. Butler. Illustrated by F. W. Frohawk. Brumby & Clarke. *Hull. pp. [VIII] + VIII + 317. 60 col. pl. large 8vo.*

The first edition of this work on cage-birds was issued in 4to format in 1894—96 with hand-coloured plates by Frohawk. In this edition the plates are executed in chromo-lithography (litho'd by Brumby & Clarke). It is Butler's most important work in this, his favourite, field, and deals with eighty foreign cage-birds, their distribution, appearance, song, and behaviour in captivity, about which so much information is given that on that account alone the work acquires a special importance, though it is not otherwise planned on strictly scientific lines ; for instance, all the birds treated in it are not really finches.

With some alterations the families are arranged in accordance with the 'Catalogue of the birds in the British Museum', 1874—98 (70), and many of the descriptions are slightly altered reproductions of those by R. Bowdler Sharpe.

CABANIS, J. L.

1845—46. Untersuchungen über die Fauna Peruana von J. J. von Tschudi. Ornithologie ... mit Anmerkungen von J. Cabanis. *See Tschudi, J. J. von.*

1853—93. See Journal fuer Ornithologie.

1869. Baron Carl Claus von der Decken's Reisen in Ost-Afrika ... 1859—65. Vol. III ... Erste Abtheilung ... < *pp. 19—52:* Vögel. Bearbeitet von J. Cabanis. Mit ... Tafeln, nach der Natur gezeichnet von M. Th. von Heuglin >. C. F. Winter. *Leipzig. 18 col. pl. (numb. I—XVIII). large 8vo.*

The report, of which a part is cited here, was published in four volumes (in 6) in 1869—79.

In the pages quoted Cabanis describes the birds collected by the expedition, while Finsch and Hartlaub in the next volume on Decken's journeys deal with East African avifauna as a whole (143).

Altogether 126 species are mentioned, some of which are figured on the accompanying beautiful chromo-lithographs (Art. Anst. v. Th. Fischer, Cassel).

CALIFORNIA ACADEMY OF SCIENCES.

1893. Occasional Papers. III. Evolution of the colors of North American land birds. *See Keeler, C. A.*

CALIFORNIA UNIVERSITY. SEMICENTENNIAL PUBLICATIONS.

1918. The game birds of California. Contribution from the University of California, Museum of Vertebrate Zoology. *See Grinnell, J.*

CANADA. DEPARTMENT OF MINES. GEOLOGICAL SURVEY.

1919. Memoir 104. No. 3. Biological series. Birds of Eastern Canada. *See Taverner, P. A.*

CARNEGIE INSTITUTION OF WASHINGTON.

1907. Research in China. Vol. I. Part II. pp. 479 —507: Section V. Zoology. *See Blackwelder, E.*

CASSIN, J.

1853—56. Illustrations of the birds of California, Texas, Oregon, British and Russian America. Intended to contain descriptions and figures of all North American birds not given by former American authors, and a general synopsis of North American ornithology. By John Cassin. 1853—55. J. B. Lippincott & Co. *Phila-delphia. pp. VIII + 298. 50 col. pl. (numb. 1—50). 4to.*

This work was published in ten parts in 1853—55, while the preface, contents, and index did not appear until 1856, the year printed on the title-page. Fasc. 1 was actually issued for the first time in 1852 (588, p. 280 ; 723) with the following title on the paper cover, 'Illustrations of the birds of California, Texas and British and Russian America. Intended to comprise all the species of North America except Mexico, not figured by former American authors, and to serve as a supplement to the octavo edition of Audubon's Birds of America. By John Cassin ... and Henry L. Stevens'.

This part, which contains five plates, drawn and lithographed by Henry L. Stephens, was, however, suppressed, and in the final work, 1853—55, the bird portraits (lithographs coloured by hand) are drawn by Geo. G. White, drawn on stone by Wm. E. Hitchcock, and lithographed, printed, and coloured by J. T. Bowen.

The work was intended by Cassin as a general revision of the ornithology of the United States, and he expresses the hope that he may be able to issue two additional volumes or series ; however, no more than this one volume ever appeared ; in it 50 species are described and figured, while à number of others are treated in the Synopsis of North American birds which is inserted in several places in the text. The book contains a number of data on the life of the birds in nature, based on observations made by different contributors, such as George A. McCall, J. P. McCown, A. L. Heermann, and others.

Cassin is here, in 1854, the first American ornithologist to use trinomials to designate geographical races, the word *Variety,* however, being inserted in front of the third name (874, pp. 72 —73).

The work was re-issued in 1862 and 1865.

1856. Narrative of the expedition of an American **93.** squadron to the China Seas and Japan ... 1852—54, under the command of Commodore M. C. Perry ... Vol. II. < - - *pp. 215—248:* Birds. By John Cassin >. Beverley Tucker. (Senate Ex. Doc., No. 79). *Washington. 6 col. pl. (numb. 1—6). 4to.*

This expedition, the whole report on which was published in three volumes, had not been planned or equipped for exploring or scientific purposes but was intended exclusively for the naval and diplomatic services. Nevertheless, a good deal of material of interest to natural history was collected by different members of the expedition, among whom the artist William Heine deserves special mention as he secured the greater part of the zoological collections. The birds were collected partly in Japan — on Hokkaido — partly in China, the Loo Choo Islands, the islands of Singapore and Ceylon, and on the coast of California. The coloured plates (lithographs coloured by hand) are executed by Wm. E. Hitchcock, Philadelphia.

1858. Reports of explorations and surveys ... for a railroad from the Mississippi River to the Pacific Ocean ... 1853—56. Vol. IX ... Birds. *See Baird, S. F.*

1860. The birds of North America ... *See Baird, S. F.*

CATESBY, M.

1749—76. Sammlung verschiedener ausländischer und seltener Vögel ... [Catesby and Edwards]. *See Seligmann, J. M.*

1754. The natural history of Carolina, Florida, and **94.** the Bahama Islands: containing the figures of birds, beasts, fishes, serpents, insects and plants: particularly the forest-trees, shrubs, and other plants, not hitherto described, or very incorrectly figured by authors. Together with their descriptions in English and French. To which are added, observations on the air, soil, and waters: with remarks upon agriculture, grain, pulse, roots, &c. To the whole is prefixed a new and correct map of the countries treated of. By Mark Catesby.

Revis'd by Edwards. C. Marsh. *London. 2 vols. 109 col. pl. birds. large fol.* Added title. in French. — Vol. I. *pp.* [IV] + VII + 100. 100 col. pl. (birds) (numb. 1—100). Vol. II. *pp.* [IV] + 100 + 20 + [1] + XLIV + [6]. 100 + 20 col. pl. (9 pl. birds (numb. 1, 3, 5, 8, 10, 12—14, 16)). 1 map.

This is a new edition, by Geo. Edwards, of the work which was published for the first time in London in 1731—43. The text is printed in English and French in parallel columns, and gives a brief description of the figures on the plate which bears the number corresponding to the page. On the ornithological plates a plant which constitutes the food of the bird, or with which it has some other connection, is figured in addition to the bird.

The bird portraits of Vol. II are found in an appendix (pp. 1—20). The last section of this volume (pp. I—XLIV) consists of 'An account of Carolina, and the Bahama Islands'.

The drawings for the plates have been executed by Catesby, with a few exceptions from living specimens of the birds; it is almost exclusively the males that are figured, owing to their more generally brilliant plumage. Catesby engraved the plates personally, and he also coloured all the first copies, while the remainder were executed under his personal supervision. A new, third, edition of the work appeared in 1771 (95).

The plates were copied by J. M. Seligmann in his work 'Sammlung verschiedener ausländischer und seltener Vögel', etc., which was issued in several languages. The German edition just mentioned and the French edition are listed in the present catalogue (462 ; 463). Furthermore, a somewhat enlarged Dutch edition of the German adaptation appeared in 1772—81 (462, note).

1768—76. Recueil de divers oiseaux étrangers et peu communs qui se trouvent dans les ouvrages de messieurs Edwards et Catesby ... *See Seligmann, J. M.*

95.   *1771.* The natural history of Carolina, Florida, and the Bahama Islands: containing the figures of birds, beasts, fishes, serpents, insects, and plants: particularly, those not hitherto described, or incorrectly figured by former authors, with their descriptions in English and French. To which is prefixed, a new and correct map of the countries; with observations on their natural state, inhabitants, and productions. By Mark Catesby. Revised by Edwards. To the whole is now added a Linnæan index of the animals and plants. Benjamin White. *London. 2 vols. 109 col. pl. birds. large fol.* Added title in French. — Vol. I. *pp.* ⌊IV⌋ + VII + XLIV + 100 + 2. 100 col. pl. (birds) (numb. 1—100). 1 map. Vol. II. *pp.* [IV] + 120 + [1] + 2. 120 col. pl. (9 pl. birds (numb. 1, 3, 5, 8, 10, 12—14, 16)).

This edition differs from that of 1754 (94) in that the appendix to Vol. II has no separate pagination. Moreover the map and the 'Account of Carolina, and the Bahama Islands', 44 pages, are found in Vol. I of this edition.

CHALLENGER, Voyage of H. M. S.

1880. Report on the birds collected during the voyage of H. M. S. Challenger ... 1873—76. *See Sclater, P. L.*

CHAMBERLAIN, M.

1884—87. See Auk.

CHAPMAN, F. M.

1894—1911. See Auk.

96.   *1917.* Bulletin of the American Museum of Natural History. Vol. XXXVI. Editor J. A. Allen. The distribution of bird-life in Colombia; a contribution to a biological survey of South America. By Frank M. Chapman. Published by order of the Trustees. *New York. pp. X + 729. text-figs. 36 pl. (32 phot. pl., 4 col. pl. birds (numb. XXXVII—XL)). 5 maps. (plates and maps numb. I—XLI). 8vo.*

This volume has been produced on the basis of material collected on eight expeditions sent out by the American Museum in the years 1910—1915.

The first section of the work (pp. 3—169) is more general in character and, including a review of Colombian ornithology deals with the American Museum's expeditions to Colombia, the life-zones of the Colombian Andes, and the various climatic zones of the country and their faunas. The last part of the work consists chiefly of a distributional list of the birds collected (pp. 170—639), in which 1285 species and subspecies are enumerated, or a considerable part of the total number of forms — about 1700 — known from Colombia.

Of the forms listed, twenty-two species, and one hundred and fifteen subspecies are described as new, the majority of them having been treated in previous volumes of the Bulletin.

The coloured plates (three-colour prints) are executed from drawings by L. A. Fuertes, who was a member of two of the expeditions.

1926. Bulletin of the American Museum of Natural History. Vol. LV. The distribution of bird-life in Ecuador. A conrtibution to a study of the origin of Andean bird-life. By Frank M. Chapman. Published by order of the Trustees. *New York. pp. XIII + 784. text-figs. 27 pl. (22 phot. pl., 5 col. pl. birds (numb. XXV—XXIX)). 3 maps. (plates and maps numb. I—XXX). 8vo.*

This work is based on the results of a number of expeditions sent out by the American Museum in the period 1913—1925. Chapman himself took part in several of these expeditions. A large part of the work, however, was carried out by collectors such as George K. Cherrie and others.

Through these expeditions and in other ways the Museum gradually obtained a total of somewhat over 13,500 specimens of the birds of Ecuador.

In the first section of the work (pp. 1—133) subjects of a more general character are treated, such as the history of Ecuadorean ornithology, general climatic conditions, and the life-zones of Ecuador and their bird-life. Part II consists chiefly (pp. 134—702) of a systematic survey of the birds which have hitherto been found in the country. Altogether 1357 species and 151 subspecies are treated, all of which, except 33, are represented in the collections of the Museum.

The coloured plates (three-colour prints), executed from drawings by L. A. Fuertes, show figures of eleven forms.

CHENU, J. C.

[1852—54]. Encyclopédie d'histoire naturelle ... Par Chenu. Oiseaux. Avec la collaboration de M. Des Murs. Marescq et Co. *Paris. 6 vols. text-figs. 240 pl. (numb. 1—40 in each vol.). 4to.*

This is the ornithological section of the large encyclopædia which was issued in altogether 22 volumes and 9 supplementary volumes. It was originally published in 1850—61, several later editions of the different volumes being found.

In each volume, in the section on the birds, of which only a fragment is extant, there are 40 plates, the figures of which are reproduced from plates by Gould and Audubon, and others.

CHERNEL ZU CHERNELHÁZA, S. von.

1916—21. See Aquila.

CHERRIE, G. K.

1930. The birds of Matto Grosso, Brazil ... With field notes by George K. Cherrie. *See Naumburg. E. M. B.*

CHICAGO ACADEMY OF SCIENCES.
1867—69. Transactions of the Chicago Academy of Sciences. Vol. I. Parts I—II. Published by the Academy. *Chicago. 1 vol. 12 col. pl. birds (numb. XVI—XIX, XXVII—XXXIV). 4°.*
The publication of this periodical was stopped in 1870 after the first part of Vol. II had been issued. Ornithological contributions to the present first volume have been made by S. F. Baird and William Stimpson, and others. These two papers are illustrated with plates executed in lithography coloured by hand (Edwin Sheppard del.; Bowen & Co. lith., Phila.).

CHICAGO. FIELD MUSEUM OF NATURAL HISTORY. *See Field Museum of Natural History. Chicago.*

CHILDREN, J. G.
1824—26. See Zoological Journal, The, 1824—35.
1826—35. Illustrations of ornithology ... Vols. I—III. *See Jardine, W.,* 1826—43.

CHUBB, C.
1913. The birds of South America. *See Brabourne, W. W. K.-H., Third Baron,* 1913—17.
1916—21. The birds of British Guiana, based on the collection of Frederick Vavasour McConnell. By Charles Chubb. With a preface by Mrs. F. V. Mc Connell. Bernard Quaritch. *London. 2 vols. 20 col. pl. birds. 8vo.* — Vol. I. 1916. *pp. LIII + 528. text-figs. 27 pl. (10 col. pl. birds (numb. I—X)). 1 map.* Vol. II. 1921. *pp. XCVI + 615. text-figs. 18 pl. (10 col. pl. birds (numb. I—X)).*
McConnell spent several years in British Guiana and, taking a great interest in ornithology, he secured a large collection of the birds of the country, some of which he obtained on two long expeditions to the interior. Death prevented him from completing a catalogue of the collection then in preparation, and Mrs. McConnell induced Ch. Chubb, who had assisted in the working up of the catalogue, to prepare the present work on the basis of the collection; however, its completion was delayed by the War.
Vol. I contains an itinerary, which seems to be due to F. V. McConnell, of the first expedition in 1894, while the itinerary found in Vol. II is concerned with the second expedition, which took place in 1898, and was written by John J. Quelch, one of the members of the expedition.
The work describes families, genera, and species, whose breeding season and range in British Guiana are given. It further contains descriptions of nests and eggs, and accounts of the habits of the birds. The drawings for the coloured plates were executed by H. Grønvold, and are reproduced in Vol. I (chromo-lithographs) by John Bale, Sons, and Danielsson, in Vol. II (three-colour prints) by the Sun Engraving Company.

COLLIN, J. S.
1872—79. Skandinaviens Fugle ... Med over 600 kolorerede Figurer. *See Kjærbølling, N.*
1875—77. Skandinaviens Fugle ... *See Kjærbølling, N.*
1877. Ornithologiske Bidrag til Danmarks Fauna af Jonas Collin. Udgivet som Supplement til 'Skandinaviens Fugle'. L. A. Jørgensen. *Kjøbenhavn. pp. 28. 8vo.*
During his revision of the text for the new edition of Kjærbølling's work (251) Collin had received much information about the occurrence of rare birds. This had come to hand too late that he could not include it in the revised text. These data were therefore published in the present first supplement, in which 102 species are mentioned.

1888. Bidrag til Kundskaben om Danmarks Fugle- 102. fauna. Af Jonas Collin. Udgivet som 2det Supplement til 'Skandinaviens Fugle'. Gyldendal. *Kjøbenhavn. pp. 119. 8vo.*
In this little volume the author gives a series of data on the Danish avifauna which had come to hand since the publication in 1877 of his first supplement to 'Skandinaviens Fugle' (101).
A great part of the matter concerning the 237 species or varieties mentioned had previously been published in other places. It is stated in the preface that a new plate for the atlas (250) is under preparation. This plate was issued the same year (103), and in the text reference is made to its figures.
[1888]. [Ny Tavle (III) til 'Skandinaviens Fugle'. 103. Udgivet af Jonas Collin. (Gyldendal). *Kjøbenhavn]. 1 col. pl. fol.*
This plate (marked 'Ny Tavle III') with figures of four species was issued in connection with the second supplement to Kjærbølling's 'Skandinaviens Fugle' (102), published the same year by Collin. The bird portraits (coloured by hand) were executed in lithography by C. Cordts from drawings by H. Grønvold, whose first work as a bird painter they represent. The total number of Kjærbølling's plates is thus increased to 107. For the other plates, see the works of Kjærbølling (247; 249; 250).
This new plate, the remainder of which is in the possession of a second-hand bookseller in Copenhagen, is not cited in 'Dansk Bogfortegnelse'.
The present copy is bound up with the first edition of Kjærbølling's plates (247).
1895. Faunistiske og biologiske Meddelelser om 104. danske Fugle. Samlede af Jonas Collin. Udgivet som 3die Supplement til 'Skandinaviens Fugle'. Gyldendal. *Kjøbenhavn. pp. [V] + 120 + [4]. 8vo.*
This is the last of Collin's supplements to 'Skandinaviens Fugle', the first of which was issued in 1877 (101) and the second in 1888 (102). It does not differ in construction from its predecessors, the same nomenclature being retained, but in this supplement the Danish vernacular names are given.
Altogether 219 species and varieties are dealt with, but the treatment of the information collected is hardly so critical as in the preceding supplements, a fact noted by Collin himself in the preface.

COLLINS, C.
[1736]. [Twelve engravings of British birds]. Thos. 105. Bowles. *[London]. 12 col. pl. (numb. 1—12). large (obl.) fol.*
These plates (engravings coloured by hand), engraved by H. Fletcher and J. Mynde, contain 115 figures of 58 species of British birds. Each plate shows a picture of a landscape in which are placed 9—11 figures of birds.

CONTRIBUTIONS TO ORNITHOLOGY.
1848—53. Contributions to ornithology for 1848—52. *See Jardine, W.*

COOPER, J. G.
1859. The natural history of Washington Territory, 106. with much relating to Minnesota, Nebraska, Kansas, Oregon, and California, between the thirty-sixth and forty-ninth parallels of latitude, being those parts of the final reports on the survey of the northern Pacific Railroad route, containing the climate and physical geography, with full catalogues and descriptions of the plants and animals collected from 1853 to 1857. By J. G. Cooper and G. Suckley ... < Part III. - - Zoological report. - - *pp. 140—291:* No. 3. Report upon the

15

birds collected on the survey. Chapter I. Land birds, by J. G. Cooper. - - Chapter II. Water birds, by G. Suckley >. Baillière Brothers. *New York. 10 pl. (8 col.) (numb. XI, XVI, XXVIII, XXI, XXIII—XXV, VII, XXXVIII, VIII). 4to.*

The government edition of this work appeared in 1859 as a supplement to Vol. I of the Pacific Railroad Reports (preface p. XII), while at the beginning of the preface the present volume is designated as 'those parts of the eleventh of these reports, which describe the natural condition and products of the country traversed by the Surveying Expedition near the 47th and 49th parallels of latitude'.

The different editions of this work are enumerated in the Catalogue of the Library of the British Museum (Natural History) (552, V, p. 2045).

The present special edition contains a new preface, giving a sketch of the explorations, a classified table of contents, and the latest additions by the authors.

The plates (lithographs coloured by hand) are marked: Bowen & Co. lith. & col. Plates VII and VIII, which are not registered in the list of illustrations, have been prepared for this volume. The exact technical descriptions of the birds are borrowed from those by Baird, Cassin and Lawrence in Vol. IX, Pacific Railroad Reports (22), but the authors, who were the collectors of the party, have added to Baird's scientific descriptions many notes on the habits of the different species. The treatise concludes (pp. 288—291) with a 'List of birds heretofore reported as found in the northwest part of America, but of which no specimens have been procured by recent explorers'.

The volume contains (pp. 391—399) an Index to the zoological report.

The same plates as are found in this work occur in a slightly altered form in Baird, Cassin and Lawrence's 'The birds of North America', 1860 (24).

107.   *1860. Reports of explorations and surveys, to ascertain the most practicable and economical route for a railroad from the Mississippi River to the Pacific Ocean ... 1853—5 ... Vol. XII. Book II. < - - Parts II and III of the narrative and final report by Isaac I. Stevens ... upon the route near the forty-seventh and forty-ninth parallels. - - Zoological report. - - pp. 140—291: No. 3. Report upon the birds collected on the survey. Chapter I. Land birds, by J. G. Cooper. - - Chapter II. Water birds, by G. Suckley >. Thomas H. Ford. (Senate Ex. Doc.), Washington. 8 col. pl. (numb. XI, XVI, XXVIII, XXI, XXIII—XXV, XXXVIII). 4to.*

Another edition of Cooper and Suckley's Birds, which does not contain Plates VII and VIII, found in the special edition of 1859 (106). The two plates occur in a somewhat altered shape in another report of this series issued by A. L. Heermann in 1859 (199).

COQUILLE, LA, Voyage of the [French corvette].
    1826—31. Voyage autour du monde ... sur la corvette ... la Coquille ... 1822—25 ... Zoologie. *See Lesson, R. P.*

CORDEAUX, J.
    1897. British birds with their nests and eggs. Vol. IV. Order Anseres. *See Butler, A. G., 1896—98.*

COUAILHAC, J. J. L.
    1842. Le Jardin des Plantes ... *See Bernard, P.*

COUES, E.
    1874. A history of North American birds. Land birds. [Tables and glossary]. *See Baird, S. F.*
    1884—87. See Auk.

COURCELLES, A. P. J. R. de. *See Knip, A. P. J. R.*

COWARD, T. A.
    1910—13. The British bird book ... *See Kirkman, F. B. B.*
    1920. The birds of the British Isles and their eggs. By T. A. Coward. First series comprising families Corvidæ to Sulidæ. With 242 accurately coloured illustrations by Archibald Thorburn and others reproduced from Lord Lilford's work 'Coloured figures of the birds of the British Islands' and 65 photographic illustrations by Richard Kearton and others. Second impression. Frederick Warne & Co. *London. pp. VII + 376. 159 pl. (numb. 1—159; 96 col.). small 8vo.*

This popular pocket guide to British birds was printed in 1919 and first published in February, 1920, while the second impression dates from March of the same year.

Lord Lilford's work, from which the coloured illustrations of the birds are reproduced, appeared in 1885—98, a second edition in 1891—98 (308). The illustrations of eggs are selected from Hewitson's 'Coloured illustrations of the eggs of British birds', which was first published under this title in 1842—46. A second series of the present work appeared in 1920 (109).

    1920. The birds of the British Isles and their eggs. By T. A. Coward. Second series comprising families Anatidæ to Tetraonidæ. With 213 accurately coloured illustrations by Archibald Thorbrun and others ... and 69 photographic illustrations by E. L. Turner, R. Kearton and others. Frederick Warne & Co. *London. pp. VII + 376. 159 pl. (numb. 1—159; 96 col.) small 8vo.*

The coloured illustrations in this second volume are chiefly due to A. Thorburn. A supplementary volume — third series — comprising migration and habits, and observations on rarer visitants to the British Isles, was issued in 1926, with 69 coloured illustrations by A. Thorburn and others.

CRETZSCHMAR, P. J.
    1826. Atlas zu der Reise im nördlichen Afrika. Erste Abtheilung. Zoologie ... Vögel. Bearbeitet von Ph. J. Cretzschmar. *See Rueppell, É. W. P. S.*

CSÖRGEY, T.
    1905. Ornithologische Fragmente aus den Handschriften von Johann Salamon von Petényi. Deutsch bearbeitet von Titus Csörgey ... *See Petényi, J. S. von.*
    1915, 1922 → *See Aquila.*

CURAÇOA, Voyage of H. M. S.
    1873. Jottings during the cruise of H. M. S. Curaçoa among the South Sea Islands in 1865 ... pp. 353—394: Birds. *See Gray, G. R.*

CUVIER, G. F.
    1816—30. Dictionnaire des sciences naturelles ... *See Dictionaries, 1816—41.*

CUVIER, G. L. C. F. D.
    1801. La Ménagerie du Muséum Nationale d'Histoire Naturelle ... *See Lacépède, B. G. É. de la V.*
    [1827—] 1829. The animal kingdom arranged in conformity with its organization, by the Baron Cuvier, with additional descriptions of all the species hitherto named, and of many not before noticed, by Edward Griffith, and others. Vols. VI—VIII. - - The class aves arranged by the Baron Cuvier, with specific

descriptions by Edward Griffith and Edward Pidgeon. The additional species inserted in the text of Cuvier by John Edward Gray. Whittaker, Treacher, and Co. *London. 3 vols. 8vo.* — Vol. VI. [I]. *pp.* [*VIII*] + *548. text-fig. 32 pl. (28 col.).* Vol. VII. [II]. *pp.* [*VII*] + *586. 60 pl. (57 col.).* Vol. VIII. [III]. *pp.* [*VI*] + *690. 68 pl. (63 col.).*

Cuvier's famous review of the animal kingdom, 'Le règne animal distribué d'après son organisation', etc., appeared for the first time in 1817 (Paris, 4 vols., 2 pl. birds, 8vo) or more correctly at the end of 1816 (571, 18, p. 18), while the second edition was issued in 1829—30 (Paris, 5 vols., 2 pl. birds, 8vo). In this work, based on the author's great knowledge of the structure of recent and fossil animals, the whole animal kingdom is divided into four main groups. As regards the birds, however, the work showed no particular advance. The description of the species was quite brief, and the other information about them is minimum. The present edition, which consists of altogether 16 volumes and one volume 'Index', is the most comprehensive of the English translations. It differs somewhat from the French original, containing, as it does, a great amount of new matter, such as descriptions of species not described by Cuvier and, notably, the large supplements to the different orders or larger groups of them, in which many contributions are made to the illustration of the zoology of birds, especially of their natural habits.

The whole work was issued in parts in 1827—35. It was completed with a volume containing 'A classified index and synopsis of the animal kingdom'. In the alphabetical index the class aves is given on pp. 49—129, while the birds in the section 'A tabular view of the classification of animals' is found on pp. XIII—XXV. A chapter, 'Observations on several of the genera and species of the order Passeres of Cuvier', by William Swainson fills Vol. VIII, pp. 677—690.

The coloured plates (coloured by hand; Griffith and others sc.), each with a single figure of a bird, were executed from drawings by C. Hamilton Smith, H. Kearsley, and others. According to the dates of publication given on them, they were published from November 1, 1827, to January, 1830, and the publication of the three volumes cited here would seem to have been completeed at the end of 1829 or possibly at the beginning of 1830.

1829—38. Iconographie du Règne Animal de Mr. le Baron Cuvier ... *See Guérin-Méneville, F. E.*

[*1838—43*]. Le règne animal distribué d'après son organisation, pour servir de base à l'histoire naturelle des animaux, et d'introduction à l'anatomie comparée, par Georges Cuvier. Edition accompagnée de planches gravées, représentant les types de tous les genres, les caractères distinctifs des divers groupes et les modifications de structure sur lesquelles repose cette classification. Par une réunion de disciples de Cuvier, MM. Audouin, Blanchard, Deshayes, Alcide d'Orbigny, Doyère, Dugès, Duvernoy, Laurillard, Milne Edwards, Roulin et Valenciennes. < - - [II]. Les oiseaux. Avec un atlas, par Alcide d'Orbigny >. Fortin, Masson et Cie. *Paris. 2 vols. in 1. 4to.* — < Texte >. *pp. V* + *370.* < Atlas >. *102 pl. (numb. 1—2, 1—100; 95 col. (numb. 3, 7—100)) with descriptive letterpress.*

This edition, by pupils of Cuvier (the "Disciples' edition"), was published in 1836—49 in 262 livraisons, which together constitute eleven vols. text and eleven vols. atlas with nearly 1000 coloured plates. The section on the birds consists of 27 livraisons, and was supplied, like the other parts, with the plates plain or printed in colours and retouched by hand. Eight of the plates (Vertébrés ovipares 1—2, Oiseaux 1—6) are anatomical, while the remaining plates (numb. 7—100) show coloured portraits of the birds, as well as smaller uncoloured figures of the beaks and feet of birds, their crania and their breastbones. As a rule two birds, more rarely one, are figured on each plate. The figures, printed in beautiful and vivid

colours, are drawn by E. Traviès and engraved by A. Fournier, Guyard, Oudet, and others (N. Rémond imp.).

CYMMRODORION SOCIETY.
1761—66. The British zoology. Class I. Quadrupeds. II. Birds. Published under the inspection of the Cymmrodorion Society ... pp. 57—162: Class II. Birds. *See Pennant, T.*

D'ALEMBERT, J. LE R. *See Alembert, J. Le R. d'.*

DALMAN, J. W.
1825. Svensk zoologi. Part 12. *See Palmstruch, J. W., 1806—25.*

DAM, D. C. van.
1867—68. Recherches sur la faune de Madagascar et de ses dépendances, d'après les découvertes de ... D. C. van Dam. 2me Partie. Mammifères et oiseaux. *See Schlegel, H.*

DANMARK, Danish exploring vessel.
1910. Danmark-Ekspeditionen til Grønlands Nordøstkyst 1906—08 under Ledelse af L. Mylius-Erichsen. Vol. V. The terrestrial mammals and birds of North-East Greenland. pp. 93—199: Birds. *See Manniche, A. L. V.*

DANSKE VIDENSKABERNES SELSKAB. KØBENHAVN.
1772. Vice-Lavmand Eggert Olafsens og Land-Physici Biarne Povelsens Reise igiennem Island, foranstaltet af Videnskabernes Sælskab i Kiøbenhavn ... *See Olafsson, E.*

DARWIN, C. R.
1838—41. The zoology of the voyage of H. M. S. Beagle ... 1832—1836 ... Edited and superintended by Charles Darwin. Part III. Birds. *See Gould, J.*

DAUBENTON, E. L.
1770—86. Histoire naturelle des oiseaux. [Planches enluminées]. *See, Buffon, G. L. L. de.*

DAUBENTON, L. J. M.
1751—77. Encyclopédie, ou dictionnaire raisonné des sciences ... *See Encyclopædias.*

DAUDIN, F. M.
1800. An VIII. Traité élémentaire et complet *112.* d'ornithologie, ou histoire naturelle des oiseaux; Par F. M. Daudin. Chez l'auteur (Vol. II: Buisson). *Paris. 2 vols. 29 pl. 4to.* — Vol. I. *pp. VII* + [*I*] + *9— 474. 8 pl. (numb. 1—8).* Vol. II. *pp. 473. 21 pl. (numb. IX—XXIX).*

The first volume of this work is a general ornithology, which deals with the anatomy, physiology, reproduction, song, and biology of birds, their nomenclature and classification, and also includes a chapter on taxidermy.

The author has based certain sections on data supplied by Cuvier, Duméril, and Dufresne.

The contents of the second volume are of a systematic character.

The plates (engravings) were drawn by Barraband and engraved by Pérée, L. Duval, and several others. The plates

15*

in Vol. I contain anatomical figures (of skeletons), while those in Vol. II contain portraits of birds. The work was also issued with coloured plates.

1802. Histoire naturelle ... Des oiseaux. Vol. LXIV. pp. 159—341: Exposition méthodique d'ornithologie. Méthodes d'ornithologie. Par Brisson, Lacépède, Latham. (Rédigées par F. M. Daudin). *See Buffon, G. L. L. de,* 1800—02.

DAVID, A.
113.   *1877.* Les oiseaux de la Chine. Par Armand David et E. Oustalet. Avec un atlas de ... planches, dessinées et lithographiées par Arnoul et coloriées au pinceau. G. Masson. *Paris. 1 vol. text, 8vo, and 1 vol. Atlas, large 8vo. —* (Texte). *pp. [III] + VII + 573. Atlas. pp. [VI] + [I]. 124 col. pl. (numb. 1—124).*

In this important review of the birds of the Chinese Empire 807 species are dealt with, 249 of which are supposed to be peculiar to the Chinese fauna. The text contains the most important synonyms with a brief description of the birds and remarks on their distribution and other features of their history.

The plates have been printed by Becquet, Paris; they are finely drawn and coloured.

DECKEN, C. C. von der.
1869—70. Baron Carl Claus von der Decken's Reisen in Ost-Afrika ... 1859—65.

Vol. III. 1869. Erste Abtheilung. pp. 19—52: Vögel. *See Cabanis, J.*

Vol. IV. 1870. Die Vögel Ost-Afrikas. *See Finsch, F. H. O.*

DECKER, J. M.
114.   *1774—85.* Naturgeschichte der Vögel aus den besten Schriftstellern [zusammengetragen von J. M. Decker und F. A. Weber] mit Merianischen und neuen Kupfern. - - Naturgeschichte aus den besten Schriftstellern mit Merianischen und neuen Kupfern. Ecke-brecht. *Heilbronn. 12 parts in 2 vols. pp. 1338 + title-pages, preface, and indices. 59 pl. (numb. I—LIX) fol.*

Issued in parts with a continuous pagination. Each part has a separate title-page, from which the latter of the above titles is taken, and is provided with an index of the names of the birds treated in it.

The publishers owned Merian's plates to Johnstone's 'Historiæ naturalis', etc., an edition of which they had issued (237). These old copperplates were then printed again, while Johnstone's text, which must have appeared too obsolete, was replaced by a compilation of more recent authors of natural science.

This whole 'Naturgeschichte' was issued in 1772—85, and, in addition to birds, treats also of quadrupeds, trees, and butterflies, the last section, however, being provided with 'ganz neuen Kupfern', while the plates in the chapter on birds — as in the section on quadrupeds — are in all essentials the same as those found in Johnstone's work; they have, however, been renumbered, some few new figures have been added, while others, notably of fabulous birds, have been omitted. The frontispiece is identical with the corresponding one in the editions of Johnstone's 'Historiæ naturalis de avibus', 1650 (234) and 1756 (237).

The text of Parts 1—8 in the section on birds is stated to have been written by J. M. Decker (618, II, p. 294), who also wrote the text of the section on the quadrupeds, while the text of the last parts is stated to have been prepared by F. A. Weber (617, X, p. 793). The main source of this is Buffon's 'Histoire naturelle des oiseaux', whose text has been abridged by the compilers, the remaining portion having been sometimes altered, though in many cases it has been translated literally.

However, the authors have had recourse to other sources also, notably Brisson.

Such a procedure, combined with the re-issue of the obsolete figures of the old plates, must necessarily provoke criticism, which indeed did not fail to appear (see e. g. Allgemeine deutsche Bibliothek, 46, 1781, p. 220, and Anhang 3, 1785, pp. 1679 —1680).

DE KAY, J. E.
1844. Natural history of New York. D. Appleton & Co. *New York. 1843.* - - Zoology of New-York, or the New-York fauna; comprising detailed descriptions of all the animals hitherto observed within the State of New-York, with brief notices of those occasionally found near its borders, and accompanied by appropriate illustrations. By James E. De Kay. Part II. Birds. Printed by Carroll and Cook. *Albany. 1844. pp. XII + 380 + [1]. 141 col. pl. (numb. 1—141). 4to.*

The entire work on the natural history of New York consists, in the present copy, of 30 volumes (in 28), which were issued in 1842—94 [1895]. The zoology (6 vols. in 5) was written by De Kay, and appeared in 1842—44.

The present ornithological part contains a systematic survey of the species of birds, with synonyms, characteristics, descriptions, and remarks on the geographical distribution, habits, and occurrence in the state under consideration, together with brief diagnoses of genera, families, and orders.

On each of the hand-coloured plates (Lith. of Endicott, New York; Pls. 9 (?), 10, 53, and 76: V. Balch sc.) are figured two or three species drawn by J. W. Hill. Some of Hill's original water-colour drawings for this work are now in the Edward E. Ayer Ornithological Library of the Field Museum of Natural History, Chicago.

DERBY, E. S. S., Thirteenth Earl of.
1846. Gleanings from the menagerie and aviary at Knowsley Hall. *See Gray, J. E.*

DERHAM, W.
1738. A natural history of birds ... To which are added, notes and observations by W. Derham. *See Albin, F.*

1750. Histoire naturelle des oiseaux ... augmentée de notes & de remarques curieuses, par W. Derham. *See Albin, E.*

DESMAREST, A. G.
1805 [—07]. An XIII. Histoire naturelle des tangaras, des manakins et des todiers, par Anselme-Gaëtan Desmarest; Avec figures imprimées en couleur, d'après les dessins de Mademoiselle Pauline de Courcelles, élève de Barraband. Garnery. *Paris. pp. [V] + 8 + [68] + 12 + [48]. 72 col. pl. large fol.*

This work was published in 12 livraisons, the first four of which, according to Sherborn (583, Sectio II, I, 1922, p. XLIII), appeared in 1805, the next six in 1806, and the last two in 1807. The contents of the plates and text of the different livraisons are given on the last printed leaf of the volume in an 'Avis servant de table'.

Under the individual forms figured on the beautifully executed plates the text contains a diagnosis in French and Latin, further synonyms, a description, brief or long, information of the geographical occurrence and other data of interest.

DES MURS, M. A. P. Œ.
1852—54. Encyclopédie d'histoire naturelle ... Oiseaux. *See Chenu, J. C.*

DEUTSCHE ORNITHOLOGEN-GESELL-SCHAFT.

1850—58. See Naumannia.
1854—58. See Journal fuer Ornithologie. Jahrgang II—VI.

DEUTSCHE ORNITHOLOGISCHE GESELL-SCHAFT.

1868—75, 1896 →See Journal fuer Ornithologie. Jahrgang XVI—XXIII, XLIV →

DICTIONARIES.

1803—04. An XI—XII. Nouveau dictionnaire d'histoire naturelle, appliquée aux arts, principalement à l'agriculture et à l'économie rurale et domestique. Par une société de naturalistes et d'agriculteurs. Avec des figures tirées des trois règnes de la nature. Deterville. *Paris. 24 vols. plates. 8vo.*

The present, first, edition of this work was issued with 'Discours préliminaire' by J. J. Virey, who in collaboration with Sonnini treated the subjects: l'homme, les quadrupèdes, les oiseaux, les cétacés.

The ornithological plates were drawn by Deseve, some few by J. G. Prêtre, and engraved by Tardieu, Letellier, Voysard, and others. An atlas comprising 236 coloured plates in 4to was published in 1805 (564, I, 1846, p. 161).

A new edition of this dictionary was issued in 1816—19 in 36 volumes, 8vo.

1816—41. Dictionnaire des sciences naturelles, dans lequel on traite méthodiquement des différens êtres de la nature ... Suivi d'une biographie des plus célèbres naturalistes ... Par plusieurs professeurs du Jardin du Roi, et des principales écoles de Paris. F. G. Levrault. *Strasbourg. 1816—30. 60 vols. plates. 8vo.*
— Supplément. Ch. Pitois. *Paris. 1840—41. 1 vol. plates. 8vo.*

The first five volumes and some few copies of Vol. VI of this 'Dictionary' were published in 1804—06. By means of supplements, to be found at the end of each of the volumes, these first volumes were brought up-to-date in the present edition, and the work was concluded, after which supplements were again added from 1840.

Of this later supplement a copy is at hand (Tome I (A-Aye)), dated 1840, while there is another copy (Tome I (A-Aye + A-Bel)) in an original paper-cover dated 1841. The plates in the supplement appeared in two livraisons, of ten plates each. The ornithological plates in this supplement were drawn by J. G. Prêtre and engraved by Pardinel and Visto.

The plates for the work, which — apart from the supplements — were published under the superintendence of Turpin in 61 cahiers of 20 plates each, were also issued in colour, and copies with double figures and a few with the plates in 4to are found. In the present copy only a fraction of the total number of plates is found, including 79 with figures of birds. Like those of the 'Dictionary', they have been drawn by Prêtre but engraved by Coutant, Guyard, Massard, and others.

The editor of the work proper was Fréd. Cuvier, while the supplement was edited by Ducrotay de Blainville assisted by P. Gervais.

Among the collaborators was Georges Cuvier, who wrote a 'Prospectus' for it. Charles Dumont was the ornithological collaborator.

Copies of some of the plates were issued in 1835—44 by J. F. Schouw and D. F. Eschricht (136).

DIDEROT, D.

1751—77. Encyclopédie, ou dictionnaire raisonné des sciences ... *See Encyclopædias.*

DISCOVERY. Antarctic Expedition.

1907. National Antarctic Expedition 1901—04. Natural history. Vol. II. Zoology. II. Aves. *See Wilson, E. A.*

DIXON, C.

1909. The bird-life of London. By Charles Dixon. **119.** With illustrations in colour and black and white. William Heinemann. *London. pp. XII + 335. 24 pl. (8 col.). 8vo.*

A popular account, based on observation of the bird-life of London for many years. The species dealt with are all that are found resident within the fifteen-mile radius, all that visit the area either as summer or winter guests, and finally the casual wanderers that occur at irregular intervals. The pictures of the birds (three-colour prints) were drawn by John Duncan.

DOFLEIN, F. J. T.

1910—14. Tierbau und Tierleben ... *See Hesse, R.*

D'ORBIGNY, A. D. *See Orbigny, A. D. d'.*

DRESSER, H. E.

1871—96. A history of the birds of Europe, in- **120.** cluding all the species inhabiting the western Palæarctic region. By H. E. Dresser. Published by the author. *London. 9 vols. 722 pl. (720 col.). large 4to.* — Vols. I—VIII. 1871—81 [—82]. 84 parts. 633 pl. (numb. consecutively in the indices; 631 col.). — Vol. I. pp. XIII + XLVI + 102. Vol. II. pp. VIII + [644]. text-figs. 95 col. pl. (Nos. 1—95). Vol. III. pp. VIII + [620]. text-figs. 86 col. pl. (Nos. 96—181). Vol. IV. pp. VIII + [635]. text-figs. 92 col. pl. (Nos. 182—273; 91 col. (Nos. 182—261, 263—273)). Vol. V. pp. VIII + [668]. text-figs. 90 col. pl. (Nos. 274—363). Vol. VI. pp. VIII + [708]. text-figs. 92 col. pl. (Nos. 364—455). Vol. VII. pp. VIII + [660]. text-figs. 89 pl. (Nos. 456—544; 88 col. (Nos. 456—484, 486—544)). Vol. VIII. pp. VIII + [666]. text-figs. 89 col. pl. (Nos. 545—633). Vol. IX. Supplement. 1895—96. pp. XXV + [441]. 89 col. pl. (numb. 634—722).*

The first part of this monumental work was issued in March, 1871, and the publication of the 84 parts constituting the eight volumes of which the original work consisted seems, in spite of the dates on the title-pages, not to have been finished until 1882 (574, p. 179; Parts 83 and 84 were reviewed in the 'Ibis', July 1882). The supplementary volume was issued in nine parts, from January, 1895, to November 1896.

The plates in Vols. II—VIII are unnumbered, and the text is without continuous pagination; the pages and numbers in the above collation are therefore cited from the indices.

Publication originally took place in co-operation with R. B. Sharpe; however, he assisted only in the preparation of the first twelve parts, although his name was retained on the title pages of the parts up to Part 17; but he also prepared the synonymy for Part 13 before his partnership with Dresser was dissolved. Part of the synonymy was elaborated by Lord Walden (the Marquis of Tweeddale).

The entire work, including the supplement, deals with 736 species. The drawings for the plates were executed chiefly by J. G. Keulemans, though Joseph Wolf drew a number of the birds, some few were drawn by E. Neale and some in the supplement by A. Thorburn. The plates (lithographs coloured by hand) were printed by M. and N. Hanhart, Walter, and Mintern Brothers, and the colouring was entrusted to Mr. Smith and W. Hart, while the hand-colouring of the plates in the supplement was executed by H. Piffaretti.

A selection of the plates was reproduced in Bonhote's 'Birds of Britain', 1907 (50).

1876. Reprint of Eversmann's Addenda ad celeberrimi Pallasii Zoographiam Rosso-Asiaticam. *See Eversmann, E. F.*

121.   [*1905*—] *1910.* Eggs of the birds of Europe, including all the species inhabiting the western Palæarctic area. By H. E. Dresser. Published by the author at the office of the Royal Society for the Protection of Birds. *London. 2 vols. 4to.* — Vol. I. Letter-press. *pp. XX + 837. text-figs.* Vol. II. Plates. *106 col. pl. with explanation. Wrappers.*

The text of this work, which is a kind of continuation of the author's 'Birds of Europe', 1871—96 (120), has references to figures in other publications, states the vernacular names of the birds, discusses their breeding ranges, habits, notes and times of incubation, describes their nests, which are often figured from photographs, and their eggs.

According to the original covers of the numbers, the work was issued in 24 parts, which appeared from August, 1905, to November, 1910.

The letterpress up to p. 505 requires to be rearranged and repaged throughout according to the full table of the contents in Volume I.

The plates have been executed by the three-colour photographic process direct from the eggs, without the intervention of an artist, by André and Sleigh, and are fine examples of the efficiency of this procedure.

Subsequently twenty-two of the plates were used in H. Kirke Swann's 'A synopsis of the Accipitres', etc., 1921—22 (497).

DREYER, J. W.
   1900—04. Vor Klodes Dyr. *See Bøving-Petersen, J. O.*

DUBOIS, A. J. C.
122.   *1905.* État indépendant du Congo. Annales du Musée du Congo. Publiées par ordre du secrétaire d'état. Zoologie. Série IV. Remarques sur l'ornithologie de l'État indépendant du Congo suivies d'une liste des espèces recueillies jusqu'ici dans cet état. Par Alph. Dubois. Vol. I. Fasc. I. Spineux et Cie. *Bruxelles. pp. [VII] + 36. text-fig. 12 col. pl. (numb. I—XII). large 4to.*

In the first section of this work ('Partie descriptive') a number of new or but slightly known species and subspecies are described; four species are listed as new.

In the last section ('Relevé des oiseaux observés dans l'État indépendant du Congo') 483 species and subspecies, found in the collections of the Musée du Congo at Tervueren, or in Musée Royal d'Histoire Naturelle de Belgique, are listed in systematical order with indication of their localities.

The plates (three-colour prints) are beautifully executed (Établts. Jean Malvaux sc.) from originals by L. Cuvelier.

DU BUS DE GISIGNIES, B. L.
123.   *1845—48.* Esquisses ornithologiques; descriptions et figures d'oiseaux nouveaux ou peu connus; par Bernard Du Bus. A. Vandale (Part IV: C. Muquardt). *Bruxelles. 4 parts in 1 vol. 20 col. pl. large 4to.* — Part I. 1845. *pp. [12]. 5 col. pl. (numb. 1—5).* Part II. 1846. *pp. [12]. 5 col. pl. (numb. 6—10).* Part III. 1847. *pp. [14]. 5 col. pl. (numb. 11—15).* Part IV. 1848. *pp. [12]. 5 col. pl. (numb. 16—20).*

The four livraisons cited here contain all that was published of the text for this work. Seventeen additional plates were, however, issued up to 1850.

The plates are executed in lithography coloured by hand, chiefly by G. Severeyns, some few, however, by J. Dekeghel.

DUCROTAY DE BLAINVILLE, H. M. *See Blainville, H. M. D. de.*

DUMONT DE SAINTE-CROIX, C. H. F.
   1816—41. Dictionnaire des sciences naturelles ... [Oiseaux]. *See Dictionaries.*

DUMONT D'URVILLE, J. S. C.
   1830—33. Voyage de ... l'Astrolabe ... 1826—29, sous le commandement de J. Dumont d'Urville. Zoologie. Oiseaux. *See Quoy, J. R. C.*

DUPERREY, L. I.
   1826—31. Voyage autour du monde ... sur la corvette ... la Coquille ... 1822—25. Par L. I. Duperrey. Zoologie. *See Lesson, R. P.*

EDWARDS, A. MILNE. *See Milne Edwards, A.*

EDWARDS, G.
   1743—51. A natural history of birds. Most of 1 which have not been figur'd or describ'd, and others very little known from obscure or too brief descriptions without figures, or from figures very ill design'd ... By George Edwards. Printed for the author. *London. 4 vols. 189 col. pl. birds. fol.* — Vol. I. 1743. *pp. XXIV + 1—53. 52 col. pl. (numb. 1—52; 50 pl. birds).* Vol. II. 1747. *pp. IV + 53—128 + LIII—CV + 26. 56 pl. (54 col. (front. + Nos. 53—105); 50 pl. birds).* Added title-page in French, dated 1748. Vol. III. 1750. *pp. [IV] + 106—157. 52 col. pl. (numb. 106—157).* Vol. IV. 1751. *pp. [VIII] + 158—248. 53 col. pl. (numb. 158—210; 37 pl. birds).*

A work in four parts, whose title is here cited from the title-page of Part I. A general title to the four parts is cited as 'A natural history of uncommon birds, and of some other rare and undescribed animals', etc. Two editions of the work are said to have been issued with the same dates on the title-pages. The author's 'Gleanings of natural history' (126) is a sequel to it, the two books constituting a work of seven parts, which was re-issued in 1802—05.

In addition to the plates and the accompanying text Part I contains a dedication, a preface, addenda, 'Names of the generous encouragers of this work', and, on p. 53, a catalogue of the names of the birds. In Part II there is also a dedication, to the foregoing work, by way of illustration', and on pp. 125 —128, a catalogue of the names of the birds, etc., mentioned 'in this work', in Latin and English. Pp. LIII—CV and the last 26 pages of Vol. II contain a French translation of Part II (125). In Part III is found an advertisement concerning the continuation of the work, while Part IV, in addition to the zoological text, contains a preface, and the names of the 'encouragers of this work', which have been added since the publication of the former parts, 'A brief and general idea of drawing' (pp. 212—217), 'Some thoughts on the passage of birds' (pp. 218—220), additions, instructions for etching and engraving, and finally 'A catalogue of the names of all the birds, beasts, etc., contained in the four parts of this Natural history, ranged in a generical order' and 'A catalogue of the names of the birds, beasts, etc., described in the third and fourth parts of this work; in Latin and English'.

A list of the species treated in this work, with English and Latin names, was issued by Linnæus, 1776 (311).

The plates are executed from drawings by Edwards himself, who also himself engraved and for the most part coloured them. Among the figures may be noted the first good coloured plate of the Great Auk (Pl. 147).

Edwards' plates were later copied by Seligmann in the work 'Sammlung verschiedener ausländischer und seltener Vögel', etc., which was issued in several languages. In the present catalogue the above-mentioned German edition is listed, as well as the French one (462; 463). In 1772—81 a somewhat enlarged Dutch edition of the German adaptation was issued (462, note).

1745—51. Histoire naturelle de divers oiseaux, qui n'avoient point encore été figurez ni décrits, ou qui n'étoient que peu connus d'après des descriptions obscures ou abrégées sans figures, ou d'après des figures mal dessinées ... Par George Edwards. Traduit de l'anglois par M. D. de la S. R. Imprimé pour l'auteur. *Londres. 4 parts in 2 vols. 189 col. pl. birds. fol. General title to the 4 parts, in Vol. I:* Histoire naturelle d'oiseaux peu communs: et d'autres animaux rares & qui n'ont pas été décrits, consistant en quadrupèdes, reptiles, poissons, insectes, etc. représentés sur cent dix planches en taille douce, avec une ample & exacte description de chaque figure. A laquelle on a ajouté quelques reflexions sur les oiseaux de passage; & un supplément à plusieurs des sujets qui sont décrits dans cet ouvrage. En quatre parties. Par George Edwards. Imprimé pour l'auteur. *Londres. 1751.* — Part I. 1745. *pp. [VIII] + XXI + I—LII + [1]. 54 pl. (53 col. (front. + Nos. 1—52); 50 pl. birds).* Part II. 1748. *pp. [IV] + LIII—CV + 26. 53 col. pl. (numb. 53—105; 50 pl. birds).* Part III. 1751. *pp. [VII] + CVI—CLVII. 53 pl. (52 col. (numb. 106—157)).* Part IV. 1751. *pp. [III] + CLVIII—CCX + 211— 236. 53 col. pl. (numb. 158—210; 37 pl. birds).*
This translation of Edwards' 'A natural history of birds' (124) was made by David Durand, and deviates somewhat from the English original published in 1743—51. Part I contains an engraved portrait of Edwards, dated 1763 (Gosset, Cerâ delin., J. Miller sc.), and the coloured frontispiece, which is found in Part II of the above-mentioned copy of the English edition. The portrait of the Samoyed is lacking in Part II, while in Vol. II (Part III) there is an engraved portrait of Edwards, dated 1754 (Dandridg pinx, J. S. Miller sculp.). The 'idea of drawing' and the instructions for etching and engraving are lacking in Part IV. A sequel to this French edition is found in the author's 'Gleanings of natural history', 1758—64 (126).

1749—76. Sammlung verschiedener ausländischer und seltener Vögel ... [Catesby and Edwards]. *See Seligmann, J. M.*

1754. The natural history of Carolina, Florida, and the Bahama Islands ... By Mark Catesby. Revis'd by Edwards. *See Catesby, M.*

1758—64. Gleanings of natural history, exhibiting figures of quadrupeds, birds, insects, plants, etc. most of which have not, till now, been either figured or described. With descriptions of ... different subjects, designed, engraved, and coloured after nature, on ... copper-plate prints. By George Edwards. Printed for the author. *London. 3 vols. 128 col. pl. birds. fol. Added title-page in French.* — Vol. I. 1758. *pp. [VII] + 1—108. 51 pl. (50 col. (numb. 211—60); 37 pl. birds).* Vol. II. 1760. *pp. [XII] + XXXV + 109— 220. 50 col. pl. (numb. 261—310; 41 pl. birds).* Vol. III. 1764. *pp. [VIII] + VII + 221—347. 52 col. pl. (numb. 311—362). 50 pl. birds).*
The text of this work is printed in English and French in parallel columns. Parts I and II have been translated from the English by J. Du Plessis, Part III by Edmond Barker. The numbers of the plates are in continuation of the numbers in 'A natural history of birds', 1743—51 (124), the two works together being thought to constitute a work in seven parts. At the end of Part II there is a catalogue in English, French, and Latin, arranged according to the numbers of the plates

and giving the names of the birds, beasts, fishes, insects, etc., figured in the Gleanings; it is continued at the end of Part III, where it is followed by 'A catalogue of the names of the birds, beasts, fishes, insects, plants, etc. contained in Edward's [sic] Natural history of birds, and his Gleanings of natural history, in a generical order'.
A list of the species dealt with in this work. with English and Latin names, was issued by Linnæus in 1776 (311).
The majority of the plates were drawn and engraved on the copper plates direct from the natural objects they represent; many of them are coloured after nature.
For some of the plates, nearly all of which were engraved by Edwards himself, use was made of pictures from the collection of drawings of Indian animals and plants which Gideon Loten had had executed in India, nearly all of which are due to the native artist P. C. de Bevere.
Another edition of this work is said to have been issued with some alterations in the text, but with unaltered title-pages, while a third edition was issued together with 'A natural history of birds', 1802—05. In Vol. I of the present copy the engraved portrait of Edwards in 1754 and the following dedication are found: 'To Miss Crisp Present from her Most Humble Servant the Author'.
The plates of this work were copied in J. M. Seligmann's 'Sammlung verschiedener ausländischer und seltener Vögel', etc., which was issued in several languages. In the present catalogue the above-mentioned German edition is listed, as well as the French one (462; 463). A somewhat enlarged Dutch edition of the German adaptation was issued in 1772—81 (462, note).
A kind of supplement to the 'Gleanings' and its precursor was issued by Peter Brown under the title 'New illustrations of zoology', 1776 (72).

1768—76. Recueil de divers oiseaux étrangers et peu communs qui se trouvent dans les ouvrages de messieurs Edwards et Catesby ... *See Seligmann, J. M.*

1771. The natural history of Carolina, Florida, and the Bahama Islands ... By Mark Catesby. Revised by Edwards. *See Catesby, M.*

1776. [Supplement to Edwards' Natural history]. *See Brown, P.*

1776. A catalogue of the birds, beasts, fishes, insects, plants, &c. contained in Edwards's Natural history. *See Linnæus, C.*

1776. Some memoirs of the life and works of **127.** George Edwards. (Addenda. [A reprint of the papers which he communicated to the Royal Society]). J. Robson. *London. pp. 38. 5 pl. (3 fold.; 2 pl. birds). 4to.*
Pp. 1—26 contain a biographical sketch of Edwards, which must be ascribed to the bookseller James Robson who on May 1, 1769, bought all the remaining copies of Edwards' Natural History, together with all his copperplates, letterpress, and every article in Edwards' possession relative to it. The purpose of the work was to serve as a supplement to Edwards' Natural History; the last section, pp. 27—38, contains in addition to the reprints two addenda to the accounts of the objects on Plates 211 and 212 in the 'Gleanings of natural history', 1758—64 (126), and a brief addition to Linnæus' 'Catalogue of the birds ... contained in Edwards's Natural History', 1776 (311). One of the plates is Miller's engraving of Edwards, dated 1754, while the remaining plates, which are of a zoological character, were engraved by J. Lodge from drawings by Edwards.

ELLIOT, D. G.

[*1864—*] *1865.* A monograph of the Tetraoninæ, **128.** or family of the grouse. By Daniel Giraud Elliot. Published by the author. *New York. pp. [XX] + [50]. 27 col. pl. (numb. I—XXVII in 'List of plates'; 2 pl. eggs). large fol.*
In this monograph, which was published in five parts, the first two of which appeared in 1864, 25 forms are treated in

figures and text. The latter contains synonyms, data on the geographical distribution and the habits of the birds, illustrated by quotations from other authors, and most often a description of the birds and their different plumages.

The plates are executed in lithography coloured by hand (Bowen & Co. lith. et col. Philada), the bird portraits from drawings by the author and a single plate (Falcipennis Hartlaubii: Pl. XI) from a drawing by J. Wolf. The two plates with figures of eggs (Pl. XXVI & XXVII, numb. on plates: I—II) were executed from drawings by William S. Morgan. The drawings of birds were lithographed by C. F. Tholey.

129.　　[*1866*—] *1869.* The new and heretofore unfigured species of the birds of North America. By Daniel Giraud Elliot. Published by the author. *New York.* 2 vols. *in 1. large fol.* — Vol. I. *pp. [XXXI]* + [57]. *text-figs.* 29 col. pl. (numb. I—XXIX). Vol. II. pp. [IV] + [87]. text-figs. 43 col. pl. (numb. XXX—LXXII).

This work is probably intended to be a kind of supplement or sequel to Wilson's 'American ornithology', 1808—14 (533), and Audubon's 'The birds of America', 1827—38 (17), and gives life-size representations of various little known species of the birds of North America.

It was published in 15 parts, of which I and II appeared in 1866; III—VIII in 1867; IX—XII in 1868; and XIII—XV in 1869.

In the introduction a 'recapitulation of the birds necessary to be considered in this work' is given, in which 114 forms are cited, or 33 more than are contained in the text itself.

In the latter, synonymy, remarks on the geographical distribution and the habits of the birds, and a brief description are given under the individual forms figured.

The plates are executed in lithography coloured by hand (Bowen & Co. lith. & col. Philada.) from drawings chiefly by the author and by J. Wolf, a single one by Edwin Sheppard. According to the signatures, some of the plates were lithographed by C. F. Tholey.

130.　　[*1870*—] *1872.* A monograph of the Phasianidæ, or family of the pheasants. By Daniel Giraud Elliot. Published by the author. *New York.* 2 vols. 81 pl. (numb. in 'List of plates'; 79 col.). large fol. — Vol. I. pp. [III] + XXX + [IX] + [76]. 33 pl. (Nos. I—XXXII, XXIXbis; 31 col. (Nos. III—XXXII, XXIX bis)). Vol. II. pp. [III] + [109]. 48 col. pl. (Nos. I—XLVII, XIIIbis).

This monograph was published in six parts from June, 1870, to October, 1872.

The introduction (Vol. I, pp. V—XXX) gives a general account of the bird group in question, a statement of the literature of the family (pp. VII—XII), a treatment of the classification, genera, geographical distribution, and refers briefly to the rearing of young pheasants. Under the individual forms we also find synonymy, mostly information about the habits of the birds with quotations from other authors, their geographical distribution, and description.

The beautiful coloured plates, which are among the best ever produced for Elliot's monographs, are executed in lithography coloured by hand. (J. Wolf & J. Smit, or: J. Wolf & J. G. Keulemans del. & lith.; some: M. & N. Hanhart imp., others: P. W. M. Trap, Leiden, exc.). The colouring was done by J. D. White.

Wolf's 79 original charcoal drawings for the plates of this work are now in the Blacker Library of Zoology, McGill University, Montreal (588, pp. 331 and 505).

131.　　1873. A monograph of the Paradiseidæ, or birds of paradise. By Daniel Giraud Elliot. Printed for the subscribers by the author. [*London*]. *pp.* XXXII + [I] + [87]. 37 pl. (numb. I—XXXVII in 'List of plates'; 36 col. (Nos. II—XXXVII)). large fol.

This monograph was published in seven parts. The introduction (pp. IX—XXVIII) consists of a general account of the group under headings such as 'Literature of the family' (pp. IX—XV), 'Classificatio', 'Genera', 'Review of the family', and 'Geographical distribution'.

In the text accompanying the plates synonymy, information

about the habits and geographical distribution of the birds, and a description, are given under each form.

The beautiful plates were executed in lithography coloured by hand (M. & N. Hanhart imp.) from drawings by J. Wolf. The drawings are lithographed by J. Smit, and the colouring of the plates was done by J. D. White.

1874. The life and habits of wild animals ... *See Wolf, Joseph.*

ENCYCLOPÆDIAS.

1751—77. Encyclopédie, ou dictionnaire raisonné des sciences, des arts et des métiers par une société de gens de lettres. Mis en ordre & publié par Diderot; & quant à la partie mathématique par D'Alembert ... Briasson. *Paris.* (Supplément: M. Rey. *Amsterdam*). *28 vols. (11 vols. pl.)* + *5 suppl. vols. (1 vol. pl.). fol.* — Recueil de planches ... avec leur explication. Vol. VI. 1768. - - < Histoire naturelle. Suite du règne animal. Oiseaux >. *pp. 11. 22 pl. (numb. XXX—Lbis).*

A 'Table analytique et raisonnée des matières' (by Mouchon) to this immense Encyclopædia was issued in 1780 (2 vols., fol.).

Several expert collaborators were connected with this great literary undertaking, for instance natural history was treated, notably by L. J. M. Daubenton and Chevalier de Jaucourt. Brisson's classification of the birds is followed in the atlas, for the plates of which (Benard fecit) the drawings were executed by Martinet, as far as possible from life.

1770—80. Encyclopédie, ou dictionnaire universel raisonné des connoissances humaines. Mis en ordre par de Felice. *Yverdon. 58 vols. (10 vols. pl.). 4to.* — Planches. Vol. VI. 1777. - - < I. Histoire naturelle >. *pp. 48. 29 pl. birds (numb. 31—59).*

This is a rather inaccurate edition of Diderot's and d'Alembert's great Encyclopædia which appeared in 1751—77 (132), revised and enlarged by Professor de Felice and others.

The plates (engravings) are not signed.

1782—1823. Encyclopédie méthodique, ou par ordre de matières; par une société de gens de lettres, de savans et d'artistes. Précédée d'un vocabulaire universel. - - Histoire naturelle des animaux. Panckoucke (from 1792: Veuve Agasse). *Paris. 4to.* — Vol. I. 1782. - - < pp. 321—691: Ornithologie, par Mauduyt >. Vol. II. 1784. - - < pp. 1—544: [Oiseaux] >.
— Tableau encyclopédique et méthodique des trois règnes de la nature. Ornithologie. Par Bonnaterre, et continuée par L. P. Vieillot. 1790—1823. 4 vols. 4to. — Vol. I. 1790 [—1820]. *pp. XCVII + 1—402.* Vol. II. [1820—]1823. *pp. 403—902.* Vol. III. 1823. *pp. 903—1460.* Vol. IV. [1790—] 1823. Planches. *240 pl. (numb. 1—240).*

The ornithological section of this immense undertaking (comprising altogether 205 parts in 196 vols., published 1782—1812), whose only rival is Ersch and Gruber's unfinished German Encyclopædia, was originally evolved by P. J. E. Mauduyt de la Varenne.

The later revision by Bonnaterre and Vieillot has the character of an independent work, of which Bonnaterre issued the plates (to No. 230?) and the text in Vol. I up to p. 320. After Bonnaterre's death Vieillot completed the work during the years 1820—23, and published the remaining part of the text and possibly the last ten plates, representing birds not known till after 1800.

According to Sherborn and Woodward (870) the part of the work issued by Bonnaterre is in livraisons 37, 38, 40, 47, and 51, which appeared in 1790—91 [—92], while the part by Vieillot is in livraisons 89, 91, and 93, which appeared in [1820] 1821—23. According to an 'Avis' at the beginning of the volumes, that, with the plates should contain seven anatomical plates from Recueil des planches, Vol. VII, livraison

32, ('Méthode pour la connoissance des oiseaux par le bec et par les pattes'), which correspond to the section 'Sur la nature des oiseaux' in Mauduyt's work ('Histoire naturelle', Vol. I).

The plates (engravings) each contain four or more portraits of birds; most of them (1—230) are marked: Benard direxit, the remainder: Deseve del. et dir., Barrois, Pierron, Mlle Cornu, Drouet sc.

35. [*1788*—]*1797*. Encyclopædia Britannica; or, a dictionary of arts, sciences, and miscellaneous literature ... The third edition ... A Bell and C. Macfarquhar. *Edinburgh. 20 vols. 45 pl. birds. 4to.*

The first edition of this famous Encyclopædia appeared in 1768—71 and consisted of 3 vols. in quarto, while the second edition was issued in 1777—84 and occupied ten quarto vols.

The publication of the present edition (18 vols. text, 542 plates in two vols.) was begun in 1788 and was completed in 1797. A supplement in two volumes was issued in 1801. In this, as in the previous editions, the plates (engravings) whose bird portraits are of no very great value, were engraved by A. Bell, one of the original owners of this valuable asset, while Colin MacFarquhar was the editor until his death in 1793, when Vol. 12 was almost completed, after which Bell appointed George Gleig editor.

Much useful information is stated to have been communicated occasionally by the ornithologist John Latham.

1852—*54.* Encyclopédie d'histoire naturelle ... Oiseaux. *See Chenu, J. C.*

ENCYCLOPÉDIE PRATIQUE DU NATURALISTE.

XX. 1925. La faune des lacs, des étangs et des marais. pp. 255—280: Chapitre X. Les oiseaux. *See Germain, L. A. P.*

XXVI—XXVII. 1932—34. Les oiseaux de France. Vols. I—II. *See Ménégaux, H. A.*

ENTRECASTEAUX, J. A. B. d'.

1800. Relation du voyage à la recherche de La Pérouse ... 1791—94. *See Labillardière, J. J. H. de.*

EREBUS, Voyage of H. M. S.

1844—*75.* The zoology of the voyage of H. M. S. Erebus & Terror ... 1839—43 ... Birds. *See Gray, G. R.*

ERICHSEN, L. MYLIUS. *See Mylius-Erichsen, L.*

ERMAN, A. G.

1835. Reise um die Erde durch Nord-Asien und die beiden Oceane ... 1828—30 ausgeführt von Adolph Erman. Naturhistorischer Atlas ... pp. 1—18: I. Vögel. *See Nordmann, A. von.*

ESCHRICHT, D. F.

5. [*1835*—] *1844*. Afbildninger af Dyr og Planter efter Dictionnaire des sciences naturelles, ved J. F. Schouw og D. F. Eschricht. Gyldendal. *Kjøbenhavn. pp. [VIII] + [195]. 8 col. pl. birds (numb. 3, 11, 19, 43, 44, 57, 58, 67). large 8vo.*

This work was published in twelve parts, each containing eight plates, almost all coloured, with accompanying explanatory letterpress on unpaginated leaves, on which the birds and other natural objects figured are described. The animals are evidently treated by Eschricht; they are mentioned under their Danish vernacular and their Latin names; a few data are also given on their native localities and their habits.

The plates, engraved by various engravers from the plates in the French work issued in 1816—30 (118), are engravings

coloured by hand; several of the ornithological plates are signed: J. D. Petersen sc.

In 1851—52 the text and plates were again offered for subscription.

EVANS, A. H.

1890—*99.* Aves Hawaiienses: The birds of the Sandwich Islands. *See Wilson, S. B.*

1901—*12. See Ibis.*

EVERSMANN, E. F.

1876. Reprint of Eversmann's Addenda ad cele- **137.** berrimi Pallasii Zoographiam Rosso-Asiaticam. Edited by H. E. Dresser. Published by the editor. *London. pp. II + 32 + 16 + 19. 8vo.*

This addition to a well-known work (387) was originally issued at Kazan in three parts which were published in 1835 (Part 1), 1841 (Part 2), and 1842 (Part 3).

The original edition is very rare, and Dresser therefore issued the present reprint of the three fascicules in which a series of birds and some few mammals are treated.

EXPLORATION SCIENTIFIQUE DE L'ALGÉRIE ... 1840—42.

1849—*67.* Sciences physiques. Zoologie. Vol. IV. [Histoire naturelle des oiseaux]. Atlas. *See Loche, V.*

EYDOUX, J. F. T.

1841. Voyage autour du monde exécuté ... 1836— **138.** 37 sur la corvette la Bonite commandée par Vaillant. Publié par ordre du Roi (Atlas: Publié par ordre du gouvernement) sous les auspices du département de la marine. Zoologie (Atlas: Histoire naturelle. Zoologie). Par Eydoux et Souleyet. Arthus Bertrand. *Paris.* — Vol. I. 1841. - - <*pp. 69*—*132:* Oiseaux>. *8vo. Atlas.* - - < *Oiseaux >. 10 col. pl. (numb. 1—10). large fol.*

The ornithological portion of these travels, which appeared in its entirety in 1840—66 in 15 volumes text (in 11), 8vo, and 3 volumes atlas, large folio. The text on zoology comprises two volumes, which were published in 1841—52 (869, p. 391).

The preparation of the zoological section of the report was begun by Eydoux, after whose death Souleyet carried on the task. To the ornithological section de Blainville has contributed 'Remarques zoologiques et anatomiques sur le Chionis', etc. Information of interest to ornithology is found in certain parts of the introduction to the zoological section of the report. This introduction is found in the present volume.

The handsome plates (engravings printed in colour; N. Rémond, imp.) are in some cases retouched by hand. The originals are due to Prévost, a single one to Werner, while the engravers are Melle Massard and Visto.

EYTON, T. C.

1838. A monograph on the Anatidæ, or duck tribe. **139.** By T. C. Eyton. Longman, Orme, Brown, Green, & Longman. *London. pp. [X] + 178 + [5]. text-figs. 24 pl. (numb. 1—24 in 'List of plates'; 6 col. (Nos. 19—24)). 4to.*

A review of the group, based chiefly on anatomical and morphological characters. In the first section an account is given of the external and anatomical characters of the family, the sub-families, and the genera in English and Latin, the affinities of these groups being discussed. A synopsis specierum, with descriptions, synonyms, and remarks on the geographical distribution follow in the last section of the work.

In an introductory chapter the divisions of the animal kingdom are discussed, notably with reference to the problem of species and varieties, for instance 'the universal distribution

16

of animals after the Deluge' and the resulting influence of various local circumstances are included in the considerations.

The plates are executed in lithography, printed by C. Hullmandel; the anatomical plates were drawn by G. Scharf and T. C. E[yton], while the six hand-coloured plates with bird portraits were executed from drawings by Edward Lear.

Another edition of this work was issued without the plates in 1869 under the title 'A synopsis of the Anatidæ, or duck tribe' (Wellington, 4to).

1838—41. The zoology of the voyage of H. M. S. Beagle ... *1832—1838* ... *See Gould, J.*

1849—53. Contributions to ornithology ... *See Jardine, W., 1848—53.*

FALCK, J. P.

140.   *1786.* Johann Peter Falk Beyträge zur topographischen Kenntniss des russischen Reichs. Vol. III, welcher Beyträge zur Thierkenntniss und Völkerbeschreibung enthält. *< -- pp. 326—410:* Zweite Klasse. Vögel. Aves >. *Gedruckt bey der Kayserl.* Akademie der Wissenschaften. *St. Petersburg. 11 pl. (numb. XXI —XXXI). 4to.*

The ornithological section of a work in three volumes issued in 1785—86 by J. G. Georgi on the basis of Falck's notes of a journey in the Russian Empire in 1768—73 on the occasion of the transit of Venus in 1769. It was originally planned to be published in two volumes but, owing to the increase in the amount of the subject-matter, the second volume had to be divided into two. In Vol. III, therefore, the numbering of the sheets and the pagination are continued from Vol. II. The zoological section constitutes the fifth part of these 'Beyträge', whose ornithological part, which follows the 12th edition, 1766, of Linnæus' 'Systema naturæ', deals with altogether 222 forms of birds, some of which are figured on the accompanying plates (unsigned engravings).

FARREN, W.

1910—13. The British bird book ... *See Kirkman, F. B. B.*

FAUNE DE LA RUSSIE ... Rédigée par N. V. Nasonov.

1916. Oiseaux (Aves). Vol. VI. Falconiformes. Part I. *See Menzbir, M. A.*

FELICE, F. B. de

1770—80. Encyclopédie, ou dictionnaire universel ... *See Encyclopædias.*

FIELD MUSEUM OF NATURAL HISTORY. CHICAGO.

1930. Abyssinian birds and mammals ... Published by Field Museum of Natural History. *See Fuertes, L. A.*

FINLEY, W. L.

1936. Birds of America ... *See Pearson, T. G.*

FINSCH, F. H. O.

141.   *1867.* Beitrag zur Fauna Centralpolynesiens. Ornithologie der Viti-, Samoa- und Tonga-Inseln von O. Finsch und G. Hartlaub. *H. W. Schmidt. Halle. pp. XXXIX + [I] + 290. 14 col. pl. (numb. I—XIV). 8vo.*

In this valuable contribution to the avifauna of Polynesia G. Hartlaub has prepared the preface, the introduction (found also as a separate copy), and the diagnoses, the remaining part of the text being written by Finsch.

The work is based chiefly on material collected by Dr. E. Gräffe, but deals with all birds known from the area in question, — altogether 99 species as well as ten doubtful ones.

The hand-coloured plates (O. Finsch del. & lith.), five of which represent eggs, are not all of them equally successful. The artist therefore complains 'Die von mir gemalten Bilder wurden meist sehr mittelmässig und schlecht wiedergeben' (718).

1867—68. Die Papageien, monographisch bear- 142 beitet von Otto Finsch. E. J. Brill. *Leiden. 2 vols. 8vo.*
— Vol. I. 1867. *pp. XII + 561 + [1]. 1 pl. (fold.; numb. 1). 1 map.* Vol. II. 1.—[2.]Haelfte. 1868. *pp. VII + [I] + 21 + 996 + [3]. 5 col. pl. (numb. 2—6).*

In the first section of Vol. I of this comprehensive monograph the author describes the general natural history of the birds, beginning with a historical and literary survey of the subject, followed by a treatment of the habits, geographical distribution, morphology, feathers, anatomy, and systematics of parrots. The remaining part of the work is devoted to the special natural history of parrots, containing a detailed synonymy and elaborate descriptions of the individual genera and species.

The plates (lithographs coloured by hand; O. Finsch del. & lith.) are not particularly good.

1870. Baron Carl Claus von der Decken's Reisen 14 in Ost-Afrika ... *1859—65.* Vol. IV. - - Die Vögel Ost-Afrikas. Von O. Finsch und G. Hartlaub. *C. F. Winter. Leipzig. pp. VIII + [II] + 897. 11 col. pl. (front. + Nos. I—X). large 8vo.*

The present volume of these travels, which is described in more detail under J. Cabanis, 1869 (91), was published in March.

In a paper in the preceding volume Cabanis had discussed the birds collected (91); in the present volume the authors treat the avifauna of East Africa as a whole. Altogether 457 species from this area and 87 species from other parts of Africa are described with the addition of a detailed synonymy; several other species are mentioned, too.

The preface, the introduction, and the text relating to 61 species marked with an asterisk, were prepared by Hartlaub, while O. Finsch was responsible for the remaining part of the text; the latter also supplied drawings for the plates (chromolithographs; Art. Anst. v. Th. Fischer i. Cassel).

1871. Nachträge und Berichtigungen zur Ornithologie Nordost-Afrika's ... Mit Beiträgen von O. Finsch. *See Heuglin, M T von, 1869—74.*

1880. Report on the birds collected during the voyage of H. M. S. Challenger ... *1873—76. See Sclater, P. L.*

FISHER, A. K.

1893. U. S. Department of Agriculture. Division 1 of Ornithology and Mammalogy. Bulletin No. 3. The hawks and owls of the United States in their relation to agriculture. Prepared under the direction of C. Hart Merriam by A. K. Fisher. *Published by authority of the Secretary of Agriculture. Government Printing Office. Washington. pp. 210. 26 col. pl. (numb. 1—26). 8vo.*

An account of the economic importance of the different species of birds of prey in the United States. An attempt to shed light on this subject by examination of the contents of the stomachs of about 2700 of these birds. It was found that only six of the 73 species and subspecies of hawks and owls occurring in this area are harmful, three of these being, moreover, very rare. Of the 2212 stomachs of the non-injurious species no less than 56 per cent. contained portions of mice and other small animals, while 27 per cent. contained portions of insects.

During the discussion of the different species and subspecies of rapacious birds mention is made of their occurrence and distribution, their habits, notably their food habits, the species are briefly described, and the result of the examination of the stomachs is tabulated.

The plates (chromo-lithographs) were executed from drawings by J. L. Ridgway and R. Ridgway.

FITZROY, R.
1838—41. The zoology of the voyage of H. M. S. Beagle, under the command of Captain Fitzroy ... 1832—36 ... Part III. Birds. *See Gould, J.*

FITZSIMONS, F. W.
5. 1923. The natural history of South Africa. By F. W. Fitzsimons ... Birds. Longmans, Green and Co. *London. 2 vols. 8vo. —* Vol. I. *pp. XVI + [I] + 288. text-figs. 7 pl. (5 col. (numb. I—V)).* Vol. II. *pp. VII + 323. text-figs. 5 col. pl. (numb. VI—X).*

The first volume of this popular work deals mainly with the economic aspect of bird life, while the second volume contains a systematically arranged list of the birds of South Africa with notes on their diet, a list of the birds figured accompanied by brief descriptions and remarks on their distribution and habits, and finally another systematic list containing the scientific, vernacular, and native names of the species.

The coloured plates (three-colour prints) are reproduced from the plates in Layard and Sharpe's 'Birds of South Africa' (281) with the exception of one reproduced from 'The Ibis'.

FLOERICKE, K. E.
6. [1906—] 1907. Deutsches Vogelbuch für Forst- und Landwirte, Jäger, Naturfreunde und Vogellieb- haber, Lehrer und die reifere Jugend und für alle Ge- bildeten des deutschen Volkes gemeinverständlich ge- schildert von Kurt Floericke. Mit ... Tafeln in Bunt- druck nach Originalaquarellen des Tiermalers Albert Kull. Kosmos, Gesellschaft der Naturfreunde. *Stutt- gart. pp. [VIII] + 403 + [2]. text-figs. 30 col. pl. (numb. 1—30). 8vo.*

A popular account of German avifauna, which was intended to replace K. G. Lutz's 'Der Vogelfreund', 1901. It was issued in eleven Lieferungen with coloured plates (chromo-litho- graphs), each containing four figures. A second and third edi- tion appeared in 1922 and 1924 respectively, with 54 plates (53 col., 50 pl. birds) by Karl Neunzig.

[1912]. Taschenbuch zum Vogelbestimmen. Prak- tische Anleitung zum Bestimmen unserer Vögel in freier Natur nach Stimme, Flug, Bewegungen usw. nebst Tabellen zur Bestimmung toter Vögel, der Nester und Eier. Von Kurt Floericke. Mit ... farbigen Dop- peltafeln von W. Heubach, 1 Doppeltafel mit dem Flugbilderschema der Raubvögel und mit vielen Text- bildern von H. Kuttner. Zweite Auflage. Kosmos, Ge- sellschaft der Naturfreunde. *Stuttgart. pp. 260 + [12]. text-figs. 10 pl. (numb. 1—8, 11—12; 9 col. (numb. 1—7, 11—12)). 8vo.*

A popular pocket book for the identification of German birds with a table for identification of the species and an account of the birds, which are divided into winter guests, summer guests, and birds inhabiting the area during the summer and the winter. The volume further contains tables for the identification of birds' eggs and nests, and of birds from their song and other sounds, flight and other charac- teristic movements, and for the identification of the feet of birds of prey. A brief chapter deals with the foot-prints of birds.

The coloured plates (fold.) are executed by the three- colour process.

Many new editions of the book have been issued (39. Auf- lage, 1936).

FORBES, A. *See Forbes, H. O., 1897—98.*

FORBES, H. O.
1897—98. [With Anna Forbes]. British birds with their nests and eggs. Vols. III, IV, VI. Orders Stega- nopodes, Herodiones, Odontoglossæ, Gaviæ. *See But- ler, A. G., 1896—98.*

FORBES, J.
1834—35. Oriental memoirs. A narrative of seven- *148.* teen years residence in India. By James Forbes. Second edition, revised by his daughter, the Countess de Mon- talembert. Richard Bentley. *London. 2 vols. text, 8vo, and 1 vol. Illustrations, 4to. —* Vol. I. 1834. *pp. XIX + 550. 1 pl.* Vol. II. 1834. *pp. VIII + 552. 1 pl.* Il- lustrations to Oriental memoirs. With explanatory no- tices. 1835. *pp. 24. 8 col. pl. birds (numb. I, II, IX, X, XXXIX—XLI, LXVIII in 'Explanation of the plates').*

The first edition of this work appeared in 1813 in four volumes, in 4to, with 93 partly coloured plates. It is based on a series of letters, written during the author's sojourns and journeys in foreign parts of the world, especially India, when he observed nature and human life, and amused himself by draw- ing many of the things he saw. Sundry information on bird life is found in the text. The above-mentioned drawings are used for the illustration of the present work, the hand-coloured plates in which are also marked W. Hooker, fecit. The volume of plates in the present edition contains altogether 83 plates, 24 of which are coloured.

FORBES, W. A.
1880. Report on the birds collected during the voyage of H. M. S. Challenger ... 1873—76. *See Scla- ter, P. L.*

FORBUSH, E. H.
1936. Birds of America ... *See Pearson, T. G.*

FORSTER, J. R.
1795. Indische Zoologie, in welcher zu finden sind, *149.* I. Beschreibungen einiger seltenen in Kupfern vorge- stellten Thiere; II. Bemerkungen über den Umfang und die Beschaffenheit des Himmelstriches, des Bo- dens, und der Meere von Indien; letztlich III. auch eine indische Fauna, oder ein so viel möglich vollstän- diges Verzeichniss aller Thierarten von Indien. Aus- gefertigt von Johann Reinhold Forster. Zweyte sehr vermehrte Auflage. Johann Jacob Gebauer. *Halle. pp. [VIII] + IV + 42 + 38. 14 col. pl. birds (numb. II—XII; 3 unnumb.). fol.* Added title-page in Latin.

This volume contains 15 coloured plates, one of which (No. I) represents a mammal. The first edition of the work appeared in 1781 as a reproduction of Pennant's 'Indian zoology', which had been issued in 1769 (395). The latter contained 12 plates and these, together with the text and three more unpublished plates, engraved at Pennant's expense, were handed over to Forster, who translated the text into German and Latin and added a description of India and of the animals, among which were three shown, figured on the new plates, a chapter on the bird of paradise and the phoenix, and finally a brief list of the animals of India by Pennant. Forster's addi- tions were inserted in the second edition of Pennant's English work which appeared in 1791 (dated 1790), to which was added a new list of the 'Animals of India' or 'Faunula Indica', evolved chiefly by J. Latham and H. Davies. This list, in a somewhat altered form, is also found in the present new edition of Forster's work, of which it occupies the last 38 pages. An independent edition of the 'Faunula' appeared in the same year. Apart from this part of the work, the text is printed in German and Latin in parallel columns.

16*

The drawings for the plates (engravings coloured by hand, engraved by P. Mazell) are copies by Sydney Parkinson from Gideon Loten's collection of natural history pictures, executed in India by the native artist P. C. de Bevere.

FRANCE. COMMISSION D'ÉGYPTE.
Description de l'Égypte ... Histoire naturelle.
1809. Vol. I. Part I. pp. 63—114: Système des oiseaux de l'Égypte et de la Syrie. *See Savigny, M. J. C. L. de.*
1826. Vol. I. Part IV. pp. 251—318: Explication sommaire des planches d'oiseaux de l'Égypte et de la Syrie, publiées par Jules-César Savigny ... *See Audouin, J. V.*
1883. Audouin's Explication sommaire des planches d'oiseaux de l'Égypte et de la Syrie. Publiées par Jules-César Savigny. *See Audouin, J. V.*

FRANCE. Voyages, expeditions, etc.
1776. Voyage à la Nouvelle Guinée ... *See Sonnerat, P.*
1777. Sonnerat's Reise nach Neuguinea ... *See Sonnerat, P.*
1783. Reise nach Ostindien und China ... 1774—81. Vol. II. pp. 116—173: Fünftes Buch ... Zweiter Abschnitt. Von den Vögeln. *See Sonnerat, P.*
1797. Voyage de La Pérouse autour du monde ... rédigé par M. L. A. Milet-Mureau. *See Lapérouse, J. F. de G. de.*
1800. Relation du voyage à la recherche de La Pérouse ... 1791—94. *See Labillardière, J. J. H. de.*
1806. Voyage aux Indes Orientales et à la Chine... 1774—81 ... *See Sonnerat, P.*
1826—31. Voyage autour du monde ... sur la corvette ... la Coquille ... 1822—25 ... Zoologie. *See Lesson, R. P.*
1830—33. Voyage de ... l'Astrolabe ... 1826—29 ... Zoologie. Oiseaux. *See Quoy, J. R. C.*
1835—47. Voyage dans l'Amérique méridionale ... 1826—33 ... Oiseaux. *See Orbigny, A. D. d'.*
1841. Voyage autour du monde exécuté ... 1836—37 sur la corvette la Bonite ... Zoologie ... Oiseaux. *See Eydoux, J. F. T.*
1849—67. Exploration scientifique de l'Algérie ... 1840—42 ... Sciences physiques. Zoologie. Vol. IV. [Histoire naturelle des oiseaux]. Atlas. *See Loche, V.*

FRANKFURT AM MAIN. SENCKENBERGISCHE NATURFORSCHENDE GESELLSCHAFT. *See Senckenbergische Naturforschende Gesellschaft. Frankfurt am Main.*

FRANKLIN, J.
1831. Fauna Boreali-Americana ... containing descriptions of the objects of natural history collected on the late northern land expeditions under command of Captain Sir John Franklin. Part II. The birds. *See Swainson, W.*

FRASER, L.
150. [1845—]1849. Zoologia typica, or figures of new and rare mammals and birds described in the Proceedings, or exhibited in the Collections of the Zoological Society of London. By Louis Fraser. Published by the author. *London. pp. VIII + [139]. 42 col. pl. birds (numb. 29—70 in 'List of plates'). fol.*
This collection of altogether 70 handsome plates was issued in parts (734), each with a page or a leaf with a brief text. The edition was limited to 250 copies and, according to the original plan, the work was to supply figures of every new and rare mammal and bird described in the Proceedings, or exhibited in the collections of the society mentioned in the title, of which figures had not appeared in any other publication. However, publication was stopped before this had been achieved, as the Proceedings of the Zoological Society of London, the issue of which had been commenced in 1831 (547), were illustrated from 1848.
The plates (lithographs coloured by hand), on which forty-six species of birds are figured, were executed by Charles Couzens and H. N. Turner, jun.

FRAUENFELD, G. von.
1868. Neu aufgefundene Abbildung des Dronte *1.* und eines zweiten kurzflügeligen Vogels, wahrscheinlich des Poule Rouge au bec de Bécasse der Maskarenen in der Privatbibliothek S. M. des verstorbenen Kaisers Franz. Erläutert von Georg Ritter von Frauenfeld. Herausgegeben von der K. K. zoologisch-botanischen Gesellschaft. *Wien. pp. [V] + 16 + [1]. 4 pl. (numb. 1—4; 2 col. (numb. 1—2)). large fol.*
In the library cited above two volumes were found, each containing 90 plates with pictures of various animals painted in oils on parchment.
One of the volumes contained paintings of birds, the majority of which were very faithfully depicted and artistically executed. The paintings are ascribed to the Dutch painter J. Hoefnagel, who is supposed to have painted most of them from living specimens in the menagerie of the Emperor Rudolf II.
The figures of the Dodo and another extinct bird, reproduced in chromo-lithography, are derived from this collection of pictures, while the two uncoloured plates (lithographs) represent in outline all figures of short-winged Mascarene birds known at the time.
The plates were executed by: Art. lith. Institut v. Ant. Hartinger, Wien.

FREDERICK II, Emperor of Germany. *See Friedrich II.*

FRIČ, A. J.
1870—71. Naturgeschichte der Vögel Europa's. Von Anton Fritsch. Verlag des Verfassers. *Prag. 1 vol. text, 8vo, and 1 vol. Atlas, fol. —* [Text]. 1870. *pp. [IV] + XV + 506 + [11].* [Atlas]. 1871. *pp. [12]. 61 col. pl. (numb. 1—61).*
This work was published in 16 parts in the years 1852—71. The text-volume opens with a systematic survey of the birds of Europe; then follow diagnosis, description, and a detailed treatment of the individual species, whose names are given in Latin, German, Czech, and French, with the addition of some of the most important Latin synonyms. In an index of names the nomenclature of the birds is in the three first-mentioned languages. The volume of plates opens with a systematically arranged list of the birds figured, in which the names are given in Latin, German, English, and French. The plates (chromo-lithographs) contain more than 700 small figures of birds.
The work was also issued in Czech, and the plates were published at London in 1877. A new German edition of the text (3. Auflage) was issued at Prague in 1898.

FRIEDRICH II, Emperor of Germany.
1896. Des Hohenstaufen-Kaisers Friedrich II Bücher von der Natur der Vögel und der Falknerei mit den Zusätzen des Königs Manfred. Aus dem Lateinischen übersetzt und versehen mit Originalzeichnungen,

sowie einem Wörterbuch der Falknereisprache von H. Schöpffer. Mit ... Tafeln und 40 Textabbildungen. Paul Parey. *Berlin. pp. XVI + 212. text-figs. 8 pl. (numb. I—VIII). fol.*

The greater part of this book is a German translation of the work by the Emperor Frederick II, who was much interested in nature and hunting, entitled 'De arte venandi cum avibus', which he wrote after 30 years of observing birds, and in which he also sets forth original remarks on ornithological subjects. His son, King Manfred of Naples and Sicily, contributed to its preparation, and the work is still extant in illustrated manuscripts. Printed editions of it were issued in 1596 and, by J. G. Schneider, in 1788—89. It falls into two parts, a book on the nature of birds, and another on falconry.

The present translation was issued by C. Schöpffer, and is provided with an introduction by the translator, a chapter on the species of falcons employed in hunting by the ornithologist Ernst Schaeff, who assisted in the preparation, a survey of the history of falconry in the nineteenth century, a dictionary of the German falconers' language, and an annotated list of the literature on falconry.

The figures of the plates represent various species of falcons and are reproduced from drawings by the translator.

FRISCH, F. H.

1819. Verzeichniss der in ... Vorstellung der Vögel in Deutschland ... abgebildeten Säugethiere und Vögel ... *See Frisch, Johann L., 1733—63.*

FRISCH, JOHANN L.

4. *1733—?* Johann Leonhard Frisch, Vorstellung der Vögel in Teutschland und beÿläuffig auch einiger fremden mit ihren natürlichen Farben, aus seinem desswegen von vielen Jahren her gesammleten Vogel-Cabinet, zur Verbesserung der bisher davon herausgekommenen Abbildungen; wobey den Kleinern ihre eigene Grösse geblieben, bey den Grössern aber das Maass bemercket worden ... bey dem Auctore (from Class V: bey des Auctoris Sohn F. H. Frisch). *Berlin. 10 parts in 1 vol. 103 col. pl. (numb. 1—67, 69—104). fol.* Text unpaged. Pl. 68 und ad 31 missing; Pl. 102—104 of bats.

A fragment of the author's 'Vorstellung der Vögel Deutschlandes', which appeared in its entirety in 1733—63 (155). The title is cited from the title-page to Part I. Of the ten special title-pages which the volume contains only the first six are dated and, as the dates on these title-pages and on the 'Kurzen Nachrichten' vary considerably in the different copies of the work (633, p. 59), they are given here: Class I, Part 1: 1733; Class I, Part 2: 1734; Class I, Part 3: 1735; the 'Kurtze Nachrichten' belonging to Class I: 1736; Class II: 1736; Class III: 1739; Class IV: 1742; and 'Fortsetzung einer kurzen Nachricht', to Class IV: 1743.

5. *[1733—] 1763.* Vorstellung der Vögel Deutschlandes und beyläufig auch einiger Fremden; nach ihren Eigenschaften beschrieben von Johann Leonhard Frisch, in Kupfer gebracht, und nach ihren natürlichen Farben dargestellt von Ferdinand Helfreich Frisch. Gedruckt bey Friedr. Wilhelm Birnstiel. *Berlin. 14 parts and a supplement, in 2 vols. 256 pl. (front. + 255 col. pl. (numb. 1—241, ad 31, 114 B, ad No 212, Supplement p. 28, 31, 33, 106, 107, 109, 152, 157, 165, 185 A, 185 B; 252 pl. birds (pl. 102—104 of bats)). fol.* Text unpaged.

This is a complete copy of Frisch's work, which was finished in 1763, as shown by the date given on the final title-page. Publication actually commenced in 1733 (cf. the fragment cited above (154)), but in the present copy the special title-page to Part I ('bey des Auctoris Sohn') is dated 1736, 'Kurtze Nachrichten' to Class I is dated 1739, the title-page to Class III 1740, while the text to Class IV, as in the preceding copy, bears the date 1743. All the other title-pages are undated.

The birds are divided into 12 classes and the plates (engravings coloured by hand), which contain altogether 307 figures, are accompanied by a brief text divided according to the classes into sections, the subtitles of which open with the words 'Kurtze Nachricht' or 'Fortsetzung einer kurtzen [kurzen] Nachricht'.

After the death of J. L. Frisch the publication was continued by his sons, of whom Just Leopold Frisch prepared the text, assisted, chiefly at the end, by Baron Friedrich Aug. von Zorn, who also compiled the comprehensive index, while Ferdinand Helfreich Frisch, with his brother Philipp Jacob Frisch, engraved and coloured most of the plates for the work, which are rather fine. The last thirty plates were executed by Ferd. Helfreich's son Johann Christoph Frisch.

At the end of the second volume is inserted a list entitled: 'Verzeichniss der in Ferdinand Helfreich Frisch Vorstellung der Vögel in Deutschland ... abgebildeten Säugethiere und Vögel, nach der 13ten Ausgabe des von J. F. Gmelin bearbeiteten Linné'schen Natursystems geordnet'. (Nicolai, Berlin 1819, pp. [11], fol.), for in 1817 the 'Nicolaische Buchhandlung' issued a new edition of the plates for Frisch's large work on birds. A number, 150, of the original drawings for the plates are found, according to Schalow (633, p. 60), in Jacob Moyat's library at Mainz. These drawings are said to be somewhat sharper in detail than the figures on the plates, and certain deviations from the final prints may similarly occur.

1805. Gemeinnützige Naturgeschichte Deutschlands ... Zweyte Auflage. Vol. II. *See Bechstein, J. M.*

FRISCH, JUST L.

1733—63. Vorstellung der Vögel Deutschlandes... *See Frisch, Johann L.*

FRITSCH, A. *See Frič, A. J.*

FROHAWK, F. W.

1919. British Museum (Natural History). Economic Series. No. 9. Birds beneficial to agriculture. By F. W. Frohawk. Printed by order of the Trustees of the British Museum. *London. pp. VI + 47. 22 pl. (numb. I—XXII). 8vo.*   156.

A small guide-book containing a selection of species believed to be beneficial to agriculture. The book is produced in connection with an exhibition of such species in the Museum. The plates are reproduced from originals drawn for the purpose by the author.

FUEHRER, L. von.

1896. Materialien zu einer Ornis Balcanica ... Vol. IV. Montenegro. *See Reiser, O., 1894—1905.*

FUERTES, L. A.

1930. Abyssinian birds and mammals. Painted from life by Louis Agassiz Fuertes. Published by Field Museum of Natural History Chicago. Through the generosity of C. Suydam Cutting. *Chicago. pp. [IV]. 28 col. pl. birds (numb. 1—28 in 'List of subjects'). 4to.*   157.

An album in a portfolio with altogether 32 plates, four of which represent mammals, issued as a special publication of the Field Museum of Natural History. The title cited is printed on the portfolio.

The plates are reproductions in chromo-lithography (offset) in eight, sometimes nine, colours of the finest of the 108 paintings which Fuertes executed as a member of the Field Museum-Chicago Daily News Abyssinian Expedition in 1926—27. The album is provided with an introduction by Wilfred H. Osgood, and a brief descriptive text is printed on the back of each plate. The 108 original paintings are now in the possession of the Field Museum.

FUNKE, K. P.

[1805—06]. Kupfer-Sammlung besonders zu Funke Naturgeschichte und Technologie aber auch zu je-   158.

dem andern Lehrbuche der Naturgeschichte brauchbar. Zur allgemeinen Schulencyklopädie gehörig. Schulbuchhandlung. *Braunschweig. pp. 90. 5 col. pl. birds (numb. VI—IX, XXIV). obl. 4to.*

Funke's popular hand-book and text-book of natural history and technology was first published in 1790—92 in three volumes, 8vo, several new editions being issued in rapid succession, thus evidencing the popularity of the work. To keep down the price the first edition was not accompanied by plates; these were only added to the second and later editions. The present volume, which belongs to the fifth edition of the natural history contains altogether 24 plates. The plates are of no particular value. They were engraved by Sellier from drawings by Maréchal.

GADOW, H. F.
1883—84. Catalogue of the birds in the British Museum. Vols. VIII, IX. *See British Museum (Natural History),* 1874—98.

1891. Remarks on the structure of certain Hawaiian birds ... *See Wilson, S. B.,* 1890—99.

1899. Further remarks on the relationships of the Drepanididæ. *See Wilson, S. B.,* 1890—99.

GAIMARD, J. P.
1830—33. Voyage de ... l'Astrolabe ... 1826—29 ... Zoologie. Oiseaux. *See Quoy, J. R. C.*

GARDINER, L.
1923. Rare, vanishing & lost British birds ... *See Hudson, W. H.*

GARNOT, P.
1826. Description de quelques espèces nouvelles d'oiseaux. *See Lesson, R. P.,* 1826—31.

GARROD, A. H.
1880. Report on the birds collected during the voyage of H. M. S. Challenger ... 1873—76. *See Sclater, P. L.*

GAZELLE, Voyage of S. M. S.
1889. Die Forschungsreise S. M. S. 'Gazelle' ... 1874—76 ... Vol. III. Zoologie und Geologie. *See Studer, T.*

GEBAUER, C. A. (H. REBAU).
159. [*1837*—] *1838.* Volksnaturgeschichte oder gemeinfassliche Beschreibung der merkwürdigsten, nützlichsten und schädlichsten Thiere, Pflanzen und Mineralien. Nebst einer ausführlichen Anweisung, Säugthiere, Vögel und deren Eier und Nester, Amphibien, Fische, Käfer, Schmetterlinge, Würmer, Pflanzen, Mineralien u. s. w. zu sammeln und aufzubewahren. Nach den besten Quellen und Hilfsmitteln bearbeitet von Heinrich Rebau. <- - *pp. 326—488:* Zweite Klasse. Vögel >. Weise & Stoppani. *Stuttgart. 6 col. pl. (numb. 21—26). 8vo.*

The German author and poet who wrote this popular work is best known by his pen-name Heinrich Rebau.

The account of the birds opens with a general review (pp. 326—349), after which comes a systematic treatment of the group, in which the birds are mentioned by their vernacular names. The volume contains 40 plates in all, executed in lithography and coloured by hand (C. Schach lith.).

The popular work was issued in a series of editions: 2nd edition (40 col. pl.), 1841; 3rd edition, (48 col. pl.), 1844;

4th edition, revised by Traug. Bromme (48 col. pl.), 1857; the later editions under the title 'Naturgeschichte für Schule und Haus': 5th edition, revised by Traug. Bromme (45 col. pl.), 1864—66; 6th edition (34 col. pl.), 1869—70; 7th edition, revised by G. Jäger, H. Wagner, and O. Fraas (48 col. pl.), 1875.

GEOGRAPHISCHE GESELLSCHAFT. ST. PETERSBURG.
1863. Reisen im Süden von Ost-Sibirien ... 1855—59 ... Vol. II. Die Festlands-Ornis des südöstlichen Sibiriens. *See Radde, G. F. R.*

GEORGI, J. G.
1786. Beyträge zur topographischen Kenntniss des russischen Reichs. Vol. III ... pp. 326—410: Zweite Klasse. Vögel. *See Falck, J. P.*

GERMAIN, L. A. P.
1925. La faune des lacs, des étangs et des marais. Par Louis Germain. <- - *pp. 255—280:* Chapitre X. Les oiseaux >. Paul Lechevalier. (Encyclopédie pratique du naturaliste XX). *Paris. text-figs. 6 col. pl. (numb. 13—18). small 8vo.*

The ornithological section of a small book of 315 pages provided with altogether 20 coloured plates printed on ten leaves (three-colour prints) and 225 figures in the text. It gives a general review of all the fresh-water fauna, and is intended for amateurs.

Some of the plates in the section on birds were executed from drawings by N. Boadarel.

GERMANY. Voyages, expeditions, etc.
1824—25. Avium species novæ, quas in itinere per Brasiliam annis 1817—20 ... collegit et descripsit ... *See Spix, J. B. von.*

1826. Atlas zu der Reise im nördlichen Afrika. Erste Abtheilung. Zoologie ... Vögel ... *See Rueppell, E. W. P. S.*

1834. Supplementum I, sistens F. J. F. Meyenii observationes zoologicas, in itinere circum terram institutas ... pp. 59   124: Beiträge zur Zoologie, gesammelt auf einer Reise um die Erde. Vierte Abhandlung. Vögel. *See Meyen, F. J. F.*

1835. Reise um die Erde durch Nord-Asien und die beiden Oceane ... 1828—30 ... Naturhistorischer Atlas ... pp. 1—18: I. Vögel. *See Nordmann, A. von.*

1869—70. Baron Carl Claus von der Decken's Reisen in Ost-Afrika ... 1859—65.

Vol. III. Erste Abtheilung. 1869. pp. 19—52: Vögel. *See Cabanis, J.*

Vol. IV. 1870. Die Vögel Ost-Afrikas. *See Finsch, F. H. O.*

1889. Die Forschungsreise S. M. S. 'Gazelle' ... 1874—76 ... Vol. III. Zoologie und Geologie. *See Studer, T.*

GERVAIS, F. L. P.
1840—41. Dictionnaire des sciences naturelles ... Supplément. *See Dictionaries,* 1816—41.

1842. Le Jardin des Plantes ... *See Bernard, P.*

GILL, T. N.
1874. A history of North American birds. Land birds. [Introduction, part]. *See Baird, S. F.*

GINANNI (ZINANNI), G.

51.   *1737.* Delle uova e dei nidi degli uccelli, libro primo, del Giuseppe Zinanni. Aggiunte in fine alcune osservazioni, con una dissertazione sopra varie spezie di Cavallette. Antonio Bortoli. *Venezia. pp. [VIII] +
130 + [I] + 55 + [I]. front. 22 pl. eggs (numb. I—XXII). 4to.*
    A work consisting of two parts, of which the last one, 'Osservazioni giornali sopra le Cavalette' (title, pp. 55 + [1]), contains eight plates with figures of grasshoppers.
    The ornithological section of the volume, an early work with figures of birds' eggs, divides the birds into three groups ('uccelli terrestri non rapaci', 'uccelli terrestri rapaci', and 'uccelli aquatici'), and contains a brief account of the forms whose eggs are figured, their nests, breeding time, and eggs. The plates (engravings) in this work, previously much in demand, are comparatively well executed, and show figures of the eggs of 106 species in as many pictures.

GLADDEN, G.
    1936. Birds of America ... *See Pearson, T. G.*

GMELIN, S. G.

52.   *[1770—] 1774.* Samuel Gottlieb Gmelins Reise durch Russland zur Untersuchung der drey Natur-Reiche. Gedruckt bey der Kayserl. Academie der Wissenschaften. *St. Petersburg. 3 vols. 38 pl. birds. 4to. —*
Vol. I. [1770]. *pp. [VIII] + 182. 11 pl. birds (numb. I, X—XVI, XXX—XXXII). 1 map.* Vol. II. 1774. *pp. VIII + 260. 15 pl. birds (numb. 9, 10, 13—22, 24—26). 5 maps.* Vol. III. 1774. *pp. 508. 12 pl. birds (numb. XII, XVI—XX, XXVI, XXVII, XXXVII—XXXIX, XLII).*
    A fourth volume of this work was issued by P. S. Pallas in 1784. The three present volumes contain 39, 38, and 51 plates respectively.
    One of the expeditions undertaken by command of the Empress Catherine II with the object of observing the transit of Venus in 1769. The first volume describes the journey from St. Petersbourg to the Don area in 1768—69, while the second deals with the journey to and the period in Astrakhan in 1769—70.
    In 1700—72 Gmelin travelled in Northern Persia and was the first naturalist to explore part of this country. Some of his results from these regions are embodied in Vol. III of his travels in which, as in the preceding volumes, he himself describes the part of the material concerning the plants and animals collected, including a number of birds.

GODMAN, F. D.
    1879—1904. Biologia Centrali-Americana. Aves. *See Salvin, O.*
    1907—10. A monograph of the petrels (order Tubinares). By Frederick Du Cane Godman. With hand-coloured plates by J. G. Keulemans. Witherby & Co. *London. pp. LV + 381. 106 col. pl. (numb. 1—103, 5 A, 98 A, 102 A). 4to.*
    This work appeared in five parts from December, 1907, to May, 1910. The number of copies was limited to 225, of which the present one is No. 143. The origin of this monograph is to be found in the fact that Osbert Salvin, after having completed his part, 'Tubinares', of Vol. XXV of the Catalogue of the birds in the British Museum (70), intended to publish a fuller account of the petrels illustrated by coloured figures of each species. Some forty plates were prepared, the work being carried on after Salvin's death by Godman, who with the assistance of R. B. Sharpe carried out the work on the lines indicated by Salvin.
    Pp. XV—XXI contain a chapter by W. P. Pycraft, 'On the systematic position of the petrels'. The classification is almost identical with that of Salvin in the above-mentioned

catalogue. The nomenclature is binomial, and under each species synonymy, history, information about the life history, and distribution are given.
    Altogether 122 species, belonging to 25 genera, are discussed. The plates (lithographs coloured by hand) show figures of 104 species. The majority were drawn and lithographed by J. G. Keulemans (Hanhart, some few Mintern Bros., imp.), but a few were executed by H. Grønvold (Witherby & Co. imp.), while the colouring of the plates was entrusted to Dr. Sharpe's daughters.

GOELDI, E. A.

    1894 [—1900]. As aves do Brasil por Emilio Au-   *164.* gusto Goeldi. Livraria Classica de Alves & C. *Rio de Janeiro. pp. 664 + 82. small 8vo.*
    Published in two parts, Part 1 (pp. 1—311), 1894, and Part II (pp. 311 (duplicate) — 664 + 1—82), 1900. The title-page to the second part and p. 311 (1894) are missing in the present volume. The last 82 pages contain an alphabetical index to the work which, otherwise, gives a popular account of the birds of Brazil, whose number of species is estimated by the author at 1610.
    A supplement to this work, 'Album de aves Amazonicas' was issued in 1900—06 (165).

    1900—06. Museu Goeldi (Museu Paraense) de   *165.* Historia Natural e Ethnographia. Album de aves Amazonicas organisado pelo Emilio A. Goeldi ... Desenhos do sñr Ernesto Lohse, desenhista-lithographo do Museu Goeldi. Supplemento illustrativo a' obra 'Aves do Brazil' pelo Emilio A. Goeldi. *(Belem (Pará)). 3 fasc. in 2 vols. 4to. — Fasc. I. 1900. 12 col. pl. (numb. 1—12).* Fasc. II. 1902. *12 col. pl. (numb. 13—24).* Fasc. III. 1905—06. *pp. [V] + 46 + [II]. 24 col. pl. (numb. 25—48).*
    This collection of plates with its pictures of tropical scenery is a popular description, like the work which it is intended to illustrate in the form of a supplement, Goeldi's 'Aves do Brazil' (164). Each plate shows several birds against a background of natural scenery, by which the artist, the museum draughtsman Ernst Lohse, has increased the pictorial effect of his water-colours, which are reproduced in chromo-lithography by the Polygraphisches Institut, Zürich.
    The plates are accompanied by explanations — partly on loose covers, partly collected on pp. 1—46 — a guide to the final numbering of the plates, and two indexes, one with the scientific and one with the popular names.

GOETZ, G. F.

    1782. Naturgeschichte einiger Vögel, von Georg   *166.* Friedrich Götz. mit [sic] ... ausgemalten Kupfertafeln. Bei dem Verfasser. *Hanau. pp. [XXIII] + 119 + [I]. 6 col. pl. (numb. I—VI). 8vo.*
    A description of some rare birds, such as the Gold Pheasant and the Silver Pheasant, some from specimens in the princely pheasantry and in the cabinet of natural curiosities of Princess Marie Friederike of Hessen. The cabinet had been started by the author, who was also its custodian. The small volume was produced on the basis of some articles published by the author in the Hanau Magazine, and is illustrated by hand-coloured plates (engravings) somewhat uncertain in colouring, drawn and engraved by J. J. Müller.

GOLDSMITH, O.

    1832. A history of the earth and animated nature.   *167.* By Oliver Goldsmith. With copious notes, embracing accounts of new discoveries in natural history. To which is subjoined an appendix ... By Thomas Brown. A. Fullarton & Co. *Glasgow, 4 vols. plates. 12mo. —*
Vol. III. - - < *pp. 1—439:* A history of birds >. *30 pl. (numb. XXVI, XXVIII, XXIX, XXXII—XXXIV, XXXVI—XLVIII, XXVI,* XXX,*

XXXII,* XXXVII,* XXXIX,* XL,* XLII,*
XLVII,* XXIX,** XXXVII,** XXIX,** missing
pl. XXIX*). Vol. IV. - - < pp. 526—595: Birds >.
4 pl. (numb. XXV,* XXVII, XXX, XXXV).

The first edition of this popular work by the famous author appeared in 1774 and was succeeded by a number of editions in which the account was improved and enlarged by means of corrections, notes, and additions.

The appendix to the present edition (Vol. IV, pp. 429—654) contains a survey of the animal kingdom with explanations of technical terms and an outline of the Cuvierian and other systems. The birds are arranged according to Temminck's system of classification.

The engravings were executed by R. Scott, many birds being figured on each of the ornithological plates.

Several bird books with coloured plates, based entirely or partially on Goldsmith's work, have appeared, for instance a work in two volumes in 1815 under the title 'The natural history of birds; from the works of Oliver Goldsmith', etc., with altogether 152 coloured plates, and a volume in 1838 with the title 'Goldsmith's history of British and foreign birds' with 46 coloured plates.

GOULD, J.

168.   *[1831—] 1832. A century of birds from the Himalaya Mountains. By John Gould. London. pp. [XI] + [143]. 80 col. pl. (numb. I—LXXX in text). large fol.*
The first of the long series of Gould's pictorial works in large folio.

The leaf of text accompanying each, or in a few cases two or three of the plates, contains the diagnosis in Latin of the bird or birds figured on the plate, an indication of the measures, and some few other data of interest, such as notes on the history, habitat, and habits of the species. The greater part of this text was apparently written by N. A. Vigors, who is thanked in an advertisement in the following words, 'by him not only the nomenclature, but also the accompanying letterpress descriptions were liberally contributed'.

The plates contain altogether 102 figures, two of which, however, represent birds figured twice; thus the 100 birds referred to in the title are actually figured.

The plates (drawn from nature and on stone by E. Gould) from sketches by J. Gould, are executed in lithography coloured by hand (printed by C. Hullmandel). In the present copy the backgrounds of the plates are coloured; however, the work also occurs with these backgrounds uncoloured.

169.   *[1832—] 1837. The birds of Europe. By John Gould. Published by the author. London. 5 vols. 448 col. pl. (numb. consecutively in 'List of plates'). large fol. — Vol. I. Raptores. pp. XII + [II] + 4 + [I] + [99]. 50 col. pl. (Nos. 1—50). Vol. II. Insessores. pp. [IV] + [197]. 99 col. pl. (Nos. 51—149). Vol. III. Insessores. pp. [IV] + [185]. 93 col. pl. (Nos. 150— 242). Vol. IV. Rasores. Grallatores. pp. [IV] + [205]. 103 col. pl. (Nos. 243—345). Vol. V. Natatores. pp. [IV] + [205]. 103 col. pl. (Nos. 346—449; Figs. 447 and 448 on one plate).*
This work was published in 22 parts, the issue of which was commenced on June 1, 1832. Each volume contains a 'List of plates' in which the plates of the particular volume are numbered.

In the introduction (pp. IX—XII) questions relative to migration are briefly dealt with, and an outline is given of the plan of the work.

The brief text which accompanies each plate by way of explanation gives a characterization of the genera, while the individual form is treated with regard to its geographical distribution, habitat, habits, and other facts of interest, and is briefly described.

The plates are executed in lithography coloured by hand. The greater number were drawn and lithographed by Mrs. E. Gould from sketches and designs by the author, taken from nature. The remainder of the plates were drawn and litho-

graphed by E. Lear. All the plates were coloured under the direction of Mr. Bayfield. Finally, the printing was done by C. Hullmandel.

[1833—] 1834 [—35]. A monograph of the Ram- 17(phastidæ, or family of toucans. By John Gould. Published by the author. London. pp. [XX] + [74]. 34 pl. (33 col.). large fol.

This work — Gould's first monograph — was issued in three parts. The introduction contains a general review of the history of the group and of the geographical distribution, habits, and classification of the birds. The explanatory text accompanying each of the plates gives in Latin the specific characters of the form figured, and also the description, measurements, synonyms, and, in a different type, information about the iconography, special characters, habitat, etc., of the birds.

The plates (lithographs coloured by hand, printed by C. Hullmandel) were mostly drawn and lithographed by J. & E. Gould, though some were executed by E. Lear.

The work has a final four-page chapter with the title 'Observations on the anatomy of the toucan' by Richard Owen, illustrated with figures on an uncoloured plate drawn and lithographed by G. Scharf.

A new edition of this work, with 52 plates, was issued in 1852—54 (in three parts?),' while a supplement was published in 1855 (180).

A German edition (four parts, 38 plates, folio) was issued at Nürnberg in 1841—47.

[1836?—] 1838. A monograph of the Trogonidæ, or 17 family of trogons. By John Gould. Published by the author. London. pp. [V] + VII + [III] + [71]. 36 col. pl. (numb. 1—36 in 'List of plates'). large fol.

Published in three parts, the first of which possibly appeared in 1836.

The present work is Gould's second monograph, in which altogether 34 species are treated, Gould having added to the 22 species known hitherto 12 others new to science.

The introduction, dealing with general conditions relative to the group, is succeeded by a 'Synopsis specierum'. The text accompanying each plate contains a diagnosis in Latin and also a description, measurements, and synonyms, of the bird figured on the particular plate, to which is added some information on the history, habitat, and iconography of the bird.

The plates (drawn from nature and on stone by J. & E. Gould) are executed in lithography coloured by hand (printed by C. Hullmandel).

Another, revised, edition of this work (4 parts, 47 col., pl., large fol.) was issued in 1858—75.

1837—38. Icones avium, or figures and de- 17 scriptions of new and interesting species of birds from various parts of the globe. By John Gould. Forming a supplement to his previous works. Published by the author. London. 2 parts. 18 col. pl. large fol. — Part I. 1837. pp. [19]. 10 col. pl. Part II. Monograph of the Caprimulgidæ. Part I. 1838. pp. [15]. 8 col. pl.

The present two parts were the only ones of this work to appear, their covers being dated August, 1837, and August, 1838, respectively, after which publication was stopped owing to Gould's journey to Australia.

Each plate is accompanied by a leaf of text, containing a diagnosis in Latin of the form figured, description, synonyms, and information about the history and geographic distribution of the bird, etc.

The plates (printed by C. Hullmandel) are executed in lithography coloured by hand (drawn from nature & on stone by J. & E. Gould).

[1838—] 1841. The zoology of the voyage of H. 1 M. S. Beagle, under the command of Captain Fitzroy ... 1832—1836. Published with the approval of the Lords Commissioners of her Majesty's Treasury. Edited and superintended by Charles Darwin. Part III. Birds, by John Gould. Smith, Elder and Co. Lon-

don. pp. [VII] + II + 3—156 + [8]. 50 col. pl. (numb. 1—50). 4to.

The ornithological section of the report on the zoological collections from the famous voyage round the world of the 'Beagle', in which Darwin participated as zoologist, and during which he conceived the idea of his theory of evolution. The whole zoological report (five parts, Part III: Birds) appeared in 1838—43, and was issued in numbers, of which 3, 6, 9, 11, and 15 contained the ornithological section (863).

The subtitle of this section runs as follows: 'Birds, described by John Gould, with a notice of their habits and ranges, by Charles Darwin, and with an anatomical appendix, by T. C. Eyton'. In the advertisement Darwin states that Gould had prepared the descriptions of the new species and supplied those already known with names, but that his manuscript was so incomplete that G. R. Gray had to come to his assistance with information as to some parts of the general arrangement and the use of proper generic terms, while Darwin himself enlarged some of Gould's descriptions which were too brief.

The main part of the work (pp. 3—146) is taken up with a description of the comprehensive material, after which follows (pp. 147—156) the appendix by Eyton, while the last eight pages contain an 'Index to the species'.

The plates (lithographs coloured by hand) are made from sketches by J. Gould, and executed on stone by Mrs. E. Gould.

[1840—] 1848. The birds of Australia. By John Gould. Published by the author. London. 7 vols. 600 col. pl. (numb. in the lists of plates). large fol. — Vol. I. pp. [XVIII] + V—CII + 13 + [I] + [71]. text-figs. 36 col. pl. (Nos. 1—36). Vol. II. pp. [IV] + [207]. 104 col. pl. (Nos. 1—104). Vol. III. pp. [IV] + [193]. 97 col. pl. (Nos. 1—97). Vol. IV. pp. [IV] + [207]. 104 col. pl. (Nos. 1—104). Vol. V. pp. [IV] + [183]. 92 col. pl. (Nos. 1—92). Vol. VI. pp. [IV] + [163]. 82 col. pl. (Nos. 1—82). Vol. VII. pp. [IV] + [169]. 85 col. pl. (Nos. 1—85).

In 1837—38 Gould issued two parts of a work with the title 'The birds of Australia, and the adjacent islands' (20 plates, text, large fol.). Owing to lack of material, however, he did not go on with the work, but went to Australia to collect the material on which the present work is based. This was published in 36 parts, the first of which was dated December 1, 1840, the last December 1, 1848.

Vol. I, in addition to the material concerning individual forms, contains a general index to the whole work, a preface (pp. V—XII) with information about the origin of the work, and a long introduction (pp. XIII—CII) with a general account of the avifauna of Australia, consisting chiefly of a synoptic table with references to the volumes in which the respective plates are to be found. This is followed by a table of the range or distribution of the species (pp. 1—13), in which the species are arranged in the same order as in the work itself. These parts of Vol. I (preface and introduction with the table of the range) were also issued separately in 1848, 8vo, under the title 'An introduction to the birds of Australia'.

Each volume contains a 'List of plates'. The treatment of the subject is otherwise as in Gould's other works in large folio, a brief explanatory text accompanying each plate.

The plates (J. Gould and H. C. Richter del. et lith., or J. & E. Gould del.) are executed in lithography coloured by hand (Hullmandel & Walton, or C. Hullmandel, imp.).

A supplement to the work was issued by Gould in 1851—59 (179), the text of the main work and the supplement being published in 1865 in an enlarged form under the title 'Handbook to the birds of Australia' (London, 2 vols., 8vo).

1843—44. The zoology of the voyage of H. M. S. Sulphur, under the command of Captain Sir Edward Belcher ... 1836—42. Published under the authority of the Lords Commissioners of the Admiralty. Edited and superintended by Richard Brinsley Hinds. No.

III (IV). Birds, by John Gould. Smith, Elder and Co. London. 2 parts. 16 col. pl. fol. — Part I. 1843. pp. 37—44. 8 col. pl. (numb. 19—26). Part II. 1844. pp. 45—50. 8 col. pl. (numb. 27—34).

This expedition made studies and scientific investigations on the shores and among the islands of the Pacific Ocean. The zoological results were published in 12 parts in 1843—45.

The present section on birds appeared as Nos. III and IV, as stated in the still extant covers of the parts of the present copy, which are dated October, 1843, and January, 1844, respectively. The above title is taken from these covers. A total of 16 species is dealt with, all of which are figured and eleven of which, described as new, have also been treated by Gould in the Proceedings of the Zoological Society of London, Parts X and XI, 1842—43.

The majority of the plates (lithographs coloured by hand, printed by C. Hullmandel) are signed: drawn by J. Gould, on stone by B. Waterhouse Hawkins.

[1844—] 1850. A monograph of the Odontopho- 176. rinæ, or partridges of America. By John Gould. Published by the author. London. pp. 23 + [1] + [63]. 32 col. pl. large fol.

Published in three parts appearing in succession in 1844, 1846, and 1850 respectively. Altogether 35 species are described, of which three are more closely treated in the introduction. This gives a general account of the group, especially as regards classification.

Each of the 32 forms figured is treated in detail in the text, which accompanies the individual plates and contains a brief diagnosis in Latin, description — sometimes of both male and female —, measurements, and synonyms, and also data of the appearance, habits, and habitats, of the birds, and information about the figures on the plates.

The plates (J. Gould and H. C. Richter del. et lith.) are executed in lithography coloured by hand (Hullmandel & Walton, or C. Hullmandel, imp.).

[1849—] 1861. A monograph of the Trochilidæ, 177. or family of humming-birds. By John Gould. Published by the author. London. 5 vols. 360 col. pl. (numb. in the lists of plates). large fol. — Vol. I. pp. [IX] + V—CXXVII + [81]. 41 col. pl. (Nos. 1—41). Vol. II. pp. [III] + [149]. 75 col. pl. (Nos. 42—116). Vol. III. pp. [III] + [175]. 87 col. pl. (Nos. 117—203). Vol. IV. pp. [III] + [159]. 80 col. pl. (Nos. 204—283). Vol. V. pp. [III] + [153]. 77 col. pl. (Nos. 284—360).

This work was published in 25 parts. Each volume contains a 'List of plates' giving the numbers of the plates of the particular volume.

In addition to the matter concerning the birds figured Vol. I contains a preface (pp. V—VIII), dated September 1, 1861, and a long introduction (pp. IX—CXXVII) with a general review of the group, including a synopsis of the classification and a review of the individual forms, including also nomenclature. The introductory chapters conclude with lists of generic and specific names. These introductory chapters (preface, introduction, and list of names) were issued separately in 1861 under the title 'An introduction to the Trochilidæ, or family of humming birds' (London, 8vo).

The explanatory text about the birds figured contains synonyms, history, and, in addition to other information of interest, a brief description.

The plates (J. Gould and H. C. Richter, del. et lith.) are executed in lithography coloured by hand (Hullmandel & Walton (some few: Walter & Cohn) imp.), while Mr. Bayfield, who is thanked in the preface, seems to have been concerned in the colouring.

A supplement to the present work was issued under the same title as this work in 1880—87 (182).

1850—53. Contributions to ornithology ... See Jardine, W., 1848—53.

1850—83. The birds of Asia. By John Gould. De- 178. dicated to the honourable East India Company. Pub-

lished by the author. *London. 7 vols. 530 col. pl.
(numb. in the lists of plates). large fol.* — Vol. I. *pp.*
[VII] + *9* + *[1]* + *[151]. 76 col. pl. (Nos. 1—76).*
Vol. II. *pp. [IV]* + *[149]. 75 col. pl. (Nos. 1—75).*
Vol. III. *pp. [IV]* + *[155]. 78 col. pl. (Nos. 1—78).*
Vol. IV. *pp. [IV]* + *[143]. 72 col. pl. (Nos. 1—72).*
Vol. V. *pp. [IV]* + *[165]. 83 col. pl. (Nos. 1—83).*
Vol. VI. *pp. [IV]* + *[149]. 75 col. pl. (Nos. 1—75).*
Vol. VII. *pp. [IV]* + *[141]. 71 col. pl. (Nos. 1—71).*

This work was published in 35 parts, of which the last
three were issued after Gould's death by R. Bowdler Sharpe,
whose contributions are marked with the initials 'R. B. S.'.
He also wrote the preface and the introduction to the work.
Each volume contains a 'List of plates' which states in which
part the particular plate is published and when that part appeared.

The introduction contains a general review of the history
of Asiatic ornithology during the time the work was published.

As in Gould's other works, each plate is accompanied by
a leaf of descriptive text giving synonymy, history, description, and other information of interest regarding the form
figured on the particular plate.

The plates, executed in lithography coloured by hand, were
drawn and lithographed by J. Gould in collaboration with W.
Hart or H. C. Richter, or by the latter in collaboration with
J. Wolf, or — in the parts issued after Gould's death — by
W. Hart. The plates were printed by Hullmandel & Walton,
T. Walter, or Walter & Cohn.

Plates from this work were reproduced in Gould's unfinished
paper 'A monograph of the Pittidæ', etc. (London 1880, 1
part, 10 (13 ?) col pl., large folio).

179.   *[1851—] 1869. The birds of Australia. By John
Gould. Supplement. Published by the author. London.
5 parts. 81 col. pl. (numb. 1—81 in 'List of plates').
large fol.* — Part I. 1851. *pp. [31]. 16 col. pl.* Part II.
1855. *pp. [35]. 17 col. pl.* Part III. 1859. *pp. [29]. 16
col. pl.* Part IV. 1867. *pp. [31]. 16 col. pl.* Part V.
1869. *pp. [31]* + *IV* + *[4]. 16 col. pl.*

In 1840—48 Gould had issued his work 'The birds of
Australia' (174), to which the present treatise forms a supplement. The five parts, which are in the original covers, deal
with a number of the forms belonging to the area and discovered after the conclusion of the main work cited above.

The plates are executed in lithography coloured by hand
(J. Gould & H. C. Richter, del. et lith.; Parts I—III: Hullmandel & Walton, imp., Parts IV—V: Walter, imp.).

The text of this work was re-issued in 1865, as stated in
the note on the main work (174).

180.   *1855. Supplement to the first edition of A monograph of the Ramphastidæ, or family of toucans. By
John Gould. Published by the author. London. pp.
7—26* + *[41]. 20 col. pl. large fol.*

This supplement was issued in two parts. The work to
which it belongs appeared in 1833—35 (170), a new and
enlarged edition being issued in 1852—54. The supplement,
which was intended to balance the two editions, therefore deals
with the forms which are found in the second edition but not
in the first.

The introduction — a reprint of the introduction to the
second edition of the work — treats of the group in general,
principally as regards history and habits — illustrated by quotations from various authors — and classification.

The text accompanying the plates, as in the main work,
gives under each form the specific character in Latin and
English, measurements, and other data of the birds.

The plates (Gould & Richter, del. (or del. et lith.)) are
executed in lithography coloured by hand (Hullmandel &
Walton, imp.).

181.   *1875—88. The birds of New Guinea and the adjacent Papuan Islands, including many new species recently discovered in Australia. By John Gould. Completed after the author's death by R. Bowdler Sharpe.*

Henry Sotheran & Co. *London. 5 vols. 320 col. pl.
(numb. in the 'Contents'). large fol.* — Vol. I. *pp. [III]*
+ *III* + *[I]* + *[109]. 56 col. pl. (Nos. 1—56).* Vol.
II. *pp. [III]* + *[115]. 58 col. pl. (Nos. 1—58).*
Vol. III. *pp. [IV]* + *[143]. 72 col. pl. (Nos. 1—72).*
Vol. IV. *pp. [III]* + *[117]. 59 col. pl. (Nos. 1—59).*
Vol. V. *pp. [IV]* + *[149]. 75 col. pl. (Nos. 1—75).*

The present copy of this work consists of the 25 parts in
which it was issued, the contents of which are distributed among
the individual volumes as stated above.

The individual parts may be briefly described as follows:—
Part I, 1875, (Dec. 1), *pp. [25]. 13 col. pl.;*
Part II, 1876, (Jan. 1), *pp. [25]. 13 col. pl.;*
Part III, 1876, (May 1), *pp. [25]. 13 col. pl.;*
Part IV, 1877, (Jan. 1), *pp. [25]. 13 col. pl.;*
Part V, 1877, (June 1), *pp. [25]. 13 col. pl.;*
Part VI, 1878, (Febr. 1), *pp. [25]. 13 col. pl.;*
Part VII, 1878, (June 1), *pp. [25]. 13 col. pl.;*
Part VIII, 1878, (Oct. 1), *pp. [23]. 12 col. pl.;*
Part IX, 1879, (March 1), *pp. [23]. 12 col. pl.;*
Part X, 1879, (Sept.), *pp. [23]. 13 col. pl.;*
Part XI, 1880, (Febr.), *pp. [25]. 13 col. pl.;*
Part XII, 1881, *pp. [25]. 13 col. pl.;*
Part XIII, 1882, *pp. [25]. 13 col. pl.;*
Part XIV, 1883, *pp. [25]. 13 col. pl.;*
Part XV, 1883, *pp. [25]. 13 col. pl.;*
Part XVI, 1884, *pp. [25]. 13 col. pl.;*
Part XVII, 1884, *pp. [25]. 13 col. pl.;*
Part XVIII, 1884, *pp. [25]. 13 col. pl.;*
Part XIX, 1885, *pp. [25]. 13 col. pl.;*
Part XX, 1885, *pp. [25]. 13 col. pl.;*
Part XXI, 1886, *pp. [25]. 13 col. pl.;*
Part XXII, 1886, *pp. [25]. 13 col. pl.;*
Part XXIII, 1887, *pp. [25]. 13 col. pl.;*
Part XXIV, 1888, *pp. [25]. 13 col. pl.;*
Part XXV, 1888, *pp. [19]* + *title-pages, preface, introduc-
tion, and contents. 10 col. pl.*

After Gould's death the work was continued and finished
by R. Bowdler Sharpe who is responsible for the last thirteen
parts, as is evidenced by the initials (R. B. S.) appended at the
foot of each article. Sharpe further prepared the preface and
the sketch of the zoological work carried out in New Guinea
and the Moluccas, which constitutes the introduction (pp. I—
III).

The explanatory text which accompanies each plate contains
synonymy, description, and other information about the bird
figured on the plate.

The plates are executed in lithography coloured by hand,
those in Parts I XII, some in Part XIII, and a few in the
subsequent parts, being signed: J. Gould & W. Hart, del. et
lith., while the remainder of the plates are signed: W. Hart,
del. et lith. The printing of the plates in Parts I—XV and
of some in Part XVI was done by Walter, Mintern Bros.
printing the rest.

*[1880—] 1887. A monograph of the Trochilidæ
or family of humming-birds. By John Gould. Completed after the author's death by R. Bowdler Sharpe.
Supplement.* Henry Sotheran & Co. *London. pp.
[VII]* + *[199]. 58 col. pl. large fol.*

In 1849—61 Gould issued his work 'A monograph of
the Trochilidæ' (177), to which the present forms a supplement; it was issued in five parts, which appeared in 1880,
1881, 1883, 1885, and 1887 respectively.

After Gould's death, which occurred before the publication
of Part II, the continuation of the work was entrusted to
Sharpe, whose contributions are marked with his initials (R.
B. S.). In the preface Sharpe thanks Osbert Salvin 'for his
advice in planning the present work and for having supervised
the proofs of each Part'. A large number of species are included
in the supplement without accompanying plates, Sharpe having
included descriptions of all the species of Trochilidæ discovered
since 1861, when Gould's monograph was finished.

The plates are executed in lithography coloured by hand.
Most of the drawings for the plates were executed while Gould
was alive, while the finishing of the plates was entrusted

W. Hart. The majority of them are therefore signed : J. Gould
& W. Hart del. et. lith., some of the supplementary plates being
signed : W. Hart del. et lith. The plates were printed by
Walter or Mintern Bros.

GRAESER, K.

1904. Der Zug der Vögel. Eine entwicklungsge-
schichtliche Studie von Kurt Graeser. Hermann Wal-
ther. *Berlin. pp. 96. text-figs. 5 col. pl. 8vo.*

An attempt to explain the origin of the migration of the
birds on the basis of the theory of evolution by assuming the
development of a migratory instinct in all species and its decline
or disappearance in some of them.

The plates (three-colour prints, by J. S. Preuss, Berlin)
were executed from original water-colours by E. Bade.

The second edition of the book appeared in 1905, the third
edition in 1911.

GRANT, W. R. O.- *See Ogilvie-Grant, W. R.*

GRANVIK, S. H.

1923. Journal für Ornithologie. 71. Jahrgang.
<- - Sonderheft. Contributions to the knowledge of the
East African ornithology. Birds collected by the Swedish Mount Elgon Expedition 1920. By Hugo Granvik >. Deutsche Ornithologische Gesellschaft. *Berlin.*
pp. [III] + 280 + [1]. text-figs. 10 pl. (numb. 1—
10; 5 col. (numb. 1—5)). 1 map. (numb. 11). 8vo.

A report, issued on February 15, 1923, on the ornithological
results of the Swedish expedition, carried in the title, carried
out under the leadership of S. A. Lovén.

The first section, the general part, deals with the itinerary
of the expedition, system and nomenclature, the route of the
expedition, and the ornithology of Mount Elgon and surrounding regions.

The systematic part, in which the birds are arranged in
accordance with the system of classification of Reichenow's
work 'Die Vögel Afrikas' (416), discusses the material collected,
which consists of 1517 specimens, distributed over 330 forms,
ten of which are described as new.

The coloured plates (three-colour prints) were executed from
drawings by Erich Schröder.

GRAY, G. R.

1838—41. The zoology of the voyage of H.
M. S. Beagle ... 1832—1826 ... Part III. Birds. *See*
Gould, J.

1844—75. The zoology of the voyage of H. M. S.
Erebus & Terror, under the command of Captain
Sir James Clark Ross ... 1839—43. By authority of
the Lords Commissioners of the Admiralty. Edited by
John Richardson and John Edward Gray. Vol. I.
Mammalia, birds. - - Birds. By George Robert Gray
and R. Bowdler Sharpe. E. W. Janson. *London. pp.*
39. 37 col. pl. (numb. 1—35, 1, 11*, 20*, XXI*,*
missing Nos. 12 and 22). 4to.

The special title-page for the ornithological section of the
report of this expedition is dated 1846—75. The section is
divided into two parts, of which Part 1, 'Birds of New Zealand', pp. 1—20, was written by G. R. Gray. Pp. 1—8 of
this part were published in 1844, while pp. 9—20 were published in 1845 (328, VII, p. 484). The appendix (pp. 21—39),
which appeared in 1875, was written by R. B. Sharpe. It ends
with a list of the plates originally issued and those now issued. In this list numbers 12 and 22 are missing. The plates
are executed in lithography coloured by hand. The plates in
the latter series, however, are marked : Wolf del. et lit., printed
by Hullmandel and Walton, while the former are marked :
C. Hullmandel's Patent Lithotint.

1873. Jottings during the cruise of H. M. S. Cura- *186.*
çoa among the South Sea Islands in 1865. By Julius
L. Brenchley. <- - *pp. 353—394:* Birds. By G. R.
Gray >. Longmans, Green, and Co. *London. 21 col.*
pl. (numb. 1—21). 8vo.

This work, the ornithological section of which is cited here,
may be briefly described as follows: pp. XXVIII + 487, text-
figs., 60 pl. (44 col.).

The section on birds was prepared on the basis of material
collected by Brenchley during the cruise of the frigate 'Curaçoa'
in the western Pacific. Only birds new to science or particularly
rare are noted.

The bird portraits were drawn and lithographed by J. Smit,
and the plates (lithographs coloured by hand) impressed by
Mintern Bros.

GRAY, J. E.

1827—29. The animal kingdom ... by the baron
Cuvier ... Vols. VI—VIII. The class aves ... The ad-
ditional species inserted in the text of Cuvier by John
Edward Gray. *See Cuvier, G. L. C. F. D.*

1830—35. Illustrations of Indian zoology; chiefly *187*
selected from the collection of Major-General Hardwicke. By John Edward Gray. Treuttel, Wurtz, Treuttel, jun., and Richter. *London. 2 vols. 90 col. pl. birds.*
large fol.

This work was published in altogether 20 parts, of which,
however, only the first twelve are found in the present copy,
which may be briefly described as follows, the ornithological
plates only being mentioned :

    Vol. I, 1830—32, *pp. (VI). front. 58 col. pl. birds*
                (numb. 14—71 in the list of plates).
    Part XI (1832) *4 col. pl. birds (numb. V—VIII on cover).*
    Part XII (1832) *4 col. pl. birds (numb. VI—IX on cover).*

The list of subscribers is missing in Vol. I.

A summary of the approximate date of publication and
the contents of each part was given by Zimmer (589, pp.
272—273) from N. B. Kinnear (773). In its complete form
the work contains 202 coloured plates for, as planned, each
part was to consist of 10 plates. The plates themselves are not
provided with numbers but are numbered in the 'Directions for
arranging the plates' appended to each volume. Vol. I is composed of Parts I—X, Vol. II of Parts XI—XX.

After the appearance of Part XII publication was interrupted for more than a year. In the present copy Parts XI
and XII are found in their original covers, whose title runs
as follows: 'Illustrations of Indian Zoology, consisting of
coloured plates of new or hitherto unfigured Indian animals,
from the collection of Major-General Hardwicke. Selected and
arranged by John Edward Gray. Dedicated, by permission, to
the honourable court of directors of the East India Company'.
On the back of the cover there is a 'Prospectus', in which
among other announcements is the statement that 'shortly will
be published ... Part I, containing the Mammalia of Prodromus
Faunæ Indicæ, or a synopsis of Indian vertebrated animals,
containing the generic and specific characters of all recorded
Indian Vertebrated Animals ... This Synopsis will form a Text
to the »Illustrations«', and 'will be complete in four parts'. However, this work was never issued. The Prospectus furthermore
gives information about the material possessed by General
Hardwicke, on the basis of which the present work was prepared,
and of which are mentioned 'Drawings made upon the spot,
and chiefly from living specimens of Animals ... executed by
English and native Artists, constantly employed for this purpose, under his [Hardwicke's] own immediate superintendence'.
This collection of water-colour drawings was bequeathed by
Hardwicke to the British Museum ; it consists of 32 volumes
(552, II, p. 903 ; 677, I, pp. 37—38 ; II, pp. 169—170 ; II.
Appendix, p. 54). The figures of birds, of which 76 are said
to be due to T. W. Lewin, amount to a total of 1735 which,
however, do not all represent Indian birds.

Not all of the plates in the present work were, however,
executed from drawings in the collection mentioned above ;

17*

some are derived from other sources, such as drawings which Gray caused to be made from specimens in the British Museum. The plates (drawn & lith. (or lith.) by Waterhouse Hawkins) are coloured by hand (printed by Engelmann & Co., W. Day, or Graf & Soret).

188. *1831.* The zoological miscellany. To be continued occasionally. By John Edward Gray. Treuttel, Wurtz and Co. *London. pp. 40. 4 pl. (3 col. pl. birds). 8vo.*

This is a copy in the original cover of the first part of a work, of which six parts only appeared, and which stopped in 1844 after the publication of altogether 86 pages and the four unsigned plates (engravings, the ornithological ones coloured by hand) in Part 1.

1844—75. The zoology of the voyage of H. M. S. Erebus & Terror ... 1839—43 ... Edited · by John Richardson and John Edward Gray ... Birds. *See Gray, G. R.*

189. *1846.* Gleanings from the menagerie and aviary at Knowsley Hall. *Knowsley. pp. [III] + [10]. 9 col. pl. birds (numb. 8—15, one pl. unnumb. [= 16]). large fol.*

The work whose ornithological plates are cited here consists of two parts, the first of which, whose text is collated above, contains 17 plates, while the other part (Hoofed quadrupeds, dated 1850), which in the present copy is bound together with the first part, may be described as follows: pp. [III] + 76, 62 pl. (partly col.).

The text for the ornithological plates, pp. [4—10], consists mainly of extracts from notes by Lord Derby, whose collection of living animals at Knowsley Hall had served as a. basis for the execution of the drawings from which the plates (lithographs) of the present work were produced. The ornithological plates were executed from drawings by Edward Lear, lithographed by J. W. Moore (pl. 15 : in lithotint by D. Mitchell), and coloured by Bayfield (printed by Hullmandel & Walton).

GREAT BRITAIN AND IRELAND. Voyages, expeditions, etc.

1831. Fauna Boreali-Americana ... containing descriptions of the objects of natural history collected on the late northern land expeditions under command of Captain Sir John Franklin. Part II. The birds. *See Swainson, W.*

1838—41. The zoology of the voyage of H. M. S. Beagle ... 1832—1836 ... Part III. Birds. *See Gould, J.*

1839. The zoology of Captain Beechey's voyage ... in H. M. S. Blossom ... 1825—28 ... pp. 13—40: Ornithology. *See Vigors, N. A.*

1843—44. The zoology of the voyage of H. M. S. Sulphur ... 1836—42 ... (Nos. III—IV). Birds. *See Gould, J.*

1844—75. The zoology of the voyage of H. M. S. Erebus & Terror ... 1839—43 ... Birds. *See Gray, G. R.*

1870. Observations on the geology and zoology of Abyssinia, made during the progress of the British expedition to that country in 1867—68. pp. 285—443: Class aves. *See Blanford, W. T.*

1873. Jottings during the cruise of H. M. S. Curaçoa among the South Sea Islands in 1865 ... pp. 353—394: Birds. *See Gray, G. R.*

1880. Report on the birds collected during the voyage of H. M. S. Challenger ... 1873—76. *See Sclater, P. L.*

1886. The cruise of the Marchesa to Kamschatka & New Guinea, with notices of Formosa, Liu-Kiu,

and various islands of the Malay Archipelago ... *See Guillemard, F. H. H.*

1907. National Antarctic Expedition 1901—04. Natural history. Vol. II. Zoology ... II. Aves. *See Wilson, E. A.*

1910. Zoological results of the Ruwenzori Expedition, 1905—06. pp. 253—480: Part 4 ... Aves ... *See Ogilvie-Grant, W. R.*

1915 & 1916. Report on the birds collected by the British Ornithologists' Union Expedition and the Wollaston Expedition in Dutch New Guinea. *See Ogilvie-Grant, W. R.*

GRIFFITH, E.

1827—29. The animal kingdom ... by the baron Cuvier ... Vols. VI—VIII. The class aves ... with specific descriptions by Edward Griffith ... *See Cuvier, G. L. C. F. D.*

GRINNELL, J.

1918. Semicentennial Publications of the University of California. The game birds of California. Contribution from the University of California, Museum of Vertebrate Zoology. By Joseph Grinnell, Harold Child Bryant, and Tracy Irwin Storer. University of California Press. *Berkeley. pp. X + 642. text-figs. 16 col. pl. (numb. 1—16). 8vo.*

This work on the status of the game birds of California gives in its introductory sections a summary of some general questions relative to the subject, such as the decrease of game, the natural enemies of game birds, attempts to introduce non-native game birds, and game propagation and legislation. The large systematic section gives a description of the individual species and a brief characterization of field marks, voice, nest, eggs, and distribution, while the habits, the life-histories and the economic importance of the birds are treated at greater length.

The line-drawings in the text are due to Frieda Lueddemann, while the plates (three-colour prints) were executed from drawings by L. A. Fuertes (altogether 12) and Allan Brooks (4 plates).

GRØNVOLD, H.

1915—17. The birds of South America. Vol. II. Illustrations of the game birds and water fowl of South America. *See Brabourne, W. W. K.-H., Third Baron, 1913—17.*

GROUSE.

1912. The Grouse in health and in disease ... *See Leslie, A. S.*

GUÉNEAU DE MONTBEILLARD, P.

1770—83. Histoire naturelle des oiseaux. *See Buffon, G. L. L. de, 1770—86.*

GUENTHER, F. C.

1772. Sammlung von Nestern und Eyern verschiedener Vögel ... Erstes Heft. *See Wirsing, A. L., 1772—86.*

GUÉRIN-MÉNEVILLE, F. E.

[1829—38]. Iconographie du Règne Animal de Mr. le Baron Cuvier, ou représentation, d'après nature, de l'une des espèces les plus remarquables, et souvent non encore figurée, de chaque genre d'animaux. Ouvrage pouvant servir d'atlas à tous les traités de zoologie. Dédié à Mr. le Baron Cuvier et à Mr. La-

treille. Par F. E. Guérin. [Vol. I]. (Mammifères Oiseaux). J. B. Baillière. *Paris. 70 col. pl. birds (numb.
1—67, 22bis, 23bis, 36bis). 4to.*
According to Quérard (579, III, 1829, p. 509) five livraisons of this work appeared at the end of 1829 (livraison V
appeared in 'Bibliographie de la France', January 23, 1830),
while Brunet (558, II, column 1786) states that the total number
of 450 plates were published in 45 livraisons (of 10 pl.) from
1830 to 1838. Then followed, in livraisons 46—50, an explanatory text to the plates, by which the work was completed in 1844. The above title is cited from a wrapper.
Both text and plates were issued in two formats, 8vo and
4to, and parts of the various sections were published in each
livraison.
In a report to the Académie des Sciences Cuvier recommended the work as being very useful for people who wanted
to know the multifarious animal forms, and he also said that
the figures were 'as accurate as they were elegant'.
The plates (Impr. de Rémond, some few Langlois) were
engraved by Giraud, a single one by Canu, printed in colour
and retouched by hand, from drawings by Guérin, mostly in
collaboration with E. Traviès; some few were executed from
drawings by Bévalet and Prêtre. Each plate contains 2—4
coloured figures of birds and uncoloured figures of beaks and
feet. A few figures of feathers are given.

GUILLEMARD, F. H. H.
1886. The cruise of the Marchesa to Kamschatka
& New Guinea, with notices of Formosa, Liu-Kiu, and
various islands of the Malay Archipelago. By F. H. H.
Guillemard. With maps and numerous woodcuts,
drawn by J. Keulemans, C. Whymper, and others, and
engraved by Edward Whymper. John Murray. London. *2 vols. 8vo. — Vol. I. pp. XVII + [I] + 284.
text-figs. 1 col. pl. bird. (front.). 5 maps. Vol. II.
pp. XVI + [I] + 399. text-figs. 7 pl. birds (1 col.
(front.). 9 maps.*
This voyage was made in an auxiliary screw schooner yacht
of 420 tons, owned by Mr. C. T. Kettlewell, and started from
England on January 8, 1882, where it ended again on April
14, 1884.
The present report of the voyage contains much information about the physical conditions of the regions visited. A
large collection of objects of natural history was brought home,
especially from the Malay and Papuan regions, including
about 3000 specimens of birds, which the author treated in
a series of papers in the Proceedings of the Zoological Society
of London for 1885. One of the main objects was to become
acquainted with the Birds of Paradise in their native forests,
and a total number of seventeen different species of these birds
was obtained.
The two volumes are abundantly illustrated and contain
11 and 20 plates respectively; the ornithological plates (the
coloured ones in lithography coloured by hand) were executed
from drawings by J. G. Keulemans, who also drew the originals
for the ornithological illustrations in the text. A second edition
of this work appeared in 1889.

GUNNISON, J. W.
1859. Reports of explorations and surveys ... for a
railroad from the Mississippi River to the Pacific
Ocean ... 1853—56. Vol. X. Report of Lieut. E. G.
Beckwith ... upon explorations ... near the 38th and
39th parallels of north latitude, by Captain J. W.
Gunnison ... 1854. Zoological report. 1857. pp. 11—
16: No. 2. Report on birds collected on the survey.
See Baird, S. F.

GYLLING, C. O.
1911—26. Nordens fåglar ... Vol. II. Tavlor av
Olof Gylling. *See Jägerskiöld, A. K. E. L.*

HAACKE, J. W.
1891—92. Brehms Thierleben ... Dritte ... Auflage. Vols. IV—VI. Die Vögel ... Unter Mitwirkung
von Wilh. Haacke ... *See Brehm, A. E.*
1893. Die Schöpfung der Tierwelt. Von Wilhelm **193.**
Haacke. Mit 1 Karte und 469 Abbildungen im Text
und auf 20 Tafeln in Farbendruck und Holzschnitt
von R. Koch, W. Kuhnert und G. Mützel. Bibliographisches Institut. *Leipzig. pp. X + 557 + [4], text-
figs. 6 col. pl. birds. 4to.*
A popular account of the evolution of animals, divided
into a general part and a special part, in which the evolution
of the individual main groups of the animal kingdom is treated.
The account is based chiefly on the works of Lamarck, Ernst
Haeckel, and other evolutionary theorists.
The coloured plates with figures of birds were executed
from drawings by W. Kuhnert.

HACHISUKA, M.
1935. Report of the First Scientific Expedition to
Manchoukuo ... June-October 1933. Section V. Division II. Part III. Birds of Jehol. *See Taka-Tsukasa, N.*

HAHN, C. W.
[1830—] 1835. Fauna Boica, oder gemeinnützige **194.**
Naturgeschichte der Thiere Bayerns bearbeitet und
herausgegeben von Jakob Ernst von Reider und Carl
Wilhelm Hahn. Zweite Abtheilung. Vögel. Mit ... fein
ausgemalten Tafeln. - - Deutschlands Vögel in Abbildungen nach der Natur mit Beschreibungen, von
Carl Wilhelm Hahn ... E. H. Zeh. *Nürnberg. 2 vols.
182 col. pl. (numb. 1—182 in 'Systematische Uebersicht'). 8vo. — Vol. I. Landvögel. pp. LXII + [358].
110 col. pl. (Nos. 1—110). Vol. II. Sumpf- und Wasservögel. pp. [230]. 72 col. pl. (Nos. 111—182).*
The ornithological section of a work on the fauna of Bavaria, which appeared in 1830—35 in 6 Abtheilungen with
altogether 29 Lieferungen, of which Nos. 2, 8, 12, 29, 16—18,
20, and 22—27 constitute the present section (552, IV,
p. 1672).
The text (unpaginated) deals with the species in a
systematical order, the matter under each species being as
a rule grouped under the following headings:— 'Art-Kenn-
zeichen', 'Beschreibung', 'Aufenthalt', 'Nahrung', 'Fortpflanzung',
'Eigenheiten und Sitten', 'Schaden', 'Nutzen', 'Feinde', 'Namen'.
Part I, pp. III—LXII, consists of a 'Systematische Übersicht der Vögel', in which the number of figures on the plates
(some lithographs and some engravings, coloured by hand),
which represent all the forms treated in the text, is stated to
be 301.

HAMBURG.   NATURWISSENSCHAFTLICHER
VEREIN. *See Naturwissenschaftlicher Verein in
Hamburg.*

HAMONVILLE, J. C. L. T. d'.
1898. Atlas de poche des oiseaux de France, Bel- **195.**
gique et Suisse utiles ou nuisibles. Suivi d'une étude
d'ensemble sur les oiseaux. Par L. d'Hamonville. Paul
Klincksieck. *Paris. 2 vols. 164 pl. (144 col.). small
8vo. — Série I. (Bibliothèque de poche du naturaliste.
VII). pp. VII + 152 + [I] + 16. 76 pl. (72 col.
(numb. 1—72); 4 uncol. (numb. A—D)). Série II.
(Bibliothèque de poche du naturaliste. IX). pp. VI +
[I] + 157 + 16. text-fig. 88 pl. (72 col. (numb. 1—
72); 16 uncol. (numb. I—XVI)).*
These two small popular volumes are each divided into

a systematic and a general section. The former gives brief information about the species figured, principally their life history, their economic importance, and biological conditions.

Series I treats of 70 species of birds, while Series II deals with 72 species. In addition to birds, eggs and nests are figured. The plates (chromo-lithographs) were executed from drawings by G. Denise.

HANCOCK, J.

196. *1874*. Natural History Transactions of Northumberland and Durham; being papers read at the meetings of the Natural History Society of Northumberland, Durham, and Newcastle-upon-Tyne, and the Tyneside Naturalists' Field Club, 1873. Vol. VI. <- - A catalogue of the birds of Northumberland and Durham. By John Hancock >. Williams & Norgate. *London. pp. XXV + 174 + [3]. 14 pl. (front. + Nos. 1—13). 8vo.*

This systematically arranged list comprises 265 species, ninety-one of which are resident forms. It is illustrated with 14 photographic copperplates, from drawings by the author. The list was re-issued separately in 1874.

HARDWICKE, T.

1826—35. Illustrations of ornithology ... Vols. I—III. *See Jardine, W.,* 1826—43.

1830—35. Illustrations of Indian zoology ... *See Gray, J. E.*

HARGITT, E.

1890. Catalogue of the birds in the British Museum. Vol. XVIII. *See British Museum (Natural History),* 1874—98.

HARRIMAN, E. H.

1902. Harriman Alaska Expedition ...
Vol. I. pp. 1—118: Narrative of the expedition. *See Burroughs, J.*
Vol. II. pp. 205—234: Days among Alaska birds. *See Keeler, C. A.*

HARTERT, E. J. O.

1892. Catalogue of the birds in the British Museum. Vol. XVI. *See British Museum (Natural History),* 1874—98.
1894—1933. See Novitates Zoologicæ.
1910—13. The British bird book ... *See Kirkman, F. B. B.*

HARTING, J. E. F.

1880. Glimpses of bird life ... *See Robert, L. P. S.*

HARTLAUB, C. J. G.

1850—53. Contributions to ornithology ... *See Jardine, W.,* 1848—53.

197. *1852*. Abhandlungen aus dem Gebiete der Naturwissenschaften herausgegeben von dem naturwissenschaftlichen Verein in Hamburg. Vol. II. Part II. <- - *pp. 1—56:* Beitrag zur Ornithologie Westafrica's, von G. Hartlaub >. Herold. *Hamburg. 11 col. pl, (numb. I—XI). 4to.*

A study on the birds of West Africa, based on a zoological collection sent in two shipments to the Hamburg Museum by the traveller Carl Weiss. The collection included 59 species of birds, eleven of which are described as new in the present paper, which consists principally of a list of all the birds

hitherto observed in the area (pp. 14—44); 501 species are enumerated, seven of them in a 'Nachtrag' (p. 44).

The plates are engravings coloured by hand (L. Reichenbach del., E. Lange sc.).

A 'Zweiter Beitrag zur Ornithologie Westafrica's' by G. Hartlaub was published in the same volume and in the same part of the periodical, pp. 57—68.

1867. Beitrag zur Fauna Centralpolynesiens. Ornithologie der Viti-, Samoa- und Tonga-Inseln. *See Finsch, F. H. O.*

1870. Baron Carl Claus von der Decken's Reisen in Ost-Afrika ... 1859—65. Vol. IV. Die Vögel Ost-Afrikas. *See Finsch, F. H. O.*

HATCHER, J. B.

1904—28. Reports of the Princeton University expeditions to Patagonia, 1896—1899. J. B. Hatcher in charge ... Vol. II. Ornithology. *See Scott, W. E. D.*

HAY, A., Ninth Marquis of Tweeddale. *See Tweeddale, A. H., Ninth Marquis of.*

HAYES, W.

[1771?—] 1775. A natural history of British birds, &c. with their portraits, accurately drawn, and beautifully coloured from Nature, by Hayes. S. Hooper. *London. pp. [III] + 24. 40 col. pl. (numb. I—XL in text). large fol.*

This work seems to have been published in parts; the dedication (engraved) refers to 'this first part of the portraits of British birds'.

The species described and figured — altogether 47 — are not all indigenous; several imported forms, for instance pheasants, are treated.

The text, which is without any great value, describes each of the birds figured, giving its nar e in English, Latin, and French, a brief diagnosis in Latin, and a description and other information in English. The latter part of the text is printed in parallel coloumns.

The plates, of no particularly prominent quality, were executed in engravings coloured by hand from drawings by the author, who also engraved several of them, while some were engraved by Gabr. Smith.

HEERMANN, A. L.

1859. Reports of explorations and surveys, to ascertain the most practicable and economical route for a railroad from the Mississippi River to the Pacific Ocean ... 1853—6 ... Vol. X. <- - Report of explorations for a railroad route near the 32d parallel of north latitude, lying between Dona Ana, on the Rio Grande, and Pimas Villages, on the Gila, by Lieutenant John G. Parke ... 1855. - - Zoological report. - - *pp. 9—20 + [1]:* No. 1. Report upon birds collected on the survey. By A. L. Heermann >. Beverley Tucker. (Senate Ex. Doc., No. 78). *Washington. 3 col. pl. (numb. I, IV, VI). 4to.*

This paper, belonging to a report commenced in Vol. VII, 1857, of the series, treats of 25 species and gives specific characters and field notes. Reference is also made to the page in the general report on birds, Vol. IX of the series (22), on which the bird in question is more closely described.

The plates (lithographs coloured by hand) are reproduced with some alterations in Baird, Cassin, and Lawrence's 'The birds of North America' (24).

1859. Reports of explorations and surveys, to ascertain the most practicable and economical route for a railroad from the Mississippi River to the Pacific Ocean ... 1853—6 ... Vol. X. <- - Report of explorations in California for railroad routes to connect with the routes near the 35th and 32d parallels of north latitude. By Lieutenant R. S. Williamson ... 1853. - - Part IV. - - Zoological report. - - *pp. 29—80: No. 2.* Report upon birds collected on the survey. By A. L. Heermann >. Beverley Tucker. (Senate Ex. Doc., No. 78). *Washington. 7 col. pl. (numb. II—III, V, VII—X). 4to.*

In this treatise, which belongs to a report commenced in Vol. V, 1856, of the series, a great number of species are enumerated with the addition of field notes.

The plates (lithographs coloured by hand) are reproduced with some alterations in Baird, Cassin, and Lawrence's 'The birds of North America' (24).

HEILMANN, G. V. E.

[1926] 1928—30. Danmarks Fugleliv. Af Gerhard Heilmann og A. L. V. Manniche. Hage & Clausen. [Gyldendal]. *København. 3 vols. text-figs. 92 pl. (71 col.). 4to. —* Vol. I. [1926—] 1928. Indledning, Dykkere, Stormfugle, Storkefugle, Andefugle, Rovfugle. Med 155 Tekstbilleder og ... Tavler. *pp. [VIII] + 312. 36 pl. (numb. 1—36; 26 col. (numb. 1, 2, 7, 9—16, 18, 19, 22—24, 26, 28—36)).* Vol. II. [1928—] 1929. Hønsefugle, Tranefugle, Spovefugle. Gøgefugle, Skrigefugle. Med 148 Tekstbilleder og ... Tavler. *pp. [VI] + 322. 34 pl. (numb. 37—70; 24 col. (numb. 37—40, 43, 46—52, 54—56, 58, 59, 61, 62, 65, 66, 68—70)).* Vol. III. [1929—] 1930. Spurvefugle. Med 155 Tekstbilleder og ... Tavler. *pp. [VI] + 244 + [32]. 22 pl. (numb. 71—92; 21 col. (numb. 71, 73—92)).*

This popular handbook on the birds of Denmark, in which most attention is paid to the description of biological conditions, was published in 40 parts, which are cited in 'Dansk Bogfortegnelse' from October, 1926, to December, 1930.

The introduction, with general remarks upon the zoological conditions of the bird group, notably its classification and biology, was prepared by Heilmann, who wrote the chapter on the cuckoos, composed the text for the figures, and drew the figures for the plates and by far the greater number of the text-figures.

The systematic part, in which the individual species of birds are treated, was prepared by Manniche, largely on the basis of personal observation of the life conditions and habits of the birds. In addition to biology, the geographical distribution is briefly mentioned, while descriptions of the birds are reduced to a minimum, the portraits on the plates (three-colour prints, executed by Charles Hansen, printed by Oscar Fraenckel & Co.) forming a substitute.

The systematic arrangement chiefly follows Gadow in Bronn's 'Klassen und Ordnungen des Thier-Reichs', while the nomenclature employed agrees in all essentials with the earlier one used by H. Winge in his list of the birds of Denmark (914).

HEINROTH, M.

1924—33. Die Vögel Mitteleuropas ... *See Heinroth, O. A.*

HEINROTH, O. A.

[1924—33]. Die Vögel Mitteleuropas in allen Lebens- und Entwicklungsstufen photographisch aufgenommen und in ihrem Seelenleben bei der Aufzucht vom Ei ab beobachtet von Oskar und Magdalena Heinroth. Herausgegeben von der Staatl. Stelle für Naturdenkmalpflege in Preussen. Hugo Bermühler. *Berlin. 4 vols. 511 pl. (159 col.). 4to. —* Vol. I. [1924—

26]. Sperlingsvögel. Rackenvögel. Kuckuck. Spechte. *pp. VIII + 339. 170 pl. (53 col. (numb. I—LII, XXXVa); 117 uncol. (numb. 1—111, 3a, 66a, 68a, 69a, 69b, 93a)).* Vol. II [1926—27]. Eulen. Tauben. Raubvögel. Ruderfüsser. Sturmvogel. Reiher-Storchgruppe. *pp. IV + 160. 99 pl. (27 col. (numb. LIII—LXXIX); 72 uncol. (numb. 112—181, 114a, 156a)).* Vol. III. [1927—28]. Die Nestflüchter: Regenpfeifer- und Schnepfenvögel. Möwen. Rallen, Kranich. Trappe. Entenvögel. Hühner. Steissfüsse. *pp. X + 286. 140 pl. (49 col. (numb. LXXX—CXXVIII); 91 uncol. (numb. 182—267, 2?7a, 228a, 248a, 254a, 254b)).* Vol. IV. [1931—33]. Nachtrag. *pp. [IV] + 127 + [1]. 102 pl. 30 col. (numb. I—XXX); 72 uncol. (numb. 1—72)).*

This work was issued in 80 parts, the first of which appeared in June, 1924. They are found in the various volumes as follows:—

Vol. I (= Parts 1—33), Vol. II (= Parts 34—46), Vol. III (= Parts 47—60). The final Lieferung appeared in October, 1928. The supplementary volume (Vol. IV. Nachtrag) was issued in 20 parts.

The authors were collecting the particular material on which this work is based for more than twenty years before the work began to appear. During this time they reared a number of the breeding birds of Germany, either from individuals collected when a few days old, or from the egg. Later on — in 1908 — they also began to photograph the objects of their study, to illustrate in this way the bodily and mental development of the birds. They thus succeeded in examining nearly all the breeding birds of Germany, and figured them in their different stages of development in the several thousand pictures with which the work is illustrated.

The matter is as far as possible systematically arranged, and the text aims especially at throwing light on the bodily and mental development of the birds during their infancy, alterations in their weight, mental life and instinctive acts, changes of plumage, and special features of their habits, such as the way in which they collect their food, etc.; or mainly such things as had not previously received much attention, the object being to give a biological interpretation of the observations.

For purposes of comparison, the life of the birds in their natural environment was also studied. Their distribution is stated, subspecies are noted, and trinomials used in order to distinguish between geographical forms.

The arrangement of the matter in the supplementary volume agrees with that of the preceding parts of the work.

The coloured plates, which in Vols. I—III contain more than 765 figures, represent the eggs, the young bird just hatched, the inside of the mouth, and the bird at various ages. Mode of reproduction: faint impressions of the photographs were coloured by Erich Schröder from living birds or from skins from the Zoological Museum of Berlin. They were reproduced by the four-colour process; the blocks were made by Carl Schütte, Berlin, and the plates printed by Förster & Borries, Zwickau i. S.

Some of the coloured plates of the work are reproduced in the book 'Die heimischen Singvögel', 1934 (484).

HELMS, O.

1924. O. Helms Danske Fugle ved Hus og i Have. 203. Med ... farvetrykte Tavler af Ingeborg Frederiksen. G. E. C. Gad. *København. pp. 109 + [4]. text-figs. 14 col. pl. (numb. 1—14). 4to.*

A popular account intended as a guide in a convenient form for people who wish to identify the birds, chiefly song birds, generally met with near houses and in gardens. Such characteristics as can be observed in the bird in the open, its shape and colour, its song and whole behaviour, are therefore emphasized. The food and breeding habits of the different species are also briefly treated and a description given of their nests. The information about the life of the birds is based on the author's own observations. The systematic section is divided into breeding birds and winter birds and is succeeded by a chapter on how to protect birds and attract them to human habitations.

Altogether 42 species are treated, all of which are figured on the plates, somewhat weak in colour (three-colour prints), executed by Egmont H. Petersen. The plates contain 70 portraits of birds, painted from observations in the open, from birds in captivity, from birds just killed, or from stuffed specimens.

The work was issued in a second edition in 1924, in a third edition in 1932.

204. *1927.* O. Helms Danske Fugle ved Stranden. Med... farvetrykte Tavler efter Akvareller af Ingeborg Frederiksen. G. E. C. Gad. *København. pp. 97 + [3]. textfigs. 16 col. pl. (numb. 1—16). 4to.*

Another volume of the author's work on Danish birds written on the same principles as the book 'Danske Fugle ved Hus og i Have' (203) published in 1924. Of the species of birds which are commonly observed as breeding birds or as migratory birds on the Danish shores, 43 are treated in the text and figured on the plates (three-colour prints, executed by Egmont H. Petersen), which contain altogether 82 figures of birds.

The main stress is laid upon the account of the biological conditions, which is based on the author's own experience. The text concludes with a chapter on the protection of shore-birds.

205. *1930.* O. Helms Danske Fugle i Skov, Mark og Mose. Med ... farvetrykte Tavler efter Akvareller af Ingeborg Frederiksen. G. E. C. Gad, *København. pp. 107 + [9]. text-figs. 16 col. pl. (numb. 1—16). 4to.*

The third and last volume of the author's work on Danish birds and, like the preceding ones, a guide to the species which are of common occurrence in the localities mentioned in the title, in this case woods, fields, and bogs. Grallatorial and natatorial birds, with which the author is especially familiar, occupy a prominent place, and special prominence is given to the description of their biological conditions. The volume ends with an alphabetical index of the Danish and Latin bird names in all three volumes, of which the two preceding ones appeared in 1924 (203) and 1927 (204) respectively.

The plates (three-colour prints, executed by Egmont H. Petersen), as in the two preceding works of this series, are somewhat pale in colour. They contain altogether 81 figures of birds, which are distributed over 52 species treated in the text.

HEMPELMANN, F.
1911—13. Brehms Tierleben ... Vierte ... Auflage. Vols. VI—IX. Die Vögel ... See *Brehm, A. E.*

HENNICKE, C. R.
1896—1905. Naumann, Naturgeschichte der Vögel Mitteleuropas ... Herausgegeben von Carl R. Hennicke. See *Naumann, J. A.*

206. *1903.* Die Raubvögel Mitteleuropas ... Tafeln in feinem Chromo- und ... Tafeln in Schwarzdruck nebst Abbildungen im Text nach Originalen der Maler Goering, Keulemans, Kleinschmidt, de Maes, v. Nécsey und Rhamm, mit erklärendem Text von Carl R. Hennicke. Fr. Eugen Köhler. *Gera-Untermhaus. pp. VIII + 230 + [2]. text-figs. 62 pl. (front + Nos. 1—61; 53 col. (numb. 1—10, 12—17, 19—26, 28, 30, 32— 34, 36—50, 52—56, 58—61)). 8vo.*

This volume was prepared on the basis of Vol. V, 1898— 99, of the Jubilee edition 1896—1905 of Naumann's 'Naturgeschichte der Vögel Mitteleuropas' (356), which was edited by Hennicke.

In the text the families, subfamilies, and genera are briefly described while the species are treated at greater length, with descriptions and notes on their geographical distribution, occurrence in Germany, ecology and behaviour in captivity, and their importance as beneficial or harmful animals.

The coloured plates, reduced reproductions of the plates in Vol. V of Naumann's work cited above, are executed in chromolithography (printed by Fr. Eugen Köhler, Gera-Untermhaus) chiefly from drawings by Keulemans, but some few from originals by O. von Riesenthal, who is not mentioned in the title. The plain plates (feet of birds of prey) are likewise derived from Naumann's work.

HENRICHSEN, M. V. See *Vahl, M.*

HENSHAW, H. W.
1875. Engineer Department, United States Army. Report upon geographical and geological explorations and surveys west of the One Hundredth Meridian, in charge of First Lieut. Geo. M. Wheeler ... under the direction of Brig. Gen. A. A. Humphreys ... Published by authority of Wm. W. Belknap ... Vol. V. Zoology. *<-- pp. 131—508:* Chapter III. Report upon the ornithological collections made in portions of Nevada, Utah, California, Colorado, New Mexico, and Arizona ... 1871—74, by H. W. Henshaw >. Government Printing Office. *Washington. 15 col. pl. (numb. I—XV). 4to.*

Vol. V. includes also a list of the plates in the present report (p. 9: 'Birds') and pp. 977—989 'Index to report on ornithology'; the opening chapters (pp. 13—21) also contain information of importance to the ornithological report.

The entire report on the investigations west of the One Hundredth Meridian was published in seven volumes and one supplement in 1874—89.

The present ornithological report is based on a material of about 3000 specimens of birds, collected by various collectors. Altogether 296 species are enumerated, with field notes, synonymies and tables of data regarding the collection of the different specimens and their measurements, chiefly to illustrate geographical variation.

The classification and nomenclature of the land-birds follow those employed by Baird, Brewer, and Ridgway in 'A history of North American birds. Land birds', 1874 (25), while those of the water-birds follow Coues' 'Check list of North American birds', 1873—74.

The fine plates, executed in chromo-lithography (T. Sinclair & Son, lith., Phila.), contain 18 portraits of birds, drawn by R. Ridgway.

Chapter III was also issued separately, contemporaneously with Vol. V.

1888. Report upon the natural history collections made in Alaska between ... 1877 and 1881 ... Edited by Henry W. Henshaw ... *pp. 19—226:* Part I. Birds of Alaska ... See *Nelson, E. W.,* 1887.

HERKLOTS, J. A.
1854—58. Fauna van Nederland ... See *Schlegel, H.*

HERMAN, O.
1894—1914. See Aquila.
1905. Ornithologische Fragmente aus den Handschriften von Johann Salamon von Petényi ... Mit einer Einleitung von Otto Herman. See *Petényi, J. S. von.*

HESSE, R.
1910—14. Tierbau und Tierleben in ihrem Zusammenhang betrachtet von Richard Hesse und Franz Doflein. B. G. Teubner. *Leipzig. 2 vols. 7 pl. birds (6 col.). large 8vo.* — Vol. I. 1910. - - Der Tierkörper als selbständiger Organismus von Richard Hesse. Mit 480 Abbildungen im Text und 15 Tafeln ... *pp. XVI*

+ 789 + 16. text-figs. 4 pl. birds (numb. I, VI, X, XIII; 3 col. (numb. I, VI, X)). Vol. II. 1914. - - Das Tier als Glied des Naturganzen von Franz Doflein. Mit 740 Abbildungen im Text und 20 Tafeln ... pp. XV + 960 + 8. text-figs. 3 col. pl. birds (numb. XII A, XII B, XIII B).

A comprehensive biological account of the animal kingdom assuming no previous knowledge of zoology on the part of the reader.

An account of the connection between the form of an animal and its habits of life, and of the agreement between the structure of an organ and its function, must necessarily derive some material from birds; and this is in fact the case in the present work, Volume I of which deals with subjects of a more physiological character, such as the movements of animals — with a section on the flight of birds — metabolism, reproduction and heredity, nervous system, and sense organs. Vol. II deals with such questions as the relation of animals to their surrounding inanimate and animate environment, considerable space being allotted to birds, for instance in the chapters on the sexual life of animals, animal migrations, and the care of their young, in which a section on the building of nests and breeding habits of birds occurs.

The coloured plates (three-colour prints) with figures of birds in Vol. I were executed from drawings by W. Kuhnert, E. L. Hoess, and O. Vollrath, while Bruno Liljefors is responsible for the coloured plates in Vol. II.

A new edition, without plates, of Vol. I of this work was issued by Hesse in 1935. The appearance of the second volume within a few years has been promised.

HEUGLIN, M. T. von.

1869—74. Ornithologie Nordost-Afrika's, der Nilquellen- und Küsten-Gebiete des Rothen Meeres und des nördlichen Somal-Landes von M. Th. von Heuglin. Mit 51 Tafeln Abbildungen (nach der Natur gezeichnet vom Verfasser) und mit einer zoo-geographischen Karte. Theodor Fischer. Cassel. 2 vols. in 4. 8vo. — Vol. I. Part I. 1869. pp. [V] + XII + [IV] + CVIII + A—H + 1—416. 16 col. pl. (numb. I—IV, VI, VII, VII VIIIa, VIIIb, IX—XI, XIIa, XIIb, XIII, XIV). Vol. I. Part II. 1871. pp. [III] + 417—851. 17 col. pl. (numb. XV—XVII, XX, XXI, XIXa, XVIII, XIX, XIX, XXIa, XXIII, XXIIIb, XXIV, XXVb, XXVI—XXVIII). Vol. II. Part I. 1873. pp. 853—1261. 7 col. pl. (numb. XXIX—XXXV). Vol. II. Part II. 1873. pp. 1263—1512. Nachträge und Berichtigungen zur Ornithologie Nordost-Afrika's von M. Th. von Heuglin. Mit Beiträgen von Dr. O. Finsch. 1871. pp. [III] + CCCXXV + [1]. 11 col. pl. (numb. XXXVI—XL, XLIII, XLII, XLVIII—LI). 1 map.

Published in 57 parts which appeared at irregular intervals so that, according to Zimmer (589, I, p. 302), the work was not finished until 1874 or even 1875.

Based partly on the author's own observations and collections during a twelve years' stay in Western Asia, and Northeast and Central Africa, the work gives a systematic synopsis of all the birds observed up to the date of publication in Northeast Africa and the adjacent districts, with detailed synonymies and descriptions in Latin of the specifically African species. In addition much information, based on the author's own observations, is given as to the habits and reproduction of the birds, and especially as to their zoogeography and migrations.

The plates are executed in chromo-lithography (Art. Anst. Th. Fischer) from the drawings of the author, as stated in the title.

HILL, J.

1752. An history of animals. Containing descriptions of the birds, beasts, fishes, and insects, of the several parts of the world; and including accounts of the several classes of animalcules, visible only by the assistance of microscopes. In these the characters, qualities, and forms of the several creatures are described, the names by which they are commonly known, as well as those by which authors, who have written on the subject, have called them are explained: And each is reduced to the class to which it naturally belongs. Illustrated with figures. By John Hill. <- - pp. 318—514: Part V. Of birds>. Thomas Osborne. London. 8 col. pl. (numb. 17—24). fol.

This is the ornithological section of Vol. III of this very prolific author's work 'A general natural history: Or new and accurate descriptions of the animals, vegetables, and minerals, of the different parts of the world', etc. The two preceding volumes are 'A history of fossils', 1748, and 'A history of plants', 1751, and both these volumes have the general title quoted above, which is missing in Vol. III.

Like so many other literary productions by this author the present ornithological section is chiefly a compilation, though the matter concerning British birds includes many personal observations. It is arranged according to Linnæus' system of classification, and is divided into the final six orders of that classification, or classes, as they are termed by the author, with descriptions, notes on the geographical distribution, and on biological conditions, especially food habits.

The plates are engravings coloured by hand (B. Cole sculp.). They contain altogether 111 figures of as many species, and do not surpass the text in quality. The work was also issued with uncoloured plates.

HINDS, R. B.

1843—44. The zoology of the voyage of H. M. S. Sulphur ... 1836—42 ... Edited and superintended by Richard Brinsley Hinds. (Nos. III—IV). Birds. See Gould, J.

HOESLIN, J.

1781. Des Ritters Carl von Linné Lehr-Buch über das Natur-System so weit es das Thierreich angehet ... Vol. I. pp. 187—475: Zwote Classe. Die Geschichte der Vögel. See Mueller, P. L. S.

HOLLAND. NATUURKUNDIGE COMMISSIE IN INDIË.

1839—44. Verhandelingen over de natuurlijke geschiedenis der Nederlandsche overzeesche bezittingen ... [Aves]. See Mueller, S.

HOLTEN, J. S.

1806. Zoologia Danica seu animalium Daniæ et Norvegiæ rariorum ac minus notorum descriptiones et historia. Vol. IV ... See Mueller, O. F.

HØRRING, R.

1911—26. Nordens fåglar ... See Jägerskiöld, A. K. E. L.

1931. Danmarks Fugle ... Vol. III ... Bindet fuldført af R. Hørring ... See Schiøler, E. L. T. L., 1925—31.

HORSBRUGH, B. R.

1912. The game-birds & water-fowl of South Africa. By Boyd Horsbrugh. With coloured plates by C. G. Davies. Witherby & Co. London. pp. XII + 159. 211.

18

67 col. pl. (numb. 1—45, 46a, 46B--C, 47—65).
4to.
This work was issued in four parts, the first of which appeared in March, 1912.

The birds dealt with in the work are found south of a line running from east to west through the Zambesi River. The text is brief, consisting of synonymies, local names, descriptions, information about geographical distribution, field-notes by the author and Sergeant C. G. Davies, of the Cape Mounted Riflemen, and a brief mention of the breeding habits with descriptions of the eggs (colour and dimensions). These descriptions are in most cases derived from W. Sclater and A. C. Stark's work 'The fauna of South Africa', 1900—06, whence also the notes on the general distribution of the birds are largely derived; other information is based on Layard and Sharpe's 'The birds of South Africa', 1875—84 (281).

The parts of the notes which deal with the habits of the species in Pondoland and Griqualand are based on observations by C. G. Davies, who also drew the originals for the coloured plates. These plates (three-colour prints, Witherby & Co., imp.) each contain one or two figures of birds (Pl. 37: three heads of Guinea fowls), and are almost without exception faultless both as regards drawing and colour.

HORSFIELD, T.

212.   [1821—] 1824. Zoological researches in Java, and the neighbouring islands. By Thomas Horsfield. Kingsbury, Parbury & Allen. London. pp. [V] + [318]. 32 col. pl. birds, 7 pl. (uncol.) partly birds. 4to.

Eight parts in the original covers, dated 1821 (Parts 1 and 2), 1822 (Parts 3, 4, and 5), 1823 (Part 6), and 1824 (Parts 7 and 8). The times of delivery for the successive unpublished parts do not seem to have been observed.

The material was collected chiefly in Java in 1811—17, during which period the island was under British rule.

Each part contains four coloured plates with figures of birds and four with figures of mammals. There is an accompanying explanatory text which gives for each species of birds the corresponding order in Cuvier, Temminck, Linnæus, and Illiger, and also generic characters, a brief diagnosis in Latin, synonymy, native names, description, and brief information about the habits of the birds.

Several genera and species are designated as new.

At the end of Part 8 there is a 'General catalogue of Javanese birds, arranged in the Museum of the honourable East India Company', the first column of which contains the bird names from the author's 'Arrangement and description of birds from the island of Java', read before the Linnean Society of London, April 18, 1820 (758).

Altogether 33 species are described and figured in the 36 birds shown on the plates (830), the greater number of which were drawn on stone by Auguste Pelletier (printed by C. Hullmandel), who also superintended the colouring. Other plates are engravings coloured by hand, engraved by W. Taylor from drawings by John Curtis, who engraved some of the plates himself. In each of Parts 1—7 there is a 'plate of illustrations', the figures on which include beaks and feet of birds.

1826—35. Illustrations of ornithology ... Vols. I—III. See Jardine, W., 1826—43.

HOUTTUYN, M.

1773. Des Ritters Carl von Linné ... vollständiges Natursystem ... Part II. Von den Vögeln. See Mueller, P. L. S.

1789—1829. Nederlandsche vogelen ... See Nozeman, C., 1770—1829.

HOWARD, H. E.

213.   1907—14 [—15]. The British warblers; a history with problems of their lives. By H. Eliot Howard. Illustrated by Henrik Grönvold. R. H. Porter. London. 2 vols. in 10 parts. large 8vo.

These are the ten parts (original covers, numb. 1—9, 9*) in which the present work was issued. The volumes formed by them are composed in the present complete copy as follows:—
Vol. I [1908—15]. pp. XV + [203]. 47 pl. (numb. 1—25, 28—49 in 'List of plates'; 17 col. (Nos. 1, 8, 11, 12, 21, 28—30, 33—38, 45, 46, 48); 30 photograv.). 4 maps (Nos. 26, 27, 50, 51).
Vol. II. [1907—15]. pp. X + [260]. 39 pl. (numb. 1—11, 14—18, 21—27, 30—42, 45—47 in 'List of plates'; 18 (3 pl. eggs) col. (Nos. 1—6, 10, 18, 21, 23, 27, 30—32, and (egg pls. I—III) 45—47); 21 photograv.). 8 maps (Nos. 12, 13, 19, 20, 28, 29, 43, 44).

The plates are unnumbered, but, as stated above, they have, together with the maps, been assigned numbers in the 'List of plates' found in each volume, which also contains a 'Collation of letterpress', in which the final pagination is stated; the text to each of the forms treated was originally paginated separately.

A complete survey of the history of publication and of the contents of the separate parts is found in Zimmer (589, I, p. 309) and in Mullens and Swann (574, p. 299).

The monograph deals with 26 species, giving synonymies, names in different languages, descriptions of the plumage, an account of the geographical distribution, and finally a detailed description of the life history of the forms breeding in England, which Howard was able to study during the period of reproduction. The behaviour in the breeding season is especially discussed, on the basis of Howard's ideas about a particular 'breeding territory' for each male. A concluding chapter, 'General summary and concluding remarks', is found in Vol. II, pp. 193—220 (final pagination).

The coloured plates, executed in chromo-lithography (Litho., W. Greve, Berlin; some few: C. Hodges & Son, Lith., London), are excellent, and the same applies to the photogravures (Swan Electric Engraving Co.).

1929. An introduction to the study of bird behaviour by H. Eliot Howard. The University Press. Cambridge. pp. XII + 136. text-figs. 11 pl. birds (front. + Nos. I—X). 4to.

A study based on observations of the behaviour of birds during the breeding season. This is described in detail as regards two species, the Reed-Bunting and the Yellow Bunting, after which the subject is analysed and discussed, experience of the life history of other English warblers during the period of reproduction being included in the discussion.

The plates are beautifully executed (Emery Walker, ph. sc.) from drawings by G. E. Lodge, and show the birds in different situations during the period treated in the work.

HUDSON, W. H.

1919. Birds in town & village. By W. H. Hudson. With pictures in colour by E. J. Detmold. J. M. Dent & Sons. London. pp. IX + 274. text-figs. 8 col. pl. 8vo.

This very popular account of bird life in the localities mentioned in the title is mainly a reprint, though with omissions, corrections, and additions, of Hudson's 'Birds in a village' (London 1893, 8vo) which was the author's first book on bird life in England.

In its present shape the book falls into three main sections, 'Birds in a village', 'Essays', five in number, and 'Birds in a Cornish village'. The third part replaces the concluding portion of the earlier book.

Ten species are figured on the coloured plates (three-colour prints).

A special American edition was issued at New York in 1920. The work also appeared in Hudson's 'Collected works' 1923; new edition 1924, and in 'Works', 1935.

1920. Birds of La Plata. By W. H. Hudson. With ... coloured illustrations by H. Gronvold [sic]. J. M. Dent & Sons. London. 2 vols. 22 col. pl. 8vo. — Vol. I. pp. XVI + [I] + 244. 11 col. pl. Vol. II. pp. IX + 240. 11 col. pl.

The matter of this work is derived from Hudson and

Philip Lutley Sclater's 'Argentine ornithology', which appeared in two volumes in 1888—89, with 20 coloured plates by Keulemans. In the latter work Sclater had prepared the descriptions and synonymies, while Hudson had contributed the account of the birds' habits. This part of the earlier work has been reproduced in the present book, though Sclater's contribution has been omitted; in this way a collection of popular bird biographies has been obtained, with additional brief descriptions of the species treated, 23 of which are figured on the coloured plates (three-colour prints).

On the back of the title-pages of both volumes the following statement is found 'There have been printed of this Edition 1500 Copies for England and 1500 Copies for United States of America, also a Large Paper Edition of 200 Copies, and the type then distributed'.

The work also appeared in Hudson's 'Collected works' 1923.

1923. Rare, vanishing & lost British birds, compiled from notes by W. H. Hudson, by Linda Gardiner. With ... coloured plates by H. Gronvold [sic]. J. M. Dent & Sons. *London. pp. XIX + 120. 25 col. pl. 8vo.*

Before his death Hudson had contemplated the publication of an enlarged edition of his paper 'Lost British Birds', 1894, (Society for the Protection of Birds, 14). In it he described thirteen species which in his opinion could hardly still be regarded as British breeding birds. He therefore left several notes in pen and pencil on the subject, and he had further commissioned the artist to paint pictures of twenty-five species for the new edition which, after Hudson's death, was issued by L. Gardiner on the basis of the available material, with additions in smaller type of some extracts from the literature. A brief chapter, 'Allusions in poetry', is found pp. 110—114.

Twenty-five species are treated in the book and figured on the coloured plates (three-colour prints).

HUMBOLDT, F. H. A. von.

1811 [1812]—33. Voyage de Humboldt et Bonpland. Deuxième partie. Observations de zoologie et d'anatomie comparée. - - Recueil d'observations de zoologie et d'anatomie comparée, faites dans l'Océan Atlantique, dans l'intérieur du Nouveau Continent et dans la Mer du Sud ... 1799—1803; par Al. de Humboldt et A. Bonpland. F. Schoell (Vol. II: J. Smith). *Paris. 2 vols. 6 pl. birds (1 col.). 4to.*

This is the zoological portion of Humboldt and Bonpland's immense report 'Voyage aux Régions équinoxiales du Nouveau Continent, fait en 1799—1804', etc., which was issued in 30 volumes in 1805—37.

Part of the zoological section appeared for the first time in 1805—09, but was later replaced by the present two volumes; the part previously issued corresponds to pp. 1—309 in the first of these volumes.

Three articles, all by A. Humboldt, are concerned with birds:—

Vol. I, pp. 1—13: Mémoire sur l'os hyoïde et le larynx des oiseaux, des singes et du crocodile, 3 pl. (numb. I—III) ;

Vol. I, pp. 26—45: Essai sur l'histoire naturelle du Condor, ou du Vultur gryphus de Linné, 2 pl. (numb. VIII—IX, 1 col. (numb. VIII)) ;

Vol. II, pp 139—144: Mémoire sur le Guacharo de la caverne de Caripe, nouveau genre d'oiseaux nocturnes de la famille des passereaux, 1 pl. (numb. XLIV).

The plates are engravings. The coloured plate representing the Condor, was drawn by Humboldt (Barraband perf.) and engraved by Bouquet (Langlois imp.), who also engraved the plate, IX, representing the head and foot of this bird, while the plate, XLIV, with figures (head, feet, and feathers) of the Steatornis was drawn by Huet (after Humboldt) and engraved by Coutant.

HUNGARIAN ORNITHOLOGICAL CENTRAL-BUREAU. *See Magyar Ornithologiai Központot.*

HUTCHINSON AND CO. (publishers).

1924. Hutchinson's Animals of all countries ... Vol. II. pp. 775—1200: Birds. *See Pycraft, W. P.*

IBIS.

1859 → The Ibis, a magazine of general ornithology (from New Series, I, 1865: a quarterly journal of ornithology). Edited by Philip Lutley Sclater (1859—64), Alfred Newton (1865—70), Osbert Salvin (1871—76), Osbert Salvin and Philip Lutley Sclater (1877—82), Philip Lutley Sclater and Howard Saunders (1883—88), Philip Lutley Sclater (1889—94), Philip Lutley Sclater and Howard Saunders (1895—1900), Philip Lutley Sclater and A. H. Evans (1901—12), William Lutley Sclater (1913—27), William Lutley Sclater and Herbert C. Robinson (1928), William Lutley Sclater (1929—30), C. B. Ticehurst (1931 →). N. Trübner and Co. (1859—64), John van Voorst (1865—86), Gurney and Jackson (1887—1903), R. H. Porter (1904—13), British Ornithologists' Union (1914 →). (Sold by William Wesley & Son (1914—20), Wheldon & Wesley (1921—29), Taylor and Francis (1930 →)). *London. Vol. I →. text-figs. maps. col. plates. 8vo.*

One of the leading, and doubtless the most prominent, of the current ornithological periodicals. Though one of the first British journals of its kind and one of the earliest of all to appear it is surpassed in age by 'Journal für Ornithologie' (239), which was started in 1853.

The decision as to the initiation and publication of 'The Ibis' was taken at a meeting held by British ornithologists in November, 1858, at which it was further decided to found a society, the 'British Ornithologists' Union', with a maximum of 20 members, for the purpose of obtaining funds for the publication of the periodical. The list of members contains the names of the twenty persons who must be considered to be the original promoters of the scheme. Ten ornithologists not resident in the United Kingdom were added to these in 1860 as honorary members. Among these ten original honorary members of the Union were, Spencer F. Baird, Jean Cabanis, John Cassin, Gustav Hartlaub, Alfred Russel Wallace, and J. Reinhardt, Copenhagen ; as the owner, Reinhardt has written his name in the first volumes, 1859—66, of the present copy of the periodical.

Six volumes constitute a series, and the periodical is at present (1937) in its 14th series, Vol. I, or its 79th volume. Four supplementary volumes have been issued — the two cited below, in 1915 and 1930, the Jubilee Supplement No. 1, 9th series, Vol. II, 1908, March, 1909, and a Supplementary Number, 12th series, March, 1927.

Several indices have further been published, in addition to the General Index to the individual series, 'Index of genera and species, and an index to the plates, 1859—76', published in 1879 ; 'Index of genera and species, and an index to the plates, 1877—94', published in 1897 ; 'General subject-index, 1859—1894', published in 1900 ; 'Index of genera, species, and subspecies, and to the plates, 1895—1912', published 1916 ; and 'Index of genera, species, and subspecies, and to the plates, 1913—30'.

A considerable number of ornithologists, chiefly British, have in the course of time published in 'The Ibis' a large amount of matter on bird life in all parts of the world. This has been of great importance for the development of ornithology and for the promotion of ornithological science.

The periodical has not only been important for the papers which have been published in its columns, but also for the many beautiful plates that have appeared in its considerable number of volumes. The total number of the plates exceeds 1200, the majority of which (between 800 and 900) are coloured, although plain photographic plates have gained ground in the recent volumes. The greater part of the pictures for the coloured plates were executed by J. Wolf (in the volumes of 1859—69), John Jennens (volumes 1859—69), and notably by J. G. Keulemans (volumes 1869—1909), and H. Grønvold

219.

18*

(the volumes from 1899 to date). However, several others have worked for 'The Ibis' within this field, such as J. Smit, W. C. Hewitson (plates of eggs in some of the volumes 1859—63), G. E. Lodge (some of the volumes 1900—07), and H. Goodchild (volumes 1902—06).

The greater number of the plates in the volumes 1859—1914 are lithographs coloured by hand (chiefly M. & N. Hanhart (or Hanhart) imp. (from 1859); Mintern Bros. imp. (from 1874); West, Newman (from 1907)). Other methods of reproduction have also been used, occasional chromo-lithographs having appeared. After the turn of the century, the three-colour process was employed, and it has been predominant from 1915 to this date (André & Sleigh, Bushey; Witherby & Co.; Menpes Press, Watford; Vitty & Seaborne, and others).

1915. Jubilee Supplement No. 2. Tenth series. Report on the birds collected by the British Ornithologists' Union Expedition and the Wollaston Expedition in Dutch New Guinea. *See Ogilvie-Grant, W. R.*

1930. Twelfth series. Volume VI. Supplementary Number. Review of the Genus Cisticola. *See Lynes, H.*

INDIA. [Second Yarkand Mission].
1891. Scientific results of the Second Yarkand Mission ... Aves. *See Sharpe, R. B.*

INDIA. [Western Yunnan Expedition].
1879. Anatomical and zoological researches: comprising an account of the zoological results of the two expeditions to Western Yunnan in 1868 and 1875 ... [Aves]. *See Anderson, J., 1878.*

IVES, J. C.
1859. Reports of explorations and surveys ... for a railroad from the Mississippi River to the Pacific Ocean ... 1853—6. Vol. X. Report of explorations ... near the thirty-fifth parallel of north latitude ... By Lieutenant A. W. Whipple ... assisted by Lieutenant J. C. Ives ... 1853—54. Part VI. Zoological report. pp. 19—35: No. 3. Report on birds collected on the route. *See Kennerly, C. B. R.*

JACQUIN, J. F. von.
220.   *1784.* Beyträge zur Geschichte der Vögel. Herausgegeben von Joseph Franz von Jacquin. Mit ausgemahlten Kupfertafeln. Christian Friedrich Wappler. *Wien. pp. [VIII] + 45. 19 col. pl. (numb. 1—19). 4to.*

In 1755—59 J. F. von Jacquin's father, Nicolaus Joseph Jacquin, made an expedition to the West Indies to collect plants and animals. During this work he made a number of notes on the animal world, of which the present paper is an extract.

Altogether 32 species are treated, of which nineteen are figured on the plates, whose figures have been executed 'nach dem Leben' (pl. 14: A. Amon f.; pl. 18: J. Adam fe.), several of the birds having been kept in the Royal zoological garden at Schönbrunn.

The descriptions and the figures of species No. XXXI (Colymbus subcristatus) and No. XXXII (Muscicapa atricapilla L.) were prepared by Freiherr von Wulfen.

JÄGERSKIÖLD, A. K. E. L.
1895—1902. Nordens fåglar ... *See Kolthoff, G. I.*
221.   [*1911—*] *1926.* Nordens fåglar. Av L. A. Jägerskiöld och Gustaf Kolthoff. Under medverkan av Rud. Söderberg. Med... tavlor av Olof Gylling. Andra upplagan. Albert Bonnier [Beijer]. *Stockholm. 2 vols. large 4to.* — [Vol. I. Text]. *pp. XXIX + 523. text-*

figs. [Vol. II]. Tavlor av Olof Gylling. *pp. [III]. 170 col. pl. (numb. 1—165, 28A, 31A, 51A, 95A, 113A).*

The present second edition of this work was issued in 48 parts (in 39) at irregular intervals; they seem to have appeared as follows: 1911, Part 1; 1912, Parts 2—5; 1913, Parts 6—10; 1914, Parts 11—15; 1915, Parts 16—19; 1916, Parts 20—31 (12 parts (in 6, each comprising two numbers)); 1917, Parts 32—33; 1920, Parts 34—42; 1921, Part 43; 1922, Part 44; 1926, Parts 45—48 (4 parts in 1). Up to and including Part 31 the work was published by Beijer's Bokförlagsaktiebolag. As in the original issue (270), the text is printed in double columns.

The main feature of this edition is the new plates, while the theme is limited and the subject-matter of the text arranged as in the preceding edition. The increased knowledge of the bird fauna of the land areas treated has, however, necessitated several alterations and additions.

The material concerning the avifaunæ of the neighbouring countries was edited by collaborators especially familiar with them. Thus the birds of Denmark and its dependencies and of Iceland were dealt with by Mag. sc. R. Hørring, Copenhagen; the birds of Norway by E. A. Th. Landmark, inspector of fisheries, Oslo; and the birds of Finland first by Professor J. A. Palmén, and subsequently — from and including the swans — by Professor K. M. Levander.

Kolthoff's collaboration in this edition was interrupted by his death and is in the main limited to some few new data. Dr. Rud. Söderberg assisted in the edition of the work from and including the eagles, while the lists of names of this edition were edited by Professor Dr. Elof Hellquist, and the list of references (pp. 457—493) continued by Fr. E. Ahlander, librarian.

The pictures from which the plates were prepared had been executed in distemper by Olof Gylling, who painted some of the birds in their natural surroundings on one species on each plate, while on other plates several birds are painted together. All the figures were drawn from living specimens, some in the open, and some in zoological gardens, while the colouring was taken from living or newly killed specimens, special attention being paid to such colours as change after the death of the bird.

The figures of the plates were reproduced by the four-colour process (Cederquists Graf. A.B., Stockholm). An abridged edition (pp. [IV] + 58, 170 pl., fol.) appeared in 1920 (Bonnier), the text condensed by Reinhold Ericson; it was issued in a second revised edition in 1930 (pp. 76, 165 pl., fol.).

A copy of this work, consisting of the parts in their original covers, is in the possession of the library. The title on the cover of the first part (published by Beijer) runs as follows: 'Nordens fåglar. Andra upplagan av L. A. Jägerskiöld och Gustaf Kolthoff med bilder av Olof Gylling'.

JAMESON, R.
1826—35. Illustrations of ornithology ... Vols. I—III. *See Jardine, W., 1826—43.*

JANSEN, K.
1896. Vore almindelige nyttige Fugle og deres Æg ... *See Wallengren, H. T. S.*

JAPAN. Voyages.
1935. Report of the First Scientific Expedition to Manchoukuo ... June—October 1933. Section V. Division II. Part III. Birds of Jehol. *See Taka-Tsukasa, N.*

JARDIN DES PLANTES, PARIS. *See Muséum d' Histoire Naturelle, Paris.*

JARDINE, W.
[*1826—43*]. Illustrations of ornithology. By William Jardine and Prideaux John Selby. With the co-operation of J. E. Bicheno, J. G. Children, T. Hard-

wicke, T. Horsfield, R. Jameson, T. Stamford Raffles, N. A. Vigors. W. H. Lizars. *Edinburgh. 4 vols. 4to. —* Vol. I. [1826—28]. *pp. [138]. 55 col. pl. (numb. 1— 55). 55 plain pl. (numb. 1—55).* Vol. II. [1828—30]. *pp. [143]. 55 col. pl. (numb. 56—110). 55 plain pl. (numb. 56—110).* Vol. III. [1831—35]. *pp. [99]. 44 col. pl. (numb. 106—136, 139—151). 44 plain pl. (numb. 106—134, 137—151).* Vol. IV. [1837—43]. *pp. [VI] + [119]. text-figs. 53 col. pl. (numb. I— LIII, N. S.).*

The title-page of Vol. IV bears the names of Jardine and Selby only.

The plate-numbers, 106—110, which conclude the series of numbers in Vol. II, have been repeated by mistake in Vol. III.

The work was issued in 19 parts. Information of the dates of publication is found in Zimmer (589, I, pp. 322—324), cf. C. D. Sherborn (862 a, p. 326).

The text of this famous work deals with the genera and the species figured, the latter with brief diagnoses in Latin, synonyms, history, habitat, description, and some information about habits and mode of life, while under genera, besides the particular order, are found the characters in Latin, history, notes on distribution and a general discussion succeeded by a synopsis specierum. Many new species are described and figured.

The coloured plates in Vols. I—III, coloured by hand, are accompanied by uncoloured ones. Some were engraved by W. H. Lizars (Patrick Syme col.) from drawings by Jardine, Selby, E. Lear, James Stewart, A. F. Rolfe, Thompson, John Gould, and R. Mitford. A number of the plates were executed from drawings found in General T. Hardwicke's collection (187).

1832. American ornithology ... The illustrative notes, and life of Wilson, by William Jardine. See Wilson, A.

3.   *1843 [1833]. The Naturalist's Library. Edited by William Jardine. Vols. XIV—XV. Ornithology (Vols. I—II). Humming birds. Parts I—II. By the editor. W. H. Lizars. Edinburgh. 2 vols. small 8vo. — pp. XV + 17—191. text-figs. 35 pl. (front. (plain) + 34 col. pl. birds (numb. 1—34)).* Vol. II. *pp. VIII + XIII—XV + 192. text-figs. 31 pl. (front. (plain) + 30 col. pl. birds (numb. 1—30)).*

Two volumes of Jardine's serial work cited in the title (224), which appeared as a whole in 1833—43.

The plates (Lizars sc.) represent the hand-coloured figures of birds on uncoloured backgrounds.

In addition to the ornithological matter each volume contains a biography of a naturalist with an accompanying engraved portrait (front.) , Vol. I, memoir of Linnæus (pp. 25—91), and Vol. II, memoir of Pennant (pp. 1—65).

4.   *[1833—] 1843. The Naturalist's Library.* Edited by William Jardine. Vols. XIV—XXVII. *Ornithology ... Illuminated titles:* The Naturalist's Library. Ornithology. Vols. I—XIV. W. H. Lizars. *Edinburgh. 14 vols. text-figs. 385 col. pl. small 8vo.*

The works constituting this series, the ornithological section of which is cited here, appeared for the first time in 1833—43 in 40 volumes. Besides birds various groups of animals that come under mammalogy, ichthyology, and entomology are described by different authors. When the series was concluded in 1843, each volume was provided with a title-page dated 1843 and given a serial number, as is the case with the present set.

The ornithological section of the series consists of the following separate works:

I—II. Humming birds. By the editor.	(first published)	1833.
III. Gallinaceous birds. By the editor.	— —	1834.
IV. Game birds. By the editor.	— —	1834.
V. Pigeons. By Prideaux John Selby.	— —	1835.
VI. Parrots. By Prideaux John Selby.	— —	1836.
VII—VIII. Birds of Western Africa.		
By W. Swanson	— —	1837.

IX, XI, XII, XIV. British birds. By		
the editor.	(first published)	1838—43.
X. Flycatchers. By W. Swainson.	— —	1838.
XIII. Sun-birds. By the editor.	— —	1843.

More detailed bibliographical data as to the individual volumes are found under each author.

Each volume contains a biography of a well-known naturalist in addition to the ornithological matter, which comprises a brief treatment of the individual forms with a statement of synonyms, distribution, brief descriptions and sometimes other information of interest.

The whole series contains a total of more than 4000 figures distributed over 1280 plates (steel-plate engravings, Lizars sc., with hand-coloured figures on uncoloured backgrounds), executed from drawings by different artists (cf. the individual works of the series in the present catalogue).

The popularity of the series appears from the fact that it was issued in several editions, thus (552, III, pp. 1399—1400) it was re-issued in 1845—46, and again by Bohn in 1848, for whom it was reprinted in 1852—55 (574, p. 311) ; several other editions are also mentioned. In 1836—42 a German translation of ten volumes of the series was published by C. A. Harteleben, Pest (461).

1843 [1834]. The Naturalist's Library. Edited by **225.** William Jardine. Vol. XX. Ornithology (Vol. III). Gallinaceous birds. By the editor. W. H. Lizars. *Edinburgh. pp. 232. text-figs. 31 pl. (front.(plain)+30 col. pl. birds (numb. 1—2, III, 4, V, VI, 7, 8, IX—XII, 13, XIV—XVI, 17, 18, 18*, 19—29)). small 8vo.*

A volume of Jardine's serial work cited in the title (224), which appeared as a whole in 1833—43.

The plates (Lizars sc.) show hand-coloured figures of birds on uncoloured backgrounds. Five of the plates were drawn by Stewart, who also drew the vignette title-page.

In addition to the ornithological matter the volume contains a memoir of Aristotle (pp. 17—112) with accompanying portrait (front.).

1843 [1834]. The Naturalist's Library. Edited by **226.** William Jardine. Vol. XXI. Ornithology (Vol. IV). Game birds. By the editor. W. H. Lizars. *Edinburgh. pp. [IX] + 17—197. 31 pl. (front. (plain) + 30 col. pl. birds (numb. 1—2, III, 4, V—VII, 8, IX, 10, 11, XII, 13, XIV—XVI, 17, XVIII, XIX, 20, XXI, XXII, 23—26, XXVII, 28—30)). small 8vo.*

A volume of the series 'Naturalist's Library', cited in the title (224), which was edited by Jardine in 1833—43.

Some of the plates (Lizars sc.), which have hand-coloured figures of birds on uncoloured backgrounds, were executed from drawings by P. J. Selby and J. Stewart.

In addition to ,the ornithological matter the volume contains a memoir of Sir Thomas Stamford Raffles (pp. 17—88) with an accompanying engraved portrait (front.).

Some of the plates were reproduced in 1895—97 in the volume on the game-birds by W. B. Ogilvie-Grant in 'Allen's Naturalist's Library' (371).

1843 [1838—43]. The Naturalist's Library. Edited **227.** by William Jardine. Vols. XXIV—XXVII. Ornithology (Vols. IX, XI, XII, XIV). British birds. Parts I—IV. By the editor. W. H. Lizars. *Edinburgh. 4 vols. small 8vo. —* Vol. I. *[1838]. pp. XIV + 17—315. text-figs. 35 pl. (front. (plain) + 34 col. pl. (numb. 1—34; 4 pl. eggs numb. 2, 11, 16, 25)).* Vol. II. *[1839]. pp. XII + 17—409. text-figs. 31 pl. (front. (plain) + 30 col. pl. (numb. 1—30; 3 pl. eggs (numb. 28—30)).* Vol. III. *[1842]. pp. XVI + 17— 349. text-figs. 35 pl. (front. (plain) + 34 col. pl. birds (numb. 1—34)).* Vol. IV. *[1843]. pp. XVI + 17— 313. text-figs. 32 pl. (front. (plain) + 31 col. pl. birds (numb. 1—30, 2*)).*

Four volumes of the series (224) mentioned in the title, which was edited by Jardine in 1833—43.

The plates (Lizars sc.) have hand-coloured bird portraits

on uncoloured backgrounds, and were executed from drawings by J. Stewart.

Each of the volumes contains a biography of a naturalist with an accompanying engraved portrait (front.).

The persons of whom biographies are given are, in Part I, Sir Robert Sibbald (pp. 17—67), in Part II, William Smellie (pp. 17—44), in Part III, John Walker (pp. 17—50), and in Part IV, Alexander Wilson (pp. 17—50).

Some of the plates in this work were reproduced in 1894—97 in the volumes on the birds of Great Britain by R. B. Sharpe in 'Allen's Naturalist's Library' (466).

A copy of Vol. II of the original edition (dated 1839) is in the possession of the Library.

228.   *1843. The Naturalist's Library. Edited by William Jardine. Vol. XVI. Ornithology (Vol. XIII). Sunbirds. By the editor. W. H. Lizars. Edinburgh. pp. XV + 17—277. text-figs. 31 pl. (front. (plain) + 30 col. pl. birds (numb. 1—24, 26—30, 27)). small 8vo.*

A volume of the series mentioned in the title (224) edited in its entirety by Jardine in 1833—43.

The plates (Lizars sc.) — coloured figures of birds on uncoloured backgrounds — were executed from drawings by J. Stewart.

In addition to the ornithological matter the volume contains a memoir of Francis Willughby (pp. 17—146) with an accompanying engraved portrait (front.).

229.   *1848—53. Contributions to ornithology for 1848—52. By William Jardine. W. H. Lizars. Edinburgh. 5 vols. in 3. 94 pl. (numb. in 'Notice', 1850, and 'Contents'; 80 col.). 8vo. — For 1848. 1848. pp. 63. text-figs. 10 pl. (Nos. 1—3, 5—8, 10—12; 8 col.; 2 uncol. (Nos. 3, 8)). For 1849. 1849. pp. [II] + 1—15 + 17—29 +31—138. text-figs. 27 pl. (Nos. 13—22, 24—40; 21 col.; 6 uncol. (Nos. 16 (eggs), 22, 24, 25, 39, 40). For 1850. 1850. pp. IV + 1—80 + 67— 82 + 82 + 85—160 [= 106] + 105* + 106* + 107 —153. text-figs. 22 pl. (Nos. 42—45, 48—59, 61— 66; 18 col. (3 pl. eggs (Nos. 42, 52, 57)); 4 uncol. (Nos. 53, 54, 59, 65). For 1851. 1852. pp. II + 163. 15 pl. (Nos. 67—81; 13 col.; 2 uncol. (Nos. 67, 68)). For 1852. 1853. pp. [IV] + 162. 20 col. pl. (Nos. 82—101; 4 pl. (partly) eggs (Nos. 84, 89, 91, 92)).*

A subscription work issued in parts with somewhat irregular pagination. It may therefore be regarded as a periodical publication, or the first British periodical devoted to ornithology.

The 'Contributions' for 1848 consists of three parts, for 1849 of seven parts, for 1850 of seven parts, and for 1851 of six parts.

Much ornithological matter has been published in this work, for instance the section 'Illustrations of ornithology' with descriptions and figures of beautiful and rare birds. A corresponding section, 'Illustrations of foreign oology', contains descriptions and figures of eggs. Several contributions deal with anatomical features and are accompanied by plates of them.

Among the contributors, in addition to the editor who himself supplied a large part of the subject-matter, are (from 1848) H. E. Strickland, (from 1849) T. C. Eyton and J. J. Kaup, (from 1850) John Gould and G. Hartlaub, (from 1851) Philip L. Sclater, and (from 1852) E. Blyth.

The beautiful plates, coloured by hand, are mostly marked C. D. M. S., the greater number of them having been executed by Jardine's daughter Catherine Dorcas Maule, who was married to H. E. Strickland. They seem to have been printed by P. H. De la Motte, by special use of the art of anastatic printing. This method of reproduction was called papyrography (229, 1848, pp. 18—22 ; 888). Some of the plates are executed by Jardine himself, others are marked F. Reeve or Reeve & Nichols imp., some few Lizars sc. Finally, in the volume for 1852, some of the plates are marked P. Oudart, pinxt. et lith. (Becquet frères, imp.).

The numbers lacking in the description of the plates refer to text-figures, some of which are coloured.

A re-issue of the work (1860 ?) is listed in the Catalogue of the Library of the British Museum (Natural History) (522, VI, p. 228).

JAUBERT, J. B. M.

1859 [—62]. Richesses ornithologiques du midi de 2? la France, ou description méthodique de tous les oiseaux observés en Provence et dans les départements circonvoisins, Par J.-B. Jaubert et Barthélemy-Lapommeraye. Typ. et lith. Barlatier-Feissat et Demonchy. Marseille. pp. 547. 20 col. pl. 4to.

This work, which was published in seven parts, is supposed to have been written by Jaubert, although the name of Lapommeraye, too, is found on the title-page. It gives a comprehensive survey of the birds of Southern France, which had previously been treated chiefly in an unfinished work issued in 1825—30 by Polydore Roux (431).

The introduction (pp. 7—16), dealing with the migration of birds, is succeeded by the main part of the work (pp. 17—529) 'Richesses ornithologiques du midi de la France', in which the birds are divided into eight orders according to the system of classification of Bonaparte. The individual species are treated in detail, with statement of synonyms, descriptions, and information on eggs and nests, geographical distribution, and sundry remarks on their habits.

After a 'Supplément' (pp. 531—534) there follows 'Tableau synoptique de la classification suivie dans cet ouvrage' (pp 535 —538) and a "Table des matières, avec les noms provençaux des espèces'.

The plates (lithographs coloured by hand, J. Susini del. et lith.; lith Barlatier-Feissat & Demonchy) contain coloured figures of birds on uncoloured backgrounds.

JENTINK, F. A.

1884—1913. Notes from the Leyden Museum. See Leyden. Rijks Museum van Natuurlijke Historie, 1879 —1914.

JERDON, T. C.

[1843—] 1847. Illustrations of Indian ornithology, 2 containing fifty figures of new, unfigured and interesting species of birds, chiefly from the south of India By T. C. Jerdon. Printed by P. R. Hunt. Madras. pp. [V] + II + [161]. 50 col. pl. (numb. I—XVI, XVIII—XXI, XXIII—L; pl. XVII and XXII not numb.; pl. XL, XLIX and L with numbers pasted on). 4to.

This work was issued in five parts, the first of which appeared in 1843 (preface dated November 3rd) ; the dates of publication will be found in Sherborn (583, Section II, Part I, p. LXXI).

It contains descriptions with synonyms and notes on the history, distribution, and habits of the species figured.

The lithographs, coloured by hand, were executed by native Indian artists. The ground-work and the branches of the plates were executed by a »highly talented amateur Artist« (cf. Introduction, note, p. I.), who, however, did not commence this work until Plates I—IV and XII had been printed. Thirty copies of these plates, to which the above-mentioned artist added the backgrounds, were then printed, while the colourists were entrusted with the retouching of some of the copies already finished in order to make them in keeping with the additional lithographs, as is the case with the plates of the numbers in question in the present copy.

The plates in Parts 1 and 2 (Nos. I—XXV) were printed by C. V. Kistnarajoo, while most of the remaining numbers (Leonard, Miller or R. E. B. lith.) were printed by Reeve (or Reeve Brothers), London.

The work was also issued in an 8vo edition.

JESPERSEN, P. C.
1928. Brehm Dyrenes Liv ... Vol. II. Part 3. Fuglene. *See Brehm, A. E.*

JOB, H. K.
1936. Birds of America ... *See Pearson, T. G.*

JOHNS, C. A.
1918. British birds in their haunts. By C. A. Johns. With illustrations on wood, drawn by Wolf, engraved by Whymper. Fourteenth edition, with ... coloured plates. Society for Promoting Christian Knowledge. *London. pp. XXXII + 626 + [4]. text-figs. 16 col. pl. (numb. I—XVI). 8vo.*
   The first edition of this work was issued in 1862. Several editions subsequently appeared, in which, as in the 12th edition, 1911, 16 coloured plates were added. In 1909 a revised and annotated edition by J. A. Owen (Mrs. Owen Visger) with 64 coloured plates by W. Foster appeared, and this edition was re-issued several times.
   An abridged edition was issued in 1907.
   The present volume contains a popular account of all the birds figured in the second edition of Yarrell's 'A history of British birds' (London 1845, 8vo) with the addition of some few which have been observed since the date of that publication.
   A systematic arrangement of the genera of British birds is found pp. IX—XXX, with descriptions of orders, families, and genera, while in the discussion of the species main stress is laid on the habits of the birds, though some brief descriptions are added.
   Two to four species are figured on each of the coloured plates (woodcuts printed in colour).

JOHNSEN, S.
1928. Bergens Museums Årbok 1929. Naturvidenskapelig rekke. Nr. 1. Draktskiftet hos lirypen (Lagopus lagopus Lin.) i Norge. Av Sigurd Johnsen. John Griegs Boktrykkeri. *Bergen. pp. 84 + [1]. text-figs* 14 phot. pl. (numb. 1—14; 7 col. (numb. 1—7)). 8vo.
   An investigation of the plumage changes of the Willow Grouse on the basis of a material of about 125 cocks and about 40 hens (winter birds not included), which are treated in the following chapters: plumage changes of the cock; plumage changes of the hen; changes of tail, wing, feet and claws; and general remarks, including the periodicity of the plumage-changes.
   The coloured plates (three-colour prints from çhromo-photographs of skins) were executed by A/S John Griegs Boktrykkeri, Bergen.
   Another copy of this work appears as treatise No. 24 in a volume entitled 'Bergens Jæger- og Fiskeriforening. Rypeundersøkelsen 1921—27', issued at Bergen (John Griegø Boktrykkeri) in 1928 in 100 copies, of which the present øne is No. 73.

JOHNSTONE, J.
1650. Historiæ naturalis de avibus libri VI. Cum æneis figuris Johannes Jonstonus concinnavit. Matthæus Merianus. *Francofurti ad Moenum. pp. 227 + [7]. 62 pl. (numb. I—XXIX, 30—62). fol.*
   The ornithological portion of a comprehensive, learned, but rather uncritical compilation of the works of Ulisse Aldrovandi and other earlier authors. The whole work appeared in 1650—53 in six parts, each with a separate pagination, and gives a complete view of the animal kingdom.
   The text is printed in double columns. The engraved plates, which have evidently been executed by Kaspar Merian and Matthæus Merian, junior, all contain several figures of birds, among which several fabulous birds, as for instance on Plate 62, the Phoenix, Harpy and Griffon. The same plate has a figure of the Pelican which, illustrating the accounts found in the Physiologus and the Bestiaries, is shedding its blood for its young.
   The work was much read during part of the 17th and 18th

centuries and it enjoyed a certain reputation, especially the present edition, principally on account of its figures, to which Linnæus refers in his 'Systema naturæ'. It was re-issued several times, for instance at Amsterdam in 1657—65 (ornithological section 1657 (235)), and under the title 'Theatrum universale' at Amsterdam in 1718 (236), at Heilbronn in 1755—67 (the ornithological section in 1756 (237)), and (552, II, p. 942) at Rouen in 1768. It was translated into several European languages, e. g. into English ('by a person of quality') in 1657, and into Dutch ('uit het Latyn vertaelt door M. Grausius') in 1660. The section on the birds appeared in a French version in 1773—74 as part of a work which was published in 1772—74 (238), while the plates representing mammals and birds were issued in a slightly altered form with a new text in German in 1772—85 (ornithological section 1774—85 (114)).

1657. Historiæ naturalis de avibus libri VI. Cum **235.** æneis figuris Johannes Jonstonus concinnavit. Joannes Jacobi fil. Schipper. *Amstelodami. pp. [XII] + 160. 61 pl. (numb. I—XXI, XXIII—XXIX, 30—62; pl. XXII missing). fol.*
   The ornithological portion of another, the second, edition of Johnstone's work on the natural history of animals. In this edition it consists in all of six separately paginated parts. Four of the title-pages, including the one mentioned above, the title-page of the ornithological section, are dated 1657, while two are dated 1665.
   As in the first edition of 1650 (234) the text is printed in double columns, and the engraved title and the plates contain the same figures; they have merely been redrawn and reversed, and the impressions are weaker.

1718. Theatrum universale omnium animalium **236.** piscium, avium, quadrupedum, exanguium, aquaticorum, insectorum, et angium [*sic*] ... tabulis ornatum, ex scriptoribus tam antiquis quam recentioribus, Aristotele ... à J. Jonstonio collectum ... cura Henrici Ruysch VI. partibus, duobus tomis, comprehensum. Vol. I. - - Part II. Sive historiæ naturalis de avibus libri VI. Cum enumeratione morborum, quibus medicamina ex his animalibus petuntur, ac notitia animalium, ex quibus vicissim remedia pærstantissima possunt capi, cura Henrici Ruysch. R. & G. Wetstenii. *Amstelædami. pp. [XII] + 160. 62 pl. (numb. I— XXIX, 30—62). fol.*
   H. Ruysch's edition of Johnstone's 'Historia naturalis' consists of six parts, paginated separately, in two volumes (in the present copy bound in one volume) with altogether 260 plates. The text is printed in double columns, as in the first edition of 1650 (234), the engraved title is omitted, and the plates are reversed, as in the edition of 1657 (235).

1756. Historiæ naturalis de avibus libri VI. Cum **237.** æneis figuris Joannes Jonstonus concinnavit. Matthæus Merianus. *Francofurti ad Moenum. 1650.* - - Joannis Jonstoni Theatrum universale de avibus. Tabulis ... ab illo celeberrimo Mathia Meriano aeri incisis ornatum, ex scriptoribus tam antiquis, quam recentioribus, Theophrasto ... cura conlectum et ôb raritatem denuo inprimendum suscepit Franciscus Iosephus Eckebrecht. *Heilbronna. pp. [VIII] + 238 + [9]. 62 pl. (numb. I—XXIX, 30—62). fol.*
   This volume is the ornithological portion of one of the later editions of Johnstone's 'Historia naturalis', which appeared in six volumes in 1755—67, each with a separate pagination, the text being printed in double columns.
   The present volume closely resembles the volume on birds in the original edition of 1650 (234), both as regards text and the engraved title and plates, the latter being identical in the present and the original edition.

1772 [—74]. Collection d'oiseaux les plus rares, **238.** gravés et dessinés d'après nature, pour servir d'intelligence à l'histoire naturelle et raisonnée des différens oiseaux qui habitent le globe, contenant leurs noms en différentes langues de l'Europe, leurs descriptions, les couleurs de leurs plumages, leurs dimensions, le temps de leur ponte, la structure de leurs nids, la grosseur de leurs oeufs, leur caractère, & enfin tous les usages pour lesquels on peut les employer, tant pour la médecine que pour l'économie domestique. Traduite du Latin de Jonston, considérablement augmentée, & misé à la portée d'un chacun. De laquelle on a fait précéder l'Histoire particuliere des oiseaux de la Ménagerie du Roi, peints d'après nature par le célébre Robert, & gravés par lui-même. Le tout orné de ... planches, qui renferment près de neuf cens especes différentes, & divisé en trois parties, dont la premiere traite des oiseaux de la Ménagerie Royale, la seconde & la troisieme, sont l'ouvrage & les planches même de Jonston, dont le mérite est très-connu. Pour servir de suite à l'Histoire des insectes & plantes de Mademoiselle de Merian. L. C. Desnos. *Paris. pp. [VI] + 23 + [1] + 3—64. 85 col. pl. (numb. I—XXIII, 1—62). large fol.*

The explanatory text to the plates in this volume is printed in double columns.

The first section contains Plates I—XXIII, which were painted and engraved by Nicolas Robert and coloured from the originals, which according to the introduction 'se trouvent actuellement dans le Cabinet des Estampes du Roi'. In 1676 24 plates by the same artist had been issued in two parts in folio, each containing 12 plates. The first of these parts appeared under the title 'Recüil d'oyseaux les plus rares tirez de la Ménagerie Royalle du Parc de Versailles', etc., while the continuation was entitled 'Suite des oyseaux les plus rares, qui se voyent à la Ménagerie Royalle du Parc de Versailles. Desseignès et ·gravès par Nicolas Robert'. The latter title recurs on Pl. I of the present work, so it is evidently a reproduction of the plates of the work from 1676 with which we are concerned here. The number of plates in the latter is sometimes stated to be 23 (588, p. 539).

The last two parts of the work, according to Wood (588, p. 410) published in 1773—74, consist of a French version of Johnstone's book on the birds, which first appeared in 1650 (234). However, the text is a French explanation of the plates rather than a translation of Johnstone's book.

As in the first part of the work, the plates are engravings coloured by hand.

1774—85. Naturgeschichte der Vögel aus den besten Schriftstellern mit Merianischen und neuen Kupfern. *See Decker, J. M.*

JONSTON, J. *See Johnstone, J.*

JORDAN, K.
1894 —→ See Novitates Zoologicæ.

JOURDAIN, F. C. R.
1910—13. The British bird book ... *See Kirkman, F. B. B.*

JOURNAL FUER ORNITHOLOGIE.
239.   *1853 —→* Journal für Ornithologie ... Herausgegeben von Jean Cabanis (1853—59), Jean Cabanis & Ed. Baldamus (1860—66), Jean Cabanis (1867—93), Ant. Reichenow (1894—1921), Erwin Stresemann (1922—25), Erwin Stresemann & Bernhard Rensch (1926 —→). Theodor Fischer (1853—69). *Cassel.* L. A. Kittler (1870—1921). *Leipzig.* Deutsche Ornithologische Gesellschaft (1922—28), In

Kommission bei R. Friedländer & Sohn (1929 —→) *Berlin. I. —→ Jahrgang. text-figs. col. plates. 8vo.*

According to the title-pages this periodical was in 1854—58 (Jahrgang II—VI) 'Zugleich Organ der Deutschen Ornithologen-Gesellschaft', while in 1868 —→ (Jahrgang XVI —→) it was issued 'In Verbindung mit (1894 —→ (Jahrgang XLII —→): 'Im Auftrage) der (1876—95 (Jahrgang XXIV—XLIII): Allgemeinen) Deutschen Ornithologischen Gesellschaft (1868—93 (Jahrgang XVI—XLI) : zu Berlin').

The journal is at present, 1937, in its 85th year and is one of the oldest and among the leading current ornithological periodicals.

In 1860 it absorbed the periodical 'Naumannia' (358), and in 1876—82 seven volumes of the 'Ornithologisches Centralblatt', edited by J. Cabanis and Ant. Reichenow, then discontinued, were issued as 'Beiblatt'.

A large number of well-known ornithologists, chiefly from German-speaking countries, have contributed to the long series of volumes in which a great amount of important ornithological matter has been published, a number of the larger papers in the form of 'Sonderhefte', some of which are cited in this present catalogue. The periodical further contains a series of more than 200 coloured plates for which the original figures have been supplied by artists such as Baedeker, E. de Maes, J. G. Keulemans, Georg Krause, F. Neubaur, and notably G. Mützel, Bruno Geisler, and O. Kleinschmidt.

The plates are chiefly executed in lithography (Druck von Th. Fischer in Cassel; Kunst-Anstalt v. C. Böhm, Berlin; P. Kaplaneck, Berlin; Rau & Sohn, Dresden; Eugen Köhler, Gera-Untermhaus, and others); the recent volumes contain a few three-colour prints.

1923. 71. Jahrgang. Sonderheft. Contributions to the knowledge of the East African ornithology. Birds collected by the Swedish Mount Elgon Expedition 1920. *See Granvik, S. H.*

1924. 72. Jahrgang. Sonderheft. Die Saenger (Cantores) Aegyptens. *See Koenig, A. F.*

1926. 74. Jahrgang. Sonderheft. Ein weiterer Teilbeitrag zur Avifauna Aegyptica ... *See Koenig, A. F.*

1928. 76. Jahrgang. Sonderheft. Fortsetzung und Schluss der Watvögel (Grallatores) Aegyptens. *See Koenig, A. F.*

1932. 80. Jahrgang. Sonderheft. Die Schwimmvögel (Natatores) Aegyptens. Die Ruderfüsser (Steganopodes) Aegyptens. Die Flügeltaucher (Urinatores) Aegyptens. *See Koenig, A. F.*

KAUP, J. J.
1849—53. Contributions to ornithology ... *See Jardine, W., 1848—53.*

KAY, J. E. DE. *See De Kay, J. E.*

KEARTON, R.
1908. British birds' nests, how, where, and when to 24 find and identify them. By Richard Kearton. Illustrated from photographs by Cherry and Richard Kearton. With coloured and Rembrandt plates. New edition, revised and enlarged. Cassell and Co. *London. pp. XII + 520. text-figs. 21 pl. (15 col. pl. eggs (numb. 1—15)). 8vo.*

A popular work on British birds, distinguished by the numerous reproductions of photographs taken by the author and notably by his brother Cherry, who in 1892 began to photograph birds' nests.

The first edition of this work appeared in 1895 with an introduction by R. Bowdler Sharpe, since when it has been reissued several times. A kind of supplementary volume with additional photographs and containing the results of further research appeared in 1899 under the title 'Our rarer British breeding birds'. Matter from the latter volume has been included in the present edition of the main work in which the species are arranged in alphabetical order, the subject-matter being grouped under the following headings: Description of parents birds, situation and locality, materials, eggs, time, and remarks on the birds.

The coloured plates have been printed from photographs by the three-colour process.

KEELER, C. A.

1. *1893. Occasional Papers of the California Academy of Sciences. III. - - Evolution of the colors of North American land birds. By Charles A. Keeler. California Academy of Sciences. San Francisco. pp. XII + 361. text-figs. 19 pl. (numb. I—XIX; 12 col. (numb. II, III, V—VII, XIII—XIX); 5 maps (numb. IX—XIII)). 8vo.*

This work deals with the question of the colours of the birds considered especially from the standpoint of the theoretical views of evolution. It falls into two parts, 'I. Introduction' (pp. 1—132) and 'II. The colors of North American birds' (pp. 132—336), while the remainder of the text includes a fairly comprehensive bibliography (pp. 337—343).

The first main section deals with questions of a general character, such as the inheritance of acquired characters, variation and natural selection, sexual selection, etc., while the second main section of the volume consists of chapters such as 'On modes of plumage changes', 'General principles of color in birds', 'The pattern of markings', etc., and ends with a long chapter, 'Orders, families, and genera of North American birds, considered from the standpoint of their evolution' (pp. 257—336).

The subject and the views of the author are illustrated by plates, which, in lithography and chromo-lithography (C. A. K[eeler] del.; Lith. Britton & Rey S. F.), show figures of feathers and birds, or parts of birds, and colour charts of the plumage.

2. *1902. Smithsonian Institution. Harriman Alaska Series. (Edited by C. Hart Merriam). City of Washington. 1910. - - Harriman Alaska Expedition with cooperation of Washington Academy of Sciences. Alaska ... Doubleday, Page & Co. New York. — Vol. II. - - < pp. 205—234: Days among Alaska birds. By Charles Keeler>. 11 pl. birds (8 col.; 1 phot. pl.). 8vo.*

The first and second volumes of the Harriman Alaska Series (for this and the expedition, see Burroughs, J. (87)) contain a few papers of general interest, among others the present section of Volume II which, in a popular and literary form, describes observations of the bird life of Alaska made during the expedition. Notes on birds are further found scattered through Vol. II, and the opening chapters of Vol. I (pp. XXI—XXVII) also contain information of importance for the ornithological work of the expedition.

Several figures of birds in characteristic positions from L. A. Fuertes' paintings and drawings from living or flesh specimens, are reproduced on the fine plates (photo-mechanical prints and chromo-lithographs, executed i. a. by the Heliotype Co., the Grignard Litho. Co. N. Y., and by A. Hoen & Co., Baltimore).

KENNERLY, C. B. R.

1859. Reports of explorations and surveys, to ascertain the most practicable and economical route for a railroad from the Mississippi River to the Pacific Ocean ... 1853—6 ... Vol. X. < - - Report of explorations for a railway route (near the thirty-fifth parallel of north latitude), from the Mississippi River to the Pacific Ocean. By Lieutenant A. W. Whipple ... assisted by Lieutenant J. C. Ives ... 1853—54. - - Part VI. - - Zoological report. - - pp. 19—35: No. 3. Report on birds collected on the route. By C. B. R. Ken-

nerly >. Beverley Tucker. (Senate Ex. Doc., No. 78). *Washington. 11 col. pl. (numb. XVIII—XX, XXII, XXVII, XXIX—XXXI, XXXIII, XXXVI —XXXVII). 4to.*

This article belongs to a report begun in Vol. IV, 1856, of the series. In the present paper 88 species are enumerated with the addition of brief field-notes and references to the pages in Vol. IX of the series (22) in which the particular species is described in greater detail.

The plates (lithographs coloured by hand) are, with some alterations, reproduced in Baird, Cassin, and Lawrence's 'The birds of North America' (24).

KIELLERUP, C. E.

1851. Zoologisk Haandatlas til Brug for Skoler ... See Sundevall, C. J.

KIELSEN, F. C.

1835. Icones avium. Indicem systematicum addidit F. C. Kielsen. Christian Steen. Hafniæ. pp. X. 108 pl. (numb. I—CVIII) 4to. 244.

In the same year in which this work appeared Kielsen issued six volumes of plates, containing altogether 488 plates with figures of the animal kingdom.

The engravings are unsigned and without particular value, and the bird portraits, evidently chiefly copied from Buffon's 'Planches enluminées' (76), are small, each plate containing one to four, in a single case (the humming birds) even eight, figures.

In the systematic Index (pp. III—X) the birds are divided into orders in accordance with Blumenbach, while Linnæus (13th edition of 'Systema naturæ') has been followed as regards the genera and species.

KINBERG, J. G. H.

1881—86. Svenska foglarna ... Vols. II—IV. See Sundevall, C. J., 1856—86.

KIRKMAN, F. B. B.

1910—13. The British bird book. An account of all the birds, nests and eggs found in the British Isles. Edited by F. B. Kirkman. Illustrated by two hundred coloured drawings and numerous photographs. T. C. & E. C. Jack. London. 4 vols. large 4to. — Vol. I. [1910—] 1911. pp. XII + XVIII + 449. text-figs. col. pl. 1—46, 18a. phot. pl. I—XVII. 1 map. Vol. II. 1911. pp. XII + 540. text-figs. col. pl. 47—93. egg pl. (col.) E. phot. pl. XVIII—XXXVIII. egg pl. E. Vol. III. 1912. pp. XII + 609. text-figs. col. pl. 94—135. phot. pl. XXXIX—LVIII. Vol. IV. [1912—] 1913. pp. XII + 692. text-figs. col. pl. 136—178. egg pl. (col.) A—D, F—R, V—W. phot. pl. LIX—LXXIX. egg pl. S—T. pl. U (nest feathers and down ducks).* 245.

This work is in the twelve parts in which it was issued. The dates of publication of the sections and their contents are as follows (cf. Novitates Zoologicæ, XXII, 1915, p. 386):

I, May, 1910, pp. XVIII + pp. 1—156, col. pl. 1—18, pl. I—V, egg pl. (col.) A, 1 map;

II, October, 1910, pp. 157—296, col. pl. 18a, 19—32, pl. VI—XI, egg pl. (col.) B;

III, January, 1911, pp. 297—449 + XII, col. pl. 33—46, pl. XII—XVII, egg pl. (col.) C (2 copies);

IV, April, 1911, pp. 1—170, col. pl. 47—61, pl. XVIII—XXIII, egg pl. (col.) D;

V, June, 1911, pp. 171—378, col. pl. 62—79, pl. XXIV—XXXIII;

VI, November, 1911, pp. 379—540 + XII, col. pl. 80—93, pl. XXXIV—XXXVIII, egg pl. (col.) E, egg pl. E*;

VII, February, 1912, pp. 1—194, col. pl. 94—108, pl. XXXIX XLVI, egg pl. (col.) F-J;

19

VIII, April, 1912, pp. 195—412, col. pl. 109—122, pl. XLVII
—LIII, egg pl. (col.) K, L;
IX, July, 1912, pp. 413—609 + XII, col. pl. 123—135, pl.
LIV—LVIII, egg pl. (col.) M, N;
X, December, 1912, pp. 1—188, col. pl. 136—155, pl. LIX
—LXV, egg pl. (col.) O-R;
XI, June, 1913, pp. 189—404, col. pl. 156—174, pl. LXVI—
LXXV, egg pl. S, T, pl. U, egg pl. (col.) V;
XII, November, 1913, pp. 405—692 + XII, col. pl. 175—
178, pl. LXXVI—LXXIX, egg pl. (col.) W.
Section I contains a provisional title-page to Vol. I, dated
1910, and the preface and some explanations, pages I—XVIII.
The final title-page to Vol. I was published in Section III to-
gether with the contents and list of plates, pages I—XII.
Sections VI, IX, and XII contain (pp. I—XII) title-page,
contents, and list of plates to Vols. II, III, and IV respectively.
The work is one of the most important recent publications
on British birds of which it gives, in a popular form, a detailed
account prepared by various authors, the matter concerning the
individual forms being arranged under headings such as
description, distribution, migration, nest and eggs, food, and
song period, if any.
The contributors, besides the editor, are J. L. Bonhote,
T. A. Coward, William Farren, E. Hartert, F. C. R. Jourdain,
R. B. Lodge, W. P. Pycraft, Edmund Selous, A. Landsborough
Thomson, and Emma L. Turner.
The originals for the coloured plates were executed by Wini-
fred Austen, G. E. Collins, H. Grønvold, G. E. Lodge, Alfred
Priest, A. W. Seaby, and H. Wormald. The coloured drawings
in nearly all cases were drawn from life, and reproduced by
the three-colour process. In most cases they show not merely
a portrait of the birds, but present them in their natural surroundings in some characteristic position. Not all of the reproductions are, however, of equal value. Grønvold's plates of eggs,
on which all breeding British species are represented are the
best.
The coloured plates were subsequently used in the work
'British Birds' by F. B. Kirkman and F. C. R. Jourdain, which
appeared in London in 1930 (pp. XVI + 184, 202 pl. (199
col.), 4to). Another edition of the latter work appeared in 1932.

KITTLITZ, F. H. von.

1830—35. See Académie Impériale des Sciences
de St.-Pétersbourg. Mémoires présentés ... par divers
savans.

KJÆRBØLLING, N.

246.   [1847—] 1851. Ornithologia Danica. Danmarks
Fugle i 304 Afbildninger af de gamle Hanner. Med
særskilt Text. Af N. Kjærbølling. Forfatterens Forlag
(Gyldendalske Boghandel). Kjøbenhavn. 60 col. pl.
(numb. I—XXI, XXIIa—b, XXIII—XXVII,
XXVIIIa—c, XXIX—XXXII, XXXIIIa—b,
XXXIV—XXXIX, XLa—b, XLI—L, LIa—b, LII
—LIV (Pl. LIV headed: Supplementtavle)). fol.
This is the first portion of Kjærbølling's plates which were
published in fifteen parts, each containing four plates, to which
a supplement-plate (numb. LV) was later added (247, note),
thus completing the collection in the first section of 'Ornithologia Danica'.
The first two parts with Pl. XXIII, XLVI, XI, LII, XXV,
XLII, XIII, and VII appeared in 1847, after which publication
stopped, the Schleswig wars causing an upheaval in Kjærbølling's life, as the German Baron Brockdorff of Tirsbæk, his
employer up to that time, had to leave the country. However,
up to the end of 1849 six parts are reported to have appeared
(Almindeligt dansk Forlagscatalog, 3rd Supplement, 1850, p.
52), but the last parts were not issued till 1851.
The price of each part was 1 Rigsbankdaler and 32 Skilling,
or about 3/—. The publication was aided by a considerable
Royal grant.
The figures were drawn by N. Kjærbølling who, as he himself says in the preface to 'Danmarks Fugle', 1852 (248), was
especially guided by the bird portraits in Naumann's 'Natur-

geschichte der Vögel Mitteleuropas', a second edition of which
had appeared in 1820 [1822]—44 (355). He also availed himself of live birds, and of his considerable collection of nearly
4000 specimens of birds, some stuffed, but mostly preserved
as skins, representing about 450 species. In addition he owned
a large collection of eggs which contained most of the known
birds' eggs of Europe (774).
Some of the plates are engravings (Emil Hallesen sc.), of
which a few are dated 1848 or 1849, while others are lithographs, including those of the two parts first issued. Several
of these plates bear the inscription: A. (or Andr.) Hansens
lith. Inst.
Each plate contains from one to ten rather small figures of
birds, which have been coloured by hand under the supervision
of Kjærbølling. The colouring, which is fairly good in the present copy, varies greatly in different copies. The method of
preparation employed and the position and placing of the
figures may also vary in different copies of the same plate
(247), thus testifying to the existence of two different types
of the corresponding originals. In 1851 the price of the 60
plates was 20 Rigsbankdaler (about 45/—).
One of the original covers is preserved in the present copy,
in which is also inserted the general title-page which was issued
in 1856 for the complete collection of plates (247).
A more detailed description of the work and the accompanying text is found in a paper by the present compiler (657).

[1847—] 1856. Icones ornithologiæ Scandinavicæ. 24?
Scandinaviens: Danmarks, Sverrigs, Norges, Islands
og Færøernes Fugle i 600 colorerede Afbildninger.
Med særskilt Text. Af N. Kjærbølling. Forfatterens
Forlag. Kjøbenhavn. 3 vols in 1. fol. — [Vol. I].
[1847—] 1851 [—52]. Ornithologia Danica. Danmarks Fugle i 304 Afbildninger af de gamle
Hanner. Med særskilt Text. Af N. Kjærbølling.
Forfatterens Forlag (Gyldendalske Boghandel). 61
col. pl. (numb. I—XXI, XXIIa—b, XXIII—XXVI,
XXVI [= XXVII], XXVIIIa—c, XXIX—XXXII,
XXXIIIa—b, XXXIV—XXXIX, XLa—b, XLI—L,
LIa—b, LII—LV (Pl. LIV and LV headed: Supple-
menttavle)). [Vol. II]. [1852?—] 1854. < Ornithologia Danica. Danmarks Fugle i 252 Afbildninger af
de dragtskiftende gamle Hanner, samt de fra Han-
nerne væsentligt afvigende Hunner og unge Fugle.
Af N. Kjærbølling >. 35 col. pl. (numb. I, 2—35).
[Vol. III]. [1855?]. < De i det øvrige Scandinavien:
Sverrig, Norge, paa Island og Færøerne forekommende Fuglearter, der ei ere bemærkede i Danmark. 45
colorerede Afbildninger. Af N. Kjærbølling >. 8 col.
pl. (numb. I—8).
The first section of this work, 'Danmarks Fugle i 304 Afbildninger af de gamle Hanner', consists, in this complete copy,
of 61 plates, Plate LV not having been issued till after the
publication of the text for the plates was finished in 1852
(248). Mention is not made in this text to the figures on that
plate, even though the species figured are mentioned in the text
or in the supplement, but the plate is promised in the preface
(dated February, 1852) 'in the course of this year'.
The separate title-page is unaltered, and the number of
figures stated on it does not include the eight bird portraits
on Plate LV, which increase the total number of figures to 312.
Moreover, in the production of Plates VII, XI, XXV, and XLII
another procedure or method has been employed than that in the
above-mentioned copy, and the figures in question have been
altered. As stated above (246), these four plates belong to the
eight which were published in 1847.
Soon after the completion of the pictorial work on the adult
males Kjærbølling was induced by various persons to set about
preparing supplementary plates with figures of the different
plumages of the birds according to season, age, and sex. It
was promised that these plates should be issued in six parts of
four plates each, and that one part should be published every
other month at the same price as the parts of the preceding

section of the work. Up to December, 1853, five parts of this first supplement had appeared, and the issue of the remainder was promised in three parts in the course of a few months; this section of the work with its 35 plates distributed over nine parts, which also contained Plate LV of the preceding section, was then completed in 1854. The plates (without inscription, or with the inscription: Andr. Hansens lith. Inst.; No. 29: lith. af N. Kjærbølling) are marked 'Suppl.' before the number; the number of the plate or plates they are to supplement being given in parentheses after the number of the plate itself. Possibly as early as 1855 the eight plates in the second supplement (marked before the number: 2det Suppl. Tab.) brought the work to a final though provisional conclusion, which was marked by the issue of the general title-page 'Icones ornithologiæ Scandinavicæ', etc., dated 1856.

Kjærbølling was his own publisher, and his work attained no small success, since he secured about 500 subscribers, no inconsiderable number in view of Danish conditions; and, as appears from the present catalogue, the plates have also found publishers and a ready sale right down to the present day (249; 250; 252).

8. [1851—] 1852. Danmarks Fugle, beskrevne af N. Kjærbølling. Hertil et Billedværk med 304 naturtroe, colorerede Afbildninger; udgivet med offentlig Understøttelse. Forfatterens Forlag. *Kjøbenhavn. pp.* [VI] + XXXIV + 422 + IX + [2]. 8vo.

This is the text for the first 60 plates in 'Ornithologia Danica', which was published in 1847—51 (246). It was distributed gratis to the subscribers for the plates, and appeared in three parts, of which the first two, each comprising eight sheets, were published in 1851 (in January and June respectively), while Part 3 (217 pages) appeared in February, 1852.

As Kjærbølling says himself in the preface, he has chiefly relied on Naumann's work, cited above (246, note), in the preparation of the introduction and the diagnoses of genera and species, while at the same time he has used S. Nilsson's 'Skandinavisk fauna. Foglarna', of which a new revised edition had been issued in 1835 (364, note). As regards the biological sections Kjærbølling, as has been ascertained later by O. G. Petersen (837), also derived his material from H. D. F. Zander's 'Naturgeschichte der Vögel Mecklenburgs', 1837—53, which was never completed.

In his work Kjærbølling gives the first entire description of the avifauna of Denmark. Altogether 308 species are mentioned, with brief diagnoses, descriptions, and brief notes on the habits, habitat, occurrence in Denmark, distribution, and other features of interest, such as the voices of the birds and the dates of arrival of the migratory birds. A brief description and a general account are likewise given of the genera and superior groups.

The work is written in popular form, Kjærbølling having, as he puts it himself, worked 'as a layman for laymen', but it has been of great importance in arousing an interest in the study of the avifauna of Denmark and serving as a guide to beginners and amateurs in this field.

Two copies of this work are in the possession of the Library. A completely revised edition was issued by Jonas Collin in 1875—77 (251).

(1858—65). Icones ornithologiæ Scandinavicæ. Scandinaviens: Danmarks, Sverrigs, Norges, Islands og Færoernes Fugle i 612 colorerede Afbildninger. Med særskilt Text. Af N. Kjærbølling. Forfatterens Forlag. *Kjøbenhavn. 3 vols. in 1. 104 col. pl. fol.*

The success of Kjærbølling's atlas issued in 1847—56 (247) was so great that it was soon out of print and he could then issue the plates with new title-pages, as they are found in the present copy which, besides the undated general title-page, contains new special title-pages reading as those known from the first edition. Of these new special title-pages, only those for the two sections of 'Ornithologia Danica' are dated, 1858 and 1865 respectively, while the general title-page differs from that of the preceding edition in the number of figures stated on it.

The plates in the first section with the figures of the adult males are identical with the plates in the corresponding section of the copy of the edition completed in 1856. Nor are the 35 plates in the second section, 1865, very different from the plates of the preceding edition; however, Plate 29 has been executed

by a different method (G. Hillebrandts Steentr.), and several of the other plates are inscribed: Simonsens & Andersens Steentryk.

The plates of the last section, with the figures of the species of birds occurring in the other parts of Scandinavia, do not differ from the corresponding plates in the previous edition.

The fact that Kjærbølling's plates were issued privately — for some time the sale of the plates was one of his most important sources of income — has obscured their history. Thus the present title-edition of the plates is not cited in Dansk Bogfortegnelse or by C. C. A. Gosch (567).

The variation in the prints that are available of the same plate is furthermore the reason that copies of the atlas are not infrequently composed of plates from the different issues or reprints. Its first and second separate title-pages may also be dated 1858 and 1854, respectively, if the first portion of the atlas (or its separate title-page) of the present issue is combined with the two supplements, 1854—56, of the first edition.

[1872—] 1879. Skandinaviens Fugle, med særligt **250.** Hensyn til Danmark og de nordlige Bilande. Af Dr. N. Kjærbølling. Paany udgivet af Jonas Collin. Med over 600 kolorerede Figurer. L. A. Jørgensen. *Kjøbenhavn. 106 col. pl. fol.*

The plates are numbered as in the edition of 1847—56 (247) with the exception that the first plate in the first supplement is now numbered 1. Two new unnumbered plates have been added. The plates of the first supplement bear in front of the number the inscription: 1ste Suppl. Tab., while the plates of the second supplement, as in the original edition, bear the inscription: 2det Suppl. Tab.

L. A. Jørgensen acquired the copyright of Kjærbølling's work, and in 1871 he sent out a prospectus for a new edition of the plates, which was intended to comprise 20 parts at 1 Rigsdaler each (plain at 48 Skilling), but actually 22 parts were published, of which the last one, which contained two new plates, appeared in 1879. The subscribers were later to receive gratis a new edition of the text revised by Jonas Collin, who also undertook the issue of the plates and who, in the preface to the text which appeared in 1875—77 (251), complains that he has only been able to alter and improve the figures to a slight extent. Indeed, they do not differ very much from the bird portraits in the preceding edition of 1858—65 (249), the only change being that the names of the lithographers have disappeared from the plates. However, the issue of the plates does not seem to have been commenced until 1872 (Nordisk Boghandlertidende, Maj 3, 1872), and this edition was not finally concluded until 1879 with the issue of the title-page, and of a part entitled on the cover 'To nye Tavler til Dr. Kjærbølling's Skandinaviens Fugle. Tegnede og lithographerede af C. Cordts. Kollorerede af Frøken Hallesen. Udgivet af Jonas Collin.' (Kjøbenhavn. L. A. Jørgensen). These new plates are unnumbered, and Collin refers to their figures in his revised edition of the text. Frøken Hallesen undertook the colouring of all the other plates in this edition also, of which only the concluding section, the two new plates, are cited in 'Dansk Bogfortegnelse'.

In 1879 the price of the complete copy of the plates was Kroner 42 (about 47/—).

One more plate was issued in 1888 (103), which increased the total number of Kjærbølling's plates to 107.

1875—77. Skandinaviens Fugle, med særligt Hen- **251.** syn til Danmark og de nordlige Bilande. Af N. Kjærbølling. Anden, fuldstændigt omarbeidede Udgave. ved [sic] Jonas Collin. L. A. Jørgensen. [Fr. Wøldike]. *Kjøbenhavn. pp.* [XII] + VII—LI + [1] + 838 + [2]. 8vo.

A second title-page with the inscription 'Text' is dated 1875.

The first edition of this text appeared in 1851—52 (248), and the present edition is to be regarded as the text for Collin's edition of Kjærbølling's plates in 1872—79 (250). It was issued in eleven parts, of which the first appeared in March, 1875, to be succeeded in the same year by two more. The last parts are dated 1876 on the cover, but are not cited in the 'Dansk Bogfortegnelse' until December, 1877.

19*

No great alterations have been made in the classification, but in a special chapter (pp. 750—756) Collin gives a general survey of the birds treated in accordance with C. Sundevall's 'Methodi naturalis avium disponendarum tentamen' (Stockholm 1872, 4to). Furthermore some alterations have been made in the nomenclature and, for the sake of the plates, the Norwegian and Swedish species of birds have been included in the present revision of the text in which an attempt has also been made to include the observations made and experience gained in the faunistic field since the appearance of the first edition; again, doubtful matter or such matter as in the opinion of the editor was of less value has been left out, e. g. the descriptions of the birds' voices.

Subsequently Collin issued three supplements to 'Skandinaviens Fugle', — in 1877 (101), 1888 (102), and 1895 (104).

1877. Ornithologiske Bidrag til Danmarks Fauna. Udgivet som Supplement til 'Skandinaviens Fugle'. *See Collin, J. S.*

1888. Bidrag til Kundskaben om Danmarks Fuglefauna. Udgivet som 2det Supplement til 'Skandinaviens Fugle'. *See Collin, J. S.*

[1888]. Ny Tavle (III) til 'Skandinaviens Fugle'. *See Collin, J. S.*

252.   *[1893?].* Skandinaviens Fugle med særligt Hensyn til Danmark og de nordlige Bilande. Af Dr. N. Kjærbølling. Paany udgivet af Jonas Collin. Med over 600 kolorerede Figurer. Chr. Mackeprang. *Kjøbenhavn. fol.*

Since the completion of the new edition of Kjærbølling's plates, 1872—79 (250), the rest of the stock of plates and their copyright have been held by various small publishing firms. One of these provided the plates with a new, undated, cover and title-page. The title cited above is derived from such a copy.

Since then copies of the work with this new title-page have also been sold by the present owner of the copyright, who is the owner, too, of all the old copper-plates.

The price of the work has varied somewhat; at the end of the nineties well coloured copies could be bought at a price of about 50 Kroner, but the price of such copies now is about 90 Kroner (about £ 4).

1895. Faunistiske og biologiske Meddelelser om danske Fugle. Udgivet som 3die Supplement til 'Skandinaviens Fugle'. *See Collin, J. S.*

253.   *No date. [Manuscript].* Forsøg til en Afbildning af danske Fugle tilligemed en kort Beskrivelse af N. Kjærbølling. 2. Hefte, indeholdende Skovfuglene. Tegnede efter Naturen, i naturlig Størrelse, dog ere Krageslægten og nogle andre i halv naturlig Størrelse. *pp. [14]. 4 col. pl. obl. 4to.*

This undated manuscript, or fragment of a manuscript, for which the author drew a title-page, executed with painstaking neatness, contains a description of a few common Danish birds, illustrated with coloured drawings by the author.

KLEIN, J. T.

254.   *1750.* Iacobi Theodori Klein Historiæ avium prodromus cum præfatione de ordine animalium in genere. Accessit historia muris alpini et vetus vocabularium animalium, msc. Cum figuris. Ionas Schmidt. *Lubecæ. pp. [XVI] + 238. 8 pl. 4to.*

The main part of this work, 'Ordo avium' (pp. 13—153), is a systematically arranged survey of the group of birds, which are classed into eight families.

A chapter entitled 'De origine avium' is found on pp. 1—12, and the work also contains chapters such as 'De avibus erraticis et migratoriis', 'De hybernaculis Hirundinum', and 'De hybernaculis Ciconiarum', besides a brief chapter on the natural history of the Alpine Marmot and a vocabulary of about the year 1420 with names of animals in Latin and German, as in 'Georgii Agricolæ de Animantibus subterraneis; 16 apud Froben. 1549'.

The plates, of which four contain portraits of as many birds, are of no particular importance. Three of them are marked: M. Cerulli sc. Regiom.

The work appeared in a German translation in 1760 (256).

1759. Iac. Theod. Klein Stemmata avium ... ta-   255 bulis aeneis ornata; accedunt nomenclatores: Polono-Latinus et Latino-Polonus. Geschlechtstafeln der Vögel, mit ... Kupfern erläutert. Adam Henr. Holle. *Lipsiæ. pp. [XVI] + 48. 40 pl. (numb. I—XL). 4to.*

The text is printed in Latin and German in parallel columns, except for the chapters headed 'Observatio' in the 'Stemmata avium'

The work contains a general survey of birds arranged according to Klein's system of classification, which is based on the differences in their heads, tongues, and feet. These are figured on the engraved plates, which constitute the most important part of the work; some of them are marked D. J. Gr. del., a single one J. G. Golcke del., or Deusch pinx (Fritsch sc.).

1760. Jak. Theodor Kleins Vorbereitung zu einer   25 vollständigen Vögelhistorie, nebst einer Vorrede von der Ordnung der Thiere überhaupt, und einem Zusatz der Historie des Murmelthieres, wie auch eines alten Wörterbuchs der Thiere. Aus dem Lateinischen übersetzt durch D. H. B. Jonas Schmidt. *Leipzig. pp. [XXIV] + 427. 8 pl. 8vo.*

A German translation of Klein's 'Historiæ avium prodromus', 1750 (254), made by the editor, Friedrich Daniel Behn. The plates are the same as in the original Latin edition, but owing to the smaller format they are folded.

In the same year another German translation, by Klein himself, was issued. It contains no plates, and after Klein's death was issued by Gottfried Reyger.

1766. Jacobi Theodori Klein Ova avium plurima-   2 rum ad naturalem magnitudinem delineata et genuinis coloribus picta. J. T. Klein Sammlung verschiedener Vögel Eyer in natürlicher Grösse und mit lebendigen Farben geschildert und beschrieben. Johann Jacob Kanter. *Leipzig. pp. 36. 21 col. pl. eggs (numb. I—XXI). 4to.*

The text of this work is printed in Latin and German in parallel columns.

Klein's preface is dated December 23, 1758, and the work is arranged and edited by Gottfried Reyger. It gives a brief description, arranged in accordance with Klein's system of classification, of the 145 eggs of different species figured on the plates, with scattered notes on the birds and their nidification.

The figures of eggs (engravings coloured by hand) are rather poorly executed, especially as regards the colouring. They were drawn 'von einer geschickten Hand nach dem Leben' and engraved by Gust. Phil. Trautner, Norimb.

KLEINSCHMIDT, O.

1905. Berajah, Zoographia infinita. Saxicola Borealis. Von O. Kleinschmidt. W. Schlüter. *Halle. pp. 22. 9 pl. (numb. I—IX) (6 col. pl. birds (numb. I—VI)). 4to.*

This is the first Lieferung of a serial work, or periodical, with which was associated 'Falco, unregelmässig im Anschluss an das Werk Berajah, Zoographia infinita, erscheinende Zeitschrift', Jahrgang I, 1905.

Both publications deal especially with subjects of a systematic character and questions regarding geographical variation in connection with geographical distribution. This applies to the work, chiefly written by Kleinschmidt, of which the present book is the first part. As one of the advocates of recent systematic points of view he arranges the various related forms in groups, 'Formenkreise' — the specific names of which he begins with a capital letter — so as to provide a new and truer picture of nature, claiming that 'das Bild, das Linné von der Natur hatte, war falsch, das Bild, das Darwin von der Natur entwarf, ist gleichfalls falsch'.

According to the editor's own statement, Berajah is 'ein

zoologischer, zunächst ornithologischer Bilderatlas mit begleitendem Text, der in einzelnen Heften je einen Formenkreis (eine wirkliche natürliche Art) behandelnd ausgegeben wird'. The coloured figures in the present portion of the work of which several Lieferungen have subsequently appeared, were drawn on stone by O. Kleinschmidt and printed in colours under his supervision.

1913. Die Singvögel der Heimat ... farbige Tafeln mit systematisch-biologischem Text nebst Abbildung der wichtigsten Eier- und Nestertypen letztere meist nach Naturaufnahmen in Schwarzdruck von O. Kleinschmidt. Quelle & Meyer. *Leipzig. pp. X + [I] + 107 + [17]. text-figs. 86 col. pl. (numb. 1—86; 2 pl. eggs. (numb. 85—86)). 8vo.*
A popular account of the song-birds of Germany, with the exception of the Corvidæ. The book has been written by a man who knows these birds well; he is an excellent draughtsman and has himself drawn the originals for the coloured plates (three-colour prints), which are accompanied by a brief schematic text with notes on the names, appearance, occurrence, habits and other features, of the birds.
This work has subsequently been issued in several editions (7th edition, 1934).

1934. Die Raubvögel der Heimat auf ... farbigen und ... schwarzen Tafeln in einer nach praktischen Gesichtspunkten geordneten Übersicht ihrer häufigen und ihrer seltenen Vertreter mit kurzen Erläuterungen ihres Schönheitswertes und der Grundzüge ihres Wesens und Lebens dargestellt von Otto Kleinschmidt. Quelle & Meyer. *Leipzig. pp. XV + [II] + 86 + [3]. text-figs. 80 pl. (numb. 1—80; 60 (3 pl. eggs) col. (numb. 1—46, 50—60, and (egg pl.) 47—49; 17 phot. pl. (numb. 61—77)). 8vo.*
An atlas of the birds of prey of Germany, intended for lovers of Nature. The text is divided into brief chapters, which describe in broad features the figures they accompany.
Altogether 46 forms of birds are mentioned, while a chapter, 'Allgemeines', deals with eggs, plumages, and other phenomena of interest, chiefly individual and geographical variation. The concluding chapter is entitled 'Raubvogelleben im Wechsel der Jahreszeiten'.
The coloured plates (three-colour prints) are executed from drawings by Kleinschmidt, and represent the birds in characteristic positions of rest; on most of the plates a smaller figure (very occasionally two figures) has been added showing the bird on the wing.

KNATCHBULL-HUGESSEN, W. W., Third Baron Brabourne. *See Brabourne, W. W. K.-H., Third Baron.*

KNIP, Madame A. P. J. R.
[1809—43]. Les pigeons, par Madame Knip, née Pauline de Courcelles ... Mme Knip. *Paris. 2 vols. 147 col. pl. large fol.* — Vol. I. [1809—] 1811. Le texte par C. J. Themminck [*sic*]. *pp. [III] + III + 13 + [1] + 23—41 + 128 + 30. 87 col. pl. (numb. I— XI, I—XXXII, XXXI [=XXXIII], XXXIV— LIX, I—XVI in text, 1 unnumb. [= XXVbis]. Vol. II. [1838—43]. Le texte par Florent Prévost. pp. [VI] + 114. 60 col. pl. (numb. I—V, XI [= VI], VII— LX in text).*
The two volumes of which this work consists, were published in fifteen livraisons each.
The text of the first volume was written by Temminck, as stated in the title, but during publication Madame Knip, from whose drawings the plates were executed, in 1811 appropriated the work at the ninth livraison, when she changed the covertitle of this and the subsequent livraisons and made other alterations also, for instance she published a new title-page for

the whole work in the 15th livraison. Temminck then published his text in the first volume of his 'Histoire naturelle générale des pigeons et des gallinacés', 1813—15 (501), in whose Vol. III (pp. 640—644) he gives a detailed account of his controversy with Madame Knip who, according to his statement, showed the mutilated work to 'S. M. l'Impératrice et Reine Marie Louise, et servit à obtenir des gratifications que l'ambition de Madame Knip convoitoit depuis longtemps'. In these circumstances it can be understood that during a visit to Paris Temminck failed to obtain what was due to him from the lady artist who, on the title-page of the first Volume, is designated as 'premier peintre d'histoire naturelle de S. M. l'Impératrice Reine Marie-Louise'.
The copies which Temminck received from Madame Knip, among which eight were due to him as author, were not altered, and bore the title 'Histoire naturelle générale des pigeons'. Only twelve such copies were approved by Temminck. This extraordinary controversy has also been treated by Coues (561, 4, pp. 794—798).
Simultaneously with Vol. II, which is in itself an entirely separate work, a new and somewhat altered edition (deuxième édition) of Vol. I was issued, which was to appear in 22 livraisons (579, VI, 1857, p. 81).
As stated above, the beautiful plates were executed from original paintings by Madame Knip. The plates in Vol. I were engraved by César Macret, printed in colour (Imp. de Millevoy), and retouched under the direction of the artist. Some of the plates in Vol. II are engravings, engraved by Dequevauviller or Guyard (Imp. de Gobry, or Saunier), but most of them are lithographs (Imp. de P. Bineteau).
A continuation of, or a supplement to, this work, with 55 coloured plates, written by C. L. Bonaparte, was issued in 1857 —58 under the title 'Iconographie des pigeons non figurés par Mme Knip' (Paris, large folio).

KØBENHAVN. KONGELIGE DANSKE VIDENSKABERNES SELSKAB. *See Danske Videnskabernes Selskab. København.*

KOCK, W. A.
[1912—] *1915*. Haandbog i Fjerkræavl. Af W. A. **262.** Kock. Med 215 i Teksten trykte Illustrationer og ... Farvetavler. *Schønberg. København. pp. [IV] + [VIII] + 246. text-figs (1 col.). 6 col. pl. 4to.*
This work was published in twelve parts, of which the first appeared in November, 1912, the last in January, 1915.
A comprehensive account of practical poultry-breeding, the main stress being laid on the elucidation of questions of importance to the promotion of profitable poultry-breeding, the treatment of the different races being kept in the background. The text pp. 11—174 deals with the breeding of fowls and fowl-keeping, pp. 175—198 the hygiene of poultry, especially fowls, pp. 201—214 other gallinaceous birds, pp. 215—233 natatorial birds, pp. 234—241 pigeons, and pp. 242—246 eggs and poultry as commercial products.
The coloured plates were produced by the three-colour process from drawings by F. L. Sewell.
The second edition (263) of this work appeared in 1918 (dated 1919), the third edition (without plates, 8vo) in 1919, the fourth edition (without plates, 8vo) in 1924, and a large work on the same subject in 1930—35 (264).

1919 [*1918*]. Haandbog i Fjerkræavl. Af W. A. **263.** Kock. Anden Udgave. *Schønberg. København. pp. [VIII] + 188 + [3]. text-figs. 10 col. pl. large 8vo (size as 4to).*
The second, somewhat altered, edition of this work, the first edition of which appeared in 1912—15 (262).

[1930—] *1935*. W. A. Kock Store illustrerede **264.** Haandbog i Fjerkræavl. Med 635 Tekstillustrationer og ... Bilagsbilleder. *Schønberg. København. 2 vols. 44 pl. (26 col.). 4to.* — Vol. I. *pp. [VIII] + 1—266. text-figs. (3 col.). 21 pl. (11 col.).* Vol. II. *pp. [IV] + 267—604. text-figs. 23 pl. (15 col.).*

This work was published in 18 parts (1—4, 1930; 5—10, 1931; 11—14, 1932; 15—16, 1933; 17, 1934; 18, 1935). It gives a complete account of all branches of poultry-breeding, in which the description of the fowls (pp. 27—512) occupies a prominent place. Other gallinaceous birds are treated on pp. 513—536, water-fowls on pp. 537—588, and pigeons on pp. 589—604. The coloured plates (three-colour prints) were executed from drawings by F. L. Sewell and others.

KOENIG, A. F.
265.   *1911.* Avifauna Spitzbergensis. Forschungsreisen nach der Bären-Insel und dem Spitzbergen-Archipel, mit ihren faunistischen und floristischen Ergebnissen. Herausgegeben und verfasst von Alexander Koenig. Mit 74 Textbildern, 26 Heliogravuren, ... Farbentafeln und einer Karte. *Bonn. pp. X + [III] + 294. 60 pl. (34 col. (front. + Nos. I—XXXIII; 10 pl. eggs (Nos. XXIV—XXXIII)). 4to.*

The present work is based on the results of three journeys to the area explored, in 1905, 1907, and 1908 as well as on the literature on the subject. The course of the expeditions is described by Alex. Koenig in the general part; the special part was written by Dr. Otto le Roi. The latter section (pp. 113—270) opens with 'Ornithologische Bibliographie der Bären-Insel und des Spitzbergen-Archipels', in which the bibliography goes as far back as 1598.

Then follows a list of the 36 species or subspecies of birds found in Bear Island and of the 52 found in Spitsbergen, altogether 58 forms in the area investigated having been recorded with certainty; they are described in detail, and forms that are stated in the literature to have been reported from the region are also enumerated, though they cannot be said to have been recorded with certainty.

Of the final part of the work (pp. 271—294) only the table of contents (pp. 289—294) is concerned with ornithological subjects, the remainder dealing with land Arthropods, and Phanerogams and Pteridophyta.

The originals for the coloured plates with figures of birds were executed by A. Thorburn, J. G. Keulemans, and H. Schultze, while the plates of eggs are due to G. Krause. Plates VI, XII—XXIII, and XXXI are reproduced in lithography (Kunstanstalt Wilhelm Greve, Berlin), and the remainder of the coloured plates are reproduced in facsimile-colour-collotype (Kunstanstalt Albert Frisch, Berlin). The plates executed from photographs are reproduced in photogravure (Kunstanstalt Meisenbach, Riffarth & Co., Leipzig-Reudnitz).

266.   *1924.* Journal für Ornithologie. 72. Jahrgang. <-- Sonderheft. Die Saenger (Cantores) Aegyptens. Bearbeitet von Alexander Koenig >. Deutsche Ornithologische Gesellschaft. *Berlin. pp. XIV + 277. 2 pl. (numb. I—II; 1 col. (numb. II)). 8vo.*

A section (published on September 1, 1924) of the author's work on the birds of Egypt, published in the course of many years, 'Avifauna Aegyptiaca', as he occasionally calls it himself. It is, however, merely the bird fauna along the Nile which is actually treated in this work, which deals with altogether 257 species including some subspecies under consecutive numbers.

All the sections of the work were published in 'Journal für Ornithologie', the present and succeeding parts as 'Sonderhefte', the previous sections having been published as follows (the pages of the periodical and the numbers of the species treated are given in parentheses) :

1907, 'Die Geier Aegyptens', (pp. 59—91; Nos. 1—5), 6 pl. (2 col);
1907, 'Die Falconiden Aegyptens', (pp. 391—469, 549—582; Nos. 6—38), 1 pl.;
1917 II, 'Die Eulen Aegyptens', (pp. 129—160; Nos. 39—45);
1919, 'Die Sperrschnäbler (Fissirostres) Aegyptens', (pp. 431—485; Nos. 46—57);
1920, Sonderheft. 'Die Sitzfüsser (Insessores), die Klettervögel (Scansores) und die rabenartigen Vögel (Coraces) Aegyptens', (p. 148; Nos. 58—77).;
1921, 'Die Fänger (Captores) Aegyptens', (pp. 426—456; Nos. 78—84).

Of the group of birds treated in the present section 31 genera with 62 species and 6 subspecies are found in Egypt. Under the genera diagnoses and brief descriptions of the habits and the geographical distribution are given, while under the individual forms (Nos. 85—151 [152]) the names are given in English and French, sometimes the diagnoses in Latin, together with descriptions and notes on habits and occurrence in Egypt. The plates (collotype) were executed by A. Frisch, Berlin, from drawings by F. Neubaur.

The remaining publications by Koenig in the series on the birds of Egypt were published in 1926, 1928, and 1932 (267—269).

A new edition, enlarged by additions and beautiful plates, of the section on the birds of prey (Nos. 1—45 of the list cited above) was issued under the title 'Die Vögel am Nil', etc., Vol. II, 'Die Raubvögel' (55 col. pl., 4to).

1926. Journal für Ornithologie. 74. Jahrgang. Sonderheft. <-- Ein weiterer Teilbeitrag zur Avifauna Aegyptica, ... enthaltend die Ordnungen der Kegelschnäbler (Conirostres), der Tauben (Columbæ), der Scharr- oder Hühnervögel (Rasores) und drei Vertreter aus der Ordnung der Wat- oder Sumpfvögel (Grallatores). Bearbeitet von Alexander Koenig >. Deutsche Ornithologische Gesellschaft. *Berlin. pp. 152. 6 col. pl. (numb. I—VI). 8vo.*

This is a part of the author's account of the birds of Egypt, published on October 20, 1926, and containing numbers 153—166 (Conirostres: Nos. 153—156, Columbæ: Nos. 157—159, Rasores: Nos. 160—163, Grallatores: Nos. 164—166). In addition the paper contains (pp. 3—6) a 'Berichtigung' to the preceding part of the work, 1924 (266).

The plates (Dr. F. Neubaur, Bonn fec.) are executed in collotype.

1928. Journal für Ornithologie. 76. Jahrgang. Sonderheft. <-- Fortsetzung und Schluss der Watvögel (Grallatores) Aegyptens. Mit ... farbigen Tafeln. Bearbeitet von Alexander Koenig >. Deutsche Ornithologische Gesellschaft. *Berlin. pp. 311. 3 col. pl. (in 1 (fold.); numb. I—III). 8vo.*

Koenig has found and treated 55 species of the order Grallatores, of which 52 (Nos. 167—218) are treated in the present part of the work, three being dealt with in the preceding section, 1926 (267).

The plates (collotype) are executed from originals by F. Neubaur.

1932. Journal für Ornithologie. 80. Jahrgang. Sonderheft. <-- Die Schwimmvögel (Natatores) Aegyptens. Die Ruderfüsser (Steganopodes) Aegyptens. Die Flügeltaucher (Urinatores) Aegyptens. Bearbeitet von Alexander Koenig. Schlussbeitrag zur Vogelfauna Aegyptens. Mit einem Titelbild ... farbigen und ... Schwarzdrucktafeln >. In Kommission bei R. Friedländer & Sohn. *Berlin. pp. VIII + 237. 4 pl. (numb. I—IV; 1 col. (numb. II)). 8vo.*

The final part of the author's work on the birds of Egypt, the first of which was published in 1907 (266, note). It deals with numbers 219—257 (Steganopodes: Nos. 219—250, Steganopodes: Nos. 251—254, Urinatores: Nos. 255—257).

Plates II—IV (collotype, with figures of birds or parts of birds) are executed from drawings by F. Neubaur.

KOLTHOFF, G. I.
[1895—] 1898 [—1902]. Nordens fåglar. Af Gustaf Kolthoff och L. A. Jägerskiöld. Ny utvidgad och omarbetad upplaga af C. J. Sundevalls 'Svenska foglarna'. F. & G. Beijer. *Stockholm. pp. [VII] + XV + 343 + 7 + II. text-figs. 69 col. pl. (numb. 1—69). 4to.*

This work, published in 19 parts and one supplement as well as 'Nya tillägg och rättelser' and 'Tillägg till litteraturförteckningen', was issued as follows :

1895, Parts 1—3 (pp. 1—48, 12 pl.) ;
1896, Parts 4—8 (pp. 49—128, 20 pl.) ;
1897, Parts 9—12 (pp. 129—192, 16 pl.) ;
1898, Parts 13—19 (pp. 193—343, 21 pl.) ;
1899, Supplement (pp. XV) ;
1902, 'Nya tillägg' and the supplement to the bibliography.
Parts 18 and 19 are double. The text is printed in double columns.

It is only the plates in this work that really constitute a new edition of the previous work on the birds of Sweden cited on the title-page (490), as the text is quite independent, altered and enlarged, the work being also intended to correspond to the bird fauna issued by S. Nilsson (364) and Aug. Emil Holmgren's 'Skandinaviens foglar', 1867—71.

In addition to the birds of the Scandinavian Peninsula the work deals with the birds of Denmark, Finland, Iceland, the Faroes, and Spitsbergen, the birds of Greenland only being included if they occur in Scandinavia, too. In other words, the subject is kept within about the same limits as in Collin's edition of Kjærbølling's 'Skandinaviens Fugle' (250; 251).

The work, which is intended for a wider circle of readers, opens with a survey of the structure of the birds and their conditions of life (pp. I—XV). The birds are classed according to W. Lilljeborg's system, which is based mainly on that suggested by C. J. Sundevall. Under each species are stated some few synonyms, names in the Northern languages, description, geographical distribution, and occurrence in the Scandinavian countries. There are also notes on habitat, habits, and life-history. Under the genera and more comprehensive groups, which are briefly mentioned, a table is given for identification of the subordinate groups.

Most of the observations made from life are due to Kolthoff, who also prepared the descriptions of the habits of the different species. The final revision was carried out by Jägerskiöld, who also wrote the introduction, studied the literature on the subject, and compiled the information about the distribution and occurrence of the species. The two authors co-operated in the production of descriptions of the species. Of other contributors may be mentioned Dr. Hj. Östergren, who from the 7th sheet prepared the lists of names and compiled the synonyms, while Dr. M. Rubin, librarian, prepared the fairly comprehensive bibliography which completes the work (pp. 328—343).

The figures of the plates are chiefly reproductions of those in the work of Sundevall; the colours, however, have been somewhat altered. Several of the figures are new, and, as regards drawing, apart from some few original figures, are taken from figures in Dresser's 'A history of the birds of Europe', 1871—96 (120).

The plates (chromo-lithographs, Lit. Central-Tryckeriet, Stockholm), of which each contains from four to twelve figures of birds, were executed by L. L. Ljunggren, lithographer, who also drew a number of the text-figures.

A new edition of this work was issued in 1911—26 (221).

1911—26. Nordens fåglar ... Andra upplagan. See Jägerskiöld, A. K. E. L.

KONINKLIJK ZOÖLOGISCH GENOOTSCHAP 'NATURA ARTIS MAGISTRA'. AMSTERDAM.

1848—1929. Bijdragen tot de dierkunde. Uitgegeven door het Koninklijk Zoölogisch Genootschap Natura Artis Magistra. See Bijdragen tot de dierkunde.

1860. De toerako's afgebeeld en beschreven ... Gedruckt voor rekening van het Koninklijk Zoölogisch Genootschap Natura Artis Magistra ... See Schlegel, H.

KÖRNER, M. P.

1. 1839—1846. Skandinaviska foglar. Tecknade efter naturen, lithografierade och utgifne af M. Körner. (N. P. Lundbergs Boktryckeri) [C. W. K. Gleerups sort.]. *Lund. pp. [IV] + 22 + [2]. 62 col. pl. (numb. 1—40, 42, 42—62) 4to.*

This atlas was issued in ten parts, Parts 1—9 each containing six, Part 10 eight, hand-coloured plates. The preface is dated May, 1846, the dedication June, 1846.

The text (printed 1846) contains a list of the 270 species of birds figured on the plates. These are mentioned by their vernacular names, binomial names being also given, together with information about their occurrence in Scandinavia, and reference to the page in S. Nilsson's 'Skandinavisk fauna', 1835 (364, note), in which the particular species is referred to. The figures are arranged in the same sequence as that in which the birds are mentioned in Nilsson's work.

KRUSENSTERN, A. J. von.

1810—14. Reise um die Welt ... 1803—06 auf *272.* Befehl Seiner Kaiserlichen Majestät Alexander des Ersten auf den Schiffen Nadeshda und Newa unter dem Commando des Capitains von der Kaiserlichen Marine A. J. von Krusenstern. Auf Kosten des Verfassers. *St. Petersburg. 3 vols. text, 4to, and 1 vol. atlas, large fol. — Atlas. 1814. 8 pl. birds. (numb. XVII—XVIII, XLIV, XLVI, XVII, LXXXIV—LXXXVI).*

This expedition went to Alaska, at that time Russian, one of its objects being to establish commercial connection with Japan. It was the first circumnavigation made from Russia, the expedition visiting the west coast of Hokkaido, the east coasts of Kamchatka and Sakhalin, the Kurile and Aleutian Islands.

The painter, H. Kurlandzoff, who had been engaged for the expedition, left it upon arrival at Kamchatka, so the naturalist of the expedition, W. G. Tilesius, had to make the most of his talent as a draughtsman and execute the drawings of the birds, as well as the other pictures for the atlas. The latter contains altogether 106 maps and plates (engravings by Klauber and others), 24 of which show figures of natural historical objects (742). Tilesius, however, also wrote a few zoological papers for the 3rd volume of the report of the expedition, and these were issued separately in 1813. None of them is concerned with ornithological subjects.

A Russian edition of the report on the expedition appeared at the same time, 1809—12, as this German one. Other editions, too, were published, for instance an English one in 1813 (2 vols., 4to), a French one in 1821 (2 vols, 8vo, and atlas), an abridged German edition in 1811—12 (3 vols., small 8vo), the same adapted for the young 1816 (2 vols., 8vo), and a Danish translation of the first part in 1818, 8vo.

KUHL, H.

1820. Buffoni et Daubentoni figurarum avium *273.* coloratarum nomina systematica. Collegit Henricus Kuhl. Edidit, præfatione et indicibus auxit Theodorus van Swinderen. I. Oomkens. *Groningæ. pp. [IV] + 26 + [2]. 4to.*

The main part, pp. 1—17, of this list of names consists of a list of the figures in Buffon's and Daubenton's 'Planches enluminées' (76, note), arranged according to the numbers of the plates, and printed in double columns. Then follows, pp. 18—26, a systematic index, arranged according to the system employed in J. K. W. Illiger's 'Prodromus systematis mammalium et avium', 1811. The two last pages contain a systematically arranged survey of the orders, families, and genera of birds in accordance with Illiger's classification, and an alphabetical index to Illiger's genera.

KURODA, N.

1935. Report of the First Scientific Expedition to Manchoukuo ... June—October 1933. Section V. Division II. Part III. Birds of Jehol. *See Taka-Tsukasa, N.*

LABILLARDIÈRE, J. J. H. de.

1800 (An VIII). Relation du voyage à la re- *274.* cherche de La Pérouse, fait par ordre de l'Assemblée

Constituante ... 1791 (—94). Par Labillardière. H. J. Jansen. *Paris. 2 vols. text, 4to, and 1 vol. atlas, large fol.* — *Atlas. 4 pl. birds (numb. 9—11, 39).*

This expedition under the leadership of d'Entrecasteaux with the ships 'La Recherche' and 'L'Espérance' failed to find the lost expedition mentioned in the title (276). But several results were secured, for instance a number of natural history observations were made on the journey, including some on birds, about which information is given in the present work.

The atlas contains a map and 43 plates (engravings by Perée and others), chiefly with figures of the scenery and of natives, from drawings by Piron, the painter of the expedition. It also contains many pictures of plants, Labillardière's chief interest being botany.

The figures of birds, representing the Black Swan, Blackspotted Paroquet, the Calao and the Magpie of New Caledonia, were executed from drawings by Piron and Audebert.

Another French edition with text in two volumes, 8vo, atlas in folio, is cited, and also two English translations, 1800, one in two vols., 8vo, and one in 2 vols. text, 8vo, and atlas, folio.

LACÉPÈDE, B. G. É. DE LA V.

275.   *1801* (An X). La Ménagerie du Muséum Nationale d'Histoire Naturelle, ou description et histoire des animaux qui y vivent ou qui y ont vécu; par Lacépède et Cuvier, avec des figures peintes d'après nature, par Maréchal, gravés ... par Miger. Miger. *Paris. pp. 9, and descriptive text. 4 pl. birds. large fol.*

This volume contains 41 plates, of which 3 represent mammals. Each plate is accompanied by text, chiefly by Cuvier, with separate pagination. The introduction (pp. 9) was written by Lacépède. The birds figured are the Ostrich (2 plates), the Cassowary, and the Egyptian Goose.

LACHMANN I, F. H. A.

1840—44. Malerische Naturgeschichte der drei Reiche ... pp. 166—237 ... Vögel ... *See Lindner, F. W.*

LANDMARK, E. A. T.

1911—26. Nordens fåglar ... *See Jägerskiöld, A. K. E. L.*

LAPÉROUSE, J. F. DE G. de.

276.   *1797* (An V). Voyage de La Pérouse autour du monde, publié conformément au décret du 22 avril 1791, et rédigé par M. L. A. Milet-Mureau. Imprimerie de la République. *Paris. 4 vols. text, 4to, and 1 vol. atlas, large fol.* — *Atlas. 3 pl. birds (numb. 22, 36, 37).*

In 1788 the French expedition under the leadership of Lapérouse, which set out in 1785 with the frigates 'La Boussole' and 'L'Astrolabe', disappeared in the South Sea.

The present report was prepared with the help of communications from the expedition and particularly from the journals and maps Lapérouse in 1787 sent home over land from Kamchatka by Lesseps, the interpreter of the expedition. It also contains a fairly large amount of natural historical matter, principally in Vol. IV, from observations made by the naturalists of the expedition.

Prevost oncle and Prevost le jeune were the natural historical draughtsmen of the expedition, and Duché de Vancy was the landscape-painter and figure-draughtsman. Each of these artists has drawn one of the figures of birds in the atlas, which contains altogether 69 maps and plates (engravings, executed by Le Pagelet and others).

Prevost le jeune seems, however, to have acted especially as zoological artist, for Lapérouse says in a note to the naval department (dated Macao, 3rd January, 1787; Vol. IV, pp. 166—167) that he 'a dessiné tous les oiseaux, les poissons, les coquilles ; j'ai cru devoir a son zèle la faveur de vous adresser trois de ses dessins d'oiseaux ...'.

Another edition of the work appeared in 1798 (an VI) in four volumes, 8vo, with atlas. This became the basis for editions in several foreign languages, for instance in English in 1798 (2 vols., 8vo), in German in 1799—1800 (2 vols., 8vo), and in Danish in 1799—1801 (3 vols., 8vo).

1800. Relation du voyage à la recherche de La Pérouse ... 1791—94. *See Labillardière, J. J. H. de.*

LAPOMMERAYE, C. J. B.

1859—62. Richesses ornithologiques du midi de la France ... *See Jaubert, J. B. M.*

LATHAM, J.

1781—85. A general synopsis of birds. (By John 277 Latham). Benj. White (Vol. II, Part I — Vol. III, Part II: Leigh & Sotheby). *London. 3 vols. (in 6). 106 col. pl. 4to.* — Vol. I. Part I. 1781. *pp. VI + II + I—416. 16 col. pl. (numb. 1—5, VI—XVI).* Vol. II. [= Vol. I. Part II]. 1782. *pp. 417—788 + [34]. 19 col. pl. (numb. XVII—XXXV).* Vol. II. Part I. 1783. *pp. III + I—366. 15 col. pl. (numb. XXXVI—L).* Vol. II. Part II. 1783. *pp. 367—808 + [36]. 19 col. pl. (numb. LI—LXIX).* Vol. III. Part I. 1785. *pp. I—328. 26 col. pl. (numb. LXX —XCV).* Vol. III. Part II. 1785. *pp. 329—628 + [44]. 11 col. pl. (numb. XCVI—CVI).*

In the present copy of this work the preface to Vol. II, Part I (pp. II), is bound in Vol. I, Part I, while the preface to Vol. III, Part I (pp. III) is bound in Vol. II, Part I.

According to the preface the work should contain 'a concise account of all the birds hitherto known', and may thus be considered a kind of English parallel to Brisson's French work 1760 (69) and to the ornithological section of Buffon's 'Histoire naturelle', 1770—83 (74), which was almost completed when the publication of the present work began.

The system employed is based mainly on that introduced by Linnæus, which is largely followed in the classification of genera of which, however, Latham himself adds several new ones.

In the division of the birds into two main groups, land birds and water birds, Latham follows the system of Ray as employed by him in his edition of Willughby's Ornithology, which appeared in 1678 in an English translation from the original edition in Latin, 1676 (532).

The work contains figures and descriptions of a large number of species and states briefly whence the birds are derived. The 'manners' of the birds are occasionally mentioned, too.

The vastness of the subject has given rise to several errors, thus the same species is sometimes described under different names. Latham does not employ the nomenclature introduced by Linnæus, but refers to the birds by their vernacular names ; under each species, however, a list of synonyms is added which also includes the Linnean name.

A considerable amount of material, comprising many times the number of birds known by Linnæus, was at Latham's disposal, for the present work was prepared just when the knowledge of the birds of foreign countries was increasing so considerably. It was also at this time that a large amount of ornithological material from remote regions, principally from Australia and the South Sea Islands, poured into England, where it was included in the numerous collections which had been founded, such as the British Museum and Sir Asthon Lever's collection at Leicester House.

Latham drew, etched, and coloured his pictures himself. Each plate contains a figure of a single bird, and cannot be said to be free from defects in execution.

A supplement to the present work was issued in 1787 (278), a Supplement II in 1801 or 1802, as stated in the note to the 'Supplement' 1787, while an 'Index ornithologicus' with a brief survey of the birds treated in the 'General synopsis' and the first supplement was issued in 1790 (279). After the publication of Supplement II a 'Supplementum indicis ornithologici' to it was issued, as stated in the note to 'Index ornithologicus', 1790. A German edition, by J. M. Bechstein, of the 'General synopsis', the first supplement, and the 'Index ornithologicus' (without its supplement) appeared in 1793—1812 (280). A new English edition, 1821—28, of the 'General synopsis' and the works belonging to it is mentioned under the 'Index ornithologicus', 1790 (279).

78.   *1787.* Supplement to the General synopsis of birds. (By John Latham). Leigh & Sotheby. *London. pp. III + 298 + [15]. 13 col. pl. (numb. CVII—CXIX). 4to.*

In the preface to Vol. III, Part 1 of the General synopsis, Latham had promised to supplement the information given in that work in a continuation — the present work. In addition to corrections and additions to the species previously published new ones are described, so that the whole work now comprises about 3000 species, of which 500—600 are described for the first time. Pp. 281—298 contain 'A list of the birds of Great Britain'.

In 1801 or 1802 a 'Supplement II. to the General synopsis of birds' was issued (pp. 376 + [20], 23 col. pl., 4to).

1788—97. Encyclopædia Britannica ... The third edition. *See Encyclopædias.*

1789. The voyage of Governor Phillip to Botany Bay ... *See Phillip, A.*

79.   *1790.* Index ornithologicus, sive systema ornithologiæ; complectens avium divisionem in classes, ordines, genera, species, ipsarumque varietates: Adjectis synonymis, locis, descriptionibus, &c. Studio et opera Joannis Latham. Sumptibus authoris. *Londini. 2 vols. in 1. 4to. — Vol. I. pp. XVIII + 1—466. Vol. II. pp. 467—920.*

This is a brief systematic survey of the birds treated in the 'General synopsis' (277), issued in 1781—85, and in the first supplement to this work, of 1787 (278).

The species are mentioned under binomial names ; further diagnosis, synonymy, and habitat are given under each species, sometimes with very brief information on other features, while short diagnoses are also given for genera and orders.

A continuation of this work appeared in 1801 ? (pp. 74, 4to) under the title 'Supplementum indicis ornithologici, sive systematis ornithologiæ', as an index to Supplement II, which is mentioned under Supplement to the General synopsis, 1787 (278).

Another edition of the present work by Latham himself never went beyond the stage of the manuscript. However, a new edition appeared in Paris in 1809 by E. Johanneau (pp. 444, 12mo).

A new English edition of the works of Latham mentioned here, containing the Synopsis, the two supplements to it, the Index, and a few additions and new plates, appeared under the title 'A general history of birds' (10 vols., 1821—24, and 1 vol. index, 1828 ; 193 col. pl., 4to).

80.   *1793—1811.* Johann Lathams allgemeine Uebersicht der Vögel. Aus dem Englischen übersetzt und mit Anmerkungen und Zusätzen versehen von Johann Matthäus Bechstein. Mit ... ausgemahlten Kupfertafeln ... *Illuminated titles to Vol. I, Part I—Vol. III, Part II:* John Latham's allgemeine Übersicht der Vögel mit gemalten (Vol. III, Part III: ausgemahlten) Kupfern aus dem Englischen übersetzt. Weigel und Schneider. *Nürnberg. 4 vols. in 7. 4to. — Vol. I. Part I. 1793. pp. [XIV] + 1—346 + [2]. 19 col. pl. (numb. 1—19).* Vol. I. Part II. 1793. *pp. [XIV] + 347—649 + [1]. 18 col. pl. (numb. 20—32, 35 [33], 36 [34], 35—37).* Vol. I. [Supplement]. 1793. Anhang zum ersten Bande von Lathams allgemeiner Uebersicht der Vögel, welcher Zusätze, Bemerkungen und Berichtigungen der deutschen Benennungen enthält von Johann Matthäus Bechstein. Mit ... Kupfertafeln. *pp.*

651—738. 2 col. pl. (numb. 1—II). Vol. II. Part I. 1794. *pp. [XIV] + 1—366 + [2]. 14 col. pl. (numb. 38—51).* Vol. II. Part II. 1795. *pp. [XII] + 369— 775 + [1]. 22 col. pl. (numb. 52—73).* Vol. III. Part I. 1796. *pp. [X] + 1—275 + [1]. 37 col. pl. (numb. 74—100, 79b, 80a, 80b [= 81a], 83b-c, 84b, 88b, 89b, 1 unnumb. [= 92a], 92b).* Vol. III. Part II. 1798. *pp. [VIII] + 277—548. 23 col. pl. (numb. 101 —123).* Vol. IV. Part I. 1811. Welcher die Vögel nach ihren Kennzeichen der Art nebst den Zusätzen zu obigem Werke enthält. *pp. [VII] + IV + 320.*

A copy of Bechstein's German edition of Latham's 'A general synopsis of birds', 1781—85 (277), its first supplement 1787 (278), and 'Index ornithologicus', 1790 (279). Vol. IV, Part II (pp. [VIII] + 321—576), which appeared in 1812, is missing. Vol. IV was also issued with coloured plates. An index to the whole work, by Joh. Gottfr. Rademacher, appeared in 1813.

Vol. IV, Part I, in addition to the general title-page, contains a separate one which runs as follows : 'Kurze Uebersicht aller bekannten Vögel oder ihre Kennzeichen der Art nach Lathams General Synopsis of Birds und seinem Index ornithologicus entworfen von Dr. Johann Matthäus Bechstein. Mit 44 ausgemahlten Kupfern, auch ohne dieselben ...'. The translator has added a good deal of new matter scattered throughout the volumes. The additions to the first volume, however, are chiefly to be found in the above-mentioned supplement to this volume. A collection of 'Zusätze zu allen sechs Theilen der allgemeinen Uebersicht', most of them derived from Judge Borkhausen at Darmstadt, is found in Vol. III, Part II, pp. 536—548.

The plates (engravings coloured by hand) are unsigned and are mostly copies of the plates in the English work which forms the basis of the translation.

1795. Faunula Indica. *See Forster, J. R., Indische Zoologie.*

1812. British zoology by Thomas Pennant. A new edition. Class II. Birds. *See Pennant, T.*

LAUGIER DE CHARTROUSE, M.

1820—39. Nouveau recueil de planches coloriées d'oiseaux ... *See Temminck, C. J.*

LAWRENCE, G. N.

1858. Reports of explorations and surveys ... for a railroad from the Mississippi River to the Pacific Ocean ... 1853—56. Vol. IX ... Birds. *See Baird, S. F.*

1860. The birds of North America ... *See Baird, S. F.*

LAYARD, E. L.

1875—84. The birds of South Africa, by Edgar **281.** Leopold Layard. New edition. Thoroughly revised and augmented by R. Bowdler Sharpe. Bernard Quaritch. *London. pp. XXV + [2] + 890. 12 pl. (numb. I— XII). 8vo.*

The first edition of this work appeared in 1867. In the present edition, which was issued in six parts, R. Bowdler Sharpe has omitted the descriptions of the superior groups and has only described the individual species, mentioning their habits, habitats, and distribution. In the 'Systematic list of the birds of South Africa' (pp. XVII—XXV) altogether 812 species are enumerated, 771 of which are treated in the main section of the work, while the rest have been added in an appendix (pp. 793—855) in which is included the new material that had appeared during the publication of the work.

Compared with Layard's original edition, the matter has been increased by 110 species, one of the reasons for this being that a larger land area is dealt with in the present

20

edition, the South African sub-region being extended to the Zambesi River on the east coast, and to the Quanza River on the west, while Layard had drawn the northern boundary at the 28th parellel of south latitude.

Most of the original descriptions given by Layard are retained; in some cases, however, a complete revision of the families has been made and new descriptions have been added.

The plates (lithographs) are due to J. G. Keulemans. The majority of copies of the work cited in the bibliographies are stated to have coloured plates.

LEACH, W. E.

282. *1814—17.* The zoological miscellany; being descriptions of new, or interesting animals, by William Elford Leach. Illustrated with coloured figures, (Vols. I—II: drawn from nature) (Vol. III: engraved from original drawings), by R. P. Nodder. E. Nodder & Son. *London. 3 vols. in 2. 29 col. pl. birds. small 4to. — Vol. I. 1814. pp. 144. 13 pl. birds (numb. 2, 6, 11, 16—17, 21, 31, 36, 41, 46, 51—52, 56). Vol. II. 1815. pp. 154 + [8]. 14 pl. birds (numb. 61, 66, 71, 76—77, 81, 86, 97, 101, 106, 112—113, 116—117). Vol. III. 1817. pp. V + [I] + 151 + [I]. 2 pl. birds (numb. 122—123).*

This work, which forms a continuation of 'The naturalist's miscellany', 1789—1813, by George Shaw (467) contains descriptions and figures of new or especially interesting animal species and genera. The text is very brief.

The mode of publication has been discussed by Zimmer (589, II, pp. 379—380).

The three volumes contain altogether 150 (respectively 60, 60, and 30) plates (engravings).

In the present copy the text and the plates are bound separately.

LEAR, E.

283. *[1830—] 1832.* Illustrations of the family of Psittacidæ, or parrots: the greater part of them species hitherto unfigured, containing ... lithographic plates, drawn from life, and on stone, by Edward Lear. E. Lear. *London. pp. [VII]. 42 col. pl. (numb. 1—42 in 'List of plates'). large fol.*

This work was published in twelve parts, the first of which, according to Mathews (809), is dated November 1, 1830, while the date on the title-page of the issue cited is 1832 (cf. 589, II, p. 381).

The plates, which are not accompanied by any text, are very finely executed (printed by C. Hullmandel). They are coloured by hand, though for the most part only the figures of the birds and as a rule the branches, or the parts of them which are adjacent to the bird figure, are coloured.

LECHNER, A. A. VAN PELT. *See Pelt Lechner, A. A. van.*

LEGGE, W. V.

284. *1880 [1881].* A history of the birds of Ceylon. By W. Vincent Legge. Published by the author. *London. pp. XLVI + 4 + 1237 + 1225b—1226b. text-figs. 35 pl. (34 col. (numb. I—XXXIV in 'List of plates'; 1 pl. eggs (No. XXXIV)). 1 map. 4to.*

The second edition of this work, the first edition of which was published in three parts, in November, 1878, September, 1879, and September, 1880, respectively, as stated pp. XLV—XLVI.

The present second edition contains (pp. 1225 b and 1226 b) an Appendix III, 'After-note published with second issue of book, February, 1881'. Appendices I—II (pp. 1209—1225), however, were found in the first issue also.

The work gives a comprehensive account of the birds of the area and is intended as a text-book for the local student and collector in Ceylon. Our knowledge of the avifauna of the

island is considerably increased by this work, which deals with altogether 371 species, two of which are introduced birds. The author has added 24 species to the list of the birds of Ceylon, and mentions 47 species as peculiar to the island.

The synonyms are given under each species, as well as a description of the bird as regards sex and age, and detailed information as to distribution and habits.

The fine plates, coloured by hand (lithographs), were executed from drawings by J. G. Keulemans.

LE MAOUT, J. E. M.

1842. Le Jardin des Plantes ... *See Bernard, P.*

1853. Les trois règnes de la nature. Règne animal. 2? Histoire naturelle des oiseaux, suivant la classification de M. Isidore Geoffroy-Saint-Hilaire, avec l'indication de leurs moeurs et de leurs rapports avec les arts, le commerce et l'agriculture. Par Emm. Le Maout. L. Curmer. *Paris. pp. [III] + XLVIII + 425 + [II]. text-figs. 34 pl. (15 col. (numb. 1—14; 1 unnumb.)). 4to.*

This work was first published in 50 livraisons from June to December, 1852. It contains a systematically arranged survey of the class aves which opens with a description of the anatomy and physiology of the birds and an outline of the classification of the group with a 'Tableau systématique des ordres établis par Cuvier dans la classe des oiseaux'.

The numbered coloured plates (lithographs: Imp. Hangard Mangé, Paris) are coloured by hand. Some of them are found also in the work issued by P. Bernard and others, 'Le Jardin des Plantes', etc. 1842 (39). Two of the uncoloured plates are steel-engravings the remainder woodcuts (W. H. Freeman, del.; L. Dujardin, Sargent, and others sc.). An uncoloured plate (Pélican ordinaire) is missing in the present copy. A new unaltered edition of the work appeared in 1855.

Another volume in this series, 'Règne végétal. Botanique', was issued in 1851.

LEMBKE (LEMBCKE), G.

1800—09. Teutsche Ornithologie ... *See Borkhausen, M. B.*

LEPECHIN, I. I.

1775—83. Herrn Iwan Lepechin Tagebuch der 2 Reise durch verschiedene Provinzen des russischen Reiches ... 1768 (—1771). Aus dem Russischen übersetzt von M. Christian Heinrich Hase. Richter. *Altenburg. 12 pl. birds. 4to. — Vol. II. 1775. - - < pp. 180 —211: Anhang. Beschreibung einiger Vögel, Fische und Insekten >. 7 pl. birds (numb. 2—8). Vol. III. 1783. - - < pp. 219—234: Anhang >. 5 pl. birds (numb. 7—11).*

The Russian work on which the present translation is based was issued in St. Petersburg in 1771—80 (3 vols., 4to). It is written by the leader of one of the five separate expeditions which the Russian Government sent out to the more remote parts of the empire on the occasion of the transit of Venus in 1769.

The present German translation was issued in three volumes in 1774—83. A fairly large amount of information about birds is found scattered throughout the volumes, and the appendices to Vol. II (pp. 180—190) and Vol. III (pp. 219—226) contain descriptions of several birds which are figured on the accompanying plates (engravings, signed in Vol. II: J. D. Philipp geb. Sysang sc.).

LE ROI, O.

1911. Avifauna Spitzbergensis ... *See Koenig, A. F.*

LESKE, N. G.

1784. Sammlung von Nestern und Eyern verschiedener Vögel ... Zweites Heft. *See Wirsing, A. L., 1772—86.*

LESLIE, A. S.

37. *1912.* The Grouse in health and in disease. Being
the popular edition of the report of the Committee of
inquiry on grouse disease. Edited by A. S. Leslie, assisted by A. E. Shipley. Smith, Elder & Co. *London.
pp. XX + 472. text-figs. 21 pl. (front. + Nos. II—
XX + 1 unnumb. [=XXI]; 10 col. pl. birds (front.
+ Nos. II—X)). 1 map. 8vo.*

An abridged and popularized edition of the final report
of the committee of inquiry on grouse disease, published in
1911 in two volumes, 8vo, under the title 'The Grouse in
health and in disease', with 39 coloured plates. As early as
1908 the committee, set up in 1905 by the Board of Agriculture and Fisheries, issued an interim report of its investigation of the British Grouse (Lagopus scoticus). Part of the
matter has been omitted, or is given in a more condensed
form, in the present edition in order to make the book a
practical guide to sportsmen and naturalists. The account is
divided into three sections, 'The Grouse in health' (pp. 1—112),
'The Grouse in disease' (pp. 113—320), and 'Management
of grouse moors' (pp. 321—457).

The coloured plates (signed: E. A. Wilson) are executed
by the three-colour process (Andre & Sleigh, Ltd.), and give
illustrations especially of the different plumages of the birds.

LESSON, R. P.

8. *1826—30 [—31].* Voyage autour du monde ... sur
la corvette ... la Coquille ... 1822—25. Par L. I. Duperrey. Zoologie, par Lesson et Garnot. Arthus Bertrand. *Paris.* — [Text]. *2 vols. 4to. Atlas. 44 col. pl.
birds (numb. 10—50, 21bis, 31bis, 35bis). large fol.*

The entire work on this expedition consists of seven volumes
of text and five atlases; its section 4 (Hydrographie (et physique)) is unfinished. The zoological section of the report was
published in 1826—32 (869, I, pp. 391—392). Birds are
treated in 'Zoologie, Tome I', viz. in Chapter VII (= pp.
588—613), 'Description de quelques espèces nouvelles d'oiseaux;
par M. P. Garnot', and in Chapter VIII (= pp. 614—735),
'Catalogue des oiseaux recueillis dans l'expédition de la Coquille,
avec la description de plusieurs genres nouveaux et d'un grand
nombre d'espèces inédites; Par R. P. Lesson'.

The atlas contains altogether 157 coloured plates. The
bird portraits are found in the atlas in the section entitled
'Mammifères. Oiseaux'. They were engraved by Coutant, printed
in colours by Rémond, and painted by a couple of
plates from Garnot; a few are due to Prévost and Bévalet.

9. *1828.* Manuel d'ornithologie, ou description des
genres et des principales espèces d'oiseaux; par R. P.
Lesson. Roret. *Paris. 2 vols. 18mo.* — Vol. I. *pp. 421.*
Vol. II. *pp. [III] + 448.*

A brief systematic survey of the birds of the world, in
which a number of species are treated, while genera, families,
and orders are briefly described. Vol. I opens (pp. 1—66) with
a general account of the group of birds and a survey of the
different systems of classification hitherto employed.

The volumes with the text were accompanied by an atlas
which appeared in the same year (290).

[1828]. Atlas des oiseaux, composé de ... planches,
représentant la plupart des espèces décrites dans le
Manuel d'histoire naturelle et dans le Manuel d'ornithologie. Roret. *Paris. pp. 19. 129 pl. (numb. 1—
129). 18mo.*

This atlas contains illustrations to the text of Lesson's
'Manuel d'ornithologie', 1828 (289). It was issued both with
coloured and with uncoloured plates (Deseve del., Racine,
Jourdan, Ve. Tardieu, and others sculp.).

A 'Table méthodique des planches' is found on pp. 3—11,
and a 'Table alphabétique des planches' on pp. 12—19.

[1829—30]. Histoire naturelle des oiseaux-
mouches, ouvrage orné de planches dessinées et gravées
par les meilleurs artistes ... par R. P. Lesson. Arthus
Bertrand. *Paris. 1 vol. in 2. 8vo.* — [Text]. *pp.*

XLVI + 223. [Plates]. *86 col. pl. (numb. 1—85,
48bis).*

This is Lesson's first work on humming-birds. It was succeeded by two others, — 'Histoire naturelle des colibris', 1830
—32 (293), and 'Les trochilidées', 1832—33 (294). It appeared in different issues and was published in 17 livraisons,
the last seven of which appeared in 1830.

The text opens (pp. IX—XLVI) with descriptions in
systematic order of the species figured, while the remainder of
the volume, 'Histoire naturelle des oiseaux-mouches', contains
a general account of the group as a whole and of the species
figured.

The plates are printed in colour ('tirées en couleur et
terminées au pinceau avec le plus grand soin') (Bévalet, Prêtre,
and others pinx.; Coutant sculp.; Rémond imp.).

1830[—32]. Centurie zoologique, ou choix d'ani- 292.
maux rares, nouveaux ou imparfaitement connus;
enrichi de planches inédites, dessinées d'après nature
par M. Prêtre, gravées et coloriées avec le plus grand
soin; par R. P. Lesson. F. G. Levrault. *Paris. pp.
X + 11—244. 42 pl. birds. (numb. 3—8, 11, 14,
16, 18, 19, 22, 24, 26, 27, 30, 32, 36, 38, 39, 41,
45, 47—50, 54, 58, 59—61, 65—75). 8vo.*

A collection of altogether 80 plates (engravings) with figures of rare animals (Prêtre pinx.; Mme Massard, Coutant,
Guyard, and others, sculp.; Imp. de Langlois). Each plate is
accompanied by a brief text with a description of the animal
figured.

The work was published in 16 livraisons and in different
issues — 8vo and 4to with coloured figures and, as in the
present copy, 8vo with plain figures.

[1830—32]. Histoire naturelle des colibris, suivie 293.
d'un supplément à l'histoire naturelle des oiseaux-
mouches; ouvrage orné de planches dessinées et gravées
par les meilleurs artistes. Par R. P. Lesson. Arthus
Bertrand. *Paris. 1 vol. in 2. 8vo.* — [Text]. *pp. X +
196.* [Plates]. *66 col. pl. (numb. 1—25, 12bis, 13bis;
1—39).*

With this work Lesson continues the series of volumes in
which he treats of humming-birds. Like the preceding volume,
'Histoire naturelle des oiseaux-mouches', 1829—30 (291), it
appeared in different issues. It was published in 13 livraisons, of
which Nos. 1—3 were published in 1830, 4—12 in 1831, 13
in 1832 (552, III, p. 1096). The first 12 parts contained
plates only.

The text opens (pp. 1—17) with a brief account of the
general natural history of the humming-birds, followed by brief
descriptions of the birds figured in the first section of the
atlas (Pl. 1—25, 12 bis and 13 bis, most of them with the
inscription 'Colibris'). The last section of the text (pp. 91—
192) consists of the supplement mentioned in the title; the
corresponding plates in the atlas (Nos. 1—39) bear the inscription 'Ois. mouch. suppl.'.

The plates, printed in colour, are beautifully executed (Prêtre
and Bévalet pinx.; Coutant and Teillard sculp.; Rémond
imp.).

A new edition of the work appeared in 1847 (Lorenz'
'Catalogue général de la librairie française 1840—65', III, p.
266), while a continuation of it was published in 1832—33
under the title 'Les trochilidées' (294).

[1832—33]. Les trochilidées, ou les colibris et les 294.
oiseaux-mouches, suivis d'un index général, dans lequel
sont décrites et classées méthodiquement toutes les
races et espèces du genre Trochilus. Ouvrage orné de
planches dessinées et gravées par les meilleurs artistes,
par R. P. Lesson. Arthus Bertrand. *Paris. 1 vol. in
2. 8vo.* — [Text]. *pp. IV + 171 + XLIII.* [Plates].
66 col. pl. (numb. 1—66).

The concluding section of Lesson's work on humming-
birds; the sections published previously are 'Histoire naturelle
des oiseaux-mouches', 1829—30 (291), and 'Histoire naturelle
des colibris', 1830—32 (293).

20*

The text consists (pp. 1—168) of a descriptive explanation of the plates, followed by a systematic survey (pp. I—XLIII) of 110 species of humming-birds. This section contains a special title-page, 'Index général et synoptique des oiseaux du genre Trochilus, par R. P. Lesson'. (Paris. Arthus Bertrand. 1832).

The work was issued in 14 livraisons, and appeared in the same different issues as the preceding volumes of the series.

The plates (Prêtre and Bévalet pinx.; Oudet sculp.; Rémond imp.) are printed in colour and bear the inscription: Les Trochilidées.

295.   [1832—35]. Illustrations de zoologie, ou recueil de figures d'animaux peintes d'après nature; par R.-P. Lesson. Ouvrage orné de planches dessinées et gravées par les meilleurs artistes, et servant de complément aux traités généraux ou spéciaux publiés sur l'histoire naturelle et à les tenir au courant des nouvelles découvertes et des progrès de la science. Arthus Bertrand. Paris. pp. [VII] + [209]. 20 col. pl. birds (numb. 1, 4, 5, 9, 11, 13, 17, 18, 20, 23, 25, 28, 29, 31, 45, 46, 49, 50, 52, 60). large 8vo.

This work appeared, in different issues, in twenty parts of three plates each, the first part being published in July, 1832. The descriptive letterpress accompanying the plates is unpaginated, in order that the plates may be placed as desired when bound.

The work was intended by the author to be a sequel or a supplement, to Buffon's 'Planches enluminées', 1770—?83 (76, note), to Temminck and Laugier de Chartrouse's 'Nouveau recueil de planches coloriées', 1820—39 (502; 503), and to the author's 'Centurie zoologique', 1830—32 (292); each volume was to consist of 20 parts, or 60 plates, but only one volume appeared.

The bird portraits were printed in colour and 'terminées au pinceau avec le plus grand soin' (Prêtre pinx.; Massard, and others, sculp.; Rémond imp.).

296.   [1834—35]. Histoire naturelle des oiseaux de paradis et des épimaques; ouvrage orné de planches, dessinées et gravées par les meilleurs artistes; par R. P. Lesson. Arthus Bertrand. Paris. 1 vol. in 2. 8vo. — [Text]. pp. VII + 34 + [I] + 248. [Plates]. 43 col. pl. (numb. 1—40, 11bis, 25bis, 25ter).

This work was published, in different issues, in livraisons the first four of which appeared in 1834.

The text comprises several sections of a different character, — 'Préface' (pp. V—VII), 'Synopsis des oiseaux de la famille des paradisiers et de celle des épimaques' (pp. 1—34), 'Introduction. Esquisse des contrées où vivent les oiseaux de paradis et les épimaques' (pp. 1—7), 'De la Nouvelle-Guinée ou Papuasie' (pp. 9—107), and 'De la famille des paradisiers ou oiseaux de paradis' (pp. 109—206), 'De la famille des épimaques' (pp. 207—237), and indices (pp. 241—248).

The two last main sections contain a brief account of the figures and the species figured in the atlas, the plates of which (Prêtre and Oudart pinx.; Massard and others sculp.; Rémond imp.) are printed in colours and retouched by hand, and bear the inscription 'Oiseaux de Paradis'.

LEVAILLANT [LE VAILLANT], F.

297.   [1796—]1799 (An VII) — 1808[—12]. Histoire naturelle des oiseaux d'Afrique; par François Levaillant. J. J. Fuchs (Vols. IV—VI: Delachaussée). Paris. 6 vols. in 5. 300 col. pl. large 4to. — Vol. I. An VII (1799). pp. XI + 194. 49 col. pl. (numb. 1—49). Vol. II. An VII (1799). pp. 206. 47 col. pl. (numb. 50—96). Vol. III. An X (1802). pp. 231. 54 col. pl. (numb. 97—150). Vol. IV. An XIII. 1805. pp. 141. 49 col. pl. (numb. 151—199). Vol. V. 1806. pp. 163. 48 col. pl. (numb. 200—247). Vol. VI. 1808. pp. 188. 53 col. pl. (numb. 248—300).

This work, which was published in 51 parts, is Levaillant's

most prominent work. It gives a comprehensive account of the birds of South Africa, based on Levaillant's personal experiences and the collections he made during his journeys in that region.

The style of the text is lively, and it gives descriptions not only of the birds, but also of their habits and habitats. Scientific names are not given. Altogether 284 species are dealt with, of which 71, according to the statement of the author, do not come from Africa; however, later investigations have shown that many other birds which Levaillant claims to have found in Africa do not inhabit that part of the world; some of the species depicted have proved to be artefacts, and on the whole the work contains many errors. In 1857 the work was analyzed by C. J. Sundevall in 'Kritisk framställning af fogelarterna uti äldre ornithologiska arbeten'. 2. (= pp. 16—60) (892; 831).

The plates (engravings) were printed in colour (Imp. de Langlois) and subsequently retouched by hand. J. B. Audebert is said to have assisted in the printing up to the 13th livraison.

Plates 1—103, 106—109, and 111—117 are signed: J. ('Jⁿ') Lebrecht Reinold p[inx]t.; 1—60, 67—78, 85—96, 169—198: Clde Fessard sculp.; 61—66, 79—84, 97—102: Pérée sculp.; 157—168: Bouquet direx.

The work is unfinished, representatives of several large groups of birds not being mentioned at all. Levaillant is said to have left at his death the manuscript and 52 drawings (by Reinold) for a seventh volume, in addition to 115 other drawings by the same artist for a continuation of the work (558, III, column 1034).

In the Catalogue of the Library of the British Museum (Natural History) (552, III, p. 1100) a copy is cited, the first title-page of which is dated 1796 (An IV).

An edition in large folio (298) with double plates, coloured and plain, was issued simultaneously, and an edition (1798—?) in a smaller format, 12mo, with uncoloured figures, is quoted (579, V, 1833, p. 268). As a kind of sequel to this work 'Histoire naturelle d'une partie d'oiseaux nouveaux et rares de l'Amérique et des Indes' (300) was issued in 1801—02.

An unfinished German translation by J. M. Bechstein appeared in 1797—1802 (299). Of another unfinished German translation, by Joh. Reinh. Forster, the first volume only appeared (Halle 1798, 8vo) with 18 coloured plates (Kayser's 'Bücher-Lexicon 1750—1832', III, 1835, p. 540). A Dutch edition, translated by Professor Rymvardt, was commenced in 1812; this was also unfinished.

In the present copy the text has been bound in three, and the plates in two, volumes.

298.   1796—1799—1802 (An IV—VII—X). Histoire naturelle des oiseaux d' Afrique; par François Levaillant. J. J. Fuchs. (First title-page to Vol. I: Histoire naturelle des oiseaux d'Afrique; par François Levaillant. Imprimerie de H. J. Jansen et Co. An quatrième [1796]). Paris. 3 vols. large fol. — Vol. I. An VII (1799). pp. [III] + XI + 127 + [I] + 128. 98 pl. (numb. 1—49, 1—49; 49 col.). Vol. II. An VII (1799). pp. 151. 96 pl. (numb. 50—97, 50—97; 48 col.). Vol. III. An X (1802). pp. [III] + 116. 82 pl. (numb. 98—138, 98—138; 41 col.).

This is part of a copy of the edition in large folio of this work. This edition was issued simultaneously with the 4to edition (297). According to the title-pages (second title-page in Vol. I) the present part of the folio edition was printed by H. L. Perronneau.

Like the 4to edition, it consists in its entirety of six volumes, the first three of which also occur with title-pages dated An XIII, 1805, i. e. in copies in which the last three volumes are dated XIII, 1805; XIV, 1806, and 1808 respectively, and which have been published by Delachaussée, who, as stated above (297), published Vols. IV—VI of the 4to edition. In these copies Vols. III—VI are described as follows (cf. 589, II, p. 391):

Vol. III (pp. 147, pl. 98—150); Vol. IV (pp. 104, pl. 151—199); Vol. V (pp. 124, pl. 200—247); Vol. VI (pp. 132, pl. 248—300). Possibly, then, the present fragment is the part of the work which was published by J. J. Fuchs.

Apart from the paper, the format, and the printing, the text of the work does not seem to differ in the two editions. The plates are double, each plate being found both coloured and plain.

9. *1797[—1800].* Franz le Vaillant's Naturgeschichte der afrikanischen Vögel. Aus dem Französischen übersetzt und mit Anmerkungen versehen von Johann Matthäus Bechstein. Vol. I. I. C. Monath und I. F. Kussler. *Nürnberg. pp. X + 11—168. 36 pl. (numb. I—XXXVI). 4to.*

The first six parts of a German translation of the French work, 'Histoire naturelle des oiseaux d'Afrique' (297 ; 298), which was issued in 1796 and the following years. The present parts were published as follows (cf. 'Allgemeines Verzeichniss der Bücher ... der Frankfurter und Leipziger ... messe') : Part 1, 1797 ; Part 2, 1798 ; Parts 3—4, 1799 ; Parts 5—6, 1800.

The translator has added several notes to the German edition, of which eight parts of six plates each only had appeared when the undertaking was discontinued in 1802.

The plates, which were also executed in colours, are engravings (J. Nussbiegel sculp.) made from drawings by J. Lebrecht Reinold.

). *1801 (An IX) [—02].* Histoire naturelle d'une partie d'oiseaux nouveaux et rares de l'Amérique et des Indes, par François Levaillant: Ouvrage destiné par l'auteur à faire partie de son Ornithologie d'Afrique. Vol. I. J. E. Gabriel Dufour. *Paris. pp. [III] + IV + 152. 49 col. pl. (numb. 1—49). large 4to.*

This work, with its descriptions and figures of foreign birds not included in Levaillant's 'Histoire naturelle des oiseaux d'Afrique', 1796—1812 (297 ; 298), was issued as a kind of supplement to the latter work and, like it, also appeared in large folio format with double plates, coloured and plain (301). Scientific names are not used.

The work was published in eight parts, the first four of which appeared in 1801, the last four in 1802. It deals with the groups Bucerotidæ and Cotingidæ, which are treated and figured on pp. 1—71, Pl. 1—24, and pp. 73—150, Pl. 25—49 respectively ; as originally planned the work was to comprise 240 plates.

Levaillant's 'Histoire naturelle des oiseaux de paradis', etc., 1801—06 (304), may be regarded as a sequel to the present work.

The plates are printed in colours (Imp. de Langlois). According to Quérard (579, V, 1833, p. 268), the work was issued in 4to with uncoloured, as well as with double plates, coloured and plain.

. *1801 (An IX) [—02].* Histoire naturelle d'une partie d'oiseaux nouveaux et rares de l'Amérique et des Indes, par François Levaillant: Ouvrage destiné par l'auteur à faire partie de son Ornithologie d'Afrique. Vol. I. J. E. Gabriel Dufour. *Paris. pp. [III] + III + 112. 98 pl. (numb. 1—49, 1—49; 49 col.). large fol.*

This is a copy of the large folio edition of the work, which was issued simultaneously with the 4to edition (300).

In the present copy the plates are double, coloured and plain, and the coloured plates have been retouched by hand.

. *1801—05 (An IX—XIII).* Histoire naturelle des perroquets, par François Levaillant. Levrault. *Paris. 2 vols. 145 col. pl. large 4to.* — Vol. I. An IX (1801). *pp. [VIII] + 203. 72 col. pl. (numb. 1—71, 2 (bis)).* Vol. II. An XIII (1805). *pp. [III] + 175. 73 col. pl. (numb. 72—139, 95 (bis), 98 (bis), 107 (bis), 108 (bis), 110 (bis)).*

This work was published in 24 parts as follows : Parts 1—2, 1801 ; 4—8, 1802 ; 10—16, 1803 ; 17—20, 1804 ; 22—24, 1805.

The text of this monograph consists of descriptions of the parrots figured on the plates, which are mentioned by their vernacular names. The figures have been drawn from nature by Barraband, engraved and printed in colour (Imp. de Lang-

lois) 'sous la direction de Bouquet, Professeur de dessin au Prytanée de Paris'. Some of the plates have been slightly retouched by hand.

The work was further issued in large folio (303), and, twelve copies, in a very large folio format with double plates, coloured and uncoloured.

In 1837—38 a continuation by A. Bourjot Saint-Hilaire of the work appeared as a third volume under the same title (54), and in 1857—58 C. de Souancé issued his 'Iconographie des perroquets' (479) as a second supplement.

A number of the plates were reprinted in 1842—54 in Chr. L. Brehm's 'Monographie der Papageien', etc. (75 col. pl., fol.).

In the present copy the text and the plates have been bound separately.

1801[—05] (An IX—XIII). Histoire naturelle **303.** des perroquets, par François Levaillant. Levrault. *Paris. 2 vols. 145 col. pl. large fol.* — Vol. I. An IX (1801). *pp. [VIII] + 135. 72 col. pl. (numb. 1—71, 2 (bis).* [Vol. II. An XIII (1805)]. *pp. 112 + [1]. 73 col. pl. (numb. 72—139, 95(bis), 98(bis), 107(bis), 108(bis), 110(bis)).*

A copy of the large folio edition of this work, which was issued simultaneously in 4to (302). The half-title and title are missing in Vol. II. The plates in the present copy are as a rule executed with greater care (better retouched by hand) than the plates in the copy of the 4to edition.

Bourjot Saint-Hilaire's continuation, 1837—38, too, was issued in a large folio format (55 a).

[1801—]1806. Histoire naturelle des oiseaux de **304.** paradis et des rolliers, suivie de celle des toucans et des barbus, par François Levaillant. Denné le jeune. *Paris. 2 vols. 114 col. pl. large fol.* — Vol. I. *pp. [III] + II + 153. 56 col. pl. (numb. 1—13, 16 [= 14], 15—56).* Vol. II. *pp. [III] + II + 1—34 + 41—48 [= 35—42] + 43—106 + 109—111 [= 107—109] + [1 = p. 110] + 111—133 + [1]. 58 col. pl. (numb. 1—18, 18 [= 19], A, 20—57).*

This work, which is a kind of sequel to the author's 'Histoire naturelle d'une partie d'oiseaux nouveaux et rares de l'Amérique«, etc., 1801—02 (300), was published in 19 parts which, according to Quérard (579, V, 1833, p. 268), each contained six plates. In 1806—18 'Histoire naturelle des promerops et des guêpiers', etc. (305) was issued as a sequel (Parts 20—33), and after this time the two works are cited under the following covering title 'Histoire naturelle des oiseaux de paradis, des toucans et des barbus; suivie de celle des promerops, guêpiers, et des couroucous' (558, III, column 1033), a title which, in a slightly altered form, is repeated in other bibliographies (579, V, 1833, p. 268). A half-title in the present work (Vol. I, p. 1) runs as follows, 'Histoire naturelle des oiseaux de paradis, des rolliers, et des promerops', its scope being thus indicated. The birds figured are described and mentioned under their vernacular names in a series of sections with accompanying plates, viz., in Vol. I, 'Introduction (pp. 1—7), 'Histoire naturelle des oiseaux de paradis' (pp. 9—68, Nos. 1—24), and 'Seconde partie. Des rolliers et des geais' (pp. 69—153, Nos. 25—56) ; and in Vol. II, 'Histoire naturelle des toucans' (pp. 1—46, Nos. 2—18, and Pl. 1), 'Seconde partie. Des barbus' (pp. 47—100, Nos. 19—43, and Pl. A), 'Histoire naturelle de barbacous' (pp. 101—106, Nos. 44—46), 'Histoire naturelle des jacamars' (pp. 109 [= 107]—126, Nos. 47—54), and 'Additions aux articles des barbus proprement dits' (pp. 127—133, Nos. 55—57).

The figures were drawn from nature by Barraband, and the plates engraved by Perée and Grémillier, some few by Bouquet, and printed in colours by Langlois and Rousset, and retouched by hand.

The work was also issued with double figures, coloured and plain ('avant la lettre').

[1806—] 1807 [—18 ?]. Histoire naturelle des pro-**305.** merops, et des guêpiers, par François Levaillant; faisant suite à celle des oiseaux de paradis, par le

même. Denné le jeune. *Paris. 3 parts in 1 vol. 82 col. pl. (2 pl. missing). large fol.* — Part. I. *pp. [VI] + 81. 30 col. pl. (numb. 1—2, 4—11, 13—22, 22bis [= 23], 24—32; missing pl.: 3 (not issued?) and 12).* Part II. *pp. 67. 21 col. pl. (numb. 1—20, 6bis).* Part III. *pp. 52. 31 col. pl. (numb. 1—20, A, AA, B—H, K—L).*

A continuation of the author's 'Histoire naturelle des oiseaux de paradis', etc., 1801—06 (304), which two works appeared in altogether 33 parts, the last fourteen of which (Parts 20—33) contained the present work. It appeared in different issues just as the work it was to supplement. As stated under the notice of the latter work (304), a covering title to both works is cited, and further the index to the present volume appears under the subtitle, 'Table du troisième volume'. According to Brunet (558, III, column 1033), the work was completed in 1816, while Quérard (579, V, 1833, p. 268) mentions 1818 as the year of completion.

The three sections into which the present volume is divided are 'Histoire naturelle des promerops. Première partie' (pp. 1—81, Nos. 1—32), 'Histoire naturelle des guêpiers. Seconde partie' (pp. 1—67, Nos. 1—20, and 6 bis), and 'Histoire naturelle des couroucous et des touracos. Troisième partie' (pp. 1—38, Nos. 1—20).

In addition to the 'Table' mentioned above, the volume contains, in Part III, 'Supplément aux differents genres d'oiseaux décrits dans les deux premiers volumes' (pp. 39—52, Figs. A, AA, B—H, and K—L).

As in the two preceding volumes, the birds are described and referred to under their vernacular names.

The figures in this volume were drawn from nature by Barraband, and engraved by Grémillier and Guyard fils., some few by Bouquet and Barrière. The plates are printed in colour, largely by Millevoy, and retouched by hand; some of the plates were printed by Langlois, a few by Bousset and Bourlier. According to Mullens (574, p. 401), H. L. Meÿer began in 1838 the publication of an English edition of Levaillant's 'Birds of Paradise', but this undertaking does not seem to have been perservered in.

LEVANDER, K. M.
1911—26. Nordens fåglar ... See *Jägerskiøld, A. K. E. L.*

306. LEWIN, W.
1795—1801. The birds of Great Britain, systematically arranged, accurately engraved, and painted from nature; with descriptions, including the natural history of each bird: From observations the result of more than twenty years application to the subject, in the field of nature; in which the distinguishing character of each species is fully explained, and its manner of life truly described. The figures engraved from the subjects themselves by the author, W. Lewin, and painted under his immediate direction. *J. Johnson. London. 8 vols in 4. 336 col. pl. 4to.* Added title-page in French. Half-title: The birds of Great Britain, with their eggs. — Vol. I. 1795. *pp. [22] + 21—75 + [4]. 35 col. pl. birds (front. + Nos. 1—31, *18, *19, 27); 7 col. pl. eggs (numb. 1—7).* Vol. II. 1796. *pp. 75 + [3]. 35 col. pl. birds (numb. 32—66); 7 col. pl. eggs. (numb. 8—14).* Vol. III. 1796. *pp. 75 + [3]. 35 col. pl. birds (numb. 67—97, 66, 81*, 84*, 94*); 7 col. pl. eggs. (numb. 16—22).* Vol. IV. 1797. *pp. 75 + [3]. 35 col. pl. birds (numb. 98—131, 100*); 7 col. pl. eggs. (numb. 23—27, 23 [= 28], 29).* Vol. V. 1797. *pp. 75 + [3]. 35 col. pl. birds (numb. 132—166); 7 col. pl. eggs (numb. 30—36).* Vol. VI.

1800. *pp. 77 + [3]. 36 col. pl. birds (numb. 167—202); 6 col. pl. eggs (numb. 37—42).* Vol. VII. 1800. *pp. 73 + [3]. 34 col. pl. birds (numb. [203]—236); 8 col. pl. eggs (numb. 43—50).* Vol. VIII. 1801. *pp. 71 + [4]. 33 col. pl. birds (numb. 237—267, 245); 9 col. pl. eggs (numb. 51—59).*

The second edition of a work which was first published in 1789—94 under the title 'The birds of Great Britain, with their eggs', etc.

In the present edition the text is printed in both English and French and comprises a brief description of the birds figured and a brief mention of their natural history, which is said to be composed chiefly from original observations by the author and his sons.

Adult males were generally used as models for the figures, which vary somewhat in quality and are not very good.

Most of the figures of the eggs were executed from specimens in the Duchess of Portland's collection.

In the present copy two successive volumes have been bound together.

LEYDEN. RIJKS MUSEUM VAN NATUUR-LIJKE HISTORIE.
1879—1914: Notes from the Leyden Museum. 3 (Vol. I: Notes from the Royal Zoological Museum of the Netherlands at Leyden). Edited by H. Schlegel (1879—83). Continued by F. A. Jentink (1884—1913). Edited by E. D. van Oort (1914). E. J. Brill. *Leyden.* — *Vols. I—XXXVI, and Index 1879—99. text-figs. col. plates. 8vo.*

These 'Notes' include a series of articles on birds written by well-known ornithologists, notably H. Schlegel, J. Büttikofer, O. Finsch, and E. D. van Oort, and also R. B. Sharpe, Ernst Hartert, A. B. Meyer, among many others.

Some few coloured plates (lithographs: P. W. M. Trap imp.) were published in various volumes, from Vol. VII, 1884, to Vol. XXIX, 1907—08, drawn by J. Büttikofer, Th. v. Hoytema, J. G. Keulemans, T. M. Meissner, and others.

In 1915 this periodical was replaced by 'Zoologische Mededeelingen', issued by the same museum.

LICHTHAMMER, J. W.
1800—09. Teutsche Ornithologie ... See *Borkhausen, M. B.*

LILFORD, T. L. P., Fourth Baron.
1891—97 [—'98]. Coloured figures of the birds of 3 the British Islands. Issued by Lord Lilford. Second edition. R. H. Porter. *London. 7 vols. 421 col. pl. (numb. in 'List of plates'). large 8vo.* — Vol. I. *pp. XXXV (p. XXXII numb. XXXI) + [112]. 52 pl. (front. (portrait) + [112]. col. pl. birds (numb. 1—51)).* Vol. II. *pp. IX + [120]. 54 col. pl. (numb. 1—54).* Vol. III. *pp. IX + [130]. 66 col. pl. (numb. 1—66).* Vol. IV. *pp. IX + [154]. 65 col. pl. (numb. 1—65).* Vol. V. *pp. IX + [138]. 59 col. pl. (numb. 1—59).* Vol. VI. *pp. IX + [150]. 65 col. pl. (numb. 1—65).* Vol. VII. *pp. IX + [1—144] + 145—170. 61 col. pl. (numb. 1—61).*

The present edition of the work was issued in 36 parts like the first edition, which was published in 1885—98. A description of the two editions is found in the opening section of each volume, in which the numbers and dates of the parts in which the plates of the volume appeared are stated; a complete history of the work is given by Gladstone (729). The present edition would therefore appear to have been published as follows:

Parts I—X, 1891; XI—XVIII, 1892; XIX—XXVI, 1893; XXVII—XXIX, 1894; XXX—XXXI, 1895; XXXII—XXXIII, 1896; XXXIV—XXXV, 1897; while Part XXXVI was issued in 1898 (574, p. 354). The 28th parts of the present as well as of the first edition appeared simultaneously (September, 1894), after which the remaining parts of the two editions were published together. Only Parts VII—XVII of the second edition are said to have been reprinted, when various improvements were achieved as regards the text and certain plates (574, pp. 354—355). After Lord Lilford's death the work was completed by the issue of Parts XXXIV—XXXVI, by Osbert Salvin.

The short text to each of the forms figured contains a brief synonymy, vernacular names in French, German, and Spanish, and an account of the occurrence and habits of the birds, and sometimes information about their nests and eggs.

The beautiful plates (chromo-lithographs, mostly executed by W. Greve, Berlin, some by Mintern Bros., Hanhart, and West, Newman & Co.) were chiefly made from originals by A. Thorburn, who supplied drawings for 260, and J. G. Keulemans (drawings for 125 plates, chiefly in the first parts), while drawings for some few plates were supplied by G. E. Lodge and W. Foster.

1920. The birds of the British Isles and their eggs ... With ... coloured illustrations ... reproduced from Lord Lilford's work 'Coloured figures of the birds of the British Islands' ... *See Coward, T. A.*

LILJEFORS, B. A.

1912. Ute i markerna. Reproduktioner efter taflor af Bruno Liljefors. Albert Bonnier. *Stockholm. pp. [3] + [1]. 29 col. pl. birds. obl. fol.*

A series of 33 plates in all (three-colour prints, made by Cederquist's Graf. Aktiebolag, Stockholm, and Kemigraf. Aktieb. Bengt Silfversparre, Stockholm and Gothenburg) with reproductions from paintings by the Swedish animal painter, who has written a brief introductory text to the beautiful pictures. The ability of the world-famed artist to reproduce wild animal life in its natural surroundings and to make it blend with them is well displayed in these pictures, among which sea-birds play a prominent part as subjects.

LINDNER, F. W.

1840[—44]. Malerische Naturgeschichte der drei Reiche, für Schule und Haus. Mit besonderer Beziehung auf das practische Leben bearbeitet von F. W. Lindner; unter Mitwirkung von Fr. H. A. Lachmann I. <-- *pp. 166—237: Zweite Klasse der Wirbelthiere. Vögel, Aves >.* Oehme & Müller. *Braunschweig. 4 col. pl. (numb. 12—15). large 4to.*

This popular handbook of natural history (pp. IV + IV + 458; 28 pl. (24 col.)) was issued in fifteen parts. It is of a practical nature and may therefore be called a kind of popular technological natural history.

The plates (lithographs, executed by Kunstanstalt von Oehme & Müller; C. W. F. Krämer, del.) are peculiar because a human figure or part of a human body is depicted among the numerous animal figures of each plate in order to show the proportions.

LINNÆUS, C. (LINNÉ, C. von).

1773. Des Ritters Carl von Linné ... vollständiges Natursystem ... Part II. Von den Vögeln. *See Mueller, P. L. S.*

1776. A catalogue of the birds, beasts, fishes, insects, plants, &c. contained in Edwards's Natural history, in seven volumes, with their Latin names. By C. Linnæus. J. Robson. *London. pp. 15 + [1]. small fol.*

A list of the 362 species figured in Edwards' 'A natural history of birds', 1743—51 (124) and 'Gleanings of natural

history', 1758—64 (126). The English names and the Latin binomials are arranged in parallel columns.

1781. Des Ritters Carl von Linné Lehr-Buch über das Natur-System so weit es das Thierreich angehet ... Vol. I. pp. 187—475: Zwote Classe. Die Geschichte der Vögel. *See Mueller, P. L. S.*

LINNÉ, C. von. *See Linnæus, C.*

LIVING ANIMALS OF THE WORLD.

[1907?]. pp. 385—544: Book II. Birds. *See Pycraft, W. P.*

LLOYD, L.

1867. The game birds and wild fowl of Sweden 312. and Norway; together with an account of the seals and salt-water fishes of those countries. Embellished with a map, 48 illustrations executed in chromolithography, and 65 woodcuts. By L. Lloyd. Day and Son. *London. pp. XX + 599. text-figs. 36 pl. birds (33 col.). 8vo.*

From his journeys and hunting excursions in Scandinavia, about which he had written a couple of books, Lloyd was familiar with the animal life of these regions.

This knowledge he has utilized in the present popular work, in which a particularly detailed description is given of the various devices adopted in the northern countries for the capture and destruction of birds and quadrupeds. The greater part of the volume is devoted to birds, which are dealt with on pp. 1—289 and pp. 333—371, the majority of the 52 plates containing figures of birds also. The coloured plates (Day & Son, lith.) were executed from drawings by M. Körner (a single one: W. von Wright, del.), while the drawings for the few woodcuts were executed by A. Wolf. Körner further supplied the drawings for the plates in S. Nilsson's 'Illuminerade figurer til Skandinaviens fauna', 1829—40 (365); some of the figures in the present work are reminiscent of the corresponding ones in that work.

A second edition (Frederick Warne and Co.) was issued in the same year as the first.

LOCHE, V.

1849 [—67]. Exploration scientifique de l'Algé- 313. rie ... 1840—42, publiée par ordre du gouvernement et avec le concours d'une commission académique. Sciences physiques. Zoologie. Vol. IV. <-- [Histoire naturelle des oiseaux, par Loche. Atlas]>. Arthus Bertrand. *Paris. 15 col. pl. (numb. 1—13, 1bis, 9bis). fol.*

The zoological atlas whose ornithological section is cited here contains altogether 156 coloured plates derived from the exploration work mentioned in the title, the results of which were published in 1844—67 in thirty volumes (25 vols. text and 5 vols. plates) of various formats.

The birds were described by le Commandant Victor Loche, whose text appeared in 1867, while le Commandant (later Général) Jean Levaillant who had originally described the ornithological material, but whose text never appeared, superintended the drawing of the plates. According to Sherborn and Woodward (869, II, pp. 163—164) some of the plates were issued as early as 1849.

The first mention of the ornithological material is found in V. Loche's 'Catalogue des mammifères et des oiseaux observés en Algérie', 1858, pp. 33—158.

The plates (engravings) are printed in colour by N. Rémond, and retouched by hand, and engraved by Guyard, Massard, Annedouche. Some are from paintings by Vaillant and Werner.

LODGE, R. B.

1903. Pictures of bird life. On woodland, meadow, 314. mountain and marsh. By R. B. Lodge. With numerous

colour and half-tone illustrations from photographs from life by the author. S. H. Bousfield & Co. *London. pp 376. text-figs. 8 col. pl. large 8vo.*
A copiously illustrated work, based on the experience gained by the author as a bird photographer. The matter is partly of a technical nature and partly concerned with bird life in the regions visited by the author, not only his own native country, but also other parts of Europe; this appears from chapters such as 'Bird life in Dutch marshes', 'Bird life in the Spanish marismas', 'Bird life in Denmark — on the fjord', and 'Bird life in Denmark — in the forest'.
A second edition appeared in 1904.
1910—13. The British bird book ... *See Kirkman, F. B. B.*

LOEPELMANN, M.
315.   *[1934].* Die heimischen Raubvögel. Von Martin Löpelmann. Herausgegeben von der Staatlichen Stelle für Naturdenkmalpflege. Mit ... farbigen Tafeln, 73 Abbildungen auf Kunstdrucktafeln, Naturaufnahmen von Dr. O. Heinroth, 9 Flugtafeln und 26 Abbildungen im Text .Hugo Bermühler. *Berlin-Lichterfelde. pp. 86 + [2]. text-figs. 25 pl. (9 col. (numb. I—IX), 16 phot. pl. (numb. 1—16)). 8vo.*
A special edition (popular edition) of 'Atlas der geschützten Pflanzen und Tiere Mitteleuropas', Abteilung 4, which was first published in 1927.
A brief guide for sportsmen and lovers of nature to the natural history of birds, prepared with a view to the protection of nature. Thirty-one forms are mentioned. Tables for the identification of birds of prey and their food increase the usefulness of the book.
A summary of the legislation affecting the protection of birds of prey is added.
The coloured plates are reproduced from plates in Heinroth's 'Die Vögel Mitteleuropas', 1924—33 (202), whence also some of the uncoloured plates are derived. The flight of birds of prey is illustrated by a collection of figures on pages 69—76.

LÖNNBERG, A. J. E.
1917—29. Svenska fåglar efter naturen och på sten ritade af M., W. och F. von Wright. Med text af Einar Lönnberg. *See Wright, M. von.*

LORENZ, T. (F. K.).
316.   *1887.* Beitrag zur Kenntniss der ornithologischen Fauna an der Nordseite des Kaukasus. Von Th. Lorenz. Buchdruckerei von E. Liessner & J. Romahn. *Moskau. pp. XII + 62. text-figs. 5 col. pl. (numb. I—V). large 4to.*
This treatise deals with the collection and observation of birds on the north side of the Caucasus in 1883 and the succeeding year.
The work consists of an introduction (pp. III—IX) by Lorenz, in which he describes the natural conditions of the areas visited; a preface (pp. X—XII) by Dr. Menzbier, who assisted in the preparation of the work; an analytic treatment of the material collected (pp. 1—59), dealing with 161 species and subspecies; and a 'Nachtrag' (pp. 60—62) with four forms from the Caucasus, which have been added later.
The plates are executed in heliogravure, they are coloured by hand and signed Lorenz.

LUCANUS, F. K. H. von.
317.   *1925.* Das Leben der Vögel. Von Friedrich von Lucanus. Mit ... farbigen Tafeln und 136 Textabbildungen. August Scherl. *Berlin. pp. 429 + [3]. 19 col. pl. (numb. 1—19; 3 pl. eggs (numb. 7—9)). 8vo.*
A popular account of the natural history of birds, which is treated in sections on the evolution of the group, the anatomy,

plumage, movements, and positions of birds, the egg and its development, the voice and song of birds, their sexual life and reproduction, mental life, migrations and wanderings, and their geographical distribution.
The text-figures as well as the plates, which are printed in colour, were executed from drawings by Erich Schröder.

LUTZ, K. G.
[1888]. Die Raubvögel Deutschlands. Nebst einem Anhang über Vogelschutz. Von K. G. Lutz. Mit 38 kolorierten Abbildungen auf ... Tafeln und 12 in den Text gedruckten Holzschnitten. Emil Hänselmann. *Stuttgart. pp. VIII + 171 + [4]. 16 col. pl. (numb. 1—16). 8vo.*
A popular, systematically arranged description of the birds of prey of Germany, especially intended for farmers and foresters as well as sportsmen. The last part of the volume (pp. 110—171) is occupied by the supplement, 'Vom Vogelschutz', mentioned in the title.

LYDEKKER, R.
[1916]. Wild life of the world; a descriptive survey of the geographical distribution of animals. By R. Lydekker. Illustrated with over six hundred engravings from original drawings and one hundred and twenty studies in colour. Frederick Warne and Co. *London. 3 vols. 43 col. pl. birds. large 8vo. — Vol. I. pp. XIV + 472. text-figs. 18 col. pl. birds. Vol. II. pp. XII + 440. text-figs. 11 col. pl. birds. Vol. III. pp. XI + 457. text-figs. 14 col. pl. birds.*
This work was issued in twelve sections and was in press when the author died.
It is a general natural history in which the animals are treated according to their geographical distribution, a mode of treatment with which the author was familiar from his earlier works, principally his 'A geographical history of mammals', 1896; he was also well qualified from his numerous works in natural history to write a book which, like the present, describes on a more popular basis animal life, vertebrate and invertebrate, throughout the world.
The coloured plates were executed, by the three-colour process (G. Bx. & Cp.), from paintings by W. Kuhnert.

LYNES, H.
1930. The Ibis. Twelfth series. Volume VI. Supplementary Number. Review of the genus Cisticola. [By H. Lynes]. British Ornithologists' Union. *London. 2 vols in 1. 8vo. — Text. pp. [V] + 673. Pictures. pp. [V] + VII. 19 col. pl. (numb. I—XIX, double, mostly fold.). 1 pl. maps (numb. XX, double).*
A comprehensive study of the genus mentioned in the title, based partly on museum material, and partly on observations in the open, of these predominantly African birds.
Altogether 10,355 skins, including types of 36 species, 111 subspecies and 93 synonyms were examined, and a proposal is made to classify the birds in 40 species and 154 subspecies, as against the previous 174 species and 54 subspecies. Four species and 24 subspecies are new to science.
The work, besides of the introduction and a check-list of the species and subspecies, consists in the main of a section containing descriptions of the forms with notes on their moults, identification of skins, geographical distribution, status, behaviour, breeding season, eggs and material. There are also a chapter containing a short history of the genus, an abridged bibliography, a survey of the museum material employed, and an account of the 'African Cisticola tour' made in 1926—27 by Lynes and B. B. Osmaston.
The concluding chapter, 'Index of names and types', contains in alphabetical order all the names ever used in connection with the generic Cisticola, and an abridged synonymy.

The plates, which were drawn by H. Grønvold (reproduced by H. W. Schofield in co-operation with Bale & Danielsson), are mostly coloured life-size diagrams of the birds, accompanied by an explanatory text of some length.

MAACK, R. K.
1860. Reisen und Forschungen im Amur-Lande ... 1854—56 ... Vol. I. pp. 215—567: Part II. Vögel des Amur-Landes. *See Schrenck, P. L. von.*

MACGILLIVRAY, W.
1831—39. Ornithological biography ... [the descriptions of the species, with their anatomy, by W. Macgillivray] ... *See Audubon, J. J. L.*
1856. The birds of America ... *See Audubon, J. J. L.*

MACPHERSON, H. A.
1898. British birds with their nests and eggs. Vol. VI. Order Tubinares. *See Butler, A. G., 1896—98.*

MADARÁSZ, J. von (MADARÁSZ G.).
1884—86. See Zeitschrift fuer die gesammte Ornithologie.

MAGYAR ORNITHOLOGIAI KÖZPONTOT.
[*Hungarian Ornithological Central-Bureau*].
1894 → See Aquila.
1905. Ornithologische Fragmente aus den Handschriften von Johann Salamon von Petényi ... *See Petényi, J. S. von.*

MALHERBE, A.
[*1859—*] *1863.* Monographie des picidées, ou histoire naturelle des picidés, picumninés, yuncinés ou torcols comprenant dans la première partie, l'origine mythologique, les moeurs, les migrations, l'anatomie, la physiologie, la répartition géographique, les divers systèmes de classification de ces oiseaux grimpeurs zygodactyles, ainsi qu'un dictionnaire alphabétique des auteurs et des ouvrages cités par abréviation; dans la deuxième partie, la synonymie, la description en latin et en français, l'histoire de chaque espèce, ainsi qu'un dictionnaire alphabétique et synonymique latin de toutes les espèces; par Alf. Malherbe. Typographie de Jules Verronnais. *Metz. 4 vols in 3. 123 col. pl. large fol. —* Texte. Vol. I. 1861 *pp.* [X] + LXX + 214. *text-figs.* Texte. Vol. II. 1862. *pp.* 325. Planches. Vol. III. 1861. *pp.* 8. 62 *col. pl. (numb. I—LXI, XLIIIbis).* Planches. Vol. IV. 1862. *pp.* 6. 61 *col. pl. (numb. LXII—CXXI, LXXXIVbis).*
This work was issued in 25 livraisons (cf. Catalogue annuel de la librairie française, edited by Ch. Reinwald), which were published as follows: livraison 1, 1859; 2—9, 1860; 10—21, 1861; and 22—25, 1862.
According to Zimmer (589, II, p. 415), the work was issued in 100 copies, whereas according to Journal général de l'imprimerie et de la librairie (2nd Sér. 6, Bibliographie, 1862, p. 326) it was issued in 80 copies only, all numbered.
In the present copy, Vols. I and III are numbered 41, Vols. II and IV, 77; all the plates are bound in one volume, the general title-page of which is dated 1863.
The first ten unpaginated pages of Vol. I contain 'Abréviations employées pour les noms des auteurs et ouvrages cités', while pp. I—LXX of the same volume, designated as 'première partie', contain 'Histoire générale des picidées'. The main part of the work, 'deuxième partie', consists of 'Histoire

naturelle des divers espèces de picidées'. Both volumes of text contain an index, and Vol. II in addition (pp. 303—325) a 'Catalogue alphabétique et synonymique des noms latins des picidées'.
C. J. Sundevall based his 'Conspectus avium picinarum' (Stockholmiæ 1866, 8vo), which opens with an index to the present work, on Malherbe's copious monograph.
The plates (A. Malherbe, direx. t) are lithographs coloured by hand (lith. A. Compan (Pl. I—XV: Becquet frères), Paris), and were drawn and lithographed by Mesnel, Delahaye and P. Oudart.

MANN, W. M.
1930. Smithsonian Scientific Series. Vol. 6. Wild *322.* animals in and out of the Zoo. By William M. Mann. Smithsonian Institution Series. *New York. pp.* [XIII] + [I] + 362. 22 *pl.* birds (3 *col. (numb. 6, 84, 89); 13 phot. pl.). 8vo.*
The author is Director of the National Zoological Park, and the subjects treated in his book are derived from this Zoo, mammals being dealt with principally; a single chapter, however, entitled 'Wings' is concerned with birds.
The majority of the 116 plates are reproduced from photographs. The originals for the coloured plates (three-colour prints) and several pen and ink drawings were executed by Benson B. Moore.

MANNICHE, A. L. V.
1910. Meddelelser om Grønland udgivne af Kom- *323.* missionen for Ledelsen af de geologiske og geografiske Undersøgelser i Grønland. Vol. XLV. 1912. -- Danmark-Ekspeditionen til Grønlands Nordøstkyst 1906—1908 under Ledelse af L. Mylius-Erichsen. Vol. V. <-- *pp. 1—200:* I. The terrestrial mammals and birds of North-East Greenland. Biological observations by A. L. V. Manniche. - - *pp. 93—199:* Birds >. C. A. Reitzel. *København. text-figs. 5 col. pl. (numb. II—VI, 1 pl. eggs (numb. VI)). 1 map. 8vo.*
This expedition, which cost the leader and two of his companions their lives, had for its main object the mapping of the whole unknown stretch of coast extending from the region round Cape Bismarck to Navy Cliff and the east coast of Peary Land. In addition, the land was to be explored scientifically to the greatest possible extent, including its fauna and flora. The scientific results of the expedition were published in the 'Meddelelser om Grønland', Vols. XLI—XLVI, 1909—17.
In the present ornithological section the ornithologist of the expedition discusses 38 birds observed and collected, describing their habits, principally as regards breeding. The paper was also published in Danish in a somewhat enlarged form under the title 'Nordøstgrønlands Fugle' in 'Dansk Ornithologisk Forenings Tidsskrift, V, 1911, Parts I—II (= pp. 1—114).
The plates (produced by the three-colour process, H. H. Thiele imp.) were executed from drawings by Gerhard Heilmann.
1928—30. Danmarks Fugleliv. *See Heilmann, G. V. E.*

MARCHESA, Cruise of the Yacht.
1886. The cruise of the Marchesa to Kamschatka & New Guinea, with notices of Formosa, Liu-Kiu, and various islands of the Malay Archipelago ... *See Guillemard, F. H. H.*

MARSHALL, C. H. T.
1870—71. A monograph of the Capitonidæ, or *324.* scansorial barbets. By C. H. T. Marshall and G. F. L. Marshall. The plates drawn and lithographed by J. G. Keulemans. Published by the authors. *London. pp.*

[XII] + XLI + [182] + [7]. 73 col. pl. (numb. I—
LXXIII in 'List of plates'). large 4to.
This work appeared in nine parts, which were issued in
1870 (I—V) and 1871 (VI—IX). It is provided with two
slightly different title-pages, the first of which is dated 1871,
the other 1870—71.
The monograph contains a great amount of information,
published or unpublished previously, about the family Capitonidæ; it is otherwise arranged in the same way as 'A monograph of the Alcedinidæ' (464), issued 1868—71 by R. B.
Sharpe, who assisted the authors in preparing the present work.
The general part of the work (pp. I—XLI) consists of an
introduction dealing with the origin of species, a summary of
the literary history of the family, a section on the classification
of the group, a Conspectus avium Capitonidarum, and finally
a survey of the geographical distribution of the Capitonidæ.
The last and greater part of the work is devoted to a treatment of individual forms, with a statement of synonyms, brief
diagnoses in Latin, descriptions, and information about the
habitats and habits of the birds.
The beautiful hand-coloured plates (the greater number:
P. W. M. Trap, Leiden exc.) contain figures of each of the
forms treated in the work.

MARSHALL, G. F. L.

1870—71. A monograph of the Capitonidæ, or
scansorial barbets. See Marshall, C. H. T.

MARSHALL, W. A. L.

325.   1898. Bilder-Atlas zur Zoologie der Vögel. Mit be-
schreibendem Text von William Marshall. Mit 238
Holzschnitten nach Zeichnungen von G. Mützel, Fr.
Specht, Rob. Kretschmer, W. Kuhnert, L. Beckmann,
Ch. Kröner u. a. Bibliographisches Institut. Leipzig.
pp. 194 + [4]. 134 pl. (pp. 61—194). 8vo.
The text (pp. 1—60) of this popular volume consists (pp.
11—60) of an introduction with a general account of the
group of birds and a brief description of the 17 orders into
which it is divided.
The illustrations recur as text-figures in the ornithological
section of 'Brehms Tierleben', for instance in the third edition,
1891—92 of that work (62).

1911—13. Brehms Tierleben ... Vierte ... Auflage.
Vols. VI—IX. Die Vögel ... See Brehm, A. E.

MARSIGLI, L. F.

326.   1726. Danubius Pannonico-Mysicus, observationibus geographicis, astronomicis, hydrographicis, histori-
cis, physicis perlustratus et in sex tomos digestus. Ab
Aloysio Ferd Marsili. Vol. V. <-- De avibus circa
aquas Danubii vagantibus, et de ipsarum nidis >.
P. Gosse. Hagæ Comitum. pp. [III] + 154 + [6]. 75
pl. (front. + 59 pl. birds (Nos. 1—59); 15 pl. eggs
(Nos. 60—74)). large fol.
A volume of a well-known work, which appeared in its
entirety in six volumes in 1726.
The present volume deals with the water-birds inhabiting
the regions near the Danube and the Tisa in great numbers.
The text of the work consists of an explanation of the plates
and is very brief, being limited to a description, usually in a
few lines on one side of the leaf.
The section dealing with the eggs and nests gives the position of the latter and also their composition and size, together
with the dimensions and colour of the eggs.
In his classification of the birds the author draws upon
Willughby.
The drawings for the plates (engravings) in this volume,
the figures in which are not of any great excellence, were supplied by R. Manzini. The originals are deposited in the University Library of Bologna (577, p. 42).
A French translation of the original Latin work was
published in 1744 at the Hague in six volumes, in large folio,

illustrated with the plates under the title 'Description du
Danube, depuis la montagne de Kalenberg en Autriche, jusqu'au
confluent de la rivière Jantra, dans la Bulgarie ...'.

MARTIN, W. C. L.

1861. A general history of humming-birds, or the
Trochilidæ: with especial reference to the collection
of J. Gould, F. R. S. &c. now exhibiting in the Gardens of the Zoological Society of London. By W. C.
L. Martin. H. G. Bohn. London. pp. VII + [I] +
232. 16 col. pl. (front. + Nos. 1—14, 3*). 8vo.
This small volume — popular in style — is a sort of supplement to Jardine's natural history of humming birds (223),
which first appeared in 1833 as Vols. I and II of the ornithological series of Jardine's 'The Naturalist's Library'. According to Coues (561, III, p. 676), it first appeared in 1852, and
is said to have been issued as a later volume of this series.
The text consists of a general history of humming-birds
(pp. 1—127) and a description of genera and species (pp. 128
—224), in which reference is made to the species described
by Jardine, these forms (except in one instance) not being
treated again in detail in the present volume.
The bird figures on the plates (engravings) are coloured
by hand, while the backgrounds are uncoloured.

MARTINET, F. N.

1770—86. Histoire naturelle des oiseaux. [Planches
enluminées]. See Buffon, G. L. L. de.

MARTINI, F. H. W.

1772—77. Herrn von Buffons Naturgeschichte der
Vögel. Aus dem Französischen übersetzt ... durch F.
H. W. Martini. Vols. I—VI. See Buffon, G. L. L. de,
1772—1809.

MATHEW, M. A.

1897. British birds with their nests and eggs. Vol
III. Orders Striges and Accipitres. See Butler, A. G.
1896—98.

MATHEWS, G. M.

1910—27. The birds of Australia. By Gregory M
Mathews. With hand-coloured plates. Witherby & Co
(Vols. VIII—XII, and Suppl. Nos. 2—5: H. F. & G
Witherby). London. 12 vols. + 5 suppl. in 2 vols. 600
col. pl. (numb. in text). large 4to. — Vol. I. 1910—11
pp. XIV + 301, 183*—184* (pp. 183 and 184 issued
in Part III are cancelled). text-figs. 67 col. pl. (Nos. 1
—67). Vol. II. 1912—13. pp. XIV + 527. text-figs. 57
col. pl. (Nos. 68—124). Vol. III. 1913—14. pp. XVI,
+ 512. text-figs. 75 col. pl. (Nos. 125—199). Vol. IV
1914—15. pp. XII + 334. text-figs. 34 col. pl. (Nos
200—233). Vol. V. 1915—16. pp. XI + 440. text
figs. 41 col. pl. (Nos. 234—274). Vol. VI. 1916—17
pp. XIX + 516. text-figs. 50 col. pl. (Nos. 275—
324). Vol. VII. 1918—19. pp. XII + 499. 46 col. pl
(Nos. 325—370). Vol. VIII. 1919—20. pp. XIV +
316. 29 col. pl. (Nos. 371—399). Vol. IX. 1921—
22. pp. XIV + 518. 54 col. pl. (Nos. 400—453)
Vol. X. 1922—23. pp. XI + 451. 37 col. pl. (Nos
454—490). Vol. XI. 1923—24. pp. XIII + 593. 5
col. pl. (Nos. 491—541). Vol. XII. 1925—27. pp
XII + 454. 59 col. pl. (Nos. 542—600). Suppl. Nos
1—3. 1920—24. Check list of the birds of Australia
Parts I—III. Suppl. No. 1 (= Part I). 1920. pp. II
+ 1—116. Suppl. No. 2 (= Part II). 1923. pp. XV
+ 117—156. Suppl. No. 3 (= Part III). 1924. pp

VIII + *157—244.* (Suppl. Nos. 4—5). 1925. Bibliography of the birds of Australia. Books used in the preparation of this work with a few biographical details of authors and collectors. (Parts I—II). *pp. VIII* + *149. 1 pl.*

This immense work was published in 79 parts, which appeared at somewhat irregular intervals, one to nine parts being issued annually. A complete survey of the contents of the various parts and their dates of publication is found in 'The Auk', 44 (1927), pp. 435—442.

An enormous amount of information is contained in these volumes, in which the literature concerned and the question of nomenclature are fully treated.

Under each genus synonyms, a brief diagnosis, a description, and a key to the species are given, while under each form we find a detailed synonymy, information about the distribution and, as far as possible, a description of the adult male, the adult female, the immature birds, and the nestling; the eggs and nest are also described, and the breeding-months stated. Then follows an account of the habits and life-history of the birds, including long quotations from the literature.

The comprehensive bibliography is found in Supplements 4 and 5, Supplements 1—3 containing a guide to the nomenclature of the species, in which are compiled the synonyms connected with 'The birds of Australia'. The exact day of the month of each publication is stated. 'Corrections and additions to my check list', Part II, is found in Vol. XII, pp. 429—431, while an Appendix, continued from Supplement No. II, 1923, pp. VII—XVI, is found in Vol. XII, pp. 433—434. Two further appendices are found in Vol. VII, viz. pp. 435—442, Appendix A with a list of works containing all the new names and a list of extra-limital genera described in the parts of the work hitherto published, and pp. 443—477, Appendix B with dates of publication of works dealing with ornithology and concerning the birds of Australia. An 'Addenda to Appendix B' (pp. 473—477) has been provided by C. W. Richmond.

The figures on the hand-coloured plates (lithographs; Witherby & Co.), are due to five different artists. The greater number have been executed from drawings by H. Grønvold, while J. G. Keulemans supplied a series of figures for Vols. I—III and a single one for Vol. IV; Roland Green and H. Goodchild contributed several plates to Vols. VI—VII and Vols. IV—VII respectively. Finally, the drawing for a single plate in Vol. V was supplied by G. E. Lodge.

The plates contain figures of about one hundred species not given in Gould's 'The birds of Australia' 1840—48 (174), and many subspecies. In most cases the bird figured is derived from another locality than that figured by Gould.

The edition of this work was strictly limited to 225 copies, of which this copy is No. 28.

Additions to the work are found in Mathews' 'The birds of Norfolk and Lord Howe Islands and the Australasian South Polar Quadrant', etc., (London 1928, 45 pl. (mainly coloured), 4to), with plates by Grønvold and Frohawk, while additions to the latter work and to Buller's 'A history of the birds of New Zealand' (85) are found in Mathews' 'A supplement to The birds of Norfolk and Lord Howe Islands, to which is added those birds of New Zealand not figured by Buller' (London 1936, 57 col. pl., 4to). The plates in the latter work, executed from originals by Grønvold, Frohawk, and Roland Green, complete the material of figures of Australian birds, so that all species should now be depicted in coloured figures.

MAUDUYT DE LA VARENNE, P. J. É.
1782—84. Encyclopédie méthodique ... Histoire naturelle des animaux. Vols. I—II. Ornithologie. *See Encyclopædias, 1782—1823.*

MAXIMILIAN, Prinz zu WIED-NEUWIED.
See Wied-Neuwied, M. A. P., Prinz zu.

MEDDELELSER OM GRØNLAND.
1910. Vol. XLV. 1912 ... pp. 1—200: The terrestrial mammals and birds of North-East Greenland. pp. 93—199: Birds. *See Manniche, A. L. V.*

MEINERTZHAGEN, R.
1930. Nicoll's Birds of Egypt. By R. Meinertzhagen. *See Nicoll, M. J.*

MEISNER, C. F. A.
[1808—] 1820. Museum der Naturgeschichte *329.* Helvetiens. Herausgegeben von Friedrich Meisner. Vol. I. P. P. Burgdorfer. *Bern. pp. 98. 6 col. pl. birds. 4to.*

The present zoological section of these museum publications was issued in 12 parts, which contained descriptions and figures, on altogether 13 plates, of interesting and remarkable objects in the collection. Among the subjects treated are six species of birds with accompanying hand-coloured engravings (Em. Wyss, J. Lienert, Th. Lienert del. ; M. G. Eichler, W. Hartmann sc.).

MELVILLE, A. G.
1848. The Dodo and its kindred ... *See Strickland, H. E.*

MÉMOIRES PRÉSENTÉS À L'ACADÉMIE IMPÉRIALE DES SCIENCES DE ST-PÉTERSBOURG. *See Académie Impériale des Sciences de St.-Pétersbourg.*

MÉNÉGAUX, H. A.
1932—34. Encyclopédie pratique du naturaliste *330.* XXVI—XXVII. - - Les oiseaux de France. Par A. Ménégaux. Paul Lechevalier & fils. *Paris. 2 vols. textfigs. 144 pl. small 8vo. —* Vol. I. 1932. Introduction à l'étude de l'ornithologie. Rapaces, Gallinacés, Colombins, Piciformes ... planches coloriées d'après les aquarelles de M. Mahler et de J. Eudes. 107 figures noires. *pp. CXCVII + [2] + 93, 8bis-ter, 24bis-ter, 40bis-ter, 56bis-ter + [2]. 64 col. pl. (numb. 1—64).* Vol. II. 1934. Oiseaux d'eau et espèces voisines. Colymbiformes, Alciformes, Procellariiformes, Lariformes, Charadriiformes, Ansériformes, Pélécaniformes, Ciconiiformes, Phoenicoptériformes, Gruiformes ... planches (dont 64 coloriées d'après les aquarelles de J. Eudes). 148 figures noires. *pp. (10) + CCI—DIV + [III] + 65—195 + 3. 80 pl. (numb. 65—144; 64 col. (numb. 65—72, 74—89, 91—106, 108—117, 127—134, 138—143)).*

The two first volumes of a popular hand-book on the birds of France, intended to give the amateur a practical and simple means of identifying all the birds occurring in the area. It is planned to comprise three volumes, the last of which is to contain the order Passeres.

The introduction to the first volume deals with the rules for zoological nomenclature, the geographical distribution and ecology of the birds, and the collection, preparation, and preservation of birds and birds' eggs. A section, 'Insectes parasites des oiseaux vivants', has been written by E. Séguy. The volumes further contain a survey of the classification of the groups of birds treated in them, with keys to the determination of the genera and descriptions of them and the higher groups. The part of the book paginated with Arabic numerals deals with individual forms, adding their vernacular names in several languages, their descriptions and dimensions, and a brief account of the ecology of the birds.

The plates, executed by the three-colour process, have figures on both sides.

MÉNÉTRIÉS, E.
331.   1835. Mémoires de l'Académie Impériale des
Sciences de Saint-Pétersbourg. Sixième série. Vol. III.
(Sciences naturelles. Vol. I). <-- *pp. 443—543:* Monographie de la famille des Myiotherinæ où sont
décrites les espèces qui ornent le Musée de l'Académie
Impériale des Sciences. Par E. Ménétriés >. Imprimerie de l'Académie Impériale des Sciences. *St. Péters-
bourg. 16 pl. (15 col. pl. birds (numb. 1—15)). 4°.*
    This monograph (lu le 28 février 1834), besides discussing
general questions relative to the group, treats of altogether 54
forms, giving their synonymies, brief diagnoses in Latin, descriptions, and remarks on their occurrence.
    The plates, containing altogether 30 figures of birds, are
hand-coloured lithographs (d'aprés nat. par Ménétriés, lith.
par. F. Davignon).

MENZBIR (MENZBIER), M. A.
332.   1916. Faune de la Russie et des pays limitrophes
fondée principalement sur les collections du Musée
Zoologique de l'Académie Impériale des Sciences de
Petrograd. Rédigée par N. V. Nasonov. Oiseaux
(Aves). Vol. VI. M. A. Menzbier (M. A. Menzbir).
Falconiformes. Part I. (Avec ... planches et 17 figures
dans le texte). *Petrograd. pp. [III] + II + 344. text-
figs. 5 col. pl. 8vo.* Added title-page in Russian.
    The large, as yet unfinished, work on the fauna of Rus-
sia, of which the present book dealing with birds of prey forms
a section, began to appear in 1911. The work is divided into
sections according to the main groups of the animal kingdom,
the first volume, dealing with birds (V. Bianchi's 'Colymbiformes et Procellariiformes'), appearing in 1911. The text is
printed in Russian, except the diagnoses, which are in Latin, and
the volumes are provided with both French and Russian title-
pages.
    The present livraison contains a survey of the order Falconi-
formes, with diagnosis, characterization and a list of the names
applied to the group ; further, a list of the most important
literature, tables for identification of subfamilies and genera,
and the matter concerning the genus Falco, with diagnosis,
characterization, and tables for identification of the species
and subspecies. Under each form we find synonymy, references
to the literature, a list of specimens in the museum, a diagnosis,
description, survey of its geographical distribution, and ecology.
    The coloured plates (signed B. B.) were executed by the
three-colour process.

MERREM, B.
333.   1786. Avium rariorum et minus cognitarum icones
et descriptiones collectæ et e Germanicis Latinæ factæ.
A Blasio Merrem. Io. Godofr. Müllerianus. *Lipsiæ.
2 parts in 1 vol. large 4to. — Part I. pp. [IV] + 20.
6 col. pl. (numb. I—VI). Part II. pp. [I] + p. 21—
45 + [1]. 6 col. pl. (numb. VII—XII).*
    A number of species of birds are described and figured in
this work, the text of which consists of discussions of the individual genus or species with references to the literature,
succeeded by a description of the bird figured. The title-pages
of the two parts differ somewhat.
    The plates are engravings coloured by hand (Pl. I—VI,
C. E. Eberlein, fec.; Pl. VII—XII, Eberlein, B. Merrem or
Berkenkamp del., G. G. Endner sc.).
    A German edition of the two parts had appeared in 1784—
86 under the title 'Beyträge zur besondern Geschichte der
Vögel'.

MERRIAM, C. H.
    1893. The hawks and owls of the United States in
their relation to agriculture. Prepared under the direction of C. Hart Merriam. *See Fisher, A. K.*

    1902. Smithsonian Institution. Harriman Alaska
Series. (Edited by C. Hart Merriam) ...
    Vol. I. pp. 1—118: Narrative of the expedition.
See Burroughs, J.
    Vol. II. pp. 205—234: Days among Alaska birds.
See Keeler, C. A.

MEYEN, F. J. F.
    1834. Novorum Actorum Academiæ Cæsareæ Leo-
poldino-Carolinæ Naturæ Curiosorum. Vol. XVI. Supplement I, sistens F. J. F. Meyenii observationes zoologicas, in itinere circum terram institutas, accedunt
Guil. Erichsonii et H. Burmeisteri, descriptiones et
icones insectorum a Meyenio in ista expeditione col-
lectorum *Added title-page in German.* - - < *pp. 59—
124:* Beiträge zur Zoologie, gesammelt auf einer Reise
um die Erde, von F. J. F. Meyen. Vierte Abhandlung.
Vögel >. *Vratislaviæ. 21 col. pl. (numb. VI—XXVI).
4to.*
    The report on this circumnavigation of the world was issued
in 1834—43 in four parts under the title, 'Reise um die Erde
ausgeführt auf, dem ... Seehandlungs-Schiffe Prinzess Louise,
commandirt von Captain W. Wendt ... 1830—32'. The first
two parts, 'Historischer Bericht', were issued separately in 1834
—35, while Part III, 'Zoologischer Bericht', 1834, was reprinted
from Vols. XVI—XVII, 1832—35, of the 'Nova Acta' mentioned in the above title, in which Part IV, 'Beiträge zur Botanik', was also published (in Vol. XIX, Supplement, I, 1843).
    On the recommendation of Alexander v. Humboldt, Meyen
took part in the journey as ship's surgeon. The chief places
visited were South America, the Sandwich Islands, and the
coast of China. Meyen made many observations on the physical
conditions, and collected several natural historical specimens
which, after his return, were partially treated by himself, for
instance the rather limited ornithological material dealt with
in the present section.
    The plates (lithographs coloured by hand, C. L. Müller
p[in]x., Lith. Inst.·d· K. L. C. Aca. v. Henry & Cohen in Bonn)
contain figures of altogether 24 species of birds.

MEYER, A. B.
    1887. Unser Auer-, Rackel- und Birkwild und
seine Abarten von A. B. Meyer. Mit einem Atlas
von ... colorirten Tafeln. Adolph W. Künast. *Wien.
2 vols. large 4to & (Atlas) large fol. —[Text]. pp.
XII + 95. Atlas. 17 col. pl. (numb. I—XVII in text
and on the cover and the title-page of the atlas).*
    An account of various forms of the genus Tetrao and their
gallinaceous birds, their variations and various hybrids of them,
based chiefly on the collections of the zoological museum at
Dresden.
    The plates are lithographs coloured by hand (Druck v. C.
Böhm, Berlin), executed from original water-colours by G.
Mützel, who also drew the figures on stone. M. Schneider,
Dresden, assisted in the colouring.

MEYER, B.
    1810. Taschenbuch der deutschen Vögelkunde,
oder kurze Beschreibung aller Vögel Deutschlands von
Meyer und Wolf. Friedrich Wilmans. *Frankfurt am
Main. 2 vols. 77 col. pl. 8vo. —* Vol. I, die Landvögel enthaltend. *pp. XVII + [I] + 1—310. 40 col.
pl.* Vol. II, Sumpf- und Wasservögel enthaltend. *pp.
XII + 311—614. 37 col. pl.*
    In 1809 seventeen out of a total of thirty parts had been
issued of Wolf and Meyer's large work in folio 'Naturgeschichte
der Vögel Deutschlands', etc. (Nürnberg 1805—21, 2 vols.,
and atlas, 180 col. pl.). In the present work the authors take
the advantage of their observations and experience to give a
brief survey of the birds of Germany with descriptions of

species, genera, and higher groups, and brief notes on the habits of the birds. The land-birds are treated by Wolf, while the birds dealt with in Vol. II are treated by Meyer.

The plates are hand-coloured. With the exception of the figures of birds on the frontispieces (J. M. Hergenröder pinx.; J. C. Bock and J. Nussbiegel sc.), the plates (G. P. Zwinger del.; J. C. Bock sculp.) contain only figures of heads and feet for the illustration of the distinguishing characters of the genera.

A supplement (Part III) to the present work was issued in 1822 (337).

1822. Zusätze und Berichtigungen zu Meyers und Wolfs Taschenbuch der deutschen Vögelkunde, nebst kurzer Beschreibung derjenigen Vögel, welche ausser Deutschland, in den übrigen Theilen von Europa vorkommen, als dritter Theil jenes Taschenbuchs von Bernhard Meyer. Mit einem vollständigen Register über das ganze Werk. H. L. Brönner. *Frankfurt a. M. pp. VI + 264. 8vo.*

A supplement to 'Taschenbuch der deutschen Vögelkunde', 1810 (336). It constitutes a third part of that work, to which it supplies a number of additions and corrections derived in part from C. J. Temminck, especially from his 'Manuel d'ornithologie', of the second edition of which Vols. I and II had appeared in 1820.

The volume further contains (pp. 245—264) 'Systematisches Verzeichniss der in den drei Theilen des Taschenbuchs enthaltenen Gattungen und Arten'.

MEYER, J. D.

1748—52. Angenehmer und nützlicher Zeit-Vertreib mit Betrachtung curioser Vorstellungen allerhand kriechender, fliegender und schwimmender, auf dem Land und im Wasser sich befindender und nährender Thiere, sowohl nach ihrer Gestalt und äusserlichen Beschaffenheit als auch nach der accuratest davon verfertigten Structur ihrer Scelete oder Bein-Körper, nebst einer deutlichen so physicalisch und anatomisch besonders aber osteologisch und mechanischen Beschreibung derselben nach der Natur gezeichnet, gemahlet, in Kupfer gestochen und verlegt von Johann Daniel Meyer. Gedruckt bei Johann Joseph Fleischmann. *Nürnberg. 2 vols. 100 col. pl. birds. large fol.* Title-page to Part II: Johann Daniel Meyers Vorstellungen allerley Thiere mit ihren Gerippen. — *Vol. I. 1748. pp. [VI] + 56 + [2]. 40 col. pl. birds (numb. IV—VI, X—XII, XVI—XXI, XXXII—XXXIV, XLV—XLVIII, LX—LXV, LXXV—LXXX, LXXXIV—LXXXVI, XCII—XCIV, XCVIII—C). Vol. II. 1752. pp. 28 + [2]. 60 col. pl. birds (numb. I—III, VII—IX, XIII—XV, XIX—XXI, XXV—XXX, XXXIV—XL, XLV—L, LV—LX, LXIV—LXX, LXXV—LXXX, LXXXV—XCI, XCVIII—C).*

This work, the first two parts of which are cited above, was issued in three parts in all (Part III, 1756) containing 100 (Part I), 100 (Part II), and 40 (Part III) plates (engravings coloured by hand) with figures of vertebrates, chiefly birds and mammals, the latter group having supplied the material for the figures in Part III. The figures were drawn and engraved by the editor of the work, who was a miniature painter, engraver, and art dealer at Nürnberg.

The text, printed in double columns, contains descriptions of the animals figured.

In the first two parts only a skeleton of the particular animal is shown on the same plate as the animal, or on the succeeding plate.

MICHIGAN AGRICULTURAL COLLEGE. DEPARTMENT OF ZOOLOGY AND PHYSIOLOGY.

1912. Special Bulletin. Michigan bird life ... *See Barrows, W. B.*

MIDDENDORFF, A. T. von.

1853. Reise in den äussersten Norden und Osten 339. Sibiriens ... 1843 und 1844. Mit allerhöchster Genehmigung auf Veranstaltung der Kaiserlichen Akademie der Wissenschaften zu St. Petersburg ausgeführt und in Verbindung mit vielen Gelehrten herausgegeben von A. Th. v. Middendorff. Vol. II. Zoologie. Part II. Säugethiere, Vögel und Amphibien. Bearbeitet von A. Th. v. Middendorff. <-- *pp. 124—246:* B. Vögel >. Kaiserliche Akademie der Wissenschaften. *St. Petersburg. 13 col. pl. (numb. XIII—XXV). 4to.*

This travel report was published in four volumes in 1847—75.

The present ornithological section treats of the birds collected and observed, the number of which amounts to 210 species, forty being represented by figures on the plates (lithographs, drawn from Nature by W. Pape).

MILET DE MUREAU, L. M. A. D. de.

1797. Voyage de La Pérouse autour du monde. ... rédigé par M. L. A. Milet-Mureau. *See Lapérouse, J. F. de G. de.*

MILLAIS, J. G.

1902. The natural history of the British surface- 340. feeding ducks By J. G. Millais ... Longmans, Green, and Co. *London. pp. XIV + 107. 65 pl. (41 col. (numb. I—XLI), 6 photograv.). large 4to.*

An account, based on personal observations, of the habits and modes of life of the forms of birds treated in the book and of the circumstances connected with their periodical changes of plumage.

The figures of the birds are mostly drawn from specimens in the author's own collection; a few rare forms are figured from specimens in the collection of Walter Rothschild, while Heatley Noble's collection was used for the eggs and young birds in down.

The illustrations were executed from drawings by the author or from photographs, with the exception of the water-colour drawings for eight of the coloured plates made by A. Thorburn. The coloured plates are mostly executed in chromo-lithography (Litho. W. Greve, Berlin), a few by the three-colour process (André & Sleigh, Bushey).

The present copy is No. 344 of a large paper edition, of which 600 copies were printed.

1907. Newfoundland and its untrodden ways. By 341. J. G. Millais ... Longmans, Green and Co. *London. pp. XVI + 340. 8 pl. birds (1 col.). 2 maps. large 8vo.*

An account of the author's journey and hunting experiences in Newfoundland, with many particulars of the natural history of its wild animals and birds.

The volume is illustrated with many plates, executed from photographs and from drawings by the author. To the latter category belong the plates with figures of birds.

1913. British diving ducks. By J. G. Millais ... 342. Longmans, Green and Co. *London. 2 vols. 74 pl. (39 col.). large 4to. — Vol. I. ... pp. XV + 141. 32 pl. (22 (1 pl. eggs) col.). Vol. II ... pp. XII + 164. 42 pl. (17 (1 pl. eggs) col.).*

The author studied ducks for many years with a view to collecting material for the life history of these birds and the different plumages they pass during their lifetime. These studies took a great deal of time, and necessitated several journeys. Most of the birds figured in the work were shot or collected by the author himself, while in addition, according to his own statement, a study of E. Lehn Schiøler's collection of Arctic and Palæarctic ducks at Copenhagen was of special advantage to him.

Under each form the author gives synonyms and local names, a description of the eggs and the two sexes at different ages, and an account of the distribution, breeding range and habits of the bird.

The figures of the plates were made by four artists, Archibald Thorburn, O. Murray Dixon, H. Grønvold, and the author. The coloured plates, several of which represent the adult birds in their natural surroundings, are beautiful and are excellently reproduced by Albert Frisch, Berlin (collotypes), and André & Sleigh of Bushey (three-colour prints). In addition to the coloured plates, Vol. I contains eight photogravures and two collotypes, and Vol. II six photogravures and nineteen collotypes showing the plumages of the ducks and episodes of their lives, for which the author supplied the drawings.

The work was printed in four hundred and fifty copies only, of which the present are No. 5 (Vol. I) and No. 2 (Vol. II).

MILNE EDWARDS, A.
343.   *1893.* Centenaire de la fondation du Muséum d'Histoire Naturelle 10 juin 1793 — 10 juin 1893. Volume commémoratif publié par les professeurs du muséum. <- - *pp. 187—252:* Notice sur quelques espèces d'oiseaux actuellement éteintes qui se trouvent représentées dans les collections du Muséum d'Histoire Naturelle, par A. Milne-Edwards, et E. Oustalet >. Imprimerie Nationale. *Paris. 5 col. pl. (numb. I—V). large 4to.*

The valuable collections in the Muséum d'Histoire Naturelle in Paris contain among their treasures specimens of bird forms which have become extinct in historic times. Six such species are treated in the present paper, the Bourbon Parrot (Mascarinus Duboisi), the Bourbon Starling (Fregilupus varius), the Hackled Pigeon of Mauritius (Alectroenas nitidissima), the Labrador Duck (Camptolæmus labradorius), the Black Emu (Dromaius ater), and the Great Auk (Alca impennis). The five species first mentioned are reproduced on the coloured plates (lithographs, coloured by hand; Imprimerie Nationale), drawn by J. G. Keulemans.

MITCHELL, D. W.
1856—59. Zoological sketches ... [Parts I—VII]. *See Wolf, Joseph, 1856—67.*

MONTAGU, G.
344.   *1013.* Supplement to the Ornithological Dictionary, or synopsis of British birds. By George Montagu. S. Bagster. *London. pp. VI + [I] + [47I] + [2]. 24 pl. 8vo.*

In 1802 Montagu issued his notable work, 'Ornithological dictionary; or, alphabetical synopsis of British birds' (London, 2 vols., 8vo), and in the present volume he published the results of his continued observations on the characters and habits of British birds.

The greater part of the work consists of 'Supplement to the Ornithological Dictionary', arranged, as in the main work, alphabetically according to the vernacular names of the species. Then follows an 'Appendix' and a couple of smaller sections, — 'Definition of the parts of extraordinary tracheæ, belonging to some species of aquatic birds', and 'Direction for amputating the wing of a bird in a menagerie', while the volume concludes with 'Catalogue of additions and alterations to be made in the original list of British birds'.

The plates (engravings) were drawn and engraved by Eliza Dorville.

MOQUIN-TANDON, C. H. B. A.
1841. Histoire naturelle des Îles Canaries ... Vol. II. Part II ... Ornithologie canarienne. *See Webb, P. B.*

1857. Iconographie des perroquets ... [Introduction]. *See Souancé, C. de,* 1857—58.

MORRIS, B. R.
1855. British game birds and wildfowl. By Beverley R. Morris ... Illustrated with ... coloured plates. Groombridge and Sons. *London. pp. IV + 252. 60 col. pl. 4to.* *3*

A collection of accounts of British game birds with a statement of the distribution and habits of the species and descriptions of the birds, their eggs and nests, and notes on their value as articles of food.

Most of the forms treated are figured on the hand-coloured plates (wood-engravings), made by B. Fawcett, who also printed the work, which has subsequently been issued in several editions, — 2nd edition, 1873, 3rd edition, 1881; 4th edition, revised and corrected by W. B. Tegetmeier, 1895, 2 vols.

MORRIS, F. O.
1903. A history of British birds. Fifth edition revised and brought up to date, with an appendix of recently added species, and with ... plates specially corrected for this edition, and all coloured by hand. By F. O. Morris. John C. Nimmo. *London. 6 vols. 400 col. pl. 4to.* — Vol. I. *pp. XX + 318. 63 col. pl.* Vol. II. *pp. VI + 288. 69 col. pl.* Vol. III. *pp. IV + 281. 63 col. pl.* Vol. IV. *pp. VI + 258. 68 col. pl.* Vol. V. *pp. IV + 232. 69 col. pl.* Vol. VI. *pp. IV + 252. 68 col. pl.* *3*

This comprehensive and very popular work appeared for the first time in 1850—57, has since then passed through several editions owing to its great popularity, although it suffers from defects, notably as regards accuracy.

The work deals broadly with individual species, for instance as regards their distribution, occurrence in the British Isles, and habits, the birds themselves and their eggs being also described.

The number of species included in the work increased gradually as new species were added to British avifauna; thus in the present edition a number of new species have been treated by H. Kirke Swann in an appendix in Vol. VI, pp. 200 —217.

A good feature of the work is the many figures of British birds shown on its hand-coloured plates, for which the woodblocks were originally engraved by the printer of the first edition, B. Fawcett, largely from drawings by Richard Alington. The first edition contained 357 plates, which number was increased in the 4th edition, 1895—96, to 394, while the present edition contains six extra plates.

According to Mullens and Swann (574, p. 417), the present edition was prepared by J. C. Nimmo, but issued by Routledge & Sons.

MUELLER, J.
1799—1800. Die vorzüglichsten Sing-Vögel Teutschlands mit ihren Nestern und Eyern nach der Natur abgebildet und aus eigener Erfahrung beschrieben von Johannes Müller. Mit ... ausgemahlten Kupfertafeln. Adam Gottlieb Schneider und Weigel. *Nürnberg. pp. [VII] + 72. 26 col. pl. (front. + Nos. (in text) I—XXV). 4to.*

This work was issued in four parts, each containing six (Part 4 seven) plates (inferior hand-coloured engravings) with an accompanying text which gives brief descriptions of the species figured, their habits, breeding seasons, capture, and food in captivity.

The volume opens with two title-pages, dated 1800 and 1799 respectively, and an engraved title with a life-size picture of a young nightingale.

In the volume is bound a prospectus with a list of the plates in Part 4, and a reply by the author to a review of the first Part of the present work published in 'Allgemeine Literatur-Zeitung', Jena 1799, No. 382 (columns 559—560).

MUELLER, O. F.

. *1806.* Zoologia Danica seu animalium Daniæ et Norvegiæ rariorum ac minus notorum descriptiones et historia. Vol. IV. Explicationi iconum fasciculi quarti ejusdem operis inserviens. Auctore Othone Friderico Müller. Descripserunt et tabulas dederunt P. C. Abildgaard, J. S. Holten, M. Vahl, J. Rathke. N. Christensen. *Havniæ. pp. [VI] + 46. 4 col. pl. birds (numb. CXXI—CXXII, CXXXVI, CL). fol.*

As early as 1777—80 Müller had issued two volumes, each containing forty coloured plates with drawings of rare and unknown Danish and Norwegian animal species — 'Zoologiæ Danicæ seu animalium Daniæ et Norvegiæ rariorum ac minus notorum icones' (Havniæ, folio), which was also issued with a Danish text and title. A more comprehensive text with descriptions of these plates, 'Zoologia Danica seu animalium ... descriptiones et historia', appeared in two volumes in 1779—84 (I: Havniæ et Lipsiæ, II: Lipsiæ, 8vo), but in 1776 Müller had already issued his 'Zoologiæ Danicæ prodromus', etc., which may be regarded as part of this work.

A somewhat enlarged folio edition of the first volume of the text with the accompanying plates of 'Zoologia Danica' was published in Danish in 1781 (Kiøbenhavn) and in German in 1783(Leipzig).

After Müller's death, his brother, C. F. Müller, re-issued, in 1788, the two first parts of the plates and the accompanying text in a folio edition. These two volumes were succeeded, in 1789, by a third volume by P. C. Abildgaard and later by the fourth volume cited above which, with its forty plates, brings up the total number of the plates to 160.

It is chiefly the lower animals which have been described and figured by Müller, and only the present Vol. IV contains plates with figures of birds.

Most of the drawings for the hand-coloured engravings of the plates, which in the last two parts are nearly all unsigned, are said to have been executed by O. F. Müller's brother, 'Kongelig Dessinateur og Hofkobberstikker' C. F. Müller, who is also said to have engraved part of the plates, although J. G. Friedrich, who was called to Denmark by O. F. Müller especially to engrave pictures of natural objects, engraved many of the plates in Parts 1 and 2.

Another copy of Vol. IV of this work differs from that cited here only in the colouring of the plates.

One hundred and twenty of the original drawings for the plates of this work are deposited in Det Kongelige Bibliotek of Copenhagen (Ny Kgl. Samling, 1558, folio).

MUELLER, P. L. S.

1773. Des Ritters Carl von Linné ... vollständiges Natursystem nach der zwölften lateinischen Ausgabe und nach Anleitung des holländischen Houttuynischen Werks mit einer ausführlichen Erklärung ausgefertiget von Philipp Ludwig Statius Müller. Part II. Von den Vögeln. Nebst ... Kupfertafeln. Gabriel Nicolaus Raspe. *Nürnberg.* [Text]. *pp. [XVI] + 638 + [34]. 8vo.* [Plates]. *28 pl. (numb. I—XXVIII). obl. fol.*

This work was issued in six parts and one volume containing supplements and index, 1773—76. It is based chiefly on the zoological section of M. Houttuyn's 'Natuurlyke historie, of uitvoerige beschryving der dieren, planten en mineraalen, volgens het samenstel van den Heer Linnæus', 1761—73 (the whole work : 1761—85) (Amsterdam, 8vo), and like the latter, has not much in common with the edition mentioned in 'Systema naturæ', apart from the Linnean classification.

The figures of the insignificant plates (engravings) are derived from the Dutch work mentioned above, the figures of which have chiefly been taken from other works.

The plates of the present copy have been bound with the plates for Part I, 'Von den säugenden Thieren', 1773.

1781. Des Ritters Carl von Linné Lehr-Buch über

das Natur-System so weit es das Thierreich angehet. In einem vollständigen Auszuge der Müllerischen Ausgabe. [Von Höslin]. Vol. I. <- - *pp. 187—475:* Zwote Classe. Die Geschichte der Vögel >. Gabriel Nicolaus Raspe. *Nürnberg. 6 col. pl. (numb. XI—XVI). 8vo.*

An extract from Ph. L. S. Müller's work 'Des Ritters Carl von Linné ... vollständiges Natursystem', etc., published in 1773 —76 (349).

It was issued in 1781—82 in two volumes with 42 plates (engravings) in all, in the main coloured (by hand), but poorly executed.

MUELLER, S.

1839—44. Verhandelingen over de natuurlijke ge- *351.* schiedenis der Nederlandsche overzeesche bezittingen, door de leden der Natuurkundige Commissie in Indië en andere schrijvers. Uitgegeven ... door C. J. Temminck. Zoologie. Geredigeerd door J. A. Susanna. <- - [Aves]. Door Sal. Müller en Herm. Schlegel >. In commissie bij S. en J. Luchtmans. *Leiden. pp. 72. 14 col. pl. (numb. I, II, 1—11, 4bis). fol.*

The ornithological section of a volume containing papers on the zoology of the Dutch East Indies. Besides the present volume of this work, which was issued in 1839—45, a volume entitled 'Land- en volkenkunde' and another volume, 'Botanie. Kruidkunde', were issued.

The present section consists of six papers, in which a series of birds and groups of birds, such as Buceros and Nectariniæ, are described and figured.

Of the plates (lithographs coloured by hand, A. Arnz & Co. col.) two (I—II) were executed from drawings by J. Wolf ; of the remainder of the plates a few are signed H. Schlegel, while the majority are signed A. S. Mulder in lap. del., J. M. Kierdorff, imp.

MURPHY, R. C.

1936. Oceanic birds of South America. A study *352.* of species of the related coasts and seas, including the American quadrant of Antarctica, based upon the Brewster-Sanford collection in the American Museum of Natural History. By Robert Cushman Murphy. Illustrated from paintings by Francis L. Jaques, photographs, maps, and other drawings. The American Museum of Natural History. *New York. 2 vols. 88 pl. large 8vo. — Vol. I. pp. XXII + [II] + 1—640. text-figs. 44 pl.· (6 col., 38 uncol. (numb. 1—38)). Vol. II. pp. [IV] + 641—1245 + [1]. text-figs. 44 pl. (10 col., 34 uncol. (numb. 39—72)).*

The material dealt with in the present work was procured in different ways, but mostly on a journey of collection made in 1912—17 by Rollo Howard Beck.

The work falls into two sections, of which Part I (pp. 1— 322), 'The physical environment', treats of subjects such as geographical background, hydrology in relation to oceanic birds, and an ornithological circumnavigation of South America. The remainder of the work, II, 'The oceanic birds', is devoted to a systematic account of the birds belonging to the orders Sphenisciformes, Procellariiformes, Pelecaniformes, Anseriformes, and Charadriiformes, with a detailed treatment of the higher groups and individual forms. Under the latter the vernacular names, characters, and measurements are given, and also descriptions of the eggs, with measurements, and information about the geographical distribution of the birds. In addition a number of data are given concerning each form, its history, habits, and affinities.

The coloured plates are executed by the four-colour process (engraved and printed by the Quadri-Color Company, Jamaica, L. I., New York).

The work was printed in 1200 copies, of which the present is No. 424.

MURRAY, J.
1880. Report on the birds collected during the voyage of H. M. S. Challenger ... 1873—76. *See Sclater, P. L.*

MUSÉE DU CONGO. ANNALES.
1905. Zoologie. Série IV. Vol. I. Fasc. I. Remarques sur l'ornithologie de l'État indépendant du Congo ... *See Dubois, A.*

MUSEU GOELDI (MUSEU PARAENSE) DE HISTORIA NATURAL E ETHNOGRAPHIA. BELEM (PARÁ).
1900—06. Album de aves Amazonicas ... *See Goeldi, E. A.*

MUSÉUM D'HISTOIRE NATURELLE. PARIS.
1801. La Ménagerie du Muséum Nationale d'Histoire Naturelle ... *See Lacépède, B. G. É. de la V.*

353.   *1839* —► Archives du Muséum d'Histoire Naturelle, publiées par les professeurs-administrateurs de cet établissement. (1865—1914: Nouvelles Archives ...; 1928 —►: Archives du Muséum National d'Histoire Naturelle ...). Gide (some vols.: Gide et J. Baudry) (1839—61), L. Guérin (1865—67), L. Guérin et Cie (1868—74), G. Masson (1878—93), Masson et Cie (1896 —►). *Paris. text-figs. plates. 4to.*
This serial from the Muséum d'Histoire Naturelle in Paris was begun as a continuation of the 'Annales' (Vols. I—XXI, 1802—27), 'Mémoires' (Vols. I—XX, 1815—32), and 'Nouvelles Annales' (Vols. I—IV, 1832—35) issued by the Museum.
The volumes are grouped in series, which mostly consist of ten volumes each, — : 'Archives', Vols I—X, 1839—61 ; 'Nouvelles Archives', Vols. I—X, 1865—74 ; Sér. II, Vols. I—X, 1878—88 ; Sér. III, Vols. I—X, 1889—98[—99] ; Sér. IV, Vols. I—X, 1899 [i. e. 1900]—1908 [i. e. 1909] ; Sér. V, Vols. I—VI, 1909—14 ; 'Archives', Sér. VI, Vols. I —►, 1926 —► In 1937 the publication, which had been suspended from 1915 —25, had reached volume 14 of the sixth series.
A great amount of natural historical matter has been published in this stately series of volumes, among which is also a large amount of ornithological matter, supplied by authors such as J. Verreaux, Armand David, and É. Oustalet.
These treatises are illustrated with a number (c. 70) of coloured plates with figures of birds, found in the volumes issued from 1844—1903. The plates (the early ones engravings coloured by hand, the more recent ones lithographs coloured by hand) were chiefly executed from drawings at first by Oudart and J. Werner (Guyard and Annedouche sc.), later by J. Huet and J. G. Keulemans. Most of the early ones were printed by Becquet, the recent ones by Lemercier.

1842. Le Jardin des Plantes. Description ... du Muséum d'Histoire Naturelle, de la Ménagerie ... *See Bernard, P.*

1893. Centenaire de la fondation du Muséum d'Histoire Naturelle ... pp. 187—252: Notice sur quelques espèces d'oiseaux actuellement éteintes qui se trouvent représentées dans les collections du Muséum d'Histoire Naturelle. *See Milne Edwards, A.*

MUSEUM DER NATURGESCHICHTE HELVETIENS.
1808—20. [Zoological section]. Vol. I. *See Meisner, C. F. A.*

MYLIUS-ERICHSEN, L.
1910. Danmark-Ekspeditionen til Grønlands Nordøstkyst 1906—1908 under Ledelse af L. Mylius-Erich-

sen. Vol. V. pp. 1—200: The terrestrial mammals and birds of North-East Greenland. pp. 93—199: Birds. *See Manniche, A. L. V.*

NADEŽDA, Voyage of the.
1810—14. Reise um die Welt ... 1803—06 ... auf den Schiffen Nadeshda und Newa ... *See Krusenstern, A. J. von.*

NATIONAL ANTARCTIC EXPEDITION 1901—04.
1907. Natural history. Vol. II. Zoology ... II. Aves. *See Wilson, E. A.*

NATURAL HISTORY SOCIETY OF NORTHUMBERLAND, DURHAM, AND NEWCASTLE-UPON-TYNE.
1874. Natural History Transactions of Northumberland and Durham; being papers read at the meetings of the ... Society ... 1873. Vol. VI. A catalogue of the birds of Northumberland and Durham. *See Hancock, J.*

NATURALIST'S LIBRARY, THE.
1833—43. The Naturalist's Library. Edited by William Jardine. Vols. XIV—XXVII. Ornithology ... *See Jardine, W.*

NATURALIST'S MISCELLANY, THE.
1789—1813. The naturalist's miscellany: or coloured figures of natural objects ... *See Shaw, G.*

NATURWISSENSCHAFTLICHER VEREIN IN HAMBURG.
1852. Abhandlungen aus dem Gebiete der Naturwissenschaften herausgegeben von dem ... Verein ... Vol. II. Part II. pp. 1—56: Beitrag zur Ornithologie Westafrica's. *See Hartlaub, C. J. G.*

NAUMANN, J. A.
[*1795*—] *1797—1805.* Naturgeschichte der Land- und Wasser-Vögel des nördlichen Deutschlands und angränzender Länder, nach eignen Erfahrungen entworfen, und nach dem Leben gezeichnet von Johann Andreas Naumann. Auf Kosten des Verfassers und in Kommission bei J. A. Aue. *Köthen.* [Text]. *4 vols. in 3. Nachtrag. 2 parts in 1 vol. 8vo.* [Atlas]. *165 pl. (164 col.). fol.* — Vol. I [1795—] 1797. *pp.* [*XII*] + 249 + [7]. *front. (portrait). 48 col. pl. (numb. I—XLVIII).* Vol. II. [1798—] 1799. *pp.* [*VI*] + 106 + [2]. *front. (portrait). 15 pl. (14 col.; numb. I—XI, XIII—XV, XVII (= XVI, plain); pl. XII missing).* Vol. III. 1799 [—1802]. *pp. 480. front. (portrait). 70 col. pl. (numb. I—XLIII, XLV—LXXII; pl. XLIV and LXXII missing).* Vol. IV. [1802—] 1803. *pp.* [*IV*] + 280 + [*I*]. *32 col. pl. (numb. I—XXXII).* Nachtrag. Part I [—II]. 1804 [—05]. *pp. 110.*
This work was published in 21 parts and a supplement comprising 8 parts, the last two of which appeared in 1817. The parts forming the supplements, of which only the first two are found in the present copy, consist of altogether 462 pages of text. The first three were accompanied by eight folio plates each, thus bringing the total number of plates of this

kind up to 192 (168 in the main work and 24 in the supplements). However, only three copies of the work with the full number of plates are known, in addition to a small number of more or less complete copies (788).

The last five supplemental parts were issued with eight plates in 8vo each, the plates for the whole preceding part of the work being also issued in that format. The total number of plates in this edition is therefore 232, or rather 233, since folio plate XX in the 'Nachträge' had to be reproduced on two plates in the 8vo edition.

In the present copy the first two volumes of the text have been bound in one, and the plates also in one volume without a title-page, no special title-page having ever appeared.

The parts containing the text, all of which except Vol. III, Part 9, have a separate title-page, are distributed as follows over the various volumes: Vol. I, Parts 1—6; Vol. II, Parts 1—2; Vol. III, Parts 1—9; and Vol. IV, Parts 1—4.

In addition to the above-mentioned title-page another one is found in Vol. I, and this is used both for the volume as a whole and the individual parts. It runs as follows: 'Johann Andreas Naumann's ausführliche Beschreibung aller Wald- Feld- und Wasser-Vögel, welche sich in den Anhaltischen Fürstenthümern und einigen umliegenden Gegenden aufhalten und durchziehen'

Thus the· present copy contains all the title-pages for Vol. I, although Paul Leverkühn (788, p. 61) says: 'doch giebt es kaum ein Exemplar des Werkes, das alle Doppeltitel besitzt.'

In Vol. I, Part 1, the subtitle-page is dated Leipzig, 1795, 'Auf Kosten des Verfassers und in Commission bey Friedrich Osterloh', while in Vol. I, Part 2, same place and year, it has been altered to 'Auf Kosten des Verfassers'. On the other hand, the final title-page cited above, is dated 1796 (Köthen) in these two parts.

From and including Vol. IV, Part 4, 1803, 'und Friedrich Naumann' is added after 'Johann Andreas Naumann' on the title-page.

The text describes the birds figured and their habits. The plates, engravings coloured by hand, were drawn, engraved, and coloured by J. A. Naumann's son, Johann Friedrich Naumann; Pl. I—XVI (Vol. I, Parts 1—2), however, were engraved by Osterloh (Halæ). The execution of the plates might have been better, but shows increasing ability as the work proceeds.

Two new editions of the work were issued, in 1822—60 (355) and in 1896—1905 (356).

1822—60. Johann Andreas Naumann's Naturgeschichte der Vögel Deutschlands, nach eigenen Erfahrungen entworfen. Durchaus umgearbeitet, systematisch geordnet, sehr vermehrt, vervollständigt, und mit getreu nach der Natur eigenhändig gezeichneten und gestochenen Abbildungen aller Vögel, nebst ihren Hauptverschiedenheiten, aufs Neue herausgegeben von dessen Sohne Johann Friedrich Naumann. Ernst Fleischer. *Leipzig.* (Dreizehnter Theil, Schluss: Hoffmann. *Stuttgart*). *13 vols. 404 pl. (396 col. (5 front. + Nos. 1—391)). 8vo.*

According to Paul Leverkühn (788, p. 37), the first volume of this work was originally published in 1820 by Gerhard Fleischer, while Ernst Fleischer, who published the remaining eleven volumes, published a new title-page for Vol. I or re-issued the whole volume.

After the publication of the twelfth volume in 1844 Naumann began the issue of a new supplementary volume (Dreizehnter Theil), which appeared in parts, until publication ceased at Naumann's death in 1857. The first section of this supplementary volume consists of eight parts (pp. 484 + [1]), the first seven of which (pp. 1—466) are stated to have been issued in 1845—54. It is provided with a provisional title-page which runs as follows, 'J. A. Naumann's Naturgeschichte der Vögel Deutschlands. Herausgegeben von dessen Sohne J. F. Naumann. Dreizehnter Theil: Nachträge, Zusätze und Verbesserungen.'

After Naumann's death Vol. XIII was completed by the

addition of a sequel (pp. 316; pl. 371—391) dated 1860 and entitled 'J. A. Naumann's Naturgeschichte der Vögel Deutschlands. Fortsetzung der Nachträge, Zusätze und Verbesserungen von J. H. Blasius, Ed. Baldamus und Fr. Sturm. Dreizehnter Theil, Schluss.' From Naumann's hand only six finished copper-plates, a plate not yet coloured, and drawings by hand of three forms of birds were available for this continuation. Blasius and Baldamus wrote the text, while Sturm made the designs for the other figures required. Several of the plates were also engraved by him.

As a whole this work provides a comprehensive account of the natural history of German birds. It opens with a section, 'Die Vögel im Allgemeinen', the first chapter of which (Vol. I, pp. 23—52), 'Von der eigenthümlichen Organisation der Vögel' was written by Chr. L. Nitzsch. Otherwise the text contains a brief description and notes on genera and higher groups, while under the individual forms the subject-matter has been grouped under headings such as specific characters, description, habitat, properties, food, reproduction, enemies, hunting, benefit and injury. These subjects are treated in much greater detail than in the original work, which appeared in 1795—1817 (354). The present revised edition is therefore entirely independent of the original issue.

Several of the figures in this work were used by N. Kjærbølling as an aid in preparing the plates for 'Icones ornithologiæ Scandinavicæ' (246, note).

1896—1905. Naumann, Naturgeschichte der Vögel Mitteleuropas. Neu bearbeitet von G. Berg, R. Blasius ... Wurm. Herausgegeben von Carl R. Hennicke. Fr. Eugen Köhler. *Gera-Untermhaus. 12 vols. textfigs. 449 pl. (439 col.). large 4to.* — Vol. I. [1904—] 1905. (Drosseln). *pp. XLVI + [V] + 164 + 253. 32 pl. (numb. 1—32; 30 col. (numb. 3—32; 2 pl. eggs (numb. 31—32)). Vol. II. [1897]. (Grasmücken, Timalien, Meisen und Baumläufer). pp. IV + 340. 30 col. pl. (numb. 1—28, 1a, 11a; 3 pl. eggs (numb. 26—28)). Vol. III. [1899—1900]. (Lerchen, Stelzen, Waldsänger und Finkenvögel). pp. VI + 393. 48 col. pl. (numb. 1—48; 5 pl. eggs. (numb. 44—48)). Vol. IV [1900—01]. (Stärlinge, Stare, Pirole, Rabenvögel, Würger, Fliegenfänger, Schwalbenvögel, Segler, Tagschläfer, Spechte, Bienenfresser, Eisvögel, Racken, Hopfe, Kuckucke). pp. VI + 432. 49 col. pl. (numb. 1—30, 32 [= 31], 32—49; 5 pl. eggs (numb. 45—49)). Vol. V. [1898—99]. (Raubvögel). pp. IV + 334. 75 pl. (numb. 1—75; 71 col. (numb. 1—71); 6 pl. eggs (numb. 65—66, 78—81)). Vol. VI. [1896—97]. (Taubenvögel, Hühnervögel, Reiher, Flamingos und Störche). pp. [IV] + 337. 32 pl. (numb. 1—32; 31 col. (numb. 1—26, 28—32); 1 pl. eggs (numb. 32)). Vol. VII. [1898—99]. (Ibisse, Flughühner, Trappen, Kraniche, Rallen). pp. [IV] + 207. 20 'col. pl. (numb. 1—20; 3 pl. eggs (numb. 17—19)). Vol. VIII. [1902]. (Regenpfeifer, Stelzenläufer, Wassertreter, Strandläufer). pp. [IV] + 276. 28 col. pl. (numb. 1—28; 4 pl. eggs (numb. 25—28)). Vol. IX. [1902]. (Wasserläufer, Schnepfen, Schwäne, Gänse). pp. [IV] + 408. 34 col. pl. (numb. 1—34; 4 pl. eggs (numb. 31—34)). Vol. X. [1901—02]. (Enten). pp. [IV] + 307. 29 col. pl. (numb. 1—29). Vol. XI. [1903]. (Pelikane, Fregattvögel, Tölpel, Fluss-Scharben, Tropikvögel, Möwen). pp. VI + 343. 42 col. pl. (numb. 1—42; 10 pl. eggs (numb. 33—42)). Vol. XII. [1903]. (Sturmvögel, Steissfüsse, Seetaucher, Flügeltaucher). Anhang: Über den Haushalt der nordischen Seevögel Europas. pp. [IV] + 274 + [2]. 30 pl. (numb. 1—26, 17a—d; 27 col. (numb. 1—17, 17b, 18—26; 6 pl. eggs (numb. 17b, 22—26)).*

356.

22

This new revised and enlarged edition of Naumann's classic work, of which two editions had previously been issued, in 1795—1817 (354) and 1822—60 (355) respectively, was published in 154 Lieferungen (Nos. 1—150, 149 a, 149 b, 150 a, 150 b).

The work was the result of the collaboration of a staff of about forty, and it is therefore hardly so uniform in construction as the earlier editions.

The old text from J. F. Naumann's edition in 1822—60 has been preserved unaltered, while corrections have been made by means of footnotes. The additions, which bring the account up to date, are inserted in the text in square brackets. The text of Vol. I, pp. IX—XLVI, written by Paul Leverkühn, was also issued as a reprint in 1904 under the title, 'Biographisches über die drei Naumanns und bibliographisches über ihre Werke', etc. (788), and the 'Anhang' in Vol. XII (pp. 259—269), entitled 'Über den Haushalt der nordischen Seevögel Europas', is a reprint of a work by J. F. Naumann from 1824.

The figures for all the plates (Lith. Anst. Fr. Eugen Köhler, Gera-Untermhaus) have been re-drawn, and show the birds in their natural surroundings. Among the many artists who assisted in the execution of the plates are Bruno Geisler, A. Goering, O. Kleinschmidt, J. G. Keulemans, E. de Maes, Stefan von Nécsey, and O. von Riesenthal.

In addition to birds, the eggs of all species with varicoloured eggs are figured on a series of special plates (A. Reichert, pinx.). The figures of the eggs, based on Eugène Rey's collection, were used in 1899—1905 in a work by Rey (cf. 419).

A French edition (pp. 24, 413 col. pl., fol.) by A. Bouvier was issued in Paris in 1910 under the title 'Iconographie d'oiseaux d'Europe et de leurs oeufs', etc.

On the basis of the volume on the birds of prey, Vol. V, Hennicke issued a small account of this group in 1903 (206).

NAUMANN, J. F.

1803—05. Naturgeschichte der Land- und Wasser-Vögel des nördlichen Deutschlands und angränzender Länder ... Vol. IV. Part 4, & Nachtrag, Parts 1—2. See Naumann, J. A., 1795—1805.

357. *1818—28.* Die Eier der Vögel Deutschlands und der benachbarten Länder in naturgetreuen Abbildungen und Beschreibungen nebst einer tabellarischen Uebersicht der Naturgeschichte der hier vorkommenden Vögel von Johann Friedrich Naumann und Christian Adolph Buhle. Karl August Kümmel. *Halle. 5 parts in 1 vol. 10 col. pl. small fol.* — Part I. 1818. *pp. [III] + VI + 17 + [1]. 2 col. pl. (numb. I—II).* Part II. 1823. *pp. XII + 17. 2 col. pl. (numb. III—IV).* Part III. 1826. *pp. VIII + 17. 2 col. pl. (numb. V—VI).* Part IV. *1828. pp. IX + 15. 2 col. pl. (numb. VII—VIII).* Part V. 1928. *pp. X + 17 + 4. 2 col. pl. (numb. IX—X).*

The separate parts of this work consist of two sections, the first of which, paginated with Roman numerals, treats of general subjects relative to birds, notably their breeding habits, e. g. 'Die Nester der Vögel', 'Bemerkungen über die Klasse der Vögel und die äussere Form der Eier', 'Über die Brutgeschäft der Vögel', and 'Beschreibung der inneren Theile des Eies und der Bildung des Fetus'.

The section of the parts paginated with Arabic numerals contains the text for the figures on the plates, the two opposite pages being divided into six columns with the following headings: 'Namen der Gattungen, Arten und Schriftsteller', 'Kennzeichen der Arten', 'Aufenthalt', 'Nahrung', 'Nestbau', and 'Beschreibung der Eier'.

Each of the hand-coloured plates (engravings) contains many (about 20) figures of eggs, executed by J. F. Naumann from nature.

As a sort of new edition of this work Fürchtegott Grässner issued 'Die Vögel Deutschlands und ihre Eier' (Halle 1860, pp. 215, 10 col. pl., 4to; new cheap edition in 1865; third

edition, 'Die Vögel von Mittel-Europa und ihre Eier', 1880, 24 col. pl.).

1822—60. Johann Andreas Naumann's Naturgeschichte der Vögel Deutschlands ... aufs Neue herausgegeben von dessen Sohne Johann Friedrich Naumann. See Naumann, J. A.

1896—1905. Naumann, Naturgeschichte der Vögel Mitteleuropas ... See Naumann, J. A.

NAUMANNIA.

[1850?] 1851—58. Naumannia. Archiv (Jahrgang 1855—58: Journal) für die Ornithologie, vorzugsweise Europa's. Organ der deutschen Ornithologen-Gesellschaft. Herausgegeben (Jahrgang 1855—58: Redigirt) von Eduard Baldamus. Hofbuchdruckerei Zu Guttenberg (1851—52, Part I), Hoffmann (1852, Part II — 1854). *Stuttgart.* Gebrüder Katz (1855—56). *Dessau.* Voigt & Günther (1857—58). *Leipzig. 8 vols. plates. 8vo.*

The preface to the first number of this periodical is dated September, 1849, but it does not appear in Hinrichs' 'Verzeichniss der Bücher', etc., before 1850, ([I]), p. 159).

The periodical was issued, as far as possible, in four annual parts. These contained papers by well-known ornithologists of Germany and the neighbouring countries; thus, in addition to the editor, J. F. Naumann, Chr. L. Brehm, Alfred Brehm, Th. v. Heuglin, N. Kjærbølling, Hermann Schlegel, G. Thienemann, G. Hartlaub, C. L. Bonaparte, J. H. Blasius, and others contributed.

In 1860 the periodical was merged with the 'Journal für Ornithologie' (239).

During its short lifetime a number of plates (altogether 31), mostly coloured (lithographs) were published in it. They were executed from drawings by Th. v. Heuglin, Baedeker, B. Altum, J. F. Naumann, E. Baldamus, and others (Kirn, J. Hoffmann lith.).

NAUMBURG, E. M. B.

1930. The birds of Matto Grosso, Brazil. A report on the birds secured by the Roosevelt-Rondon expedition. By Elsie M. B. Naumburg. With field notes by George K. Cherrie. Bulletin of the American Museum of Natural History. Vol. LX, 1930. The American Museum of Natural History. *New York. pp. VII + 432. text-figs. 17 pl. (5 col. pl. birds (numb. XIII—XVII)). 1 map. 8vo.*

The expedition took place in 1913—14, and Cherrie, who was its ornithologist, went to Brazil again in 1916 to make further investigations.

The present work is based chiefly on the collections brought home from the two journeys. According to the original plan they were to be treated by Cherrie; however, in his absence Mrs. Naumburg was entrusted with the writing of the systematic part, Cherrie writing the narrative part and the field notes. Material in the American Museum and in various European collections is also used as a basis for the account. Altogether 658 species and subspecies are mentioned, and to each of them are added synonymy, specimens collected, range and field notes.

The introduction contains a general account of the physical conditions of Matto Grosso, lists of species and subspecies, localities, and bibliography.

The coloured plates (three-colour prints) were executed from paintings by F. L. Jaques.

NELSON, E. W.

1887 [1888]. Report upon natural history collections made in Alaska between ... 1877 and 1881. By Edward W. Nelson. Edited by Henry W. Henshaw. No. III. Arctic series of publications in connection with the Signal Service, U. S. Army ... < pp. 19—

226: Part I. Birds of Alaska, with a partial bibliography of Alaskan ornithology. By E. W. Nelson >. Government Printing Office. (Senate Mis. Doc. No. 156). *Washington. 12 col. pl. (numb. I—XII). 4to.*

This report, which was also issued as a separate publication the same year, comprises, in addition to the narrative of the journey and the present section on birds, sections dealing with the mammals of Northern Alaska, field-notes on Alaskan fishes, and a report upon the diurnal Lepidoptera collected in Alaska; the total number of plates amounts to 21.

Nelson stayed most of the time at St. Michaels, whence he made several expeditions into Alaska, on which more than two thousand bird-skins and fifteen hundred eggs were secured.

H. W. Henshaw, L. Stejneger, and others assisted in the preparation of the ornithological section, which opens with a chapter on the general character and extent of Alaska and its faunal subdivisions.

The main part of the work (pp. 35—222) treats of about 270 species of birds from Alaska, chiefly on the basis of the author's field-notes and the specimens collected by him, though the skins of birds from Alaska in the Smithsonian collections, and the literature on that region have also been utilized in the preparation of the work, so that the report actually deals with all species of birds known to occur in Alaska.

The plates (chromo-lithographs) were executed from drawings by R. and J. L. Ridgway.

The present copy of the report has been bound with L. M. Turner's 'Contributions to the natural history of Alaska', 1886 (512). The general title-page to this volume reads, 'The Miscellaneous Documents of the Senate of the United States for the first session of the forty-ninth congress, 1885—86. Vol. 8.'

NEUNZIG, K. A.

1.   *1921.* Die fremdländischen Stubenvögel von Karl Neunzig. (Zugleich 5. Aufl. des Karl Russ'schen Handbuchs für Vogelliebhaber, Bd. I). Mit 400 Bildern im Text und ... Tafeln in Farbendruck. *Another title-page:* Dr. Karl Russ' Handbuch für Vogelliebhaber, -Züchter und -Händler von Karl Neunzig. Erster Band: Fremdländische Stubenvögel. Fünfte völlig neubearbeitete und wesentlich vermehrte Auflage ... Creutz. *Magdeburg. pp. [V] + 895. text-figs. 42 col. pl. (numb. I—XLII). 8vo.*

A new edition of an older work by Russ, of which the first volume, 'Fremdländische Vögel', which originally appeared in 1870, must be regarded as an abbreviated edition of Russ' work 'Die fremdländischen Stubenvögel', 1875—99 (436).

The present edition gives a systematically arranged synopsis of the most important foreign forms of cage-birds, altogether 1450, with discussions on the conditions of the breeding of the larger groups, brief descriptions of the genera, and more detailed descriptions of the individual forms and information about their geographical distribution, food, eggs, and other features of interest to breeders. The work includes numerous text-figures and coloured plates made from drawings by Karl Neunzig, executed by the three-colour process (Förster & Borries, Zwickau).

NEVA, Voyage of the.

1810—14. Reise um die Welt ... 1803—06 ... auf den Schiffen Nadeshda und Newa ... *See Krusenstern, A. J. von.*

NEW ZEALAND. COLONIAL MUSEUM AND GEOLOGICAL SURVEY DEPARTMENT.

1882. Manual of the birds of New Zealand. *See Buller, W. L.*

NEWBERRY, J. S.

?.   *1857.* Reports of explorations and surveys, to ascertain the most practicable and economical route for a railroad from the Mississippi River to the Pacific Ocean ... 1854—5 ... Vol. VI. <-- Report of Lieut. Henry L. Abbot ... upon explorations for a railroad route, from the Sacramento Valley to the Columbia River, made by Lieut. R. S. Williamson ... assisted by Lieut. Henry L. Abbot. 1855. - - Part IV. - - Zoological report. No. 2. Report upon the zoology of the route. By J. S. Newberry. - - *pp. 73—110:* Chapter II. Report upon the birds >. Beverley Tucker. (Senate Ex. Doc., No. 78). *Washington. 2 col. pl. (numb. XXVI, XXXIV). 4to.*

To the zoological section of this report belongs the 'Index to zoological report', pp. I—IV.

The present ornithological chapter, which is based on field-notes, mentions a number of species of birds from California and Oregon.

The plates (lithographs coloured by hand) recur in an altered form in Baird, Cassin, and Lawrence's 'The birds of North America', 1860 (24).

NEWTON, A.

1864—1907. Ootheca Wolleyana ... continued with additions by the editor Alfred Newton. *See Wolley, J.*

1865—70. See Ibis.

1882. Scopoli's ornithological papers from his Deliciæ floræ et faunæ Insubricæ (Ticini: 1786—1788). Edited by Alfred Newton. *See Sonnerat, P., 1776.*

1883. Audouin's Explication sommaire des planches d'oiseaux de l'Égypte et de la Syrie. Publiées par Jules-César Savigny. Edited by Alfred Newton. *See Audouin, J. 1809.*

NICHOLS, L. N.

1936. Birds of America ... *See Pearson, T. G.*

NICOLL, M. J.

1930. Nicoll's Birds of Egypt. By R. Meinertz-   *363.* hagen. Published under the authority of the Egyptian government. Hugh Rees Ltd. *London. 2 vols. 38 pl. (31 col.). 4to.* — Vol. I. *pp. XVI + 1—348. text-figs. 19 pl. birds (15 col. (numb. I—XV; 1 pl. eggs numb. I)). 3 maps.* Vol. II. *pp. III + 349—700. text-figs. 19 pl. (16 col. (numb. XVI—XXXI)).*

Nicoll lived for many years in Egypt and collected a large amount of material concerning the birds of that country. He intended to issue a work that was to replace Shelley's 'A handbook to the birds of Egypt', 1872 (469), which was no longer up to date. It was to contain the results obtained since the publication of Heuglin's 'Ornithologie Nordost-Afrika's', 1869—73 (209).

Nicoll had completed the manuscript dealing with two-thirds of the Passeres when he died, and on the basis of this Meinertzhagen finished the work. The latter extended its scope to include Sinai and added chapters on various relevant subjects such as 'Origin of life in Egypt' (pp. 1—37), 'Migration' (pp. 38—57), a chapter of no small interest in connection with the subject of the present catalogue, 'The birds of ancient Egypt' (pp. 58—77) by R. E. Moreau, who is thanked in the preface for his contribution on migration, and 'Bird protection in Egypt' (pp. 78—87). The main part of the work, 'Systematic list of Egyptian birds' (pp. 89—650), describes the individual forms and several plumages. It also gives brief information about the distribution, nidification, and field characters of the birds.

A number of appendices (pp. 651—681), including a full bibliography (pp. 675—680), and a detailed 'General index' (pp. 683—700) conclude the work.

The plates are executed by the three-colour process. The originals for the illustrations were supplied by G. E. Lodge, Roland Green, and H. Grønvold.

NILSSON, S.

1817—21. Ornithologia Svecica. Auctore Sv.   *364.*

Nilsson. J. H. Schubothius. *Havniæ. 2 vols. 8vo.* — Vol. I. 1817. *pp.* [*VI*] + [*I*] + *317* + [*1*]. *10 col. pl. (numb. I—IX ₁₋₂).* Vol. II. 1821. *pp. XIV* + [*I*] + *277. 2 col. pl. (numb. X—XI).*

The pioneer of the faunistic study of the animals of Sweden had done great preparatory work, especially in the form of collections and journeys, before his present work on the Swedish fauna was issued in Latin. It contains a brief description of the genera, and under each species a diagnosis, synonyms, description, and other general information.

The plates are hand-coloured engravings (one is signed Arvidsson, sculp.).

The second, and completely revised, edition of the work was issued in Swedish in two volumes (Vol. I, and Vol. II, Part I), 1824—28, under the title 'Skandinavisk fauna. II. Foglarna', that is to say, as part of Nilsson's work on the Scandinavian fauna, the ornithological section of which was re-issued later, in 1835 and 1858, under the same title.

In his preparation of his work 'Danmarks Fugle', 1851—52 (248) N. Kjærbølling evidently consulted the edition of 1835, in which reference is made to the figures so far published in Nilsson's 'Illuminerade figurer till Skandinaviens fauna', 1829—40 (365), while in the edition of 1858 reference is further made to the figures in M. P. Körner's 'Skandinaviska foglar', 1839—46 (271).

365.   [*1829*—] *1832—40.* Illuminerade figurer till Skandinaviens fauna, med text utgifne af S. Nilsson. Akademie-Boktryckeriet hos C. F. Berling. *Lund. 2 vols 4to.* — Vol. I [*1829*—] 1832. *pp.* [*XII*] + [*276*]. *75 col. pl. birds (numb. 1 a, 3 a—15 a, 16, 17 a—29 a, 30—73, 75—76, 1 unnumb.).* Vol. II. [*1832*—] 1840. *pp.* [*VI*] + [*292*]. 88 col. pl. birds (numb. 77, 79—85, 85, 87—165).

This work was issued in 20 parts, Vol. I comprising Parts 1—10, and Vol. II Parts 11—20. A second edition of Parts 1—4 appeared at Lund in 1831—32, Parts 1—8 were originally published at Stockholm (Norstedt & Söner).

The work deals only with mammals and birds, chiefly birds, and like the same author's 'Skandinavisk fauna', in particular, it has contributed to animate and increase Swedish interest in studies and observations of animal life.

The text (unpaginated) describes the forms figured, giving brief diagnoses, synonyms, descriptions, geographical distribution, and habits. A few genera and higher groups are occasionally mentioned.

Each volume contains 100 plates, Vols. I and II, in addition to the plates with figures of birds, containing 25 and 12 plates respectively with figures of mammals.

Most of the hand-coloured plates (lithographs; the greater number printed by Körner & Co., some by Gjöthström & Magnusson) with figures of birds were drawn and lithographed by M. Körner; one (Vol. II, Pl. 115) is signed, W. v. Wright.

The present copy comprises four volumes, the text and the plates of each volume having been bound separately.

NISSEN, N. P.

366.   *1922.* Naturhistoriske Billeder. II. Nordens Fugle ved N. P. Nissen ... smukt farvelagte Tavler med ca. 350 Afbildninger. J. P. Madsen Lind. *København. pp. 8. 50 col. pl. (numb. I—L). 8vo.*

A popular atlas with figures of birds printed in colour, arranged in a certain systematic order, and accompanied by a brief text concerning the main groups. The plates were executed abroad.

NITZSCH, C. L.

1822. Von der egenthümlichen Organisation der Vögel. *See Naumann, J. A., 1822—60.*

NODDER, F. P.

1789—1813. The naturalist's miscellany ... *See Shaw, G.*

NODDER, R. P.

1793—1813. The naturalist's miscellany ... *See Shaw, G., 1789—1813.*

1814—17. The zoological miscellany ... Illustrated with coloured figures ... by R. P. Nodder. *See Leach, W. E.*

NORDMANN, A. von.

1835. Reise um die Erde durch Nord-Asien und die beiden Oceane ... 1828—1830 ausgeführt von Adolph Erman. Naturhistorischer Atlas. - - Verzeichniss von Thieren und Pflanzen, welche auf einer Reise um die Erde gesammelt wurden von Adolph Erman. <- - *pp. 1—18:* I. Vögel. Beschrieben von Alexander v. Nordmann >. G. Reimer. *Berlin. 10 pl. (numb. I—X). fol.*

The results of this expedition, the actual object of which was to collect a complete series of magnetic observations, were published in 1833—48 in five volumes, 8vo, and the present natural historical atlas (pp. VI + 64, 17 pl. (2 col.)) with lists of the animals and plants collected. The zoological material was handed over to the Royal Museum in Berlin. The ornithological section of the atlas contains a list of altogether 143 birds some of which are new and represent the most important ornithological results of the expedition. Some of the species are described, and figured on the plates (lithographs).

NOTES FROM THE LEYDEN MUSEUM. *See Leyden. Rijks Museum van Natuurlijke Historie.*

NOVARA, Voyage of the [Austrian frigate].

1865. Reise der österreichischen Fregatte Novara um die Erde ... 1857—59 ... Zoologischer Theil. Vol. I ... 2. Vögel. *See Pelzeln, A. von.*

NOVITATES ZOOLOGICÆ.

1894 -→ Novitates Zoologicæ. A journal of zoology in connection with the Tring Museum. Edited by Walter Rothschild, Ernst Hartert, and K. Jordan. Issued at the Zoological Museum, Tring. Printed by Hazell, Watson, & Viney. *London. Vol. I* -→ *textfigs. plates. maps. large 8vo.*

The zoological journal of the Tring Museum, Vol. 39 of which is dated 1933—36. The essential parts of this collection, founded in 1890 by Walter Rothschild, were the birds (reaching in time about 300,000 skins and representing nearly 3,000 types) and the insects (butterflies, the largest and most complete collection in the world). The scientists in charge of these sections of the collection were Ernst Hartert, the ornithologist, 1892—1930, and Karl Jordan, the entomologist, (from 1893). The collection of birds was particularly famous, being considered in many ways to be the finest in the world, although that in the British Museum is larger. In 1932, however, the collection of birds at Tring was sold to the American Museum of Natural History, the ornithological department of which thus became the largest in the world (886).

Ornithologists from all over the world made pilgrimages to Tring, this 'Mekka of ornithologists', to study the collections in the museum. Most of the results they arrived at were published in the present periodical, which was issued by the museum and therefore plays an important part in systematic ornithology. In its columns we find contributions from a number of ornithologists principally Ernst Hartert and Walter Rothschild, but mention may also be made of O. Salvin, A. Reichenow, W. R. Ogilvie-Grant, C. E. Hellmayr, G. M. Mathews, T. Salvadori, E. Stresemann, E. C. Stuart Baker, and C. F. R. Jourdain.

The editors spared no expense over the production of the journal. A number of plates are published in the journal, including more than 100 relating to birds, the majority coloured (mostly lithographs coloured by hand; Mintern Bros., later (from 1906) West, Newman imp.), chiefly executed from drawings by J. G. Keulemans (the volumes issued from 1894—1910) and H. Grønvold (from 1903). In the recent volumes the number of the coloured plates has been reduced, and other methods of reproduction have gained ground, notably the three-colour process, and in some few cases chromo-lithography and collotype.

NOZEMAN, C.
9.   *1770—1829.* Nederlandsche vogelen; volgens hun-ne huishouding, aert, en eigenschappen beschreeven door Cornelius Nozeman, (Vols. II—V: en verder, na Zyn Ed. overlyden, door Martinus Houttuyn;) alle naer 't leeven geheel nieuw en naeuwkeurig getekend, in 't koper gebragt, en natuurlyk gekoleurd door, en onder opzicht van Christiaan Sepp en zoon. Jan Christiaan Sepp (Vols. III—V: en Zoon). Amster-dam. *5 vols. 255 col. pl. (5 front. + 250 numb. in 'Korte inhoud'). large fol. —* Vol. I. 1770. *pp. [VIII] + 1—92. 51 col. pl. (front. + Nos. 1—50; 6 pl. eggs (Nos. 5, 9, 30, 33, 42, 50)).* Vol. II 1789. *pp. II + [II] + 93—194 + IV. 51 col. pl. (front. +Nos. 51—100; 2 pl. eggs (Nos. 79, 90)).* Vol. III. 1797. *pp. [VI] + 195—294. 51 col. pl. (front. + Nos. 101—150).* Vol. IV. 1809. *pp. [VI] + 295—394 + IV. 51 col. pl. (front. + Nos. 151—200).* Vol. V. 1829. *pp. VI + 395—500. 51 col. pl. (front. + Nos. 201—250).*
This work gives in figures and text the first comprehensive account of the avifauna of Holland, all of whose members observed in the Netherlands up to the time of publication being described in the text in fairly great detail. A section under each form headed 'Aentekeningen' gives information about biological conditions and other subjects of interest.
The plates (engravings coloured by hand) are fairly good; the birds are shown in their natural surroundings and as far as possible in their natural attitudes. In addition to the special plates with figures of the eggs and nests of some forms, both are figured with the portrait or portraits of the particular bird on several of the plates in Vols. I and II. Figures of eggs similarly occur on plates with figures of birds in Vols. III and IV.
Many of the birds figured in the last two parts of the work are derived from C. J. Temminck's collection.
The first part of a French edition of the work appeared in 1778 (370).
0.   *1778.* Oiseaux de la Hollande, avec une descrip-tion de leur maniere de vivre, de leur nature, et de leurs propriétés: Version françoise, de Jaques Teis-sier, d'après l'original hollandois de Cornelius Noze-man. Le tout dessiné nouvellement, gravé en plan-ches de cuivre, et mis en couleurs naturelles; par les soins particuliers et sous les yeux de Jean Chrétien Sepp. Amsterdam. *pp. [IV] + 14. 7 col. pl. large fol.*
The first and evidently the only part issued of a French edition of Nozeman's 'Nederlandsche vogelen', 1770—1829 (369).

OATES, E. W.
1901—05. Catalogue of the collection of birds' eggs in the British Museum ... Vols. I—IV. *See British Museum (Natural History),* 1901—12.

OEHME, C. J.
1775—82. Allgemeine Historie der Natur ... Vols. IX—XI. Naturgeschichte der Vögel ... *See Buffon, G. L. L. de.*

OGILVIE-GRANT, W. R.
1892—98. Catalogue of the birds in the British Museum. Vols. XVII, XXII, XXVI. *See British Museum (Natural History),* 1874—98.
1893. Exploration of Mount Kina Balu, North Borneo ... Appendix. 2. *See Whitehead, J.*
1895—97. Allen's Naturalist's Library. Edited by *371.* R. Bowdler-Sharpe. A hand-book to the game-birds. By W. R. Ogilvie-Grant. W. H. Allen & Co. *London. 2 vols. 39 col. pl. 8vo. —* Vol. I. 1895. Sand-grouse, partridges, pheasants. *pp. XIV + [II] + 304. text-figs. 21 col. pl. (numb. I—XXI).* Vol. II. 1897. Pheasants (continued), megapodes, curassows, hoat-zins, bustard-quails. *pp. XIV + [I] + 316 + [4]. 18 col. pl. (numb. XXII—XXXIX; XXV numb. XXVI, and vice versa).*
A semi-popular account, useful for sportsmen and field-naturalists. The work is founded on Ogilvie-Grant's 'Game birds', which constitutes Vol. XXII, 1893, of the Catalogue of the birds in the British Museum (70).
The work is a small monograph of the game-birds of all parts of the world, with brief diagnoses of genera and higher groups, descriptions of the species in different plumages, and notes on their geographical distribution and habits. The majority of the birds treated belong to the order Gallinæ, the true game-birds.
The plates (chromo-lithographs; Wyman & Sons, Limited) are derived partly from earlier steel-plate engravings in Jardine's original edition of the 'Naturalist's Library' (226), and partly from contemporary artists, chiefly J. G. Keulemans; they are thus of very unequal value, as the reproductions from steel-plate engravings are not on a level with the other plates.
The work was re-issued in 1896—97 in Lloyd's 'Natural History', edited by R. Bowdler Sharpe. This edition only dif-fers from the present one in that it has six more coloured plates.
1897—1904. Biologia Centrali-Americana. Aves. Vol. III. *See Salvin, O.,* 1879—1904.
1910. Transactions of the Zoological Society of *372.* London. Vol. XIX. <-- Zoological results of the Ruwenzori Expedition, 1905—06. -- *pp. 253—480:* Part 4. Ruwenzori Expedition reports. 16. Aves. By W. R. Ogilvie-Grant. Appendix. On some points in the anatomy of Bradypterus cinnamomeus. By W. P. Pycraft >. Printed for the Society. *London. text-figs. 10 col. pl. (numb. X—XIX; 1 pl. eggs (numb. XIX)). 4to.*
This expedition to Ruwenzori, or the 'Mountains of the moon' in Equatorial Africa took place in 1905—06 under the leadership of R. B. Woosnam.
Valuable material representing both animals and plants was brought home, including a collection of 2470 specimens of birds.
The expedition was made on the initiative of Ogilvie-Grant, who organised it. In the present treatise he describes the large amount of ornithological material secured; the fieldnotes are by R. B. Woosnam. Altogether 385 species are dealt with, of which 27 are new. The majority of them had previously been briefly dealt with in the Bulletin of the British Ornithologists' Club.
Twenty-eight species of birds, and the eggs of twenty-four species, are figured on the coloured plates, executed from drawings by H. Grønvold (J. Green, Chromo lith.).
1912. Catalogue of the collection of birds' eggs in the British Museum ... Vol. V. *See British Museum (Natural History),* 1901—12.
1915. The Ibis. Jubilee Supplement No. 2. Tenth *373.* series. <-- Report on the birds collected by the British Ornithologists' Union Expedition and the Wollaston Expedition in Dutch New Guinea. By W. R. Ogilvie-Grant >. British Ornithologists' Union. *London. pp. XX + 336. text-figs. 8 col. pl. (numb. I—VIII). 2 maps. 8vo.*

The two expeditions which took place in 1909—11 and 1912 —13 respectively, secured important ornithological material, 3395 birds' skins being collected, representing 312 species and subspecies, of which 25 were new to science. The specimens collected were presented to the British Museum, which in this way obtained 37 forms new to its collections.

The ornithological results are recorded in the present paper, which is an important contribution to the ornithology of New Guinea. The main part of the treatise (pp. 1—329) consists of a 'Systematic list of the species', while the introduction (pp. V— XX) deals with the general conditions of the expeditions and their ornithological results.

A general account of the ornithological results of the B. O. U. Expedition by Ogilvie-Grant is found as Appendix A (pp. 263—302) to A. F. R. Wollaston's 'Pygmies and Papuans', 1912; it was republished in the Ibis, 1913, pp. 76—113.

The plates (three-colour prints; Menpes Press, Watford) were executed from drawings by H. Grønvold and show the twelve forms figured in their natural attitudes and environments.

A slightly altered reprint of the work appeared in 1916 (374).

374.   1916. Reports on the collections made by the British Ornithologists' Union Expedition and the Wollaston Expedition in Dutch New Guinea, 1910—13. Vol. I. <-- III. Report on the birds collected by the British Ornithologists' Union Expedition and the Wol­laston Expedition in Dutch New Guinea. By W. R. Ogilvie-Grant >. Francis Edwards. *London. pp. 240. text-figs. 8 col. pl. (numb. I—VIII). 4to.*
A reprint of a paper in 'The Ibis', Jubilee Supplement 2, 10th series, 1915 (373). The introduction, however, is somewhat altered, parts of it having been transferred to the Preface by its author, W. R. Ogilvie-Grant, the general editor of the two volumes in which these reports were published.

The edition was limited to 150 copies, of which the present is No. 51.

OKEN, L.
375.   1837. Allgemeine Naturgeschichte für alle Stände, von Oken. Vol. VII, Part I, oder Thierreich, Vol. IV, Part I. Vögel. Hoffmann. *Stuttgart. pp. IV + 685 + [1]. 8vo.*
The ornithological section of a once well-known and widely distributed popular natural history, which in the present copy consists of seven volumes (in 13), published in 90 parts in 1833—41. A volume of index, 'Universalregister zu Okens allgemeiner Naturgeschichte' appeared in 1843 (dated 1842). The animal kingdom is treated in Vols. IV—VII (8 vols., 1833 —38).

An atlas to this natural history was issued in 1834—45; the ornithological plates in 1839—43 (376).

376.   [1839—40—]1843. Abbildungen zu Oken's Allgemeine Naturgeschichte für alle Stände. Hoffmann. *Stuttgart.* — XII. Classe. Vögel. [1839—40]. *pp. [V]. 15 col. pl. (numb. 72—86).* — [Ergänzungsheft I]. 1843. [Nester und Eier]. *pp. 26. text-figs. 8 col. pl. (numb. I—II, 3—8). fol.*
The ornithological sections of an atlas with illustrations to Oken's Natural history, of which the volume on birds appeared in 1837 (375). It was issued, with altogether 164 plates (lithographs), in 19 parts and five supplementary parts in 1834—45. The present copy contains 132 plates only, as the 32 plates in the supplementary Parts 2—5 issued by Fr. Berge are missing.

The fifteen hand-coloured plates with figures of birds (Pl. 72—73: Zeichnung, Stich u. Druck v. C. Susemihl & Sohn in Darmstadt; the remainder: C. Schack and others, lith.) were published in Parts 10—12.

The figures are copied from those in various works, such as Daubenton's 'Planches enluminées' (76, note), works by Levaillant, Temminck, Wilson, etc.

As stated above, plates with figures of eggs and nests with accompanying text were published in the first supplementary part. This section was also issued separately, the same year,

under the title 'Die Nester und Eier der Vögel. Mit 304 grösstentheils nach der Natur entworfenen und genau kolorirten Abbildungen'.

OLAFSSON, E.
1772. Vice-Lavmand Eggert Olafsens og Land- *3* Physici Biarne Povelsens Reise igiennem Island, foranstaltet af Videnskabernes Sælskab i Kiøbenhavn, og beskreven af forbemeldte Eggert Olafsen, med dertil hørende 51 Kobberstøkker og et nyt forfærdiget Kart over Island. Trykt hos Jonas Lindgrens Enke. *Sorøe. 2 vols. 17 pl. birds. 4to.* — Vol. I. *pp. [XII] + 1— 618. 15 pl. birds (numb. XIII—XIV, XXI—XXIV, XXXIII—XLI). 1 map.* Vol. II. *pp. 619—1042 + [62] + 20 + [2]. 2 pl. birds. (numb. XLVI, XLVIII).*
A description of Iceland written by Olafsson chiefly on the basis of diaries written during travels in that country. After his death the work was revised and sent to press by Professors J. Erichsen and G. Schøning.

In accordance with the plan and the preparation of the work as a report of travels, the various parts of the country are described separately, the main stress being laid upon the treatment of the natural features, as regards physical, economic, and ethnographical conditions. The matter dealing with birds is therefore distributed between the two volumes.

When the work was to be sent to press a number of drawings made by different artists, most of them probably by Pålsson, were available. Only a limited number of these drawings are reproduced on the 51 plates (engravings), a special selection having been made by Professor Morten Thrane Brünnich, who is said to have corrected and improved the drawings also.

A German edition of the work was issued in 1774—75 (378), a French edition in 1802 (379). An extract from the French translation appeared in English in 1805 as Vol. II of 'A collection of modern and contemporary voyages and travels', etc.

1774—75. Des Vice-Lavmands Eggert Olafsens *3* und des Landphysici Biarne Povelsens Reise durch Island, veranstaltet von der Königlichen Societät der Wissenschaften in Kopenhagen und beschrieben von bemeldtem Eggert Olafsen. Aus dem Dänischen übersetzt. Mit 25 (Part II: Mit 26) Kupfertafeln und einer neuen Charte über Island versehen. Heinecke und Faber. *Kopenhagen. 2 parts in 1 vol. 17 pl. birds. 4to.* — Part I. 1774. *pp. [XVI] + IX—XVI + 328. 6 pl. birds (numb. XIII—XIV, XXI—XXIV). 1 map.* Part. II. 1775. *pp. VIII + 244. 11 pl. birds (numb. XXXIII—XLI, XLVI, XLVIII).*
A German edition of these travels, the Danish original of which appeared in 1772 (377).

The plates are copies of those in the Danish edition.

1802. Voyage en Islande, fait par ordre de S. M. *3* danoise, contenant des observations sur les moeurs et les usages des habitans; une description des lacs, rivières, glaciers, sources chaudes et volcans; des diverses espèces de terres, pierres, fossiles et pétrifications; des animaux, poissons et insectes, etc., etc.; avec un atlas; traduit du danois par Gauthier-de-Lapeyronie. Levrault. *Paris. 5 vols. 8vo.*
The volumes containing the text of the French edition of Olafsson's and Pålsson's travels, originally issued in Danish in 1772 (377). An extract from this French edition appeared in an English translation in 1805 (377, note).

An 'Atlas du voyage en Islande fait par ordre de S. M. danoise', 4to, with copies of the original plates, belonging to the French translation, is lacking in the present copy.

OLINA, G. P.
1622. Uccelliera overo discorso della natura, e pro- *3*

prieta di diversi uccelli e in particolare di qve' che cantano, con il modo di prendergli, conoscergli, alleuargli, e mantenergli. E con le figure cavate dal vero, e diligentemente intagliate in rame dal Tempesta, e dal Villamena. Opera di Gio. Pietro Olina. Dedicata al Sig. Cavalier dal Pozzo. Andrea Fei. *Roma. pp.* [*XI*] + *p. 1* + *pp.* [*1*] + *2—5* + *p. 7* + *p. 9* + *pp. 8—23* + *p. 27* + *pp. 25—61* + [*1*] + *62—81* + [*12*]. *66 pl. large 8vo.*

One of the earliest works with engraved plates representing birds, figures of them being found on altogether 63 of the plates.

These are whole-page figures, printed on the unpaginated backs of the text-leaves, the text to the individual plate being found, or at any rate beginning, on the opposite page.

In addition to the individual forms of birds the work further deals with different methods of catching birds, the art of keeping them in captivity, and their diseases.

A new edition of the work was issued in 1684.

OORT, E. D. van.

1914. Notes from the Leyden Museum. *See Leyden. Rijks Museum van Natuurlijke Historie,* 1879 —1914.

1. [*1918—*]*1922—35.* Ornithologia Neerlandica. De vogels van Nederland door E. D. van Oort. (Vol. V: voltooid door G. A. Brouwer). Met ... gekleurde platen. Martinus **♦**Nijhoff. *'S Gravenhage. 5 vols. 407 col. pl. large 4to.* —·Vol. I. [1918—] 1922. Colymbiformes. Procellariiformes. Pelecaniformes. Ardeiformes. Anseriformes. *pp. XII* + *250. text-figs. 87 col. pl. (numb. 1—87).* Vol. II. [1921—] 1926. Falconiformes. Galliformes. Gruiformes. Charadriiformes (Limicolæ I). *pp. VIII* + *265, 83 col. pl. (numb. 88—169, 149 A).* Vol. III. [*1922—*] 1928. Charadriiformes (Limicolæ II — Lari). Columbiformes. Cuculiformes. Coraciiformes (Striges). *pp. VIII* + *252. 80 col. pl. (numb. 170—246, 189 A—B, 240 A).* Vol. IV. [1923—] 1930. Coraciiformes (Caprimulgi. Cypseli. Coraciæ. Pici). Passeriformes (Hirundinidæ. Muscicapidæ. Turdidæ. Cinclidæ. Troglodytidæ. Motacillidæ (Motacilla)). *pp. VIII* + *256. 77 col. pl. (numb. 247—323).* Vol. V. [1927—] 1935. Passeriformes (Motacillidæ (Anthus). Alau didæ. Ampelidæ. Laniidæ. Panuridæ. Paridæ. Certhiidæ. Sittidæ. Regulidæ. Corvidæ. Oriolidæ. Sturnidæ. Fringillidæ). *pp. VIII* + *325. 80 col. pl. (numb. 324— 402, 388 A).*

This work with figures of all the forms of wild birds observed in Holland was issued in 46 parts.

The issue took place at somewhat irregular intervals, parts of the text coming out later than the plates. A survey of the history of publication up to and including 1925 (Parts 1—27) is found in Zimmer (589, II, p. 651). According to 'Brinkman's Alphabetische lijst van boeken', etc. (from 1931, 'Brinkman's Cumulatieve catalogus van boeken', etc.) and other sources, the rest of the work was issued as follows:

1926: the final section of the text to Vol. II (pp. VIII + pp. 169—265) and 30 irregularly numbered plates (Parts 28— 29?) ;
1927: Parts 30—37, 80 pl. and text Vol. III, pp. 1—64 ;
1928: Parts 38—41, 35 pl., which brought the series of plates to a provisional conclusion with altogether 405 plates ; the concluding section of the text to Vol. III ;
1930: Part 42 (January), text Vol. IV, pp. 1—88, Part 43 (August), text Vol. IV, pp. VIII + pp. 89—256 ;
1933 (January) : Part 44, text Vol. V, pp. 1—64, 1 pl. (numb. 402) ;
1935: Part 45 (January), text Vol. V, pp. 65—160, Part

46 (June), text Vol. V, pp. VIII + pp. 161—325, 1 pl. (numb. 388 A).

Since H. Schlegel issued his work 'De vogels van Nederland', 1854—58 (443), no comprehensive atlas of the birds of the Netherlands had been published. The plates in the present work (collotype, reproduced by Emrik & Binger, Haarlem) were executed from drawings by M. A. Koekkoek, and show the birds in their natural surroundings. Each plate contains several figures of birds, the sexes, different ages, and, when necessary, seasonal variations are figured.

The artist worked under the supervision of van Oort, who wrote the main part of the text, in which he gives a brief characterization of genera and higher groups, with keys to the genera under the families and to the species under the genera. Altogether 362 forms are treated, the author giving the synonyms, the most commonly used Dutch vernacular names, and the most familiar English, German, and French names. Then follow a description of the bird and information about its geographical distribution and habits. The nomenclature agrees in all essentials with that employed by van Oort in his list of the birds of the Netherlands in 'Notes from the Leyden Museum', XXX, 1908.

After van Oort's death G. A. Brouwer undertook the completion of the text. From Vol. V, p. 69 (No. 303, Parus ater L.) the latter wrote the generic diagnoses and the sections on the distribution and habits of the species.

The present copy has been bound into ten volumes, text and plates of each volume having been bound separately.

ORBIGNY, A. D. d'.

1835—47. Voyage dans l'Amérique méridionale(le *382.* Brésil, la république orientale de l'Uruguay, la république Argentine, la Patagonie, la république du Chili, la république de Bolivia, la république du Pérou), exécuté ... 1826—33, par Alcide d'Orbigny ... P. Bertrand. *Paris. large 4to.* — Vol. IV. Part III. 1835— 44 [—47]. - - <Oiseaux, par Alcide d'Orbigny >. *pp.* [*V*] + *III* + *395.* — Vol. IX. 1847. Atlas zoologique *67 col. pl. birds (numb. 1—36, 36* [= *37*], *38—66, 6bis).*

During his long journey in South America, on which he had been sent by the Muséum d'Histoire Naturelle, d'Orbigny went all over the country. On his return to France in 1834 he brought back a great many notes and valuable collections which included about 800 birds.

The report on the journey was published in 1835—47 in 90 parts, which constitute seven volumes of text and two volumes of atlases, as well as maps (866 ; 869, I, pp. 388—390).

The present ornithological section treats of the birds systematically, with brief notes on genera and superior groups. Altogether 332 species are dealt with, with synonyms, a brief diagnosis in Latin, a description, and information about distribution and habits being given for each species.

The plates (engravings, printed in colour, some by Langlois, others by Folliau, and retouched by hand) were engraved by Annedouche, Breton, François, Victor, Auguste Duménil, Corbié, Giraud, Pardinel, and a few other artists, from paintings by E. Travies.

1838—43. Le regne animal ... Les oiseaux ... par Alcide d'Orbigny. *See Cuvier, G. L. C. F. D.*

1839. Histoire physique, politique et naturelle de *383.* l'Île de Cuba par Ramon de la Sagra. Arthus Bertrand. *Paris.* — Ornithologie, par Alcide d'Orbigny. *pp. XXXI* + *336. 8vo.* Atlas (Mammifères. Oiseaux). *33 col. pl. (31 pl. birds (numb. I—XXX, XIXbis) ; 2 pl. eggs (numb. XXXI—XXXII). fol.*

This important work about Cuba was published in 12 volumes and atlases in 1838 [i e. 1839]—57. A Spanish edition in 13 volumes, folio, appeared in 1839—61.

Ramon de la Sagra took a large collection from Cuba to Paris, where several scientists worked on them, among others Alcide d'Orbigny, who described not only the birds, but also the foraminifera and the mollusca.

The text of the present ornithological section opens with the 'Introduction et généralités' (pp. I—XXXI), with a historical survey of our knowledge of the birds of Cuba and a grouping of them into six series according to their geographical distribution. The next section, 'Partie descriptive' (pp. 1—322), deals with the birds systematically and briefly mentions genera and higher groups. Under the individual forms — altogether 129 — the author gives synonyms, a brief diagnosis in Latin, a description, and information about the distribution and habits of the bird.

The plates in the atlas (engravings; Guyard, Fournier, Annedouche, Pardinel, and others, sculp.; Bougeard imp.) were executed from paintings by E. Traviès, apart from a few by Prêtre.

ORD, G.
1814. American ornithology ... Vols. VIII and IX. [Edited, with a memoir of the author, by G. Ord]. *See Wilson, A.,* 1808—24.
1824. American ornithology ... Vols. VII—VIII. *See Wilson, A.,* 1808—24.
1832. American ornithology ... *See Wilson, A.*

ORNITHOLOGICAL MISCELLANY.
1875—78. Ornithological miscellany. Edited by George Dawson Rowley. *See Rowley, G. D.*

OSGOOD, W. H.
1930. Abyssinian birds and mammals ... *See Fuertes, L. A.*

OTTO, B. C.
1781—1809. Herrn von Buffons Naturgeschichte der Vögel. Aus dem Französischen übersetzt ... durch Bernhard Christian Otto. Vols. VII—XXXV. *See Buffon, G. L. L. de,* 1772—1809.

384.   OUDEMANS, A. C.
1917. Dodo-studiën. Naar aanleiding van de vondst van een gevelsteen met Dodo-beeld van 1561 te Vere. Door A. C. Oudemans. Verhandelingen der Koninklijke Akademie van Wetenschappen te Amsterdam. (Tweede sectie). Deel XIX. No. 4. Johannes Müller. *Amsterdam. pp. VI + [I] + 140. 15 pl. (numb. I—XV). 8vo.*
An account of all that was produced in the sixteenth and seventeenth centuries about the Dodo, in print or in picture. This treatise contains a long bibliography (pp. 103— 135). The plates (Heliotype, van Leer, Amsterdam) contain altogether 41 figures, derived from various sources.

OUSTALET, J. F. É.
1877. Les oiseaux de la Chine. *See David, A.*
1893. Centenaire de la fondation du Muséum d'Histoire Naturelle ... pp. 187—252: Notice sur quelques espèces d'oiseaux actuellement éteintes ... *See Milne Edwards, A.*

OWEN, R.
1834. Observations on the anatomy of the toucan. *See Gould, J.,* 1833—35.

PAESSLER, C. W. G.
1855—63. Die Eier der europaeischen Voegel ... *See Baedeker, F. W. J.*

PALLAS, P. S.
1767—69. Petri S. Pallas Spicilegia zoologica. Vol. *38.* I. 1774. Continens quadrupedium, avium, amphibiorum, piscium, insectorum, molluscorum aliorumque marinorum. Fasciculos decem. *Separate title-page to the fasc.:* Spicilegia zoologica quibus novæ imprimis et obscuræ animalium species iconibus, descriptionibus atque commentariis illustrantur. Cura P. S. Pallas. <-- Fasc. 4—6. [Aves] >. Gottl. August Lange. *Berolini. 13 pl. 4to. — Fasc. 4. 1767. pp. 23. 3 pl. (numb. I—III). Fasc. 5. 1769. pp. [VI] + 34. 5 pl. (numb. I—V). Fasc. 6. 1769. pp. 36. 5 pl. (numb. I—V).*
The work of which the ornithological section is cited here was issued in 1767—80 in 14 parts, each with a separate title-page and separate pagination; they constitute two volumes (In one. I: Parts 1—10), which in the present copy are bound in one. Vol. I, however, has a separate title-page. The total number of the plates is 58.
A number of birds, such as Grus, Numida, Alca, Alcedo, Anser, are mentioned and described, sometimes also their anatomy, in the sections dealing with ornithology. These are illustrated with plates (engravings: A Schouman, C. Hiller, Decker del.; C. B. Glassbach, J. F. Schuster sc.) with figures of several of the birds mentioned in the text.
A great deal of Pallas' 'Miscellanea zoologica', 1766, has been inserted, in an enlarged form, in the present work, for example the chapter on Grus psophia (Fasc. IV, pp. 3—9), from the ornithological passages.
A German edition of Parts 1—11 of this work appeared in 1769—79 (Parts 4—6, 1774—76) under the title 'Naturgeschichte merkwürdiger Thiere', etc. (386), some parts of it, among them Parts 4—5, further appearing in a Dutch translation in 1767—70 which was re-issued later.

1774—76. Peter Simon Pallas, Naturgeschichte *386* merkwürdiger Thiere, in welcher vornehmlich neue und unbekannte Thierarten durch Kupferstiche, Beschreibungen und Erklärungen erläutert werden. (Sammlung 5—11: Durch den Verfasser verteutscht). <-- Sammlung 4—6. [Vögel] >. Gottlieb August Lange. *Berlin. 13 pl. 4to. — Sammlung 4. 1774.* Aus dem Lateinischen übersetzt von Johann Christian Polykarp Erxleben. *pp. 24. 3 pl. (numb. I—III). Sammlung 5. 1776. pp. 44. 5 pl. (numb. I—V). Sammlung 6. 1776. pp. 44. 5 pl. (numb. I—V).*
In all essentials a German translation of the author's 'Spicilegia zoologica', Parts 4—6, 1767—69 (385). Of this translation only Sammlung 1—11 appeared (Vol. I = Sammlung 1—10). These were issued in 1869—79, and contained altogether 48 plates (engravings). Sammlung 1—3 have been translated by E. G. Baldinger. Corrections by Pallas to the translation in Sammlung 4 are found in Sammlung 5, p. 8.
The plates in the ornithological sections are identical with those in the corresponding parts of 'Spicilegia zoologica'.

1831 [—42]. Zoographia Rosso-Asiatica, sistens *387* omnium animalium in extenso imperio Rossico et adjacentibus maribus observatorum recensionem, domicilia, mores et descriptiones, anatomen atque icones plurimorum. Auctore Petro Pallas. In Officina Cæs. Academiæ Scientiarum impress. *Petropolis. 3 vols. text, 4to, and 1 vol. plates, small fol. — Vol. I. 1831. - - < pp. 297—568:* Imperii Rossici. Aves. Pars prima >. Vol. II. 1831. - - < Imperii Rossici. Aves. Pars altera>. *pp. VII + [I] + 374.* [Plates. 1834—42]. Icones ad Zoographiam Rosso-Asiaticam. *26 col. pl. birds.*
This posthumous work by the great traveller exists with title-pages dated 1811 (Vols. I—II; Vol. III no date) and 1831. The printing of the first two volumes (mammals and birds) seems to have been completed in 1811 shortly after Pallas' death, whereas Vol. III (reptiles, Amphibia, and fishes),

enlarged by W. G. Tilesius von Tilenau, was not printed till some few years afterwards (in 1814) ; however, the work does not seem to have been published by the Academy till 1826 or 1827 (552, IV, p. 1505 ; 865).

The birds are divided into three orders with altogether 68 genera, of which 425 species are dealt with ; a brief diagnosis, synonymy, notes on distribution and habits, and a description are given, whereas the higher groups are only briefly mentioned.

The plates (engravings coloured by hand) are found in the original six parts in which they were published. Each part contains eight plates, those representing birds (several : F. Lehmann sc.) occurring in Fasc. 3—6, which contain 4, 8, 8, and 6 plates of birds respectively ; ten of these belong to the text of Vol. I, sixteen to the text of Vol. II. Pallas had handed over the original drawings to Geisler at Leipzig, so that he could engrave the plates ; this however, involved not only considerable delay, but also great expense in the publication of the plates (cf. Vol. III, Avertissement). 'Addenda' to this work, by E. F. Eversmann, were issued in 1835—42, reprinted in 1876 (137).

PALMÉN, J. A.
1879—88. Finska fogelägg ... See *Sundman, G. R.*
1911—26. Nordens fåglar ... See *Jägerskiöld, A. K. E. L.*

PALMSTRUCH, J. W.
1806—09 [—*25*]. Svensk zoologi, utgifven af J. W. Palmstruch. Tryckt hos Carl Delén. *Stockholm.* 2 *vols. 12 col. pl. birds. 8vo.* — Vol. I. 1806 [—08]. Med text börjad af C. Quensel. Och fortsatt af O. Swartz. - - < [Aves]>. *pp. 1—36. 6 col. pl. (numb. 2, 8, 14, 20, 26, 32).* Vol. II 1809 [—25]. Med text författad af O. Swartz. - - < [Aves] >. *pp. 37—59 + 91—103. 6 col. pl. (numb. 39, 44, 50, 56, 62, 68).*

The initiative in publishing this work, the ornithological part of which is cited here, was taken by G. J. Billberg, who was greatly interested in Nature and who on October 24, 1805, received a 'Privilegium Exclusivum på ett Verk öfver Svenska Djuren'.

The model for the work was the atlas, 'Svensk botanik', commenced in 1802, and also issued by Palmstruch. After the death of Palmstruch in 1811 this was taken over, together with 'Svensk zoologi' by Billberg, from whom the 'K. Vetenskaps-Akademien' bought the copyright of both works in 1822.

According to the original plan the work was to deal with all the Swedish animals, but publication ceased after the issue of the second volume. It was published in 12 parts (Vol. I (Parts 1—6, pl. 1—36) ; Vol. II (Parts 7—12, pl. 37—72)).

According to Carus and Engelmann (564, I, 1861, pp. 280 —281) the parts were issued as follows : 1806, Parts 1—2 ; 1807, Parts 3—4 ; 1808, Parts 5—6 ; 1809, Part 7, with the title-page to Vol. II ; 1810, Part 8 ; 1811, Part 9 ; 1813, Part 10 ; 1814?, Part 11 ; 1825, Part 12.

The preface was written by Billberg, who left the preparation of the text to C. Quensel. The latter wrote an introduction to the work (Vol. I, pp. I—VIII). After Quensel's death O. Swartz undertook the preparation of the text to Parts 2—10 (and 11 ?), J. W. Dalman writing the text to Part 12, which was issued by the 'K. Vetenskaps-Akademien'.

The subject-matter in the volumes is arranged according to the six classes of Linnæus, each section having separate pagination, which is continuous from Vol. I to Vol. II.

Under each of the species of birds mentioned the Latin name is given, the vernacular names in different languages, a brief description, literature, mention of the particular genus or higher systematic groups, a description of the species, its habits and distribution, the possibility of keeping it in captivity, and its practical value to mankind.

The plates (engravings coloured by hand) were executed from drawings by J. W. Palmstruch and engraved by him or by C. V. Venus or Ruckman.

PÁLSSON, B.
1772. Vice-Lavmand Eggert Olafsens og Land-

Physici Biarne Povelsens Reise igiennem Island ... See *Olafsson, E.*
1774—75. Des Vice-Lavmands Eggert Olafsens und des Landphysici Biarne Povelsens Reise durch Island ... See *Olafsson, E.*
1802. Voyage en Islande ... See *Olafsson, E.*

PARIS. ACADÉMIE DES SCIENCES DE L'INSTITUT DE FRANCE. See *Académie des Sciences de l'Institut de France. Paris.*

PARIS. MUSÉUM D'HISTOIRE NATURELLE. See *Muséum d'Histoire Naturelle. Paris.*

PARKE, J. G.
1859. Reports of explorations and surveys ... for a railroad from the Mississippi River to the Pacific Ocean ... 1853—6 ... Vol. X. Report of explorations ... near the 32d parallel of north latitude ... between Dona Ana, on the Rio Grande, and the Pimas Villages, on the Gila, by Lieutenant John G. Parke ... 1855. Zoological report. pp. 9—20: No. 1. Report upon birds collected on the survey. See *Heermann, A. L.*

PEARSON, T. G.
1936. Birds of America. Editor-in-chief T. Gilbert 389. Pearson. Consulting editor John Burroughs. Contributing editors Edward H. Forbush, Herbert K. Job, William L. Finley, L. Nelson Nichols. Managing editor George Gladden. Associate editor J. Ellis Burdick. Artists R. I. Brasher, R. Bruce Horsfall, Henry Thurston. With ... plates in full color by Louis Agassiz Fuertes. Garden City Publishing Company. *Garden City, New York. 3 parts in 1 vol. text-figs. 111 col. pl. large 8vo.* — Part I. *pp. XLIV +* [*I*] *+ 272. 46 col. pl. (41 pl. birds (numb. 1—41); 5 pl. eggs. (numb. 1—5)).* Part II. *pp. 271. 34 col. pl. (numb. 42—75).* Part III. *pp. 289. 31 col. pl. (numb. 76 —106).*

The first edition of this work, which appeared in 1917, was prepared for the University Society and was included as three volumes of their 'Nature Lovers' Library' (New York, 110 col. pl., 4to).

The book is written for bird-lovers and is in simple language that can be easily understood by the layman. It gives a complete account on the birds of North America. Each form is mentioned by its Latin name, after which the text gives, in smaller type, information under the headings : other names, general description, color, nest and eggs, and distribution. The remainder of the text concerning the individual form is printed in larger type and deals especially with the habits and behaviour of the bird.

The beautiful coloured plates were executed by the three-colour process, the plates with figures of eggs from drawings by Henry Thurston. The original paintings by Fuertes are in the New York State Museum at Albany. The 106 plates in question are derived from Elon Howard Eaton's 'Birds of New York' (Albany 1910—14, 2 vols., 4to).

PECHUEL-LOESCHE, E.
1891—92. Brehms Tierleben ... Dritte ... Auflage. Herausgegeben von Pechuel-Loesche. Vols. IV —VI. Die Vögel ... neubearbeitet von Pechuel-Loesche. See *Brehm, A. E.*

23

PELT LECHNER, A. A. van.

390. *1910 [1911]—1913 [—14].* 'Oologia Neerlandica'. Eggs of birds breeding in the Netherlands. By A. A. van Pelt Lechner. With ... plates containing 667 objects of which 617 printed in colours and 50 in collotype, taken from specimens in the author's collection. Martinus Nijhoff. *The Hague. 2 vols. 191 pl. (173 col.). 4to.* — Vol. I. *pp.* [*VI*] + [*228*]. *99 pl. eggs (numb. 1—99; 85 col. (numb. 1—75, 77—82, 89—90, 92—93)).* Vol. II *pp.* [*V*] + [*176*]. *92 pl. eggs (numb. 100—191; 88 col. (numb. 100—109, 113—119, 121—191)).*

This work was published in seven parts and was also issued in Dutch, 1910—14.

The text consists of a brief introduction to the families represented in Holland by more than one species, and also of tables showing the most important data relating to eggs and breeding habits, such as colour, average weight and texture of shell, average dimensions, shape and number of the eggs, the nest and its site, breeding season, and duration of incubation.

These tables face the plates to which they belong, the pictures of the eggs being mounted in frames sunk in thin card, thus producing a particularly pleasing effect; when coloured, the figures are reproduced by the three-colour process.

PELZELN, A. von.

391. [*1865*]. Reise der österreichischen Fregatte Novara um die Erde ... 1857—59. B. von Wüllerstorf-Urbair. Herausgegeben im Allerhöchsten Auftrage unter der Leitung der kaiserlichen Akademie der Wissenschaften. Zoologischer Theil. Vol. I. (Wirbelthiere.) 1869. [Part] 2. < -- Vögel. Von August von Pelzeln >. In Commission bei Karl Gerold's Sohn. *Wien. pp. IV + 3—176. 6 col. pl. (numb. I—VI; 1 pl. eggs. (numb. VI)). 4to* .

The route of this voyage, the ornithological results of which are published in the present work, was from Trieste via Gibraltar, Madeira, Rio de Janeiro to the Cape of Good Hope, through the Indian Ocean to Ceylon, Madras, and Singapore, hence via Java, Manila, the coast of China, and the Caroline Islands to Australia and New Zealand, and then across the Pacific, calling at Tahiti, to Valparaiso, and from here via Cape Horn and the Azores back to Trieste.

The results were issued under the above-mentioned general title in 1861—75 in eight separate parts, comprising altogether 21 volumes in 4to, of which zoology occupies two volumes (in six).

The expedition was led by Commodore v. Wüllerstorf-Urbair, with Georg Frauenfeld and Johann Zelebor as zoologists, the latter of whom collected vertebrates including ornithological specimens. He also collected several notes on the habits of birds, their occurrence, contents of stomachs, the dimensions of fresh specimens, etc. These notes have been used in the present systematic treatment of the material, which consisted of 1500 specimens of birds, 120 nests, and 250 eggs, acquired by collection, as gifts and by purchase.

Descriptions are only given of new or incompletely known species and of especially strange specimens, the main stress having been laid upon an account of the variations within the species and of its geographical distribution.

The plates (chromo-lithographs; T. F. Zimmermann, pinx.; lith. A. Hartinger or J. Strohmayer; Art. lith. Anstalt v. Ant. Hartinger & Sohn, Wien) show figures of seven species of birds and the eggs of sixteen species.

PENNANT, T.

392. [*1761*—] *1766.* The British zoology. Class I. Quadrupeds. II. Birds. Published under the inspection of the Cymmrodorion Society, instituted for the promoting useful charities, and the knowledge of nature, among the descendants of the ancient Britons. Illustrated with one hundred and seven copper plates. < -- *pp. 57—162:* Class II. Birds >. Printed by J. and J. March, on Tower-Hill, for the Society. *London. 121 col. pl. large fol.*

The ornithological section of the first edition of the work. The issue of these descriptions of mammals and birds began in 1761. Up to 1766 four parts appeared with altogether 107 plates, as stated on the title-page, 98 of which represented birds. A fifth part, or appendix, with 25 plates (23 of birds) was then issued, bringing the number of plates up to 132, eleven of which represent mammals.

The text is printed in double columns. The birds are divided into land birds and water birds, and under each species some synonyms and references to the literature are given, to which are added a brief description and remarks on the habits of the bird.

The volume further contains 'A catalogue of the British birds', etc., which enumerates 24 genera of land birds and 18 genera of water birds, with the addition of the names of the species in different languages.

The plates (engravings; P. Mazell sculp., coloured by hand by P. Paillou) were executed from original designs by P. Paillou, some few by G. Edwards, P. Brown, and C. Collins.

As will be seen, the name of the author is not found on the title-page. It did not appear until the fifth edition, 1812. The second edition of the work appeared in 8vo in 1768 (394), with the addition of Vol. III, 1769, and a supplement (third edition) 1770. The fourth edition, with 277 plates (98 of birds) was issued, both in 8vo and 4to, in 1776—77; the fifth edition appeared in 1812 (399). Another edition with 295 plates was published in 1818—21.

An edition in German and Latin in large folio was published at Augsburg in 1771—76, from the second English edition, 1768, of Vols. I—II.

In 1763 an 'Explantation of the plates contained in the first publication' was issued (393).

1763. Explanation of the plates contained in the 3 first publication of the British zoology. *London. pp. 16. 8vo.*

In this list of the 25 plates in the first part of the 'British zoology', 1761 (392), it is stated that 'the Second publication is in great forwardness', from which the latter would seem to have been published in 1763 at the earliest. A description at length of the 'Soland' Goose (Sula bassana L.) is found on pp. 8—15, otherwise the list contains names and a few references to the literature only.

1768. British zoology ... < -- *pp.* *109*—*120* + 3 *117—522 + IX:* Class II. Birds >. Benjamin White. *London. 16 pl. 8vo.* —Vol. I. *pp. 117—120 + *109 —*120 + 121—232. 4 pl. (numb. III—V + (1 to face) page *110).* Vol. II (i. e. pp. 232—522 + IX). Genus XVIII, &c. With an appendix, an essay on birds of passage, and an index. *12 pl. (numb. VI—XVII).*

The two volumes, the ornithological section of which is cited above, deal with mammals and birds and constitute the second edition of the work, the first edition was issued in 1761—66 (392).

The appendix in Vol. II consists of the following sections, 'Birds now extinct in Great-Britain, or such as wander here accidentally' (pp. 487—494 with plates XII—XVII), information about the importance of the birds as food, notably on festive occasions in earlier days (pp. 495—496), 'Additions to Class I. and II.' (pp. 497—504), and 'Of the migration of British birds' (pp. 505—522).

The plates (Mazell fecit) were executed from drawings by Paillou, G. Edwards, and Desmoulins.

In addition to the volumes containing mammals and birds Vol. III of this edition was issued (printed in Chester), containing Class III, Reptiles, and IV, Fishes, in 1769. A supplementary volume, often called the third edition of the work, appeared in 1770, with 103 plates, by which the total number of the plates in the four volumes was increased to 139.

95. [*1769*]. < Indian zoology >. [*London*]. *pp. 14.*
11 col. pl. birds (numb. II—XII). fol.
The first and only part ever to appear of a projected work
with descriptions and figures of Indian animals.
It contains 12 plates, of which Pl. I represents a mammal.
There is no title-page. The text is printed in English and
French in parallel columns, and describes the birds figured on
the plates, which are mentioned by their scientific names, and
the plants often used as backgrounds. It also gives desultory
information about the habits and occurrence of the birds in
India.
At the bottom of p. 14 the following title is found : 'Of
the Bird of Paradise : and the Phoenix' ; however, the description
of these birds was first published in the work of Forster
mentioned below.
Pennant's 'Indian Zoology' is of importance from a nomen-
clatorial standpoint because the species are described and figured
under scientific names. It has also been treated from this point
of view by A. O. Hume (761), Alfred Newton (827), and
J. A. Allen (654). Copies of this work are very rare. It is not
listed in the Catalogue of the Library of the British Museum
(Natural History).
The plates (engravings coloured by hand) were engraved
by P. Mazell. On a slip glued to page I and dated May 10,
1769, may be read :
'Indian Zoology. This work is formed from the fine collection of drawings of animals brought over by J. G. Loten,
Esq ; late governor in Ceylon, which were painted from the
life by several able hands, and communicated by him to T.
Pennant, Esq ;
Twelve prints, with descriptions of the new and unengraved
quadrupeds, birds, and fish, will be published at a time : the
whole work to be concluded in six sets, of twelve plates each.
At the end will be given a brief systematic view of the animals
of the Indies, its islands ; with some attempts to clear up the
accounts given by the antients of the animals of India'.
The plates published in this part were handed over to J. R.
Forster, who used them together with three other engraved
but as yet unpublished plates in his 'Indische Zoologie', 1781 ;
2nd edition 1795 (149), under which entry further information
is found about the work and the plates, the originals for which
are said to be copies by Sydney Parkinson from figures drawn by
the native Indian artist P. C. de Bevere.
The second edition of this work appeared in 1791, dated
1790, with 16 col. pl., 4to (149, note).

1776. New illustrations of zoology ... *See Brown, P.*
6.   1781. Genera of birds. B. White *London. pp. [VI]*
+XXV + [I] + 68 [+ 2]. 15 pl. (numb. I—III|IV,
V—XVI). 4to.
A copy of the second edition of this work, the first edition
of which, text only, was published by Robert Ramsay in 1773.
In the preface (pp. I—XXV) a general account is given
of the group of birds, concluded by a 'Table of arrangement',
in which the birds are divided into two main groups 'land-birds'
and 'water-fowl', and further subdivided into nine orders with
altogether 95 genera, which are cited under their English and
Latin names. After an explanation of the figure on the engraved
title-page there follow (pp. 1—57) a brief account of the
various orders and genera with the addition of synonyms, including the Latin names, and (pp. 59—68) an explanation of
the plates (engravings, Nos. III—IV on one plate).

7.   1785. Arctic zoology. Vol. II. Class II. Birds.
Printed by Henry Hughs. *London. pp. 187—586 +*
[12] + [1]. 15 pl. (numb. IX—XXIII). 4to.
The ornithological section of a work, the first volume of
which (Introduction and Class I. Quadrupeds) was published
in 1784. A supplementary volume, often called Vol. III, was
issued in 1787.
The work, which must be regarded as the most prominent
of Pennant's works, was originally planned as a sketch of the
zoology of North America, but was later enlarged with the
addition of descriptions of the quadrupeds and birds of the
parts of Europe and Asia lying north of latitude 60⁰ N.
The section thus added has been inserted in the text in
the form of an appendix to each genus, and is distinguished by
a *fleur-de-lis.*

A great number of species of birds are treated in the
present volume. They are cited under their vernacular names,
with the addition of synonyms, the subject-matter under each
species being otherwise grouped under such headings as description, place, manners, uses, note, nest, place and migration.
The northern countries are depicted in Vol. I in 'Introduction. Of the arctic world' (pp. I—CC + pp. [V]), in
which the description of animal life, including birds, plays an
essential part.
The plates (engravings ; P. Mazell sculp.) were executed
from drawings by Moses Griffith, P. Brown, and others.
The second edition of the work was published in 1792
(3 vols., 4to), a German edition in 1787 (398), and a French
edition, 'Le nord du globe', in 1789 (2 vols., 8vo) ; a Dutch
edition, too, exists. The work was, however, not translated into
Swedish, as claimed by Mullens (621, VI, p. 264), though
Samuel Ödmann, who contributed to the work, reviewed it in
'Uppfostrings-Sälskapets almänna tidningar', Stockholm, 1787
(Part 1, pp. 60—62, seqq.) ; this is possibly the cause of Mul-
lens' mistake.

1787. Thiergeschichte der nördlichen Polarländer. *398.*
Aus dem Englischen des Herrn Thomas Pennant, mit
Anmerkungen und Zusätzen durch E. A. W. Zimmermann. Vol. II. Naturgeschichte der Vögel. Siegfried Lebrecht Crusius. *Leipzig. pp. [VI] + 181—*
568 + [2]. 15 pl. (numb. IX—XXIII). 4to.
The ornithological section of a German edition of 'Arctic
zoology' issued in 1784—85 (397).
The present translation, like the first English edition, consists of the two volumes, or 'Theile', which both appeared in
1787.
The plates are identical with the corresponding ones in the
English edition referred to above.

1812. British zoology, by Thomas Pennant. A new *399.*
edition ... Wilkie and Robinson. *London. 96 pl. birds.*
8vo. — Vol. I. - - *pp. 189—568* and Vol. II: British
zoology. Class II. Birds. Benj. White. *London.* 1776.
— Vol. I. *pp. 189—568:* Div. I. Land birds. *49 pl.*
(numb. XVII—XXXII, XXXV, XXXIV—XXXVI,
XLI, XXXVIII—XXXIX, XLI—LIV, LVI—LIX,
*LXII, 92, App. I—V + (1 to face) page *110). Vol.
II. Div. II. Water fowl. *pp. VII + 452. 47 pl. (numb.*
App. VI—IX, LXI—LXVIII, XV, LXX—LXXXII,
LXXXIV—LXXXV, XXXI—XXXII, XXVIII,
LXXXVIII—XCV, LXXXV, XCVII—CIII).
This is the 8vo issue of the fifth edition of the work which
was originally issued in 1761—66 (392). In the present posthumous edition, the first with the author's name on the title-
page, the work was also issued in 4to, and consists of four
volumes with altogether 294 plates. It is generally said to have
been issued by Pennant's son, D. Pennant, who was assisted
by various scientists, among others John Latham, who revised
and augmented the ornithological portion.
The numbers of the plates are taken from the previous
editions ; they are re-numbered in the indices, according to which
four plates in the ornithological section are missing (Index Pl.
XVI, LII, LVII in Vol. I ; Pl. XIII in Vol. II).
The illuminated separate title-pages in the volumes are taken
from the fourth edition of the work, 1776—77.
The plates were engraved (some few by P. Mazell) from
drawings by M. Griffith, and others, e. g. by G. Edwards,
Desmoulins, P. Paillou, and Syd. Parkinson.
Vol. II contains (pp. 297—436) an appendix divided into
a series of numbers (I—XI) of diverse, though chiefly ornithological contents.

PERRAULT, C.

1757. Der Herren Perrault, Charras [*sic*] und *400.*
Dodarts Abhandlungen zur Naturgeschichte der
Thiere und Pflanzen; welche ehemals der königl. franz.
Akad. der Wissenschaften vorgetragen worden; Mit
dazu gehörigen nach dem Leben gezeichneten Kup-
23*

fern. Aus dem Französischen übersetzet. Arkstee und Merkus. *Leipzig.* 2 vols. *4to.* — Vol. I. *pp. XXVI +* [*II*] + 346 + [*14*]. 6 *pl. birds. (numb. XXXII— XXXVII).* Vol. II. *pp.* [*IV*] +378 + [*18*]. 25 *pl. birds. (numb. XLVIII—LVIII, LXV—LXVI, LXIX —LXXIV, LXXXV—XC).*
The third and last volume of this work, which includes M. Charas' description of the anatomy of the Viper and D. Dodart's natural history of plants, appeared in 1758.

Perrault based his part of the work on dissections of animals carried out by members of the 'Académie des Sciences' in Paris, an institution founded in 1666. From these he issued, in 1669, the first collection of treatises, 'Description anatomique d'un cameleon, d'un castor', etc., which, together with other papers of similar nature, was re-issued in 1671—76 in large folio under the title 'Mémoires pour servir à l'histoire naturelle des animaux', sequel (Suite, etc.).

Various editions of the work appeared subsequently and translations of it were made, including one into English.

The present German translation was made by Johann Joachim Schwabe from an edition published in Paris in 1731—34.

The sections dealing with birds are chiefly of an anatomical nature, and are found in Vol. I, pp. 245—284, and Vol. II, pp. 15—126, 191—202, 215—250, and 339—370. The plates belonging to these sections contain anatomical figures, and portraits of birds (engravings; several Cl. Duflos fecit).

PERRY, M. C.

1856. Narrative of the expedition of an American squadron to the China Seas and Japan ... 1852—54, under the command of Commodore M. C. Perry ... Vol. II. pp. 215—248: Birds. *See Cassin, J.*

PERSIAN BOUNDARY COMMISSION, Journeys.

1876. Eastern Persia. An account of the journeys of the Persian Boundary Commission 1870—72. Vol. II ... pp. 98—304: Aves. *See Blanford, W. T.*

PETÉNYI, J. S. von.

401.   *1905.* Ungarische Ornithologische Centrale. Ornithologische Fragmente aus den Handschriften von Johann Salamon von Petényi. Deutsch bearbeitet von Titus Csörgey. Mit einer Einleitung von Otto Herman. Fr. Eugen Köhler. *Gera-Untermhaus. pp. XXXVI + 400. text-figs. 5 pl. (4 col. pl. birds). 8vo.*
A biography of the author of the ornithological manuscripts, published in this work, which originate from the first half of the nineteenth century, was written by Otto Herman in the introduction (pp. V—XXII). In his fragmentary notes, often taken down on chance slips of paper, Petényi collected a considerable amount of material referring to the biology of birds, and explained many facts that had hitherto been unknown.

The coloured plates (three-colour prints) were executed from drawings by Titus Csörgey.

PHILADELPHIA. ACADEMY OF NATURAL SCIENCES. *See Academy of Natural Sciences of Philadelphia.*

PHILLIP, A.

402.   *1789.* The voyage of Governor Phillip to Botany Bay; with an account of the establishment of the colonies of Port Jackson & Norfolk Island; compiled from the authentic papers, which have been obtained from the several departments. to [*sic*] which are added the journals of Lieuts. Shortland, Watts, Ball & Capt. Marshall; with an account of their new discoveries embellished with fifty five copper plates. The maps

and charts taken from actual surveys ... John Stockdale. *London. pp.* 6 + [*I*] + *VIII* + [*XI*] + *X* + 298 + *LXXIV* + [*2*]. *19 pl. birds (numb. 5, 18 —29, 40—44, 53 in 'List of the plates'). 4to.*
The object of this journey was to found a convict settlement in Australia. The expedition, which consisted of eleven ships, left England in April, 1787, and, among other achievements, founded the city of Sydney, as the situation of the earlier convict settlement at Botany Bay was found to be unsatisfactory.

Birds are mentioned in several places in the volume, especially in the zoological sections, 'Some specimens of animals from New South Wales. Birds', pp. 152—167, and 'Supplemental account of animals. Birds', pp. 267—273 and 287—288. The ornithological sections are based chiefly on Latham, who is thanked in the advertisement (p. III) 'for having furnished many drawings and accurate descriptions, which stamp a value on the natural history contained in this work'. There are also many quotations from and references to Latham's works, for instance reference is made on p. 268 without further statement to 'the General Synopsis of Birds, Supplement' (278).

The volume is provided with an engraved title-page and contains 51 plates (engravings; the majority P. Mazell sculp.) and three maps and plans. The plates with figures of birds were chiefly executed from drawings by A. Latham.

The second edition of the work appeared in 1790 (403). In the same year the third edition was issued, while a French translation (by Millin, 8vo) was published in 1791, and abridged German editions in 1790 and 1791.

In 1793 F. A. A. Meyer issued 'Systematisch-summarische Uebersicht der neuesten zoologischen Entdeckungen in Neuholland und Afrika', which contains (Section 1) a 'Systematischsummarische Uebersicht der Neuholländischen Thiere welche der Gouverneur A. Phillip und der Wundarzt J. White beschrieben haben'.

1790. The voyage of Governor Phillip to Botany   *4* Bay ... Second edition. <-- *pp. 140—163:* Animals. Class II. Aves >. John Stockdale. *London 19 col. pl. (numb. 22—40 in 'List of the plates'). 4to.*
The ornithological section of the second edition of this work. The title of the volume reads as that of the first edition. In contrast to the first edition (402) published in 1789, the present edition has all the ornithological matter in one section and further contains (pp. LXXVII—CLXXV) an 'Appendix continued. The history of New Holland, from its first discovery in MDCXVI, to the present time. And a discourse on banishment by ... Lord Auckland', 1790.

The plates differ from those of the first edition merely in that they are coloured.

PIDGEON, E.

1827—29. The animal kingdom ... by the baron Cuvier ... Vols. VI—VIII. The class aves ... with specific descriptions by ... Edward Pidgeon ... *See Cuvier, G. L. C. F. D.*

PIESCH, D.

1784. Sammlung von Nestern und Eyern verschiedener Vögel ... Zweites Heft. *See Wirsing, A. L.*, 1872—86.

PLESKE, T. D.

[*1889—*] *1891[—92*]. Ornithographia Rossica. Die   *4* Vogelfauna des Russischen Reichs von Th. Pleske. Vol. II. Sylviinæ. Commissionaires de l'Académie Impériale des Sciences: M. Eggers et Cie. *St.-Pétersbourg. pp. 12 + [2] + 13 + LIII + 665. text-figs. 4 col. pl. (numb. I—IV). 4to.*
The text and the non-Latin part of the title of this work are printed in Russian and German in parallel columns. The work was issued in five parts (589, II, p. 493), the present volume being the only one ever issued; no Vol. I was published.

On the basis of the literature available and the collections of Russian birds in the zoological museum of the St. Petersburg Academy, the genera and species of the birds mentioned in the present volume are dealt with in detail.

According to the programme of the work, Vol. I was to contain a survey of the ornithological literature of Russia, a historical survey of the ornithological investigation of Russia, a determination and characterization of the ornithological regions of the Russian Empire, a key to the determination and a characterization of orders and families. The remaining volumes, like the present one, were to contain a key to the determination of genera, a characterization of them, keys to the determination of the species, and monographs of the individual species with the addition of a brief synonymy of the names of the species, a list of the figures of the species, references to works dealing with Russian avifauna which contain descriptions or systematic notes, popular names used by the Russian people, a brief diagnosis in Latin, a description, a brief survey of the geographical distribution, a detailed account of the distribution in the Russian Empire, depiction of the habitat and the vertical distribution, brief data on the habits of the birds, a tabular summary of the specimens deposited in the zoological museum of the St. Petersburg Academy, and a similar one of nests and eggs.

Of the plates, Pl. I belongs to Fasc. 1, Pl. II to Fasc. 2, Pl. III to Fasc. 3—4, Pl. IV to Fasc. 5. They contain altogether 25 figures of birds, and were executed in lithography (drawn and lit. by G. Mützel, printed by C. Böhm, Berlin) coloured by hand.

5. *1889—1905.* Wissenschaftliche Resultate der von N. M. Przewalski nach Central-Asien unternommenen Reisen. Auf Kosten einer von Seiner Kaiserlichen Hoheit dem Grossfürsten Thronfolger Nikolai Alexandrowitsch gespendeten Summe herausgegeben von der Kaiserlichen Akademie der Wissenschaften. Zoologischer Theil. Vol. II. Vögel. Bearbeitet von Th. Pleske. (Part 4: Bearbeitet von V. Bianchi). Commissionäre der Kaiserlichen Akademie der Wissenschaften: Eggers & Co. *St. Petersburg. pp. 1—192 + II + 193—360. 10 col. pl. (numb. I—X; 1 pl eggs (numb. V)). 4to.*

The unfinished ornithological section of the work on the zoological results of Prževal'skij's four journeys to Central Asia. These results were very valuable, and were collected and published in Lieferungen distributed over three volumes.

The present section on birds deals with the order Passeres and was published in four 'Lieferungen', of which Lieferung 1 (pp. 1—80 and Pl. I and III) appeared on December 10, 1889, Lieferung 2 (pp. 81—144, Pl. II, IV—VI) on September 20, 1890, Lieferung 3 (pp. 145—192, Pl. VIII and IX) on June 1, 1894, Lieferung 4 (pp. II + 193—360, Pl. VII and X) on May 15, 1905.

The title on the covers of the parts — no title-page was published in the four parts — is printed both in Russian (the front page of the first leaf) and in German (the back of the first leaf), the text being printed in Russian and German in parallel columns. In addition to the first three parts, Pleske also wrote the last section of the chapter on the family Motacillidæ in Part 4, which also deals with material collected by later expeditions than those led by Prževal'skij.

The work gives under each species a detailed list of the specimens collected, while the subject-matter under each species is otherwise divided into a systematic part with a detailed description of the bird in different plumages, and a part dealing with its geographical distribution and habits.

The plates are lithographs coloured by hand; I—VI (printed by C. Böhm, Berlin) were drawn and lithographed by G. Mützel, VII—X (Mintern Bros. imp. London) by J. G. Keulemans.

POLLEN, F. P. L.
1867—68. Recherches sur la faune de Madagascar et de ses dépendances, d'après les découvertes de Fran-

çois P. L. Pollen ... 2me Partie. Mammifères et oiseaux. *See Schlegel, H.*

POWYS, T. L., Fourth Baron Lilford. *See Lilford, T. L. P., Fourth Baron.*

POYNTING, F.
1895—96. Eggs of British birds, with an account 406. of their breeding-habits. Limicolæ. With ... coloured plates. By Frank Poynting. R. H. Porter. *London. pp. VIII + [254] + IX—XVI. 54 col. pl. (numb. 1—54 in the 'Contents'). 4to.*

The work was published in four parts, and the dates of publication and contents are stated on p. XVI of the volume. According to this statement Parts I and II appeared in 1895 (in October and November respectively), Parts III—IV in 1896 (February and July respectively). The text concerning each form is paginated separately, but the final paging is given in the 'Contents', pp. III—IV.

The completion of the work was prevented by the death of the author. The present section deals with the wading birds, whose habits — notably their nesting habits — are illustrated by numerous quotations from the particular literature.

The work is renowned for its reliability, which also distinguishes the beautiful plates (chromo-lithographs; litho. Wilhelm Greve, Berlin), chiefly made from originals designed by the author. The eggs of some American species which occur as accidental visitors in the British Isles, were drawn by J. L. Ridgway from specimens in the collection of the U. S. National Museum. Some few plates and figures were executed from drawings by M. Horman-Fisher from specimens in the Natural History Museum, South Kensington. Herbert Massey's collection also supplied a good deal of material for the figures on the plates, the value of which — over and above their fine execution — consists in the representation on them of several variations of the eggs of the individual form.

PRÉVOST, F.
1838—43. Les pigeons. Vol. II. *See Knip, A. P. J. R., 1809—43.*

PRINCETON UNIVERSITY.
1904—28. Reports of the Princeton University expeditions to Patagonia, 1896—1899 ... Vol. II. Ornithology. *See Scott, W. E. D.*

PROCEEDINGS OF THE ZOOLOGICAL SOCIETY OF LONDON. *See Zoological Society of London.*

PRUETZ, G.
[1884—86]. Illustrirtes Mustertauben-Buch. Ent- 407. haltend das Gesammte der Taubenzucht. Herausgegeben von Gustav Prütz. Mit ... Pracht-Farbendruck-Bildern direkt nach der Natur aufgenommen von Christian Förster und 40 Original-Text-Illustrationen. J. F. Richter. *Hamburg, pp. XV + 438. text-figs. 81 col. pl. 4to.*

Published in 40 Lieferungen, which appeared in 1884 (1—9, pp. 1—96), 1885 (10—23, pp. 97—224), and 1886 (24—40, pp. XV + pp. 225—438).

A comprehensive description of domestic pigeons and their different forms which, distributed over five groups, are dealt with on pp. 40—294, while more general subjects are treated on pp. 1—39, pp. 294—315 ('Färbung und Zeichnung der Haustauben'), pp. 316—344 ('Der Körperbau der Taube'), and pp. 344—431 ('Die Krankheiten der Tauben'). Some recent forms are mentioned and figured in a 'Nachtrag' (pp. 432—438).

The plates are executed in chromo-lithography (Lithogr. u. Druck von J. F. Richter, Hamburg).

PRUSSIA. STAATLICHE STELLE FUER NA-
TURDENKMALPFLEGE. *See Staatliche Stelle
fuer Naturdenkmalpflege in Preussen.*

PRŽEVAL'SKIJ, N. M.
   1876—78. Ornithological miscellany. Vols. II—
III. *See Rowley, G. D.*, 1875—78.
   1889—1905. Wissenschaftliche Resultate der von
N. M. Przewalski nach Central-Asien unternommenen
Reisen ... Zoologischer Theil. Vol. II. Vögel. *See
Pleske, T. D.*

PYCRAFT, W. P.
408.   [*1907?*]. < The living animals of the world. - -
pp. 385—544: Book II. Birds. By W. P. Pycraft>.
text-figs. 5 col. pl. 4to.
   The ornithological section of an abundantly illustrated
popular work in six books, in which the different groups of animals ars discussed by various authors. The title-page is lacking.
   The birds are treated in a series of chapters (I—XVII) in
which the various groups are briefly discussed. The coloured
plates (three-colour prints) are executed from photographs.
   The work was issued in an enlarged form in 1924 (409).
   1910. On the systematic position of the petrels.
See Godman, F. D., 1907—10.
   1910. On some points in the anatomy of Bradypterus cinnamomeus. *See Ogilvie-Grant, W. R.*
   1910—13. The British bird book ... *See Kirkman,
F. B. B.*
409.   *1924.* Hutchinson's Animals of all countries. 'The
living animals of the world in picture and story'. Vol.
II. < - - *pp. 775—1200:* Birds. By W. P. Pycraft >.
Hutchinson & Co. *London. text-figs. 10 col. pl. 4to.*
   This popular work was issued in 50 parts in 1923—25.
   In the present ornithological section — an enlarged revision
of a previous work (408) — the birds are described in a
series of chapters (XIII—XXXV) which not only deal with
the individual groups, but also with questions of a more general
character, such as the classification and the geographical
distribution of birds.
   The coloured plates (three-colour prints), which show the
birds in their natural surroundings, are derived from various
sources, such as photographs, and paintings by H, H, Johnston

QUENSEL, C.
   1806. Svensk zoologi ... Part 1. *See Palmstruch,
J. W.*

QUOY, J. R. C.
410.   *1830—33.* Voyage de découvertes de l'Astrolabe
exécuté ... 1826—29, sous le commandement de J.
Dumont d'Urville. Zoologie par Quoy et Gaimard.
J. Tastu. *Paris.* — Vol. I. 1830. - - < *pp. 153—259:*
Oiseaux>. *8vo.* Atlas. 1833. Voyage de la corvette
l'Astrolabe ... - - < Oiseaux>. *31 col. pl. birds (numb.
1—31). large fol.*
   The ornithological section of the report on the expedition,
which was published in its entirety in 1830—35, in 14 vols.
text and 7 vols. atlas, in 8vo, 4to, and large folio (869, II,
p. 333).
   In addition to the section cited above and the ornithological
parts of the indices in Vol. I, the general indices in Vol. III
are also of importance for the use of the ornithological matter
of the work, in which a number of new species of birds are
described.
   The three plates, on which the birds described, altogether
61, are figured, are engraved, printed in colour and, in many
cases, retouched by hand (Rémond, Ve. Drouart, Duménil,
Finot, or Langlois imp.), chiefly from originals by J. G. Prêtre,

and further by A. Prévost and Oudart, while the plates were
engraved by Massard, Mme Massard, Adèle Massard, Migneret,
Victor, Melle Coignet, Guyard, Manceau, Géraud, Goutière,
and Dequevauviller.

RADDE, G. F. R.
   1863. Reisen im Süden von Ost-Sibirien ... 1855
—1859 incl. im Auftrage der Kaiserlichen Geogra-
phischen Gesellschaft ausgeführt von Gustav Radde.
Vol. II. Die Festlands-Ornis des südöstlichen Sibiriens. Buchdruckerei von W. Besobrasoff & Co. *St.
Petersburg. pp. [VI] + 392. 15 col. pl. (numb. I—X,
11, XII—XIII, 14, XV). 4to.*
   The results of the expedition as regards mammals and birds
were discussed by Radde and issued in two volumes, of which
Vol. I (mammals) appeared in 1862. The present Vol. II
contains (pp. 7—24) a tabular list of the birds, altogether 328
species, occurring in the land area in question. This is followed (pp. 25—78) by some general remarks, an outline of
bird life in Southeast Siberia and a summary of observations
on the migrations at Tarei-nor.
   The essential part of the work (pp. 79—389) is the
description of the individual forms, altogether 270 species or
varieties.
   The plates (chromo-lithographs; Lith. Anst. v. N. Broese
in St. Petersburg) were executed from drawings by G. Radde.
   1884. Ornis Caucasica. Die Vogelwelt des Kaukasus systematisch und biologisch-geographisch beschrieben von Gustav Radde. Theodor Fischer. *Kassel.
pp. XI + [V] + 592. text-figs. 26 col. pl. (front. +
Nos. I—XXV; 1 pl. eggs (numb. XXI)). 1 map.
4to.*
   This work was published in 20 Lieferungen, of which Lieferung 1 (pp. 32 with 4 plates) contains the introduction, the
explanation of plates, and the beginning of the list of the
species of birds of the Caucasus district. This list, which ends
on p. 49, is followed by the main part of the work (pp. 51—
492), the systematic treatment of the individual forms, 367
species with 66 varieties, based on a collection of about 4400
skins, mostly collected by the author on his own expeditions.
On these he gained an insight into the habits of the birds,
of which he has taken advantage when dealing with the individual forms, the matter being divided into two sections, —
'Systematisches' and 'Lebensweise und Verbreitung'.
   The remainder of the work contains sections dealing with
the geography of the Caucasian countries (pp. 493—520), the
migrations of the birds (pp. 521—557), a compilation of data
relative to the migrations (pp. 558—587), and the first supplement to the work (pp. 588—589). The second supplement
was published in the 'Journal f. Ornithologie', 33, 1885, pp.
74—81, the third supplement in the 'Ornis', 1887, pp. 457—
500, and the fourth supplement in the 'Ornis', 1890, pp. 400—
441.
   The plates (chromo-lithographs, Artist. Anst. v. Th. Fischer,
Cassel) were executed from drawings by G. Radde.

RAFFLES, T. S. B.
   1826—35. Illustrations of ornithology ... Vols. I—
III. *See Jardine, W.*, 1826—43.

RAMSAY, R. G. W.
   1881. The ornithological works of Arthur, Ninth
Marquis of Tweeddale ... Edited and revised by ...
Robert G. Wardlaw Ramsay ... *See Tweeddale, A. H.*

RANZANI, C.
   [*1821—*] *1823—26.* Elementi di ornitologia. Di
Camillo Ranzani. Dalla Tipografia Nobili. *Bologna.
9 vols. 32 pl. (numb. I—XXXII). 8vo.*
   Vols. I—VIII are dated 1823.
   A handbook of ornithology which opens with a general
synopsis of the group of birds (Vol. I, pp. 1—86). The re-

mainder consists of a systematic treatment of the seven orders into which the birds are divided, with characterizations of them and of the other superior groups, and a description and a treatment of the individual species.

A number of the plates are signed G. Rosaspina fec.

RATHKE, J.
1806. Zoologia Danica seu animalium Daniæ et Norvegiæ rariorum ac minus notorum descriptiones et historia. Vol. IV ... *See Mueller, O. F.*

RAY (WRAY), J.
1676. Francisci Willughbeii ... Ornithologiæ libri tres ... Totum opus recognovit, digessit, supplevit Joannes Raius ... *See Willughby, F.*

4. *1767.* L'histoire naturelle, éclaircie dans une de ses parties principales, l'ornithologie, qui traite des oiseaux de terre, de mer et de riviere, tant de nos climats que des pays étrangers. Ouvrage traduit du Latin du Synopsis avium de Ray, augmenté d'un grand nombre de descriptions & de remarques historiques sur le caractere des oiseaux, leur industrie & leurs ruses. Par Salerne. Enrichi de ... figures dessinées d'après nature. Debure. *Paris. pp. XII + [IV] + 464. 31 col. pl. (numb. I. (front.), II, III, 4, 5, VI, VIII, 8, IX, 10, XI, 12—31). 4to.*

A translation of a posthumous work by Ray, 'Synopsis methodica avium', edited with a preface by W. Derham in 1713, 8vo.

The work gives synonyms, brief descriptions, the common names, and sundry information about the distribution and habits of the birds, based largely on the literature available. Salerne's share in the work has extended it far beyond the part translated from Ray, so that it is much more than a mere translation.

The plates, which contain one hundred figures of birds, are engravings, drawn and engraved by Martinet.

After Salerne's death the work was issued by A. J. Dezallier d'Argenville. It was also published with uncoloured plates, and a copy of this issue is also in the collection.

REBAU, H. *See Gebauer, C. A.*

RECHERCHE, LA, Voyage of the [French frigate].
1800. Relation du voyage à la recherche de La Pérouse ... 1791—94. *See Labillardière, J. J. H. de.*

REED, C. A.
5. *1915.* The bird book. Illustrating in natural colors more than seven hundred North American birds; also several hundred photographs of their nests and eggs. By Chester A. Reed. Doubleday, Page & Company. *New York. pp. 472 + [8]. col. illustrations. 8vo.*

A brief survey of a number (more than 768) of forms of North American birds, illustrated with coloured text-figures (three-colour prints) from the author's drawings. Several of the figures take rank as plates, as they occupy a whole page.

REICHENOW, A.
1894—1921. See Journal fuer Ornithologie.
16. *1900—05.* Die Vögel Afrikas. Von Ant. Reichenow. J. Neumann. *Neudamm. 4 vols. large 8vo.* — Vol. I. *1900—01. pp. CIV + 706. text-figs. 1 pl.* Vol. II. *1902—03. pp. XVI + 752.* Vol. III. *1904—05. pp. XXV + 880.* [Vol. IV]. Atlas. *1902. pp. 50. 30 col. pl. (numb. I—XXX in 'Übersicht der Tafeln'). 3 maps.*

Each of the volumes of this work was published in two parts, detailed information about the dates of publication being given by Zimmer (589, II, p. 516).

The introduction contains a survey of the history of the ornithological exploration of Africa (pp. VII—XXXVI), a survey of the literature (pp. XXXVII—LXXIX), and (pp. LXXXI—XCIII) some general considerations on the avifauna of Africa, especially as regards zoogeographical conditions and the habits of the birds.

The remainder of the work consists of a systematic treatment of the different forms of birds (about 2400), including descriptions of the families, genera, and species, and information about their geographical distribution and habits. Keys to the determination of genera and species are found under families and genera respectively.

The plates (lithographs coloured by hand) were executed from drawings by T. G. Meissner and Bruno Geisler (Druck v. Rau & Sohn, Dresden, and — some few — O. Hollmann, Berlin).

REID, P. S. G.
1903—05. Catalogue of the collection of birds' eggs in the British Museum ... Vols. III—IV. *See British Museum (Natural History),* 1901—12.

REIDER, J. E. von.
1830—35. Fauna Boica ... Zweite Abtheilung. Vögel. *See Hahn, C. W.*

REINHARDT, J. C. H.
1828. Pragtfugle og Pattedyr ... Part I. *See Walter, J. E. C.,* 1828—41.

REISER, O.
1894—1905. Materialien zu einer Ornis Balcanica. *417.* Herausgegeben vom Bosnisch-Hercegovinischen Landesmuseum in Sarajevo. In Commission bei Carl Gerold's Sohn (Vol. III: Adolf Holzhausen). *Wien. 3 vols. 9 col. pl. large 8vo.* — Vol. II. 1894. Bulgarien (Einschliesslich Ost-Rumeliens und der Dobrudscha). Von Othmar Reiser. *pp. XII + 204. 3 col. pl. (numb. I—III). 1 map.* Vol. III. 1905. Griechenland und die griechischen Inseln (mit Ausnahme von Kreta). Von Otmar [*sic*] Reiser. Mit ... Tafeln in Farbendruck, 5 Abbildungen in Schwarzdruck und ... Karte. *pp. XIV + 589. 4 col. pl. (numb. I—IV; 2 pl. eggs (numb. III—IV)). 1 map.* Vol. IV. 1896. Montenegro. Von Othmar Reiser 'und Ludwig v. Führer. Mit ... Tafeln in Farbendruck und ... Karte. *pp. X + 149. 2 col. pl. (numb. I—II). 1 map.*

Most of the material for the monographic account of the birds of the Balkan Peninsula, of which the present is a part, was collected on journeys undertaken by the author. Of Vol. I, which was to deal with Bosnia and Hercegovina, the first part only has been published, in 'Wissenschaftliche Mittheilungen aus Bosnien und der Hercegovina', II, 1894, pp. 662—688.

The subject-matter of the volumes is divided into a general and a special part, of which the former deals with the journeys for collection and observation and the ornithological literature on the area, concluding with a critical list of its birds, containing 303, 237 (+ 31), and 312 species or varieties in Vols. II, III, and IV respectively. The special part gives information about the forms of birds treated in it, such as their distribution within the area, their habitats and habits.

The plates with figures of birds were executed in chromolithography in Vols. II and IV, in Vol. III in handcoloured lithography (Kleinschmidt, del. et lith.). The plates showing eggs were executed by the three-colour process.

RENDAHL, C. H.
1935. Hialmar Rendahl. Fågelboken. Sveriges fåg- *418.*

lar i ord och bild. Tidens Förlag. *Stockholm. pp. XX + 546. text-figs. 16 col. pl. (numb. 1—16). large 8vo.*
This work was published in 15 parts, the last of which was actually three (numb. 15—17) and appeared in December.

It is a handbook of the birds of Sweden, in which all the birds occurring in that country are briefly and clearly described, with the addition of descriptions necessary for the identification of the species, and also the most important information about its geographical distribution, occurrence in Sweden, habits, breeding habits, and other features relating to the ecology of the bird. Genera, families, and orders, too, are briefly mentioned, with their diagnoses and information about their geographical distribution.

A considerable number of birds are figured on the plates, the figures on which are reproduced in four-colour prints from colour-photographs, some of which were taken in the open and some from stuffed museum specimens.

RENSCH, B.
1926 → See *Journal fuer Ornithologie.*

REY, J. G. C. E.
419. *1912.* Die Eier der Vögel Mitteleuropas von Eugène Rey. Mit über 1500 farbigen ·Eierabbildungen auf ... Tafeln, nach Originalen der Sammlung des .Verfassers. Zweite wohlfeile Ausgabe. Fr. Krüger. *Lobenstein. 2 vols. 8vo. —* Vol. I. Text. *pp. 681. 1 text-fig.* Vol. II. Tafeln. *128 col. pl. (numb. 1—128).*
This work was originally published in 1899—1905 in 30 Lieferungen. It is one of the best works with figures of eggs of European birds. The text describes the shape, size, and colour of the eggs while in addition the breeding area, hatching time, and nests of the particular species of birds are given ; their Latin and their vernacular names in many different languages are also stated.

Rey himself possessed a large collection of eggs, which had been used for the illustrations of the eggs in the new edition of Naumann's work (356). These figures were used in the preparation of the plates for the present work. They are executed in chromo-lithography (A. Reichert pinx.) and contain a large number of figures of birds' eggs (exclusively coloured), the variations of which are illustrated by means of a series of figures of eggs of the same species.

REYGER, G.
1766. Ova avium plurimarum ad naturalem magnitudinem delineata et genuinis coloribus picta ... See *Klein, J. T.*

RICHARD, A.
1852— ? 53. Oeuvres complètes de Buffon, mises en ordre et précédées d'une notice historique, par A. Richard ... Vols. IV—V. (Oiseaux). See *Buffon, G. L. L. de.*

RICHARDSON, J.
1831. Fauna Boreali-Americana ... containing descriptions of the objects of natural history collected on the late northern land expeditions under command of Captain Sir John Franklin. Part II. The birds. See *Swainson, W.*
1844—75. The zoology of the voyage of H. M. S. Erebus and Terror ... 1839—43 ... Edited by John Richardson and John Edward Gray ... Birds. See *Gray, G. R.*

RIDGWAY, R.
1874. A history of North American birds. Land birds. See *Baird, S. F.*

1884—87. See *Auk.*

1887. A manual of North American birds. By Robert Ridgway. Illustrated by 464 outline drawings of the generic characters. J. B. Lippincott Company. *Philadelphia. pp. XI + 631. 125 pl. (front. + 124 pl. birds on 62 leaves (numb. I—CXXIV)). large 8vo.*
A handbook of North American ornithology, limited to the smallest possible volume, everything not absolutely necessary for the determination of a specimen having been omitted.

The matter is arranged in the form of keys to the different groups, ending with the species and subspecies, with descriptions of each of these forms and a statement of the natural habitat and the character of the nest and eggs. Four new subgenera and thirty-nine new species and subspecies are given. The work was originally projected by S. F. Baird, whose death occurred just as the book was about to be issued, and a leaf (dated August 20, 1887) with an obituary of Baird has been inserted after the preface ; Baird's portrait serves as a frontispiece.

The figures in the plates (outline-drawings) were made by the author.

A second edition was issued in 1896, a popular edition in 1910, and a fourth edition in 1915.

1901—19. Smithsonian Institution. United States National Museum. Bulletin of the United States National Museum. No. 50. - - The birds of North and Middle America: A descriptive catalogue of the higher groups, genera, species, and subspecies of birds known to occur in North America, from the Arctic lands to the Isthmus of Panama, the West Indies and other islands of the Caribbean Sea, and the Galapagos Archipelago. By Robert Ridgway. Government Printing Office, *Washington. 8 vols. 222 pl. 8vo. —* Part. I. 1901. *pp. XXX + [1] + 715. 20 pl. (numb. I—XX).* Part. II. 1902. *pp. XX + 834. 22 pl. (numb. I—XXII).* Part. III. 1904. *pp. XX + 801. 19 pl. (numb. I—XIX).* Part. IV. 1907. *pp. XXII + 973. 34 pl. (numb. I—XXXIV).* Part. V. 1911. *pp. XXIII + 859. 33 pl. (numb. I—XXXIII).* Part. VI. 1914. *pp. XX + 882. 36 pl. (numb. I—XXXVI).* Part. VII. 1916. *pp. XIII + 543. 24 pl. (numb. I—XXIV).* Part. VIII. 1919. *pp. XVI + 852. 34 pl. (numb. I—XXXIV).*

This work, which was unfinished at the author's death, but may, it is supposed, be completed by two further volumes, gives a comprehensive systematic account of the birds in the lands concerned ; they are dealt with very fully within the scope of the work.

The eight volumes give full descriptions, synonymies, and geographical distribution not only of the families and higher groups, but also of 551 genera and 2,507 species and subspecies, besides 213 extralimital genera and 602 extralimital species and subspecies.

All the figures on the plates are outline-drawings illustrating the generic characters, and were drawn by the author.

RIESENTHAL, O. von.
1876 [—78]. Die Raubvögel Deutschlands und des angrenzenden Mitteleuropas. Darstellung und Beschreibung der in Deutschland und den benachbarten Ländern von Mitteleuropa vorkommenden Raubvögel. Allen Naturfreunden besonders aber der deutschen Jägerei gewidmet von O. v. Riesenthal. Theodor Fischer. *Cassel. 1 vol. text, 8vo, and 1 vol. atlas, fol. —* [Text]. *pp. XXI + 522. 1 text-fig. 6 pl. (1 unnumb. +Nos. I—V).* Atlas. *pp. [III]. 60 col. pl. (numb. I—LX).*

The text to this work was published in 12, the plates in 14, Lieferungen, as follows: Text, Parts 1—2 (pp. VII + 96) in 1876; 3—7 (pp. 97—288) in 1877; 8—12 in 1878; while of the atlas (each with four chromo-lithographs) Parts 1—2 appeared in 1876, 3—10 in 1877, and 11—14 in 1878.

The text deals with birds of prey, giving under each species synonymy, description, information about distribution and habitat, reproduction, and habits, and also methods for hunting and capture.

The plates (chromo-lithographs by Th. Fischer, Cassel) were executed from paintings by the author.

The work was also issued in an edition de luxe in large folio.

1883. Gefiederte Freunde ... Mit erläuterndem Text von O. von Riesenthal. See *Robert, L. P. S., 1880—83.*

RIJKS MUSEUM VAN NATUURLIJKE HISTORIE. See *Leyden. Rijks Museum van Natuurlijke Historie.*

ROBERT, L. P. S.

3.   1880. Glimpses of bird life. Pourtrayed with pen and pencil. By J. E. Harting and L. P. Robert. With ... coloured plates, and forty-three woodcuts and initial letters. W. Swan Sonnenschein and Allen. *London. pp. V + [40]. 20 col. pl. (numb. I—XX in 'Contents'). fol.*

The plates of this work are identical with twenty of the plates published in 1880—83 in Robert's 'Gefiederte Freunde', etc. (424) and, like the latter, are executed in chromo-lithography (imp. Lemercier & Cie.). Each of the plates is accompanied by a leaf of explanatory text, illustrated with an ornithological initial letter and a final ornithological picture.

4.   [1880—83]. Gefiederte Freunde. Bilder zur Naturgeschichte angenehmer und nützlicher Vögel Mittel-Europas. Nach der Natur gemalt von Leo Paul Robert ... chromolithographirte Tafeln in Klein-Folio. Lithographie von Thurwanger. Farbendruck von Lemercier & Co. in Paris. Mit erläuterndem Text von O. von Riesenthal. Arnoldische Buchhandlung. *Leipzig. pp. [IV]. 60 col. pl. (numb. I—LX in 'Inhalt und Eintheilung'). fol.*

These finely executed plates were published in three 'series', each comprising 20 plates, which appeared as follows: I, 1880; II, 1881; and III, 1883. Riesenthal's text volume (pp. X + 162, large 8vo) appeared in 1883.

The plates were issued in other places, too. Thus twenty of them were published in London in 1880 with text by J. E. Harting (423).

ROBERT, N.

1772. Collection d'oiseaux les plus rares ... De laquelle on a fait précéder l'Histoire particuliere des oiseaux de la Ménagerie du Roi, peints d'après nature par le célébre Robert, & gravés par lui-même ... See *Johnstone, J., 1772—74.*

ROBINSON, H. C.

1928. See *Ibis.*

ROBSON, J.

1776. Some memoirs of the life and works of George Edwards ... See *Edwards, G.*

ROCHEBRUNE, A. T. de.

5.   *[1884].* < Faune de la Sénégambie, par A. T. de

Rochebrune. Oiseaux >. [J. Durand. *Bordeaux*]. *pp. 85—459. 30 col. pl. (numb. I—XXX; 4 pl. eggs (numb. XXIV, XXVIII—XXX)). 8vo.*

A separate copy of Actes de la Société Linnéenne de Bordeaux, XXXVIII.

It is based on collections and observations made during a sojourn in Senegambia in 1875—77, the whole of the resultant work being also published separately (426).

The work deals with no fewer than 686 species, stated to belong to the fauna of Senegambia. Their places of occurrence are given and also information about their geographical distribution, together with occasional descriptions of the birds.

The plates (lithographs coloured by hand, Imp. Becquet fr. Paris) were drawn by J. Terrier.

426.   *[1884?] 1883—85.* Faune de la Sénégambie. Par A. T. de Rochebrune. Vol. I. Vertébrés. [Part 3]. Oiseaux. Octave Douin. Paris. *2 vols. large 8vo. —* Texte. *pp. 370 + 6.* Atlas. *pp. [III]. 30 col. pl. (numb. I—XXX; 4 pl. eggs (numb. XXIV, XXVIII—XXX)).*

The ornithological part of the work cited here was also published in the Actes de la Société Linnéenne de Bordeaux, XXXVIII, 1884 (425).

The entire work was issued in five parts in 1883—85, and a supplement (Fasc. I, Mammifères) in 1887. In the present copy the five original parts are bound in two volumes containing the text and the plates respectively.

ROSENIUS, J. A. M. P.

427.   *1913 →* Paul Rosenius Sveriges fåglar och fågelbon. Med fågelbilder utförda i färgljustryck efter originalmålningar av Gustaf Swenander. C. W. K. Gleerup. *Lund.* Part 1 *→ plates. large 8vo. (Size as fol.).*

This work was published in parts, 207 of which had appeared up to June, 1937. According to information mostly supplied by the publishers as regards the text and the coloured plates, they have been issued as follows:

1913, Part 1	(Vol. I, pp. 1—20);
1914, Parts 2—4	(Vol. I, pp. 21—90);
1915, Parts 5—6	(Vol. I, pp. 91—138);
1916, Parts 7—8	(Vol. I, pp. 139—186);
1917, Parts 9—11	(Vol. I, pp. 187—234);
1918, Parts 12—15	(Vol. I, pp. 235—298);
1919, Parts 16—21	(Vol. I, pp. 299—362);
1921, Parts 22—36	(Vol. I, pp. 363—412; Vol. II, pp. 1—96);
1922, Parts 37—46	(Vol. II, pp. 97—208);
1924, Parts 47—64	(Vol. II, pp. 209—368; 11 plates to Vol. I);
1925, Parts 65—75	(18 plates to Vol. I);
1926, Parts 76—95	(Vol. II, pp. 369—420; title and contents to Vol. I; 27 plates to Vol. I);
1927, Parts 96—110	(Vol. III, pp. 1—96; 15 plates to Vol. I);
1928, Parts 111—117	(Vol. III, pp. 97—144; 7 plates to Vol. II);
1929, Parts 118—139	(Vol. III, pp. 145—288; title and contents to Vol. II; 21 plates to Vol. II);
1930, Parts 140—148	(Vol. III, pp. 289—384; 5 plates to Vol. III);
1931, Parts 149—170	(Vol. III, pp. 385—423; Vol. IV, pp. 1—128; 18 plates to Vol. III);
1933, Parts 171—180	(Vol. IV, pp. 129—288);
1935, Parts 181—189	(Vol. IV, pp. 289—428);
1936, Parts 190—198	(Vol. V, pp. 1—144; title and contents to Vol. III);
1937, Parts 199—207	(12 plates to Vol. III).

The work is planned to appear in five volumes of about equal size but, up to and including June, 1937, only two volumes had been finished:

Vol. I. [1913—]1926. pp. [X] + 412. text-figs. 183 pl. (56 col. pl. birds).

Vol. II. [1921—]1929. pp. [VII] + 420. 169 pl. (43 col. pl. birds). 1 map.

Furthermore, the whole text to both the third and the fourth volume has appeared, though none of the coloured plates to the latter volume have been published and 20 coloured plates to Vol. III are still lacking.

The work is intended to give an account of the life history and habits of all the breeding birds of Sweden, especially during their breeding season, arranged in accordance with the natural interdependence of the species. Under each species the Latin and the Swedish names of the bird are given, besides an account of its habits in a popular, often semi-poetical, form.

Of coloured plates (collotype in four colours, executed by Albert Frisch, Berlin) altogether 134 have been published. In addition the work contains numerous illustrations, reproduced from photographs of the environment in which the bird breeds, the nearest surroundings of the nest, and the nest with eggs in it.

428.   *1926*. Måklappen. Fågelriket på Falsterbo rev. Av Paul Rosenius. Med 103 illustrationer efter fotografier och ... planscher efter autokromfotografier. Andra upplagan. Åhlén & Åkerlund. *Stockholm. pp. 249 + [1]. text-figs. 8 col. pl. (2 pl. eggs). large 8vo.*

The author of this work was one of the first in Sweden to begin to photograph animals in their natural surroundings. He thus secured the material for the illustrations in this book, in which he depicts in a popular narrative style the bird life on a sandy island near the southwestern headland of the Swedish province of Skåne, describing altogether sixteen species of birds.

The coloured plates are executed by the three-colour process.

ROSS, J. C.

1844—75. The zoology of the voyage of H. M. S. Erebus & Terror, under the command of Captain Sir James Clark Ross...1839—43... Birds. *See Gray, G. R.*

ROTHSCHILD, L. W.

429.   *1893—1900*. The avifauna of Laysan and the neighbouring islands: With a complete history to date of the birds of the Hawaiian possessions. By Walter Rothschild. Illustrated with coloured and black plates by Keulemans and Frohawk; and plates from photographs, showing bird-life and scenery. R. H. Porter. *London. pp. XX + XIV + 1—58 + (Di.) 1— (Di.) 21 + 59—320. text-figs. 83 pl. (numb. I— LXXXIII in 'List of plates'; 52 col. pl. birds (Nos. VIII—XIII; XXIII; XXV; XXVII—XXVIII; XXX; XXXII; XXXIX; XLII—LXXX); 3 col. pl. eggs (Nos. XL, XLI, LXXXI); 20 collotype).*

This monograph was issued in three parts : — I (pp. I—XIV, 1—58 ; 41 pl.) August 1893 ; II (pp. 59—126, 15 pl.) November 1893 ; III (pp. I—XX, (Di.) 1—(Di.) 21, 127—320, 27 pl.) December 1900, (cf. 'Contents', p. II).

In addition to the list of contents, the preface, and the list of plates, the opening chapter of the copy (pp. I—XX) contains a bibliography relating to the birds of the Hawaiian Islands (pp. V—XII) and a quite brief survey of the origin and distribution of the Hawaiian avifauna (pp. XIII—XV).

The section on the island of Laysan opens (pp. I—XIV) with a historical survey of the ornithological exploration of this island and is followed by the diary of Henry Palmer written during his stay on the island in 1891.

Palmer's journey of collection, which lasted from December, 1890, to August, 1893, and which yielded a total of 1832 birds, forms the basis of the present work. A summary of Palmer's diary dealing with his stay in the Sandwich Islands is found on pages (Di.) 1 — (Di.) 21.

The work describes, pp. 1—58, the species of birds from Laysan and the neighbouring islands, altogether 27 forms, while pp. 59—317 comprises the 'History of the birds of the Hawaiian Islands'. The complete list of the birds known from the Hawaiian possessions (pp. 313—314) comprises 116 forms.

The beautiful coloured plates are executed in hand-coloured lithography (Mintern Bros. imp.) ; the majority of them were drawn and lithographed by Keulemans.

1894 → See Novitates Zoologicæ.

1900. A monograph of the genus Casuarius. *See Zoological Society of London. Transactions, 1833 →*

1907. Extinct birds. An attempt to unite in one volume a short account of those birds which have become extinct in historical times — that is, within the last six or seven hundred years. To which are added a few which still exist, but are on the verge of extinction. By Walter Rothschild. With ... coloured plates, embracing 63 subjects, and other illustrations. Hutchinson & Co. *London. pp. XXIX + 244. 49 pl. numb. 1—42, 4A, 5A, 24A—C, 25A—B; 45 col. (pl. 24A—C, and 25B uncol.)). fol.*

A work written on the basis of a paper read before the Ornithological Congress, London, June, 1905, and illustrated with a number of drawings. The lecture was published in the 'Proceedings of the Fourth International Ornithological Congress', forming Vol. 14 of the 'Ornis', 1907.

The book gives a survey of a number of birds which have become extinct within historic times, including forms only known as fossils from the Pleistocene of New Zealand and the adjacent islands, as well as that of the Mascarene Islands and Madagascar.

The matter is arranged systematically, and a number of the species treated have been reconstructed, partly from earlier descriptions or pictures, in the figures of the coloured plates (three-colour prints), executed from drawings by J. G. Keulemans, G. E. Lodge, H. Grønvold, J. Smit, and F. W. Frohawk.

The present copy is No. 136 of the limited edition of 300 copies for the British Empire, of which 280 were for sale.

ROUX, J. L. F. P.

1825—30. Ornithologie provençale, ou description, avec figures coloriées, de tous les oiseaux qui habitent constamment la Provence ou qui n'y sont que de passage; suivi d'un abrégé des chasses, de quelques instructions de taxidermie, & d'une table des noms vulgaires. Par Polydore Roux. Levrault. *Paris. 2 vols. (in 3). 451 pl. (450 col.). 4to.* — Vol. I. 1825 [—29]. [Text]. [Parts 1—50]. *pp. LV + 388. Atlas. 394 pl. (393 col.; 348 pl. birds (numb. (partly in 'Avis au relieur') 1 (uncol.), 2—247, 249—266, 268—316, 318—335, 5bis, 53bis, 74bis, 78bis, 82bis, 104bis-ter, 112bis, 114bis, 120bis, 123bis, 124bis, 177bis, 211bis, 227bis, 263bis); 10 pl. nests (numb. I—XVII, XIIbis); 27 pl. eggs (numb. A—Æ, Aa)).* [Vol. II]. 1830. [Parts 51—56]. *pp. 48. 57 col. pl. (51 pl. birds (numb. 336—379; 7 not numb.); 6 pl. eggs (numb. Ab—Ag)).*

This work was projected in two volumes and, according to a note on the cover of the part last published (Livraison 56), which is preserved in the present copy, it was to comprise about 500 coloured plates and a text of about 600 pages ; however, it was never completed, but ceased to appear after the 56 livraisons mentioned above had been published (Livraison I, June 1, 1825).

As regards classification, Vieillot's system is followed, while the synonymy usually comprises the names given by Brisson, Buffon, Vieillot, Latham, and Temminck. The text also contains brief descriptions of genera and higher groups, of the two sexes and the age differences of the birds, and of their habits and life histories. The hand-coloured plates (Polydore Roux del. ; Lith. de Beisson à Marseille) often show figures of male and female and of the young bird.

Complete copies of this work are very rare, especially as many of the plates, notably those first published, are unnumbered. According to Engelmann (564, 1846, p. 414), each of the 56 parts contained eight plates.

ROWLEY, G. D.

[*1875—*] *1876—78*. Ornithological miscellany.

Edited by George Dawson Rowley. Trübner and Co. London. *3 vols. 104 col. pl. birds. 4to.* — Vol. I. [1875 —] 1876. *pp. VI + [X] + 321 + [11]. text-figs. 41 pl. (35 col.; 37 pl. birds (33 col.)). 3 maps.* Vol. II. [1876—] 1877. *pp. VI + [V] + 477 + [15]. text-figs. 57 pl. (45 col.; 52 pl. birds (43 col.); 1 col. pl. eggs).* Vol. III. [1877—] 1878. *pp. VI + [I] + 276 + [11]. text-figs. 37 pl. (28 col.; 26 pl. birds (25 col.); 4 pl. eggs (2 col.)).*

A work of a rather periodical character, published in parts, which were issued at irregular intervals. Altogether fourteen parts were published (Vol. I, Parts I—IV; Vol. II, Parts V—X; Vol. III, Parts XI—XIV), the dates of publication being stated in the particular volume. The original, dated, covers in the present copy have been bound in the corresponding volume.

The majority of the treatises were written by Rowley himself, while a series of other well-known ornithologists also contributed, e. g. H. E. Dresser, O. Finsch, A. Newton, N. Prževal-'skij ('On the birds of Mongolia', etc., in Vols. II and III), O. Salvin, P. L .Sclater, H. Seebohm, R. B. Sharpe, Arthur, Marquis of Tweeddale, and others.

In the list of contents the plates are numbered I—CXV. Most of the coloured plates with figures of birds (lithographs, coloured by hand) were made from drawings by J. G. Keulemans; some are signed J. Smit lith. (Mintern Bros., M. & N. Hanhart, T. Walter imp.; a few T. Walter lith.).

RUEPPELL, E. W. P. S.

1826. Atlas zu der Reise im nördlichen Afrika von Eduard Rüppell. Erste Abtheilung. Zoologie. Herausgegeben von der Senkenbergischen [*sic*] naturforschenden Gesellschaft. - - Vögel. Bearbeitet von Ph. J. Cretzschmar. Gedruckt und in Commission bei Heinr. Ludw. Brönner. *Frankfurt am Main. pp. 55. 36 col. pl. (numb. 1—36). fol.*

In the years 1822—27 Rüppell travelled in Northern Africa, including also the Red Sea in his investigations. The material collected, and especially the whole of the zoological material, was sent by Rüppell to the museum at his native town, Frankfort-on-Main, and the Senckenbergische naturforschende Gesellschaft decided therefore, even before Rüppell's return, to publish an atlas dealing with his journey in Northern Africa. This was to consist of two sections, of which, however, only the present zoological one appeared; the 'II. Abteilung' with the geographical results was never issued.

The present volume was published in 1826—28 in 20 parts, containing altogether 119 plates. It deals with five groups of animals, — mammals, birds, reptiles, fishes, and new invertebrate animals from the Red Sea.

The text of the ornithological section appears as a text to the plates; it describes the species figured, and gives diagnoses, measurements, native country, and habitats of the birds.

Most of the plates (lithographs coloured by hand; lithogr. Anstalt von B. Merck) were executed by F. C. Vogel, a few from drawings by H. v. Kittlitz.

The ornithological section of the work was continued in 1835 in a corresponding section in 'Neue Wirbelthiere zu der Fauna von Abyssinien gehörig' (434).

1835. Neue Wirbelthiere zu der Fauna von Abyssinien gehörig, entdeckt und beschrieben von Eduard Rüppell. Vögel. In Commission bei Siegmund Schmerber. *Frankfurt am Main. pp. 116. 42 col. pl. (numb. 1—42). fol.*

According to the author's preface the work of which a section is present here, was issued in 1835—40 in 13 parts, the last two of which were double. The publication was a great expense to Rüppell as the work hardly obtained sixty subscribers in the whole of Europe. Four animal groups are dealt with, mammals, birds, amphibia, and fishes from the Red Sea. The work forms a sequel to Rüppell's 'Atlas zu der Reise im nördlichen Afrika' published in 1826—28 (433).

The text of the ornithological section describes the birds figured on the plates, and is supplemented by diagnoses in Latin

and information about the occurrence in Abyssinia of the species in question.

The plates (lithographs coloured by hand, printed by P. C. Stern) were executed from drawings by F. C. Vogel.

In 1845 Rüppell continued his account of the birds of North Africa in a systematically arranged work (435).

1845. Systematische Uebersicht der Vögel Nord- 435. Ost-Afrika's nebst Abbildung und Beschreibung von fünfzig theils unbekannten, theils noch nicht bildlich dargestellten Arten. Von Eduard Rüppell. Fortsetzung der neuen Wirbelthiere, zu der Fauna von Abyssinien gehörig. In Commission der S. Schmerber'schen Buchhandlung. *Frankfurt a. M. pp. VII + [I] + 140. 50 col. pl. (numb. 1—50). 8vo.*

A continued treatment of ornithological material from Northeast Africa, which appears as a kind of sequel to the ornithological section of the author's 'Neue Wirbelthiere zu der Fauna von Abyssinien gehörig' (434), in which the birds are treated in no systematic order. In the present work, however, the matter is systematically arranged, both as regards plates and text, the text accompanying the plates as a kind of description of the figures on them, a diagnosis in Latin being added.

The beautiful plates (lithographs, showing hand-coloured figures of birds on uncoloured backgrounds) were drawn by Jos. Wolf, who by this work made his name known among ornithologists, and thus began his great career as a painter of bird figures for ornithological works.

RUSS, K. F. O.

[1875—] 1879—99. Die fremdländischen Stuben- 436. vögel, ihre Naturgeschichte, Pflege und Zucht. Von Karl Russ. Carl Rümpler. *Hannover* (Vols II & IV: Creutz. *Magdeburg*). *4 vols. 35 col. pl. 8vo.* — Vol. I. [1875—77—] 1879. Die körnerfressenden fremdländischen Stubenvögel, Hartfutter- oder Samenfresser, *pp. XXIII + 710. 14 col. pl. (numb. I—XIV).* Vol. II. [1893—] 1899. Die fremdländischen Weichfutterfresser (Insekten- oder Kerbthierfresser, auch Wurmvögel genannt, Frucht- oder Berenfresser und Fleischfresser). Mit Anhang: Tauben- und Hühnervögel. *pp. XXVIII + 928. 10 col. pl. (numb. XV—XIX, XXXI—XXXV).* Vol. III. [1878—80—] 1881. Die Papageien, ihre Naturgeschichte, Pflege, Züchtung und Abrichtung, *pp. XXVIII + 891. 10 col. pl. (numb. XXI—XXX).* Vol. IV. [1881—] 1888. Lehrbuch der Stubenvogelpflege, -Abrichtung und -Zucht. *pp. XXVI + 950. text-figs. 1 col. pl. (numb. XX).*

This work is to be regarded as an enlarged edition of the author's 'Handbuch für Vogelliebhaber, -Züchter und -Händler', which appeared in 1870—73 (Vol. I, 'Fremdländische Vögel').

It was published in Lieferungen, which according to Kayser's 'Bücher-Lexicon' were issued as follows: Vol. I: 1—4 (pp. 1—256, 8 pl.) 1875—76; 5—9 (pp. XXIII + 257—710, 6 pl.) 1877; Vol. II: 1—9 (pp. 1—368, 5 pl.) 1893—94; 10—21 (pp. 369—864) 1895—98; 22 (pp. XXVIII + 865—928, 5 pl.) 1899; Vol. III: 1—10 (10 pl.) 1878—80; Vol. IV, 1—2 (pp. 1—208, 1 pl.) 1881—82; 3—7 (pp. 209—784) 1883—86; 8 (pp. XXVI + 785—950, 1 pl.) 1888.

The work gives a comprehensive description of the cagebirds of warmer climes, and treats of their geographical distribution, habits, synonymy, and behaviour in captivity, giving also a scientific description of each species.

The plates, containing altogether 100 figures of birds, were executed from drawings by Emil Schmidt (Chrom. Lith. Th. Fischer, Cassel).

A fifth edition of 'Handbuch für Vogelliebhaber. Erster Band. Fremdländische Stubenvögel' was issued in 1921 by Karl Neunzig (361).

24*

RUSSELL, W. H.
 1881. The ornithological works of Arthur, Ninth Marquis of Tweeddale ... Together with a biographical sketch of the author by William Howard Russell. *See Tweeddale, A. H.*

RUSSIA. Voyages, expeditions, etc.
 1770—74. Reise durch Russland zur Untersuchung der drey Natur-Reiche. *See Gmelin, S. G.*
 1775—83. Tagebuch der Reise durch verschiedene Provinzen des russischen Reiches ... 1768—71 ... Vols. II—III. *See Lepechin, I. I.*
 1786. Beyträge zur topographischen Kentniss des russischen Reichs. Vol. III ... pp. 326—410: Zweite Klasse. Vögel. *See Falck, J. P.*
 1810—14. Reise um die Welt ... 1803—06 ... auf den Schiffen Nadeshda und Newa ... *See Krusenstern, A. J. von.*
 1853. Reise in den äussersten Norden und Osten Sibiriens ... 1843 und 1844 ... Vol. II. Zoologie. Part II. Säugethiere, Vögel und Amphibien. pp. 124—246: B. Vögel. *See Middendorff, A. T. von.*
 1860. Reisen und Forschungen im Amur-Lande ... 1854—56 ... Vol. I. pp. 215—567: Part II. Vögel des Amur-Landes. *See Schrenck, P. L. von.*
 1863. Reisen im Süden von Ost-Sibirien ... 1855—59 ... Vol. II. Die Festlands-Ornis des südöstlichen Sibiriens. *See Radde, G. F. R.*
 1889—1905. Wissenschaftliche Resultate der von N. M. Przewalski nach Central-Asien unternommenen Reisen ... Zoologischer Theil. Vol. II. Vögel. *See Pleske, T. D.*

RUYSCH, H.
 1718. Theatrum universale omnium animalium ... Vol. I. Part II. Sive historiæ naturalis de avibus libri VI. *See Johnstone, J.*

SAGRA, R. de la.
 1839. Histoire physique, politique et naturelle de l'Île de Cuba par Ramon de la Sagra. Ornithologie. *See Orbigny, A. D. d'.*

SAINT-HILAIRE, A. BOURJOT. *See Bourjot Saint-Hilaire, A.*

ST. PETERSBURG. ACADÉMIE IMPÉRIALE DES SCIENCES. *See Académie Impériale des Sciences de St.-Pétersbourg.*

ST. PETERSBURG. KAISERLICHE GEOGRAPHISCHE GESELLSCHAFT. *See Geographische Gesellschaft. St. Petersburg.*

SALERNE, F.
 1767. L'histoire naturelle, éclaircie dans une de ses parties principales, l'ornithologie ... Ouvrage traduit du Latin du Synopsis avium de Ray ... Par Salerne. *See Ray, J.*

SALVADORI, T. A.
 1880. Report on the birds collected during the

voyage of H. M. S. Challenger ... 1873—76. *See Sclater, P. L.*
 1891—95. Catalogue of the birds in the British Museum. Vols. XX, XXI, XXVII. *See British Museum (Natural History), 1874—98.*

SALVIN, O.
 1866—69. Exotic ornithology, containing figures and descriptions of new or rare species of American birds. *See Sclater, P. L.*
 1871—82. *See Ibis.*
 1879—1904. Biologia Centrali-Americana. Aves. By Osbert Salvin and Frederick Du Cane Godman. R. H. Porter. London. 4 vols. large 4to. — Vol. I. 1879—1904. *pp. XLIV + 512.* Vol. II. 1888—1904. *pp. 598.* Vol. III. 1897—1904. *pp. IV + 510.* Vol. IV. 1879—1904. *pp. VII. 84 col. pl. (numb. 1—79, 15a, 54a, 58a, 58b, 59a).*
 The ornithological section of the great work, edited by the authors, on the flora and fauna of Mexico and Central America. In its entirety it consists of 57 volumes, and was published in 1879—1915 in 257 parts, of which 74 contained the section relating to the birds. The last of these appeared in November, 1904.
 As Salvin died before Vol. III had been finished the work was completed by Godman with the assistance of R. B. Sharpe and W. R. Ogilvie-Grant.
 The material on which the work is based was mostly secured by the authors during several visits to Central America. The large collection of birds they thus acquired by collection and purchase they presented to the British Museum at South Kensington (more than 55,000 specimens).
 The work deals with 1413 species representing 78 families and 539 genera.
 The hand-coloured plates which show figures of 149 species were, except for a very few, which are due to E. Neale, drawn and lithographed by J. G. Keulemans (Hanhart, a few Mintern Bros., imp.).
 1880. Report on the birds collected during the voyage of H. M. S. Challenger ... 1873—76. *See Sclater, P. L.*
 1892—95. Catalogue of the birds in the British Museum. Vols. XVI, XXV. *See British Museum (Natural History), 1874—98.*
 1897—98. Coloured figures of the birds of the British Islands. Second edition. Parts XXXIV—XXXVI. *See Lilford, T. L. P., Fourth Baron, 1891—98.*

SARAJEVO. BOSNISCH-HERCEGOVINISCHES LANDESMUSEUM.
 1894—1905. Materialien zu einer Ornis Balcanica. Herausgegeben vom ... Landesmuseum ... Vols. II—IV. *See Reiser, O.*

SAUNDERS, H.
 1880. Report on the birds collected during the voyage of H. M. S. Challenger ... 1873—76. *See Sclater, P. L.*
 1883—88, 1895—1900. See Ibis.
 1895. Catalogue of the birds in the British Museum. Vol. XXV. *See British Museum (Natural History), 1874—98.*

SAVIGNY, M. J. C. L. de.
 1809. Description de l'Égypte, ou recueil des observations et des recherches qui ont été faites en Égypte

pendant l'expédition de l'armée française, publié par les ordres de sa majesté l'empereur Napoléon le Grand. Histoire naturelle. Imprimerie Impériale. *Paris.* — Vol. I. - - < [Part I]. - - *pp. 63—114:* Système des oiseaux de l'Égypte et de la Syrie, par Jules-César Savigny. Ouvrage présenté à l'assemblé générale de la commission, le 29 août 1808 >. *large 4to.* Planches. Vol. I. Zoologie. - - < Oiseaux par J. C. Savigny >. *14 col. pl. (numb. 1—14). large fol.*

This large work on observations and investigations during the expedition of the French army to Egypt in 1798—1801 was issued in 1809—30. The text appeared in 9 vols., 4to, the plates in 10 vols., large folio; these two sections are generally bound in 10 and 13 volumes respectively.

The section dealing with natural history was published in 1809—29 in 2 vols. text, and 2 vols. plates in 3 vols. (I, II and II bis).

In the present section of the Histoire naturelle, Vol. I, Part 1, Savigny commenced the treatment of the birds, giving 27 species of birds of prey with detailed synonymies and brief diagnoses of the species, as well as brief descriptions of genera and higher groups.

Reference is made to the figures of birds of prey found on Plates 1—3 and 11—12; Savigny, however, never wrote the text for the remaining figures, and the plates were therefore described by Audouin in 1826 (15). The plates (engravings printed in colour and retouched by hand) were engraved by Bouquet, and drawn for the most part by Barraband, Pl. 14, however, is by Prêtre, and a few figures are by H. J. Redouté.

SCHAEFF, E. A. F. W.
1896. Des Hohenstaufen-Kaisers Friedrich II Bücher von der Natur der Vögel und der Falknerei ... *See Friedrich II, Emperor of Germany.*

SCHAEFFER, J. C.
1779. Jacobi Christiani Schaefferi Elementa ornithologica iconibus vivis coloribus expressis illustrata. Editio secunda. Typis Breitfeldianis. *Ratisbonœ. pp. [VIII]* + *[80]. 70 col. pl. (numb. I—LXX). 4to.*

The first edition of this work appeared in 1774 with a somewhat different title-page.

The main part of the text is divided into four sections and the index, — I, 'De avium facie et structura externa', with explanation to Pl. I—IV; II, 'De avium classibús et ordinibus', with explanation to Pl. V; III, 'Tabulæ generum characteristicæ', with explanation to Pl. VI—XVI; and IV, 'Genera avium in Germania præcipve Bavaria et Palatinatu circa Ratisbonam habitantium, nidificantium et migrantium', with explanation to Pl. XVII—LXX.

The plates (engravings coloured by hand) were executed from drawings by Joh. Jos. Rotermundt (Joh. Gottl. Friedrich, some Jacob Andr. Eisenmann, Sebast. Leitner, and Andr. Hoffer sc.).

1789. Museum ornithologicum, exhibens enumerationem et descriptionem avium qvas nova prorsus ratione sibi paratas in museo suo asservat D. Iacobus Christianus Schaeffer ... tabulæ aeri incisæ et coloribus distinctæ. *Ratisbonæ. pp. [III]* + *72* + *[6]. 52 col. pl. (numb. I—LII). 4to.*

The text to this work deals with 229 forms of birds distributed over 59 genera. Each species is cited under its binomial name, with the addition of the common name in French and German, and a brief diagnosis or a description with references to the literature on the subject.

The plates (engravings coloured by hand) were engraved by Joh. Sebast. Leitner, Johann Adam Fridrich, J. C. Pemsel, J. C. Claussner, and J. M. Mansinger; a single plate is signed: Franck pinx., another: von Reicheln pinx.

SCHEEL, H. K. J.
1931. Danmarks Fugle ... Vol. III ... Bindet fuldført af ... H. Scheel ... *See Schiøler, E. L. T. L., 1925 —31.*

SCHINZ, H. R.
1818. Beschreibung und Abbildung der Eier und *441.* künstlichen Nester der Vögel, welche in der Schweiz, in Deutschland und den angränzenden nördlichen Ländern brüten. Mit illuminirten Kupfern. Von H. R. Schinz. Part I. In Commission bey Orell, Füssli und Compagnie. *Zürich. pp. IV* + *2* + *4. 6 col. pl. (3 pl. nests and birds (numb. 1—3; 3 pl. eggs (marked ℵ, numb. 1—3)). 4to.*

The first part of a work which up to 1830 was issued in 13 parts with altogether 73 plates.

The present part, the title of which is derived from the cover, is divided, like the whole work, into two sections; the first treats of nests and eggs, the other eggs.

The text gives brief information about the reproductive history of the species whose eggs or nests are figured on the plates; these are executed in hand-coloured engravings (W. Hartmann pinx & sc.).

SCHIØLER, E. L. T. L.
1925—31. Danmarks Fugle. Med Henblik paa de *442.* i Grønland, paa Færøerne og i Kongeriget Island forekommende Arter. Af E. Lehn Schiøler. Gyldendal. *København. 3 vols. 276 pl. (173 col.). fol.* — Vol. I. 1925. Indledning og Andefugle (Anseriformes). *pp.* 552. *text-figs. 98 pl. (numb. I—XCVIII; 55 (5 osteological) col., 24 phot. pl.).* Vol. II. 1926 [1927]. Oversigt over Grønlands Fugle og Andefugle (Anseriformes) II, Dykænder (Fuligulinæ). *pp.* 338. *text-figs. 86 pl. (numb. I—LXXXVI; 46 col., 27 phot. pl.). 1 map.* Vol. III. 1931. Af E. Lehn Schiøler†. Bindet fuldført af R. Hørring, H. Scheel og Å Vedel Tåning. Rovfugle (Falconiformes). *pp. 413. text-figs. 92 pl. (front. + Nos. I—XCI; 72 col., 9 phot. pl.).*

A broadly designed account of the birds of Denmark which was never completed, as the work ceased to appear on Lehn Schiøler's death.

According to information supplied by the publishers the volumes have been published as follows: — I, 8th July, 1925; II, 9th February, 1927; III, 8th March, 1931.

In addition to the preface and the indices, the volumes comprise the sections stated below: —

Vol. I contains four chapters, I (pp. 11—197) giving a brief synopsis of the ornithological literature of Denmark; II (pp. 199—226) giving an outline of the structure of the birds; III (pp. 227—255), a synopsis of the birds of Denmark, in which 324 species and subspecies are enumerated, and (pp. 244—255) the fossil birds of Denmark by H. Winge; and IV (pp. 257—523), a description of part of the order Anseriformes.

Vol. II consists of three chapters, I (pp. 11—30), a brief survey of the ornithological papers dealing with the avifauna of Greenland; II (pp. 33—59), a survey of the birds of Greenland, in which 168 species and subspecies are given; and III (pp. 61—319), a treatment of the group of Fuligulinæ.

Vol. III contains by way of introduction (pp. 11—29) a general account of the group of diurnal birds of prey, followed (pp. 30—31) by a key to the determination of the Danish genera of these birds and, finally (pp. 33—405), the account of the group.

In the systematic section of the volumes keys to the determination of the species are given under each group; the species found in the Faroes, Greenland, and Iceland are also mentioned. Under each species the author gives the synonymy, the vernacular names in different European languages, a diagnosis, brief information about the occurrence in Denmark and the

other lands concerned, a detailed description with depiction
of the various plumages, and information about the ecology
and occurrence of the species.

The coloured plates with portraits of birds (three-colour
prints) show the birds in their changing plumages; they were
executed from drawings by Johannes Larsen (all these plates
in Vols. I & II and some of the plates in Vol. III), Gerhard
Heilmann (some of the plates in Vol. III), and Henning
Scheel (some of the plates in Vol. III). The latter further
supplied the greater number of the drawings for a series of
anatomical plates. Johannes Larsen, whose drawings from an
artistic point of view rank high in ornithological illustration,
also drew sketches and vignettes for many of the text-figures,
some of which are coloured.

Two identical copies of this work are found in the collection.

SCHLEGEL, H.

1839—44. Verhandelingen over de natuurlijke geschiedenis der Nederlandsche overzeesche bezittingen...
[Aves]. *See Mueller, S.*

1844—50. Fauna Japonica ... notis, observationibus et adumbrationibus illustravit Ph. Fr. de Siebold
... Aves. *See Temminck, C. J.*

1850. Monographie des Loxiens ... *See Bonaparte,
C. L. J. L.*

443. *1854—58.* Fauna van Nederland door H. Schlegel
en J. A. Herklots. - - De vogels van Nederland beschreven en afgebeeld door H. Schlegel. P. W. M. Trap.
Leiden. 2 vols. in 3. small 8vo. — [Text]. *pp. VIII +
699 + [1].* [Atlas]. *362 col. pl. [in 2 vols., Vol. [1]:
pl. 1—185] (numb. 1—362 in 'Systematische lijst').*

The only volumes published of a projected work on the
fauna of the Netherlands. It was published in 46 parts (Brinkman's Catalogus van boeken 1850—82, p. 363), and gives a
systematic synopsis of the birds of the country, with descriptions of the individual forms and their different plumages,
and notes on their geographical distribution and habits. In
this work Schlegel uses trinomials to denote the varieties; he
had used trinomials already in 1844 in his 'Kritische Uebersicht der europäischen Vögel'. A systematic list of the birds
is found on pp. 617—642.

The plates, which show the birds in their different plumages,
were executed in lithography, coloured by hand, from drawings
by the author.

The work was re-issued, with the omission of the first title-
page, (Leyden, D. Noothoven van Goor) in 1859 (dated 1860)
(Brinkman's Catalogus van boeken 1850—82, p. 363), since
in the year first mentioned van Goor had bought it from the
original publisher, the lithographer Trap (564, 1861, p. 277).

444. *[1860].* De toerako's afgebeeld en beschreven door
H. Schlegel, onder medewerking van G. F. Westerman
... Gedrukt voor rekening van het Koninklijk Zoölogisch Genootschap Natura Artis Magistra. (Niet in
den handel). *Amsterdam. pp. 24 + [1]. 17 col. pl.
(numb. 1—17 in text). large fol.*

This work exists also with a somewhat different title-
page, dated 1860, and with double plates, coloured and uncoloured (552, IV, p. 1839).

The text, which is written in Dutch, describes the forms
figured, altogether 17, and gives synonymies, information about
the occurrence of the species and, occasionally, about other
features of interest, too. A 'Tabula synoptica specierum e genere
Musophagarum' has been inserted after the text proper.

The essential part of the work consists of the beautiful
plates, executed in lithography coloured by hand (P. W. M.
Trap excudit) from drawings by Schlegel, made from nature
and as far as possible from life (856, p. 51). The birds are
figured in life-size, which accounts for the large format.

445. *1860.* Natuurlijke historie van Nederland. De dieren van Nederland. Gewervelde dieren, door H. Schlegel. < - - De vogels. Aves >. A. C. Kruseman. *Haar-*

*lem. pp. [V] + LXXI + 263 + [106] + II. 53
col. pl. (numb. 1—18 (in 'Verklaring der tafereelen'
numb. I—XVIII), 1—35). 8vo.*

The ornithological volume of the work 'Natuurlijke historie
van Nederland', which was issued in seven parts in 1856—62
(Brinkman's Catalogus van boeken 1850—82, p. 527).

The introduction (pp. I—LXXI) gives a general account
of the group of birds, especially as regards their occurrence in
different habitats (such as shore, heath, etc.). In this chapter
278 species are enumerated as belonging to the fauna of the
country.

The main section of the book (pp. 1—256) is a systematic
synopsis of the birds occurring in the Netherlands, in which
tame birds and those that have become wild are dealt with
(pp. 243—256).

The plates, with explanatory text on alternate leaves,
are lithographs (Steendr. van P. W. M. Trap) executed from
drawings by the author and coloured by hand (Pl. XVII—
XVIII monochrome). Pl. I—XVIII belong to the introduction, and show the birds in their different habitats, while Pl.
1—35 contain figures of heads and feet.

The whole work on natural history was re-issued in 1867
—69 (G. L. Funke, Amsterdam; D. Bolle, Rotterdam), and
it is evidently the volume on birds of this edition which is
cited in the catalogue of the British Museum (Natural History)
(552, IV, p. 1839). One further edition (Tweede herz. druk,
1877—78, 2 deel) of the volume on birds is cited (Brinkman's Catalogus van boeken 1850—82, p. 1043; cf. 552, IV,
p. 1839).

1867—68. Recherches sur la faune de Madagascar
et de ses dépendances, d'après les découvertes de François P. L. Pollen et D. C. van Dam. 2me Partie. < - -
Mammifères et oiseaux par H. Schlegel et François
P. L. Pollen >. J. K. Steenhoff. *Leyde. pp. XIX +
186. 30 col. pl. birds (numb. 11—40). 4to.*

Part of a report on Pollen's and van Dam's zoological collections in Madagascar, of which six numbers appeared in 1867
—77 (Partie 1—2, 4, and 5: parts 1—3), after which publication stopped.

The present volume, published in four parts (Part IV 1868),
treats mainly of birds, most of the text pp. 30—174 dealing
with this group. The individual forms are characterized, measurements are stated, and information is given about their different plumages, habits, and distribution on the island.

The plates with figures of the birds in their different
plumages (Steendr. v. P. W. M. Trap) are coloured by hand.
Most of them are signed by J. G. Keulemans.

1879—83. Notes from the Leyden Museum. *See
Leyden. Rijks Museum van Natuurlijke Historie, 1879
—1914.*

SCHLEINITZ, G. E. G. von.

1889. Die Forschungsreise S. M. S. 'Gazelle' ...
1874—76 unter Kommando ... Freiherrn von Schleinitz ... Vol. III. Zoologie und Geologie. *See Studer, T.*

SCHOEPFFER, H.

1896. Des Hohenstaufen-Kaisers Friedrich II Bücher von der Natur der Vögel und der Falknerei ...
See Friedrich II, Emperor of Germany.

SCHOUW, J. F.

1835—44. Afbildninger af Dyr og Planter efter
Dictionnaire des sciences naturelles. *See Eschricht,
D. F.*

SCHRENCK, P. L. von.

1860. Reisen und Forschungen im Amur-Lande ...
1854—56 im Auftrage der Kaiserl. Akademie der Wissenschaften zu St. Petersburg ausgeführt und in Ver-

bindung mit mehreren Gelehrten herausgegeben von Leopold v. Schrenck. Vol. I. *(pp. 215—567)*: Part II. Vögel des Amur-Landes. Commissionäre der Kaiserlichen Akademie der Wissenschaften: Eggers und Comp *St. Petersburg. 7 col. pl. (numb. X—XVI; 1 pl. eggs (numb. XVI)). 4to.*

After the journeys in Siberia undertaken by Middendorff (339), interest centred on Eastern Siberia which, as well as Sakhalin, was visited by Schrenck during the years stated in the title (taken from the cover).

The results of the expedition were published in a work which appeared in 1858—95 in four volumes and an appendix (to Vol. III).

The present ornithological section of the work further records the results of Maack's journey in 1855, and contributions were also made by the botanist Carl Maximowicz, who took part in the expedition.

Altogether 190 species and varieties are treated of, mostly by statements of their measurements and variations, descriptions of their colours, and information about their geographical distribution.

The chapter 'Schlussfolgerungen' (pp. 519—565) contains a discussion of zoogeographic questions and the climatic colour variations; migration times observed are tabulated.

The plates (lithographs coloured by hand) were executed from drawings by W. Pape.

SCLATER, P. L.

1851—53. Contributions to ornithology ... *See Jardine, W.,* 1848—53.

3. *1857* [—*58*]. A monograph of the birds forming the tanagrine genus Calliste; illustrated by coloured plates of all the known species. By Philip Lutley Sclater. London. *pp. XVIII + 104. 45 col. pl. (numb. I—XLV in text). 1 map. 8vo.*

This work, which was published in four parts, treats of all the known, 52, species of the genus cited, giving under each species its synonymy, diagnosis in Latin, its geographical distribution, and in most cases characters by which the particular form differs from related species, and information about its habits.

The plates are lithographs coloured by hand, executed from drawings by Oudart (Lith. Becquet frères, and others).

1859—64, 1877—1912. See Ibis.

). [*1861*—] *1862*. Catalogue of a collection of American birds belonging to Philip Lutley Sclater. N. Trubner and Co. *London. pp. XIV + [II] + 367 + p. 338 [= 368]. 20 col. pl. (numb. I—XX). 8vo.*

The sheets (I—XXIII) of this work are dated from May 1, 1861, to May 16, 1862. The collection comprised about 4100 specimens — among which 386 type-specimens — referred in the catalogue to 2169 species belonging to the orders Passeres, Fissirostres, and Scansores. Thirty-two of the species are cited in a supplement (pp. 358—360) containing the names of the species added to the collection during the progress of the catalogue.

Several of the type-specimens are figured on the fine plates, which are executed in hand-coloured lithography (J. Jennens, del. et lith., M. & N. Hanhart, imp.).

1861—67. Zoological sketches ... Edited, with notes, by Philip Lutley Sclater. *See Wolf, Joseph,* 1856—67.

). [*1866*—] *1869*. Exotic ornithology, containing figures and descriptions of new or rare species of American birds, by Philip Lutley Sclater and Osbert Salvin. Bernard Quaritch. *London. pp. VI + 204. text-figs. 100 col. pl. (numb. I—C in text). fol.*

This work was published in 13 parts from October 1, 1866, to August 1, 1869 (561, II, p. 336).

The authors' original plan was that their work should form a continuation of well-known atlases, such as Buffon and

Daubenton's 'Planches enluminées', (76) and Temminck and Laugier's 'Nouveau recueil de planches coloriées', 1820—39 (502).

According to the plan, the work was to give figures and descriptions of new and rare birds from all parts of the world ; however, the authors soon limited the task to the birds of the Neotropical region.

A total number of 104 species, belonging to 51 different genera, are figured. Each plate is accompanied by a leaf of text in which the forms figured on the particular plate are treated ; thus synonyms, diagnosis in Latin, and information about the geographical distribution and history of discovery of the species are given. In addition, as regards most of the genera figured, a systematic list of all the American species of the genus is added.

The beautiful plates are hand-coloured lithographs (J. Smit lith. ; M. & N. Hanhart imp.).

1879—82. A monograph of the jacamars and puff- **451.** birds, or families Galbulidæ and Bucconidæ. By P. L. Sclater. Published for the author by R. H. Porter. *London. pp. LII + [I] + 171. text-figs. 55 col. pl. (numb. I—LV in text). 4to.*

This work was published in seven parts, which in the present copy are found in their original covers. According to these, the various parts were issued as follows and with the following contents : I (pp. 1—32, Pl. I—VIII), October, 1879 ; II (pp. 33—60, Pl. IX—XVIII), January, 1880 ; III (pp. 61—84, Pl. XIX—XXVII), May, 1880 ; IV (pp. 85—108, Pl. XXVIII —XXXV), November, 1880 ; V (pp. 109—132, Pl. XXXVI— XLIV), July, 1881 ; VI (pp. 133—160, Pl. XLV—LIV), November, 1881 ; VII (pp. I—LII + [I] + 161—171, Pl. LV), July, 1882.

The introduction to the monograph gives, among other information, a general account of the two groups of birds (pp. XI—XLIV) and a comprehensive bibliography (pp. XLV— LII). The special part of the work contains detailed synonymies, descriptions, information about geographical distribution and other facts relating to altogether 62 forms, 60 of which are figured on the beautiful plates, executed in hand-coloured lithography (J. G. Keulemans lith., Hanhart imp.).

[*1880*] *1881*. (Provisional title). Report on the **452.** scientific results of the voyage of H. M. S. Challenger ... 1873—76 under the command of Captain George S. Nares and Captain Frank Tourle Thomson. Prepared under the superintendence of C. Wyville Thomson. Zoology. Vol. II. <- - [Memoir II]. Report on the birds collected during the voyage of H. M. S. Challenger ... 1873—76. By Philip Lutley Sclater >. Published by order of Her Majesty's Government. Sold by Longmans & Co. *London. pp. 166. text-figs. 30 col. pl. (numb. I—XXX). 4to.*

The immense material brought home by the Challenger Expedition, so important for the development of oceanography, was treated in a publication, 1880—95, comprising altogether 40 volumes.

The collection of birds consisted of 903 specimens in skin and a number of sea-birds in salt and spirit, besides a collection of eggs, belonging to 170, chiefly oceanic, species.

The collection was secured under the leadership of John Murray, who through his ornithological note-book and further notes has contributed to the report on the birds, which otherwise chiefly consists of reprints of preliminary reports read before the Zoological Society of London, and published in the Society's 'Proceedings', 1877—78, the material having been distributed among various specialists, whose contributions to the report are as follows :

Pp. 5—25 : I. On the birds in the Philippine Islands. By Arthur, Marquis of Tweeddale. Pl. I—VI.

Pp. 25—34 : II. On the birds collected in the Admiralty Islands. By P. L. Sclater. Pl. VII—XI.

Pp. 34—58 : III. On the birds collected in Tongatabu, the Fiji Islands, Api (New Hebrides), and Tahiti. By O. Finsch. Pl. XII—XVII.

Pp. 58—83 : IV. On the birds collected in Ternate, Amboyna,

Pp. 84—93: V. On the birds collected at Cape York, Australia, and on the neighbouring islands (Raine, Wednesday, and Booby Islands). By W. A. Forbes.

Pp. 93—99: VI. On the birds collected in the Sandwich Islands. By P. L. Sclater. Pl. XXI—XXII.

Pp. 99—109: VII. On the birds collected in Antarctic America. By P. L. Sclater and Osbert Salvin.

Pp. 110—117: VIII. On the birds collected on the Atlantic Islands and Kerguelen Island, and on the miscellaneous collections. By P. L. Sclater. Pl. XXIII—XXIV.

Pp. 117—132: IX. On the Steganopodes and Impennes collected during the expedition. By P. L. Sclater and Osbert Salvin. Pl. XXV—XXX.

Pp. 133—140: X. On the Laridæ collected during the expedition. By Howard Saunders.

Pp. 140—149: XI. On the Procellariidæ collected during the expedition. By Osbert Salvin.

Pp. 150—152: Appendix. I. List of eggs collected during the expedition. By P. L. Sclater.

Pp. 152—154: Appendix. II. Note on the gizzard and other organs of Carpophaga latrans. By A. H. Garrod.

The plates were executed in lithography, coloured by hand (J. Smit del. et lith.; Hanhart imp.).

1886—91. Catalogue of the birds in the British Museum. Vols. XI, XIV, XV, XIX. *See British Museum (Natural History),* 1874—98.

SCLATER, W. L.

1912. The birds of Africa ... Vol. V. Part II. Completed and edited by W. L. Sclater. *See Shelley, G. E.* 1896—1912.

1913—30. See Ibis.

SCOPOLI, G. A.

1786. Specimen zoologicum exhibens characteres genericos, & specificos, necnon nomina trivialia novorum animalium, quæ clarissimus Sonnerat in China, & in Indiis Orientalibus nuper detexit. Aves. *See Sonnerat, P.,* 1776.

SCOTT, R. F.

1907. National Antarctic Expedition 1901—1904. Natural history. Vol. II. Zoology ... II. Aves. *See Wilson, E. A.*

SCOTT, W. B.

1904—28. Reports of the Princeton University expeditions to Patagonia, 1896—1899 ... Edited by William B. Scott. Vol. II. Ornithology. *See Scott, W. E. D.*

SCOTT, W. E. D.

453. *1904—27 [—28]. J.* Pierpont Morgan Publication Fund. Reports of the Princeton University expeditions to Patagonia, 1896—1899. J. B. Hatcher in charge. Edited by William B. Scott. Vol. II. Ornithology. The University. *Princeton, N. J. 1 vol. in 2 sections. 24 pl. (15 col.). 4to. —* 1. 1904—15. By William Earl Dodge Scott associated with R. Bowdler Sharpe. *pp. XII + 1—504. text-figs. 10 pl. (9 uncol. (figs. 134—136, 146—147, 157, 170, 172, 174), 1 col. (numb. I)).* 2. 1915—27 [—28]. Phalacrocoracidæ-Falconidæ. By

William Earl Dodge Scott associated with R. Bowdler Sharpe. Stridgidæ-Icteridæ. By Witmer Stone. *pp. 505—884. 14 col. pl. (numb. II—XV).*

The ornithological section of the report on the Princeton University expeditions to Patagonia in 1896—99. The main object of the expeditions was to collect fossils, but collections of birds were secured, too, and these were deposited in the museum of the Princeton University.

The present volume was published in five parts (+ titles to Vol. II, 1, contents and index), which in the present copy are in their original covers. According to a note p. XII, their dates of publication are as follows (the dates of issue as printed on the inside of the covers being added in parentheses, if different from the true dates of publication): I, August 3 (July 26) 1904; II, March 11 (March 3), 1910; III, April 1, 1912; IV, July 8, 1915; V, February 15, 1928.

The contents of the various parts are as follows: I, Rheidæ-Spheniscidæ, pp. 1—112; II, Procellariidæ-Charadriidæ, pp. 113—344, 9 pl. (figs. as stated above); III, Charadriidæ-Anatidæ, pp. 345—504, Pl. I; IV, Anatidæ-Tytodidæ, pp. 505—718; V, Psittacidæ-Icteridæ, pp. 719—857, Pl. II—XV.

The elaboration of the material was entrusted to Scott and Sharpe who, however, both died before the completion of the work, which was therefore left to Stone. According to a note in Part IV, p. 505, and to the title-page to Vol. II, 2, published in the same part, he compiled the sections Strigidæ-Icteridæ (i. e. pp. 673—857), since the manuscripts left by the original authors were practically completed to the end of the Accipitriformes.

Each form has been treated thoroughly, with statement of synonymy, a general description including measurements, and a detailed description of the colour and the different plumages, being mentioned.

The whole-page figures in Part II were executed from drawings by H. Grønvold, who also supplied the design for Pl. I, which, like the other plates (J. G. Keulemans del.) are chromolithographs (Werner & Winter, Frankfort o. M., lith.).

SEBA, A.

1734—35. Locupletissimi rerum naturalium thesauri accurata descriptio, et iconibus artificiosissimis expressio, per universam physices historiam. Opus, cui, in hoc rerum genere, nullum par exstitit. Ex toto terrarum orbe collegit, digessit, descripsit, et depingendum curavit Albertus Seba. J. Wetstenius. *Amstelædami. Vols. I—II. 38 pl. birds. large fol. —* Vol. I. 1734. *pp. [XXXVII] + 178. 27 pl. birds (numb. XXX, XXXI, XXXVI, XXXIX [=XXXVIII], XLII, XLV, XLVI, LI—LIII, LV, LVII, LIX—LXIX, LXXII, XCIX, CII, CX).* Vol. II. 1735. *pp. [XXX] + 154. 11 pl. birds (numb. III, VII, XII, XIX, XL, XLI, LXII, LXV, LXX, LXXXVII, XCVI).*

The first two volumes of a copy of the description of Seba's large collection of natural objects, a work which consists of altogether four volumes with a total of 451 plates. Figures of birds are only found in the two present volumes, of which Vol. I contains 113 plates (front. + portrait + Pl. I—CXI), Vol. II 114 plates.

The last two volumes were published after Seba's death, in 1758 and 1765 respectively.

The volumes are provided with a half-title, which reads 'Naaukeurige beschryving van het schatryke kabinet der voornaamste seldzaamheden der natuur van Albertus Seba'. Seba was assisted in the preparation of the work by several scientists, e. g. P. van Musschenbroek, P. Massuet, and H. D. Gaubius. Gaubius also undertook the translation into Latin, a language which in the present copy is combined with Dutch; the work also exists in a French-Latin edition.

Vol. I contains among the opening chapters a preface in Latin by Herman Boerhaave. An alphabetical index to all four volumes is found in Vol. IV, in Latin (pp. 129—176) and in Dutch (pp. 177—214).

The plates (engravings, some signed P. Tanjé fecit) are

remarkable for their fine and skilful execution. The plates were issued separately in Paris (and Strasbourg: Levrault) in 1827—30 under the title 'Planches du cabinet de Seba', etc., and published with the assistance of Cuvier by F. Guérin, whose text to them, however, never appeared.

SEEBOHM, H.
1881. Catalogue of the birds in the British Museum. Vol. V. *See British Museum (Natural History),* 1874—98.

[1887]. The geographical distribution of the family Charadriidæ, or the plovers, sandpipers, snipes, and their allies. By Henry Seebohm. Henry Sotheran & Co. *London. pp. XXIX + 524. text-figs. 21 col. pl. (numb. I—XXI in text). 4to.*

A comprehensive account, based on a large amount of material, of the groups of birds cited in the title, principally as regards their distribution and mutual relationship, the habits of the birds being only occasionally referred to.

The subject-matter is distributed over 30 chapters, the first eight of which deal with general questions, such as the classification and evolution of the birds, the differentiation of species, migration, etc., while the greater part of the remainder of the work (pp. 66—506) is devoted to a systematic treatment of the birds. Under each genus the author gives its diagnosis, characters, synonymy, and information about its geographical distribution, as well as a key to the species; the individual forms are treated similarly, with the addition of the literature and information about variations and nearest allies.

The plates (J. G. Keulemans lith.) are hand-coloured (Hanhart, some few Judd & Co., imp.) and show birds which have not been figured before, or of which good figures are lacking.

1893. Exploration of Mount Kina Balu, North Borneo. Appendix 4. *See Whitehead, J.*

1896. A history of British birds with notes on their classification and geographical distribution. Also ... coloured plates of their eggs. By Henry Seebohm. John C. Nimmo. *London. (Another title-page:* A history of British birds, with coloured illustrations of their eggs. By Henry Seebohm. R. H. Porter. *London.* 1883 —85*). 4 vols. 8vo.* — Vol. I. *pp. [III] + XXIII + 614. text-figs.* Vol. II. *pp. [III] + XXXII + 600. text-figs.* Vol. III. *pp. [III] + XXIV + 684. text-figs.* Vol. IV. Plates. *pp. [III] + X + 11—124. 68 col. pl. (numb. 1—68).*

The second edition of a work which was originally issued in 1882—85, as indicated, approximately, on one of the title-pages.

Largely on the basis of personal observation, the author gives a systematic account of the breeding range of each species, its habits, especially during the breeding season, migration, nesting-site, nest, and eggs.

The introduction to the first three volumes deals with questions of a more general character, thus in Vol. II, 'On the protective colour of eggs', by Charles Dixon, and Vol. III, 'The historians of British birds'. The text of Vol. IV comprises, besides the 'List of plates' (pp. 103—124), two sections, — 'Classification of birds' (pp. X + 11—52; preface dated 1895), a revised edition of an essay of 1890, and 'Geographical distribution of British birds' (pp. 53—102; preface dated 1893).

The plates, which in the first edition had been made by Hanhart, are executed in chromo-lithography (printed by Lemercier, Paris); they were re-issued in 1904 in London (Routledge) in an edition consisting of one volume, which was limited to 110 copies.

In 1896 another work by Seebohm with coloured plates of British birds' eggs was issued (457); however, its plates are different from those of the present work.

1896. Coloured figures of the eggs of British birds, with descriptive notices, by Henry Seebohm. Edited after the author's death) by R. Bowdler Sharpe. Pawson and Brailsford. *Sheffield. pp. XXIV + 304.*

61 pl. (front. (portrait) + 60 col. pl. (numb. 1—59, 58a)). 8vo.

This work, which opens (pp. V—XIV) with a memoir of Seebohm, by the editor, gives brief information about the occurrence, breeding habits, nests, and eggs of British birds. In preparing the issue Sharpe has relied on Seebohm's 'A history of British birds', 1896 (456). The text proper runs to p. 278 only, the remainder being a list of subscribers and an index.

Specimens of the eggs of nearly all the birds mentioned in the volume are figured on the plates (chromo-lithographs), which were both drawn and lithographed by the publishers of the book, and which differ from the plates in the author's 'A history of British birds', etc. (456).

[1898—] 1902. A monograph of the Turdidæ, or **458.** family of thrushes. By Henry Seebohm. Edited and completed (after the author's death) by R. Bowdler Sharpe. Henry Sotheran & Co. *London.* 2 vols. *149 col. pl. (numb. in 'List of plates'). large 4to.* — Vol. I. [1898—99]. *pp. XI + 337. 79 pl. (78 col. pl. birds (Nos. I—LXXVIII)).* Vol. II. [1899—1902]. *pp. IX + 250. 71 col. pl. (Nos. LXXIX—CXLIX).*

This work was published in 13 parts (Vol. I: Parts I— VII (VII partly)). The writing of the manuscript had been commenced by Seebohm, and nearly all the coloured plates were ready at his death, although more plates had to be added later in order to bring the work up to date. However, Seebohm's manuscript constitutes merely one-fourth of the work, so the remainder had to be written by R. Bowdler Sharpe, whose contributions are signed with his initials.

The text dealing with individual forms gives their synonymies, brief diagnoses in Latin, descriptions with other notes; and, most often, information about the geographical distribution and the habits of the birds.

The greater number of the forms mentioned are figured, while such species as it was impossible to illustrate are recorded in the 'Table of contents', and briefly dealt with in the 'Appendix' (Vol. II, pp. 227—240) or in the 'Addenda' (Vol. II, pp. 241—242).

The plates (J. G. Keulemans lith. or del.) are hand-coloured (Hanhart, some Mintern Bros. or Judd & Co., imp.).

SELBY, P. J.
1826—43. Illustrations of ornithology. *See Jardine, W.*

1843 [1835]. The Naturalist's Library. Edited by **459.** William Jardine. Vol. XIX. Ornithology (Vol. V). Pigeons. By Prideaux John Selby. W. H. Lizars. *Edinburgh. pp. IX + XIII—XV + 17—228. text-figs. 31 pl. (front. (plain) + 30 col. pl. birds (numb. 1— 30)). small 8vo.*

A volume of the series issued by Jardine and cited in the title, which appeared in 1833—43 (224).

The plates (Lizars sc.) show coloured figures of birds on uncoloured backgrounds, and are executed from drawings by E. Lear, one by Prêtre.

In addition to the ornithological matter, the volume contains a memoir of Pliny (pp. 17—82) with an accompanying engraved portrait (front.).

1843 [1836]. The Naturalist's Library. Edited by **460.** William Jardine. Vol. XVIII. Ornithology (Vol. VI). Parrots. By Prideaux John Selby. W. H. Lizars. *Edinburgh. pp. XV + 17—187 + 4. 31 pl. (front. (plain) + 30 col. pl. birds (numb. 1—30)). small 8vo.*

A volume of the series cited in the title, which was issued by Jardine, and appeared in its entirety in 1833—43 (224).

The plates (Lizars sc.), showing coloured figures of birds on uncoloured backgrounds, were executed from drawings by E. Lear.

In addition to the ornithological matter, the volume contains a memoir of Thomas Bewick (pp. 17—51) with an accompanying engraved portrait (front.).

461.   *1842.* Naturgeschichte der Papageien. Nach Prideaux-Selby. Deutsch bearbeitet von Friedrich Treitschke. Mit dem Bildnisse und der Lebensbeschreibung Le Vaillant's. Nebst ... colorirten Abbildungen und einer Vignette. C. A. Hartleben. *Pesth. pp. [VIII] + XII + 113. 31 pl. (front. (plain) + 30 col. pl. birds (numb. I—XXX in text)). small 8vo.*

A German edition of Selby's volume on the parrots in Jardine's 'Naturalist's Library', of which series ten volumes were issued in German editions in 1836—42.

Many of the plates (steel-plate engravings with hand-coloured figures of birds on uncoloured backgrounds) are signed Gebhart sc.

A biography of Levaillant is found on pp. I—XII.

SELIGMANN, J. M.

462.   *1749—76.* Sammlung verschiedener ausländischer und seltener Vögel, worinnen ein jeder dererselben nicht nur auf das genaueste beschrieben, sondern auch in einer richtigen und sauber illuminirten Abbildung vorgestellet wird (Parts II—VI: Ausgefertiget und herausgegeben) von Johann Michael Seligmann. *(Engraved title to Parts I—IV: Catesby und Edwards Sammlung seltener Vögel. Parts VII—IX with title:* Sammlung verschiedener ausländischer und seltener Vögel, und einiger anderer Seltenheiten der Natur, in richtigen und sauber illuminirten Abbildungen ... als eine Nachlese zu Georg Edwards Werken. Ausgefertigt, heraus gegeben und verlegt von Johann Michael Seeligmanns seel. Erben.) Gedruckt bey Johann Joseph Fleischmann (Parts VII—IX: zu finden bey denen Verlegern). *Nürnberg. 9 parts in 5 vols. 474 pl. (473 col.; 426 pl. birds). fol. — Part I. 1749. pp. [XVIII] + [50]. engraved title. 51 pl. (50 col. pl. birds (numb. I—L)). Part II. 1751. pp. [56]. engraved title. 52 col. pl. (numb. LI—CII; 50 pl. birds). Part III. 1753. pp. [XII] + [LIV] + [50]. engraved title. 50 col. pl. (numb. I—L). 1 map. Part IV. 1755. pp. [100]. engraved title. 64 col. pl. (numb. LI—CXIV; 59 pl. birds). Part V. 1759. pp. [IV] + [52]. 52 col. pl. (numb. I—LII). Part VI 1764 pp [70]. 53 col. pl. (numb. LIII—CV; 37 pl. birds). Part VII. 1770. pp. [IV] + [52]. 50 col. pl. (numb. I—L; 37 pl. birds). Part VIII. 1773. pp. [XVI] + [63]. 50 col. pl. (numb. LI—C; 41 pl. birds). Part IX. 1776. pp. [IV] + [56]. 52 col. pl. (numb. I—LII; 50 pl. birds).*

The nine parts of which this work consists are bound in pairs, with the exception of Part 9, which is bound separately.

It is in all essentials a translation by Georg Leonhard Huth of George Edwards' 'A natural history of birds', 1743—51, (124) and 'Gleanings of natural history', 1758—64 (126), and Mark Catesby's 'The natural history of Carolina', etc. (94; 95), provided with hand-coloured copies of the plates in these works, engraved by Seligmann.

A Dutch, somewhat enlarged, edition was issued in 1772 —81, translated by Martinus Houttuyn, under the title 'Verzameling van uitlandsche en zeldzaame vogelen', etc. A French translation of the work appeared in 1768—76 (463).

463.   *1768—76.* Recueil de divers oiseaux étrangers et peu communs qui se trouvent dans les ouvrages de messieurs Edwards et Catesby representés en taille douce et exactement coloriés par Jean Michel Seligmann. *(Engraved title to Vols. I—III: Recueil des oiseaux étrangers de Catesby et Edwards. Catesby und Edwards Sammlung seltener Vögel).* Les heritiers de Seligmann. *Nuremberg. 8 vols. 414 col. pl. (371*

pl. birds). fol. — Vol. I. 1768. pp. [XVIII] + 52. engraved title. 50 col. pl. (numb. I—L). Vol. II. 1768. pp. 56. engraved title. 52 col. pl. (numb. LI—CII; 50 pl. birds). Vol. III. 1770. pp. 50 + [2]. engraved title. 50 col. pl. (numb. I—L). Vol. IV. 1771. pp. 88 + [2]. 64 col. pl. (numb. LI—CXIV; 59 pl. birds). Vol. V. 1772. pp. 52 + [2]. 52 col. pl. (numb. LII). Vol. VI. 1773. pp. 54 + [2]. 48 col. pl. (numb. LIII—LVIII, LXI, LXIII—LXXV, LXXVII—LXXXV, LXXXVII—CV; 33 pl. birds). Vol. VII. 1774. pp. 58 + [2]. 49 col. pl. (numb. I—XI, XIII— L; 37 pl. birds). Vol. VIII. 1776. pp. 74 + [2]. 49 col. pl. (numb. LI—LV, LVII—C; 40 pl. birds).

A French edition of the German work published in 1749 —76 (462). In the present copy eight of the coloured plates are missing, the total number of coloured plates thus being 422.

SELOUS, E.

1910—13. The British bird book ... *See Kirkman, F. B. B.*

SENCKENBERGISCHE   NATURFORSCHENDE GESELLSCHAFT. FRANKFURT AM MAIN.

1826. Atlas zu der Reise im nördlichen Afrika. Erste Abtheilung. Zoologie. Herausgegeben von der Senckenbergischen naturforschenden Gesellschaft. Vögel. *See Rueppell, E. W. P. S.*

SHARPE, R. B.

1868—71. A monograph of the Alcedinidæ: or, family of kingfishers. By R. B. Sharpe. Published by the author. *London. pp. [III] + II + II + LXXI + [304] + XI. 2 text-figs. 121 pl. (120 col. (numb. I—120 in 'List of plates')). 1 map (diagram). 4to.*

This monograph, the idea of which was originally conceived by W. J. Williams, was published in fifteen parts, the contents and dates of publication of which are given in the introduction pp. II—III.

The first part of the book (pp. I—LXXI) consists, besides the introduction, of a number of chapters dealing with the group in general under the headings classification, geographical distribution, concluding remarks, and literature.

The remainder of the work (pp. 304), apart from the index (pp. I—XI), is devoted to a systematic treatment of the group, which is divided into the subfamilies Alcedininæ with 5 genera and 84 species, and Daceloninæ with 14 genera and 84 species. Under each species the author gives its synonymy, diagnosis, and habitat in Latin, description, and information from various sources about the habits of the birds.

The plates (lithographs coloured by hand) were drawn by J. G. Keulemans, while the printing and colouring, which sometimes leave much to be desired, were entrusted to P. W. M. Trap.

1871—72. A history of the birds of Europe ... Parts I—XII. *See Dresser, H. E., 1871—96.*

1874—98. Catalogue of the birds in the British Museum. Vols. I—IV, VI, VII, IX (genus Zosterops) X, XII, XIII, XVII, XXIII, XXIV, XXVI. *See British Museum (Natural History), 1874—98.*

1875. The zoology of the voyage of H. M. S. Erebus and Terror ... 1839—43 ... Birds. *See Gray, G. R., 1844—75.*

1875—84. The birds of South Africa. New edition. Thoroughly revised and augmented by R. Bowdler Sharpe. *See Layard, E. L.*

1881—87. A monograph of the Trochilidæ, or

family of humming-birds. Completed after the author's death by R. Bowdler Sharpe. Supplement. Parts II— V. *See Gould, J.*, 1880—87.

1882—83. The birds of Asia. Parts XXXIII— XXXV. *See Gould, J.*, 1850—83.

1882—88. The birds of New Guinea and the adjacent Papuan Islands ... completed after the author's death by R. Bowdler Sharpe. Parts XIII—XXV. *See Gould, J.*, 1875—88.

1891. Scientific results of the Second Yarkand Mission; based upon the collections and notes of the late Ferdinand Stoliczka. Aves. By R. Bowdler Sharpe. Published by order of the government of India. 1878 —1891. Printed by Taylor and Francis. *London. pp. XVII + 153. 24 col. pl. (numb. I—XXIV). large 4to.*

The ornithological section of a report of an expedition, published in its entirety in 14 parts in 1878—91.
The ornithological collections were first treated by Allan Hume, but his manuscript was stolen and sold as waste paper. Altogether 350 forms are described, with synonymies and extracts of notes from the diary of Dr. Stoliczka and notes given by Colonel Biddulph in manuscript to Hume. The report also includes all the species obtained by Dr. Henderson and Dr. Scully and previously treated in publications by them. The work does, therefore, deal with the whole of the material secured by the British expeditions into Central Asia. In an appendix (pp. 149—152) mention is made of some Indian birds, which are figured on Pl. XVI—XXIV.
Most of the plates (lithographs coloured by hand) were drawn by J. G. Keulemans, a few by W. Hart and — probably — J. Smit (some: Hanhart imp.).

1893. Exploration of Mount Kina Balu, North Borneo. Appendices 2 and 3. *See Whitehead, J.*

1894—97. Allen's Naturalist's Library. Edited by R. Bowdler Sharpe. A hand-book to the birds of Great Britain. By R. Bowdler Sharpe. W. H. Allen & Co. *London. 4 vols. 125 col. pl. (out of 128). 8vo.* -- Vol. I. 1894. *pp. XXII + 342. text-figs. 28 col. pl. (numb. I—XVI, XVIII—XXIX; 1 pl. (XXIX) eggs). missing pl.: XVII, XXX, XXXI.* Vol. II. 1896. *pp. XVIII + [I] + 308. text-figs. 27 col. pl. (numb. XXXII—LVIII).* Vol. III. 1896. *pp. XII + [I] + 338. 35 col. pl. (numb. LIX—XCIII).* Vol. IV. 1897. *pp. XVII + [I] + 314. text-figs. 35 col. pl. (numb. XCIV—CXXIV, CXIa—d).*

A semi-popular account, which forms a useful guide to the study of British birds, whose individual forms are treated under headings such as description of the plumages of the adult male and adult female, adult in winter plumage, immature birds, description of nestlings and young birds, discussions of the range in Great Britain, the range outside the British Islands, habits, and nests and eggs.
The plates (chromo-lithographs; Wyman & Sons, Limited) are of different origin, some being reproductions of the old steel-plate engravings in Jardine's original edition of the 'Naturalist's Library' (227), while others are executed from drawings by contemporary artists, particularly J. G. Keulemans. The latter plates are the better, and naturally vary greatly from the former.
Vols. I and II were re-issued with a few alterations in 1896 in Lloyd's Natural History, edited by R. Bowdler Sharpe, in which series Vols. III and IV also appeared, in 1896 and 1897 respectively.

1895—97. Allen's Naturalist's Library. Edited by R. Bowdler Sharpe. A hand-book to the game-birds. *See Ogilvie-Grant, W. R.*

1896. Coloured figures of the eggs of British birds ... Edited (after the author's death) by R. Bowdler Sharpe. *See Seebohm, H.*

1897—1904. Biologia Centrali-Americana. Aves. Vol. III. *See Salvin, O.*, 1879—1904.

1898—1902. A monograph of the Turdidæ, or family of thrushes. Edited and completed (after the author's death) by R. Bowdler Sharpe. *See Seebohm, H.*

1900. The natural history and antiquities of Selborne and a garden kalendar. Edited by R. Bowdler Sharpe ... *See White, G.*

1904—15. Reports of the Princeton University expeditions to Patagonia, 1896—1899 ... Vol. II. Ornithology Parts I—IV (IV partly). *See Scott, W. E. D.*, 1904—28.

1907—10. A monograph of the petrels (order Tubinares). See *Godman, F. D.*

SHAW, G.

[1789—] 1790—1813. The naturalist's miscellany: **467.** or coloured figures of natural objects; drawn and described immediately from Nature. *Engraved title to Vol. I:* Vivarium naturæ or the naturalist's miscellany. By George Shaw ... the figures by F. P. Nodder. Nodder & Co. *London. 24 vols. 1064 col. pl. (282 pl. birds). small 4to (size as 8vo).* Added title-page in Latin.

This series was published in 287 parts which, according to C. D. Sherborn (862 b), appeared monthly, from August, 1789, to June, 1813 inclusive.
The general title-page to the whole work is only found in Vol. I which, like the other volumes in the series, contains two dedicatory title-pages, in Latin and in English, which bear the names of Shaw and his co-editor, viz. in Vols. I—XII, F. P. Nodder; Vol. XIII, E. R. Nodder; Vol. XIV, E. and R. Nodder; Vols. XV—XXIV, E. Nodder.
The plates are distributed as follows over the individual volumes: I (pl. 1—37), II (38—74), III (75—110), IV (111 —146), V (147—182), VI (183—218), VII (219—254), VIII (255—300), IX (301—348), X (349—396), XI (397—444), XII (445—492), XIII (493—540), XIV (541—588), XV (589—636), XVI (637—684), XVII (685—732), XVIII (733 —780), XIX (781—828), XX (829—876), XXI (877—924), XXII (925—972), XXIII (973—1020), XXIV (1021—1064).
In Vol. XXIV have been bound 'General indexes, in Latin and English, to the subjects contained in the twenty-four volumes of the Naturalist's Miscellany; by the late George Shaw and Rich P. Nodder'. (Elizabeth Nodder & Son. London. 1813. pp. 26).
The text of the remaining part of the work is unpaged and consists of explanations to the plates, in Latin and English, containing generic and specific characters, descriptions, and information about the habitats of the animals figured, and sometimes notes on their habits.
The plates (engravings coloured by hand) in Vols. V— XXIV, at any rate a number of them, were drawn and engraved by R. P. Nodder.
As a sequel to this work, 'The zoological miscellany' by W. E. Leach and R. P. Nodder was issued in 1814—17 (282).

1790. Journal of a voyage to New South Wales ... [Birds]. *See White, J.*

1809—26. General zoology, or systematic natural **468.** history by (from Vol. IX, Part I: commenced by the late) George Shaw. With plates from the first authorities and most select specimens engraved principally by Griffith. Vol. VII, Parts I—IV, Vol. XIV, Part I. Aves. (From Vol. IX, Part I: by J. F. Stephens). G. Kearsly (Vols. VII, VIII), G. Wilkie (Vols. IX, X), J. Walker (Vol. XI), I. and A. Arch (Vol. XII—Vol. XIV, Part I). *Second title:* General zoology. (From

25·*

Vol. IX, Part I: By James Francis Stephens.) Birds. *London. 8 vols. in 15. 8vo.* — Vol. VII. Part I. 1809. *pp. XVII + [II] + 280. 36 pl. (numb. 1—36).* Vol. VII. Part II. 1809. *pp. X + [I] + 281—504. 35 pl. (numb. 37—71).* Vol. VIII. Part I. 1811 (engraved title: 1812). *pp. IX + [I] + 357. 46 pl. (numb. 1— 28, 79 [= 29], 30—45, 39*).* Vol. VIII. Part II. 1811 (engraved title: 1812). *pp. VI + [I] + 359—557. 39 pl. (numb. 46—84).* Vol. IX. Part I. 1815. *pp. XIV + [I] + 227. 50 pl. (numb. 1—40, 3*, 4*, 35*— 35*******, 36*).* Vol. IX. Part II. 1816. *pp. XVII + [II] + 229—547. 30 pl. (numb. 41—70).* Vol. X. Part I. 1817. *pp. XIX + [I] + 317. 29 pl. (numb. 1—28, 30 [= 29]).* Vol. X. Part II. 1817. *pp. XXXI + [I] + 319—765 + [I]. 31 pl. (numb. 30—60).* Vol. XI. Part I. 1819. *pp. XIV + [I] + 264. 16 pl. (numb. 1—4, 6—17).* Vol. XI. Part II. 1819. *pp. XXI + [II] + 265—646. 34 pl. (numb. 18—21, 23 —52).* Vol. XII. Part I. 1824. *pp. [IV] + 297. 35 pl. (numb. 1—35).* Vol. XII. Part II. 1824. *pp. [IV] + 264. 29 pl. (numb. 36—64).* Vol. XIII. Part I. 1826 (engraved title: 1825). *pp. [IV] + 278. 29 pl. (numb. 1—28, 30).* Vol. XIII. Part II. 1826 (engraved title: 1825). *pp. [IV] + 290. 33 pl. (numb. 31—63).* Vol. XIV. Part I. 1826. *pp. [III] + 385. 41 pl. (numb. 1—41).*

The publication of this work, comprising 14 vols. in 28, which besides birds deals with mammals, amphibia, fishes, and insects, was commenced in 1800 with the issue of the first volume of the section on mammals, and concluded in 1826 with [Vol. XIV. Part II] 'General index to the zoology, by George Shaw and James Francis Stephens', since the latter continued and concluded the publication after Shaw's death.

The ornithological section treats of the birds in a systematic order, with a brief mention of each genus and a statement of generic characters in Latin, while a more detailed account is given of the individual species.

SHELLEY, G. E.

469. *1872.* A handbook to the birds of Egypt. By G. E. Shelley. John van Voorst. *London. pp. VIII + [I] + 342. 14 col. pl. (numb. I—XIV). 8vo.*

A synopsis of the birds of Egypt, especially intended for hunters and collectors. The greater part of the matter compiled in the volume is derived from the author's personal observations on three ornithological tours in Egypt, and from a collection of almost a thousand skins which he possessed. The work deals with all the species of birds which are to be found in Egypt between the Mediterranean and the Second Cataract, giving a description of them and their measurements, and sundry notes on their habits. This matter takes up the greater part of the book (pp. 65—316), while four introductory chapters (pp. 3—64) with diary notes by the author give a picture of the nature of the country and information about the best localities for the ornithologist and sportsman to visit.

The fine plates (lithographs coloured by hand) were executed from drawings by J. G. Keulemans.

1891. Catalogue of the birds in the British Museum. Vol. XIX. *See British Museum (Natural History),* 1874—98.

470. *1896—1912.* The birds of Africa, comprising all the species which occur in the Ethiopian Region. By G. E. Shelley. Published for the author by R. H. Porter. (Vol. V. Part II: Henry Sotheran & Co.). *London. 5 vols in 7. 57 col. pl. large 8vo (size as 4to).* — Vol. I. 1896. List. *pp. VIII + 196.* Vol. II. 1900. *pp. VII + 348. 14 col. pl. (numb. I—XIV).* Vol. III.

1902. *pp. VII + [I] + 276. 14 col. pl. (numb. XV— XXVIII).* Vol. IV. Part I. 1905. *pp. V + [I] + 287. 7 col. pl. (numb. XXIX—XXXV).* Vol. IV. Part II. 1905. *pp. IV + [I] + 289—511. 7 col. pl. (numb. XXXVI—XLII).* Vol. V. Part I. 1906. *pp. [IV] + [I] + 163. 7 col. pl. (numb. XLIII—XLIX).* Vol. V. Part II. 1912. Completed and edited by W. L. Sclater. *pp. VII + [I] + 165—502. 8 col. pl. (numb. L— LVII).*

This work was published in eight parts, Vol. II appearing in two parts (Vol. II, Part I, pp. 1—160).

Vol. I contains a list of all the species known to occur in the Ethiopian Region up to the time of publication, with reference to a fine picture and to the volume and page of the catalogue of the British Museum in which the species in question is mentioned. Altogether 2534 forms of birds are listed in this 'Nomenclator avium Æthiopicarum', as it might be called.

The remainder of the work, which contains descriptions of several new genera and species, gives a systematic account of the birds, with keys to the species and higher groups, brief characterizations of the latter, and, under the individual forms, descriptions, mostly brief, and information about their geographical distribution and habits.

The beautiful plates (lithographs coloured by hand) were executed from drawings by H. Grønvold.

SHIPLEY, A. E.

1912. The Grouse in health and in disease ... Edited by A. S. Leslie, assisted by A. E. Shipley. *See Leslie, A. S.*

SIBBALD, R.

1684. Scotia illustrata, sive prodromus historiæ naturalis in quo regionis natura, incolarum ingenia & mores, morbi iisque medendi methodus, & medicina indigena accurate explicantur: Et multiplices naturæ partus in triplice ejus regno, vegetabili scilicet, animali & minerali per hancce borealem Magnæ Britaniæ partem, quæ antiquissimum Scotiæ regnum constituit, undiquaque diffusi nunc primum in lucem eruuntur, & varii eorum usus, medici præsertim & mechanici, cum ad vitæ cum necessitatem, tum commoditatem præstant, cunctis perspicue exponuntur. Cum figuris æneis ... Auctore Roberto Sibbaldo. < - - Pars secunda specialis. Tomus secundus. - - pp. 1—37: Partis secundæ liber tertius. De animalibus Scotiæ tam feris quam domesticis >. Sumptibus auctoris. *Edinburgi. 10 pl. birds (numb. 7, 9, XI—XIII, 14—16, 18, 21). fol.*

To the present zoological part of the work belongs the unpaginated 'Index II' of four pages. The whole work consists of a volume in three parts, or rather two, of which the last one is divided into two tomes, which are both further divided into two books.

The third of these is the one here cited, 'De animalibus Scotiæ', etc., which represents the first comprehensive attempt to depict the fauna of Scotland. The birds are treated in the 'Sectio tertia. De avibus' (pp. 13 (misprinted 11) —22), which section is mainly a catalogue of birds. In an appendix, 'Diatribe de Anseribus Scoticis', contains the legend about the birth of the Barnacle-Goose; the fable, however, is refuted. The work has been dealt with by W. H. Mullens (818), who gives an English translation of the greater part of the ornithological section.

Some of the plates (engravings) are signed, some Geo. Main fecit, others excud. Jo. Reid.

SIEBOLD, P. F. von.

1844—50. Fauna Japonica ... notis, observationibus et adumbrationibus illustravit Ph. Fr. de Siebold. Aves. *See Temminck, C. J.*

SJÖSTEDT, B. Y.
2. *1895.* K. Svenska Vetenskaps-Akademiens Handlingar. Ny följd. Vol. XXVII. No. 1. Zur Ornithologie Kameruns nebst einigen Angaben über die Säugetiere des Landes. Von Yngve Sjöstedt. Mit ... kolorierten Tafeln. *Stockholm. pp. 120. 10 col. pl. (numb. I—X). 4to.*

The greater part of the material treated in this paper was collected by the author on a journey of collection and observation which started in October, 1890, and lasted for fifteen months.

About 400 specimens belonging to 176 species were collected; 56 of these species proved to be new to the Cameroons, and six new to science. Three species which the author believes he observed are mentioned. Further, the author treats of material from the Cameroon mountains collected by K. Knutson and G. Valdau, and deposited in the Natural History Museum at Stockholm. Among the 52 species of this collection, 32 had not been met with by Sjöstedt in the land below the mountains, eleven had not previously been ascertained in the Cameroons, and four were new to science.

After an introductory description of the various types of landscape and vegetation and their birds and mammals, there follows a systematic account of the individual forms, arranged according to Reichenow's system in 'Die Vögel der zoologischen Gärten' (1882 and 1884), with a statement of the synonyms, measurements, and occasionally a brief description of the bird and information about its habitat and habits.

A 'Übersicht aller bis jetzt aus dem Kamerungebiet bekannten Vogelarten' (pp. 113—118) contains 316 items.

All the new species and the female of Malimbus Racheliæ are figured on the plates (chromo-lithographs, A. Ekblom pinx., G. Tholander lith., W. Schlachter, Stockholm).

A separate copy of this paper (a thesis for a doctorate, dated 1896) is in the possession of the Library. The greater number of the plates were reproduced in the report of Sjöstedt's travels published in 1904 (473).

Part of the avifauna of the Cameroons was further treated in Sjöstedt's 'Die Vögel des nordwestlichen Kamerungebietes' (Mittheilungen aus den deutschen Schutzgebieten 8 (1895) pp. 1—36).

1904. I Västafrikas urskogar. Natur- och djurlifsskildringar från en zoologisk resa i Kamerun. Af Yngve Sjöstedt. Med talrika illustrationer efter fotografier, laveringar och akvareller samt en karta. Fröléen & Comp. *Stockholm. pp. [III] + 564. text-figs. 7 col. pl. birds. (numb. 1, 2, 4—7, 11 in 'Illustrationer'). 1 map. 8vo.*

A report of Sjöstedt's travels in the Cameroons in 1890—92, in which a series of data is given about the animal life there, including bird life. The journey yielded very valuable material, more than 23,000 specimens of animals being brought home. The works on the expedition issued prior to the publication of the present volume dealt with more than 2300 different forms of animals, of which 530 were hitherto unknown.

The volume is abundantly illustrated, and contains eleven coloured plates (three-colour prints, Tullbergs Tr., Stockholm), of which those showing figures of birds have been reproduced from the plates (A. Ekblom, pinx.) in Sjöstedt's 'Zur Ornithologie Kameruns', etc., 1895 (472).

SLATER, H. H.
1898. British birds with their nests and eggs. Vol. V. Order Limicolæ. *See Butler, A. G., 1896—98.*

SLOANE, H.
1707—25. A voyage to the islands Madera, Barbados (Vol. II: Barbadoes), Nieves, S. (Vol. II: St.) Christophers, and Jamaica; with the natural history of the herbs and trees, four-footed beasts, fishes, birds, insects, reptiles &c. of the last of those islands. To which is prefix'd an introduction, wherein is an account of the inhabitants, air, waters, diseases, trade &c. of that place; with some relations concerning the neighbouring continent, and islands of America. Illustrated with the figures of the things described, which have not been heretofore engraved. In large copperplates as big as the life. By Hans Sloane. Printed (Vol. I: by B. M.) for the author. *London. 2 vols. plates. fol.*

This work was prepared on the basis of the material, chiefly plants, collected by the author during a stay in the West Indies.

A good deal of ornithological matter is found scattered through the first volume, though it is chiefly collected in the section 'Of the birds of Jamaica' in Vol. II, pp. 293—325 (Book VI, Part II), which deals with 82 birds, giving their measurements, brief descriptions, and some information about their anatomy, habits, occurrence, and other features of interest.

The work is illustrated with a number of plates, the majority of which, however, show plants.

One of the plates (engravings) in Vol. I and nineteen (Nos. 254—272) in Vol. II represent birds which, however, are rather poorly drawn. Several of the plates in the latter volume are signed M. van der Gucht scul.

SMITHSONIAN INSTITUTION. HARRIMAN ALASKA SERIES.
Vol. I. 1902. pp. 1—118: Narrative of the expedition. *See Burroughs, J.*
Vol. II. 1902. pp. 205—234. Days among Alaska birds. *See Keeler, C. A.*

SMITHSONIAN INSTITUTION. SMITHSONIAN CONTRIBUTIONS TO KNOWLEDGE.
1859. Vol. XI. North American oölogy. Part I. *See Brewer, T. M.*
1892. Vol. XXVIII. Life histories of North American birds with special reference to their breeding habits and eggs. *See Bendire, C. E.*
1895. Vol. XXXII. Life histories of North American birds, from the parrots to the grackles, with special reference to their breeding habits and eggs. *See Bendire, C. E.*

SMITHSONIAN INSTITUTION. UNITED STATES NATIONAL MUSEUM. *See United States National Museum.*

SMITHSONIAN SCIENTIFIC SERIES.
Vol. 6. 1930. Wild animals in and out the Zoo. *See Mann, W. M.*
Vol. 9. 1931. Warm-blooded vertebrates. pp. 1—166: Part I. Birds. *See Wetmore, F. A.*

SÖDERBERG, J. R.
1911—26. Nordens fåglar ... Under medverkan av Rud. Söderberg. *See Jägerskiöld, A. K. E. L.*

SONNERAT, P.
1776. Voyage à la Nouvelle Guinée, dans lequel on trouve la description des lieux, des observations physiques & morales, & des détails relatifs à l'histoire naturelle dans le règne animal & le règne végétal. Par Sonnerat. Enrichi de cent vingt figures en taille douce. Ruault. *Paris. pp. XII + [IV] + 206 + [2]. 79 pl. birds (numb. 20—55, 64—85, 95—115). 4to.* 475.

The expedition which is recorded in the present work set out from Isle de France on June 29, 1771, and went to the Philippine Islands, the Moluccas, and other neighbouring islands. A series of observations relating to natural history were made, especially as regards plants and birds, a number of which are figured and described in several of the chapters of the book, viz. in Chapter VI (pp. 51—92), 'Description de quelques nouveaux oiseaux, observés à l'Isle de Luçon', in part of Chapter VIII (pp. 109—126), 'Description de quelques oiseaux observés à Antigue', and in Chapter XII (pp. 155—181), 'Description de quelques oiseaux de la Nouvelle Guinée'. The accompanying plates with figures of birds are engravings (P. Sonnerat, pinx.; C. Baquoy, sculp.).

The birds dealt with in this work were treated in 1786 by J. A. Scopoli in the 'Deliciæ floræ et faunæ Insubricæ', etc., Pars II, pp. 85—96 : 'Specimen zoologicum exhibens characteres genericos, & specificos, necnon nomina trivialia novorum animalium, quæ clarissimus Sonnerat in China, & in Indiis Orientalibus nuper detexit. Aves.' The same paper further treats of mammals and birds from Sonnerat's 'Voyage aux Indes Orientales et à la Chine', 1782, which appeared in a new edition in 1806 (478). Together with the other ornithological sections of Scopoli's work, which appeared in three parts in 1786—88, the paper was re-issued in 1882 by The Willughby Society, edited by Alfred Newton.

An abridged English edition of Sonnerat's work appeared in 1776 (dated 1775), and was reprinted in 1781, a German translation being issued in 1777 (476).

476.   *1777. Sonnerat's Reise nach Neuguinea. Aus dem Französischen übersetzt von J. P. Ebeling. Mit dreyszig Kupfern. Weygand. Leipzig. pp. [IV] + 72. 16 pl, birds. 4to.*
A German translation of Sonnerat's work, 'Voyage à la Nouvelle Guinée', etc., issued in 1776 (475), with the addition of the scientific names of several of the species treated. The subtitle reads, 'Reisen nach dem neuentdeckten Guinea, nebst einer Beschreibung der philippinischen Inseln und Molukken'. A number of the bird-figures in the French work are reproduced on the plates, each of which contain several figures.

477.   *1783. Reise nach Ostindien und China, auf Befehl des Königs unternommen ... 1774—81. Von Sonnerat. Vol. II. < - - pp. 116—173: Fünftes Buch. Neu entdeckte Gegenstände aus der Naturgeschichte. Zweiter Abschnitt. Von den Vögeln >. Orell. Zürich. 29 pl. (numb. 94—122). 4to.*
Part of a German translation in two volumes, with 140 plates, of a work, the French original of which appeared in Paris in 1782 under the title, 'Voyage aux Indes Orientales et à la Chine', etc., in an edition in two volumes, 4to, and in another in 3 vols., 8vo. A new French edition was issued in 1806 (478), and several smaller ones were published, e. g. in English 1788—89, and in German 1783 and 1784 ; a 'Supplément au voyage de Sonnerat dans les Indes Orientales et à la Chine, par un ancien marin (Foucher d'Obsonville)' appeared in Amsterdam and in Paris in 1785.

In the present edition the main part of the ornithological matter is collected in the above-cited section of Vol. II, in which a large number of birds are described and figured. Binomial names are not used. The plates are engravings (P. Sonnerat, pinx., the majority, J. J. Avril, sculp.), and recur in the French edition mentioned above.

The birds as well as the mammals in this work were treated on the basis of the French original edition in 1786 by J. A. Scopoli (cf. 475, note).

478.   *1806. Voyage aux Indes Orientales et à la Chine, fait par ordre de Louis XVI ... 1774—1781; dans lequel on traite des mœurs, de la religion, des sciences et des arts des Indiens, des Chinois, des Pégouins et des Madégasses; suivi d'observations sur le Cap de Bonne-Espérance, les îles de France et de Bourbon, les Maldives, Ceylan, Malacca, les Philippines et les Moluques, et de recherches sur l'histoire naturelle de ces pays, etc., etc. Par Sonnerat. Nouvelle édition, revue*

et rétablie d'après le manuscrit autographe de l'auteur; augmentée d'un précis historique sur l'Inde, depuis 1778 jusqu'à nos jours, de notes et de plusieurs mémoires inédites, par Sonnini. Dentu. *Paris. text, 8vo, and atlas, 4to.* — [Text]. Vol. IV. - - < *pp. 143—383: Livre V. Histoire naturelle de l'Inde. § II. Des oiseaux, amphibies, poissons, insectes et vers >.* [Atlas]. Collection de planches pour servir au voyage aux Indes Orientales et à la Chine. *pp. 8. 29 pl. birds (numb. 94—122).*
Part of a new edition of a work which appeared for the first time in 1782, and of which several editions in other languages are extant (cf. 477, note).

The present copy consists in its entirety of four volumes text, 8vo, and an atlas with altogether 140 plates. As compared with the first edition it has been enlarged by additions derived from manuscripts by Sonnerat, and some written by Sonnini. The latter additions are denoted by square brackets. The ornithological matter of the text is chiefly in the section of Vol. IV mentioned above, in which a number of birds are treated, with comprehensive additions by Sonnerat.

The plates are engravings (P. Sonnerat pinx.; the majority, J. J. Avril, sculp.). They are identical with the plates in the German edition of the work from 1783 (477) ; the individual numbers in the two editions do not, however, correspond.

SONNINI DE MANONCOURT, C. N. S.

1800—02. Histoire naturelle ... Nouvelle édition ... rédigé par C. S. Sonnini. Vols. XXXVII—LXIV ... Des oiseaux. *See Buffon, G. L. L. de.*

1803—04. Nouveau dictionnaire d'histoire naturelle ... L'homme, les quadrupèdes, les oiseaux, les cétacés. [Par] Sonnini et Virey. *See Dictionaries.*

1806. Voyages aux Indes Orientales et à la Chine ... Nouvelle édition ... augmentée ... par Sonnini. See Sonnerat, P.

SOUANCÉ, C. de.

1857 [—58]. Iconographie des perroquets non figurés dans les publications de Levaillant et de M. Bourjot Saint-Hilaire. Par Charles de Souancé. Avec la coopération de S. A. le prince Bonaparte et de Émile Blanchard. Histoire naturelle des perroquets. P. Bertrand. *Paris. pp. [VII] + [48]. 48 col. pl. (numb. I—XLVII, LXXIX). large 4to.*
This work constitutes the fourth volume of the work 'Histoire naturelle des perroquets', the first two volumes of which were issued by Levaillant in 1801—05 (302), the third by Bourjot Saint-Hilaire in 1837—38 (54).

The introduction (dated May 15, 1857) was written by A. Moquin-Tandon. The forms figured are treated briefly in the text, which gives the synonymies, descriptions, habitats, and, occasionally, information about the habits of the birds.

Of the fine plates (lithographs coloured by hand), Pl. I—XV, on which both birds and branches are coloured, are signed E. Blanchard pinx. et lith. (or del.) (Imp. Lemercier, Paris), while the remaining ones (Lith.ie Juliot à Tours), with uncoloured branches, are signed J. Daverne, del. et lith.

Like the works to which it forms a sequel, this one was further issued in a large folio edition. It appeared in 12 livraisons, each containing four plates and the accompanying text. The price of each livraison was 16 and 13 francs respectively. The work should have consisted of 30 livraisons, but publication was stopped after the issue of the 12th.

In 1866 the publishers J. B. Baillière et fils acquired the proprietory rights of the work and reduced the price to 100 francs for the folio edition and 70 francs for the quarto edition. At the same time they issued the unpublished Pl. XLVIII and a 'table des planches' (cf. Lorenz, 'Catalogue général de la librairie française, 1840—65', IV, p. 421). The text to Pl.

XLVIII deals with Platycercus adelaidæ, Gould, while Pl.
LXXIX occurring in the present volume represents Cyanoramphus malherbi, Souancé.

SOULEYET, F. L. A.

1841. Voyage autour du monde exécuté ... 1836—
37 sur la corvette la Bonite ... Zoologie. Oiseaux. *See
Eydoux, J. F. T.*

SOWERBY, G. B.

1824—26. See Zoological Journal, The, 1824—35.

SOWERBY, J.

[1804—] 1806. The British miscellany: or coloured
figures of new, rare, or little known animal subjects;
many not before ascertained to be inhabitants of the
British Isles; and chiefly in the possesion of the author,
James Sowerby. Printed by R. Taylor & Co.; and sold
by the author. *London. 2 vols in 1. 7 col. pl. birds.
8vo. —* Vol. I. *pp. VI + 136. 4 col. pl. birds (numb.
6, 10, 17, 21).* [Vol. II]. *pp. 31. 3 col. pl. birds (numb.
62, 69, 70).*
A series of 76 plates (Vol. I, Pl. 1—60; Vol. II, Pl. 61—
76) with figures and accompanying descriptions of rare animals
of Great Britain.
Generic and specific characters, synonyms, a description, and
a brief mention of habitat and occurrence are given under
each form.
The work was issued in twelve parts, the first five of which
contained four plates, the remainder eight plates each.
The plates are dated October 1, 1804, to August 1, 1806,
and the covers in agreement herewith as follows: No. 1, 1804;
No. 2, January 1805; No. 3, February 1805; No. 4, March
1805; No. 5, April 1805; No. 6, June 1805; No. 7, August
1805; No. 8, October 1805; No. 9, December 1805; No. 10,
February 1806; No. 11, June 1806; No. 12, August 1806
(574, p. 554).
Later the stock was bought by Mr. Quaritch, who (1875 ?)
had a new title-page printed without the statement 'Vol. I',
and enlarged the index to comprise the published part of
Vol. II.
The plates (engravings coloured by hand) were executed by
the author.

SOWERBY, J. de C.

1824—26. See Zoological Journal, The, 1824—35.

SPARRMAN, A.

1786—89. Museum Carlsonianum, in quo novas et
selectas aves, coloribus ad vivum brevique descriptione
illustratas, suasu et sumtibus generosissimi possessoris,
exhibet Andreas Sparrman. Ex Typographia Regia.
Holmiæ. 4 fasc. 100 col. pl. fol. — Fasc. I. 1786.
pp. [VII] + [49]. 25 col. pl. (numb. 1—25). Fasc.
II. 1787. *pp. [V] + [49]. 25 col. pl. (numb. 26—50).*
Fasc. III. 1788. *pp. [V] + [49]. 25 col. pl. (numb.
51—75).* Fasc. IV. 1789. *pp. [V] + [49]. 25 col. pl.
(numb. 76—100).*
In addition to the plates in the present copy, mention is
sometimes made (565, p. 10) of twenty more plates ('Fasc.
V sine anno et textu, Tabb. 101—120'), which have probably
been printed but never published.
The text is, as a rule, limited to a brief diagnosis in Latin,
which accompanies each of the figures on an unpaged leaf,
on which the number of the species is stated in Roman
numerals.
The work is the earliest sumptuous ornithological work to
be published in Scandinavia, and is the first work of this kind
which exclusively applies Linnæus' method in its nomencla-

ture. It is therefore of importance owing to the new species
cited in it.
The hand-coloured engravings were executed from drawings
by J. Carl Linnerhielm (Fr. Akrel sc.) (cf. the preface, and
the Vecko-skrift för läkare och naturforskare 8 (1787) pp. 19
—22, 303—310; 9 (1788) pp. 308—313). Some of the figures,
a large number of which represent foreign species, recur in
Sparrman's 'Svensk ornithologie', 1806—17 (482).
Part of the collection was presented by Carlson to the
Swedish Academy of Sciences whence, together with other
parts of the collection, they were deposited in the Natural
History Museum at Stockholm. Owing to the importance of
the work, C. J. Sundevall later tried to identify the birds it
dealt with in his 'Kritisk framställning af fogelarterna uti äldre
ornithologiska arbeten' (892, pp. 3—15).

1806 [—17]. Svensk ornithologie. Med efter natu- *482.*
ren colorerade tekningar. Utgifven af Anders Sparrman. Tryckt i Kongl. Tryckeriet. *Stockholm. pp. [IV]
+ 44. 61 col. pl. fol.*
Of this unfinished work by the well-known Swedish traveller altogether eleven parts appeared, after which publication
was stopped (593, 1822, p. 278). The present copy contains the
whole text published and most of the plates, of which 68 are
usually referred to (576, p. 71), while the copy in the possession of the Royal Swedish Library is stated to contain 70
plates (565, p. 11). The text, which is printed in double
columns, treats of the species in systematic order, giving brief
characteristics of the genera, the species being dealt with in
greater detail, with enumeration of names in different languages,
descriptions, information about the habits and economic importance of the birds, and other features of interest.
Some of the plates (engravings coloured by hand, some:
J. P. Boström del. & sculp., Fr. Akrel sc.) are identical with
those found in the author's 'Museum Carlsonianum', 1786—
89 (481).

SPIX, J. B. von.

1824—25. Avium species novæ, quas in itinere *483.*
per Brasiliam annis 1817—20 jussu et auspiciis Maximiliani Josephi I Bavariæ regis suscepto collegit et
descripsit J. B. de Spix. Tabulæ ... a M. Schmidt
Monacensi depictæ (Vol. II: sculptæ). Typis Franc.
Seraph. Hübschmanni. *Monachii. 2 vols. large 4to. —*
[Vol. I]. 1824. *pp. [VI] + 90. 104 col. pl. (numb.
I—XCI, I a—d, III a, IV a, VIII a—c, IX a, X a,
XIV a, XXXII a, XXXVIII a; one plate numb.
LXXVI—LXXVII).* Vol. II. 1825. *pp. [VI] + 85.
118 col. pl. (numb. I—CIX, VIII a, XXXI a,
LXII a, LXVII a, LXXV a, LXXVI a—c, LXXIII a).*
In the years stated in the title Spix, in company with the
botanist Karl Friedrich Philipp von Martius, travelled in Brazil,
from where the two explorers brought back to the museum at
Munich large collections, including 350 birds. The zoological
material was worked up by Spix and others in large works, of
which the present one contains descriptions and figures of
birds, while to each species is added a brief diagnosis and
information about its habitat. About 220 species are described
as new or under new names, though only a little over a hundred
of these have been maintained (cf. C. E. Hellmayr's 'Revision
der Spix'schen Typen brasilianischer Vögel' (Abh. mat.-phys.
Kl. Bayer. Akad. Wiss., XXII, III Abt., 1906, pp. 561—
726)).
The plates (lithographs coloured by hand) were evidently
printed by J. B. Dressely (cf. Vol. II, Tab. CIX: Depictæ
et in lapide sculptæ a M. Schmid, impressæ a J. B. Dressely
Monachii).
In the present copy the table of contents to Vol. I and
an additional page, 47, of the same volume (cf. 552, V, p. 1992)
are missing.

STAATLICHE STELLE FUER NATURDENK-MALPFLEGE IN PREUSSEN.

1924—33. Die Vögel Mitteleuropas ... Herausgegeben von der Staatl. Stelle für Naturdenkmalpflege in Preussen. *See Heinroth, O. A.*

1934. Die heimischen Raubvögel ... Herausgegeben von der Staatlichen Stelle für Naturdenkmalpflege ... *See Loepelmann, M.*

484.   [1934]. Die heimischen Singvögel. Herausgegeben von der Staatlichen Stelle für Naturdenkmalpflege. Mit ... farbigen Tafeln, 60 Abbildungen auf Kunstdrucktafeln. Naturaufnahmen von Dr. O. Heinroth, 5 Karten und 11 Abbildungen im Text. Hugo Bermühler. *Berlin. pp. [III] + 116. text-figs. 28 pl. (14 col. (numb. I—XIV), 14 phot. pl. (numb. 1—14)). 8vo.*

A separate copy (cheap popular edition) of the 'Atlas der geschützten Pflanzen und Tiere Mitteleuropas', Abt. 5, 1—2, of which Part I appeared in 1928.

Like the original edition, the volume is divided into two parts (pp. 1—60: Part I), in which the birds in question, 115 forms, are dealt with in a brief text with the addition of 'Gesetzliche Massnahmen zum Schütze der Vogelwelt' with 'Nachtrag' and a 'Tafel der Schutzzeiten'.

The coloured plates are reproduced from Heinroth's 'Die Vögel Mitteleuropas' (202), whence also several of the plain plates are derived.

STANLEY, E. S., Thirteenth Earl of Derby. *See Derby, E. S. S., Thirteenth Earl of.*

STEJNEGER, L. H.

485.   1885. Department of the Interior: U. S. National Museum. Serial number 39. Bulletin No. 29 of the United States National Museum. Published under the direction of the Smithsonian Institution. - - Results of ornithological explorations in the Commander Islands and in Kamtschatka. By Leonhard Stejneger. Government Printing Office. *Washington. pp. 382. text-figs. 8 pl. (numb. I—VIII; 7 col. (numb. I—IV, VI—VIII)). 1 map. 8vo.*

This report of the ornithological results of an expedition to the land areas stated in the title, in 1882—83, is a significant work on the avifauna of Kamchatka.

The report is divided into three parts, viz. I, 'Review of the species of birds collected or observed by me on the Commander Islands and at Petropaulski, Kamtschatka, 1882—1883'; II, 'Synopsis of the birds reported to inhabit Kamtschatka'; and III, 'Conclusions'.

Part I (pp. 9—310) treats of 140 species, giving their synonymies and nomenclature as well as information about their habits and occurrence. Part II enumerates 186 species, while two more are mentioned in an appendix (pp. 327—331) after B. Dybowski and L. Taczanowski. In Part III (pp. 333—358) the composition of the avifauna of the two localities is discussed.

The plates (chromo-lithographs, L. Stejneger, ad nat. pinx.; Julius Bien & Co. Lith.) contain a number of figures finely executed, showing the heads of several of the birds.

STEPHENS, J. F.

1815—26. General zoology ... Vols. IX—XIV. *See Shaw, G., 1809—26.*

STEVENS, I. I.

1860. Reports of explorations and surveys ... for a railroad from the Mississippi River to the Pacific Ocean ... 1853—5 ... Vol. XII. Book II. Parts II and III of the ... report by Isaac I. Stevens ... upon the route near the forty-seventh and forty-ninth parallels. Part III. Zoological report. pp. 140—291: No. 3.

Report upon the birds collected on the survey. *See Cooper, J. G.*

STOCKHOLM. K. SVENSKA VETENSKAPS-AKADEMIEN. *See Svenska Vetenskaps-Akademien. Stockholm.*

STONE, W.

1912 → *See Auk.*

1915—28. Reports of the Princeton University expeditions to Patagonia, 1896—1899 ... Vol. II. Ornithology. Parts IV (partly) — V. *See Scott, W. E. D., 1904—28.*

STORER, T. I.

1918. The game birds of California ... *See Grinnell, J.*

STRASSEN, O. K. L. zur.

1911—13. Brehms Tierleben ... Vierte ... Auflage herausgegeben von Otto zur Strassen. Vols. VI—IX. Die Vögel ... *See Brehm, A. E.*

STRESEMANN, E.

1922 → *See Journal fuer Ornithologie.*

STRICKLAND, H. E.

1848. The Dodo and its kindred; or the history, affinities, and osteology of the Dodo, Solitaire, and other extinct birds of the islands Mauritius, Rodriguez, and Bourbon. By H. E. Strickland and A. G. Melville. Reeve, Benham, and Reeve. *London. pp. [IX] + I—IV + 5—141 + 12. text-figs. 15 pl. birds (front. + Nos. II, III, V—XV, IX*; 2 col. (front. + No. III)). fol.*

In this work the subject in question is thoroughly treated. Part I (pp. 1—65), 'History and external characters of the Dodo, Rodriguez, and other extinct brevipennate birds of Mauritius, Rodriguez, and Bourbon', was written by Strickland, while Melville wrote Part II (pp. 67—122), 'Osteology of the Dodo and Solitaire'. The book further contains two appendices, A (pp. 123—126) with translations of foreign extracts in Part I, and B (pp. 127—134) with a bibliography of the Didinæ.

The work contains altogether 18 plates, the greater number of which are lithographs executed by various artists. Plates II, III, III*, IV, and IV* are examples of various applications of anastatic printing; a special method of this art has been applied in the production of the plates III, III*, and IV*, viz. the process of papyrography invented by Strickland (cf. the note to Jardine's 'Contributions to ornithology', 1848—53 (229)).

1848—53. Contributions to ornithology ... *See Jardine, W.*

STUDER, T.

1889. Die Forschungsreise S. M. S. 'Gazelle' ...

1874—76 unter Kommando ... Freiherrn von Schleinitz herausgegeben von dem hydrographischen Amt des Reichs-Marine-Amts. Vol. III. Zoologie und Geologie. [Von Th. Studer]. Ernst Siegfried Mittler und Sohn. *Berlin. pp. VI + 322. 8 pl. birds (numb. 10—17; 5 col. (numb. 10—13, 15)). 4to.*

This expedition of a party of German astronomers to the Kerguelen Island, where they were to study the transit of Venus in December, 1874, also made several other scientific investigations.

The results were published in five volumes in 1888—90.

The present one includes the ornithological observations, which had previously been dealt with in papers by Cabanis and Reichenow in the 'Journal für Ornithologie', 1875, 1876, and 1877.

The plates, six of which concern the development of the birds, are executed in chromo-lithography by C. F. Schmidt from drawings by O. Bay and — a single one — G. Mützel.

STURM, J.

1829—30. Jacob Sturm's Deutschlands Fauna in Abbildungen nach der Natur mit Beschreibungen. II. Abtheilung. Die Vögel. Bearbeitet von J. H. C. F. und J. W. Sturm. Jacob Sturm. *Nürnberg. 2 parts in 1 vol. small 8vo.* — Part. I. 1829. *pp. [20]. 6 col. pl.* Part. II. 1830. *pp. [22]. 6 col. pl.*

There is no title-page; the title cited is taken from the covers of the parts.

Part of the illustrated work on the fauna of Germany commenced in 1797 by Jacob Sturm. The section dealing with birds, was prepared by Sturm's two sons. Besides the two present parts, a third one appeared in 1834 with six coloured plates.

The matter is arranged quite unsystematically.

The text, which is unpaged, gives the names of each species in German and Latin, as well as synonyms, diagnosis, a description, and a brief mention of the various plumages, information about the geographical distribution and habits, and the various German names of the bird.

In Part II Parus lugubris and Columba livia are treated by Dr. C. Michahelles.

The plates (engravings coloured by hand) are signed Fr. Sturm ad. nat. pinx. et sc.

STURM, J. H. C. F.

1829—30. Deutschlands Fauna ... II. Abtheilung. Die Vögel. Parts I—II. *See Sturm, J.*

1860. J. A. Naumann's Naturgeschichte der Vögel Deutschlands. Fortsetzung der Nachträge, Zusätze und Verbesserungen. *See Naumann, J. A.,* 1822—60.

STURM, J. W.

1829—30. Deutschlands Fauna ... II. Abtheilung. Die Vögel. Parts I—II. *See Sturm, J.*

SUCKLEY, G.

1859. The natural history of Washington Territory ... Part III. Zoological report. pp. 140—291: No. 3. Report upon the birds ... *See Cooper, J. G.*

1860. Reports of explorations and surveys ... for a railroad from the Mississippi River to the Pacific Ocean ... 1853—5 ... Vol. XII. Book II ... Part III. Zoological report. pp. 140—291: No. 3. Report upon the birds ... *See Cooper, J. G.*

SULPHUR, Voyage of H. M. S.

1843—44. The zoology of the voyage of H. M. S. Sulphur ... 1836—42 ... (Nos. III—IV). Birds. *See Gould, J.*

SUNDEVALL, C. J.

1851. Zoologisk Haandatlas til Brug for Skoler. Figurerne tegnede af Ferdinand v. Wright under Vejledning af Prof. Carl J. Sundevall. Texten tillæmpet til Brug for de danske Skoler. Efter andet forøgede Oplag. < - - *pp. 9—17: Fugle >.* Gyldendal. *Kjøbenhavn. 7 pl. (numb. 7—13). 8vo.*

A translation, with alterations and additions by C. E. Kielerup, of the second edition, 1851 (i. e. 1850), of Sundevall's 'Zoologisk handatlas för skolor, eller figurer till Lärobok i zoologien'.

Bird Books

The plates (Lith. och tr. af M. Körner i Lund) with their finely drawn figures were executed from the drawings by F. v. Wright mostly made from nature.

1856—86. Svenska foglarna, med text af Carl J. **490.** Sundevall, tecknade och lithographierade af Peter Åkerlund. Tryckt hos J. & A. Riis. [Levertin & Sjöstedt]. *Stockholm. 4 vols. text, and 1 vol. atlas with title as Vol. I. obl. 4to.* — [Vol. I]. 1856 [—71]. *pp.* [V] + 352 + [2]. Vol. II. [1881—] 1883 [—86]. *pp.* 353—755. Vol. III. 1885 [—86]. *pp. 757—1188.* Vol. IV. 1886. *pp. 1189—1570.* [Atlas. 1856—69]. Lith. & tr. hos A. J. Salmson. *84 col. pl. (numb. I—LXXXIV).*

Title from Vol. I; Vols. II—IV, published by F. & G. Beijer, with title, 'Svenska foglarna av Carl J. Sundevall, fortsättning av J. G. H. Kinberg'.

This work, whose text is printed in double columns, was issued in 40 parts, of which the first twenty-one contained all the plates, four in each part. According to a publisher's note on the cover to Part 21, preserved in Vol. I of the present copy, this part appeared in August 1869. Part 22 (pp. 285—352) was published in 1871, and concluded Vol. I. A survey of the dates of publication of these first twenty-two parts is found in Zimmer (589, II, p. 610). In the annual catalogue of the Swedish booksellers the remaining parts are cited as stated below.

1883 : Parts 23—28 (pp. 353—755), or the text to Vol. II. The sheets in this volume are dated 1881, 1881—82, and 1881—83, the title-page is printed in 1886.

1885 : Parts 29—34 (pp. 757—1164), or the greater part of the text to Vol. III, the sheets of which are dated 1881 —83, 1881—84, and 1881—85, and the title-page of which is dated 1885.

1886 : Parts 35—40 (pp. 1165—1570) or the end of the text to Vol. III and the text to Vol. IV, the sheets dated 1881—85 and 1881—86, while the title-page is dated and printed 1886.

After Sundevall's death the work was continued (Parts 23—40) by Professor J. G. Kinberg. The text was issued as publication of the plates had commenced and was written by Sundevall chiefly with a view to the classification of the birds, as to which he had his own ideas. Otherwise he treats the higher systematic divisions in fairly great detail, while the individual species are briefly characterized, and some information is given about geographical distribution or about some natural historical point or other. The individual species are more fully treated in the part of the work written by Kinberg.

The figures, which are coloured by hand, are rather small, and several are arranged on each plate. The figures on the same plate are drawn to the same scale, which is given below on the plate. Pl. LXV—LXXXIV are marked : Bihang Pl. I—II, 3—20, and most of plates Nos. LXXI —LXXXIV are signed Paulina Sjöholm.

The figures in this work were later used in Kolthoff and Jägerskiöld's 'Nordens fåglar', 1895—1902 (270).

SUNDMAN, G. R.

1879 [—88]. Finska fogelägg. Tecknade af G. **491.** Sundman. Finska Litteratur-Sällskapets Tryckeri. *Helsingfors. pp.* [IV] + [48]. *25 col. pl. obl. 4to.* Added title in Finnish.

This work — the first chromo-lithographic atlas published in Finland — was issued in nine parts. The first two of these were published in 1879, the last two in 1888. Each of the first seven parts contained three plates, the last two contained two plates each. The introduction to the work and the text to the plates were written by J. A. Palmén, but this text seems, as in the present copy, to have been interrupted after the issue of Part 5. Besides the present edition, the work was issued in an edition with German as well as English text, 40 pages, and title — 'Finnische Vögeleier' or 'Eggs of Finnish birds'.

The text is printed in Swedish and Finnish in parallel columns; it gives brief information about the breeding habits, breedings places, and eggs of the birds. Of these last the plates contain altogether 234 figures, which are good both as regards drawing, colour, and execution. Both in the text and on the plates the names of the particular species are given in Latin, Swedish, and Finnish.

SUSEMIHL, J. C.

492.   [1821—26]. Abbildungen aus dem Thierreiche. In Kupfer gestochen von J. C. Susemihl. Ornithologie. Parts 1—4. C. W. Leske. Darmstadt. 20 pl. fol.

The ornithological section, or Parts 1, 3, 5, and 6, of a work which was to show figures from the animal kingdom, chiefly of such animals as were indigenous to Germany. The present copy contains the six parts that were issued; Part 2 contains Amphibia, Part 4 insects.

Each part contains five leaves of text. On the cover from which the title cited is derived the name of each bird is printed in Latin, German, French, Italian, and English. The bird's length and a reference to the papers in which a detailed description of the bird is found are also included. The work was also supplied with painted engravings.

SVENSKA VETENSKAPS-AKADEMIEN. STOCKHOLM.

1825. Svensk zoologi. Part 12. See Palmstruch, J. W., 1806—25.

Handlingar.

1895. Ny följd. Vol. XXVII. No. 1. Zur Ornithologie Kameruns nebst einigen Angaben über die Säugetiere des Landes. See Sjöstedt, B. Y.

SWAINSON, W.

1829. The animal kingdom ... Vol. VIII. pp. 677 —690: Observations on several of the genera and species of the order Passeres of Cuvier. See Cuvier, G. L. C. F. D., 1827—29.

493.   1831. Fauna Boreali-Americana; or the zoology of the northern parts of British America: containing descriptions of the objects of natural history collected on the late northern land expeditions under command of Captain Sir John Franklin. Part II. The birds. By William Swainson and John Richardson. John Murray. London. pp. LXVI + 523 + [1]. text-figs. 50 col. pl. (numb. 21 73). 4to.

The ornithological section (second volume) of a work which was issued in its entirety in 1829—37 in four volumes written by John Richardson, assisted by William Swainson and William Kirby. The present volume treats of the avifauna of the British American fur countries, dealing with birds which have been found in North America north of the 48th parallel of latitude. It deals with 238 species, many of which are new to science. Dr. Richardson accompanied John Franklin as surgeon and naturalist on his two land expeditions to northern North America, and spent seven summers and five winters in the area. He has written those passages of the text which concern the habits of the birds and the descriptions of the species. He also wrote the introduction, in which he gives an account of the previous investigation of the ornithological fauna in the region observed, of whose birds, for instance, 42 were previously described and figured by Edwards in his 'Natural history' (124; 126). Richardson's collaborator William Swainson undertook the arrangement of most of the birds and gave the synonyms; he also wrote the introductory observations on the natural system, a preface, and the two appendices.

Swainson also drew the designs for the plates (lithographs coloured by hand). To the publication of them and to the remaining plates of the work the government made a grant of £ 1000. This may therefore boast of being the first zoological work published with the support of the British government. It also exists with uncoloured plates.

494.   [1834—] 41. A selection of the birds of Brazil and Mexico. The drawings by William Swainson. Henry

G. Bohn. London. pp. 4. 78 col. pl. (numb. 2—10, 12, 14—59, 61—66; pl. 1, 11, 13, 60 and 69—78 unnumb.; pl. 67 numb. 72; pl. 68 numb. 73). 8vo.

This work is cited by Engelmann (564, I, 1846, p. 415) under the title 'Ornithological drawings, being figures of the rarer and most interesting birds of Brazil', as being issued in seven parts in 1834—41. He also cites the present edition under the title given above this note, and dates it 1841. Zimmer (589, II, p. 616) assumes that the work was originally issued in 1834 —36, possibly in six parts.

Of text the volume merely contains (pp. 1—4) a 'List of plates in Swainson's Birds of Brazil', which gives the names in English and Latin of the 78 species figured. These names are also stated on most of the plates, which are carefully executed hand-coloured lithographs.

1843 [1837]. The Naturalist's Library. Edited by William Jardine. Vols. XXII—XXIII. Ornithology. (Vols. VII—VIII). Birds of Western Africa. Parts I— II. By W. Swainson. W. H. Lizars. Edinburgh. 2 vols. text-figs. small 8vo. — Vol. I. pp. XV + 17—286. text-figs. 33 pl. (front. (plain) + 32 col. pl. birds (numb. 1—32)). Vol. II. pp. XVI + 17—263. text-figs. 33 pl. (front. (plain) + 32 col. pl. birds (numb. 1—32)).

Two volumes of the series cited in the title, which was edited by Jardine in 1833—43 (224).

The plates (Lizars sc.), showing coloured bird portraits on uncoloured backgrounds, were executed from drawings by Swainson.

In addition to the ornithological matter each of the volumes contains a biography of a naturalist, with an accompanying engraved portrait (front.), viz. in Part I (pp. 17—84) 'Memoir of Bruce', and Part II (pp. 17—31) 'Memoir of Le Vaillant'.

1843 [1838]. The Naturalist's Library. Edited by William Jardine. Vol. XVII. Ornithology. (Vol. X). Flycatchers. By W. Swainson. W. H. Lizars. Edinburgh. pp. XIV + 15—256. 32 pl. (front (plain) + 31 col. pl. birds (numb. 1—31)). small 8vo.

A volume of the series edited by Jardine and cited in the title, published in 1833—43 (224).

The plates (Lizars sc.) show coloured bird portraits on uncoloured backgrounds; they were executed from drawings by Swainson.

Besides the ornithological matter the volume contains a 'Memoir of Baron Haller' (pp. 15—63) with an accompanying engraved portrait (front.).

SWANN, H. K.

1915—17. The birds of South America. Vol. II. Illustrations of the game birds and water fowl of South America. By H. Grönvold. See Brabourne, W. W. K.-H., Third Baron.

[1921—22]. A synopsis of the Accipitres (diurnal birds of prey). Comprising species and subspecies described up to 1920, with their characters and distribution. By H. Kirke Swann. Second edition revised and corrected throughout. Privately printed for the author. London. pp. X + 233 + [3]. 22 col. pl. eggs. (numb. 1—22 in 'Plates of eggs'). 4to.

A new revised edition, with additions and corrections, of Swann's 'A synoptical list of the Accipitres', etc. (London 1919 —20, 8vo). According to the original covers preserved in the present copy the work was published in four parts, as follows: Part I (Vultur to Accipiter) September 28, 1921; Part II (Erythrotriorchis to Lophoaëtus) January 3, 1922; Part III (Herpetotheres to Pernis) February 16, 1922; Part IV (Microhierax to Pandion) May 20, 1922.

The present copy is No. 10 of 28 copies privately printed on large paper, each having 22 coloured plates of eggs (three-colour prints; André & Sleigh, Ltd.), while an edition in 8vo without plates was issued simultaneously. The plates are derived from Dresser's 'Eggs of the birds of Europe', etc., 1905—10 (121), and are reproduced directly from photographs of the eggs.

SWARTZ, O.
1806 [—?14]. Svensk zoologi ... Parts 2—?11. *See Palmstruch, J. W.*

SWEDEN. Voyages, expeditions, etc.
1895. Zur Ornithologie Kameruns ... *See Sjöstedt, B. Y.*
1905. I Västafrikas urskogar. Natur- och djurlifsskildringar från en zoologisk resa i Kamerun. *See Sjöstedt, B. Y.*
1923. Contributions to the knowledge of the East African ornithology. Birds collected by the Swedish Mount Elgon Expedition 1920. *See Granvik, S. H.*

TAKA-TSUKASA, N.
1935. Report of the First Scientific Expedition to Manchoukuo under the leadership of Shigeyasu Tokunaga, June—October 1933. Section V. Division I. Part III. Birds of Jehol by N. Taka-Tsukasa, M. Hachisuka, N. Kuroda, Y. Yamashina, S. Uchida. *pp.* [II] +91 + [I]. 28 *col. pl. (numb. I—XXVIII).* 8vo. Added title in Japanese.
   A report in two languages (Japanese pp. 1—61, English pp. 63—91), based on the specimens of birds procured in Jehol by the members of the zoological division of the First Scientific Expedition to Manchoukuo. On the cover and the title-page the report is dated April (p. 91 : 30th April) 1935. The specimens of birds collected were handed over to the Ornithological Society of Japan for identification and report.
   The orders Galli to Upupæ (pp. 1—32, English text pp. 63—76) are reported by N. Taka-Tsukasa and M. Hachisuka, and the order Passeres (pp. 32—61, English text pp. 76—91) by N. Kuroda and Y. Yamashina. The English summary was written by S. Uchida, who also supervised the execution of the plates.
   The collection comprises 13 orders, 27 families, 53 genera, and 70 forms, among which is a new subspecies. In the section of the work printed in English the locality of the specimens collected is stated under each species and information is given about the distribution in and outside Manchuria ; occasionally special remarks are added.
   The plates (three-colour prints) are signed S. Kobayashi.

TÅNING, Å. V.
1931. Danmarks Fugle ... Vol. III ... Bindet fuldført af ... Å. Vedel Tåning ... *See Schiøler, E. L. T. L., 1925—31.*

TAVERNER, P. A.
1919. Canada. Department of Mines. Geological Survey. Memoir 104. No. 3. Biological series. Birds of Eastern Canada. By P. A. Taverner. J. de Labrouquerie Taché. *Ottawa. pp. III + 297. text-figs. 50 col. pl. (pp. 223—272; numb. I—L). 8vo.*
   A handbook on the birds which may generally be observed between the Atlantic coast and the prairies north of the International Boundary, an area which constitutes a natural zoological area. It is a nearly complete check-list of the birds of the region. Only species that are dubious, very rare, or occur but occasionally have been omitted.
   The introduction (pp. 1—39) deals with a number of subjects of a more general character, such as classification, migration, etc., and contains a 'Key to the birds of Eastern Canada' and a systematic index. In the main part of the book (pp. 41—221), 'Descriptive ornithology', altogether 766 forms are treated.

Brief descriptions of them are given (distinctions, field marks) and also information about nesting and distribution, and the habits and economic status of the birds.
   The plates (three-colour prints) are signed F. C. Hennessey. As stated above, they are paginated, and contain figures on both sides of the leaf, two small figures on each page.
   A new edition of this work appeared in 1922, and a complementary work, 'Birds of Western Canada', was issued in 1926 (Canada. Department of Mines. Museum Bulletin No. 41), and re-issued in 1928. The matter from both works was in 1934 embodied by Taverner in 'Birds of Canada' (Ottawa, 87 col. pl., 8vo).

TEGETMEIER, W. B.
1897—98. British birds with their nests and eggs. Vols. IV—V. Orders Columbæ, Pterocletes, Gallinæ, Fulicariæ and Alectorides. *See Butler, A. G.*, 1896 —98.
1911. Pheasants, their natural history and practical management. By W. B. Tegetmeier. Fifth edition, enlarged. Illustrated from life by J. G. Millais, T. W. Wood, P. Smit, and F. W. Frohawk. Horace Cox. *London. pp. XII + 276. text-figs. 22 pl. (6 col.). 8vo.* **500.**
   The first edition of this favourite book, to whose popularity a number of editions testify, appeared in 1873. The different sections of the work deal with the natural history of pheasants, their management in preserves and in confinement, and the diseases of these birds ; they also describe all the different species adapted to the covert and to the aviary.
   The coloured plates (three-colour prints) were executed from drawings by F. W. Frohawk.

TEISSIER, J.
1778. Oiseaux de la Hollande ... Version française, de Jaques Teissier ... *See Nozeman, C.*

TEMMINCK, C. J.
1809—11. Les pigeons. Vol. I. *See Knip, A. P. J. R.*, 1809—43.
1813. Histoire naturelle générale des pigeons et des **501.** gallinacés, par C. J. Temminck. Ouvrage en trois volumes, accompagné de planches anatomiques. J. C. Sepp & fils. *Amsterdam. Vol. I. pp. 499 + [1]. 1 pl.* 8vo.
   The first volume of this work, which appeared in its entirety in three volumes in 1813—15, is cited here, as the main part of the text had been published previously by Mme Knip in the first volume of the work 'Les pigeons', 1809—11 (261). Unknown to Temminck and without his consent this lady artist had altered the title, thus bestowing on herself the main honour for the work, which she altered in other ways, too. For the text of Vols. II and III, dealing with gallinaceous birds, Temminck had had 160 figures made by Prêtre. It was his intention to publish these together with the text in folio format as a sequel to his work on pigeons ; but on account of the controversy with Mme Knip Temminck decided to issue the work in the present smaller format (cf. Vol. III, pp. 640—44 ; 561, III, pp. 794—798).

[1820—] 1838 [—39]. Nouveau recueil de **502.** planches coloriées d'oiseaux, pour servir de suite et de complément aux planches enluminées de Buffon, édition in-folio et in-4° de l'Imprimerie Royale, 1770; publié par C. J. Temminck, et Meiffren Laugier de Chartrouse , d'après les dessins de MM. Huet et Prêtre. F. G. Levrault. *Paris. 5. vols. (in 9). 600 col. pl. fol.* — [Text]. Vol. I. *pp. [VI] + 11 + [2] + 109 + [240].* Vol. II. *pp. [III] + [280].* Vol. III. *pp. [III] + [403].* Vol. IV. *pp. [III] + [304].* Vol. V. *pp. [III] + [412].* [Plates]. [Vol. I]. *150 col. pl. (numb. 1—150).* [Vol. II]. *150 col. pl. (numb. 151—*

26*

*300). [Vol. III]. 150 col. pl. (numb. 301—450).
[Vol. IV]. 150 col. pl. (numb. 451—600).*
This large work, which forms a kind of continuation to Buffon's 'Histoire naturelle des oiseaux', 1770—86 (76), and its accompanying plates were issued both in a large folio format (503) and, as in the present copy, in a smaller folio format. As stated in a postscript, it was issued in 102 livraisons, and a survey of their dates of publication has been compiled by Zimmer (589, II, p. 627; cf. 884).
The work was first published by Gabr. Dufour, later by Levrault. In addition to the text dealing with the birds, which consists chiefly of technical matter, Vol. I contains a Prospectus (pp. 11) by Cuvier, an unpaginated leaf with a Postscriptum, published in Livraison 101, and a 'Tableau méthodique suivant lequel les Planches enluminées de Buffon et les Planches coloriées du présent Ouvrage peuvent être combinées et classées, d'après le système etabli dans la seconde édition du Manuel d'Ornithologie, par M. Temminck' (pp. 109).
The plates (engravings coloured by hand) contain altogether about 800 figures of birds, said to represent 661 species.
A kind of sequel to this work was issued in 1845—49 by M. A. P. Œ. Des Murs under the title 'Iconographie ornithologique'; Maximilian, Prince zu Wied's 'Abbildungen zur Naturgeschichte Brasiliens', 1822—31 (530) was also intended as a sort of supplement to it.

503. *[1820—] 1838 [—39]*. Nouveau recueil de planches coloriées d'oiseaux, pour servir de suite et de complément aux planches enluminées de Buffon, édition in-folio et in-4° de l'Imprimerie Royale, 1770; publié par C. J. Temminck, et Meiffren Laugier de Chartrouse, d'après les dessins de MM. Huet et Prêtre. *F. G. Levrault. Paris. 5 vols. 600 col. pl. large fol. —* Vol. I. *pp. [III] + 8 + [256]. 102 col. pl. (numb. 1 —102).* Vol. II. *pp. [III + [232]. 101 col. pl. (numb. 103—203).* Vol. III. *pp. [III] + [228]. 96 col. pl. (numb. 204—299).* Vol. IV. *pp. [III] [314]. 119 col. pl. (numb. 300—418).* Vol. V. *pp. [III] + [440] + 81 + [7]. 182 col. pl. (numb. 419—600).*
A copy of the edition in large folio format of this work, which was issued simultaneously in a smaller format (502). Vol. I, which contains Cuvier's 'Prospectus' (pp. 8), consists of Livraisons I—XVII, while the remaining parts are distributed over the other volumes as follows: Vol. II, XVIII—XXXIV; Vol. III, XXXV—L; Vol. IV, LI—LXX; Vol. V, LXXI—CII.
1826—42. Atlas des oiseaux d'Europe d'après C.J. Temminck. See *Werner, J. C.*
1839—44. Verhandelingen over de natuurlijke geschiedenis der Nederlandsche overzeesche bezittingen … Uitgegeven … door C. J. Temminck … [Aves]. See *Mueller, S.*
504. *1844—50.* Fauna Japonica, sive descriptio animalium, quæ in itinere per Japoniam, jussu et auspiciis superiorum, qui summum in India Batava Imperium tenent, suscepto … 1823—30 collegit, notis, observationibus et adumbrationibus illustravit Ph. Fr. de Siebold. Conjunctis studiis C. J. Temminck et H. Schlegel pro vertebratis atque W. de Haan pro invertebratis elaborata. Regis auspiciis edita. < - - Aves>. *Arnz et Socii. Lugduni Batavorum. pp. [III] + 141. 120 col. pl. (numb. I—LXXXIX, IB, IVB—VIIB, IXB, XVIIB—E, XXB—C, XXIB—D, XXXIB—C, XXXVIIIB—XXXIXB, LIVB, LVIB, LIXB, LXB —D, LXXVIIIB, LXXXIIB—C, LXXXIIIB— LXXXIVB, A—B). fol.*
The whole work, the ornithological section of which is cited here, appeared in six volumes in 1833—50.
The present volume was issued in twelve parts; their contents and dates of publication can be found in Sherborn and Jentink (868). The text, which is printed in French, was written by Temminck and Schlegel, and treats of a collection of Japanese birds, secured chiefly by Siebold, and described mostly in connection with the figures of the plates, on which a large number of the species cited are shown. The varieties are denoted with trinomials, evidently on the initiative of Schlegel (cf. 443, note).
Of the plates (lithographs coloured by hand), the first ones (I—XX) are signed by J. Wolf, the remainder are unsigned (Schlegel?).

TERROR, Voyage of H. M. S.
1844—75. The zoology of the voyage of H. M. S. Erebus & Terror … 1839—43 … Birds. See *Gray, G. R.*

THAYER, A. H.
1918. Concealing-coloration in the animal kingdom … being a summary of Abbott H. Thayer's disclosures … See *Thayer, G. H.*

THAYER, G. H.
1918. Concealing-coloration in the animal king- 5(dom. An exposition of the laws of disguise through color and pattern: being a summary of Abbott H. Thayer's disclosures. By Gerald H. Thayer. With an introductory essay by A. H. Thayer. New edition with a new preface. Illustrated by Abbott H. Thayer, Gerald H. Thayer, Richard S. Meryman and others and with photographs. The Macmillan Company. *New York. pp. XIX + 260. 42 pl. birds (8 col. (numb. I— IV, VI, VIII—X), 34 phot. pl.). 8vo.*
The first edition of the work appeared in 1909 with a slightly different title. It gives a detailed account in text and figures of A. H. Thayer's much disputed theory that most animals possess a sort of 'camouflage' which serves to protect them; and which he defines as follows: 'Concealing coloration means coloration that matches the background'.
The work is provided with 16 coloured plates (collotype; A. Hoen & Co., Baltimore), of which the majority of those concerning birds were executed from sketches by A. H. Thayer.

THIENEMANN, F. A. L.
1825—38. Systematische Darstellung der Fort- 5 pflanzung der Vögel Europa's mit Abbildung der Eier. Im Vereine mit Ludwig Brehm, Georg August Wilhelm Thienemann herausgegeben von Friedrich August Ludwig Thienemann. Johann Ambrosius Barth. *Leipzig. 5 parts in 1 vol. 28 col. pl. 4to. —* Part I. 1825. Raubvögel—Krähenarten. *pp. XII + 47. 4 col. pl. (numb. I—IV).* Part II. 1826. Insectenfresser. *pp. 76. 4 col. pl. (numb. V—VIII).* Part III. 1829. Körnerfresser. *pp. 96. 4 col. pl. (numb. IX—XII).* Part IV. 1830. Körnerfresser. Sumpfvögel. *pp. 54. 6 col. pl. (numb. XIII—XVIII).* Part V. 1838. Wasservögel. Vom Herausgeber allein bearbeitet. *pp. 67. 10 col. pl. (numb. XIX—XXVIII).*
This work was actually planned to appear in six parts (cf. Vorwort, p. VI), but was completed in five, after which a general title-page to the five parts, which are all provided with their own title-page, was issued. The editor ascribes to himself alone the authorship of Part V. The text deals with the breeding places, nests, and eggs of European birds, while the plates (engravings coloured by hand, L. Thienemann del., gest. v. Fr. Ed. Müller in Leipzig) show figures of a considerable number of eggs.
1845—54 [—56]. < Einhundert Tafeln colorirter $ Abbildungen von Vogeleiern. Zur Fortpflanzungsgeschichte der gesammten Vögel von Friedrich August

Ludwig Thienemann. Ausgearbeitet ... 1845—54 >.
*pp. XVII + [II] + 432. 100 pl. (numb. I—C; 95
col.). 4to.*
The text of this work is unfinished, the author having been
prevented by illness from completing it (cf. the preface, dated
October, 1856, Dresden).
The work was issued in ten parts, and their contents and
dates of publication have been compiled in the catalogue of
the books in the British Museum (Natural History) (552, V,
p. 2094). In its arrangement and treatment of material it is
in accord with Thienemann's work on the birds of Europe cited
above, the distribution of the birds, their habits, especially
breeding habits, nests, and eggs being mentioned under each
species. A 'Namenverzeichniss der abgebildeten Vogeleier" is
found on pp. V—XVII, while an unpaginated leaf contains a
list of the 'Nidi avium et ova quæ collegit L. Thienemann'.
The plates (lithographs coloured by hand) contain about
1800 figures of the eggs of nearly 900 species of birds from
Thienemann's collection.

THIENEMANN, G. A. W.
1825—30. Systematische Darstellung der Fortpflanzung der Vögel Europa's ... Parts I—IV. *See
Thienemann, F. A. L.,* 1825—38.

THOMSON, A. L.
1910—13. The British bird book ... *See Kirkman,
F. B. B.*

THOMSON, C. W.
1880. Report on the scientific results of the voyage
of H. M. S. Challenger ... 1873—76 ... Prepared
under the superintendence of C. Wyville Thomson.
Zoology. Vol. II. [Memoir II]. Report on the birds ...
See Sclater, P. L.

THORBURN, A.
1915—18. British birds. Written and illustrated by
A. Thorburn. With eighty plates in colour, showing
over four hundred species. Longmans, Green and Co.
London. 4 vols., and supplement. 82 col. pl. 4to. —
Vol. I. 1915. *pp. VIII + 143. 20 col. pl. (numb. I—
20).* Vol. II. 1915. *pp. VI + 72. 20 col. pl. (numb.
21—40).* Vol. III. 1916. *pp. VI + 87. 20 col. pl.
(numb. 41—60).* Vol. IV. 1916. *pp. VII + 107. 20
col. pl. (numb. 61—80).* Supplementary Part. 1918.
pp. 11. 2 col. pl. (numb. 80A, 80B).
The essential part of this work is the beautiful coloured
sketches of British birds, made from life. Among these are
also species which are rarely met with as casual visitors to
the British Isles.
The text is mainly a compilation from other works with
brief notes on the appearance, distribution, nests and eggs,
food, song, and habits of the birds.
The plates (three-colour prints) each contain several figures
of birds, which are therefore rather small.
This popular work has been issued later in new editions
in 1918—19 and 1925—26, the latter with 192 plates, so that
the number of figures on each plate could be somewhat reduced.

1919. A naturalist's sketch book. By Archibald
Thorburn. With sixty plates twenty-four of which are
in colour, and thirty-six in collotype. *< - - pp. 1—60:*
[Birds] >. Longmans, Green and Co. *London. 48 pl.
(numb. 1—48; 17 col. (numb. 1, 2, 4, 9, 12, 14, 16,
23, 25, 27, 29, 30, 32, 33, 35, 40, 44)). 4to.*
The water-colour and pencil sketches which are reproduced
in this work were drawn, mostly direct from life, in many
parts of the British Islands during a period of some thirty
years. The rather sketchy character of the figures renders it

possible to distinguish several details of the movements and
positions of the birds.
A brief description is helpful in the identification of the
various species figured on the plates. The coloured plates
(three-colour prints) were executed by the Sun Engraving
Co., Watford, the others by Emery Walker.

TICEHURST, C. B.
1931 → See Ibis.

TOKUNAGA, S.
1935. Report of the First Scientific Expedition to
Manchoukuo under the leadership of Shigeyasu Tokunaga, June-October 1933. Section V. Division II.
Part III. Birds of Jehol. *See Taka-Tsukasa, N.*

**TRANSACTIONS OF THE CHICAGO ACA-
DEMY OF SCIENCES.** *See Chicago Academy
of Sciences.*

**TRANSACTIONS OF THE ZOOLOGICAL SO-
CIETY OF LONDON.** *See Zoological Society
of London.*

TRÉMEAU DE ROCHEBRUNE, A. *See Rochebrune, A. T. de.*

TRING. ZOOLOGICAL MUSEUM.
1894 → Novitates Zoologicæ ... Issued at the Zoological Museum, Tring. *See Novitates Zoologicæ.*

TRISTRAM, H. B.
1884. The survey of Western Palestine. The fauna
and flora of Palestine. By H. B. Tristram. *< - - pp. 30
—139:* Aves>. Published by the Committee of the
Palestine Exploration Fund. *London. 7 col. pl. (numb.
VII—XIII). 4to.*
An account of the natural products of Palestine, based
chiefly on the author's own observations and collections secured
during four visits to the country.
In the section on birds 348 species are enumerated, with
the addition of brief notes on their occurrence and geographical
distribution. The plates are beautiful hand-coloured lithographs
(J. Smit lith., Hanhart imp.). The copy is marked 'Special
Edition. No. 111'.

TSCHUDI, J. J. von.
1845—46. Untersuchungen über die Fauna Peruana von J. J. von Tschudi. *< - - Ornithologie.
Bearbeitet von J. J. von Tschudi mit Anmerkungen
von J. Cabanis.* 1845 und 1846 >. Scheitlin und Zolli-
kofer. *St. Gallen. pp. 316. 36 col. pl. (numb. I—
XXXVI). large 4to.*
On a journey in Peru lasting for nearly five years Tschudi
had collected a fairly considerable number of new vertebrates,
which gave rise to the issue of the work whose ornithological
section is cited here. The whole work was published in twelve
parts and in addition to birds deals with mammals (pp. 262,
18 col. pl.), reptiles and Amphibia (pp. 80, 12 col. pl.),
and fishes (pp. 35, 6 col. pl.).
A conspectus dealing with the three higher classes had
previously been published by Tschudi in the 'Wiegmann's
Archiv für Naturgeschichte', 1843—46; the birds being treated
in that periodical Vols. IX, 1843; X, 1844; and XI, 1845.
The ornithological section consists of a 'Vorwort' (pp.
3—14), 'Systematische Zusammenstellung der aus Peru bekannten Vögel' (pp. 15—56), and the text proper, which
describes the species, occasionally with additional notes on

510.

511.

their habits and occurrence. Cabanis' contribution to the text and the notes are marked with his name.

The plates (hand-coloured lithographs, marked: Lith. Inst. v. J. Tribelhorn in St. Gallen) were executed from drawings by Jos. Dinkel (I—II), Schmidt, Berlin (III—VI, VIII), and J. Werner. In several of the plates the bird figures only are coloured, while the branches and backgrounds are uncoloured. A label bearing the correct names has been pasted over the names of the birds on Pl. I and Pl. XIV, Fig. 1, (cf. the footnote pp. 87 and 193).

TURNER, E. L.
       1910—13. The British bird book ... *See Kirkman, F. B. B.*

TURNER, L. M.
512.   *1886.* Contributions to the natural history of Alaska. Results of investigations made chiefly in the Yukon District and the Aleutian Islands; conducted under the auspices of the Signal Service, United States Army, extending from May, 1874, to August, 1881. Prepared under the direction of Brig. and Bvt. Maj. Gen. W. B. Hazen ... by L. M. Turner. No. II. Arctic Series of publications issued in connection with the Signal Service, U. S. Army...*<pp. 115—196: Part V. Birds>.* Government Printing Office. (Senate Mis. Doc. No. 155). *Washington. 11 col. pl. (numb. I—XI). 4to.*
       This report (pp. 226, 26 pl.), which consists of six parts, is based in all essentials on the author's field-notes collected during his sojourn in the Territory of Alaska. The ornithological section is therefore chiefly the result of the author's own observations in the field, and includes in its treatment several species new to North American fauna, while several of the other species dealt with are very rare.
       These notes are accompanied by an appendix (pp. 184 —196) containing a list of all the birds known to occur in Alaska.
       The plates (chromo-lithographs, produced by Giles Litho. & Liberty Printing Co. N.Y.) were executed from drawings by R. and J. L. Ridgway.
       The present copy of the report is bound together with E. W. Nelson's 'Report upon natural history collections made in Alaska 1877—81', 1887 (360). The general title-page to this volume reads, 'The Miscellaneous Documents of the Senate of the United States for the first session of the forty-ninth congress, 1885—86. Vol. 8.'.

TWEEDDALE, A. H., Ninth Marquis of.
       1871—82. A history of the birds of Europe ... *See Dresser, H. E.,* 1871—96.
       1880. Report on the birds collected during the voyage of H. M. S. Challenger ... 1873—76. *See Sclater, P. L.*
513.   *1881.* The ornithological works of Arthur, Ninth Marquis of Tweeddale ... Reprinted from the originals, by the desire of his widow. Edited and revised by his nephew, Robert G. Wardlaw Ramsay. Together with a biographical sketch of the author by William Howard Russell. For private circulation. Printed by Taylor and Francis. *London. pp. [III] + LXIV + 760. text-figs. 22 col. pl. birds. 2 maps. 4to.*
       An exact copy of the original writings, apart from the correction of misprints and orthographical errors, or alterations based on corrections in the author's hand-writing.
       In addition to the reprint of the ornithological papers which have been published in various scientific publications, 1844 —79, the volume contains the biographical sketch (pp. XIII— LXII) mentioned in the title, and an Appendix (pp. 653— 676) comprising five sections of different contents.
       The plates (lithographs coloured by hand, Hanhart imp., the greater number J. Smit lith., one J. G. Keulemans lith.)

are chiefly derived from the Transactions of the Zoological Society of London, but one is from Rowley's 'Ornithological Miscellany', 1875—78 (432).

A plate with a portrait of the author serves as a frontispiece.

TYNESIDE NATURALISTS' FIELD CLUB.
       1874. Natural History Transactions of Northumberland and Durham; being papers read at the meetings of ... the Tyneside Naturalists' Field Club, 1873. Vol. VI. A catalogue of the birds of Northumberland and Durham. *See Hancock, J.*

UCHIDA, S.
       1935. Report of the First Scientific Expedition to Manchoukuo ... June—October, 1933. Section V. Division II. Part III. Birds of Jehol. *See Taka-Tsukasa, N.*

UNITED STATES. DEPARTMENT OF AGRICULTURE. BIOLOGICAL SURVEY.
       1911. Bulletin No. 37. Food of the woodpeckers of the United States. *See Beal, F. E. L.*

UNITED STATES. DEPARTMENT OF AGRICULTURE. DIVISION OF ORNITHOLOGY AND MAMMALOGY.
       1893. Bulletin No. 3. The hawks and owls of the United States in their relation to agriculture. *See Fisher, A. K.*

UNITED STATES. GEOGRAPHICAL AND GEOLOGICAL EXPLORATIONS AND SURVEYS WEST OF THE ONE HUNDREDTH MERIDIAN.
       1875. Vol. V. Zoology. pp. 131—508: Chapter III. Report upon the ornithological collections ... 1871 —74. *See Henshaw, H. W.*

UNITED STATES NATIONAL MUSEUM. BULLETIN.
       1885. No. 29. Results of ornithological explorations in the Commander Islands and in Kamtschatka. *See Stejneger, L. H.*
       1901—19. No. 50. Parts I—VIII. The birds of North and Middle America ... *See Ridgway, R.*
       1919. 107. Life histories of North American diving birds. Order Pygopodes. *See Bent, A. C.*
       1921. 113. Life histories of North American gulls and terns. Order Longipennes. *See Bent, A. C.*

UNITED STATES NATIONAL MUSEUM. SPECIAL BULLETIN.
       1892. No. 1. Life histories of North American birds with special reference to their breeding habits and eggs. *See Bendire, C. E.*
       1895. No. 3. Life histories of North American birds, from the parrots to the grackles, with special reference to their breeding habits and eggs. *See Bendire, C. E.*

UNITED STATES. PACIFIC RAILROAD SURVEY.
       Reports of explorations and surveys ... for a rail-

road from the Mississippi River to the Pacific Ocean
... 1853 (—6). — Vol. VI. Report of ... Henry L.
Abbot ... Part IV. Zoological report. No. 2. Report
upon the zoology of the route. pp. 73—110: Chapter
II. Report upon the birds. 1857. *See Newberry, J. S.*
Vol. IX. Part II. General report upon the zoology of
the several Pacific Railroad routes. Birds. 1858. *See
Baird, S. F.* Vol. X. Report of ... E. G. Beckwith ...
Zoological report. pp. 11—16: No. 2. Report on birds
collected on the survey. 1859. *See Baird, S. F.* Vol. X.
Report ... by ... A. W. Whipple ... Part VI. Zoo-
logical report. pp. 19—35: No. 3. Report on birds
collected on the route. 1859. *See Kennerly, C. B. R.*
Vol. X. Report ... by ... John G. Parke ... Zoological
report. pp. 9—20: No. 1. Report upon birds collected
on the survey. 1859. *See Heermann, A. L.* Vol. X.
Report ... by ... R. S. Williamson ... Part IV. Zoo-
logical report. pp. 29—80: No. 2. Report upon birds
collected on the survey. 1859. *See Heermann, A. L.*
Vol. XII. Book II ... report by Isaac I. Stevens ...
Part III. Zoological report. pp. 140—291: No. 3.
Report upon the birds collected on the survey. 1860.
See Cooper, J. G.

UNITED STATES, Voyages, expeditions, etc.
1856. Narrative of the expedition of an American
squadron to the China Seas and Japan ... 1852—54,
under the command of Commodore M. C. Perry ...
Vol. II. pp. 215—248: Birds. *See Cassin, J.*
1885. Results of of ornithological explorations in
the Commander Islands and in Kamtschatka. *See
Stejneger, L. H.*
1886. Contributions to the natural history of
Alaska. Results of investigations made ... from May,
1874, to August, 1881 ... No. II ... pp. 115—196:
Part V. Birds. *See Turner, L. M.*
1888. Report upon natural history collections made
in Alaska between ... 1877 and 1881 ... No. III ...
pp. 19—226: Part I. Birds of Alaska ... *See Nelson,
E. W.,* 1887.
1902. Harriman Alaska Expedition ...
Vol. I. pp. 1—118: Narrative of the expedition
See Burroughs, J.
Vol. II. pp. 205—234: Days among Alaska birds.
See Keeler, C. A.
1904—28. Reports of the Princeton University expeditions to Patagonia, 1896—1899 ... Vol. II. Ornithology. *See Scott, W. E. D.*
1907. Research in China. Vol. I. Part II. pp. 479
—507: Section V. Zoology. *See Blackwelder, E.*

URBAIR, B. VON WÜLLERSTORF. *See Wuellerstorf-Urbair, B. von.*

VAHL, M. (properly HENRICHSEN, M. V.).
1806. Zoologia Danica seu animalium Daniæ et
Norvegiæ rariorum ac minus notorum descriptiones et
historia. Vol. IV ... *See Mueller, O. F.*

VAILLANT, A. N.
1841. Voyage autour du monde exécuté ... 1836
—37 sur la corvette la Bonite commandée par Vaillant ... Zoologie ... Oiseaux. *See Eydoux, J. F. T.*

VAN DAM, D. C. *See Dam, D. C. van.*

VAN OORT, E. D. *See Oort, E. D. van.*

VAN PELT LECHNER, A. A. *See Pelt Lechner, A.
A. van.*

VIEILLOT, L. J. P.
1800—02. Oiseaux dorés ... *See Audebert, J. B.*
1805[— ?]. Histoire naturelle des plus beaux oise- 514.
aux chanteurs de la zone torride: Par L. P. Vieillot.
J. E. Gabriel Dufour. *Paris. pp. [III] + 112 + 52* +
52**. 72 col. pl. (numb. I—LXX, XXVIII*,
XXVIII**). large fol.*
This work, which contains descriptions and figures of a
number of tropical finches, weaver-birds, and other birds, was
issued in 12 livraisons, the first six of which appeared in
1805—08 (552, V, p. 2216); however, much uncertainty prevails
as regards the time of its completion (cf. 589, II, p. 654).
The text dealing with the individual forms often gives information about the way in which the birds should be treated in
captivity.
The plates are engravings coloured by hand (printed by
Langlois) engraved by Bouquet from drawings by Prêtre and
retouched by hand.
1807[—08]. Histoire naturelle des oiseaux de 515.
l'Amérique septentrionale, contenant un grand nombre
d'espèces décrites ou figurées pour la première fois.
Par L. P. Vieillot. Desray. *Paris. 2 vols in 1. 131 col.
pl. large fol.* — Vol. I. *pp. [III] + pp. [III] + IV + 90. 60 col.
pl. (numb. I—57, 2bis, 3bis, 10bis, 14bis).* Vol. II.
*pp. [III] + II + 74. 70 col. pl. (numb. 57bis, 58—
124, 68bis, 90bis).*
This work, which contains descriptions and figures of a
number of birds of North America, was originally planned to
comprise 40 livraisons, each with six plates; however, only
22 livraisons appeared (the present two volumes) before the
work ceased to appear, possibly in 1808 (579, X, p. 150). The
history of the publication of the work is discussed in Zimmer
(589, II, p. 655).
The work was published in different issues, — with figures
in black and white, with plates printed in colour, 'cartonnés
à la Bradel' and on 'Grand papier colombier vélin'; of the
last named only twelve copies are said to have been produced
(579, X, p. 150).
The plates (Prêtre pinxt.) are engravings printed in colour
(Bouquet sculpt., Langlois imp.), and retouched by hand.
1820—23. Encyclopédie méthodique ... Tableau
encyclopédique et méthodique des trois règnes de la
nature. Ornithologie. Par Bonnaterre, et continuée par
L. P. Vieillot. *See Encyclopædia,* 1782—1823.
[1823—26]. Ornithologie française, ou histoire 516.
naturelle, générale et particulière des oiseaux de Fran-
ce. Par L. P. Vieillot; dessiné d'après nature par P.
Oudart. Motte. *Paris. pp. 55 + 8. 48 col. pl. (numb.
I—II, IX, XXII, XXXII, XXXVI, LIV, LXIII—
LXIV, LXXV—LXXVII, LXXX, LXXXIII,
LXXXV, XCI, XCVI—XCVII, CVI—CVII,
CXIII, CXXIV, CXXIVbis, CXL—CXLI, CXLV,
CLX, CLXXIV, CLXXXI—CLXXXII, CLXXXIV,
CLXXXVI, CLXXXVI, CXCI, CCXVI, CCLIV,
CCLXXII, CCLXXXVI—CCLXXXVIII, CCXCIV,
CCCXXXII, CCCLXX, CCCLV, CCCLXIX—
CCCLXX, and (egg pl.) A—B). 4to.*
The title is derived from the cover of the parts; no title-
page exists.
The present copy consists of the first eight livraisons of a
work, of which twelve livraisons appeared in 1823—30, each
containing a sheet of text and six plates. Livraisons 1—4 ap-
peared in 1823, 5—7 in 1825, 8 in 1826, and 9—12 in 1830.

Publication then ceased ; but in 1907 a series of altogether 100 plates was issued (552, V, p. 2216).

In the present copy the covers of the livraisons are preserved and, with the exception of the cover to Livraison 1, which serves as a title-page, are bound at the end of the volume. They are undated and their numbers have been written on them in ink.

The text (pp. 1—55) is a systematically arranged synopsis of the group of birds ('Classe seconde de la zoologie'), with diagnoses of orders, families, and genera, while the remainder of the text (pp. 1—8) contains the beginning of the account of the 'Histoire naturelle des Accipitres, ou oiseaux de proie', with descriptions to Pl. I and II and the beginning of the text to Pl. III and IV.

The plates are executed in lithography coloured by hand (lith. de C. Motte).

VIGORS, N. A.

1826—35. Illustrations of Ornithology ... Vols. I—III. *See Jardine, W.,* 1826—43.

1827—35. See Zoological Journal, The, 1824—35.

1831—32. A century of birds from the Himalaya Mountains. *See Gould, J.*

517.   *1839.* The zoology of Captain Beechey's voyage; compiled from the collections and notes made by Captain Beechey, the officers and naturalist of the expedition, during a voyage to the Pacific and Behring's Straits performed in H. M. S. Blossom, under the command of Captain F. W. Beechey ... 1825—28, by J. Richardson, N. A. Vigors ... Illustrated with upwards of fifty finely coloured plates by Sowerby. Published under the authority of the Lords Commissioners of the Admiralty. < - - *pp. 13—40:* Ornithology; by N. A. Vigors >. Henry G. Bohn. *London.* 12 *col. pl. (numb. III—XIV). 4to.*

This volume (pp. XII + 186, 44 col. pl., 3 maps), in addition to the ornithological section written by Vigors, contains a series of other chapters in which other groups of the animal kingdom are treated by various authors.

The ornithological section describes several new species, and supplies contributions to the comparative anatomy of many species, derived from the notes of the ship's officers.

The plates (coloured by hand) were executed from drawings by E. Lear (most of them Zeitter sc.).

VIREY, J. J.

1800—02. Histoire naturelle ... Des oiseaux. [With notes by J. J. Virey]. *See Buffon, G. L. L. de.*

1802. Histoire naturelle ... Des oiseaux. Vol. LXIV. pp. 129—158: Vues générales sur les quadrupèdes vivipares, les oiseaux, et sur la nature organisée, par J. J. Virey. *See Buffon, G. L. L. de,* 1800—02.

1803—04. Nouveau dictionnaire d'histoire naturelle ... L'homme, les quadrupèdes, les oiseaux, les cétacés. [Par] Sonnini et Virey. *See Dictionaries.*

VOYAGES. *See* under names of countries.

WALDEN, Lord. *See Tweeddale, A. H., Ninth Marquis of.*

WALLENGREN, H. T. S.

518.   *1896.* Vore almindelige nyttige Fugle og deres Æg ... farvetrykte Plancher med Afbildninger af 34 Arter. Populær Text tildels efter H. Wallengren ved Knud Jansen. Lehmann & Stage. *København. pp. 30 + [2]. 20 col. pl. (numb. 1—20). 8vo.*

The text to the unsigned coloured plates (chromo-lithographs) is popular and, like the plates, is derived from the corresponding Swedish book, Hans Wallengren's 'Våra vanligaste nyttiga fåglar och deras ägg' (Lund 1896, 8vo). Alterations necessitated by the difference between the Swedish and the Danish avifauna have, however, been made.

WALTER, J. E. C.

1828 [—29]. Vögel aus Asien, Africa, America 519 und Neuholland in colorirten Abbildungen, in Kupfer gestochen und herausgegeben von Joh. Ernst Christ. Walter. Gedruckt in Fabritius de Tengnagels Buchdruckerei. *Kopenhagen.* 3 *parts in 1 vol. pp. [III] + 19. 24. col. pl. (marked Taf. 1—24). large 8vo.*

The first three parts, in the original covers, of a work which besides the title-page to Part I — the only title-page issued — and an unpaginated leaf with a dedication, consists of 33 unpaged leaves of text and 144 plates. According to Gosch (567, III, p. 328), the work was issued in 18 parts in two series of eight and ten parts respectively, each of which contained eight plates.

The first eight parts were published in 1828 — October, 1831, the numbers of the second series in February, 1838 — March, 1841. The parts and plates of each series are numbered separately, but it is not stated to which series they belong. The plates of the second series lack the word 'Taf.' in front of the number.

From and including Part III the text is dated on the first page which, from and including Part II, is numbered and provided with the heading 'Vögel aus Asien, Africa, America und Neuholland von J. E. C. Walter. The title of the cover is the same as that of the title-page.

The text contains a brief account of the birds figured on the plates (engravings coloured by hand, rather finely executed), copied from the 'vorzüglichsten französischen Kupferwerken', such as Audebert and Vieillot's 'Oiseaux dorés, 1800 —02 (14), Temminck and Laugier's 'Nouveau recueil de planches coloriées d'oiseaux', 1820—39 (502; 503), Levaillant's 'Histoire naturelle des oiseaux de paradis', 1801—06 (304), and others.

1828 [—41]. Pragtfugle og Pattedyr i colorerede 520 Afbildninger. Stukne i Kobber og udgivet af Johann Ernst Christian Walter. Trykt hos Jacob Behrend. *Kjöbenhavn. pp. [I] + [20]. 23 col. pl. birds (numb. I—VIII, XIII—XV, XIX—XXII, XXV—XXVIII, XXXI—XXXIV). fol.* Added title in German.

Only the title on the cover exists, a title-page was never issued.

This work, which contains altogether 36 plates, was published in six parts; the covers to the first four of these are preserved in the present copy. Each part contains six plates.

Parts III—VI appeared in 1839—41 in the old covers, the dates on which, 1828, were sometimes corrected in ink.

The text of Part I and possibly of Part II is said to have been written by J. C. H. Reinhardt. It is printed in Danish and German in parallel columns and in Parts III—VI it is reduced to a minimum, since each of these parts contains one leaf of text only, while each of the first two parts contains three leaves of text.

The plates (engravings coloured by hand) are generally fairly well executed, especially in the first three parts. The figures in the first part are mostly copies of figures in Levaillant's 'Histoire naturelle des oiseaux de paradis', 1801—06 (304) and the same author's 'Histoire naturelle des perroquets', 1801—05 (302; 303), or Temminck and Laugier's 'Nouveau recueil de planches coloriées d'oiseaux', 1820—39 (502; 503), whereas many of the figures in the later parts have, or purport to have, been executed from specimens in the Royal Museum, Copenhagen, or in the collection of the Natural History Society of that city. The cause of this seems to be (cf. 567, II, 2, p. 17) that a reviewer had recommended Walter to draw original figures from specimens of new or native species instead of producing copies. This presumably also gave the impetus to the publication of Walter's 'Nordisk Ornithologie', 1828—41 (521), which appeared as a kind of sequel to the present work.

There is a second copy of the plates, I—XII, of the first two parts of the work in the collection in the Library.

*1.   1828 [—41]. Nordisk Ornithologie, eller trovær-dige efter Naturen egenhændig tegnede, stukne og colorerede Afbildninger af danske, færøiske, grønland-ske og islandske Fugle med tydsk og dansk Beskrivelse, udgivet af Johann Ernst Christian Walter. Kjøben-havn. 3 vols. in 1. 249 col. pl. fol. Added title in German. — [Vol. I]. 1928. pp. [IV] + [50]. 60 col. pl. (marked Tab. I—LX). Ny Følge. Trykt hos Peter Nicolay Jørgensen. 1832 [—33]. pp. [III] + [13]. 22 col. pl. (numb. 2—7, 10, 12, 15—16, 18, 30, 32, 34, 38, 41, 45, 47—48, 52—54). Nyeste Følge. Trykt hos Directeur Jens Hostrup Schultz. 1835[—41]. pp. [III] + [55]. 167 col. pl. (numb. 1.:.—107.:., 109.:.—165.:., 164.:. [= 166], 167.:.—168.:.).

This work, which purports to be a continuation of the author's 'Pragtfugle og Pattedyr', 1828—41 (520), was issued in parts, in three series (567, III, pp. 329—332). The first, which in complete copies comprises 60 pl. and 35 unpaginated leaves of text besides the title-page, appeared in eight parts (Nos. I—VII, IX—X), of which the first (Nos. I—II) was double. The second series, which consists as a whole of a title-page to Part I — the only title-page that was issued to this series — one unpaged leaf with a dedication, 17 leaves of text, and 60 plates, appeared in eight parts (Nos. I—IV, VI—VIII, X) of which VI and VIII were double. The third series consists altogether of the title-page to Part I, 30 unpaginated leaves of text, and 168 plates, and was issued in 27 parts (Nos. I—VIII, X—XXVIII). The text is printed in Danish and German in parallel columns with the exception of the references to the literature found before the mention of each species. The Nordic and German vernacular names are rare. Most of the figures on the plates (engravings coloured by hand) are stated to have been executed from nature or from life.

While the text is of no very great value, several of the plates are fairly well executed. Complete copies of the work are rare. Most of the figures (engravings coloured by hand) are stated to have been executed from nature or from life.

Another copy of the first 42 plates of Vol. I is in the possession of the Library.

WASHINGTON ACADEMY OF SCIENCES. ALASKA.

Vol. I. 1902. pp. 1—118: Narrative of the expedi-tion. See Burroughs, J.

Vol. II. 1902. pp. 205—234: Days among Alaska birds. See Keeler, C. A.

WEBB, P. B.

2.   [1841]. Histoire naturelle des Îles Canaries. Par P. Barker-Webb et Sabin Berthelot. Ouvrage publié sous les auspices de M. Guizot. Vol. II. Part II. Contenant la zoologie. < - - [II]. Ornithologie cana-rienne. Par P. B. Webb, S. Berthelot, et Alfred Mo-quin-Tandon >. Béthune. Paris. pp. 48. 4 col. pl. (numb. 1—4). 4to.

This large work on the natural history of the Canary Islands, of which the part cited above is the ornithological section, was issued in 1835—44 in 106 parts (552, V, p. 2276), and consists in its entirety of three volumes of text, more than four hundred plates, an atlas in folio with geographical maps, and plates relating to geology and to the geography of plants.

The ornithological matter is arranged according to Tem-minck's system and comprises 108 species, among which are five new ones; they are described briefly in the text, which

further gives synonymies, habitats, and several observations relat-ing to the birds.

Each of the ornithological plates contains two figures of birds, representing altogether five species (four of the five new, and the Canary).

The figures are beautiful and were drawn by E. Traviès and engraved by Oudet, Guyard, and Annedouche (Pl. 3, how-ever, Blanchard, Bienvenu lith.).

WEBER, F. A.

1774—85. Naturgeschichte der Vögel aus den besten Schriftstellern mit Merianischen und neuen Kupfern. See Decker, J. M.

WERNER, J. C.

[1826—]1842. Atlas des oiseaux d'Europe d'après   523. C.-J. Temminck, et dessinés par J.-C. Werner. H. Cousin. Paris. pp. [III] + 27. 530 col. pl. in 3 vols. 8vo.

The figures on these plates were intended as illustrations to Temminck's 'Manuel d'ornithologie', second edition, 1820 —40, a handbook on the birds of Europe.

The plates were issued in livraisons, each comprising ten plates, according to which the number of livraisons seems to be 53. Engelmann (564, 1846, p. 416) mentions Livraisons 1—50, and according to Quérard (579, X, 1839, p. 502) the work was intended to comprise 55 livraisons. The cover-title cited by him reads as follows: 'Atlas des oiseaux d'Europe, pour servir de complément au Manuel d'ornithologie de M. Tem-minck, par J. C. Werner', and the work may be found under this title.

A later edition (dated 1848) is cited under the title 'Les oiseaux d'Europe décrits par C. J. Temminck ... Atlas de 530 planches dessinées par J. C. Werner' (552, V, p. 2294).

The only text of the work is a 'Tables de l'Atlas des oiseaux d'Europe', in which reference is made to the place (volume and page) in 'Manuel d'ornithologie' in which the particular species is mentioned.

The plates (lithographs coloured by hand) were chiefly executed on stone by Langlumé (orders 1—8) and A. Belin (orders 9—15).

WESTERMAN, G. F.

1860. De toerako's afgebeeld en beschreven ... onder medewerking van G. F. Westerman ... See Schlegel, H.

WETMORE, F. A.

1931. Smithsonian Scientific Series. Vol. 9. Warm-   524. blooded vertebrates. < - - pp. 1—166: Part I. Birds. By Alexander Wetmore >. Smithsonian Institution Series. New York. text-figs. 70 pl. (5 col., 62 phot. pl.). 8vo.

A volume of this series of 'volumes for popular sale', in which the birds are treated in twelve chapters dealing with subjects such as their relation to man, flying, colour, ancestors, migration, homes, eggs, young birds, voice, food, and the kinds of birds.

The coloured plates (three-colour prints) were executed from drawings by Allan Brooks.

WHEELER, G. M.

1875. Report upon geographical and geological explorations and surveys west of the One Hundreth Meridian, in charge of First Lieut. Geo. M. Wheeler ... Vol. V. Zoology. pp. 131—508: Chapter III. Report upon the ornithological collections ... 1871—74. See Henshaw, H. W.

WHIPPLE. A. W.

1859. Reports of explorations and surveys ... for a railroad from the Mississippi River to the Pacific Ocean ... 1853—6 ... Vol. X. Report of explorations ... near the thirty-fifth parallel of north latitude ... By Lieutenant A. W. Whipple ... 1853—54. Part VI. Zoological report. pp. 19—35: No. 3. Report on birds collected on the route. *See Kennerly, C. B. R.*

WHITAKER, J. I. S.

525.   *1905.* The birds of Tunisia; being a history of the birds found in the regency of Tunis. By J. I. S. Whitaker. R. H. Porter. *London. 2 vols. large 8vo.* — Vol. I. *pp. XXXII + 294. 15 pl. (13 col. pl. birds). 1 map.* Vol. II. *pp. XVIII + 410. 4 pl. (2 col. pl. birds). 1 map.*

This work deals with about 365 species and subspecies of the Tunisian avifauna. Most of the descriptions are based on specimens in the author's own collection, and the greater part of the information given under the various species relating to their occurrence and life is the result of the author's personal observations in Tunis.

Some of the most interesting species are figured on the coloured plates (lithographs coloured by hand, drawn by H. Grønvold, printed by Mintern Brothers).

The edition of this book consisted of two hundred and fifty copies, of which this is No. 43.

A supplement to the present work was issued in 1924 by Louis Lavauden, A. Blanchet, and P. Bédé under the title 'Contributions à l'ornithologie tunisienne', etc. (Tunis, 1 pl., 8vo).

WHITE, G.

526.   *1900.* The natural history and antiquities of Selborne and a garden kalendar. By Gilbert White. Edited by R. Bowdler Sharpe, with an introduction to the garden kalendar by S. Reynolds Hole, and numerous illustrations by J. G. Keulemans, Herbert Railton, and Edmund J. Sullivan. S. T. Freemantle. *London. 2 vols. 45 pl. birds. small 4to.* — Vol. I. *pp. XXIII + 427. text-figs. 20 pl. birds.* Vol. II. *pp. XV + 443. text-figs. 25 pl. birds.*

This immortal work appeared for the first time in December, 1788 (the title-page dated 1789), in the only edition published during the lifetime of the author. It was an immediate success and has since been issued in a number of editions and reprints — more than 100 are cited by Mullens and Swann (574, pp. 633—647).

It consists mainly of a series of letters written by White some in the years 1767—80 to Thomas Pennant, and some in the period 1769—87 to the Hon. Daines Barrington, on whose inducement White was persuaded to publish the correspondence. The section of the work on natural history, which contains a considerable amount of matter regarding bird life, consisted in the first edition of forty-four letters to Pennant and sixty-six to Barrington. The letters — in any case those to Pennant — were, however, not published in their original form, but were revised by the author before publication. Of the 'Letters to Pennant' the first nine had never been addressed to him, but were evidently written by White as a kind of introduction to the actual correspondence, which commences with No. X.

The number of letters to Pennant mentioned above are found in the present edition (Vol. I, pp. 1—185). Then follow (Vol. I, pp. 187—421) 'A garden kalendar' for the years 1751—71 and two appendices (pp. 422—427).

Sixty-five letters to Daines Barrington are found in Vol. II (pp. 1—205), they are followed by 'The antiquities of Selborne' (pp. 207—316), five appendices to the antiquities (pp. 317—345), a bibliography by C. Davies Sherborn (pp. 347—364), and a copious index to the two volumes (pp. 365—443).

These contain altogether 99 (50 and 49 respectively) finely drawn and reproduced plates, which were also issued separately in a case. The ornithological plates were executed from drawings by J. G. Keulemans. The impression of the present edition was limited to 160 copies, for which reason the text was also published separately (2 vols., 8vo).

WHITE, J.

1790. Journal of a voyage to New South Wales 52 with sixty-five plates of non descript animals, birds, lizards, serpents, curious cones of trees and other natural productions. By John White. I. Debrett. *London. pp. [XVII] + 299 + [35] + [4]. 29 pl. birds. 4to.*

While the main part of this work, pp. 1—218, consists of 'White's Journal of a voyage to New South Wales' (650), the plants and animals collected are treated in a section entitled 'Natural history', pp. 219—297. The birds are said to have been treated by G. Shaw who, together with John Hunter and J. E. Smith, is mentioned in the advertisement.

The bird portraits on the plates (engravings) were drawn by Miss S. Stone from specimens in the Leverian Museum. Some of the plates in this work were executed from Th. Watling's original water-colour drawings of objects from the neighbourhood of Port Jackson, New South Wales. (552,, V, p. 2271).

A systematic summary of the birds of New Holland treated in this work was issued by F. A. A. Meyer in 1793 (402, note).

WHITEHEAD, J.

1893. Exploration of Mount Kina Balu, North 52 Borneo. By John Whitehead. With coloured plates and original illustrations. Gurney and Jackson. *London. pp. X + [II] + 317. text-figs. 6 col. pl. birds. 4to.*

During his journeys in the East, which lasted for nearly five years, Whitehead not only visited North Borneo but also spent several months on the islands of Java and Palawan, also making an expedition into the State of Malacca.

The main object of these expeditions was ornithological, and the main part of the book, pp. 1—192, the author's report on the journeys, therefore contains a good deal of ornithological matter. The appendix, pp. 193—307, contains an almost complete account of the zoological collections formed by the author, with descriptions of the new species obtained. It consists of a series of ten papers written by various authors and published in the journals of various societies, including three (Nos. 2—4) dealing with birds; the first and longest of these, pp. 200—248, 'On the birds of North Borneo' by R. B. Sharpe and John Whitehead, is derived from a series of papers published in the 'Ibis' during the years 1887—90, and here arranged in a connected form. Altogether 324 species are enumerated, 43 of which are described as new by R. B. Sharpe, while a single new species is described by Ogilvie-Grant (70, XVII, p. 501). The author's field-notes on the species are given in brackets.

The next ornithological section pp. 249—257, 'On the birds of Palawan', is derived from two papers published in the 'Ibis', by Sharpe, 1888, and the author, 1890, respectively. It deals with a total of 157 species, nine of which are described as new, seven by Sharpe and two by Whitehead.

The third ornithological section, 'Notes on a collection of birds from Eastern Java' (pp. 258—263) by the author, contains a list of 67 species with a few field-notes and descriptions of two new species by Seebohm (from the Bulletin of the British Ornithologists' Club, V).

The plates (coloured by hand) were lithographed by the author from his own water-colour sketches. The attitudes of several of the birds were taken from drawings by J. G. Keulemans in the 'Ibis'.

WHYMPER, C.

1909. Egyptian birds; for the most part seen in 52

the Nile Valley. By Charles Whymper. Adam and
Charles Black. *London. pp. X + 221 + [2]. text-figs.
51 col. pl. small 4to.*

A popular account of the Egyptian birds to be found in
the valley of the Nile, with a brief description of each of
the species dealt with and information about their occurrence
in the country, their habits, and other facts of interest.

The coloured plates (three-colour prints) are executed from
drawings by the author, and show the birds in characteristic
attitudes and situations.

WIED-NEUWIED, M. A. P., Prinz zu.

0.   *1822—31.* [Abbildungen zur Naturgeschichte Brasiliens. Landes-Industrie-Comptoir. *Weimar]. 5 col. pl.
birds. large fol.* [Added title in French].

A title-page is lacking, the title is given from Engelmann
(564, 1846, p. 303).

The work was issued in 15 parts, each consisting of six
coloured copper-plates and six leaves with a descriptive text in
German and French. The animals figured are mentioned in
the author's 'Reise nach Brasilien ... in 1815—17', 1820—21,
or in his 'Beiträge zur Naturgeschichte von Brasilien', 1825
—33, and the plates, of which some of the ornithological ones
were engraved by H. Hessen, were intended to supplement
Buffon's 'Planches enluminées' (cf. 76) and Temminck and
Laugier de Chartrouse's 'Nouveau recueil de planches coloriées',
1820—39 (502; 503).

WIEN. AKADEMIE DER WISSENSCHAFTEN.
See Akademie der Wissenschaften. Wien.

WIESE, V. H. F.

1.   *1894—96.* V. Wiese: Tropefuglenes Liv i Fan-
genskab. Haandbog i Fuglenes Røgt, Pleje og Opdræt.
Brødr. Backhausen. *Aarhus. 2 vols. 22 pl. (18 col.).
large 8vo. — < Part I. Tropefuglenes Beskrivelse >.
1894. pp. 599. 18 col. pl. (numb. I—XVIII). < Part
II. Tropefuglenes Behandling >. 1896. pp. 241 + 10
+ [6]. 4 pl. (numb. I—IV).*

A handbook of tropical cage-birds, their life in captivity,
and their management and care.

The first part of the work contains descriptions of the
species and notes on their geographical distribution, habits,
and other behaviour, while the second part contains a guide
to the care of the birds, with a description of bird-rooms,
aviaries, and cages, a description of arrangements for seed and
water, etc.

The coloured plates (chromo-lithographs, each containing
several figures) were executed from paintings by the author
from living or stuffed birds, and printed by Backhausen Bros.,
Aarhus.

WILLIAMSON, R. S.

Reports of explorations and surveys ... for a railroad from the Mississippi River to the Pacific Ocean
... 1853—56. — Vol. VI. 1857. Report ... upon explorations ... from the Sacramento Valley to the
Columbia River, made by Lieut. R. S. Williamson ...
1855. Part IV. Zoological report. No. 2. Report upon
the zoology of the route. *pp. 73—110:* Chapter II.
Report upon the birds. *See Newberry, J. S.* Vol. X.
1859. Report of explorations in California ... near the
35th and 32d parallels of north latitude. By Lieutenant R. S. Williamson ... 1853. Part IV. Zoological
report. *pp. 29—80:* No. 2. Report upon birds collected on the survey. *See Heermann, A. L.*

WILLUGHBY, F.

1676. Francisci Willughbeii ... Ornithologiæ libri *532.*
tres: in quibus aves omnes hactenus cognitæ in me-
thodum naturis suis convenientem redactæ accuratè
describuntur, descriptiones iconibus, elegantissimis &
vivarum avium simillimis, æri incisis illustrantur.
Totum opus recognovit, digessit, supplevit Joannes
Raius. Sumptus in chalcographos fecit illustriss. D.
Emma Willughby, vidua. Impensis Joannis Martyn.
*Londini. pp. [X] + 307 + [5]. text-figs. 77 pl.
(numb. I—LXXVII). large 4to (size as fol.).*

This work, fundamental for systematic ornithology, was
published after Willughby's death by John Ray on the basis
of the material left by Willughby. The descriptions of the birds
of the two main groups into which they are divided, viz.
'land-fowl' and 'water-fowl', constitute the last two of the
three parts of the work, since they are dealt with on pp. 25—
198 and pp. 199—295 respectively, while birds in general are
treated in the first part of the work, pp. 1—23. This concludes, with a Catalogus avium Britannicum, pp. 17—23. A
table showing the classification of the main groups has been
inserted at p. 25 ('Avium terrestrium tabula') and p. 199
('Avium aquaticarum tabula') while pp. 297—307 contain an
'Appendix, continens aves suspectas vel nimis breviter minusve
accurate descriptas. E Joannis Eusebii Nierembergii Historiæ
Naturæ libro decimo'.

Each of the plates (engravings, some signed F. H. van
Houe, W. Faithorne, or W. Sherwin sc.) contains several,
2—9, figures.

The originals are derived from various sources (cf. p. 20),
and the figures, as will be understood, are rather small and
not very good, which is also due to the fact that Ray did not
live in London, where the copper-plates were made, so that
his guidance in the execution of the engravings had to be
made by letter.

There is another copy of the work in the possession of the
Library. It differs from that cited above in that it is printed
on paper of a poorer quality and of a smaller format; it
also has a different title-page, which is printed in black, instead
of in red and black; it lacks the words 'Sumptus in Chalcographos fecit illustriss. D. Emma Willughby, Vidua', and
is not adorned with the engraving of Willughby's coat of arms
which is found on the title-page of the copy mentioned above.

A somewhat enlarged and revised English translation appeared in 1678 under the title 'The ornithology of Francis
Willughby', etc. (London, 80 pl., 4to (size as fol.)).

WILLUGHBY SOCIETY, THE, for the Reprinting
of Scarce Ornithological Works.

At a meeting of ornithologists held on May 7, 1879, Professor Newton in the chair, it was decided to form an association
for the purpose of reprinting certain ornithological works which
were of interest on account of their utility or rarity. The
society was given the name cited above; however, after the
publication of twelve volumes with reprints of older works, the
society was dissolved in 1884 owing to lack of support.

1882. Scopoli's ornithological papers from his
Deliciæ floræ et faunæ Insubricæ (Ticini: 1786—
1788). Edited by Alfred Newton. *See Sonnerat, P.,*
1776.

1883. Audouin's Explication sommaire des planches d'oiseaux de l'Égypte et de la Syrie. Publiées par
Jules-César Savigny. *See Audouin, J. V.*

WILSON, A.

1808—14 [—24]. American ornithology; or, The *533.*
natural history of the birds of the United States:
illustrated with plates engraved and colored from
original drawings taken from nature. By Alexander
Wilson. Bradford and Inskeep. (Vols. VII—VIII:

27*

Samuel F. Bradford). *Philadelphia. 9 vols. in 3. 76 col. pl. fol.* — Vol. I. 1808. *pp. VI + 158. 9 col. pl. (numb. 1—9).* Vol. II. 1810. *pp. XII + 13—167. 9 col. pl. (numb. 10—18).* Vol. III. 1811. *pp. XVI + 17—120. 9 col. pl. (numb. 19—27).* Vol. IV. 1811. *pp. XII + 13—100. 9 col. pl. (numb. 28—36).* Vol. V. 1812. *pp. XII + 13—122. 9 col. pl. (numb. 37—45).* Vol. VI. 1812. *pp. XX + 13—102. 9 col. pl. (numb. 46—54).* Vol. VII. 1824. *pp. XII + 13—138. 9 col. pl. (numb. 55—63).* Vol. VIII. 1824. *pp. XI + 13—162. text-figs. 9 col. pl. (numb. 64—72).* Vol. IX. 1814. *pp. LVII + [I] + 61—133 + [19]. 4 col. pl. (numb. 73—76).*

This classical work of American ornithological literature was first issued in 1808—14 in nine volumes, the last two of which were edited after Wilson's death by George Ord, who wrote the text to Vol. IX, for which Wilson had only left the drawings for four plates and some brief notes and hasty sketches.

A 'Biographical sketch of Alexander Wilson' by George Ord is found in Vol. IX (pp. XIII—XLVIII).

Vols. VII and VIII of the present series are from a new edition of the last three volumes which was issued by Ord in 1824—25 (715). These volumes in the original edition may, according to Coues (561, I, p. 597) be described as follows: Vol. VII. 1813. pp. XII + pp. 13—132. 9 col. pl. (numb. 55—63); Vol. VIII. 1814. pp. XI + pp. 13—146. text-figs. 9 col. pl. (numb. 64—72).

In 1825—33 Bonaparte issued his 'American ornithology, or, The natural history of birds inhabiting the United States, not given by Wilson' (47), an independent work designed on the same principles as that by Wilson, and therefore regarded as a kind of sequel to that work, for which reason the two works were issued together in several subsequent editions.

In addition to the aforesaid edition of Vols. VII—IX several editions of Wilson's work appeared later, viz. 1828—29 (by Ord, 3 vols. text, 1 vol. atlas, 8vo); 1831 (by Jameson, 4 vols., 8vo; contains Bonaparte's work; was reprinted the same year); 1832 (by Jardine (534), 3 vols., 8vo; contains 'Bonaparte'); 1840 (by Brewer, 1 vol., 8vo; contains 'Bonaparte'; re-issued 1853 and 1854); c. 1871 (Philadelphia, Porter and Coates, 3 vols. text, 8vo, 2 vols. atlas, fol.); 1876 (by Jardine, 3 vols., 4to; contains 'Bonaparte', re-issued 1877 in 3 vols., 8vo); 1878 (Popular edition, 3 vols., 8vo; contains 'Bonaparte').

The plates (engraved by A. Lawson, J. G. Warnicke, G. Murray, and B. Tanner) were executed from figures 'drawn from nature by A. Wilson'.

534.   1832. American ornithology; or, The natural history of the birds of the United States. By Alexander Wilson; with a continuation by Charles Lucian Bonaparte. The illustrative notes, and life of Wilson, by William Jardine. Whittaker, Treacher, & Arnot. *London. 3 vols. 97 col. pl. 8vo.* — Vol. I. *pp. CVII + 408. 28 pl. (27 col. pl. birds (numb. 1—27)).* Vol. II. *pp. VII + 390. 33 col. pl. (numb. 28—60).* Vol. III. *pp. VIII + 523. text-figs. 37 col. pl. (numb. 61—76, 1—21).*

The main part of this work consists of a reprint of Wilson's 'American ornithology', 1808—14 (533), which was completed by Ord, and the first three volumes of Bonaparte's 'American ornithology', 1825—28 (47), whose fourth and last volume did not appear till 1833. Wilson's contribution to the work constitutes Vol. I, pp. 1—408, Vol. II, and Vol. III, pp. 1—257, while Bonaparte's 'Continuation of Wilson's American ornithology' is found in Vol. III, pp. 259—507. Copious notes are given by Jardine, who also contributed the chapter 'Life of Alexander Wilson' (Vol. I, pp. IX—CVII).

The plates (engraved by W. H. Lizars) are copies from the originals drawn by A. Wilson (Pl. 1—76) and in Bonaparte's 'Continuation' by Titian R. Peale and A. Rider.

WILSON, E. A.
1907. National Antarctic Expedition 1901—1904. 53 Natural history. Vol. II. Zoology. (Vertebrata: Mollusca: Crustaca). < - - II. Aves. By Edward A. Wilson >. Printed by order of the Trustees of the British Museum. *London. pp. 121. 36 pl. (13 col. (numb. I— XIII; 2 pl. eggs (numb. VI—VII), 18 phot. pl.). large 8vo (size as 4to).*

Part of the report dealing with natural history of the 'Discovery' expedition to the Antarctic, 1901—04, under the leadership of R. F. Scott. The whole section dealing with natural history appeared in 1907—12 (Vols. I—VI). Wilson joined the expedition as assistant surgeon and naturalist and wrote the present section, which treats of a number of birds collected or observed during the expedition.

The coloured plates (chromo-lithographs, E. A. Wilson pinx; Bale & Danielsson, lith.) represent chiefly the heads and feet of the birds, especially penguins.

WILSON, S. B.
1890—99. Aves Hawaiienses: The birds of the 53 Sandwich Islands. By Scott B. Wilson, assisted by A. H. Evans. R. H. Porter. *London. pp. I—IIIe + V—XXV + [I] + [257]. text-figs. 70 pl. (64 col., 3 photograv.). 1 map. 4to.*

This important monograph appeared in eight parts, the first of which was issued in December, 1890, the last in 1899. This contains table of contents, list of plates, and index. A survey of the dates of publication and an analysis of the contents of the first seven parts are given in the table of contents, which also contains a pagination of the text, which is not paginated continuously.

Besides the introduction (pp. VII—XXV) and the text treating of the individual forms (pp. 1—217), the volume contains a paper by Hans Gadow, 'Remarks on the structure of certain Hawaiian birds', etc. (pp. 219—249), illustrated with plates I—III. Part II of Gadow's paper (pp. 243—249) is entitled 'Further remarks on the relationships of the Drepanididæ'.

The coloured plates have been executed in lithography coloured by hand (F. W. Frohawk del. et lith.; West, Newman imp.).

WINGE, A. H.
1925. Danmarks Fugle ... Vol. I. pp. 244—255; Oversigt over Danmarks jordfundne Fugle. *See Schiøler, E. L. T. L., 1825—31.*

WIRSING, A. L.
1772 [—86]. Sammlung von Nestern und Eyern 53 verschiedener Vögel, aus den Cabineten des ... Herrn Geheimen Hofrath Schmidels und des Herrn Verfassers. Gestochen und herausgegeben durch Adam Ludwig Wirsing. Hinlänglich beschrieben und abgehandelt von Friedrich Christian Günther (Part II: [von N. G. Leske und Dav. Piesch]). Adam Ludwig Wirsing. *Nürnberg. 2 vols. 84 col. pl.* — [Vol. I]. 1772. [Text. Part I]. *pp. XII + 90. 50 col. pl. (numb. I— L).* [Vol. II]. [1784]. [Text. Part II]. *pp. 91—133. 34 col. pl. (numb. LI—LXXXIV).*

The plates in this work, which is of no great value, were issued in four parts of 25 plates each. Altogether 101 plates were published, of which the fifty contained in the first two parts are described in the accompanying text, which also deals with the birds concerned. No text has been published to the plates in Parts 3 and 4.

The first plate in each part is dated, 1767, 1771, 1775, and 1786 respectively, while Leske's preface to Part 2 is dated 1784.

A French translation of Part 1 appeared in 1777 under

the title 'Collection de figures de nids et d'oeufs de différents oiseaux', etc. (564, 1846, p. 400; 558, II, column 830).
A prospectus, illustrated with plates, concerning this work and B. C. Vogel's 'Sammlung meistens deutscher Vögel', etc., the plates for which were engraved and edited by A. L. Wirsing, was issued in 1770 (552, V, p. 2340).
Another copy of this work, also containing 84 plates, is bound in one volume.

WOLF, JOHANN.
1810. Taschenbuch der deutschen Vögelkunde ... *See Meyer, B.*
8.   [*1816—*] *1818.* Abbildungen und Beschreibungen merkwürdiger naturgeschichtlicher Gegenstände von Johann Wolf. Conrad Tyroff. *Nürnberg. pp. 168 +* [*4*]. *11 col. pl. birds (numb. I, II, V, XV—XVII, XXII, XXIII, XXV, XXIX, XXXV). 4to.*
The first volume of a work which consists in its entirety of two volumes, each with 36 plates. It was issued in 1816—22 in 27 parts, most of which contain two sheets of text and three plates. The text gives a diagnosis and a description of the birds figured, and deals with their distribution and habits. The plates (Fleischmann, A. Gabler, J. C. Bock, Nussbiegel sc.) were executed chiefly from drawings by L. C. Tyrof and A. Gabler.
1822. Zusätze und Berichtigungen zu Meyers und Wolfs Taschenbuch der deutschen Vögelkunde ... *See Meyer, B.*

WOLF, JOSEPH.
9.   [*1856—*] *1861—67.* Zoological sketches by Joseph Wolf. Made for the Zoological Society of London, from animals in their vivarium, in the Regent's Park. Edited, with notes, by Philip Lutley Sclater. Henry Graves & Company. *London.* 2 vols. *39 col. pl. birds (numb. in text). large fol. —* [Vol. I]. 1861. *17 col. pl. birds (Nos. XXXIII—XLIX).* [Vol. II]. Second series. 1867. *22 col. pl. birds (Nos. XXVIII—XLIX).*
Each volume of this work contains fifty plates (lithographs coloured by hand and chromo-lithographs) executed from original designs by Joseph Wolf. Each plate is accompanied by a brief explanatory text occupying one page or even less.
The work was originally issued by D. W. Mitchell, Secretary to the Society, who in 1856—59 published Parts I—VII and wrote the accompanying temporary letterpress. After Mitchell's death P. L. Sclater undertook the completion of the work, selecting the subjects and writing the temporary letterpress which was to accompany the plates. He also wrote the permanent letterpress, which was issued with the thirteenth and concluding part of the work.
10.   *1874.* The life and habits of wild animals illustrated by designs by Joseph Wolf. Engraved by J. W. & Edward Whymper. With descriptive letter-press by Daniel Giraud Elliot. Alexander Macmillan & Co. *London. pp.* [*IX*] *+ 72. 6 pl. birds (numb. II, V, VIII, XI, XIV, XVIII). 4to.*
This volume is said to contain on its twenty plates (woodcuts) with figures showing the life and habits of mammals and birds 'the last series of illustrations which will be drawn by Mr. Wolf either upon wood or upon stone'. The plates constitute the essential part of the work as compared with the descriptive text, which was written for the general public.

WOLLASTON, A. F. R.
1915 & 1916. Report on the birds collected by the British Ornithologists' Union Expedition and the Wollaston Expedition in Dutch New Guinea. *See Ogilvie-Grant, W. R.*

WOLLEY, J.
1864—1907. Ootheca Wolleyana: an illustrated *541.* catalogue of the collection of birds' eggs, begun by the late John Wolley, jun., and continued with additions by the editor Alfred Newton. R. H. Porter (Vol. I, Part I: John van Voorst). *London.* 2 vols. *8vo. —* Vol. I. 1864—1902. *pp. XXXIX + 531 +* [*2*]. *1 text-fig. 27 pl. (front. + Pl. I—XIII (eggs, col.), A—M (1 (C) col.)).* Vol. II. 1905—07. *pp. VI + 665 +* [*2*] *+ 96. 2 text-figs. 11 pl. (XIV—XXI (eggs, col.), N—P (1 (N) col.)).*
Each of the volumes in this work consists of two parts with the following contents and dates of publication. Part I, 1864, Accipitres, pp. 1—180 + [2], Pl. I—IX, A—I; II, 1902, Picariæ-Passeres, pp. 181—531 + XXXIX, front., Pl. X—XIII, J—M; III, 1905, Columbæ-Alcæ, pp. 1—384 + [1], Pl. XIV —XXI; IV, 1907, Alcæ-Anseres; with supplement and appendix, pp. 385—665 + [1] + 96, Pl. N—P, 1 map.
After Wolley's death his oological collection was transferred to the editor who, on the basis of Wolley's note-books, subsequently published a complete catalogue of the contents of his egg-cabinet. However, this catalogue further includes an account of such specimens as had been acquired later by the author. Newton's additions are in all cases distinguished from Wolley's text by being shown in brackets.
Besides the text dealing with the individual specimens Vol. I also contains a memoir on Wolley (pp. IX—XXXIX), and Vol. II (pp. 96) an appendix of sixty items, 'The publications on natural history of John Wolley, except those included in the body of the work'.
The plates with figures of eggs are executed in chromolithography (Vol. I : J. T. Balcomb, del., Hanhart, lith.; Vol. II : H. Grønvold, pinx., Bale & Danielsson, lith.). Two coloured plates with figures of birds were executed from drawings by J. Wolf.

WRIGHT, F. von.
1917—29. Svenska fåglar efter naturen och på sten ritade af ... F. von Wright. *See Wright, M. von.*

WRIGHT, L.
[*1873*]. The illustrated book of poultry. With prac- *542.* tical schedules for judging, constructed from actual analysis of the best modern decisions. By Lewis Wright. Illustrated with ... coloured portraits of prize birds, painted from life by J. W. Ludlow. Cassell Petter & Galpin. *London. pp. VIII + 591 +* [*4*]. *text-figs. 50 col. pl. 4to.*
This work is a thorough and practical exposition of poultry and of poultry-keeping in its various branches.
Chapters I—XVII (pp. 1—207) are on more general conditions relating to the subject, such as 'Feeding and general treatment of fowls', 'Eggs and incubation', 'Diseases of poultry', etc., while Chapters XVIII—XXXVII deal with the various forms of poultry, their breeding and management. The last chapter of the book, XXXVII, discusses some possible additions to the poultry-yard.
The plates are executed in chromo-lithography, most of them by Vincent Brooks Day & Son, London.
Several of the illustrations in this work were reproduced in G. S. Bricka's 'Illustreret Haandbog i Fjerkræavl', 1883—84 (68).

WRIGHT, M. von.
1828 [*—38*]. Svenska foglar efter naturen och på *543.* sten ritade af M. och W. von Wright. Tryckte af C. von Schéele. *Stockholm. 179 col. pl. obl. fol.*
This series of plates without text was issued at the expense of Count Nils Bonde, and appeared in 30 parts, as follows: Parts 1—3, 1828; 4—7, 1829; 8—17, 1830; 18—21, 1831; 22—25, 1832; 26, 1834; 27, 1835; 28—29, 1837; 30, 1838.

Part 26 contained five plates, all the others six (cf. 'Svenskt boklexikon', II, 1884, p. 867). Part 31, which increased the number of the plates to 184, was never issued.

Each plate contains one figure of a bird, though two contain two figures each. On the 184 plates altogether 137 species are shown, which are thus represented by 186 figures. The plates (lithographs coloured by hand) were printed by C. von Schéele, O. Sundel, and Gjöthström & Magnusson.

A new edition (544) with text by Einar Lönnberg and additions of plates executed from paintings by M., W. and F. von Wright and Bror Hallberg was issued in 1917—29.

544.   [1917—] 1924—29. Svenska fåglar efter naturen och på sten ritade af M., W. och F. von Wright. Med text af Einar Lönnberg. Ivar Baarsen (Vols. II—III: Förlaget Svenska Fåglar). Stockholm. 3 vols. 364 col. pl. large 4to (size as fol.). — Vol. I. [1917—] 1924. pp. 9 + [1] + 1—295. text-figs. 146 col. pl. Vol. II. 1929. pp. 9 + 295—546. text-figs. 109 col. pl. Vol. III. 1929. pp. 16 + 547—902. text-figs. 109 col. pl.

According to 'Arskatalog för svenska bokhandeln' this work was published in 105 parts, many of which are double, and which appeared as follows: 1917—20, Parts 1—13, pp. 1—104, 30 pl.; 1921—24, 14/15—64/65; 1925, 66/67—68/69; 1926, 70/71—76/77; 1927, 78/79—90/91; 1928, 92/93—96/97; 1929, 98/99—104/105.

The hand-coloured plates by M. and W. von Wright, which appeared in 1828—38 under the title 'Svenska foglar', etc. (543), form the basis of this work. The original intention was that the present new edition should contain reproductions of the 184 old plates and of 44 original paintings executed by the brothers von Wright and in the possession of the Kungl. Vetenskapsakademien.

After publication had commenced reproductions from original paintings of birds, made by M. and W. von Wright and by Ferdinand von Wright, of which more than a hundred were deposited in the University Library at Helsingfors, were included among the plates of the work. In addition, several important species which had never been figured by the brothers von Wright, have been reproduced from figures made by the Swedish artist Bror Hallberg, so the work contains figures of the majority of the birds found in Sweden, such forms as rarely appear, or have only appeared a few times in that country, not being represented.

The text deals with all the species of birds, about 355, occurring in Sweden, casual visitors included, making brief mention of genera and higher groups, and descriptions of the individual forms, with an account of their different plumages, occurrence in Sweden, geographical distribution, habits, breeding places, and nests and eggs.

The plates were made at A. Börtzell's printing-establishment Stockholm.

A biography of the brothers von Wright is found pp. 899—902.

WRIGHT, W. von.
    1828—38. Svenska foglar efter naturen och på sten ritade ... af W. von Wright. See Wright, M. von.
    1917—29. Svenska fåglar efter naturen och på sten ritade af ... W. ... von Wright. See Wright, M. von.

WUELLERSTORF-URBAIR, B. von, Baron.
    1865. Reise der österreichischen Fregatte Novara um die Erde ... 1857—59 ... Zoologischer Theil. Vol. I. ... 2. Vögel. See Pelzeln, A. von.

YAMASHINA, Y.
    1935. Report of the First Scientific Expedition to Manchoukuo ... June—October 1933. Section V. Division II. Part III. Birds of Jehol. See Taka-Tsukasa, N.

ZEITSCHRIFT FUER DIE GESAMMTE ORNI-THOLOGIE.
    1884—86. Zeitschrift für die gesammte Ornitho- 54 logie. Herausgegeben von Julius von Madarász. Jahrgang I—III. Budapest. 3 vols. col. plates. 8vo.
    This journal, which was issued in four numbers annually, ceased to appear after the publication of the fourth volume, in 1888.
    It contains several contributions by well-known ornithologists, for instance the editor, Wilh. Blasius, O. Finsch, Herman Schalow, and others. The three present volumes contain a total of 51, chiefly coloured, plates (lithographs coloured by hand: I. Schubert, L. Stejneger, and notably Madarász del.; Hofkunstanst. J. Pataki and especially Grund V. lith., or W. Grund imp.).

ZIMMERMANN, E. A. W. von.
    1787. Thiergeschichte der nördlichen Polarländer. Aus dem Englischen ... mit Anmerkungen und Zusätzen durch E. A. W. Zimmermann. Vol. II. Naturgeschichte der Vögel. See Pennant, T.

ZINANNI, G. See Ginanni, G.

ZOOLOGICAL JOURNAL, THE.
    [1824—] 1825—35. The Zoological Journal. Con- 54 ducted by Thomas Bell, John George Children, James de Carle Sowerby, and G. B. Sowerby (I—II: 1824—26). Edited by N. A. Vigors (III—V: 1827—35). W. Phillips. London. Vols. I—V, and Supplementary plates, Parts 1—5. 6 vols. text-figs. plates. 8vo.
    This is all that appeared in this periodical, in which much valuable material was published. It was issued in twenty parts, four of which constituted a volume, and five parts containing supplemental plates.
    To begin with the parts were issued fairly regularly, but gradually the publication took place at rather irregular intervals. The true dates of publication of the various parts have been given by Mathews (328, VII, p. 473). According to a note found after the 'Contents', Part 4 of the numbers with supplemental plates was issued at the same time as No. XIX of the work, and Part 5 with No. XX: 'these form the conclusion of the Vth Vol. and of the Work'.
    Among the ornithological contributors may be mentioned N. A. Vigors, John Gould, C. L. Bonaparte, W. Swainson, W. Yarrell and P. J. Selby.
    In addition several plates, about 150, were published in the journal, including many coloured (lithographs coloured by hand), twenty-one of which represent birds.

ZOOLOGICAL MISCELLANY, THE. See Leach, W. E., 1814—17.

ZOOLOGICAL MISCELLANY, THE. See Gray, J. E., 1831.

ZOOLOGICAL SOCIETY OF LONDON.
    1833 → Proceedings of the Zoological Society of 54 London (1861—90: Proceedings of the scientific meetings of the Zoological Society of London; 1891 →: Proceedings of the general meetings for scientific business of the Zoological Society of London). Vol. I → Printed for the Society. London. text-figs. plates. maps. 8vo.
    The society was founded in 1826, and in 1831 it commenced the publication of its 'Proceedings' under the title 'Proceedings of the committee of science and correspondence', etc., Parts I and II, 1830 [1831]—32 [1833], which were continued in a volume appearing each year under the above titles.
    In the large number of volumes, of which only those dated 1833—60 are numbered (Parts I—XXVIII), a great amount

of important zoological matter has been published, including a great deal relating to ornithology. Among the contributors are a number of, chiefly English, ornithologists, of whom mention may be made of J. Gould, N. A. Vigors, W. Yarrell, T. C. Eyton, H. E. Strickland, C. L. Bonaparte, Th. Horsfield, G. Hartlaub, P. L. Sclater, W. B. Tegetmeier, D. G. Elliot, A. Newton, Osbert Salvin, H. E. Dresser, H. Schlegel, O. Finsch, T. Salvadori, E. L. Layard, W. V. Legge, R. B. Sharpe, A. B .Meyer, Henry Seebohm, Howard Saunders, Arthur Tweeddale, J. H. Gurney, E. Oustalet, H. Berlepsch, T. L. Lilford, H. Gadow, G. E. Shelley, J. G. Millais, W. R. Ogilvie-Grant, W. Rothschild, W. L. Sclater, E. Hartert, and several others.

The first volumes, up to and including Part XV, 1847, are not illustrated. L. Fraser, in his 'Zoologia typica', etc., 1845—49 (150), had, however, published figures of mammals and birds described in the Proceedings, or exhibited in the collections of the society. From and including 1848 a number of beautiful coloured plates, over six hundred of them with figures of birds, were published; they were executed from drawings by the best bird painters, such as J. Wolf, H. C. Richter, J. Jennens, J. Smit, J. G. Keulemans, F. W. Frohawk, G. E. Lodge, H. Goodchild, and H. Grønvold. The greater number of the plates are found in the volumes prior to 1900. Most of them are hand-coloured lithographs (M. & N. Hanhart (later: Hanhart) and Mintern Bros., imp.); in some few cases chromo-lithography has been employed.

48   [1833] 1835 → Transactions of the Zoological Society of London. Printed for the Society. London Vol. I → text-figs. plates. maps. 4to.

Published at irregular intervals; up to August, 1937, Vols. I—XXII, four parts of Vol. XXIII, and a volume General index to Vols. I—X (1835—79), 1881, had been published.

A considerable number of important zoological papers have been published in this periodical, among them several dealing with birds, written by ornithologists such as W. Yarrell, J. Gould, E. Rüppell, J. H. Gurney, P. L. Sclater, H. E. Strickland, A. Newton, O. Finsch, Arthur Tweeddale, Osbert Salvin, W. R. Ogilvie-Grant, and W. Rothschild who in Vol. XV, 1901, published an especially profusely illustrated treatise ('A monograph of the genus Casuarius' 1900, 18 col. pl. (numb. XXII—XXXIX) by Keulemans).

The papers are illustrated with a series of beautiful plates, of which about 150 contain figures of birds, executed in hand-coloured lithography from drawings by prominent bird painters such as J. & E. Gould, F. C. Vogel, J. Wolf, J. Smit, J. G. Keulemans, and H. Grønvold (C. Hullmandel, M. & N. Hanhart (Hanhart) and Mintern Bros., imp.).

1910. Vol. XIX. Zoological results of the Ruwenzori Expedition, 1905—06. pp. 253—480: ... 16. Aves ... *See Ogilvie-Grant, W. R.*

ZORN VON PLOBSHEIM, F. A.
1733—63. Vorstellung der Vögel Deutschlandes ... *See Frisch, Johann L.*

ZUR STRASSEN, O. K. L. *See Strassen, O. K. L. zur.*

BIBLIOGRAPHY

The numbers of the titles are in continuation of the numbers in the catalogue.

GENERAL AND COMPREHENSIVE BIBLIOGRAPHIES.

549. Catalogue général des livres imprimés de la Bibliothèque Nationale. Auteurs. Paris 1897 →
550. British Museum. Catalogue of printed books. London 1881—1905.
551. British Museum. General catalogue of printed books. I → London 1931 →
552. Catalogue of the books, manuscripts, maps and drawings in the British Museum (Natural History). I—VII → London 1903—33 →
553. Catalogue of the printed books and pamphlets in the library of the Linnean Society of London. New edition. London 1925.
554. Catalogue of the scientific books in the library of the Royal Society. [I—II]. London 1881—83.
555. Catalogue of the library of the Zoological Society of London. Fifth edition. London 1902.

556. *Agassiz,* L.: Bibliographia zoologiæ et geologiæ. A general catalogue of all books, tracts, and memoirs on zoology and geology. Edited by H. E. Strickland (Vol. IV: and William Jardine). I—IV. London 1848—54.
The Ray Society.
557. *Benzing,* J.: Der Buchdruck des 16. Jahrhunderts im deutschen Sprachgebiet. Eine Literaturübersicht. Leipzig 1936.
Zentralblatt f. Bibliothekswesen. Beiheft 68.
558. *Brunet,* J. C.: Manuel du libraire et de l'amateur de livres. Cinquième édition. Paris 1860—80. 6 vols., and 2 suppl. vols.
Carus, J. V. *See Engelmann,* W.
559. *Childs,* J. B.: Sixteenth century books. A bibliography of literature describing books printed between 1501 and 1601. Reprinted from the Papers of the Bibliographical Society of America. Chicago 1925.
560. *Choulant,* L.: Graphische Incunabeln für Naturgeschichte und Medicin. Leipzig 1858.
Reprinted from Archiv f. die zeichnende Künste 3 (1857). Neudruck. München 1924.
561. *Coues,* E.: [Ornithological bibliography]. Washington 1878. 4 parts. 8vo.
Part I. 1878. List of faunal publications relating to North American ornithology.
In Miscellaneous Publications U. S. Geological Survey of the Territories 11, pp. 567—784.

Parts II—III. 1879—80. Second [and] third instalment of American ornithological bibliography.
In Bulletin of the U. S. Geological and Geographical Survey of the Territories 5, pp. 239—330, 521—1066.
Part IV. 1880. Fourth instalment of ornithological bibliography: being a list of faunal publications relating to British birds.
In Proceedings of the U. S. National Museum 2 (1879) pp. 359—482.
562. *Dahl,* S.: Bibliotheca zoologica Danica 1876—1906. København 1910.
563. *Dryander,* J.: Catalogus bibliothecæ historico-naturalis Josephi Banks. Vol. II. Zoologi. Londoni 1796.
564. *Engelmann,* W.: Bibliotheca historico-naturalis. Verzeichniss der Bücher über Naturgeschichte welche ... 1700—1846 erschienen sind. Leipzig 1846.
Continued as: Carus, J. V., and W. Engelmann: Bibliotheca zoologica. Verzeichniss der Schriften über Zoologie, welche ... 1846—1860 ... erschienen sind. Leipzig 1861. 2 vols.
Continued as: Taschenberg, O.: Bibliotheca zoologica II. Verzeichniss der Schriften über Zoologie welche ... 1861—1880 ... erschienen sind. Leipzig 1887—1923. 8 vols.
565. *Friesen,* J. O. von: Öfversigt af Sveriges ornithologiska litteratur. Stockholm 1860.
566. *Giebel,* C. G.: Thesaurus ornithologiæ. Repertorium der gesammten ornithologischen Literatur. I. Leipzig 1872.
567. *Gosch,* C. C. A.: Udsigt over Danmarks zoologiske Literatur. I—III. Kjøbenhavn 1870—78.
568. *Graesse,* J. G. T.: Trésor de livres rares et précieux ou nouveau dictionnaire bibliographique. Dresden 1859—69. 6 vols., and 1 suppl. vol.
569. *Hulth,* J. M.: Öfversikt af faunistiskt och biologiskt vigtigare litteratur rörande Nordens fåglar. (Särtryck ur 'Nordens fåglar'). Stockholm 1899.
Jardine, W. *See Agassiz,* L.
Jourdain, F. C. R. *See Mullens,* W. H.
570. *Legendre,* M.: Bibliographie des faunes ornithologiques des régions françaises.

28

In Revue française d'ornithologie 18 (1926) pp. 80—87, 182—191, 264—279, 372—382; 19 (1927) pp. 60—71, 153—161.
571. *Mathews, G. M.*: On some necessary alterations in the nomenclature of birds. Parts I—II.
In Novitates Zoologicæ 17 (1910) pp. 492—503; 18 (1911) pp. 1—22.
572. *Mathews, G. M.*: Dates of ornithological works.
In The Austral Avian Record 4 (1920) pp. 1—27.
A reprint of Mathews' 'The birds of Australia', Vol. VII, Appendix B, with additions and corrections.
573. *Meisel, M.*: A bibliography of American natural history; the pioneer century, 1769—1865. I—III. Brooklyn, N. Y. 1924—29.
574. *Mullens, W. H.*, and H. Kirke Swann: A bibliography of British ornithology from the earliest times to the end of 1912. London 1917.
575. *Mullens, W. H.*, H. Kirke Swann, and F. C. R. Jourdain: A geographical bibliography of British ornithology from the earliest times to the end of 1918. Arranged under counties. London 1920.
576. *Nilsson, R.*: Förteckning över Sveriges ornitologiska litteratur rörande svenska fågelfaunan. Lund 1920.
577. *Nissen, C.*: Schöne Vogelbücher. Ein Überblick der ornithologischen Illustration nebst Bibliographie. Wien 1936.
Also in Philobiblon 8 (1935) under the title: Die ornithologische Illustration. Ein Überblick nebst einer Bibliographie schöner Vogelbücher.
578. *Phillips, J. C.*: American game mammals and birds. A catalogue of books 1582 to 1925. Boston 1930.
579. *Quérard, J. M.*: La France littéraire, ou dictionnaire bibliographique. Paris 1827—64. 10 vols., and 2 suppl. vols.
Continued as: La littérature française contemporaine, 1827—1849. Paris 1842—57. 6 vols.
580. *Schaanning, H. T. L.*: Bibliotheca ornithologia Norvegica 1591—1924.
In Norsk ornithologisk Tidsskrift 2nd Ser. 6 (1925—26) pp. 57—131.
581. *Schiøler, E.* Lehn: Kortfattet Oversigt over Danmarks ornithologiske Litteratur.
In Schiøler: Danmarks Fugle I (1925) pp. 11—197.

582. *Schiøler, E.* Lehn: Kortfattet Oversigt over ornithologiske Skrifter, behandlende Grønlands Fuglefauna.
In Schiøler: Danmarks Fugle II (1926) pp. 11—30.
583. *Sherborn, C. D.*: Bibliography.
In Sherborn: Index animalium. Sectio prima (Cantabrigiæ 1902) pp. XI—LVI. — Sectio secunda (London 1922) pp. XV—CXXXI. — Epilogue, additions to bibliography, additions and corrections, and index to trivialia (June, 1932) pp. CXXXIII—CXLVII.
584. *Stone, W.*: American ornithological literature 1883—1933.
In Fifty years' progress of American ornithology 1883—1933. Published by the American Ornithologists' Union. (Revised edition) (Lancaster, Pa., 1933) pp. 29—49.
Strickland, H. E. See Agassiz, L.
585. *Sudhoff, K.*: Deutsche medizinische Inkunabeln. Leipzig 1908.
Studien zur Geschichte der Medizin 2—3.
Swann, H. Kirke. See Mullens, W. H.
Taschenberg, O. See Engelmann, W.
586. *Tschusi zu Schmidhoffen: V. Ritter v.*: Bibliographia ornithologica. Verzeichniss der gesammten ornithologischen Literatur der österreichisch-ungarischen Monarchi.
In Verhandlungen der k.-k. zoologisch-botanischen Gesellschaft in Wien 28 (1879) pp. 491—544.
587. *(Wiegendruck-Gesellschaft:)* Der Buchdruck des 15. Jahrhunderts. Eine bibliographische Übersicht herausgegeben von der Wiegendruck-Gesellschaft. Berlin 1929—36.
588. *Wood, C. A.*: An introduction to the literature of vertebrate zoology. London 1931.
589. *Zimmer, J. T.*: Catalogue of the Edward E. Ayer Ornithological Library. Parts I—II. Chicago 1926.
Field Museum of Natural History. Publication 239—240. Zoological Series 16.
590. Zoological Record. 1864 → London 1865 → Nos. 1—6 (1865—70) as The Record of zoological literature; Nos. 43—51 (1908—16) as International catalogue of scientific literature. N. Zoology.

GENERAL AND COMPREHENSIVE WORKS RELATING TO THE HISTORY OF ART AND ORNITHOLOGY.

591. *Alcalde del Rio, H.*, H. Breuil and L. Sierra: Les oiseaux dans l'art paléolithique.
In Alcalde del Rio, Breuil and Sierra: Les cavernes de la région cantabrique (Espagne) (Peintures et gravures murales des cavernes paléolithiques) (Monaco 1911) pp. 230—237.
592. *Allen, J. A.*: Progress of ornithology in the United States during the last century.

In The American Naturalist 10 (1876) pp. 536—550.
593. Årsberättelser om vetenskapernas framsteg, afgifne af K. Vetenskaps-Akademiens embetsmän. Stockholm 1822—53. — Ornithological sections: 1821—28 by J. W. Dalman; 1829—31 by S. Nilsson; 1832—36 by B. F. Fries; 1837—50 by C. J. Sundevall.

Becker, F. See Thieme, U.

. *Boubier, F.*: L'évolution de l'ornithologie. Nouvelle édition. Paris 1932.

Breuil, H. See Alcalde del Rio, H.

. (*British Ornithologists' Union*) Biographical notices of the original members of the British Ornithologists' Union, of the principal contributors to the first series of 'The Ibis', and of the officials.
In The Ibis. Jubilee Supplement. 9th Ser. 2. 1908 (1909) pp. 71—232.

. *Carlsson, J.* G.: Faunistiska uppgifter i äldre landskaps- och sockenbeskrifninger. I. Blekinge.
In Fauna och Flora 12 (1917) pp. 137—140.

. *Carus, J.* V.: Geschichte der Zoologie. München 1872.

. (*Cooper Ornithological Club*) First exhibition of paintings of American bird artists. Assembled by the Cooper Ornithological Club on the occasion of its first annual meeting. Los Angeles Museum. April 1926.

. *Cuvier,* G.: Histoire des progrès des sciences naturelles, depuis 1789 jusqu'à ce jour. I—V. Paris 1826—36.

. *Cuvier,* G.: Histoire des sciences naturelles, depuis leur origine jusqu'à nos jours. Complétée, rédigée, annotée et publiée par M. Magdaleine de Saint-Agy. I—V. Paris 1841—45.

Dörnhöffer, F. See Graul, R.

. *Dunlap,* W.: History of the rise and progress of the arts of design in the United States. New edition. Edited, with additions, by Frank W. Bayley and Charles E. Goodspeed. I—III. Boston 1918.

. *Fatio,* V.: Introduction aux oiseaux.
In Fatio: Faune vertébrés de la Suisse. II. Histoire naturelle des oiseaux. I (Genève 1899) pp. I—XXXVI.

. *Friedländer, M.* J.: Die Lithographie. Berlin 1922.

. *Friedländer, M.* J.: Der Holzschnitt. Dritte Auflage. Berlin 1926.
Handbücher der staatlichen Museen zu Berlin. [16].

. *Gerstinger,* H.: Die griechische Buchmalerei. Wien 1926.

. *Graul,* R., and F. Dörnhöffer: Die Lithographie von ihrer Erfindung bis zur Gegenwart. Wien 1903.
Die vervielfältigende Kunst der Gegenwart 4.

. *Gurney, J.* H., *junior:* Early annals of ornithology. London 1921.

Hamberger, G. C. *See Meusel,* J. G.

. *Harris,* H.: Examples of recent American bird art.
In The Condor 28 (1926) pp. 191—206.

. *Hartert,* E.: Über die Entwicklung und die Fortschritte der Ornithologie seit 1910.
In Verhandlungen des VI. internationalen Ornithologen-Kongresses in Kopenhagen 1926 (Berlin 1929) pp. 35—51.

. *Helms,* O.: Kort Udsigt over dansk Ornithologi fra de ældste Tider til omkring Aar 1900.

In Dansk ornithologisk Forenings Tidsskrift 26 (1932) pp. 81—102.

611. *Helms,* O.: Grønlands Ornithologi fra de ældste Tider til omkring Aar 1900.
In Dansk ornithologisk Forenings Tidsskrift 29 (1934) pp. 1—14.

612. *Jourdain, F.* C. R.: Progress in ornithology during the past halfcentury.
In South Eastern Naturalist (1935) pp. 43—51.

613. *Kömstedt,* R.: Vormittelalterliche Malerei. Die künstlerischen Probleme der Monumental- und Buch-Malerei in der frühchristlichen und frühbyzantinischen Epoche. Augsburg 1929.

614. *Kristeller,* P.: Kupferstich und Holzschnitt in vier Jahrhunderten. Vierte Auflage. Berlin 1922.

615. *Lippmann,* F.: Der Kupferstich. Sechste Auflage. Berlin 1926.
Handbücher der staatlichen Museen zu Berlin. [3].

616. *Macalister, R.* A. S.: A text-book of European archæology. I. The Paleolithic period. Cambridge 1921.

617. *Meusel, J.* G.: Das gelehrte Teutschland oder Lexikon der jetzt lebenden teutschen Schriftsteller. Angefangen von Georg Christoph Hamberger. Fünfte Ausgabe. 1—21. Lemgo 1796—1827.

618. *Meusel, J.* G.: Lexikon der vom Jahr 1750 bis 1800 verstorbenen teutschen Schriftsteller. 1—15. Leipzig 1802—16.

619. *Miall, L.* C.: The early naturalists, their lives and work (1530—1789). London 1912.

620. *Moreau, R.* E.: The birds of ancient Egypt.
In Meinertzhagen, R.: Nicoll's Birds of Egypt (London 1930) I, Chapter III (= pp. 58—77).

621. *Mullens, W.* H.: Some early British ornithologists and their works.
In British Birds 2 (1908—09).
pp. 5—13: I. William Turner (circa 1500—1568).
pp. 109—118, 151—163: III. Christopher Mertett (1614—1695).
pp. 259—266: VI. Thomas Pennant (1726—1798).
pp. 290—300: VII. John Ray (1627—1705) and Francis Willughby (1635—1672).
pp. 351—361: VIII. Thomas Bewick (1753—1828) and George Montagu (1751—1815).
pp. 389—399: IX. William Macgillivray (1796—1852) and William Yarrell (1784—1853).

622. *Murray,* D.: Museums, their history and their use. I—III. Glasgow 1904.

623. *Newton,* A.: A dictionary of birds (London 1893—96) pp. 1—120: Introduction.

624. *Palmer, T.* S.: A brief history of the American Ornithologists' Union.
In Fifty years' progress of American ornithology 1883—1933. Published by the American Ornithologists' Union. (Revised edition) (Lancaster, Pa. 1933) pp. 7—27.

625. *Reichenow, A.*: Geschichte der ornithologischen Erforschung Afrikas.
In Reichenow: Die Vögel Afrikas I (Neudamm 1900—01) pp. V—LXXIX.

626. *Reichenow, A.*: Über die Fortschritte und den gegenwärtigen Stand der Ornithologie.
In Verhandlungen des V. internationalen Ornithologen-Kongresses in Berlin 1910 (Berlin 1911) pp. 117—132.

627. *Reinach, S.*: L'art et la magie à propos des peintures et des gravures de l'âge du renne.
In L'Anthropologie 14 (1903) pp. 257—266.

628. *Reinach, S.*: Répertoire de l'art quaternaire. Paris 1913.

629. *Renvall, T.*: Grunddragen af den systematiska ornitologins utveckling. (Efter utländska källor). Åbo 1904.

630. *Röttinger, H.*: Der Frankfurter Buchholzschnitt 1530—1550. Strassburg 1933.
Studien zur deutschen Kunstgeschichte 293.
Saint-Agy, M. M. de. See *Cuvier*, G.

631. *Salomonsen, F.*: Den færøiske Ornithologis Historie indtil Aar 1800.
In Dansk ornithologisk Forenings Tidsskrift 28 (1934) pp. 79—114.
Supplement.
In Dansk ornithologisk Forenings Tidsskrift 29 (1935) pp. 67—100.

632. *Salomonsen, F.*: Zoology of the Faroes. Aves (Copenhagen 1935) pp. 1—20: [Historical introduction].

633. *Schalow, H.*: Beiträge zur Vogelfauna der Mark Brandenburg (Berlin 1919) pp. 19—45: Versuch einer Geschichte der faunistischen Ornithologie in Brandenburg; pp. 46—137: Bibliographie; pp. 507—594: Biographische Versuche.

634. *Schenk, J.*: Übersicht der Geschichte der Ornithologie in Ungarn.
In Aquila 25 (1918) pp. 31—88.
The Hungarian text with the Latin translation was published as the ornithological section of the work. A magyar birodalom állatvilága ... Madarak (Fauna Regni Hungariæ ... Aves). Budapest 1917.

635. *Schlegel, H.*: Verhandeling over de vereischten van natuurkundige afbeeldingen. Ene door Teylers Tweede Genootschap in het jaar 1847 bekroonde prijsvraag. Haarlem 1849.
Verhandelingen, uitgegeven door Teyler's Tweede Genootschap. Vijf en twintigste stuk.

636. *Schreiber, W. L.*: Die Kräuterbücher des XV. und XVI. Jahrhunderts.
In Hortus sanitatis (Mainz 1485) Faksimileausgabe. München 1924.

637. *Sclater, P. L.*: A short history of the British Ornithologists' Union.
In The Ibis. Jubilee Supplement. 9th Ser. 2. 1908 (1909) pp. 19—69.

638. *Sclater, W. L.*: Notes on the early sources of our knowledge of African ornithology.
In Journal f. Ornithologie. Ergänzungsband II (1929). Festschrift Ernst Hartert ... gewidmet. pp. 184—196.
Sierra, L. See Alcalde del Rio, H.

639. *Sirks, M. J.*: Indisch natuuronderzoek. Een beknopte geschiedenis van de beoefening der natuurwetenschappen in de Nederlandsche koloniën. Amsterdam 1915.
Koloniaal Instituut te Amsterdam. Mededeeling No. VI.

640. *Stone, W.*: Some early American ornithologists.
In Bird Lore 7 (1905).
pp. 126—129: 1. Mark Catesby.
pp. 162—164: 2. William Bartram.
pp. 193—194: 3. Benjamin Smith Barton.
pp. 265—268: 4. Alexander Wilson.

641. *Stresemann, E.*: Die Anfänge ornithologischer Sammlungen.
In Journal f. Ornithologie 71 (1923) pp. 112—127.

642. *Stresemann, E.*: Beiträge zu einer Geschichte der deutschen Vogelkunde.
In Journal f. Ornithologie 73 (1925) pp. 594—628.

643. *Stresemann, E.*: Stand und Aufgaben der Ornithologie 1850 und 1925.
In Journal f. Ornithologie 74 (1926) pp. 225—232.

644. *Sutton, G. M.*: Fifty years of progress in American bird-art.
In Fifty years' progress of American ornithology 1883—1933. Published by the American Ornithologists' Union. (Revised edition) (Lancaster, Pa. 1933) pp. 181—197.

645. *Swainson, W.*: Taxidermy; with the biography of zoologists, and notices of their works. London 1840.

646. *Thieme, U.*, und F. Becker (editors): Allgemeines Lexikon der bildenden Künstler von der Antike bis zur Gegenwart. I → Leipzig 1907 →

647. *Thienemann, F. A. L.*: Geschichtlicher Abriss der Ornithologie.
In Rhea 2 (1849) pp. 13—120.

648. *Winge, H.*: Grønlands Fugle. 1898. [Historical introduction].
In Meddelelser om Grønland 21, I (1899) pp. 1—37.

SPECIAL WORKS.

649. *Ahlenius, K.*: Olaus Magnus och hans framställning af Nordens geografi. Upsala 1895.

650. *Alexander, W. B.*: White's Journal of a voyage to New South Wales.

In The Emu 23 (1924) pp. 209—215.

651. *Alexander, W. B.*: Sonnerat's voyage to New Guinea.
In The Emu 23 (1924) pp. 299—305.

. *Allen, E. G.*: Some sixteenth century paintings of American birds.
In The Auk 53 (1936) pp. 17—21.

. *Allen, E. G.*: New light on Mark Catesby.
In The Auk 54 (1937) pp. 349—363.

. *Allen, J. A.*: Pennant's 'Indian Zoology'.
In Bulletin of the American Museum of Natural History 24 (1908) pp. 111—116.

. *Allen, J. A.*: Collation of Brisson's genera of birds with those of Linnæus.
In Bulletin of the American Museum of Natural History 28 (1910) pp. 317—335.
American Museum of Natural History. See Elliot, D. G.

. *Anderson, R. M.*: The work of Bernhard Hantzsch in Arctic ornithology.
In The Auk 45 (1928) pp. 450—466.

. *Anker, J.*: Kjærbøllings Fugleværk.
In Dansk ornithologisk Forenings Tidsskrift 30 (1936) pp. 5—16.

3a. *Arthur, S. C.*: Audubon; an intimate life of the American woodsman. New Orleans 1937.

3b. *Audubon, J. J.*: Audubon and his Journals, edited by Maria R. Audubon, with zoological and other notes by Elliott Coues. I—II. New York 1897.

9. *Audubon, J. J.*: Journal of John James Audubon made during his trip to New Orleans in 1820—1821. Edited by H. Corning. Boston 1929.
Club of Odd Volumes.

0. *Audubon, J. J.*: Journal of John James Audubon made while obtaining subscriptions to his 'Birds of America', 1840—1843. Edited by H. Corning. Boston 1929.
Club of Odd Volumes.

1. *Audubon, L.*: The life of John James Audubon, the naturalist; edited by his widow, with an introduction by Jas. Grant Wilson. New York 1869. — New edition 1902.
Audubon, M. R. See Audubon, J. J.
Aurivillius, C. See Lönnberg, E.

2. *Baer, K. E.* von: Lebensgeschichte Cuvier's. Herausgegeben von Ludwig Stieda. Braunschweig 1897.
Reprinted from Archiv f. Anthropologie 24 (1897) pp. 227—275.

3. *Baldacci, A.*, and *others:* Intorno alla vita e alle opere di Ulisse Aldrovandi. Bologna 1907.

4. *Baldamus, E.*: Die drei Naumanns.
In Daheim 2 (1866) pp. 333—337.

5. *Balss, H.*: Albertus Magnus als Zoologe. München 1928.
Münchener Beiträge zur Geschichte und Literatur der Naturwissenschaften und Medizin 11 .—12.

6. *Balss, H.*: Über die Deutung von weniger bekannten Fabeltieren in wissenschaftlichen Drucken des 15. bis 17. Jahrhunderts.
In Philobiblon 8 (1935) pp. 289—294.

7. *(Banks, J.)* Sir Joseph Banks and the Royal Society. A popular biography. London 1844.

8. *Beaufort, W. H. de*: Coenraad Jacob Temminck

(31 Maart, 1778—30 Januari, 1858) uit zijne brieven geschetst.
In Ardea 9 (1920) pp. 34—43.

669. *Bechstein, L.*: Dr. Johann Matthäus Bechstein und die Forstacademie Dreissigacker. Ein Doppel-Denkmal. Meiningen 1855.

670. *(Belon, P.)* A la mémoire de Pierre Belon, du Mans.
In La Belgique horticole (1885) pp. 5—29.

671. *Berlioz, J.*: D'Orbigny, ornithologiste.
In Commémoration du voyage d'Alcide d'Orbigny en Amérique du Sud 1826—1833 (Paris 1933) pp. 67—74.

672. *Berthold, C.*: Die Forschungsreisen des französischen Missionärs und Naturforschers Armand David. Würzburg 1878.

673. *Bewick, T.*: A memoir of Thomas Bewick, written by himself. [Edited by J. B., i. e. Jane Bewick]. Newcastle-on-Tyne 1862.

674. *(Bonaparte, C. L.:)* Notice sur les ouvrages zoologiques du prince Ch.-L. Bonaparte.
In Revue et Magazin de Zoologie pure et appliquée 2nd Ser. 2 (1850) pp. 614—619.

675. *Braislin, W. C.*: An American edition of Audubon's 'Ornithological Biography'.
In The Auk 35 (1918) pp. 360—362.

676. *(Das)* Brehmbuch. Herausgegeben von der Brehm Gesellschaft. Berlin 1929.

677. *(British Museum (Natural History))*. The history of the collections contained in the natural history departments of the British Museum. I—II & II. Appendix. London 1904—12.

678. *British Museum (Natural History)*. Special guide. No. 9. A short history of the collections. London 1931.

679. *Brolén, C. A.* and *E. Lönnberg*: Linnés avhandling 'Migrationes avium' 1757.
In Svenska Linné-Sällskapets årsskrift 18 (1935) pp. 23—58.

680. *Bruinvis, C. W.*: De familiën Seba, Marcus en Muilman.
In Algemeen Nederlandsch familieblad 4 (1887) pp. 80—82.

681. *Buchanan, R.*: Life and adventures of Audubon, the naturalist. London 1868. — Reprinted 1913.

682. *Bultingaire, L.*: Les origines de la collection des vélins du Muséum et ses premiers peintres.
In Archives du Muséum d'Histoire Naturelle 6th Ser. 1 (1926) pp. 129—149.

683. *Bultingaire, L.*: Les peintres du Jardin du Roy au XVIIIᵉ siècle.
In Archives du Muséum National d'Histoire Naturelle 6th Ser. 3 (1928) pp. 19—36.

684. *Bultingaire, L.*: Les peintres du Muséum à l'époque de Lamarck.
In Archives du Muséum National d'Histoire Naturelle 6th Ser. 6 (1930) pp. 49—56.

685. *Bultingaire, L.*: L'art au Jardin des Plantes.
In Archives du Muséum National d'Histoire Naturelle 6th Ser. 12 (1935) pp. 665—678.

686. *Burns, F. L.*: Alexander Wilson. Parts 1—8.
In The Wilson Bulletin 20—22 (1908—10).

687. *Burns, F. L.*: Miss Lawson's recollections of ornithologists.
In The Auk 34 (1917) pp. 275—282.
688. *Burns, F. L.*: The mechanical execution of Wilson's 'American Ornithology'.
In The Wilson Bulletin 41 (1929) pp. 19—23.
689. *Burroughs, J.*: John James Audubon. Boston 1902.
690. *Busken Huet, C.*: François Valentyn.
In Litterarische fantasien en kritieken 11 (Haarlem 1881) pp. 3—36.
Reprinted from Nederland 3 (1879) pp. 325 seqq.
691. *Capparoni, P.*: Profili bio-bibliografici di medici e naturalisti celebri italiani dal sec. XV⁰ al sec. XVIII⁰. I. Roma 1926.
692. *Casares, J.*: William Henry Hudson y su amor a los pajaros.
In El Hornero 4 (1929) pp. 277—289.
693. *Cassin, J.*: ... Extract from a letter ... to Mr. P. L. Sclater.
In The Ibis New Ser. 1 (1865) pp. 116.
694. *Chapman, F. M.*: Autobiography of a birdlover. New York 1933.
Cheney, R. F.. See May, J. B.
695. *Chesnel de la Charbouclais, L. F. F. A.* de: Vie de Buffon. Paris 1843.
696. *Chmelarz, E.*: Georg und Jakob Hoefnagel.
In Jahrbuch der kunsthistorischen Sammlungen des A. H. Kaiserhauses 17 (1896) pp. 275—290.
697. *Christy, B. H.*: Alexander Lawson's bird engravings.
In The Auk 43 (1926) pp. 47—61.
698. Codices Græci et Latini photographice depicti. Tom. X. Dioscurides. Codex Aniciæ Julianæ picturis illustratus, nunc Vindobonensis Med. Gr. I. Pars altera. Lugduni Batavorum 1906.
699. *Collett, A.*: Familien Collett og Christianialiv i gamle dage. Kristiania 1915.
Corning, H. See Audubon, J. J.
Coues, E. See Audubon, J. J.
700. *Crosslund, C.*: An eighteenth-century naturalist: James Bolton. Halifax 1910.
701. *Cummings, B. F.*: A biographical sketch of Col. George Montagu (1755—1815). English field zoologist.
In Zoologische Annalen 5 (1913) pp. 308—325.
702. *Dahl, O.*: Biskop Gunnerus' Virksomhed fornemmelig som Botaniker tilligemed en Oversigt over Botanikens Tilstand i Danmark og Norge indtil hans Død. I—II. Trondhjem 1892—94. III. Johan Ernst Gunnerus. Tillæg II. Uddrag af Gunnerus' Brevveksling, særlig til Belysning af hans videnskabelige Sysler. 1—11.
In Det K. norske Videnskabers Selskabs Skrifter 1896—1911.
703. *Dahl, S.*: Peder Syvs Optegnelser om danske Fugle.
In Dansk ornithologisk Forenings Tidsskrift 3 (1908—09) pp. 100—112.
704. *Dahl, S.*: Peder Syv som Zoolog.
In Danske Studier (1909) pp. 51—68.

705. *Dall, W. H.*: Spencer Fullerton Baird. A biography. Philadelphia 1915.
706. *Davois, G.*: Bibliographie Napoléonienne française I (Paris 1909).
707. *Dimier, L.*: Buffon. Paris 1919.
708. [*Druitt, Mrs.*:] Lord Lilford ... A memoir by his sister, with an introduction by the Bishop of London. London 1900.
709. *Ducati, P.*: Marsili. Milano 1930.
710. *Duvernoy, G. L.*: Notice historique sur les ouvrages et la vie de M. le b.on Cuvier. Paris 1833.
711. *(Elliot, D. G.)* Daniel Giraud Elliot. A brief biographical sketch on the occasion of his eightieth birthday to emphasize his long devotion to scientific work and his services to the Museum.
In The American Museum Journal 15 (1915) pp. 133—141.
712. *Erhard, H.*: Georges Cuvier (zu seinem hundertsten Todestag).
In Bulletin de la Société fribourgeoise des Sciences Naturelle 32 (1935) pp. 32—64.
713. *Fantuzzi, G.*: Memorie della vita di Ulisse Aldrovandi. Bologna 1774.
714. *Fantuzzi, G.*: Marsili, Conte Luigi Ferdinando.
In Notizie degli scrittori Bolognesi 5 (Bologna 1786) pp. 286—327.
715. *Faxon, W.*: Early editions of Wilson's 'Ornithology'.
In The Auk 18 (1901) pp. 216—218.
716. *Ferguson, D.*: Joan Gideon Loten and Willem Hendrik de Beveren.
In De Indische Mercuur 29 (1906) pp. 187—188.
717. *Ferguson, D.*: Joan Gideon Loten, F. R. S.; the naturalist governor of Ceylon (1752—57), and the Ceylonese artist de Bevere.
In Journal of the Ceylon Branch of the Royal Asiatic Society 1906 19 (1907) pp. 217—271.
718. *Finsch, O.*: Systematische Uebersicht der Ergebnisse seiner Reisen und schriftstellerischen Thätigkeit (1859—1899). Berlin 1899.
719. *Fitzinger, L. J.*: Versuch einer Geschichte der Menagerien des österreichisch-kaiserlichen Hofes.
In Sitzungsberichte der mathematisch-naturwissenschaftlichen Classe der K. Akademie der Wissenschaften 10 (Wien 1853) pp. 300—403, 626—710.
720. *Flourens, M. J. P.*: Analyse raisonnée des travaux de Georges Cuvier. Précédée de son Éloge historique [de Georges Cuvier. Lu à la séance publique de l'Académie des Sciences du 29 dec. 1834]. Paris 1841.
Several re-issues with altered title.
721. *Flourens, M. J. P.*: Buffon. Histoire de ses travaux et de ses idées. Deuxième édition. Paris 1850.
722. *Flourens, M. J. P.*: Des manuscrits de Buffon. Paris 1859.
723. *Fox, W. J.*: The so-called cancelled fasciculus of Cassin's Illustrations.
In The Auk 18 (1901) pp. 291—292.

724. *Fries,* T. M.: Linné. Lefnadstecking. I—II. Stockholm 1903.
725. *Fuertes,* L. A., and W. H. Osgood: Artist and naturalist in Ethiopia. New York 1936.
726. *Gaillard,* C.: Identification de l'oiseau Ama figuré dans une tombe de Béni-Hassan.
Archives du Muséum d'Histoire Naturelle de Lyon 14 (1934) Mémoire 2.
727. *Gaillard,* C.: Sur une figuration coloriée du Pluvier armé, relevée dans une tombe de Béni-Hassan.
Archives du Muséum d'Histoire Naturelle de Lyon 14 (1934) Mémoire 4.
Gaillard, C. See Lortet, L. C.
728. *Gengler,* J.: Die Klein'schen Vogelbilder.
In Journal f. Ornithologie 60 (1912) pp. 570—591; 61 (1913) pp. 205—228.
729. *Gladstone,* H. S.: Handbook to Lord Lilford's Coloured figures of the birds of the British Islands. London 1917.
730. *Goldman,* E. A.: Edward William Nelson — naturalist, 1855—1934.
In The Auk 52 (1935) pp. 135—148.
731. *Goode,* G. B.: Bibliographies of American naturalists. I. The published writings of Spencer Fullerton Baird 1843—1882. Washington 1883. [Including Biographical sketch of Spencer Fullerton Baird].
Bulletin of the U. S. National Museum 20.
732. *Goode,* G. B.: A bibliography of the published writings of Philip Lutley Sclater, 1844—96. Washington 1896.
Bulletin of the United States National Museum 49.
733. *Gosse,* E.: The life of Philip Henry Gosse by his son. London 1890.
734. *Griffin,* F. J.: On the dates of publication and contents of the parts of Fraser (L.), 'Zoologia Typica', 1845—1849.
In Proceedings of the Zoological Society of London (1932) pp. 93—96.
Griffin, F. J. See Sherborn, C. D.
735. *Grosart,* A. B.: Memoir and literary remains of Alexander Wilson, the American ornithologist. I—II. Paisley 1876.
736. (*Gunnerus,* J. E.) Johan Ernst Gunnerus 1718—26. febr. 1918. Mindeblade utg. av Det K. norske Videnskabers Selskab. Trondhjem 1918.
Gunther, R. W. T. See Ray, J.
737. *Gurney,* J. H.: Biographical sketch [of Charles John Andersson. Translated from 'Svenska Jägarförbundets nya tidskrift. 1868].
In Andersson: Notes on the birds of Damara Land. Arranged and edited by John Henry Gurney (London 1872) pp. III—XXIII.
738. *Gurney,* J. H., *junior:* Rambles of a naturalist in Egypt and other countries. London 1876.
739. *Hanhart,* J.: Conrad Gessner. Winterthur 1824.
740. *Harris,* H.: Robert Ridgway a bibliography of his published writings and fifty illustrations.
In The Condor 30 (1928) pp. 1—119.
741. *Hartert,* E.: The Brehm Collection. Introduction.

In Novitates Zoologicæ 8 (1901) pp. 38—39.
742. *Hartert,* E.: On the birds figured in the atlas to Krusenstern's voyage round the world.
In Novitates Zoologicæ 23 (1916) pp. 94—95.
743. *Hartert,* E., and *others:* Zu Johann Friedrich Naumanns 150. Geburtstag.
In Beiträge zur Fortpflanzungsbiologie der Vögel 6 (1930) pp. 1—9.
744. *Haymann,* C.: Kurzgefasste Geschichte der vornehmsten Gesellschaften der Gelehrten von den ältesten Zeiten an bis auf die gegenwärtige. I. Leipzig 1743.
745. *Heinroth,* O.: Joh. Friedr. Naumann im Lichte der heutigen Forschung.
In Journal f. Ornithologie 65 (1917) pp. 116—120.
746. *Helms,* O.: Frederik Faber. 21. April 1796—9. Marts 1828.
In Naturens Verden 12 (1928) pp. 145—160.
Reprinted with some alterations in Dansk ornithologisk Forenings Tidsskrift 22 (1928) pp. 33—49.
747. *Helms,* O.: Otto Fabricius.
In Fabricius: Fauna Groenlandica. Pattedyr og Fugle. Oversat og forsynet med Indledning og Kommentarer af O. Helms (København 1929) pp. 5—26.
Det grønlandske Selskabs Skrifter 6.
748. *Helms,* O.: Frederik Faber: an early Danish ornithologist (1796—1828).
In The Ibis 13th Ser. 4 (1934) pp. 723—731.
749. *Helms,* O.: Ornithologen Johann Dieterich Petersen (1717—1786), hans Liv og Arbejder. Mit einer deutschen Zusammenfassung.
Reprinted from Dansk ornithologisk Forenings Tidsskrift 30 (1926) 2—3.
750. *Henshaw,* H. W.: Autobiographical notes.
In The Condor 22 (1920) pp. 3—10, 55—60, 95—101.
751. *Herman,* O.: J. S. v. Petényi, der Begründer der wissenschaftlichen Ornithologie in Ungarn. 1799 bis 1855. Ein Lebensbild, unter Mitwirkung von J. v. Madarász, St. v. Chernel und G. v. Vastagh. Budapest 1891.
Zweiter internationaler ornithologischer Kongress.
752. *Herrick,* F. H.: Audubon the naturalist; a history of his life and time. I—II. New York 1917.
753. *Herrick,* F. H.: Audubon's bibliography.
In The Auk 36 (1919) pp. 372—380.
754. *Hertling,* G. von: Albertus Magnus. Beiträge zu seiner Würdigung. Zweite Auflage.
Beiträge zur Geschichte der Philosophie des Mittelalters 14 (1914) 5—6.
755. *Hildebrandt,* H.: Christian Ludwig Brehm: a German ornithologist.
In The Ibis 13th Ser. 2 (1932) pp. 308—316.
756. *Hildebrandt,* H.: Johann Matthaeus Bechstein: the German ornithologist (1757—1822).
In The Ibis 13th Ser. 3 (1933) pp. 219—228.
757. *Holt-White,* R.: The life and letters of Gilbert White of Selborne, written and edited by his great-grand-nephew. I—II. London 1901.
758. *Horsfield,* T.: Systematic arrangement and description of birds from the island of Java.

In The Transactions of the Linnean Society of London 13 (1822) pp. 133—200.

759. *Hortling, I.*: Johan Axel Palmén.
In Ornis Fennica 3 (1926) pp. 42—49.

760. *Houten, P. J.* van: Twee Indische natuurlief-hebbers uit de XVIIIe eeuw.
In De Indische Mercuur 28 (1905) pp. 365—367; 29 (1906) pp. 169—170; 31 (1908) pp. 362.

Humbert-Bazile, M. See Nadault de Buffon, H.

761. *Hume, A. O.*: Pennant's Indian Zoology.
In Stray Feathers 7 (1878) pp. 506—508.

762. *Iredale, T.*: George Forster's paintings.
In The Australian Zoologist 4 (1925—27) pp. 48—53.

Iredale, T. See Mathews, G. M., and Sherborn, C. D.

763. (*James, M. R.*:) The Bestiary; being a reproduction in full of the manuscript Ii. 4. 26 in the University Library, Cambridge, with supplementary plates from other manuscripts of English origin, and a preliminary study of the Latin bestiary as current in England. Edited for the Roxburghe Club by M. R. James. Oxford 1928.

Jardine, W. See Strickland, Mrs. H. E.

Jensen, A. S. See Kornerup, B.

764. *Jensen, J. V.*: Johannes Larsen og hans Billeder. København 1920.

Jentink, F. A. See Sherborn, C. D.

765. *Johansson, K. F.*: Solfågeln i Indien. En religionshistorisk-mytologisk studie.
Uppsala Universitets årsskrift 1910.

766. *Kantorowicz, E.*: Kaiser Friedrich der Zweite. Zweite unveränderte Auflage. Berlin 1928. — Ergänzungsband, & dritte unveränderte Auflage 1931.

767. *Karwath, J.*: Zwei pharmazeutische Kostbarkeiten der Wiener Nationalbibliothek.
In Pharmazeutische Monatshefte 5 (1924) pp. 61 68.

768. *Killermann, S.*: Die Vogelkunde des Albertus Magnus. Regensburg 1910.

769. *Killermann, S.*: A. Dürers Pflanzen- und Tierzeichnungen und ihre Bedeutung für die Naturgeschichte. Strassburg 1910.
Studien zur deutschen Kunstgeschichte 119.

770. *Killermann, S.*: Die Miniaturen im Gebetbuche Albrechts V. von Bayern (1574). Ein Beitrag zur Geschichte der Insekten- und Pflanzenkunde. Strassburg 1911.
Studien zur deutschen Kunstgeschichte 140.

771. *Killermann, S.*: Der Waldrapp Gesners (Geronticus eremita L.).
In Zoologische Annalen 4 (1912) pp. 268—279.

772. *Killermann, S.*: Die ausgestorbenen Maskarenenvögel.
In Naturwissenschaftliche Wochenschrift 30 (Neue Folge 14) (1915) pp. 353—360, 369—378.

773. *Kinnear, N. B.*: The dates of publication of the plates of the birds in Gray and Hardwicke's 'Illustrations of Indian Zoology', with a short account of General Hardwicke.
In The Ibis 12th Ser. 1 (1925) pp. 484—489.

774. *Kjærbølling, N.*: Mittheilungen über meine literarische, sammlerische und beobachtende Thätigkeit im Gesellschaftsjahre 1853—54.
In Naumannia (1854) pp. 304—310.

775. *Knappen, P.*: Some additional Audubon copper-plates. In The Auk 51 (1934) pp. 343—349.

776. *Köhler, W.*: Johann Friedrich Naumann. Sein Leben und sein Werk. Biographische Skizze. Gera-Untermhaus 1899.

777. *Kornerup, B.*, C. W. Schultz-Lorentzen and A. S. Jensen: Biskop Dr. theol. Otto Fabricius. Et Mindeskrift i Hundredaaret for hans Død.
In Meddelelser om Grønland 62 (1923) pp. 215—400.

778. *Krause, E.*: Alfred Edmund Brehm.
In Brehms Tierleben. Dritte Auflage I (Leipzig 1890) pp. XVII—XLIV.
Reprinted in Vierte Auflage I (1918) pp. XLIII—LVIII.

779. *Kruseman, A. C.*: J. C. Sepp & Zoon.
In Kruseman: Bouwstoffen voor een geschiedenis van van den Nederlandschen boekhandel II (Amsterdam 1887) pp. 339—342.

780. *Kuentz, C.*: L'Oie du Nil (Chenalopex ægyptica) dans l'antique Égypte.
Archives du Muséum d'Histoire Naturelle de Lyon 14 (1934) Mémoire 1.

Lankester, E. See Ray, J.

781. *Lauchert, F.*: Geschichte des Physiologus. Strassburg 1889.

782. *Lauterborn, R.*: Das Vogel-, Fisch- und Thierbuch des Strassburger Fischers Leonhard Baldner.
In Mitteilungen des Fischerei-Vereins für die Provinz Brandenburg 2 (1901).
Reprinted in Naturwissenschaftliche Wochenschrift 16 (1901) pp. 432—437.

783. *Lauterborn, R.*: Das Vogel-, Fisch- und Thierbuch des Strassburger Fischers Leonhard Baldner aus dem Jahre 1666. Herausgegeben, mit einer Einleitung u. erläuternden Anmerkungen versehen. Ludwigshafen am Rhein. 1903.

784. *Lebasteur, H.*: Buffon. Paris 1888.

785. *Leemann-van Elck, P.*: Der Buchschmuck in Conrad Gessners naturgeschichtlichen Werken.
Der Schweizer Sammler und Familienforscher 8 (1934).

786. *Legré, L.*: Pierre Belon.
In Legré: La botanique en Provence au XVIe siècle. Louis Anguillara, etc. (Marseille 1901) pp. 35—66.

787. *Lemoine, P.*: Le Muséum National d'Histoire Naturelle. Son histoire, Son état actuel.
In Archives du Muséum National d'Histoire Naturelle 6th Ser. 12 (1935) pp. 1—79.

788. *Leverkühn, P.*: Biographisches über die drei Naumanns und bibliographisches über ihre Werke nebst den Vorreden zur zweiten Auflage der Naturgeschichte der Vögel Deutschlands. Sonderabdruck aus Naumanns Naturgeschichte

der Vögel Mitteleuropas, I. Gera-Untermhaus 1904.
789. *Ley, W.*: Konrad Gesner. Leben und Werk. München 1929.
790. *Lindberg, V.*: v. Wrightarna på Haminanlaks. Helsingfors 1926.
791. *Lindström, A.*: Taiteilijaveljekset von Wright. Helsinki 1932.
792. *Loisel, G.*: Histoire des ménageries de l'antiquité à nos jours. I—III. Paris 1912.
793. *Longhena, M.*: Il conte L. F. Marsili, un uomo d'arme e di scienze. Milano 1930.
794. *Lönnberg, E.*: The ornithological collection of the Natural History Museum in Stockholm. In The Auk 43 (1926) pp. 434—446.
795. *Lönnberg, E.*: Bröderna von Wright. Några biografiska notiser. In Wright, M. W., and F. von: Svenska fåglar, med text af Einar Lönnberg III (Stockholm 1929) pp. 899—902.
796. *Lönnberg, E.*: De Rudbeckska fågelbilderna och deras betydelse. In Rudbecksstudier. Festskrift vid Uppsala Universitets minnesfest (Uppsala 1930) pp. 211—248.
797. *Lönnberg, E.*: Olaf Rudbeck, Jr., the first Swedish ornithologist. In The Ibis 13th Ser. 1 (1931) pp. 302—307.
798. *Lönnberg, E.*: Linnæi anteckningar efter Olof Rudbeck d. y:s föreläsningar om svenska fåglar. In Svenska Linné-Sällskapets årsskrift 15 (1932) pp. 41—75.
799. *Lönnberg, E.*, and C. Aurivillius: Carl von Linné såsom zoolog. Uppsala 1907. Carl von Linnés betydelse såsom naturforskare och läkare. Skildringar utgifna af K. Vetenskapsakademien i anledning af tvåhundraårsdagen af Linnés födelse. II.
Lönnberg, E. See Brolén, C. A.
800. *Loomis, L. M.*: A forgotten volume. In The Auk 8 (1891) p. 230.
801. *Lortet, L.*, and C. Gaillard: La faune momifiée de l'ancienne Égypte et recherches anthropologiques. 3rd. Ser. 9. Oies de Meidoum. In Archives du Muséum d'Histoire Naturelle de Lyon 10 (1909) Mémoire 2, pp. 95—99.
802. *Macgillivray, W.*: Memoir of Ulysses Aldrovandi. In The Naturalist's Library. Edited by William Jardine. 13 (Edinburgh 1843) (Mammalia 7. British quadrupeds) pp. 17—58.
803. *MacGillivray, W.*: Life of William MacGillivray. With a scientific appreciation by J. Arthur Thomson. London 1910.
804. *Maiden, J. H.*: Sir Joseph Banks, the 'Father of Australia'. London 1909.
805. *Mantuani, J.*: Die Miniaturen im Wiener Kodex Med. Græcus I. In Codices Græci et Latini photographice depicti. Tom. X. Dioscurides. Codex Aniciæ Julianæ picturis illustratus, nunc Vindobonensis Med. Gr. I. Pars prior (Lugduni Batavorum 1906) pp. 210—283.

806. *Marchant, J.*: Alfred Russel Wallace; letters and reminiscences. I—II. London 1911.
807. *Martin, E. A.*: A bibliography of Gilbert White, the naturalist and antiquarian of Selborne; with a biography and a descriptive account of the village of Selborne. London 1934.
808. *Masarey, A.*: Die Vogelwelt des Vierwaldstättersees im siebzehnten Jahrhundert. Nach einer Beschreibung des Johann Léopold Cysat. In Der Ornithologische Beobachter (L'Ornithologiste) 20 (1922—23).
809. *Mathews, G. M.*: Dates of issue of Lear's Illustr. Psittacidæ. In The Austral Avian Record 1 (1912) pp. 23—24.
810. *Mathews, G. M.*: Notes on Vol. VIII. of the 'United States Exploring Expedition', by Titian R. Peale, published in 1848. In The Ibis 12th. Ser. 5 (1929) pp. 690—700.
811. *Mathews, G. M.*: John Latham (1740—1837): an early English ornithologist. In The Ibis 13th Ser. 1 (1931) pp. 466—475.
812. *Mathews, G. M.*, and T. Iredale: Captain Thomas Brown, ornithologist. In The Austral Avian Record 4 (1922) pp. 176—194.
813. *Mathews, G. M.*, and T. Iredale: Thomas Watling, artist. In The Austral Avian Record 5 (1922) pp. 22—32.
814. *May, J. B.*: Edward Howe Forbush: a biographical sketch. With a list of the writings of Edward Howe Forbush. By R. F. Cheney. In Proceedings of the Boston Society of Natural History 39 (1928—31) pp. 33—72.
815. *Merian, P.*: Nachrichten über Felix Platers Naturaliensammlung. In Bericht über die Verhandlungen der naturforschenden Gesellschaft in Basel 4 (1840) pp. 93—102.
816. *Meyer, A. B.*: Index zu L. Reichenbach's ornithologischen Werken. Berlin 1879.
817. *Mitchell, P. C.*: Centenary history of the Zoological Society of London. London 1929.
818. *Mullens, W. H.*: Robert Sibbald and his Prodromus. In British Birds 6 (1912—13) pp. 34—57.
819. *Mullens, W. H.*: Some museums of old London. I. The Leverian Museum. In The Museums Journal 15 (1915—16) pp. 123—129, 162—172.
820. *Muschamp, E. A.*: Audacious Audubon; the story of a great pioneer, artist, naturalist and man. New York 1929.
821. *Nadault de Buffon, H.*: Correspondance inédite de Buffon. I—II. Paris 1860.
822. *Nadault de Buffon, H.*: Buffon, sa famille, ses collaborateurs et ses familiers. Mémoires par M. Humbert-Bazile, son secrétaire. Paris 1863.
823. *Neumann, R. W.*: Brehms Leben. Mit einem Geleitwort von Ludwig Heck. Berlin 1929.
824. *Neviani, A.*: Luigi Ferdinando Marsili e le sue collezioni zoologiche.

In Atti della Pontificia Accademia delle Scienze Nuovi Lincei 84 (1931) pp. 376—463.

825. *Neviani,* A.: Luigi Ferdinando Marsili e la seconda donazione del 1727.
In Atti della Pontificia Accademia delle Scienze Nuovi Lincei 85 (1932) pp. 49—72.

826. *Newberry,* P. E.: Beni Hasan. Parts I—II. London 1893—94.
Archæological Survey of Egypt. Edited by F. L. Griffith.

827. *Newton,* A.: [Letter on Pennant's 'Indian Zoology'].
In Stray Feathers 8 (1879) pp. 414—415.

828. *Newton,* A.: Gilbert White of Selborne. 1899.
Reprint of article for Dictionary of National Biography.
Newton, A. See Tunstall, M.

829. *Nilsson,* S.: Critiska anmärkningar öfver Rudbecks fogelbok.
In K. Vetenskaps Academiens handlingar (1816) pp. 21—42, (1817) pp. 128—136.

830. *Oberholser,* H. C.: Notes on Horsfield's 'Zoological Researches in Java'.
In Proceedings of the Biological Society of Washington, D. C. 34 (1921) pp. 163—166.

831. *Olphe-Galliard,* L.: Les oiseaux d'Afrique de Levaillant. Critique de cet ouvrage par C. Sundevall. Traduit de suédois.
In Revue et Magasin de Zoologie (1865) pp. 153—159 seqq.

832. *Ord,* G.: Biographical sketch of Alexander Wilson.
In Ord: Supplement to the American Ornithology of Alexander Wilson (Philadelphia 1825 pp. 13—210.
Osgood, W. H. See Fuertes, L. A.

833. *Palmer,* A. H.: Life of Joseph Wolf, animal painter. London 1895.

834. *Peabody,* W. B. O.: Alexander Wilson.
In Library of American biography, edited by Jared Sparks II (New York 1856) pp. 1—169.

835. *Peattie,* D. C.: Singing in the wilderness; a salute to John James Audubon. New York 1935.

836. *Pennant,* T.: The literary life of the late Thomas Pennant. By himself. London 1793.

837. *Petersen,* O. G.: En lille Litteratur-Bemærkning.
In Dansk ornithologisk Forenings Tidsskrift 2 (1907—08) pp. 158—166.

838. *Phillips,* J. C.: Leonhard Baldner, seventeenth century sportsman and naturalist.
In The Auk 42 (1925) pp. 332—341.

839. *Quennerstedt,* A. W.: Olaus Magnus såsom skildrare af Nordens djurlif. Föredrag vid nedläggandet af rektoratet d. 1. Juni 1899. Lund 1899.

840. *(Ray,* J.) Memorials of John Ray. Edited by Edwin Lankester. London 1846.
The Ray Society.

841. *Ray,* J.: The correspondence of John Ray. Edited by Edwin Lankester. London 1848.
The Ray Society.

842. *Ray,* J.: Further correspondence of John Ray.

Edited by Robert W. T. Gunther. London 1928.
The Ray Society 144.

843. *Reiber,* F.: L'histoire naturelle des eaux strasbourgeoises de Léonard Baldner (1666).
In Bulletin de la Société d'Histoire Naturelle de Colmar 27—29 (1888) pp. 1—114.

844. *Rhoads,* S. N.: More light on Audubon's folio 'Birds of America'.
In The Auk 33 (1916) pp. 130—132.

845. *Rhoads,* S. N.: Note on Bonaparte's continuation of Wilson's Ornithology.
In The Auk 40 (1923) pp. 341—342.

846. *Rivier,* L.: Le peintre Léo Paul Robert. Neuchâtel 1927.

847. *Robinson,* R.: Thomas Bewick, his life and times. Newcastle 1887.

848. *Roman,* J.: Le peintre Pierre Gourdelle 1555—1588. Paris 1888.
Réunion des Sociétés des Beaux-Arts des départements.

849. *Roule,* L.: Notice biographique sur Alcide Dessalines d'Orbigny (1802—1857), professeur de paléontologie au Muséum.
In Commémoration du voyage d'Alcide d'Orbigny en Amérique du Sud 1826—1833 (Paris 1933) pp. 7—13.

850. *Rourke,* C. M.: Audubon. New York 1936.
Royal Society of London. See Banks, J.

851. *Rudolphi,* K. A.: Peter Simon Pallas. Ein biographischer Versuch.
In Beyträge zur Anthropologie und allgemeinen Naturgeschichte (Berlin 1812) pp. 1—78.

852. *St. John,* Mrs. H.: Audubon, the naturalist of of the new world: his adventures and discoveries. London 1856.
Several American editions.

853. *Salvadori,* T.: Della vita a delle opere dell' ornitologo inglese John Gould.
In Atti della R. Accademia delle Scienze di Torino 16 (1880—81) pp. 789—810.

854. *Salvadori,* T.: Le date della pubblicazione della 'Iconografia della Fauna Italica' del Bonaparte ed Indice delle specie illustrate in detta opera.
In Bollettino dei Musei di Zoologia ed Anatomia comparata della R. Università di Torino 3 (1888) No. 48.

855. *Schalow,* H.: Ein seltenes ornithologisches Bilderwerk.
In Journal f. Ornithologie 58 (1910) pp. 190—196.

856. *Schlegel,* G.: Levensschets van Hermann Schlegel.
In Jaarboek van de K. Akademie van Wetenschappen (Amsterdam 1884) pp. 1—97.

857. *Schramm,* A.: Die Drucke von Johann Baemler in Augsburg. Leipzig 1921.
Der Bilderschmuck der Frühdrucke 3.
Schultz-Lorentzen, C. W. See Kornerup, B.

858. *Schuster,* J.: Geschichte und Idee des naturwissenschaftlichen Museums. Vortrag bei der Gründungs-Tagung des 'Bundes der deutschen naturwissenschaftlichen Museen'.
In Archiv f. Geschichte der Mathematik, der

Naturwissenschaften und der Technik 11 (1929) pp. 178—192.

859. *Sclater, W. L.*: François Le Vaillant, 1753—1824: an early French ornithologist.
In The Ibis 13th Ser. 1 (1931) pp. 645—649.

860. (*Seba, A.*) Memoria Alberti Seba.
In Acta physico-medica Academiæ Cæsareæ Leopoldino-Carolinæ Naturæ Curiosorum 6 (1742) Appendix pp. 239—252.

861. *Sharpe, R. B.*: An analytical index to the works of the late John Gould. With a biographical memoir and portrait. London 1893.

862 a. *Sherborn, C. D.*: Dates of publication of Jardine and Selby's 'Illustrations of Ornithology'.
In The Ibis 6th Ser. 6 (1894) p. 326.

862 b. *Sherborn, C. D.*: On the dates of Shaw and Nodder's 'Naturalist's Miscellany'.
In The Annals and Magazine of Natural History 6th Ser. 15 (1895) pp. 375—376.

863. *Sherborn, C. D.*: Notes on the dates of 'The Zoology of the »Beagle«.'
In The Annals and Magazine of Natural History 6th Ser. 20 (1897) pp. 483.

864. *Sherborn, C. D.*: Dates of publication of catalogues of natural history (post 1850) issued by the British Museum.
In The Annals and Magazine of Natural History 10th Ser. 13 (1934) pp. 308—312.

865. *Sherborn, C. D.*: On the dates of Pallas's 'Zoographia Rosso-Asiatica'.
In The Ibis 13th Ser. 4 (1934) pp. 164—167.

866. *Sherborn, C. D.*, and F. J. Griffin: On the dates of publication of the natural history portions of Alcide d'Orbigny's 'Voyage Amérique méridionale'.
In The Annals and Magazine of Natural History 10th Ser. 13 (1934) pp. 130—134.

867. *Sherborn, C. D.*, and T. Iredale: J. F. Miller's Icones.
In The Ibis 11th Ser. 3 (1921) pp. 302—309.

868. *Sherborn, C. D.*, and F. A. Jentink: On the dates of the parts of Siebold's 'Fauna Japonica', etc.
In Proceedings of the Zoological Society of London (1895) pp. 149—150.

869. *Sherborn, C. D.*, and B. B. Woodward: Notes on the dates of publication of the natural history portions of some French voyages. Parts I—II.
In The Annals and Magazine of Natural History; Part I: 7th Ser. 7 (1901) pp. 388—392; Part II: 7th Ser. 8 (1901) pp. 161—164, 333—336, 491—494.

870. *Sherborn, C. D.*, and B. B. Woodward: On the dates of publication of the natural history portions of the 'Encyclopédie méthodique'.
In The Annals and Magazine of Natural History 7th Ser. 17 (1906) pp. 577—582.

871. *Simmler, J.*: Vita Conradi Gesneri. Tiguri 1566.

872. *Snouckaert van Schauburg, R. C. E. G. J.*: Onze oude ornithologen.

In Orgaan der Club van Nederlandsche Vogelkundigen 1 (1928—29) pp. 116—132.

873. *Stadler, H.* Albertus Magnus: De animalibus libri XXVI. Nach der Cölner Urschrift. Münster 1916—20.
Beiträge zur Geschichte der Philosophie des Mittelalters 15—16.

874. *Stejneger, L.*: On the use of trinominals in American ornithology.
In Proceedings of the United States National Museum 7, 1884 (1885) pp. 70—80.

Stieda, L. See Baer, K. E. von.

875. *Stone, W.*: A bibliography and nomenclator of of the ornithological works of John James Audubon.
In The Auk 23 (1906) pp. 298—312.

876. *Stone, W.*: Editions of Baird, Cassin, and Lawrence's 'Birds of North America'.
In The Auk 36 (1919) pp. 428—430.

877. *Stone, W.*: Mark Catesby and the nomenclature of North American birds.
In The Auk 46 (1929) pp. 447—454.

878. *Stone, W.*: The work of William, son of John Bartram.
Bartonia 1931 (Special issue) pp. 20—23.

879. *Storm, G.*: Om Peder Claussøn Friis og hans Skrifter.
In Claussøn Friis: Samlede Skrifter. Udgivne ... af Gustav Storm (Kristiania 1881) pp. I—LXXXIII.

880. *Storm, G.*: Om Forfatteren af Beskrivelserne over Lofoten og Vesteraalen (1591) og over Namdalen (1597).
In Historisk Tidsskrift udgivet af Den Norske Historiske Forening 2nd Ser. 4 (1884) pp. 189—196, 303—304.

881. *Strand, E.*: Der norwegische Naturforscher Hans Ström (1726—1797) und seine zoologischen Schriften. Ein Blatt aus der Geschichte der norwegischen Zoologie.
In Archiv f. Naturgeschichte Abt. A 83 6 (1919) pp. 27—46.

882. *Strand, E.*: Die zoologischen Werke von Pontoppidan (1753), Leem (1767) und Wilse (1779, 1790—1792). Aus der Geschichte der norwegischen Zoologie.
In Archiv f. Naturgeschichte Abt. A 83 7 (1919) pp. 150—156.

883. *Stresemann, E.*: Was wussten die Schriftsteller des XVI. Jahrhunderts von den Paradiesvögeln? Ein Beitrag zur Geschichte der Ornithologie.
In Novitates Zoologicæ 21 (1914) pp. 13—24.

884. *Stresemann, E.*: Erscheinungsdaten von Temminck und Laugiers Planches Coloriées.
In Anzeiger der Ornithologischen Gesellschaft in Bayern 7 (1922) pp. 54—55.

885 a. *Stresemann, E.*: Herman Shalows ornithologischer Werdegang.
In Journal f. Ornithologie 74 (1926) pp. 175—187.

885 b. *Stresemann, E.*: Zur Bibliographie der Schriften F. A. von Pernau's und H. F. von Göchhausen's.

In Journal f. Ornithologie 74 (1926) pp. 688 —691.

885c. *Stresemann, E.*: Die Entwickelung der Begriffe Art, Varietät, Unterart in der Ornithologie. In Mitteilungen des Vereins sächsischer Ornithologen 2 (1927) pp. 1—8.

886. *Stresemann, E.*: Die Vogelsammlung des Tring-Museums, ihr Aufbau und ihr Ende. In Ornithologische Monatsberichte 40 (1932) pp. 65—73.

887. *Stresemann, E.*: The Formenkreis-theory. In The Auk 53 (1936) pp. 150—158.

888. *Strickland, H. E.*: Anastatic printing. In The Athenæum. Journal of literature, science, and the fine arts (1848) pp. 172 and 276.

889. *Strickland, Mrs. H. E., and W. Jardine*: Memoirs of Hugh Edwin Strickland. London 1858.

890. *Strohl, J.*: Conrad Gessners zoologische Werke als charakteristische Zeichen einer neuen Betrachtungsweisse der Natur. In Verhandlungen der Schweizerischen naturforschenden Gesellschaft 115 (1934) pp. 440 —441.

891. *Strzygowski, J.*: Der Bilderkreis des griechischen Physiologus, des Kosmas Indikopleustes und Oktateuch. Leipzig 1899. Byzantinisches Archiv 2.

892. *Sundevall, C. J.*: Kritisk framställning af fogelarterna uti äldre ornithologiska arbeten. K. Svenska Vetenskaps-Akademiens handlingar. Ny följd 2 (1860) No. 3, 1857.

893. *Sundevall, C. J.*: Die Thierarten des Aristoteles. Stockholm 1863.

894. *Sundevall, C. J.*: Om Rudbecks fogelbok. Upsala 1872. Nova Acta Regiæ Societatis Scientiarum Upsaliensis, 3rd Ser. 8, No. VII.

895. *Taylor, H. J.*: Alexander Wilson: a sketch. In The Wilson Bulletin 40 (1928) pp. 75—84.

896. *Taylor, H. J.*: Dr. Elliott Coues — a sketch. In The Wilson Bulletin 41 (1929) pp. 219—228.

897. *Thomson, D. C.*: The life and works of Thomas Bewick. London 1882.

898. *Thomson, D. C.*: The water-colour drawings of Thomas Bewick. London 1930.

899. *Thunberg, C. P.*: Museum Naturalium Academiæ Upsaliensis. Upsaliæ 1787—1827.

900. *Tunstall, M.*: Tunstall's Ornithologia Britannica [1771]. Edited by Alfred Newton. London 1880. The Willughby Society.

901. *Vaz, Z.*: A vide e os trabalhos de Emilio Goeldi. In Boletim biologico, São Paulo, 2 (1934) pp. 3—16.

902. *Vrolik, W.*: Levensberigt van Coenraad Jacob Temminck. In Jaarboek van de K. Akademie van Weten-

schappen (Amsterdam. April 1857—April 1858) pp. 65—80.

903. *Wallace, A. R.*: My life; a record of events and opinions ... with facsimile letters, illustrations and portraits. I—II. London 1905.

904. *Waterhouse, F. H.*: On the dates of publication of the parts of Sir Andrew Smith's 'Illustrations of the Zoology of South Africa'. In Proceedings of the scientific meetings of the Zoological Society of London for the year 1880, pp. 489—491.

905. *Waterhouse, F. H.*: The dates of publication of some of the zoological works of the late John Gould. London 1885.

906. *Wedderburn, W.*: Allan Octavian Hume C. B.: 'Father of the Indian National Congress', 1829 —1912. London 1913.

907. *Wegener, H.*: Das grosse Bilderwerk des Carolus Clusius in der Preussischen Staatsbibliothek. In Forschungen und Fortschritte 12 (1936) pp. 374—376.

908. *Weicker, G.*: Der Seelenvogel in der alten Litteratur und Kunst. Eine mythologisch-archaeologische Untersuchung. Leipzig 1902.

909. *Weld, C. R.*: A history of the Royal Society. I—II. London 1848.

910. *Wellmann, M.*: Der Physiologos. Eine religionsgeschichtlich-naturwissenschaftliche Untersuchung. Leipzig 1930. Philologus. Supplementband 22, I.

911. *Wibeck, E.*: John Wolleys fågelfaunistiska arbete i svenska och finska lappmarken 1853—1857. In Fauna och Flora 25 (1930) pp. 193—202, 241—254.

912. *Williams, G. A.*: Robert Havell, Junior, engraver of Audubon's 'The Birds of America'. In Print-Collectors Quarterly 6 (1916) pp. 225 —257.

913. *Wilson, J. S.*: Alexander Wilson; the poet-naturalist — a study of his life, with selected poems. New York 1906.

914. *Winge, H.*: Fortegnelse over Danmarks Fugle. In Dansk ornithologiske Forenings Tidsskrift 1 (1906—07) pp. 5—25.

915. *Wissmüller, C.*: Der Geograph Luigi Ferdinando Graf Marsigli (1658—1730). Nürnberg 1900. Inaug. Diss. Erlangen.

916. *Wollaston, A. F. R.*: Life of Alfred Newton. London 1921.

917. *Wood, C. A.*: James Graham Cooper (1830—1902): a Pacific coast ornithologist. In The Ibis 13th Ser. 2 (1932) pp. 632—638. *Woodward, B. B. See Sherborn*, C. D.

918. *Zaunick, R.*: Peter Simon Pallas (1741—1811), der Begründer der paläarktischen Wirbeltierkunde. Ein bio-bibliographische Studie. In Pallasia 3 (1925) pp. 1—37.

INDEX OF NAMES

The numbers in parentheses refer to the numbers of the titles in the catalogue. The names of artists, engravers, lithographers, etc., are marked by an asterisk. The names of process-engravers and printers are marked by two asterisks.

Rumphius, Georg Eberhard (1627—1702) 22
** Rusch, Adolf (c. 1467) 6
* Ruspi, Carolus (c. 1830) 102 (48)
Russ, Karl Friedrich Otto (1833—99) 171 (361), 187 (436)
Russell, Alexander (1715 ? —68) 26
Russell, William Howard (1820—1907) 206 (513)
Ruysch, Henricus (—1727) 143 (236)
Ryff, W. (c. 1545) 9
Rymvardt (c. 1812) 156 (297)

S

Sagra, Ramon de la (1801—71) 175 (383)
Saint Hilaire, see Bourjot Saint Hilaire
St. John, Oliver Beauchamp Coventry (1831—91) 101 (45)
Salerne, François (—1760) 20, 183 (414)
Salomonsen, Finn (1909—) 76
Salvadori, Tommaso Adlardo (1835—1923) 54—55, 66, 102
    (48), 106—107 (70), 172 (368), 192 (452), 215 (547)
Salvin, Osbert (1835—98) 63, 67, 68, 106 (70), 127 (163),
    130 (182), 139 (219), 159 (308), 172 (368), 187 (432),
    188 (437), 192 (452), 215 (547), 548)
'*Salzmann, Wilhelm (fl. 1785—1800) 98 (30)
Sæmundsson, Bjarni (1867—) 76
Sandys, Edwyn William (1860—) 82
Sanford, Leonard Cutler (1869—) 83
* Sargent, Alfred Louis (1828— ?) 154 (285)
Sars, Georg Ossian (1837—1927) 72
Saunders, Howard (1835—1907) 57, 106 (70), 139 (219), 192
    (452), 215 (547)
* Savery, Roelant (c. 1576—1639) 14
Savi, Paolo (1798—1871) 54
Savigny, Marie Jules César Lelorgne de (1777—1851) 94
    (15, 16), 188—189 (438)
Schaanning, Hans Thomas Lange (1878—) 73
* Schach, C. (fl. 1820—40) 126 (159), 174 (376)
Schaeff, Ernst Ascan Friedrich Wilhelm (1861—1921) 125
    (153)
Schaeffer, Jacob Christian (1718—90) 36, 189 (439, 440)
Schalow, Herman (1852—1925) 49, 50, 214 (545)
* Schan, Lukas (fl. 1526 -50) 10
* Scharf, George (1788—1860) 122 (139), 128 (170)
* Scheel, Henning Knud Jørgen (1889—) 189—190
    (442)
Schinz, Heinrich Rudolf (1777—1861) 53, 189 (441)
Schiøler, Eiler Lauritz Theodor Lehn (1874—1929) 75, 165
    (342), 189—190 (442)
Schlegel, Hermann (1804—84) 44, 48, 50, 52, 55, 100 (41),
    102 (49), 158 (307), 167 (351), 170 (358), 175 (381),
    190 (443—446), 204 (504), 215 (547)
Schleinitz, Georg Emil Gustav von (1834—1910) 200 (487)
Schmidel, Casimir Christoph (1718—92) 212 (537)
* Schmidt (c. 1845) 206 (511)
* Schmidt, C. F. (c. 1889) 201 (487)
* Schmidt, E. (c. 1863) 104 (62)
* Schmidt, Emil (c. 1875—1900) 187 (436)
* Schmid(t), M[atthias? (1749—1823)] 199 (483)
Schneider, Johann Gottlob (1750—1822) 125 (153)
* Schneider, M. (c. 1887) 164 (335)
Schödler, Friedrich Karl Ludwig (1813—84) 104 (62)
** Schöffer, Peter (c. 1485) 8
Schön, see Schan
Schöpffer, C. (c. 1896) 125 (153)

Schöpffer, H. (c. 1890) 125 (153)
Schøning, Gerhard (1722—80) 174 (377)
Schönneböl, Erik Hansen (c. 1540—c. 1592) 16
* Schouman, Aart (1710—92) 176 (385)
Schouteden, Henri (1881—) 56
Schouw, Joakim Frederik (1789—1852) 121 (136)
Schrenck, Peter Leopold von (1826—94) 190—191 (447)
* Schröder, Erich (c. 1920) 131 (184), 135 (202), 160 (317)
Schrön, see Schan
* Schubert, I. (c. 1880) 214 (545)
* Schultze, H. (c. 1910) 150 (265)
* Schuster, J. F. (c. 1765—70) 176 (385)
Schwabe, Johann Joachim (c. 1757) 180 (400)
* Schwaniz (c. 1830) 105 (66)
Schwenckfeld, Caspar (1563—1609) 16
Sclater, Philip Lutley (1829—1913) 61, 63, 67, 68, 106 (70),
    108 (76), 139 (216, 219), 142 (229), 187 (432), 191—
    192 (448—452), 213 (539), 215 (547, 548)
Sclater, William Lutley (1863—) 67, 68, 69, 138 (211),
    139 (219), 215 (547)
Scopoli, Giovanni Antonio (1723—87) 198 (475)
* Scott, R[obert? (1771—1841)] 128 (167)
Scott, Robert Falcon (1868—1912) 64, 212 (535)
Scott, William Berryman (1858—) 192 (453)
Scott, William Earl Dodge (1852—1910) 85, 192 (453)
Scully, Dr. 195 (465)
* Seaby, Allen William (1867—) 146 (245)
Seba, Albert (1665—1736) 22, 192—193 (454)
Seebohm, Henry (1832—95) 58, 62, 64, 106 (70), 187 (432),
    193 (455—458), 210 (528), 215 (547)
Séguy, E. (c. 1932) 163 (330)
Selby, Prideaux John (1788—1867) 57—58, 61, 140 (222),
    141 (224, 226), 193—194 (459—461), 214 (546)
Selenka, Emil (1842—1902) 49
* Seligmann, Johann Michael (1720—62) 21, 24, 112 (94),
    118 (124), 119 (126), 194 (462, 463)
* Sellier, [? Louis (1757—c. 1835)] 126 (158)
Selous, Edmund (c. 1910) 146 (245)
Selys Longchamps, Michel Edmond, Baron de (1813—1900)
    56
* Senefelder, Aloys (1771—1834) 43
* Sepp, Christiaan (—1775) 36, 173 (369)
Sepp, Jan 36
* Sepp, Jan Christiaan (1739—1811) 36, 173 (369, 370)
* Seton, Ernest Thompson (1860—) 80, 96 (20)
* Sève, Jacques de (fl. 1742—88) 108 (74—76), 109 (80)
* Sévereyns, G. (c. 1845) 118 (123)
* Sewell, F. L. 149 (262), 150 (264)
Sharpe, Richard Bowdler (1847—1909) 35, 58, 60, 61—62,
    63, 64, 65, 66, 69, 85, 93 (10), 106—107 (70, 71), 111
    (89), 117 (120), 123 (144), 127 (163), 130 (178, 181,
    182), 131 (185), 138 (211), 144 (240), 153 (281), 158
    (307), 162 (324), 173 (371), 187 (432), 188 (437),
    192 (453), 193 (457, 458), 194—195 (464—466), 210
    (526), 210 (528), 215 (547)
Shaw, George (1751—1813) 29, 34, 35, 154 (282), 195—196
    (467, 468), 215 (547)
Shelley, George Ernest (1840—1910) 62, 68, 106 (70), 171
    (363), 196 (469, 470), 215 (547)
* Sheppard, Edwin (—1904) 82, 113 (99), 120 (129)
Sherborn, Charles Davies (1861—) 210 (526)
* Sherwin, William (c. 1645—c. 1711) 211 (532)
Shipley, Arthur Everett (1861—1927) 155 (287)

GEOGRAPHICAL INDEX

32

São Paulo 51
Sardinia (Sardegna) 37
Savoie (Savoy) 46
Scandinavia 3, 16, 26—28, 38—39, 63, 69—76 (19th and 20th
    centuries), 140 (221), 146—147 (247), 147—148 (249—
    252), 150—151 (270, 271), 172 (364—366)
Scotland 16, 57, 71, 76, 100 (42), 196 (471)
Selborne 25, 35, 210 (526)
Senegambia 31, 39, 185 (425, 426)
Shanghai 64
Siam 70
Siberia 26, 52—53, 64, 86, 165 (339), 182 (411), 191 (447)
Sicily 4
Silesia 16
Simla 65
Sinai 171 (363)
Singapore, Island of 111 (93)
Skåne 186 (428)
Somaliland 137 (209)
Søndmør 27
South Africa 39, 40, 51, 69
    Birds in general 123 (145), 153—154 (281), 156 (297,
    298), 157 (299)
    Game-birds and water-fowl 137—138 (211)
South America 18, 28, 33, 41, 46, 50—51, 53, 56, 63, 68, 81,
    84, 85, 164 (334)
    Birds in general 103 (56), 139 (218), 175 (382)
    Cotingidæ 157 (300, 301)
    Oceanic birds 167 (352)
Spain 3, 17, 53, 160 (314)
Spitsbergen 41, 50, 71, 150 (265), 151 (270)
Stavanger 73
Stockholm 71
Strasbourg 6, 9, 11, 19, 20
Sudan 76
Suffolk 57
Sumatra 51
Sweden 26, 29—31, 39, 63, 69—72 (19th and 20th centuries),
    146—147 (247), 147 (249), 151 (270), 159 (312), 171—
    172 (364, 365), 177 (388), 183—184 (418), 185—186
    (427), 199 (482), 201 (490), 213—214 (543, 544)
Switzerland (Helvetia) 16, 53—54 (19th and 20th centuries),
    133—134 (195), 163 (329), 189 (441)
Sydney 66, 180 (402)
Syria 5, 26, 94 (15, 16)

T

Tahiti 28, 191 (452)
Tanganyika Territory 69
Tarei-nor 182 (411)
Tasmania 66
Ternate 191 (452)
Texas 111 (92)
Theiss, see Tisa
Thorshavn 17

Tian-Shan 51
Tierra del Fuego 68
Timor 51
Tisa (Theiss) 162 (326)
Tonga (Friendly) Islands 122 (14)
Tongatabu 191 (452)
Toscana 12, 54
Tring 48, 49, 66, 98 (31), 172 (368)
Trinidad 46
Tunis 69, 210 (525)
Tyrol 18

U

Uganda 70
United States 21, 76—86 (19th and 20th centuries)
    Birds in general 94—95 (17—20), 101 (47), 111 (92),
    211—212 (533, 534)
    Explorations west of the One Hundredth Meridian 136
    (207)
    Hawks and owls 122—123 (144)
    Pacific Railroad Survey 96 (22, 23), 113 (106), 114
    (107), 134 (199, 200), 145 (243), 171 (362)
    Woodpeckers 97 (28)
Urubamba Valley, Peru 85
Uruguay 85, 175 (382)
Utah 80, 136 (207)

V

Venice 7
Versailles 14
Vesteraalen 16
Vienna 5, 14, 15, 86
Virgin Islands 85
Viti, see Fiji

W

Wales 57
Washington Territory 113 (106)
Wednesday 192 (452)
West Africa 69, 134 (197)
West Indies 20, 21, 36, 67, 84—85, 140 (220), 197 (474)
Woodstock 14

Y

Yarkand 64, 65, 195 (465)
Yukon District 206 (512)
Yunnan 64, 93 (10)

Z

Zambesi 69, 138 (211), 154 (281)
Zürich 10

32·

NATURAL SCIENCES IN AMERICA

An Arno Press Collection

Allen, J[oel] A[saph]. **The American Bisons,** Living and Extinct. 1876

Allen, Joel Asaph. **History of the North American Pinnipeds:** A Monograph of the Walruses, Sea-Lions, Sea-Bears and Seals of North America. 1880

American Natural History Studies: The Bairdian Period. 1974

American Ornithological Bibliography. 1974

Anker, Jean. **Bird Books and Bird Art.** 1938

Audubon, John James and John Bachman. **The Quadrupeds of North America.** Three vols. 1854

Baird, Spencer F[ullerton]. **Mammals of North America.** 1859

Baird, S[pencer] F[ullerton], T[homas] M. Brewer and R[obert] Ridgway. **A History of North American Birds:** Land Birds. Three vols., 1874

Baird, Spencer F[ullerton], John Cassin and George N. Lawrence. **The Birds of North America.** 1860. Two vols. in one.

Baird, S[pencer] F[ullerton], T[homas] M. Brewer, and R[obert] Ridgway. **The Water Birds of North America.** 1884. Two vols. in one.

Barton, Benjamin Smith. **Notes on the Animals of North America.** Edited, with an Introduction by Keir B. Sterling. 1792

Bendire, Charles [Emil]. **Life Histories of North American Birds** With Special Reference to Their Breeding Habits and Eggs. 1892/1895. Two vols. in one.

Bonaparte, Charles Lucian [Jules Laurent]. **American Ornithology:** Or The Natural History of Birds Inhabiting the United States, Not Given by Wilson. 1825/1828/1833. Four vols. in one.

Cameron, Jenks. **The Bureau of Biological Survey:** Its History, Activities, and Organization. 1929

Caton, John Dean. **The Antelope and Deer of America:** A Comprehensive Scientific Treatise Upon the Natural History, Including the Characteristics, Habits, Affinities, and Capacity for Domestication of the Antilocapra and Cervidae of North America. 1877

Contributions to American Systematics. 1974

Contributions to the Bibliographical Literature of American Mammals. 1974

Contributions to the History of American Natural History. 1974

Contributions to the History of American Ornithology. 1974

Cooper, J[ames] G[raham]. **Ornithology.** Volume I, Land Birds. 1870

Cope, E[dward] D[rinker]. **The Origin of the Fittest:** Essays on Evolution and **The Primary Factors of Organic Evolution.** 1887/1896. Two vols. in one.

Coues, Elliott. **Birds of the Colorado Valley.** 1878

Coues, Elliott. **Birds of the Northwest.** 1874

Coues, Elliott. **Key To North American Birds.** Two vols. 1903

Early Nineteenth-Century Studies and Surveys. 1974

Emmons, Ebenezer. **American Geology:** Containing a Statement of the Principles of the Science. 1855. Two vols. in one.

Fauna Americana. 1825-1826

Fisher, A[lbert] K[enrick]. **The Hawks and Owls of the United States in Their Relation to Agriculture.** 1893

Godman, John D. **American Natural History:** Part I — Mastology and **Rambles of a Naturalist.** 1826-28/1833. Three vols. in one.

Gregory, William King. **Evolution Emerging:** A Survey of Changing Patterns from Primeval Life to Man. Two vols. 1951

Hay, Oliver Perry. **Bibliography and Catalogue of the Fossil Vertebrata of North America.** 1902

Heilprin, Angelo. **The Geographical and Geological Distribution of Animals.** 1887

Hitchcock, Edward. **A Report on the Sandstone of the Connecticut Valley,** Especially Its Fossil Footmarks. 1858

Hubbs, Carl L., editor. **Zoogeography.** 1958

[Kessel, Edward L., editor]. **A Century of Progress in the Natural Sciences:** 1853-1953. 1955

Leidy, Joseph. **The Extinct Mammalian Fauna of Dakota and Nebraska,** Including an Account of Some Allied Forms from Other Localities, Together with a Synopsis of the Mammalian Remains of North America. 1869

Lyon, Marcus Ward, Jr. **Mammals of Indiana.** 1936

Matthew, W[illiam] D[iller]. **Climate and Evolution.** 1915

Mayr, Ernst, editor. **The Species Problem.** 1957

Mearns, Edgar Alexander. **Mammals of the Mexican Boundary of the United States.** Part I: Families Didelphiidae to Muridae. 1907

Merriam, Clinton Hart. **The Mammals of the Adirondack Region,** Northeastern New York. 1884

Nuttall, Thomas. **A Manual of the Ornithology of the United States and of Canada.** Two vols. 1832-1834

Nuttall Ornithological Club. **Bulletin of the Nuttall Ornithological Club:** A Quarterly Journal of Ornithology. 1876-1883. Eight vols. in three.

[Pennant, Thomas]. **Arctic Zoology.** 1784-1787. Two vols. in one.

Richardson, John. **Fauna Boreali-Americana;** Or the Zoology of the Northern Parts of British America, Containing Descriptions of the Objects of Natural History Collected on the Late Northern Land Expeditions Under Command of Captain Sir John Franklin, R. N. Part I: Quadrupeds. 1829

Richardson, John and William Swainson. **Fauna Boreali-Americana:** Or the Zoology of the Northern Parts of British America, Containing Descriptions of the Objects of Natural History Collected by the Late Northern Land Expeditions Under Command of Captain Sir John Franklin, R. N. Part II: The Birds. 1831

Ridgway, Robert. **Ornithology.** 1877

Selected Works By Eighteenth-Century Naturalists and Travellers. 1974

Selected Works in Nineteenth-Century North American Paleontology. 1974

Selected Works of Clinton Hart Merriam. 1974

Selected Works of Joel Asaph Allen. 1974

Selections From the Literature of American Biogeography. 1974

Seton, Ernest Thompson. **Life-Histories of Northern Animals: An Account of the Mammals of Manitoba.** Two vols. 1909

Sterling, Keir Brooks. **Last of the Naturalists:** The Career of C. Hart Merriam. 1974

Vieillot, L. P. **Histoire Naturelle Des Oiseaux de L'Amerique Septentrionale,** Contenant Un Grand Nombre D'Especes Decrites ou Figurees Pour La Premiere Fois. 1807. Two vols. in one.

Wilson, Scott B., assisted by A. H. Evans. **Aves Hawaiienses:** The Birds of the Sandwich Islands. 1890-99

Wood, Casey A., editor. **An Introduction to the Literature of Vertebrate Zoology.** 1931

Zimmer, John Todd. **Catalogue of the Edward E. Ayer Ornithological Library.** 1926